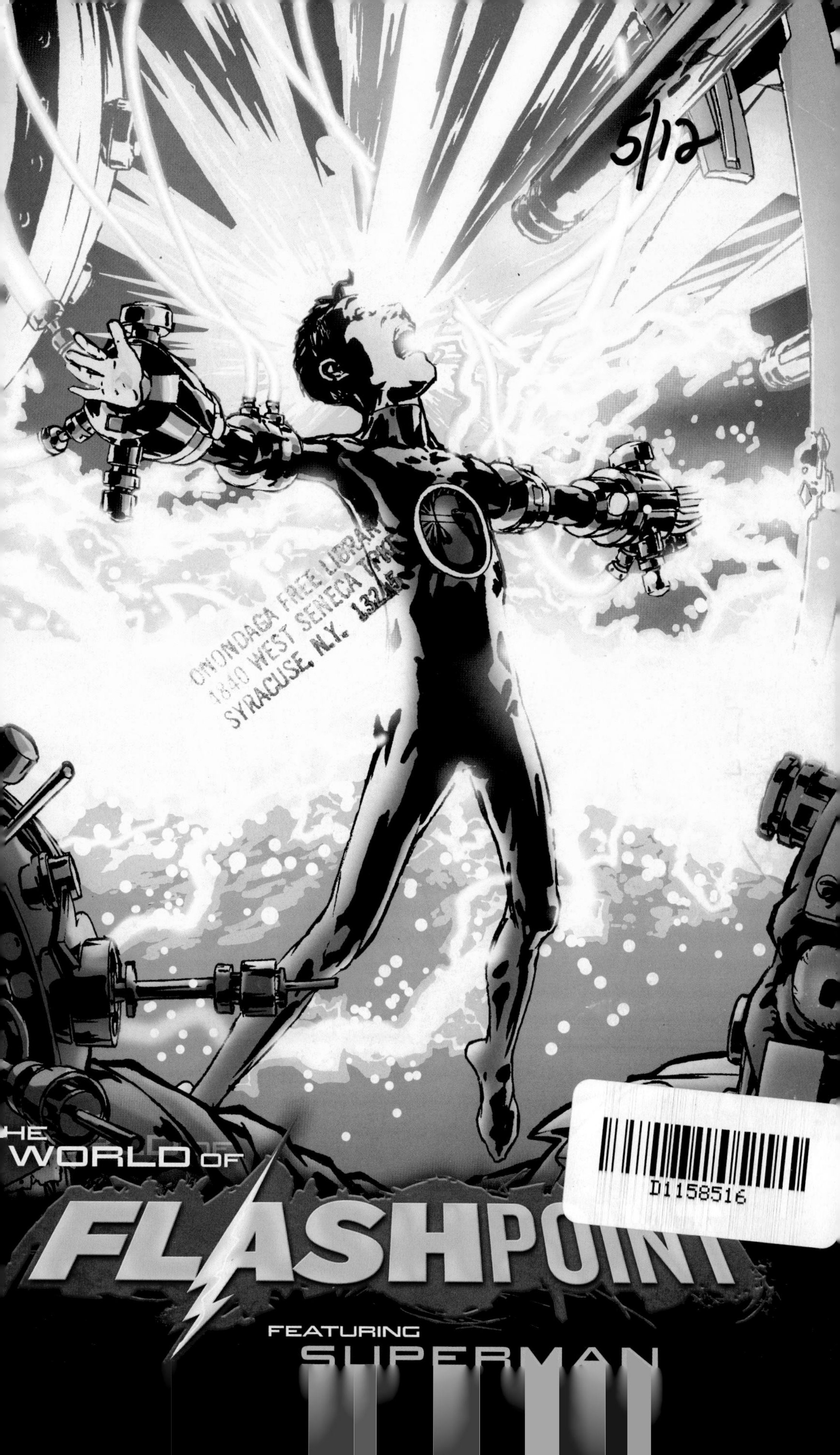
5/12
HE WORLD OF
FLASHPOINT
FEATURING
SUPERMAN

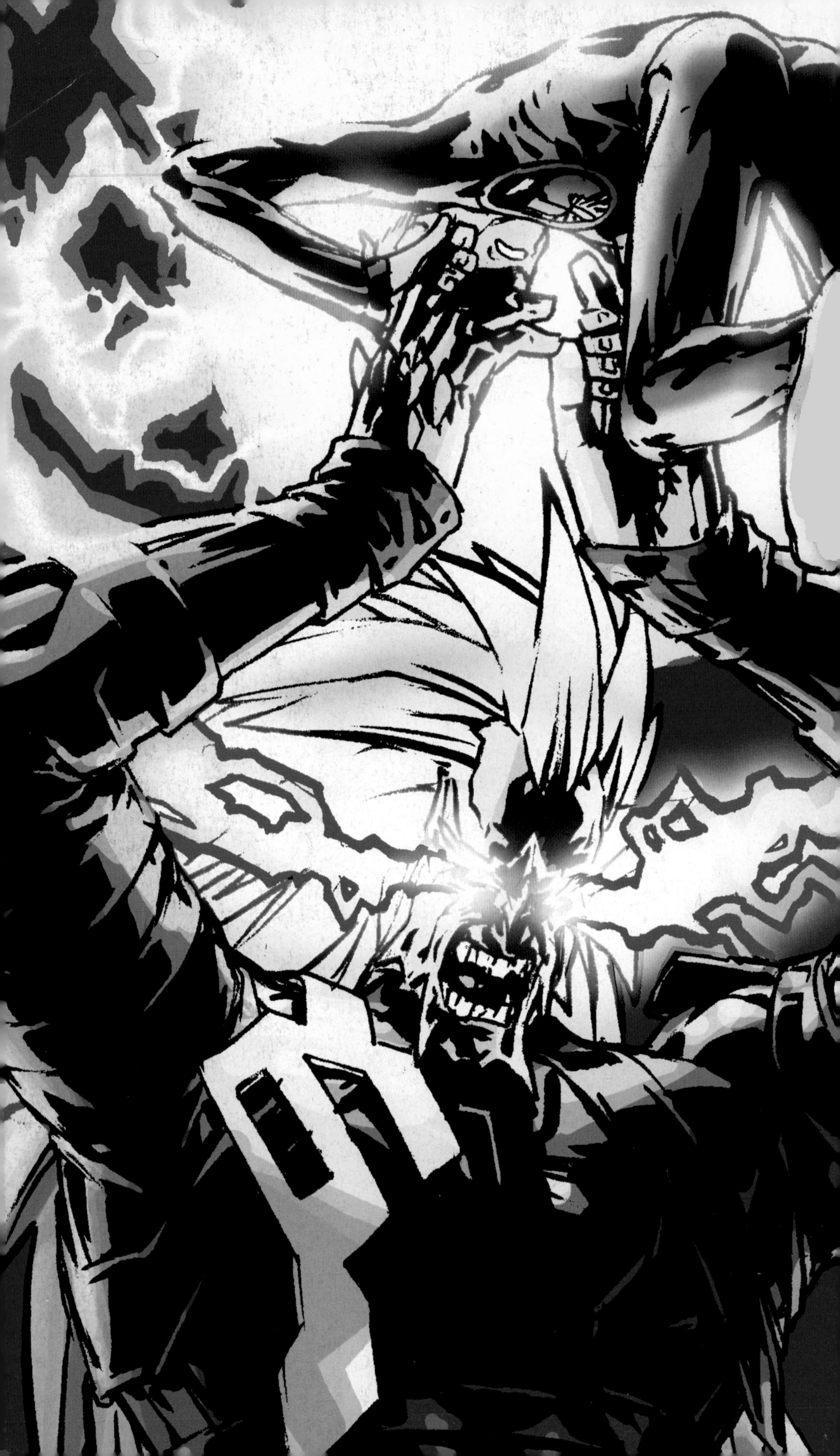

THE WORLD OF

FLASHPOINT

FEATURING SUPERMAN

PROJECT SUPERMAN

SCOTT SNYDER & LOWELL FRANCIS writers
GENE HA artist
ART LYON colorist
ROB LEIGH letterer

Superman created by JERRY SIEGEL and JOE SHUSTER

WORLD OF FLASHPOINT

REX OGLE writer
EDUARDO FRANCISCO PAULO SIQUEIRA ROLAND PARIS artists
STEFANI RENEE colorist
TRAVIS LANHAM letterer

BOOSTER GOLD: TURBULENCE

DAN JURGENS writer
DAN JURGENS RICK LEONARDI IG GUARA
NORM RAPMUND RUY JOSÉ DON HO artists
HI-FI DESIGNS colorist
CARLOS M. MANGUAL DAVE SHARPE letterers

Booster Gold created by DAN JURGENS

THE CANTERBURY CRICKET

MIKE CARLIN writer
RAGS MORALES RICK BRYANT artists
NEI RUFFINO colorist
ROB LEIGH letterer

Collection Cover by GENE HA

Barry Allen awoke in a world he barely recognizes, but it isn't a trick or a parallel Earth. Something or someone has altered time, replacing Barry's world with this one. And this new world is not a safe place.

The planet is on the brink of destruction as Wonder Woman and the Amazons wage war with Aquaman and the Atlanteans without any regard for the powerless masses caught in the middle. As a result, most of Europe is either destroyed or occupied territory, and the rest of the world lives in constant fear. A few motley heroes are mounting a resistance, but in this world heroes are hard to come by. No one has ever heard of the Flash, or the Justice League, or Superman. Hal Jordan was never given a Green Lantern ring, and Bruce Wayne was killed in Crime Alley when he was just a little boy.

Without his powers or his friends to aid him, Barry reaches out to a new Batman, Bruce's father Thomas Wayne, who survived in this reality while his son did not. Now they are working together to put the world right. If they fail, they'll never escape from this twisted, tragic world.

Welcome to...

REX OGLE
PAT McCALLUM
EDDIE BERGANZA
Editors – Original Series

SEAN MACKIEWICZ
Assistant Editor – Original Series

IAN SATTLER
Director – Editorial, Special Projects
and Archival Editions

ROBIN WILDMAN
Editor

ROBBIN BROSTERMAN
Design Director – Books

ROBBIE BIEDERMAN
Publication Design

EDDIE BERGANZA
Executive Editor

BOB HARRAS
VP – Editor-in-Chief

DIANE NELSON
President

DAN DIDIO and JIM LEE
Co-Publishers

GEOFF JOHNS
Chief Creative Officer

JOHN ROOD
Executive VP – Sales, Marketing
and Business Development

AMY GENKINS
Senior VP – Business and Legal Affairs

NAIRI GARDINER
Senior VP – Finance

JEFF BOISON
VP – Publishing Operations

MARK CHIARELLO
VP – Art Direction and Design

JOHN CUNNINGHAM
VP – Marketing

TERRI CUNNINGHAM
VP – Talent Relations and Services

ALISON GILL
Senior VP – Manufacturing
and Operations

DAVID HYDE
VP – Publicity

HANK KANALZ
Senior VP – Digital

JAY KOGAN
VP – Business and Legal Affairs,
Publishing

JACK MAHAN
VP – Business Affairs, Talent

NICK NAPOLITANO
VP – Manufacturing Administration

SUE POHJA
VP – Book Sales

COURTNEY SIMMONS
Senior VP – Publicity

BOB WAYNE
Senior VP – Sales

Certified Chain of Custody
At Least 25% Certified Forest Content
www.sfiprogram.org
SFI-01042
APPLIES TO TEXT STOCK ONLY

SUSTAINABLE
FORESTRY
INITIATIVE

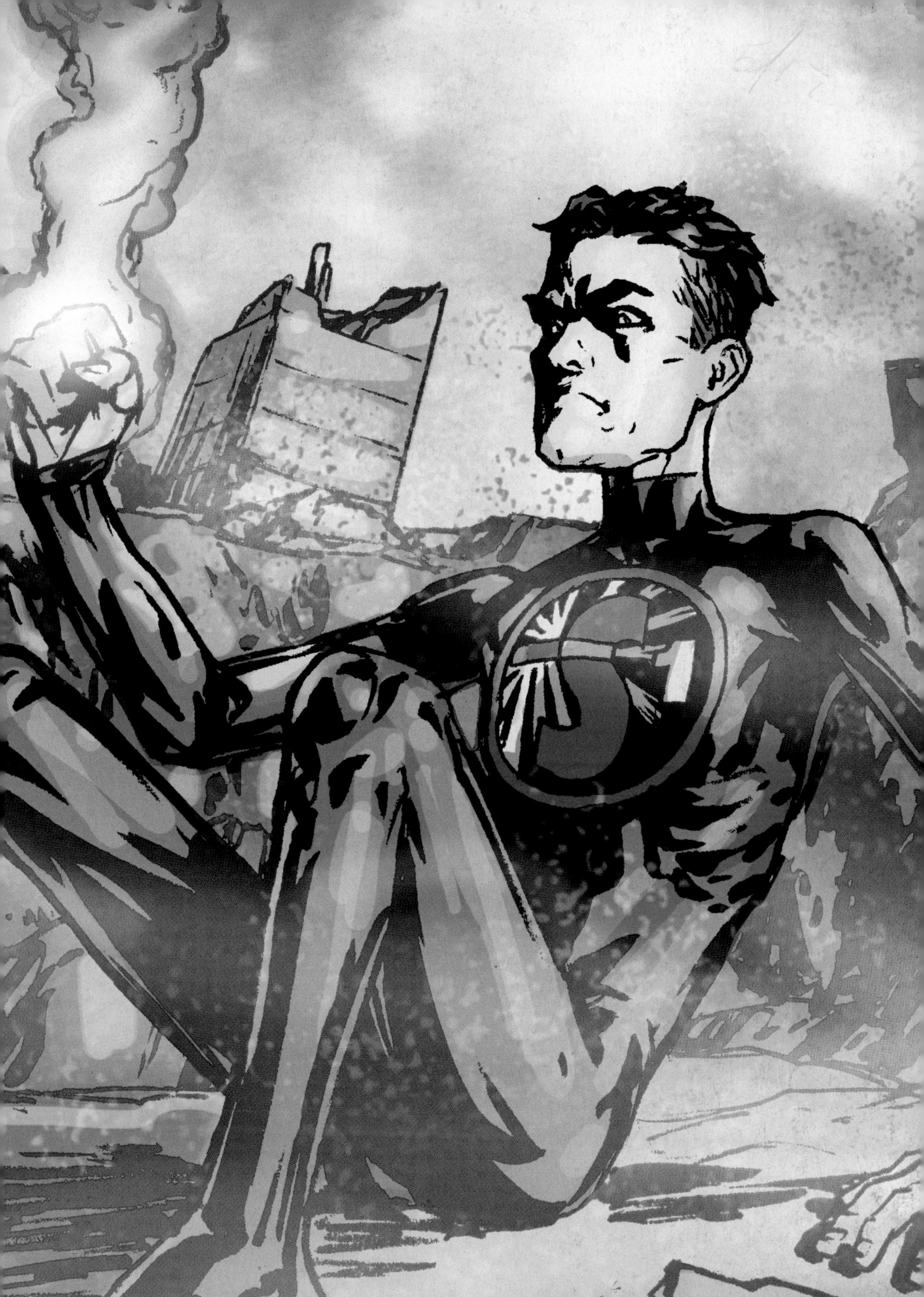

PROJECT SUPERMAN

SCOTT SNYDER
Plot

LOWELL FRANCIS
Co-Plot & Script

GENE HA
Art & Covers

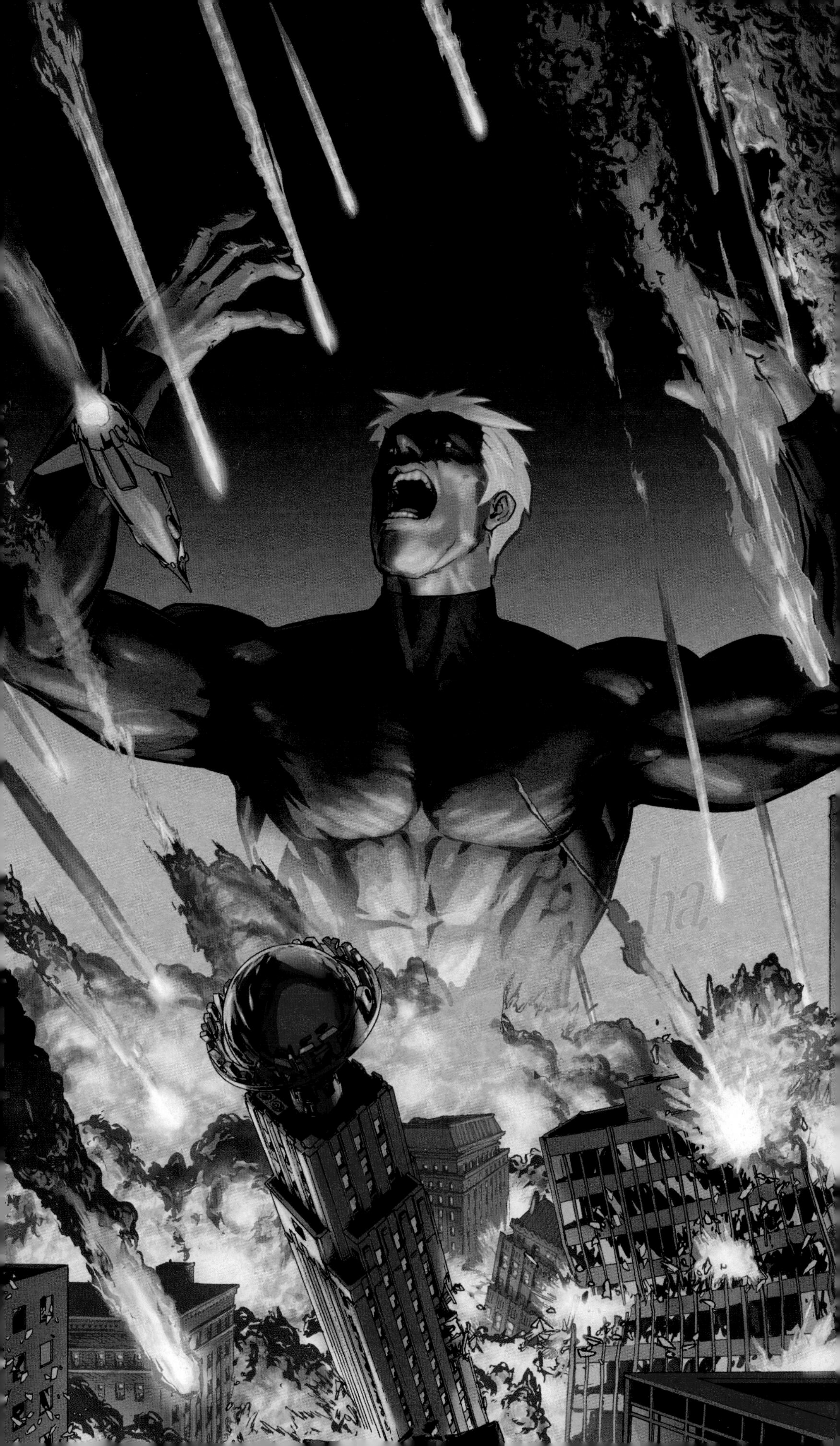
ha!

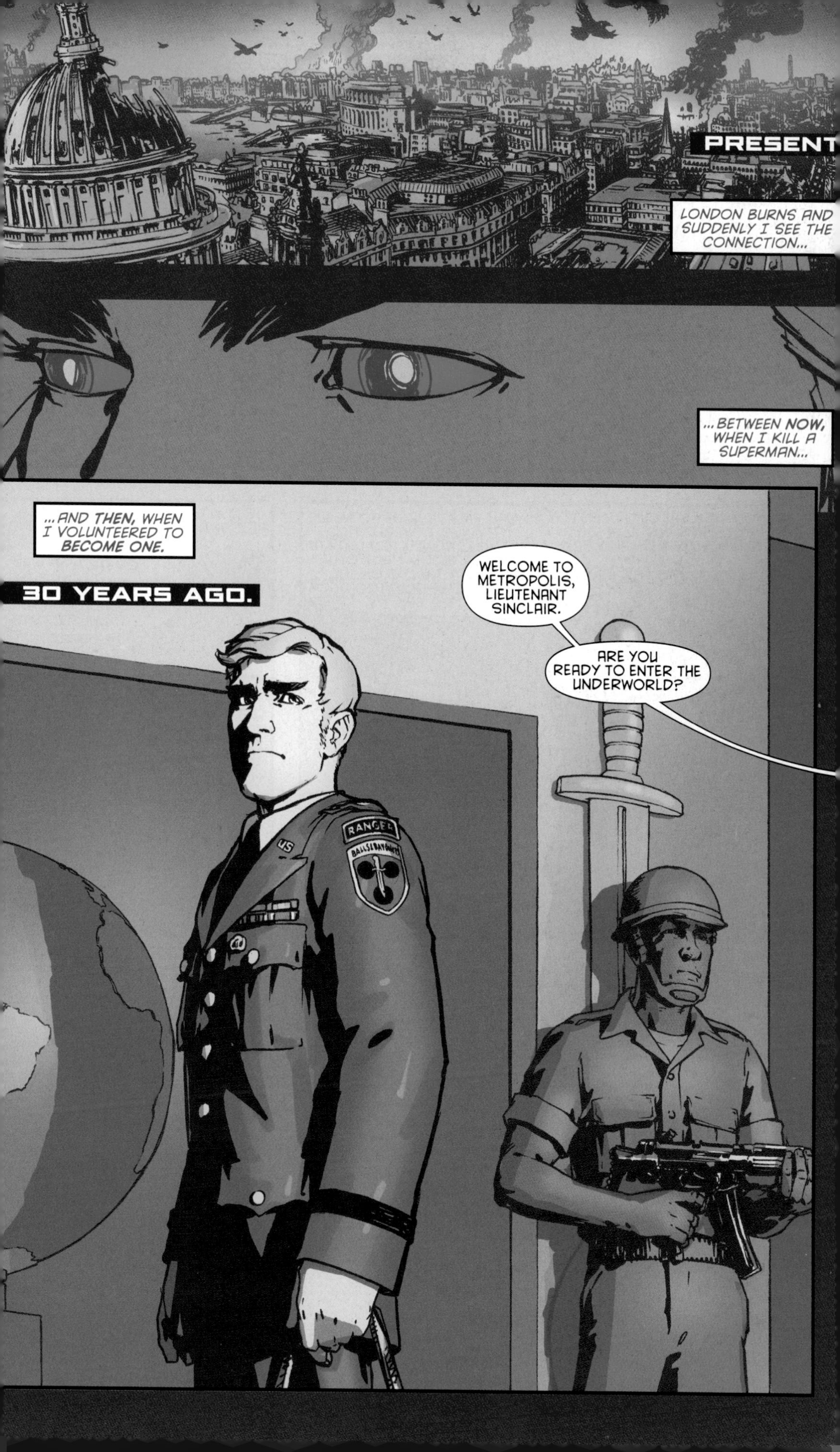
PRESENT
LONDON BURNS AND SUDDENLY I SEE THE CONNECTION...
...BETWEEN NOW, WHEN I KILL A SUPERMAN...
...AND THEN, WHEN I VOLUNTEERED TO BECOME ONE.
30 YEARS AGO.
WELCOME TO METROPOLIS, LIEUTENANT SINCLAIR.
ARE YOU READY TO ENTER THE UNDERWORLD?
RANGER
US

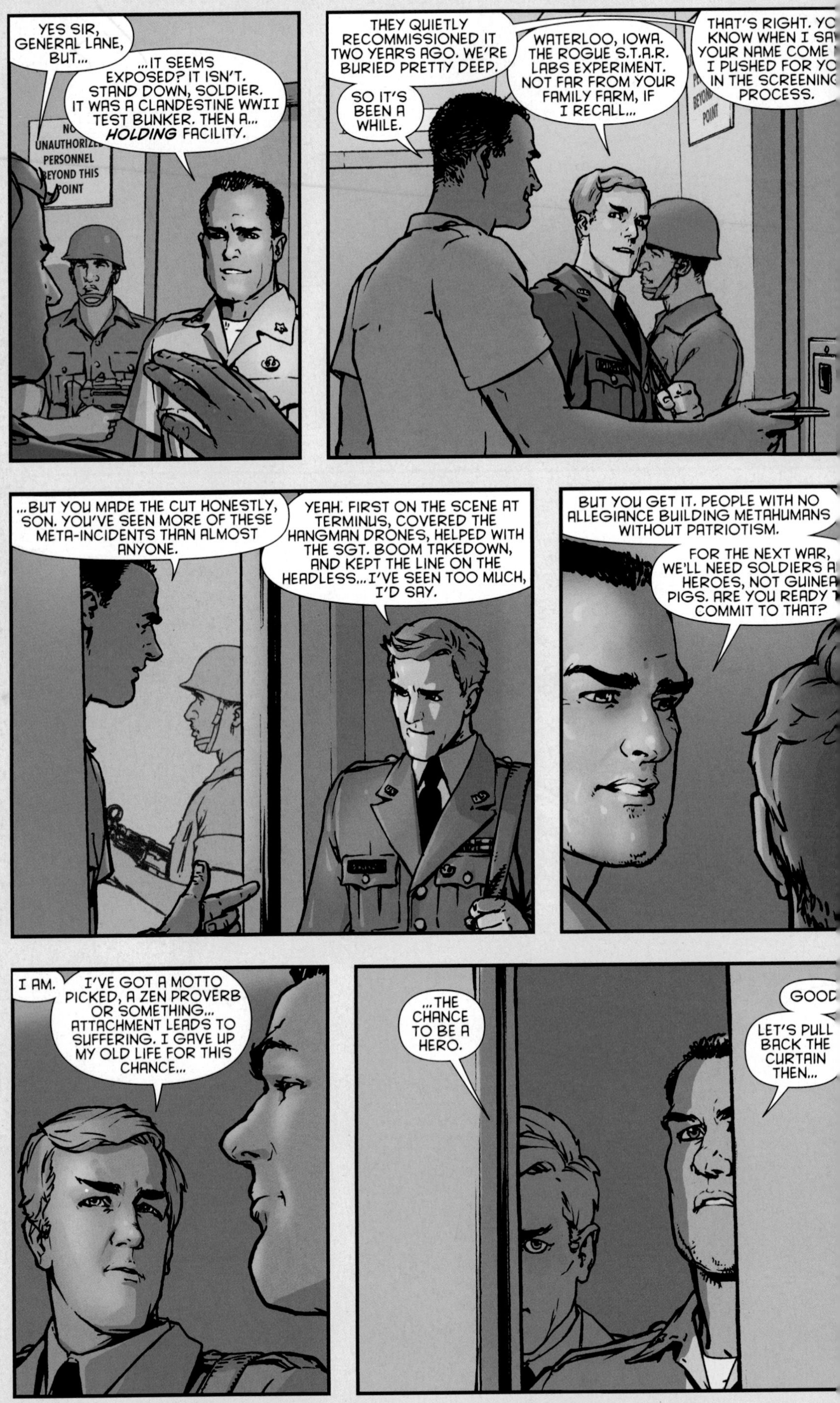

YES SIR, GENERAL LANE, BUT...
...IT SEEMS EXPOSED? IT ISN'T. STAND DOWN, SOLDIER. IT WAS A CLANDESTINE WWII TEST BUNKER. THEN A... HOLDING FACILITY.
NO UNAUTHORIZED PERSONNEL BEYOND THIS POINT
THEY QUIETLY RECOMMISSIONED IT TWO YEARS AGO. WE'RE BURIED PRETTY DEEP.
SO IT'S BEEN A WHILE.
WATERLOO, IOWA. THE ROGUE S.T.A.R. LABS EXPERIMENT. NOT FAR FROM YOUR FAMILY FARM, IF I RECALL...
THAT'S RIGHT. YO KNOW WHEN I SA YOUR NAME COME I PUSHED FOR YO IN THE SCREENING PROCESS.
...BUT YOU MADE THE CUT HONESTLY, SON. YOU'VE SEEN MORE OF THESE META-INCIDENTS THAN ALMOST ANYONE.
YEAH. FIRST ON THE SCENE AT TERMINUS, COVERED THE HANGMAN DRONES, HELPED WITH THE SGT. BOOM TAKEDOWN, AND KEPT THE LINE ON THE HEADLESS... I'VE SEEN TOO MUCH, I'D SAY.
BUT YOU GET IT. PEOPLE WITH NO ALLEGIANCE BUILDING METAHUMANS WITHOUT PATRIOTISM.
FOR THE NEXT WAR, WE'LL NEED SOLDIERS A HEROES, NOT GUINEA PIGS. ARE YOU READY T COMMIT TO THAT?
I AM.
I'VE GOT A MOTTO PICKED, A ZEN PROVERB OR SOMETHING... ATTACHMENT LEADS TO SUFFERING. I GAVE UP MY OLD LIFE FOR THIS CHANCE...
...THE CHANCE TO BE A HERO.
GOOD
LET'S PULL BACK THE CURTAIN THEN...

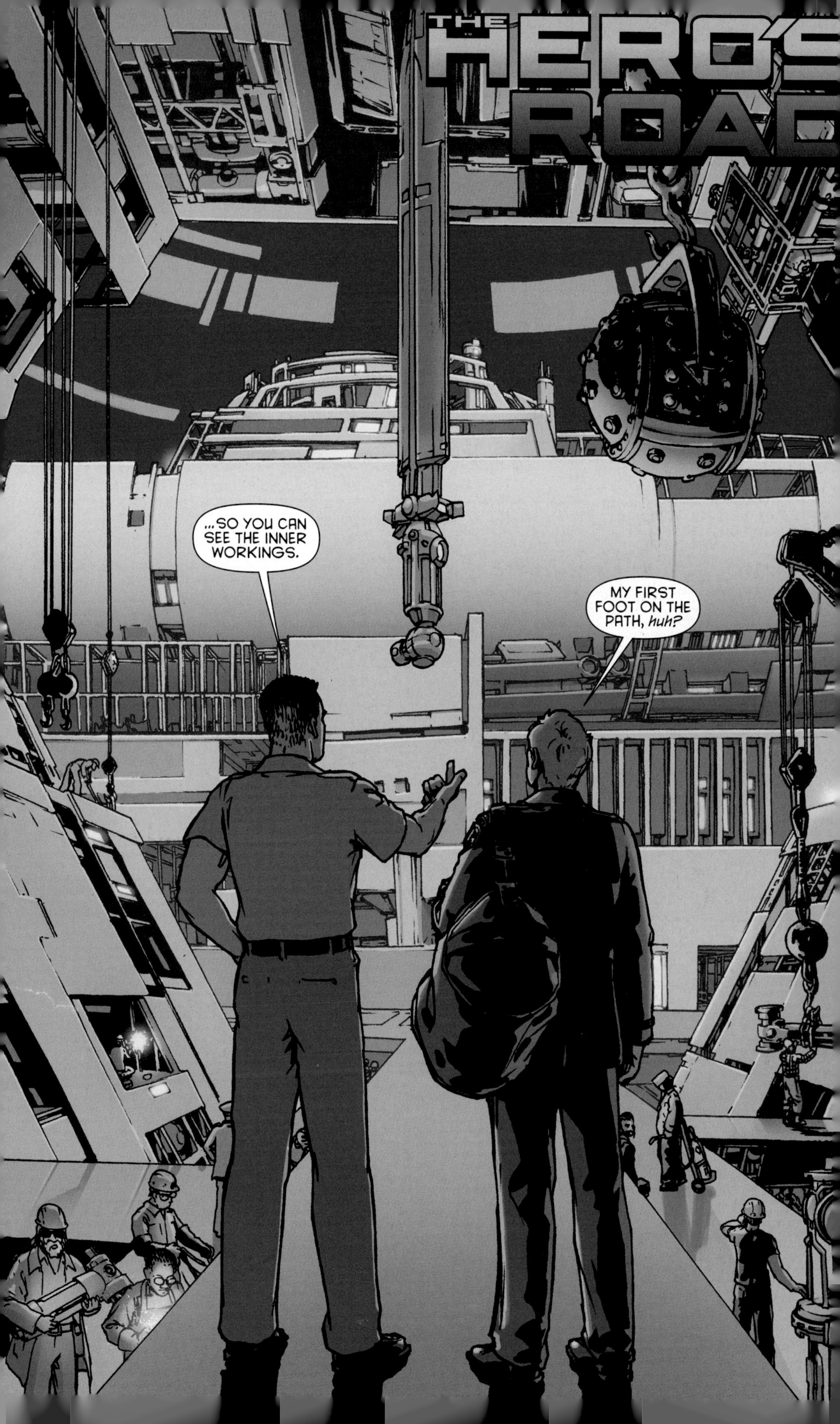
THE HERO'S ROAD
...SO YOU CAN SEE THE INNER WORKINGS.
MY FIRST FOOT ON THE PATH, *huh?*

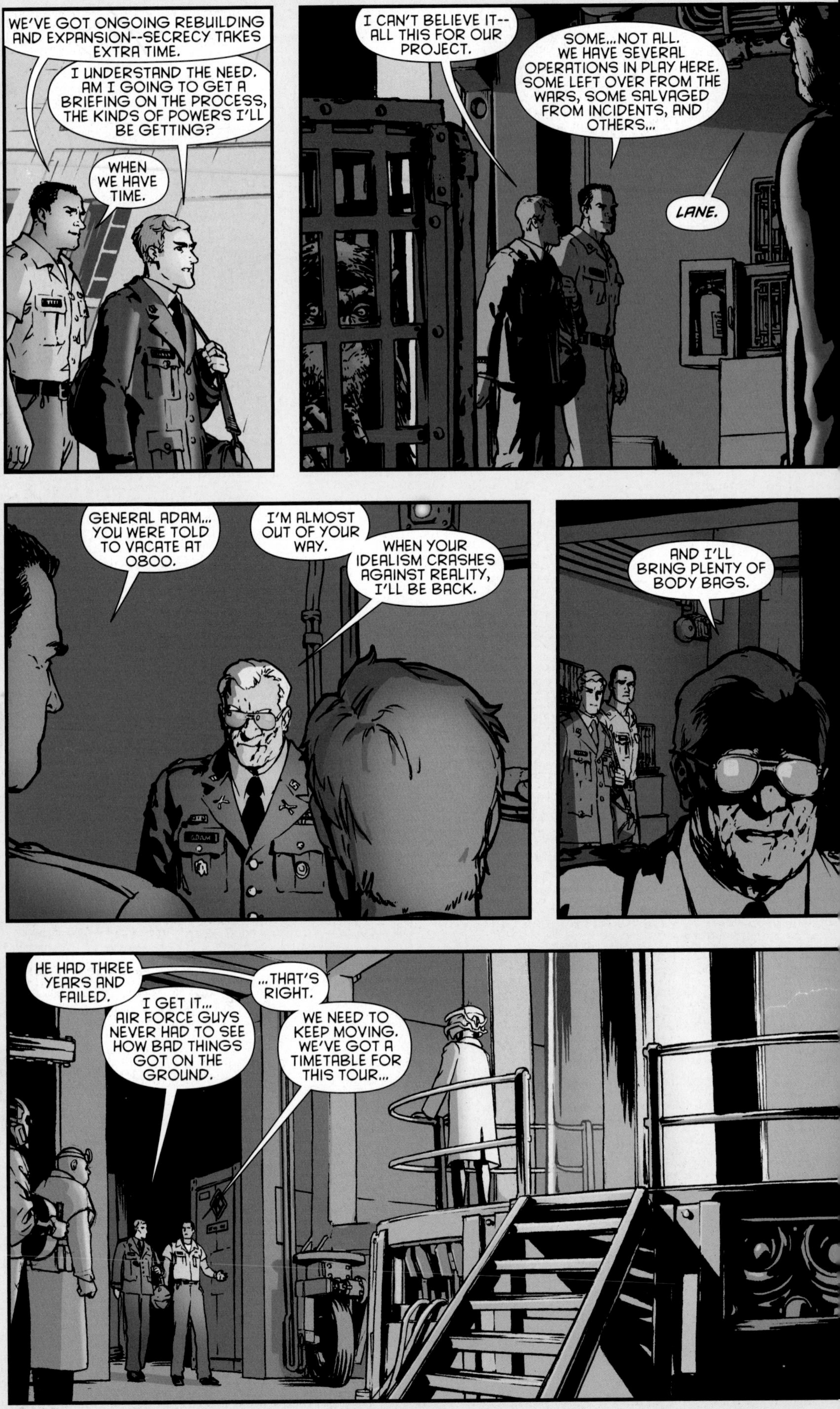
WE'VE GOT ONGOING REBUILDING AND EXPANSION--SECRECY TAKES EXTRA TIME.
I UNDERSTAND THE NEED. AM I GOING TO GET A BRIEFING ON THE PROCESS, THE KINDS OF POWERS I'LL BE GETTING?
WHEN WE HAVE TIME.
I CAN'T BELIEVE IT-- ALL THIS FOR OUR PROJECT.
SOME...NOT ALL. WE HAVE SEVERAL OPERATIONS IN PLAY HERE. SOME LEFT OVER FROM THE WARS, SOME SALVAGED FROM INCIDENTS, AND OTHERS...
LANE.
GENERAL ADAM... YOU WERE TOLD TO VACATE AT 0800.
I'M ALMOST OUT OF YOUR WAY.
WHEN YOUR IDEALISM CRASHES AGAINST REALITY, I'LL BE BACK.
AND I'LL BRING PLENTY OF BODY BAGS.
HE HAD THREE YEARS AND FAILED.
...THAT'S RIGHT.
I GET IT... AIR FORCE GUYS NEVER HAD TO SEE HOW BAD THINGS GOT ON THE GROUND.
WE NEED TO KEEP MOVING. WE'VE GOT A TIMETABLE FOR THIS TOUR...

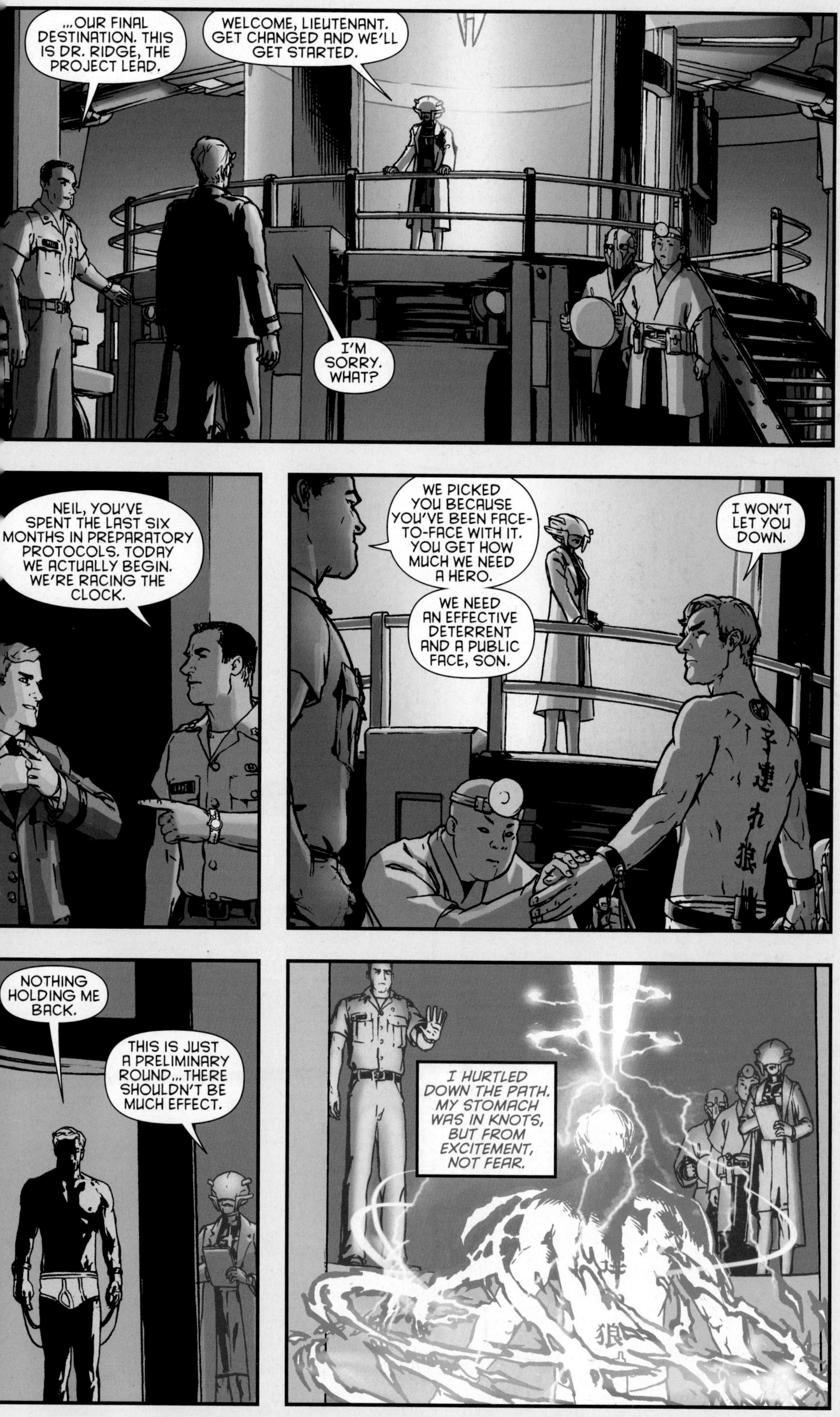
...OUR FINAL DESTINATION. THIS IS DR. RIDGE, THE PROJECT LEAD.
WELCOME, LIEUTENANT. GET CHANGED AND WE'LL GET STARTED.
I'M SORRY. WHAT?
NEIL, YOU'VE SPENT THE LAST SIX MONTHS IN PREPARATORY PROTOCOLS. TODAY WE ACTUALLY BEGIN. WE'RE RACING THE CLOCK.
WE PICKED YOU BECAUSE YOU'VE BEEN FACE-TO-FACE WITH IT. YOU GET HOW MUCH WE NEED A HERO.
WE NEED AN EFFECTIVE DETERRENT AND A PUBLIC FACE, SON.
I WON'T LET YOU DOWN.
NOTHING HOLDING ME BACK.
THIS IS JUST A PRELIMINARY ROUND...THERE SHOULDN'T BE MUCH EFFECT.
I HURTLED DOWN THE PATH. MY STOMACH WAS IN KNOTS, BUT FROM EXCITEMENT, NOT FEAR.

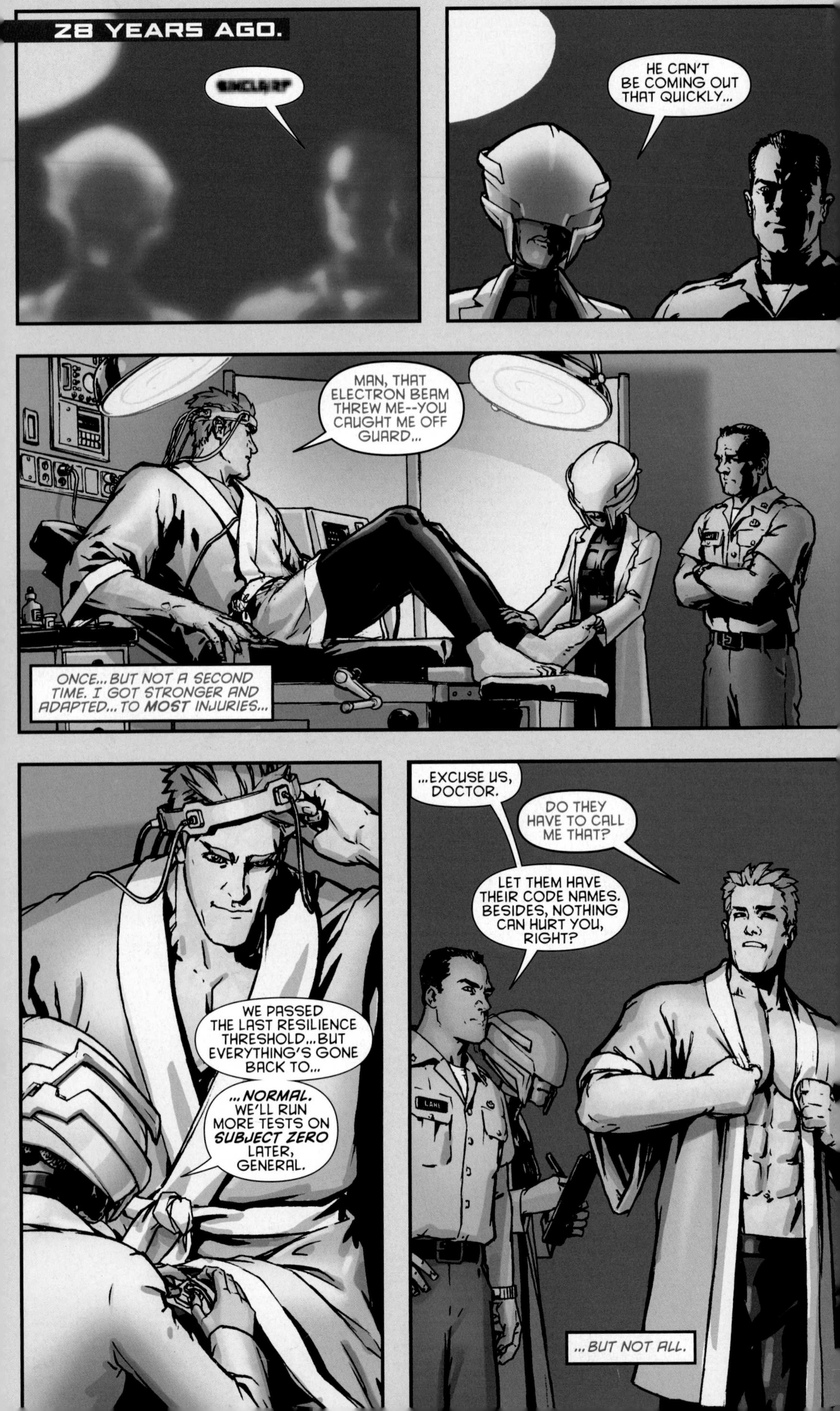
28 YEARS AGO.
HE CAN'T BE COMING OUT THAT QUICKLY...
MAN, THAT ELECTRON BEAM THREW ME--YOU CAUGHT ME OFF GUARD...
ONCE... BUT NOT A SECOND TIME. I GOT STRONGER AND ADAPTED... TO MOST INJURIES...
WE PASSED THE LAST RESILIENCE THRESHOLD... BUT EVERYTHING'S GONE BACK TO...
...NORMAL. WE'LL RUN MORE TESTS ON SUBJECT ZERO LATER, GENERAL.
...EXCUSE US, DOCTOR.
DO THEY HAVE TO CALL ME THAT?
LET THEM HAVE THEIR CODE NAMES. BESIDES, NOTHING CAN HURT YOU, RIGHT?
...BUT NOT ALL.

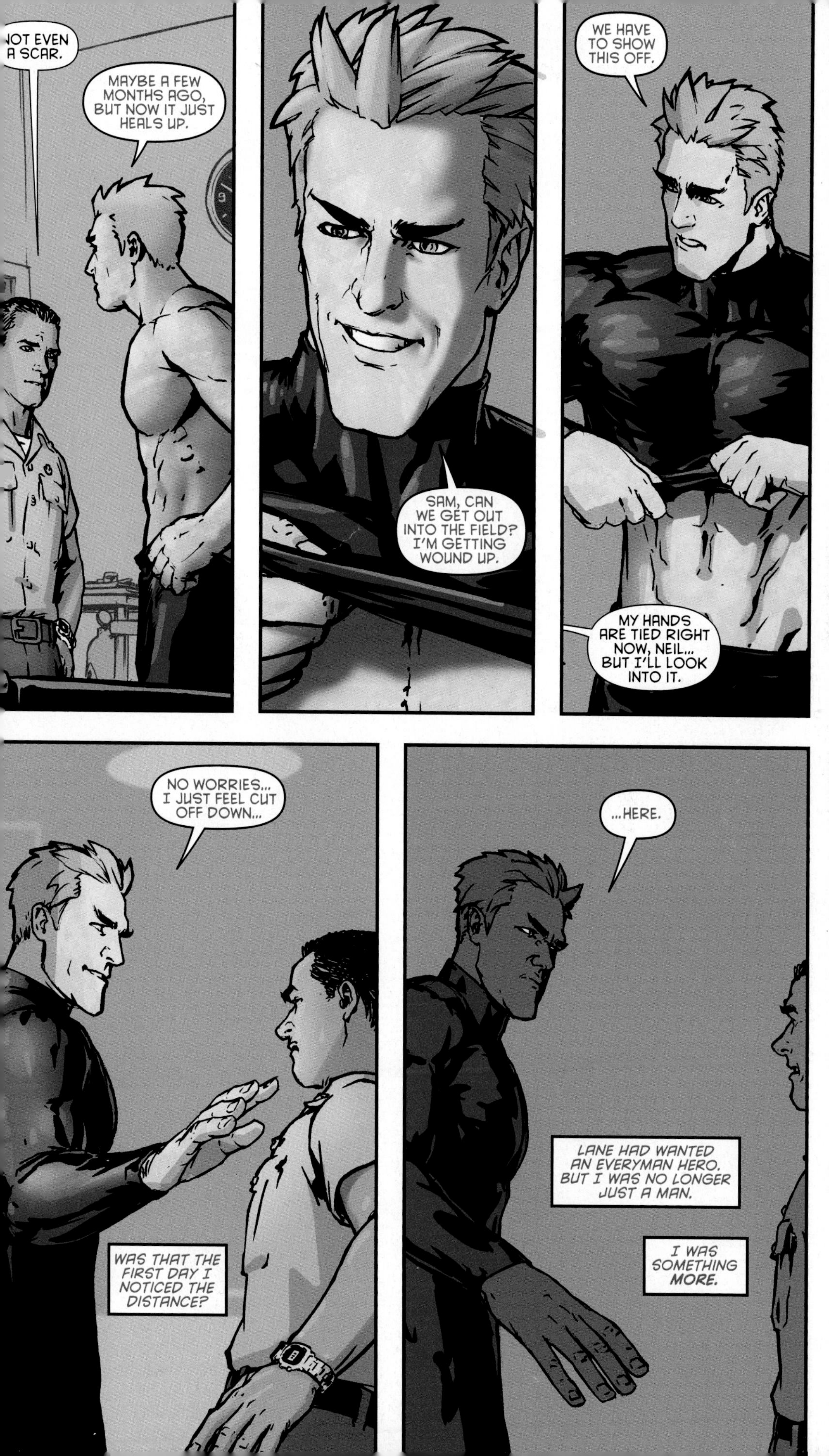
NOT EVEN A SCAR.
MAYBE A FEW MONTHS AGO, BUT NOW IT JUST HEALS UP.
SAM, CAN WE GET OUT INTO THE FIELD? I'M GETTING WOUND UP.
WE HAVE TO SHOW THIS OFF.
MY HANDS ARE TIED RIGHT NOW, NEIL... BUT I'LL LOOK INTO IT.
NO WORRIES... I JUST FEEL CUT OFF DOWN...
WAS THAT THE FIRST DAY I NOTICED THE DISTANCE?
...HERE.
LANE HAD WANTED AN EVERYMAN HERO. BUT I WAS NO LONGER JUST A MAN.
I WAS SOMETHING MORE.

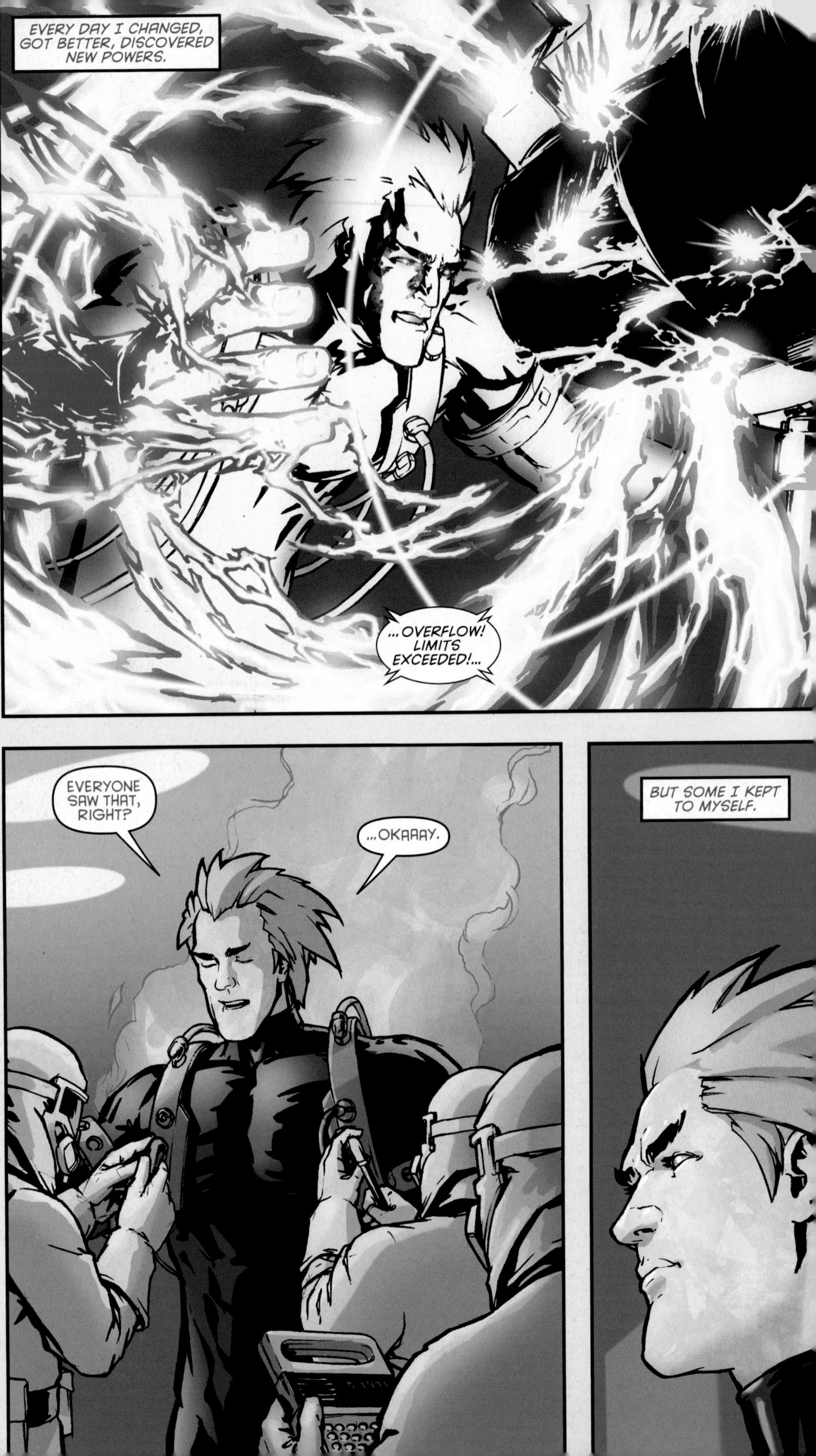
EVERY DAY I CHANGED, GOT BETTER, DISCOVERED NEW POWERS.
...OVERFLOW! LIMITS EXCEEDED!...
EVERYONE SAW THAT, RIGHT?
...OKAAAY.
BUT SOME I KEPT TO MYSELF.

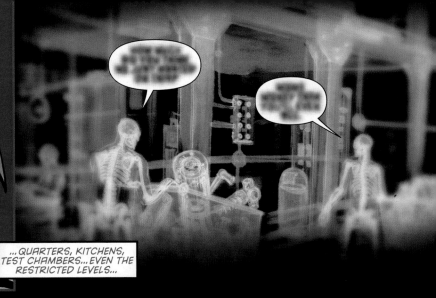

IF THEY KNEW I COULD SEE EVERYTHING...

...QUARTERS, KITCHENS, TEST CHAMBERS...EVEN THE RESTRICTED LEVELS...

CREEPY KEEPS LOOKING

WHICH MIGHT HAVE BEEN BETTER.

THEY MIGHT FIND A WAY TO BLOCK IT.

...SPECULATE HOW MUCH FURTHER THIS WILL GO, DR. RIDGE.

FIRST, UNDERSTAND THAT THE INTERACTIONS BETWEEN THE HUMAN AND *PROJECT SIX ALIEN DNA* ARE ADAPTIVE, NOT UNSTABLE, GENERAL.

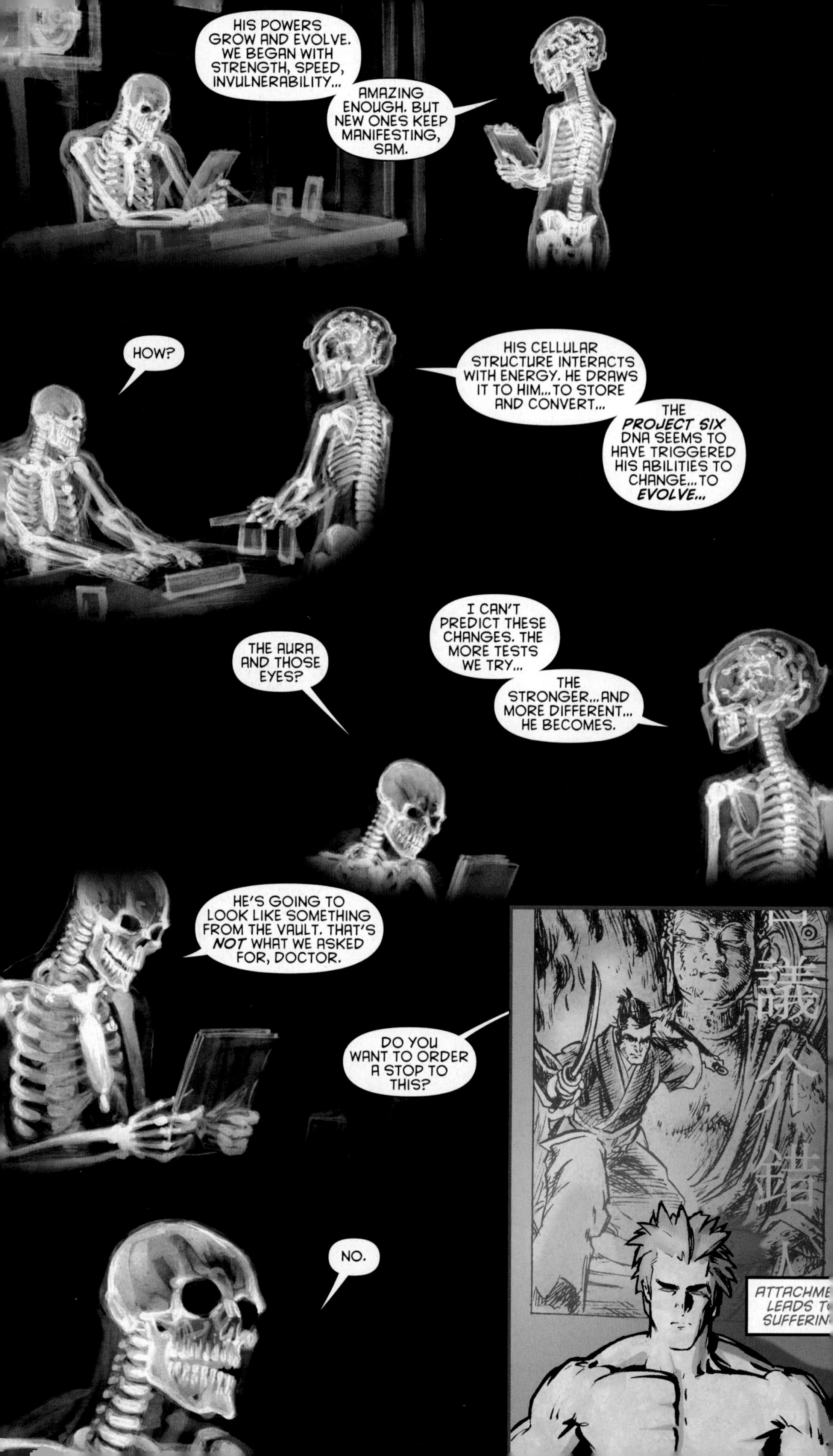
HIS POWERS GROW AND EVOLVE. WE BEGAN WITH STRENGTH, SPEED, INVULNERABILITY...
AMAZING ENOUGH. BUT NEW ONES KEEP MANIFESTING, SAM.
HOW?
HIS CELLULAR STRUCTURE INTERACTS WITH ENERGY. HE DRAWS IT TO HIM...TO STORE AND CONVERT...
THE *PROJECT SIX* DNA SEEMS TO HAVE TRIGGERED HIS ABILITIES TO CHANGE...TO *EVOLVE...*
THE AURA AND THOSE EYES?
I CAN'T PREDICT THESE CHANGES. THE MORE TESTS WE TRY...
THE STRONGER...AND MORE DIFFERENT... HE BECOMES.
HE'S GOING TO LOOK LIKE SOMETHING FROM THE VAULT. THAT'S *NOT* WHAT WE ASKED FOR, DOCTOR.
DO YOU WANT TO ORDER A STOP TO THIS?
NO.

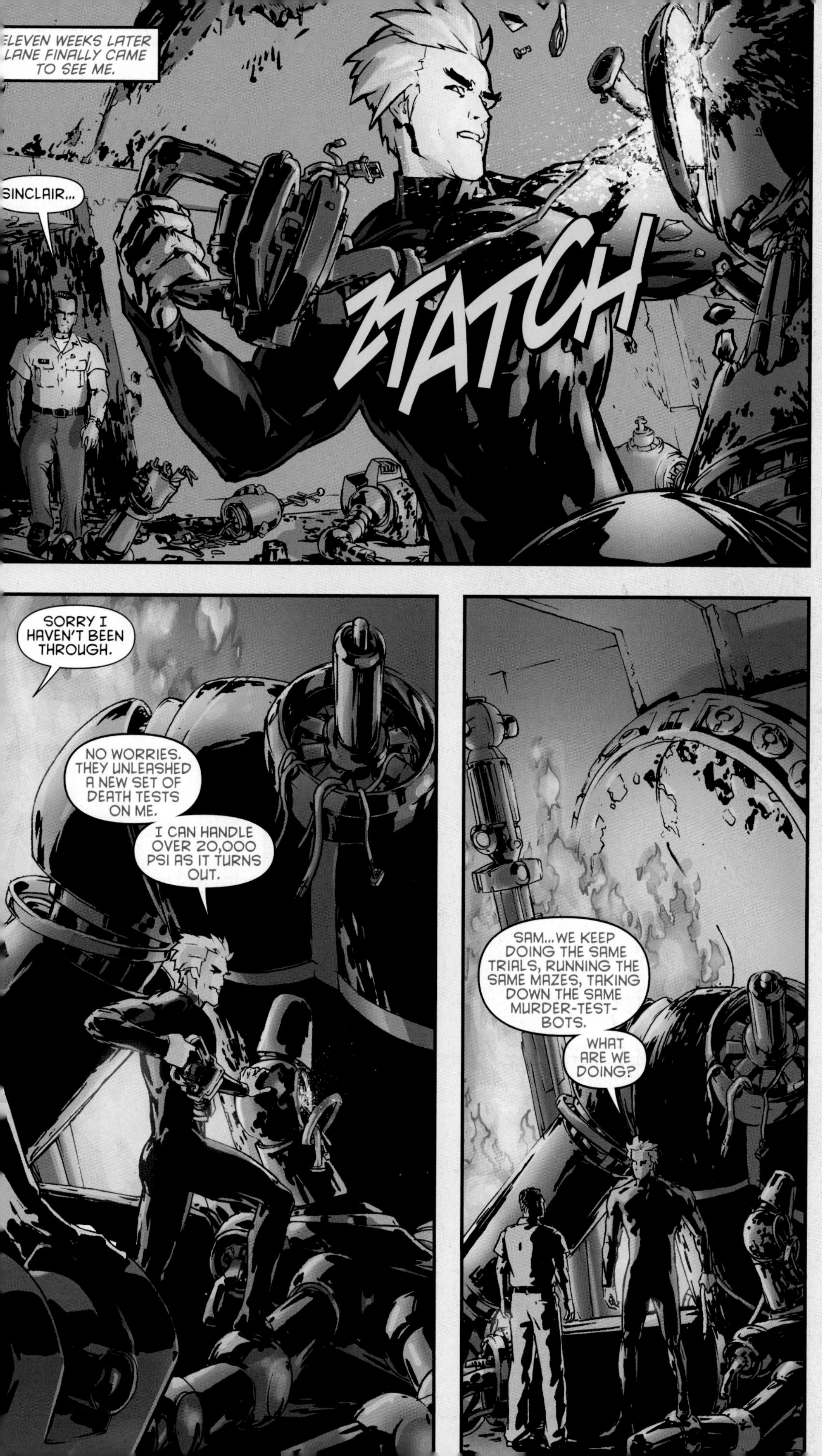
ELEVEN WEEKS LATER LANE FINALLY CAME TO SEE ME.
SINCLAIR...
ZTATCH
SORRY I HAVEN'T BEEN THROUGH.
NO WORRIES. THEY UNLEASHED A NEW SET OF DEATH TESTS ON ME.
I CAN HANDLE OVER 20,000 PSI AS IT TURNS OUT.
SAM...WE KEEP DOING THE SAME TRIALS, RUNNING THE SAME MAZES, TAKING DOWN THE SAME MURDER-TEST-BOTS.
WHAT ARE WE DOING?

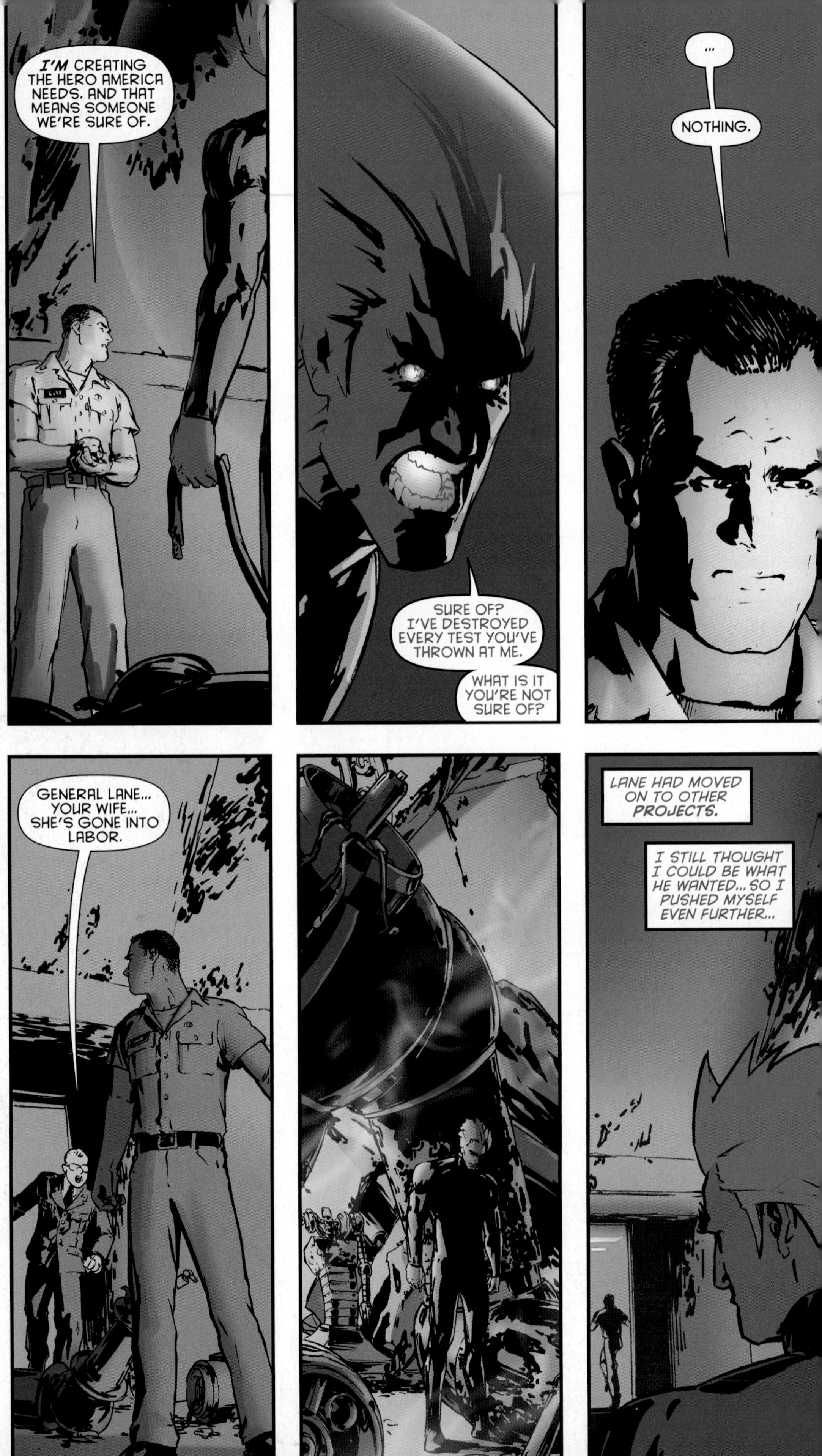
I'M CREATING THE HERO AMERICA NEEDS. AND THAT MEANS SOMEONE WE'RE SURE OF.
SURE OF? I'VE DESTROYED EVERY TEST YOU'VE THROWN AT ME.
WHAT IS IT YOU'RE NOT SURE OF?
...
NOTHING.
GENERAL LANE... YOUR WIFE... SHE'S GONE INTO LABOR.
LANE HAD MOVED ON TO OTHER PROJECTS.
I STILL THOUGHT I COULD BE WHAT HE WANTED... SO I PUSHED MYSELF EVEN FURTHER...

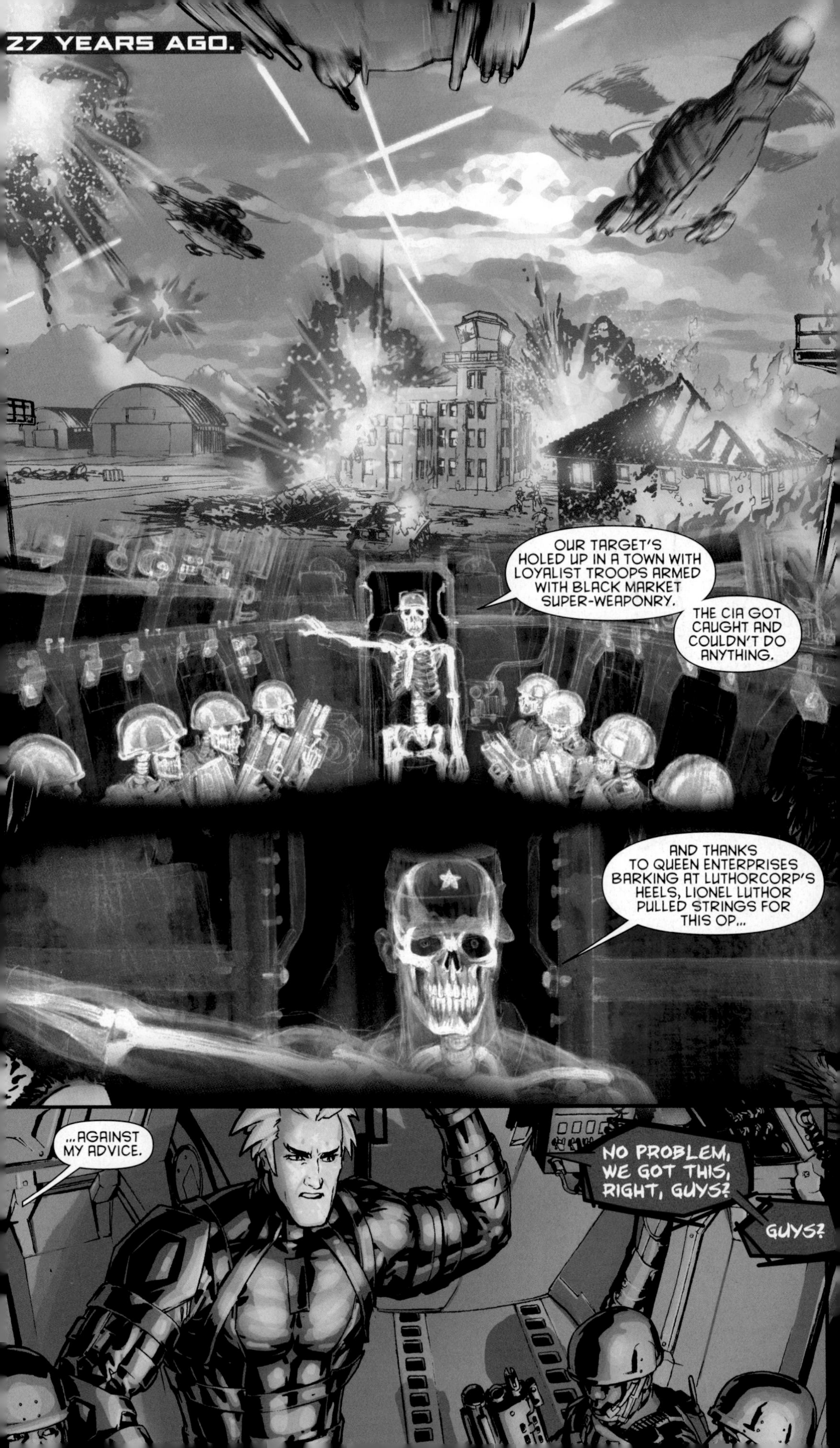
27 YEARS AGO.
OUR TARGET'S HOLED UP IN A TOWN WITH LOYALIST TROOPS ARMED WITH BLACK MARKET SUPER-WEAPONRY.
THE CIA GOT CAUGHT AND COULDN'T DO ANYTHING.
AND THANKS TO QUEEN ENTERPRISES BARKING AT LUTHORCORP'S HEELS, LIONEL LUTHOR PULLED STRINGS FOR THIS OP...
...AGAINST MY ADVICE.
NO PROBLEM, WE GOT THIS, RIGHT, GUYS?
GUYS?

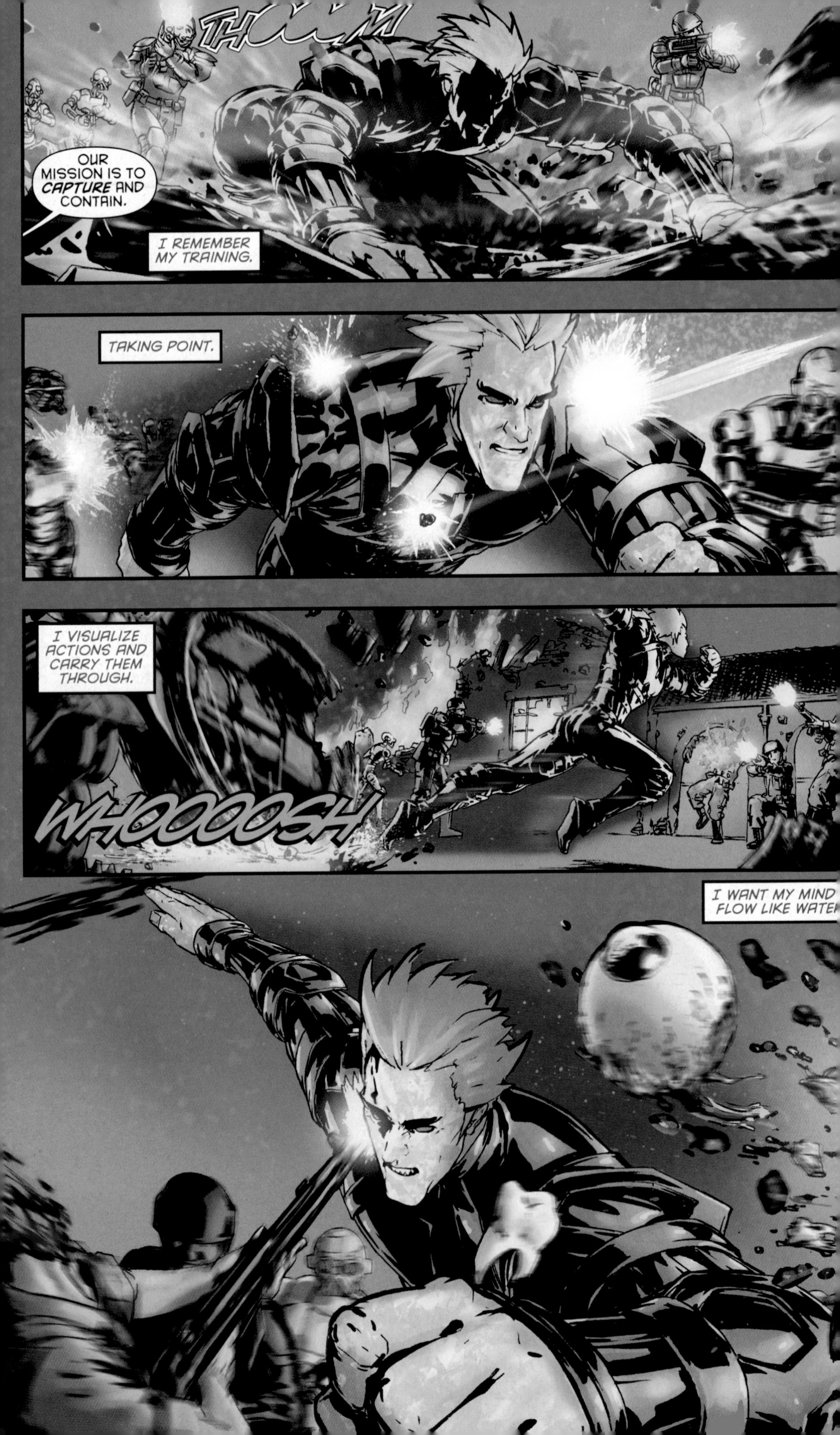
THOOM
OUR MISSION IS TO CAPTURE AND CONTAIN.
I REMEMBER MY TRAINING.
TAKING POINT.
I VISUALIZE ACTIONS AND CARRY THEM THROUGH.
WHOOOOSH
I WANT MY MIND FLOW LIKE WATER

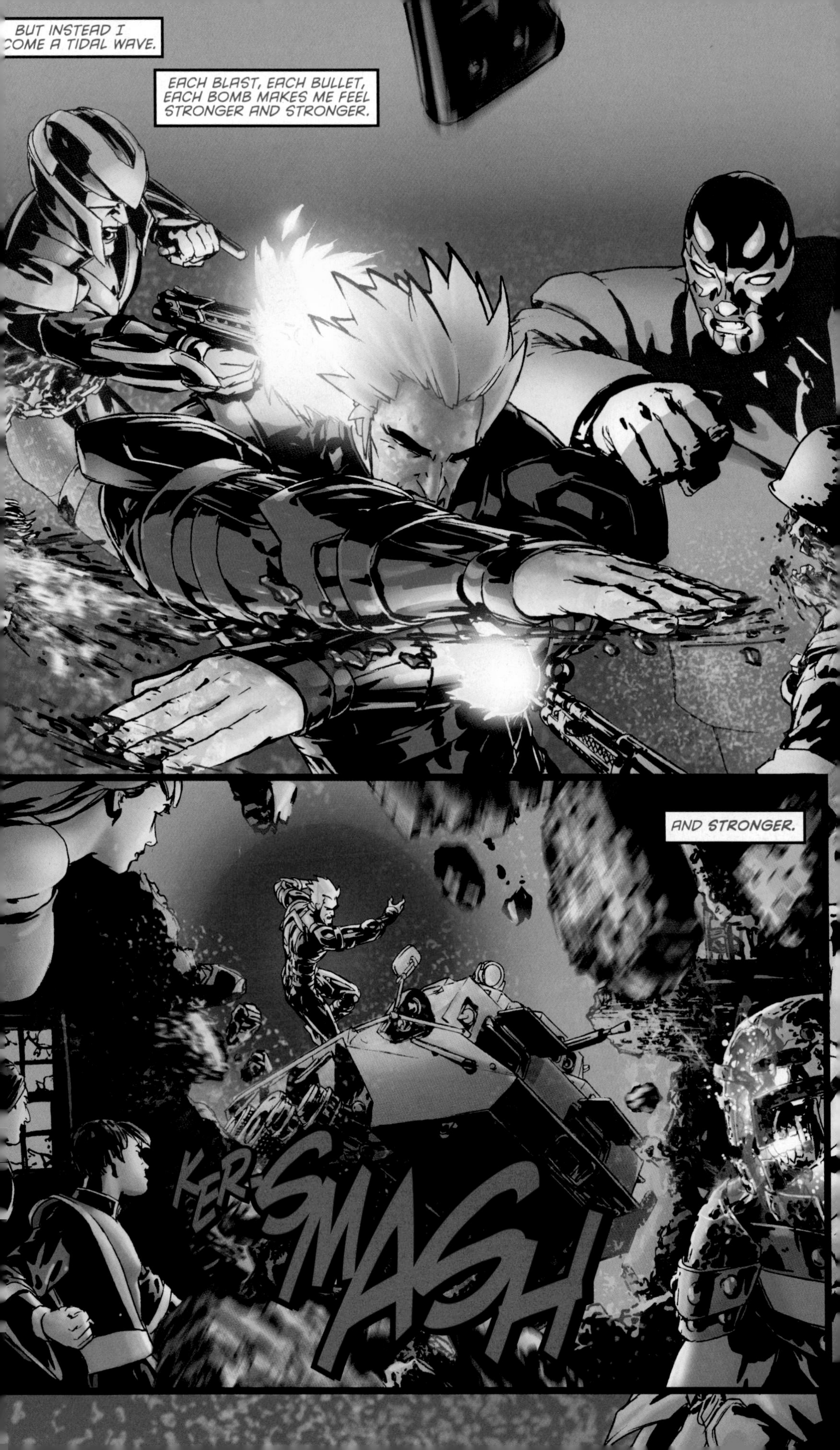

BUT INSTEAD I COME A TIDAL WAVE.
EACH BLAST, EACH BULLET, EACH BOMB MAKES ME FEEL STRONGER AND STRONGER.
AND STRONGER.
KER SMASH

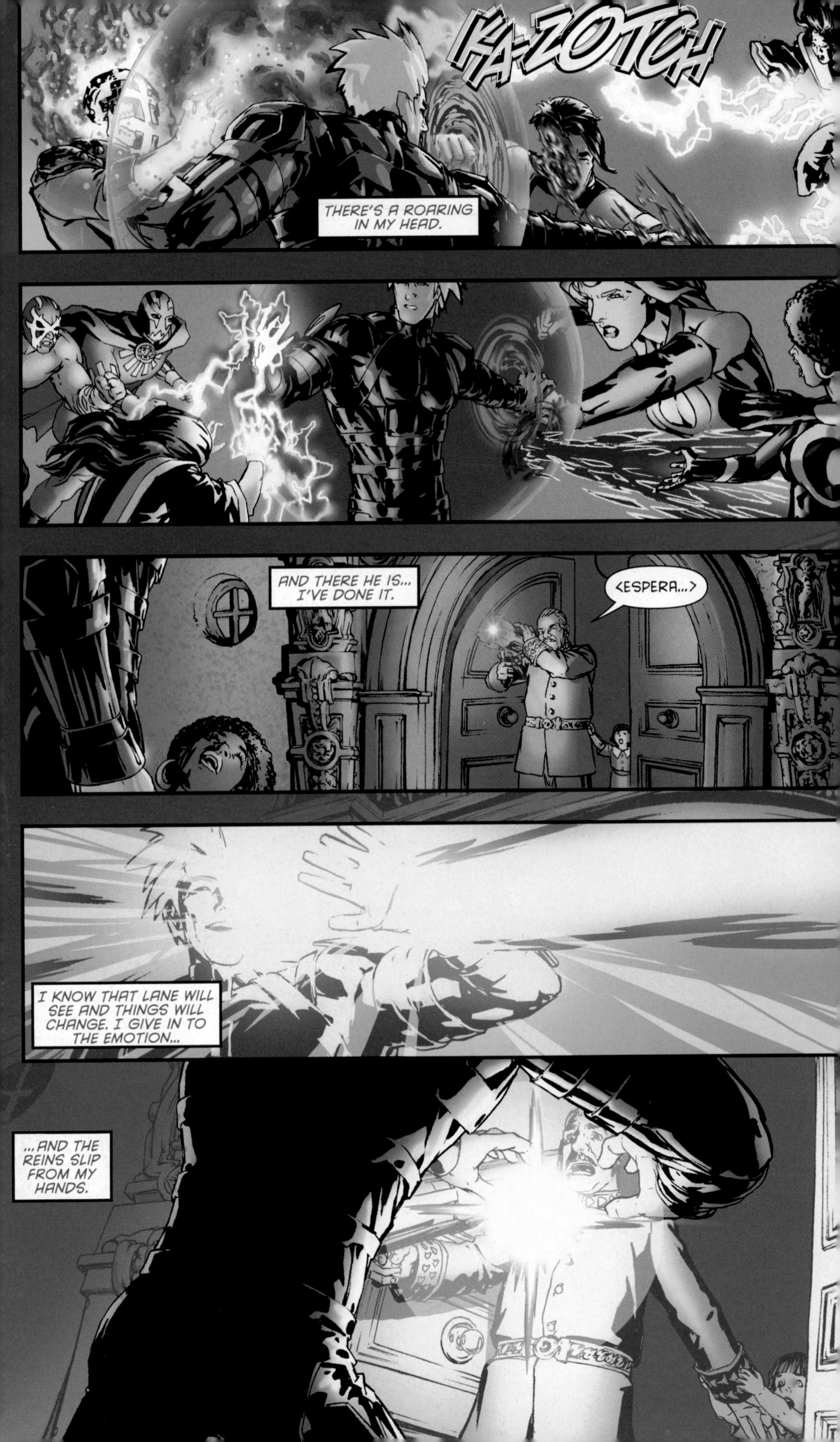
KA-ZOTCH
THERE'S A ROARING IN MY HEAD.
AND THERE HE IS... I'VE DONE IT.
<ESPERA...>
I KNOW THAT LANE WILL SEE AND THINGS WILL CHANGE. I GIVE IN TO THE EMOTION...
...AND THE REINS SLIP FROM MY HANDS.

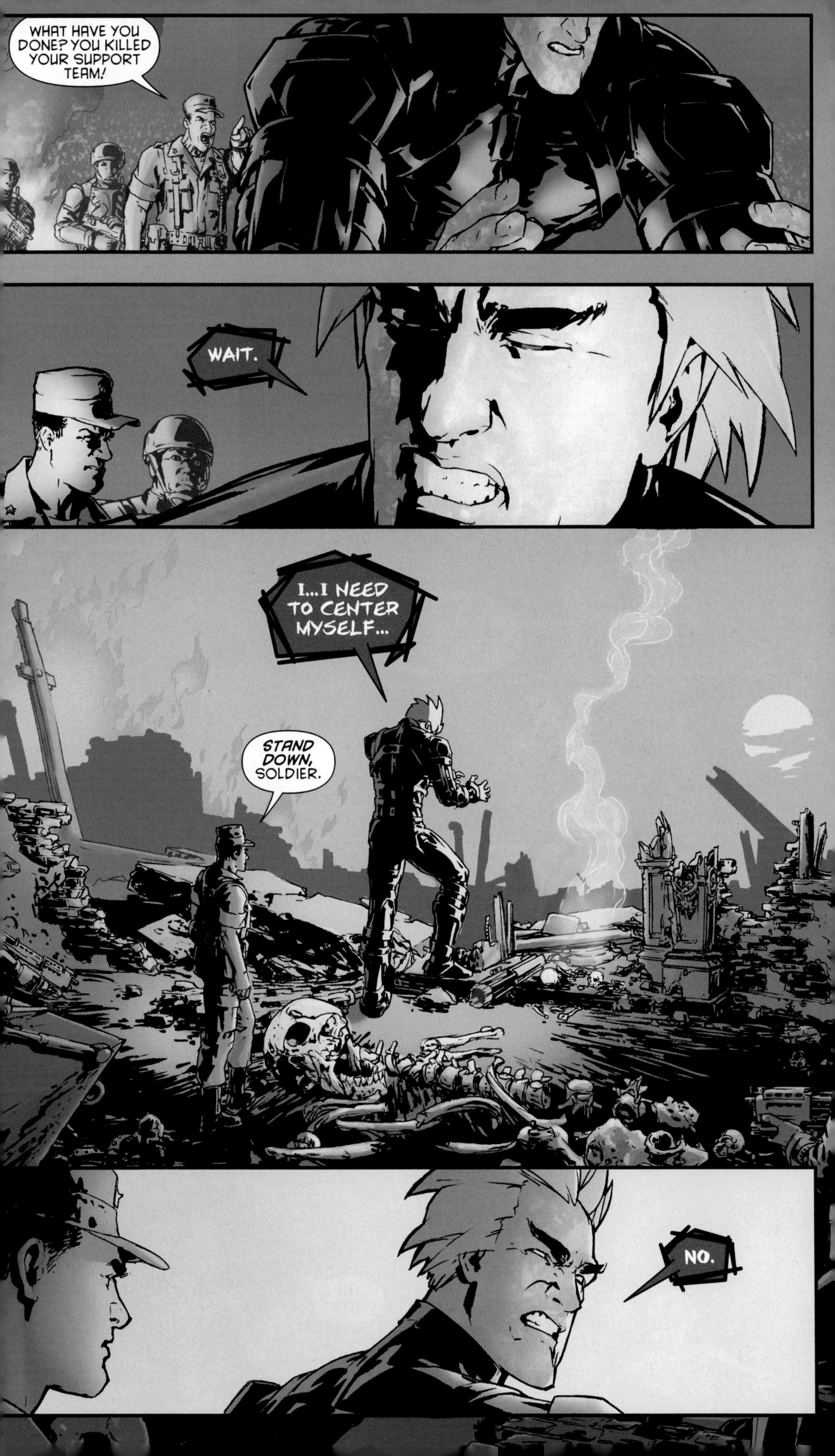
WHAT HAVE YOU DONE? YOU KILLED YOUR SUPPORT TEAM!
WAIT.
I...I NEED TO CENTER MYSELF...
STAND DOWN, SOLDIER.
NO.

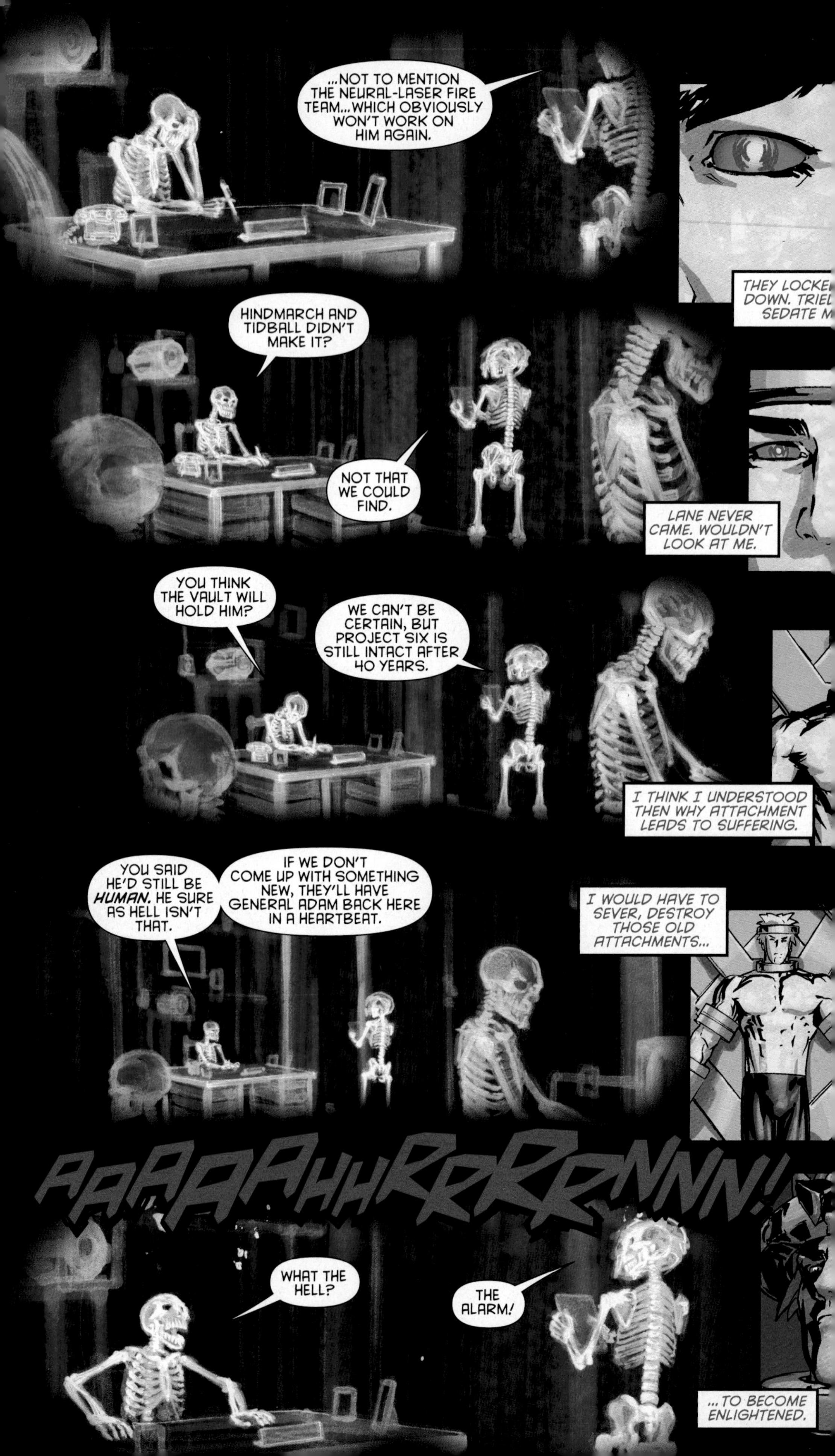
...NOT TO MENTION THE NEURAL-LASER FIRE TEAM...WHICH OBVIOUSLY WON'T WORK ON HIM AGAIN.
HINDMARCH AND TIDBALL DIDN'T MAKE IT?
NOT THAT WE COULD FIND.
YOU THINK THE VAULT WILL HOLD HIM?
WE CAN'T BE CERTAIN, BUT PROJECT SIX IS STILL INTACT AFTER 40 YEARS.
YOU SAID HE'D STILL BE HUMAN. HE SURE AS HELL ISN'T THAT.
IF WE DON'T COME UP WITH SOMETHING NEW, THEY'LL HAVE GENERAL ADAM BACK HERE IN A HEARTBEAT.
AAAAAHHHRRRRNNNN!
WHAT THE HELL?
THE ALARM!
LANE NEVER CAME. WOULDN'T LOOK AT ME.
I THINK I UNDERSTOOD THEN WHY ATTACHMENT LEADS TO SUFFERING.
I WOULD HAVE TO SEVER, DESTROY THOSE OLD ATTACHMENTS...
...TO BECOME ENLIGHTENED.

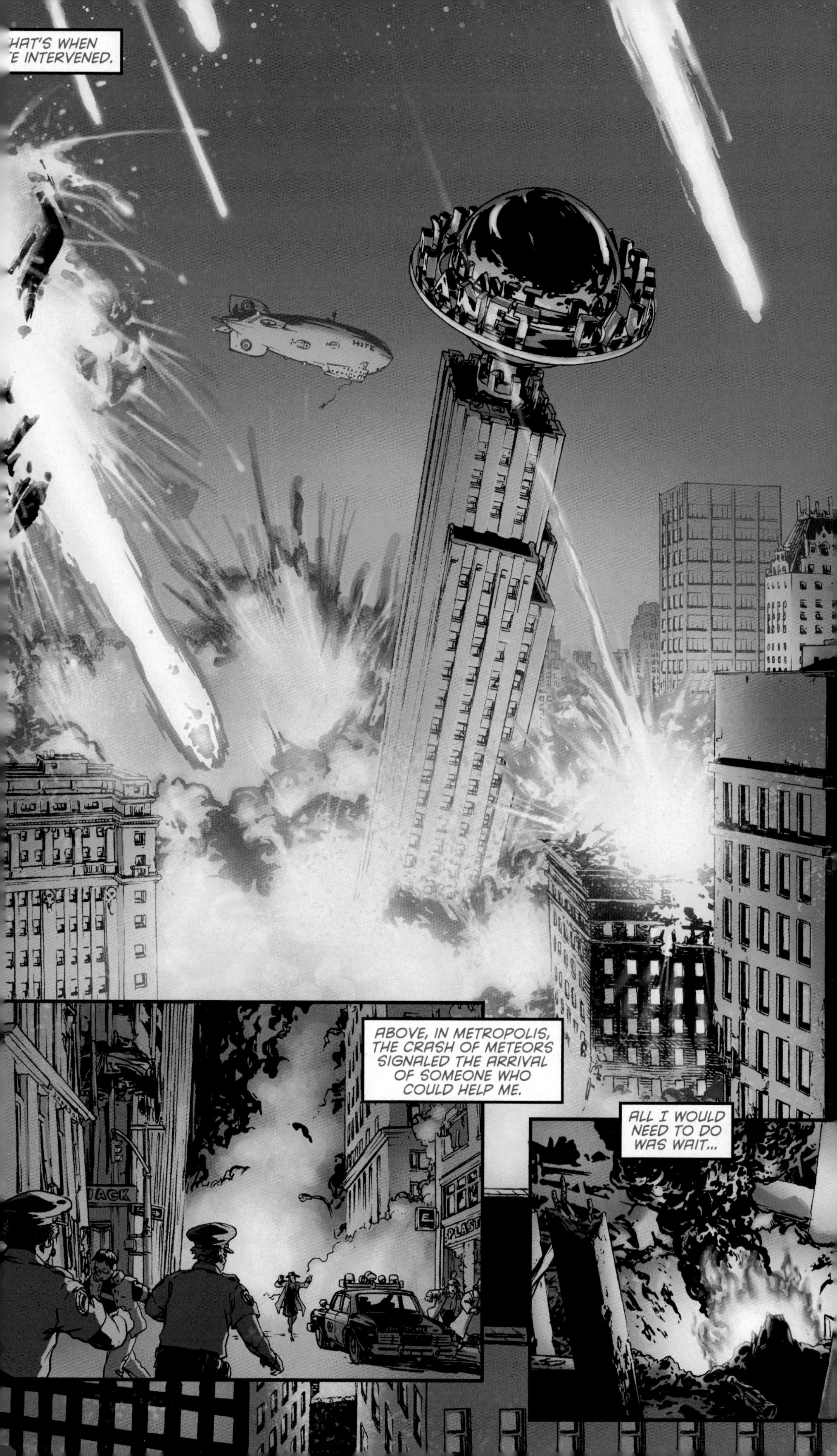
HAT'S WHEN
E INTERVENED.
HITE
ABOVE, IN METROPOLIS, THE CRASH OF METEORS SIGNALED THE ARRIVAL OF SOMEONE WHO COULD HELP ME.
ALL I WOULD NEED TO DO WAS WAIT...

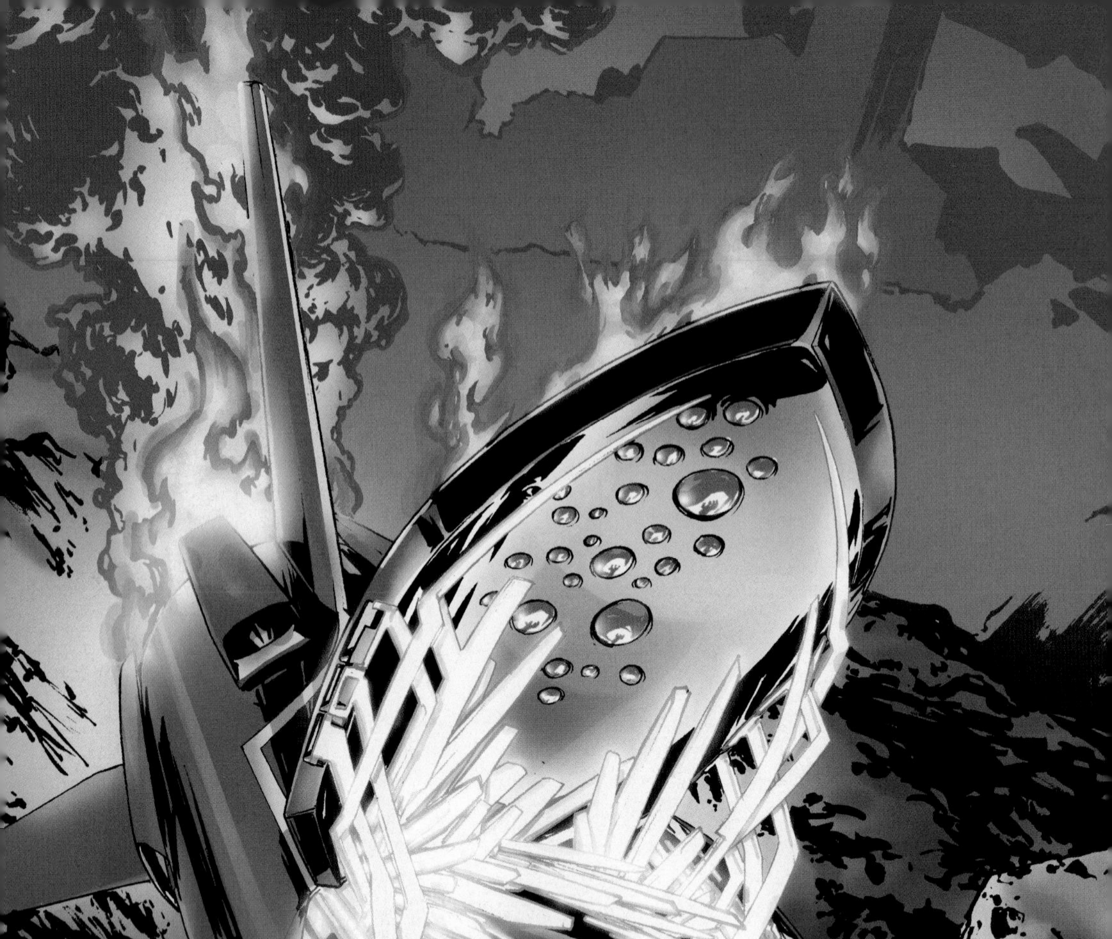
...AFTER ALL, TIMING IS EVERYTHING.

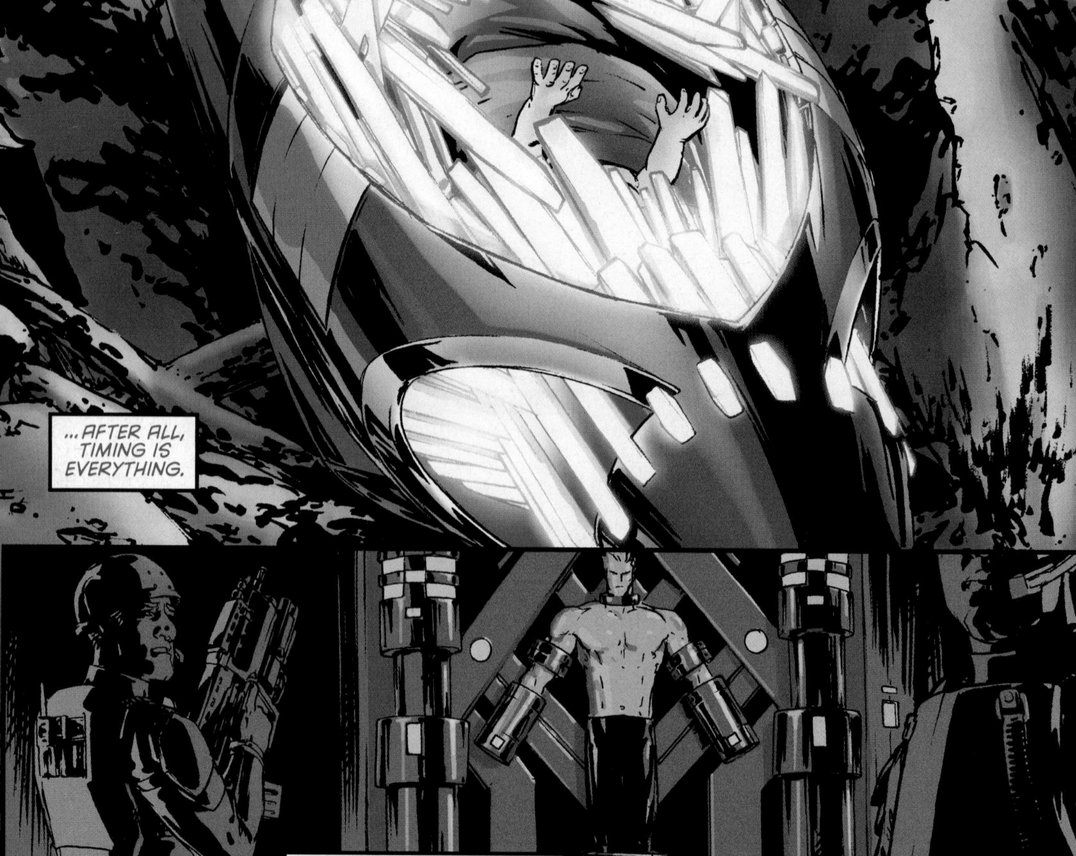
SOON, I WOULD SHOW GENERAL LANE THE TRUTH.

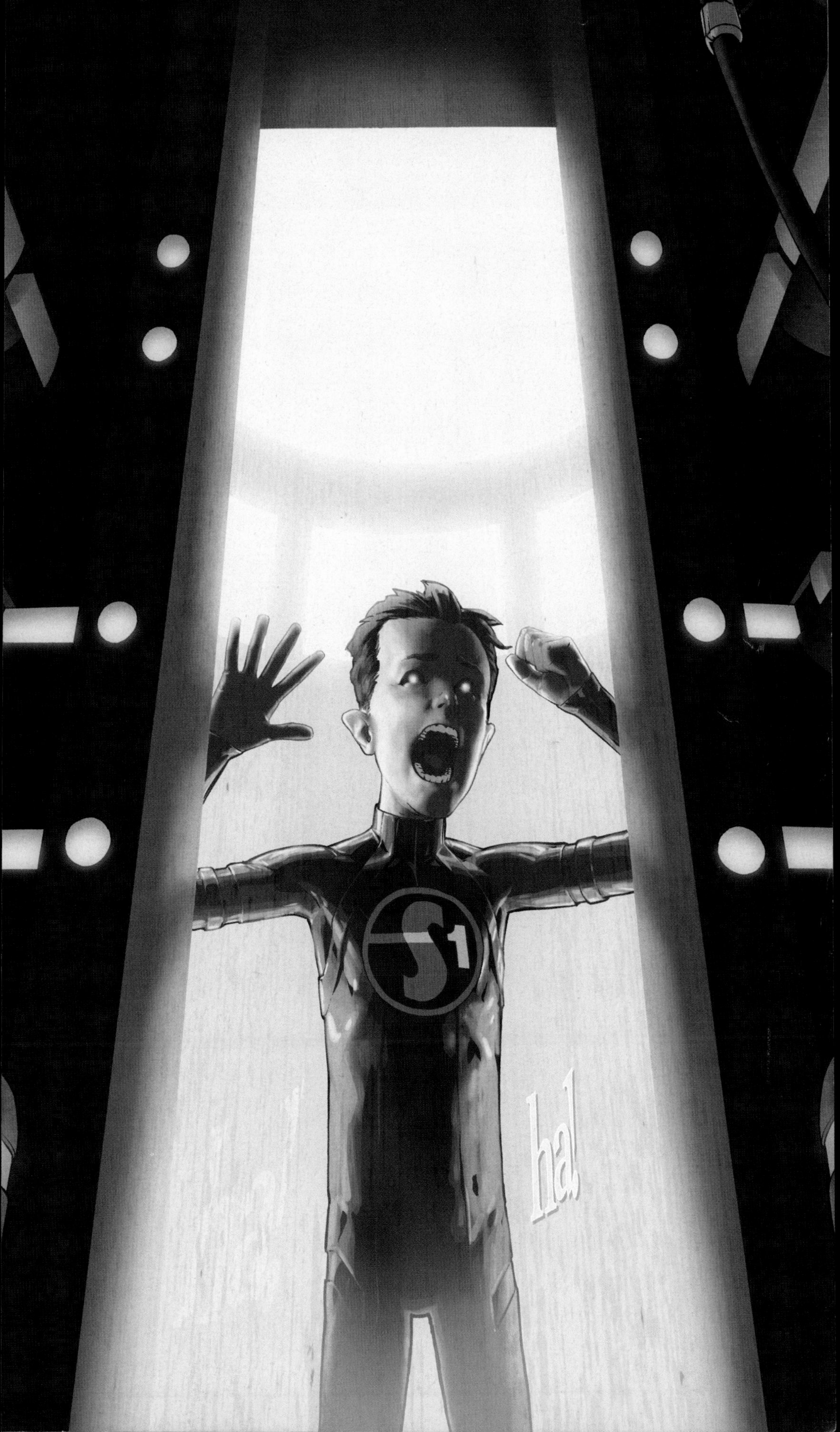
ha!

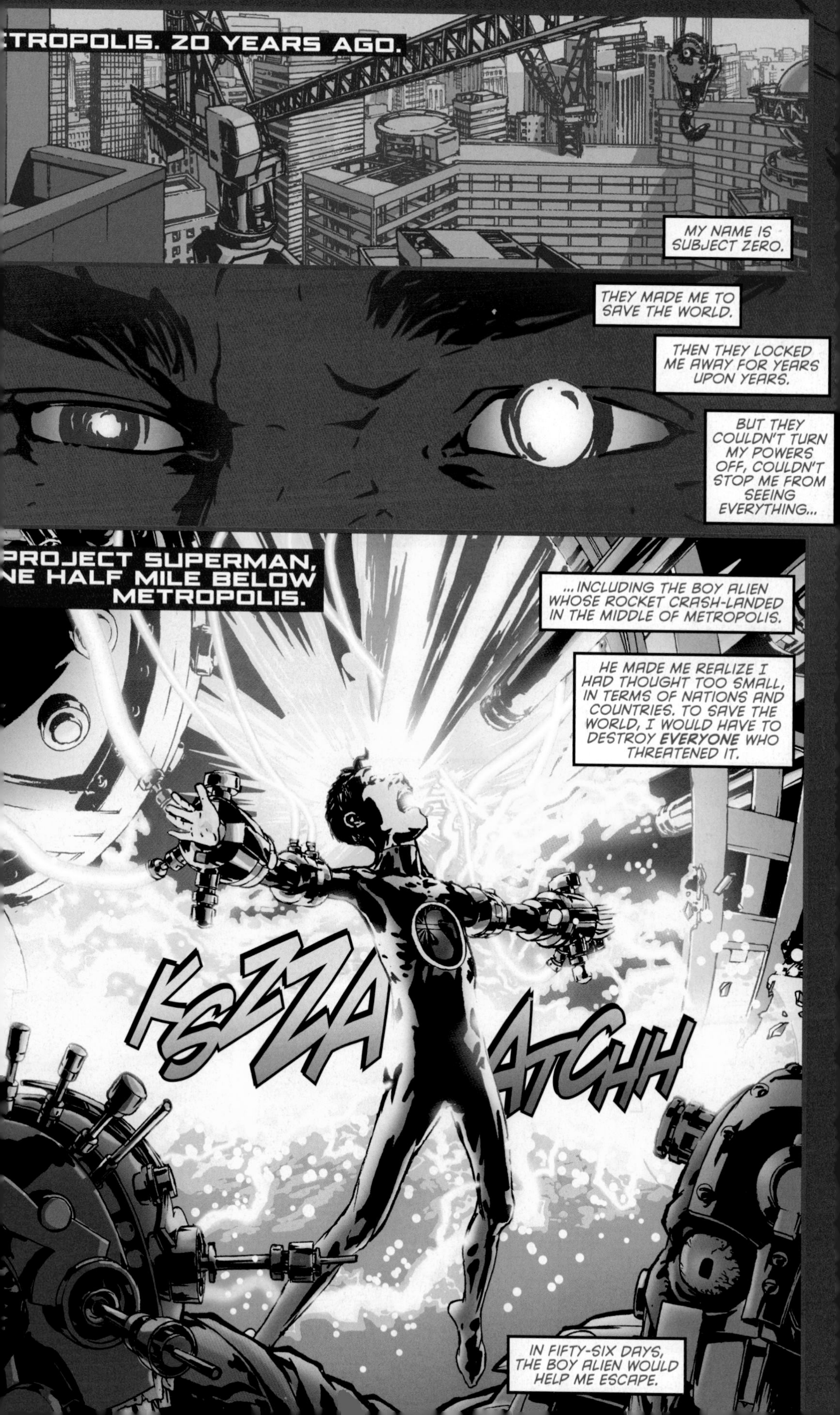

TROPOLIS. 20 YEARS AGO.
MY NAME IS SUBJECT ZERO.
THEY MADE ME TO SAVE THE WORLD.
THEN THEY LOCKED ME AWAY FOR YEARS UPON YEARS.
BUT THEY COULDN'T TURN MY POWERS OFF, COULDN'T STOP ME FROM SEEING EVERYTHING...
PROJECT SUPERMAN, NE HALF MILE BELOW METROPOLIS.
...INCLUDING THE BOY ALIEN WHOSE ROCKET CRASH-LANDED IN THE MIDDLE OF METROPOLIS.
HE MADE ME REALIZE I HAD THOUGHT TOO SMALL, IN TERMS OF NATIONS AND COUNTRIES. TO SAVE THE WORLD, I WOULD HAVE TO DESTROY EVERYONE WHO THREATENED IT.
KSZZA
ATCHH
IN FIFTY-SIX DAYS, THE BOY ALIEN WOULD HELP ME ESCAPE.

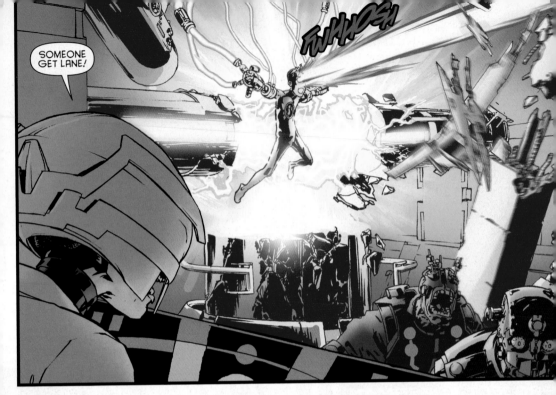

SOMEONE GET LANE!

FWHHOSH

IN THESE SMALL HANDS

GET THE FORCE DEUS SQUAD IN HERE, NOW!

NO!

I SAW MANY THINGS FROM MY PRISON CELL.

KAL, YOU KNOW ME... SAM LANE... YOU NEED TO CONTROL YOURSELF...

I WATCHED LANE CHANGE.

JUST CONCENTRATE...

AAAGH!

FROM THE GENERAL WH HATED MONSTERS...

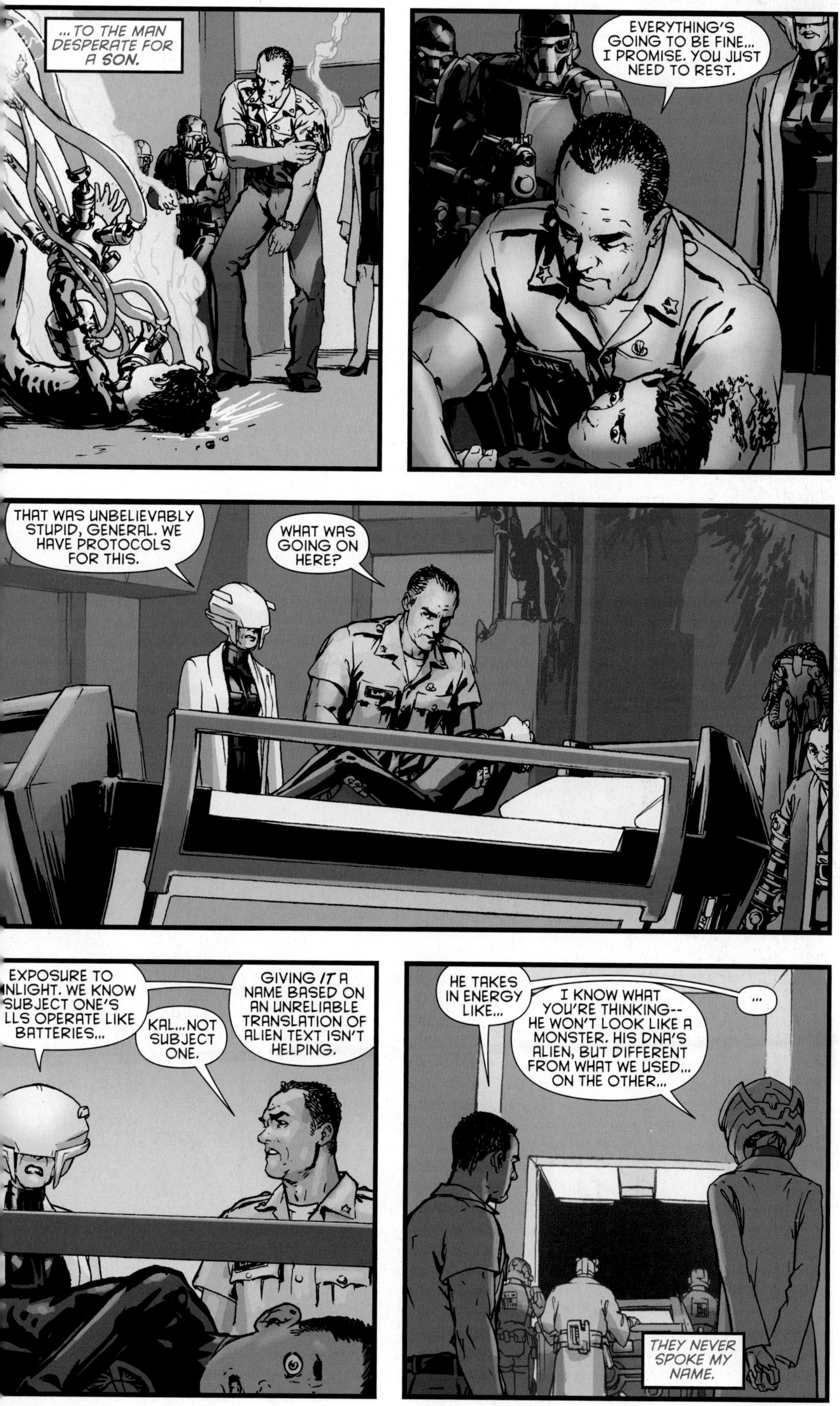
...TO THE MAN DESPERATE FOR A SON.
EVERYTHING'S GOING TO BE FINE... I PROMISE. YOU JUST NEED TO REST.
THAT WAS UNBELIEVABLY STUPID, GENERAL. WE HAVE PROTOCOLS FOR THIS.
WHAT WAS GOING ON HERE?
EXPOSURE TO NLIGHT. WE KNOW SUBJECT ONE'S LLS OPERATE LIKE BATTERIES...
KAL...NOT SUBJECT ONE.
GIVING IT A NAME BASED ON AN UNRELIABLE TRANSLATION OF ALIEN TEXT ISN'T HELPING.
HE TAKES IN ENERGY LIKE...
I KNOW WHAT YOU'RE THINKING-- HE WON'T LOOK LIKE A MONSTER. HIS DNA'S ALIEN, BUT DIFFERENT FROM WHAT WE USED... ON THE OTHER...
...
THEY NEVER SPOKE MY NAME.

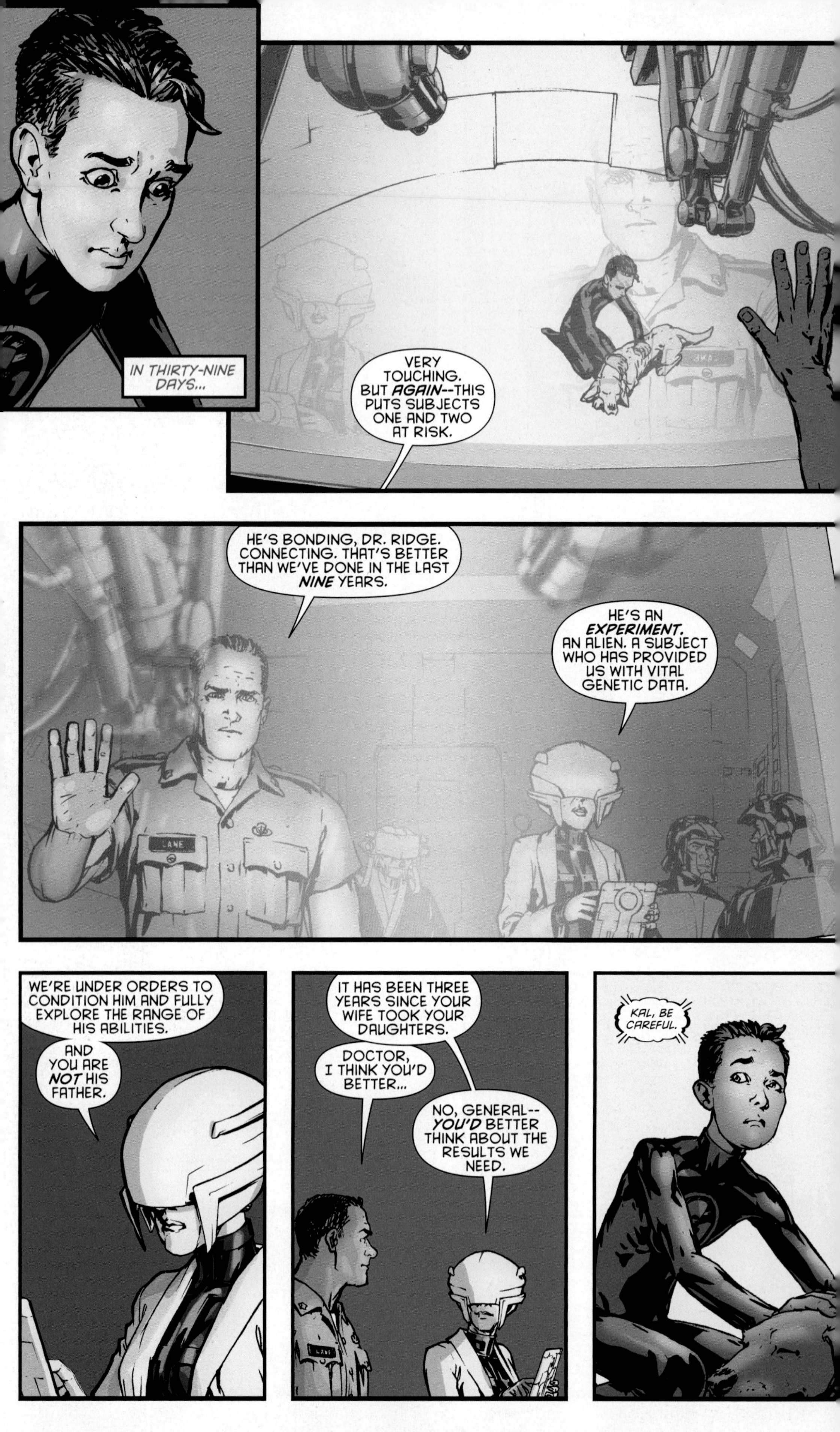

IN THIRTY-NINE DAYS...
VERY TOUCHING. BUT AGAIN--THIS PUTS SUBJECTS ONE AND TWO AT RISK.
HE'S BONDING, DR. RIDGE. CONNECTING. THAT'S BETTER THAN WE'VE DONE IN THE LAST NINE YEARS.
HE'S AN EXPERIMENT. AN ALIEN. A SUBJECT WHO HAS PROVIDED US WITH VITAL GENETIC DATA.
WE'RE UNDER ORDERS TO CONDITION HIM AND FULLY EXPLORE THE RANGE OF HIS ABILITIES.
AND YOU ARE NOT HIS FATHER.
IT HAS BEEN THREE YEARS SINCE YOUR WIFE TOOK YOUR DAUGHTERS.
DOCTOR, I THINK YOU'D BETTER...
NO, GENERAL--YOU'D BETTER THINK ABOUT THE RESULTS WE NEED.
KAL, BE CAREFUL.

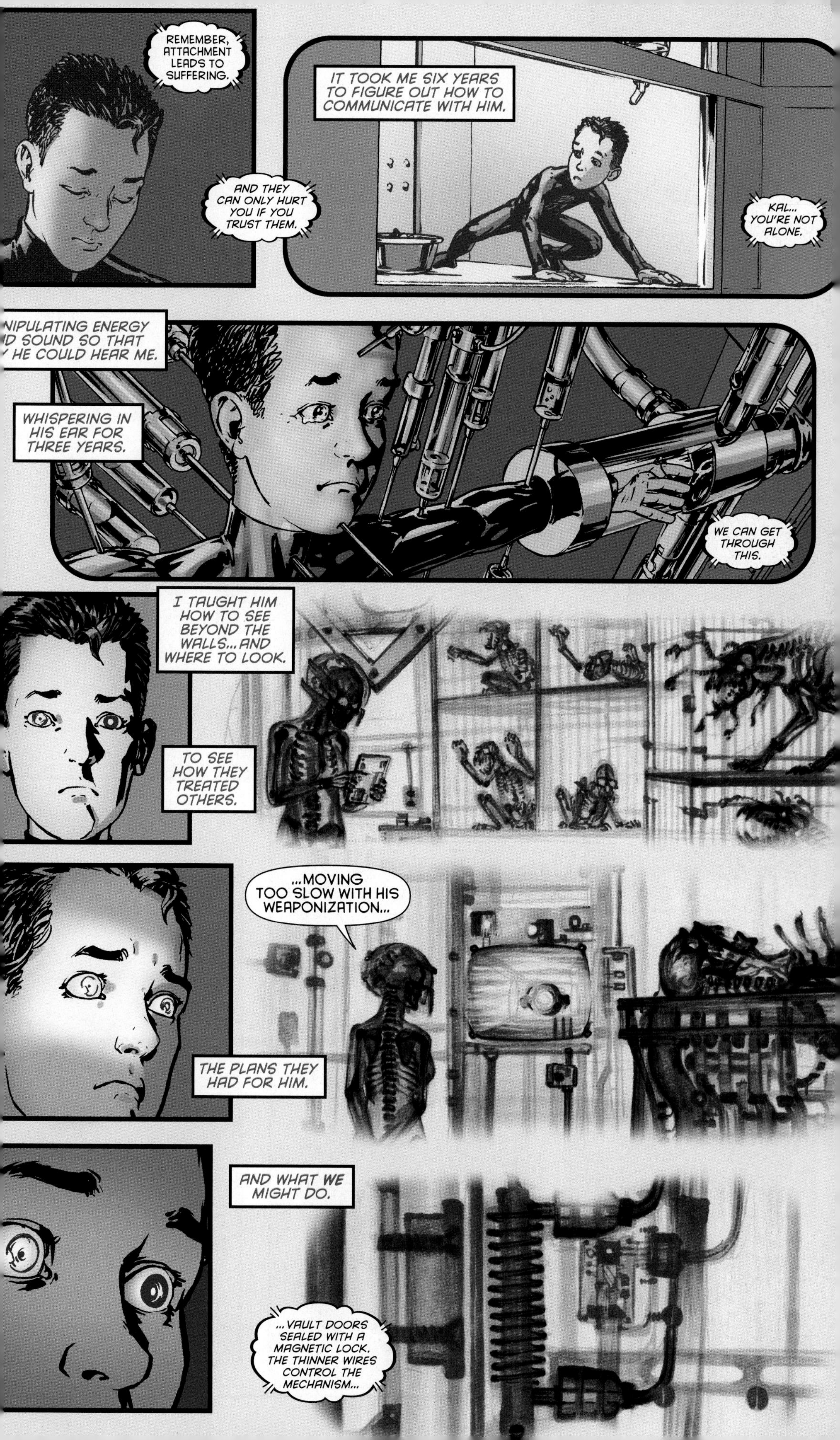
REMEMBER, ATTACHMENT LEADS TO SUFFERING.
AND THEY CAN ONLY HURT YOU IF YOU TRUST THEM.
IT TOOK ME SIX YEARS TO FIGURE OUT HOW TO COMMUNICATE WITH HIM.
KAL... YOU'RE NOT ALONE.
NIPULATING ENERGY D SOUND SO THAT HE COULD HEAR ME.
WHISPERING IN HIS EAR FOR THREE YEARS.
WE CAN GET THROUGH THIS.
I TAUGHT HIM HOW TO SEE BEYOND THE WALLS... AND WHERE TO LOOK.
TO SEE HOW THEY TREATED OTHERS.
...MOVING TOO SLOW WITH HIS WEAPONIZATION...
THE PLANS THEY HAD FOR HIM.
AND WHAT WE MIGHT DO.
...VAULT DOORS SEALED WITH A MAGNETIC LOCK. THE THINNER WIRES CONTROL THE MECHANISM...

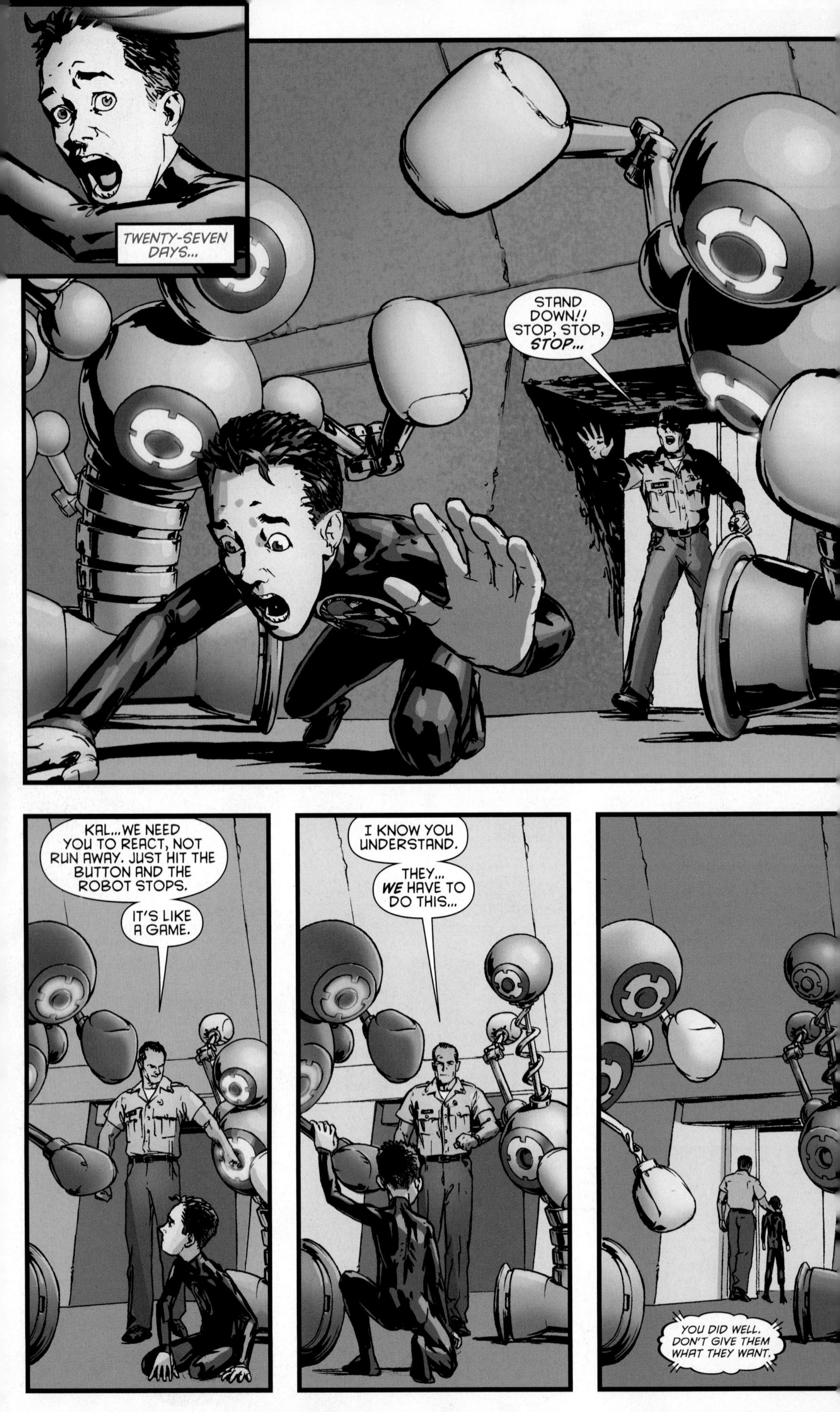
TWENTY-SEVEN DAYS...
STAND DOWN!! STOP, STOP, STOP...
KAL...WE NEED YOU TO REACT, NOT RUN AWAY. JUST HIT THE BUTTON AND THE ROBOT STOPS.
IT'S LIKE A GAME.
I KNOW YOU UNDERSTAND.
THEY... WE HAVE TO DO THIS...
YOU DID WELL. DON'T GIVE THEM WHAT THEY WANT.

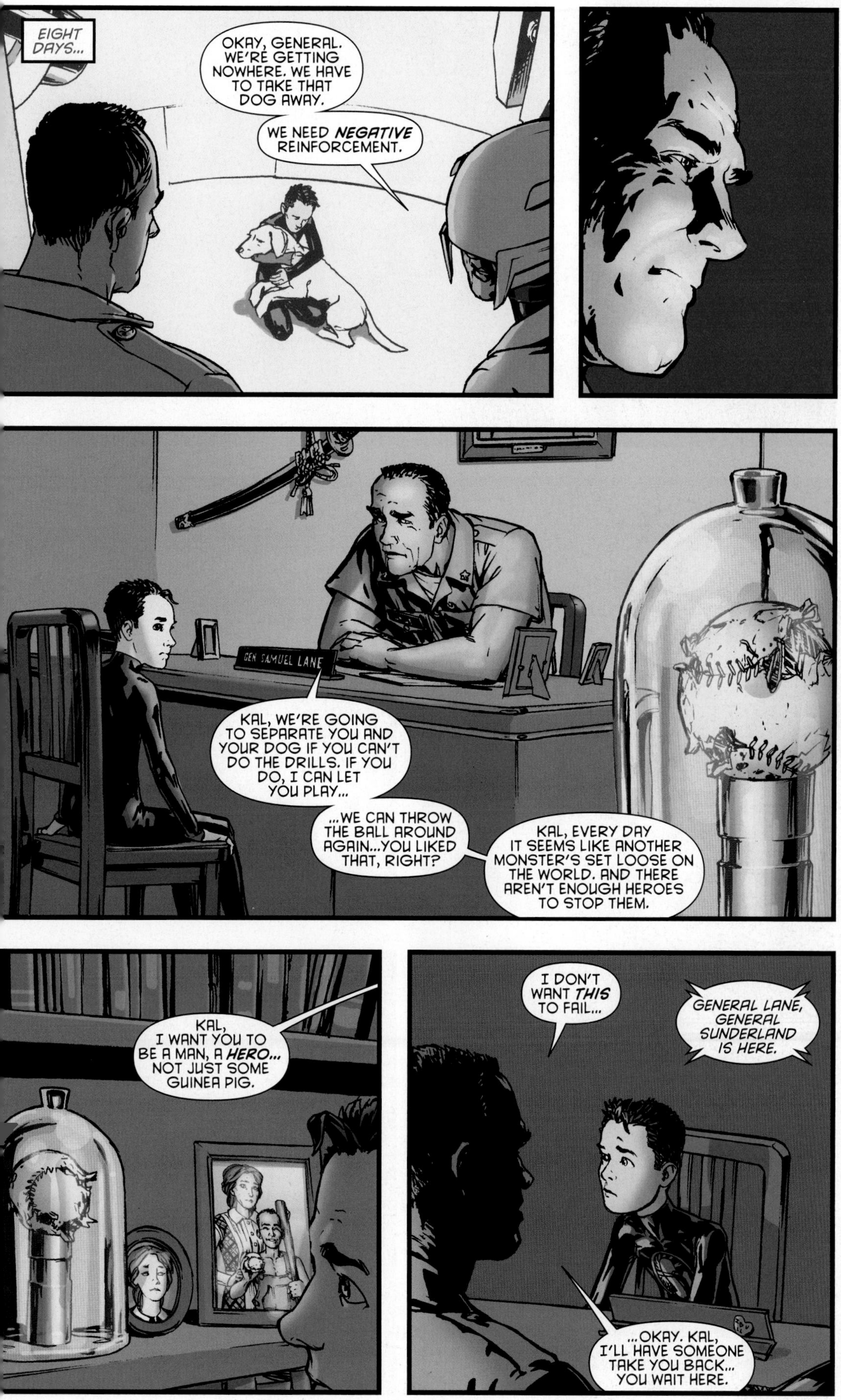
EIGHT DAYS...
OKAY, GENERAL. WE'RE GETTING NOWHERE. WE HAVE TO TAKE THAT DOG AWAY.
WE NEED NEGATIVE REINFORCEMENT.
GEN SAMUEL LANE
KAL, WE'RE GOING TO SEPARATE YOU AND YOUR DOG IF YOU CAN'T DO THE DRILLS. IF YOU DO, I CAN LET YOU PLAY...
...WE CAN THROW THE BALL AROUND AGAIN...YOU LIKED THAT, RIGHT?
KAL, EVERY DAY IT SEEMS LIKE ANOTHER MONSTER'S SET LOOSE ON THE WORLD. AND THERE AREN'T ENOUGH HEROES TO STOP THEM.
KAL, I WANT YOU TO BE A MAN, A HERO... NOT JUST SOME GUINEA PIG.
I DON'T WANT THIS TO FAIL...
GENERAL LANE, GENERAL SUNDERLAND IS HERE.
...OKAY. KAL, I'LL HAVE SOMEONE TAKE YOU BACK... YOU WAIT HERE.

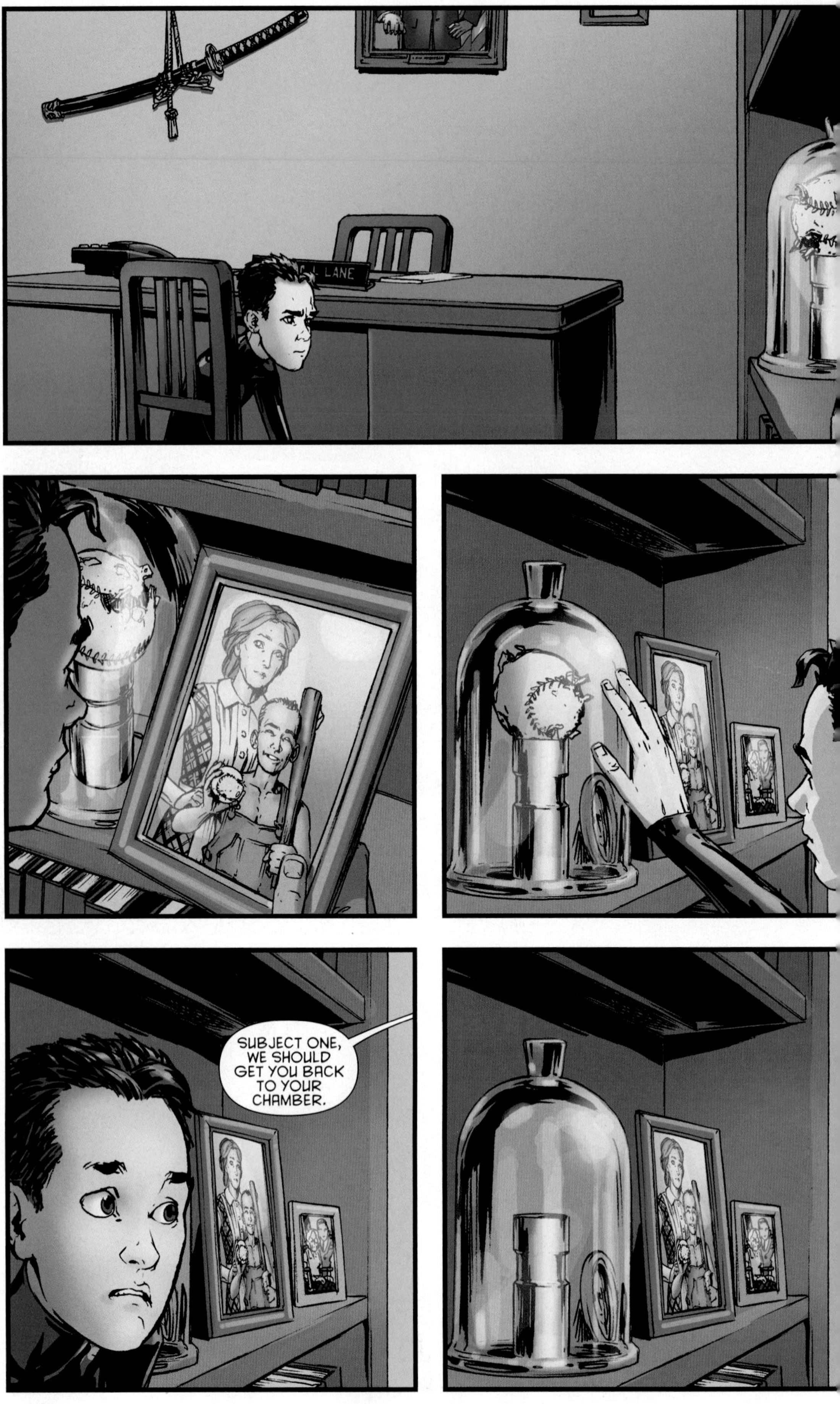
LANE
SUBJECT ONE, WE SHOULD GET YOU BACK TO YOUR CHAMBER.

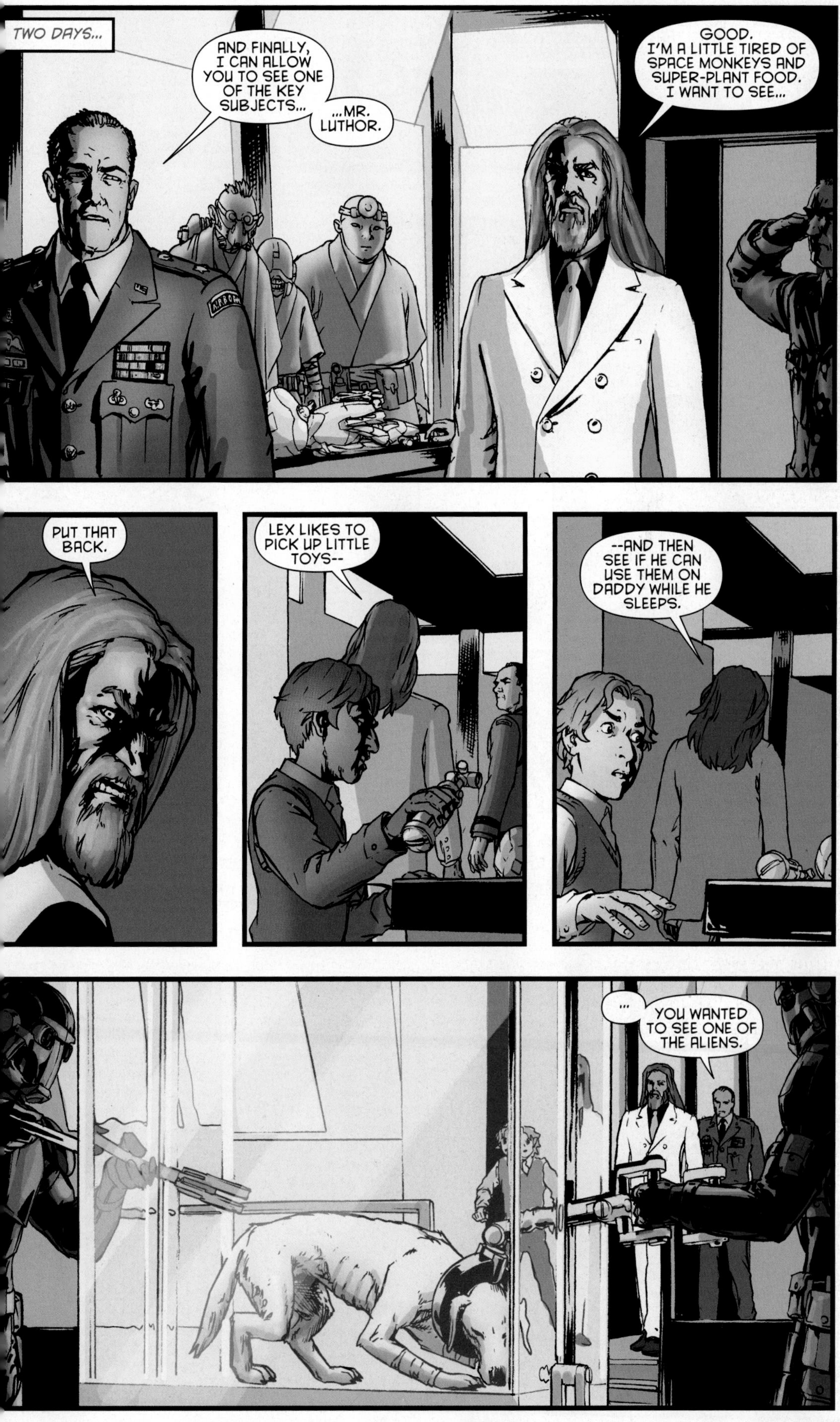
TWO DAYS...
AND FINALLY, I CAN ALLOW YOU TO SEE ONE OF THE KEY SUBJECTS...
...MR. LUTHOR.
GOOD. I'M A LITTLE TIRED OF SPACE MONKEYS AND SUPER-PLANT FOOD. I WANT TO SEE...
PUT THAT BACK.
LEX LIKES TO PICK UP LITTLE TOYS--
--AND THEN SEE IF HE CAN USE THEM ON DADDY WHILE HE SLEEPS.
...
YOU WANTED TO SEE ONE OF THE ALIENS.

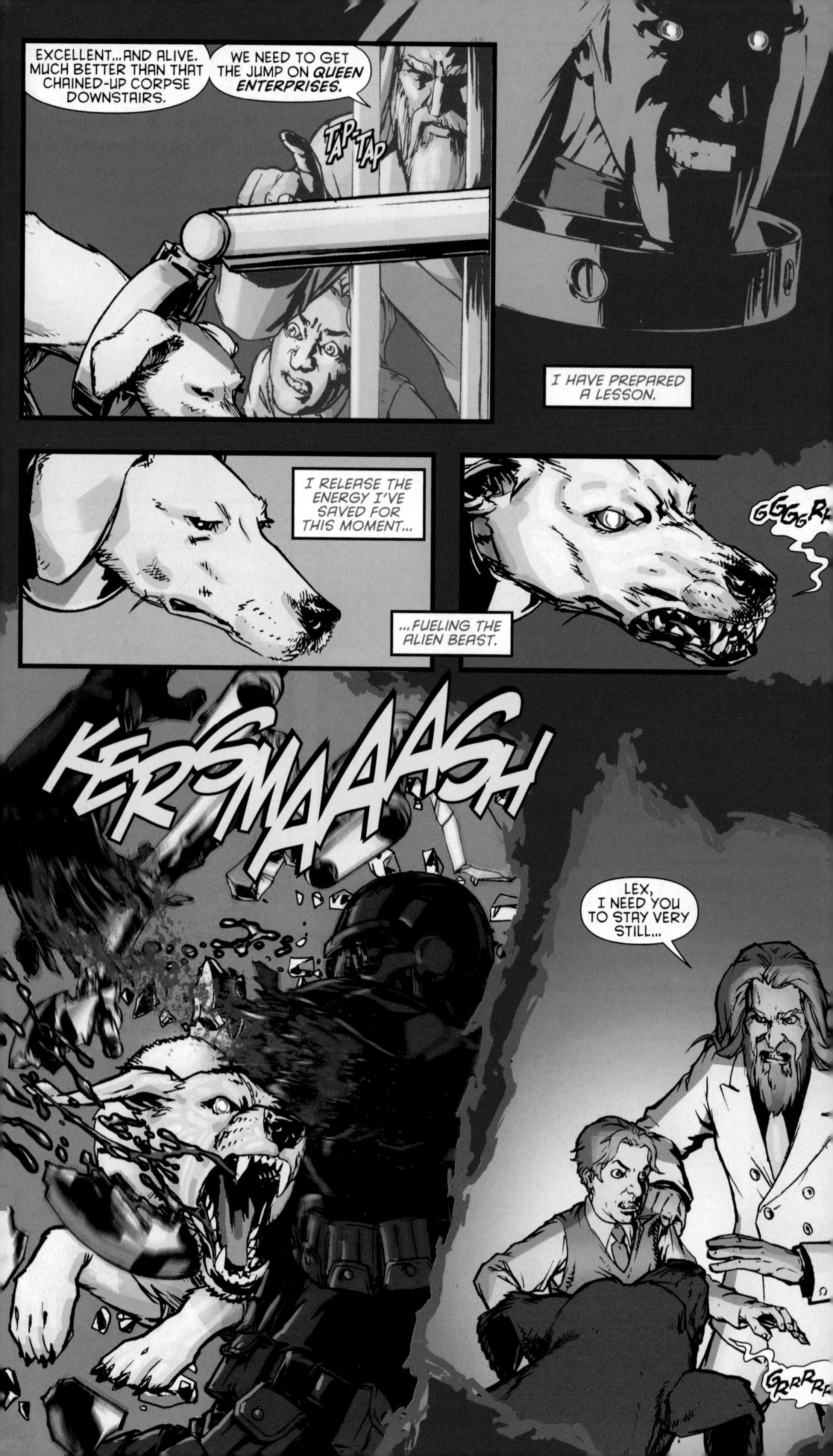
EXCELLENT...AND ALIVE. MUCH BETTER THAN THAT CHAINED-UP CORPSE DOWNSTAIRS.
WE NEED TO GET THE JUMP ON QUEEN ENTERPRISES.
TAP-TAP
I HAVE PREPARED A LESSON.
I RELEASE THE ENERGY I'VE SAVED FOR THIS MOMENT...
...FUELING THE ALIEN BEAST.
KERSMAAASH
LEX, I NEED YOU TO STAY VERY STILL...

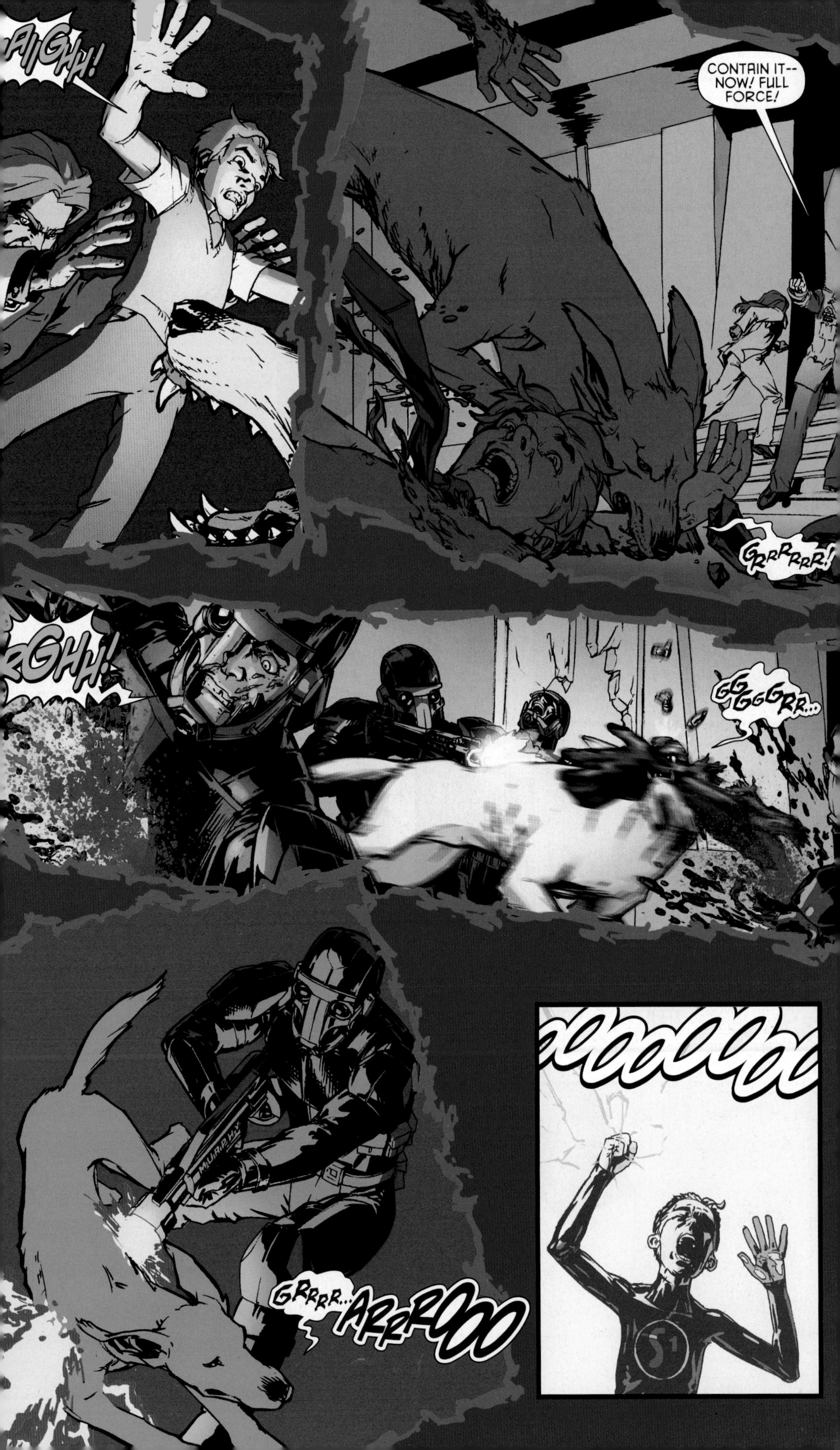
AIIGHH!
CONTAIN IT-- NOW! FULL FORCE!
GRRRRRR!
RGHH!
GGGGGRR...
GRRRR...ARRROOO
OOOOOOOO

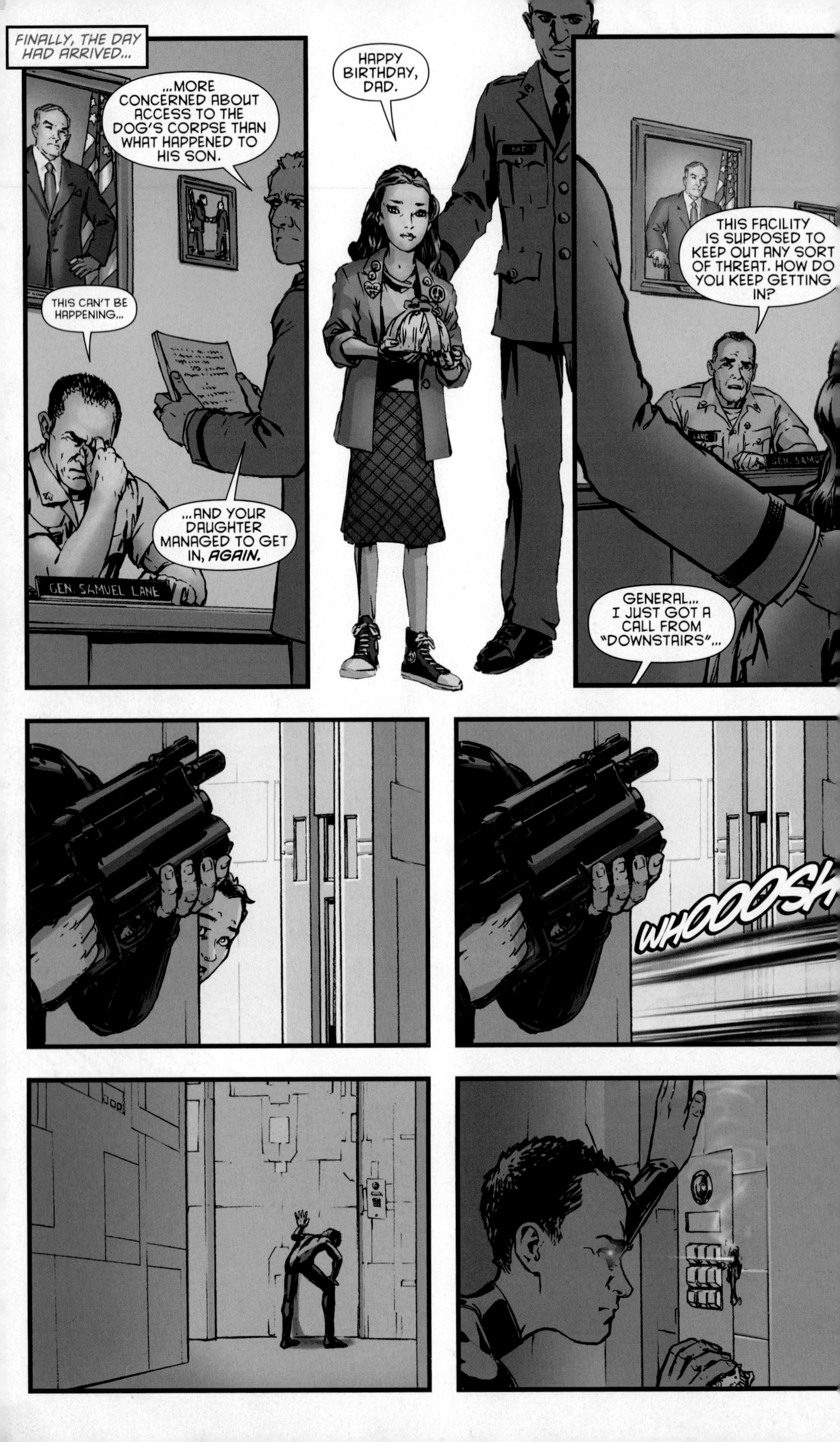
FINALLY, THE DAY HAD ARRIVED...
...MORE CONCERNED ABOUT ACCESS TO THE DOG'S CORPSE THAN WHAT HAPPENED TO HIS SON.
THIS CAN'T BE HAPPENING...
...AND YOUR DAUGHTER MANAGED TO GET IN, AGAIN.
GEN. SAMUEL LANE
HAPPY BIRTHDAY, DAD.
THIS FACILITY IS SUPPOSED TO KEEP OUT ANY SORT OF THREAT. HOW DO YOU KEEP GETTING IN?
LANE
GENERAL... I JUST GOT A CALL FROM "DOWNSTAIRS"...
WHOOOOSH

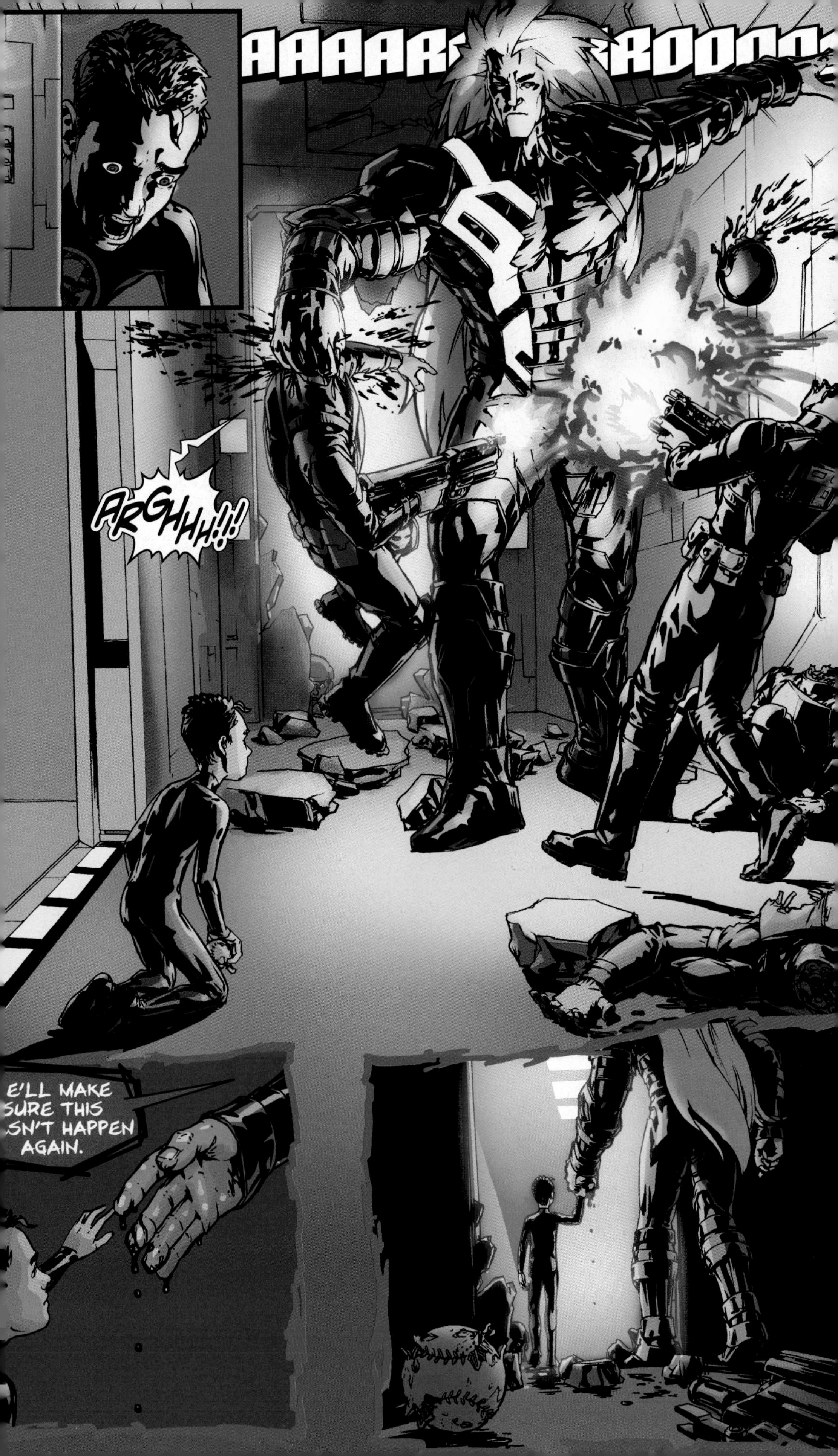
AAAAAR
RROOOO
ARGHHH!!!
E'LL MAKE
SURE THIS
SN'T HAPPEN
AGAIN.

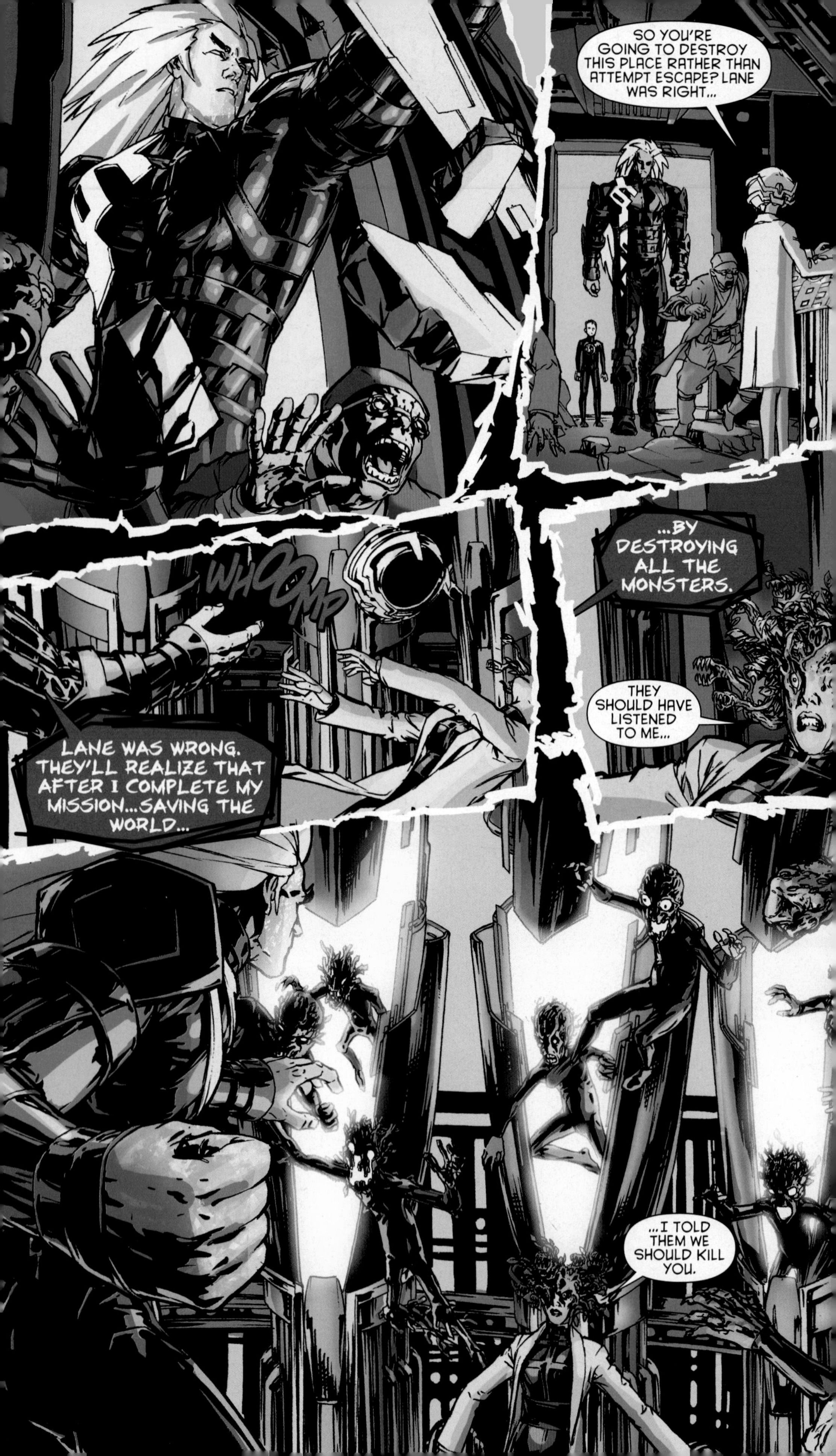

SO YOU'RE GOING TO DESTROY THIS PLACE RATHER THAN ATTEMPT ESCAPE? LANE WAS RIGHT...
WHOOMP
LANE WAS WRONG. THEY'LL REALIZE THAT AFTER I COMPLETE MY MISSION...SAVING THE WORLD...
...BY DESTROYING ALL THE MONSTERS.
THEY SHOULD HAVE LISTENED TO ME...
...I TOLD THEM WE SHOULD KILL YOU.

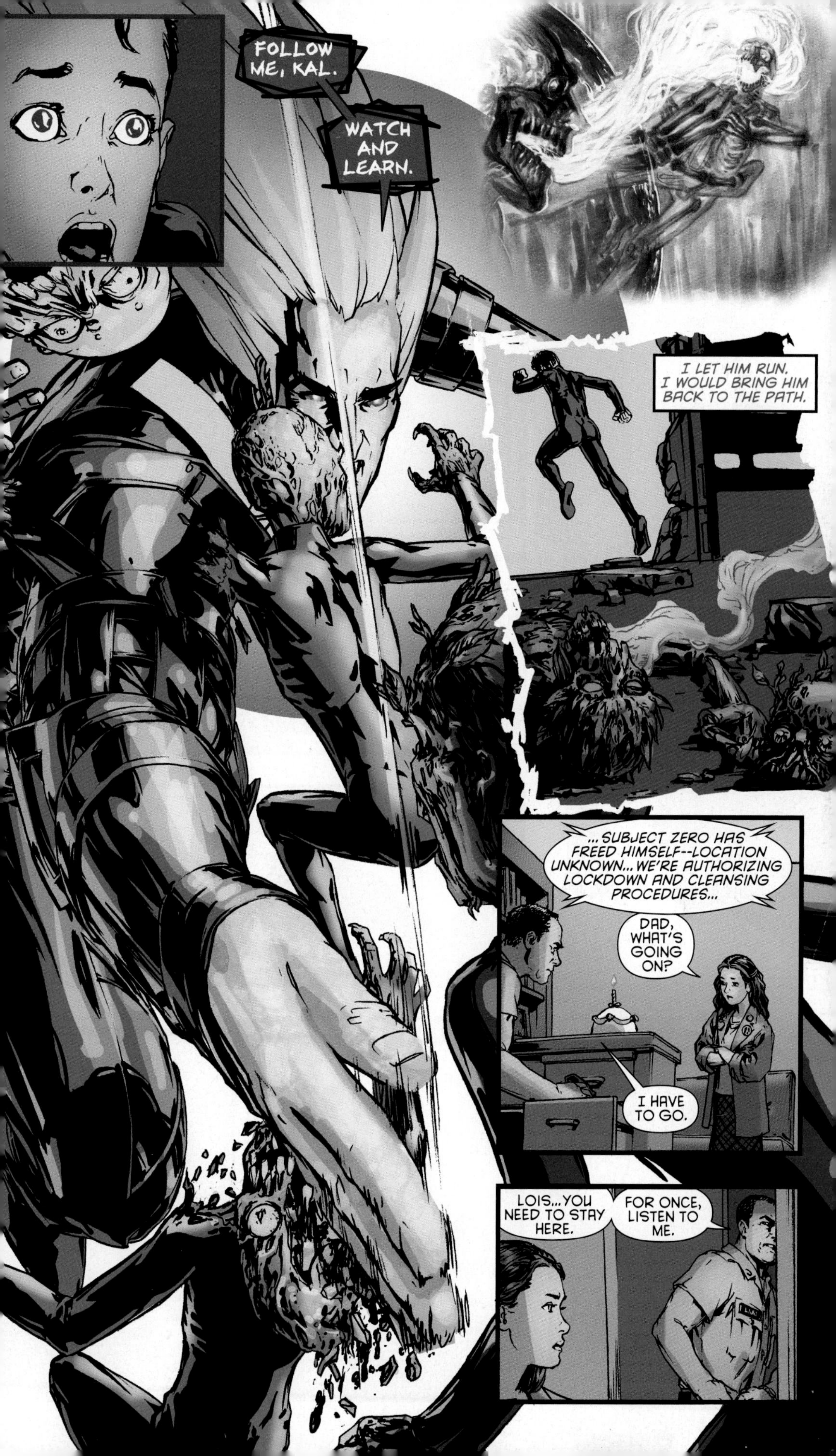
FOLLOW ME, KAL.
WATCH AND LEARN.
I LET HIM RUN. I WOULD BRING HIM BACK TO THE PATH.
... SUBJECT ZERO HAS FREED HIMSELF--LOCATION UNKNOWN... WE'RE AUTHORIZING LOCKDOWN AND CLEANSING PROCEDURES...
DAD, WHAT'S GOING ON?
I HAVE TO GO.
LOIS... YOU NEED TO STAY HERE.
FOR ONCE, LISTEN TO ME.

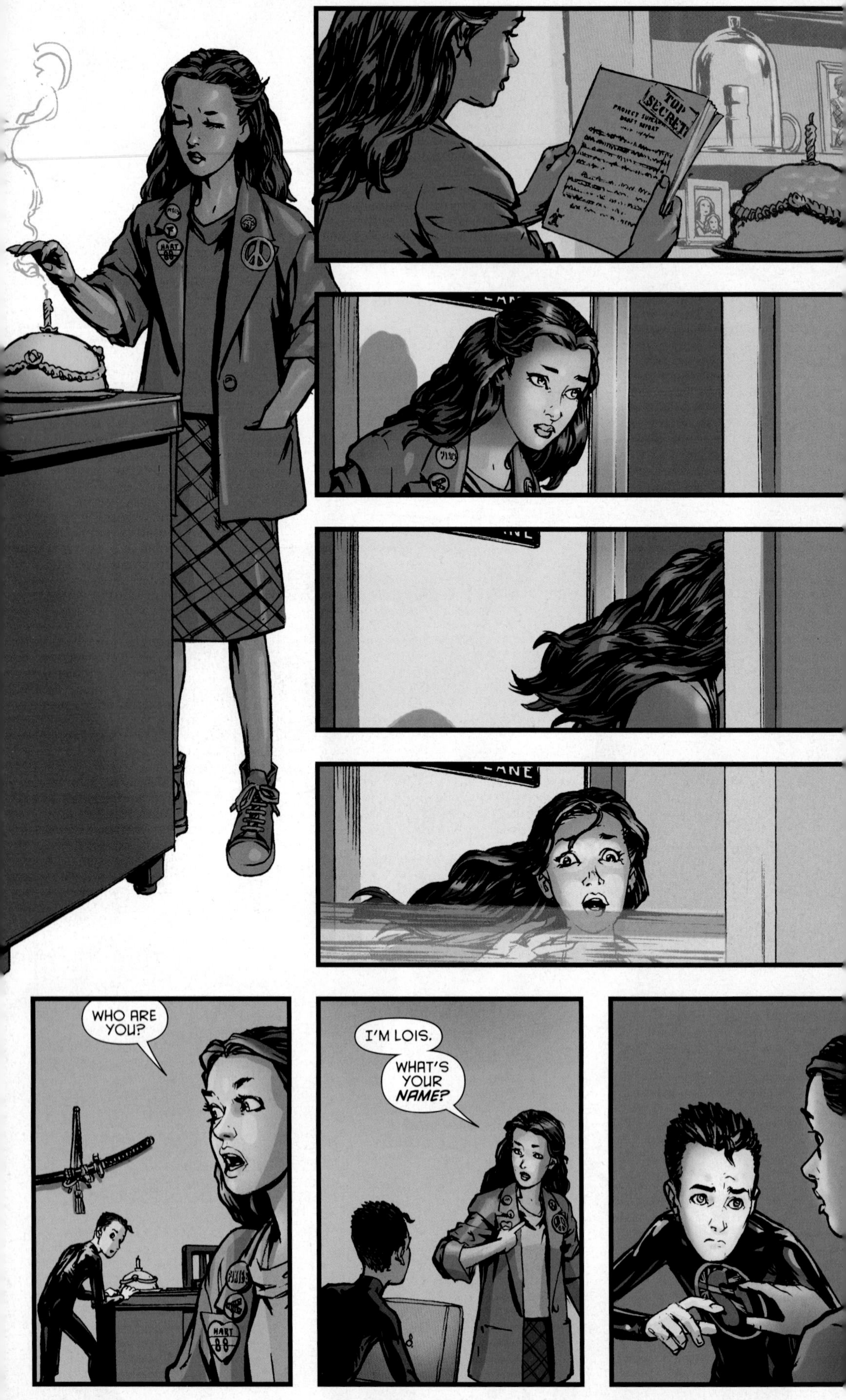
TOP SECRET
WHO ARE YOU?
I'M LOIS.
WHAT'S YOUR *NAME?*

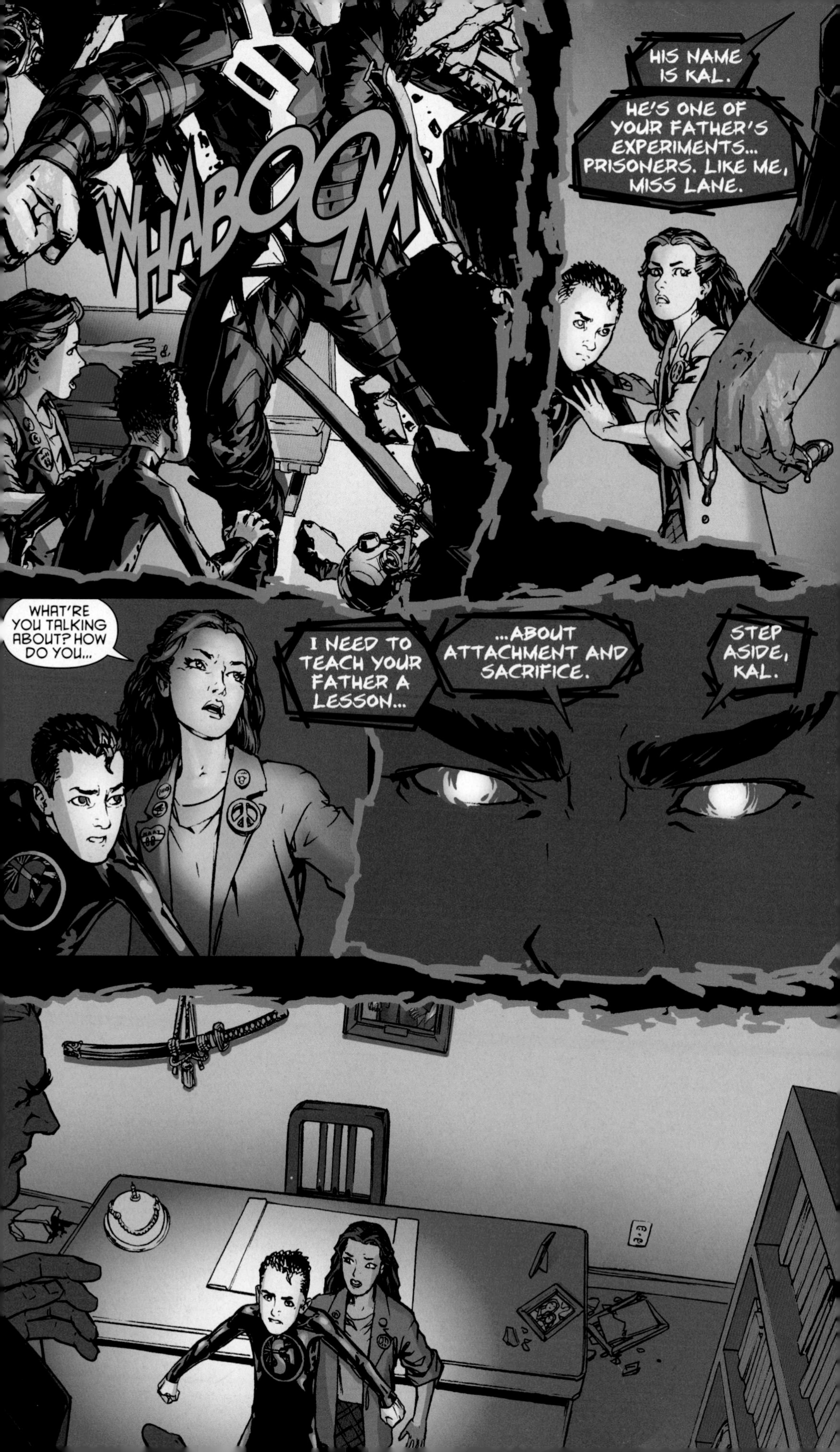
WHABOOM
HIS NAME IS KAL.
HE'S ONE OF YOUR FATHER'S EXPERIMENTS... PRISONERS. LIKE ME, MISS LANE.
WHAT'RE YOU TALKING ABOUT? HOW DO YOU...
I NEED TO TEACH YOUR FATHER A LESSON...
...ABOUT ATTACHMENT AND SACRIFICE.
STEP ASIDE, KAL.

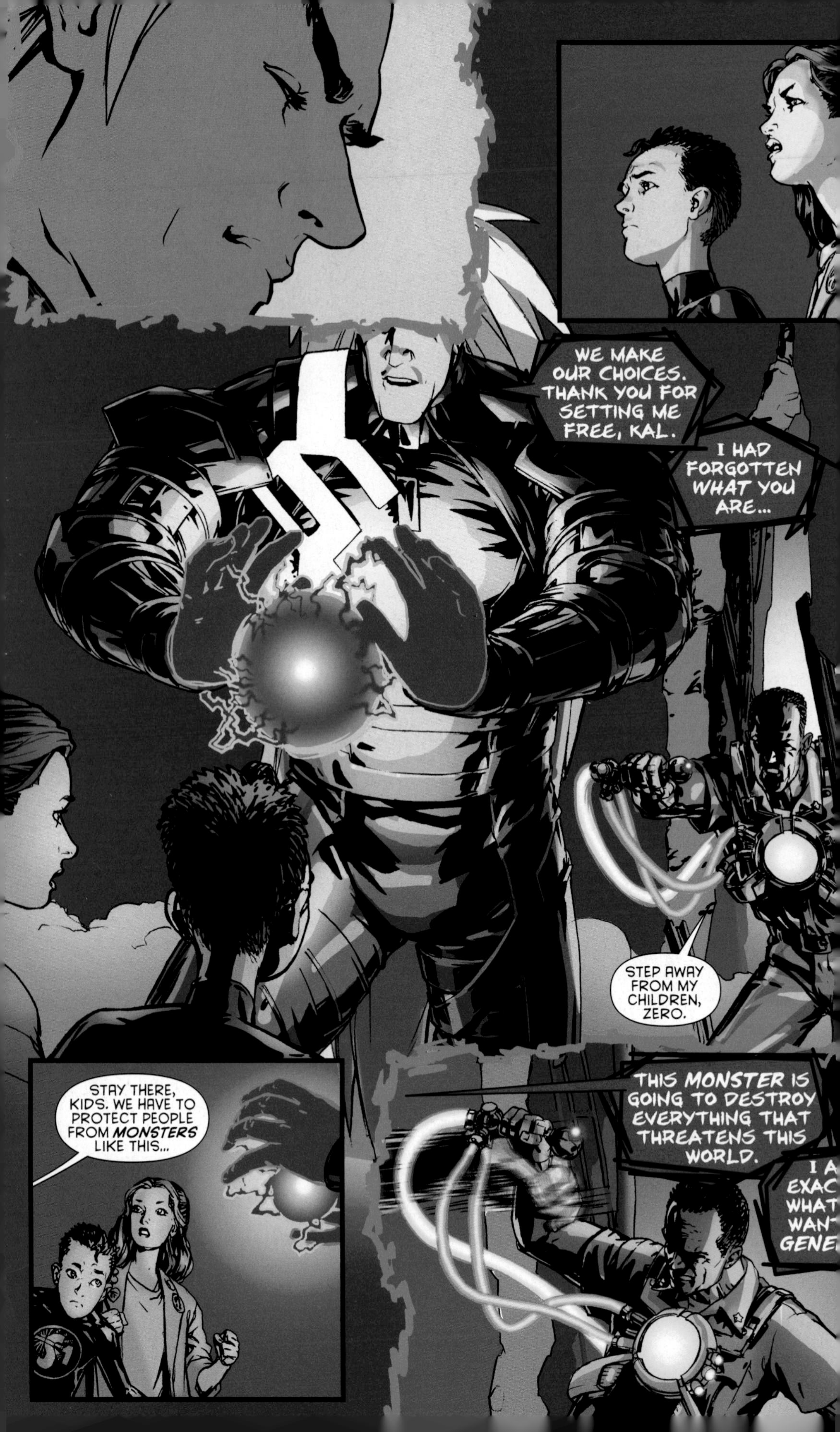
WE MAKE OUR CHOICES. THANK YOU FOR SETTING ME FREE, KAL.
I HAD FORGOTTEN WHAT YOU ARE...
STEP AWAY FROM MY CHILDREN, ZERO.
STAY THERE, KIDS. WE HAVE TO PROTECT PEOPLE FROM MONSTERS LIKE THIS...
THIS MONSTER IS GOING TO DESTROY EVERYTHING THAT THREATENS THIS WORLD.

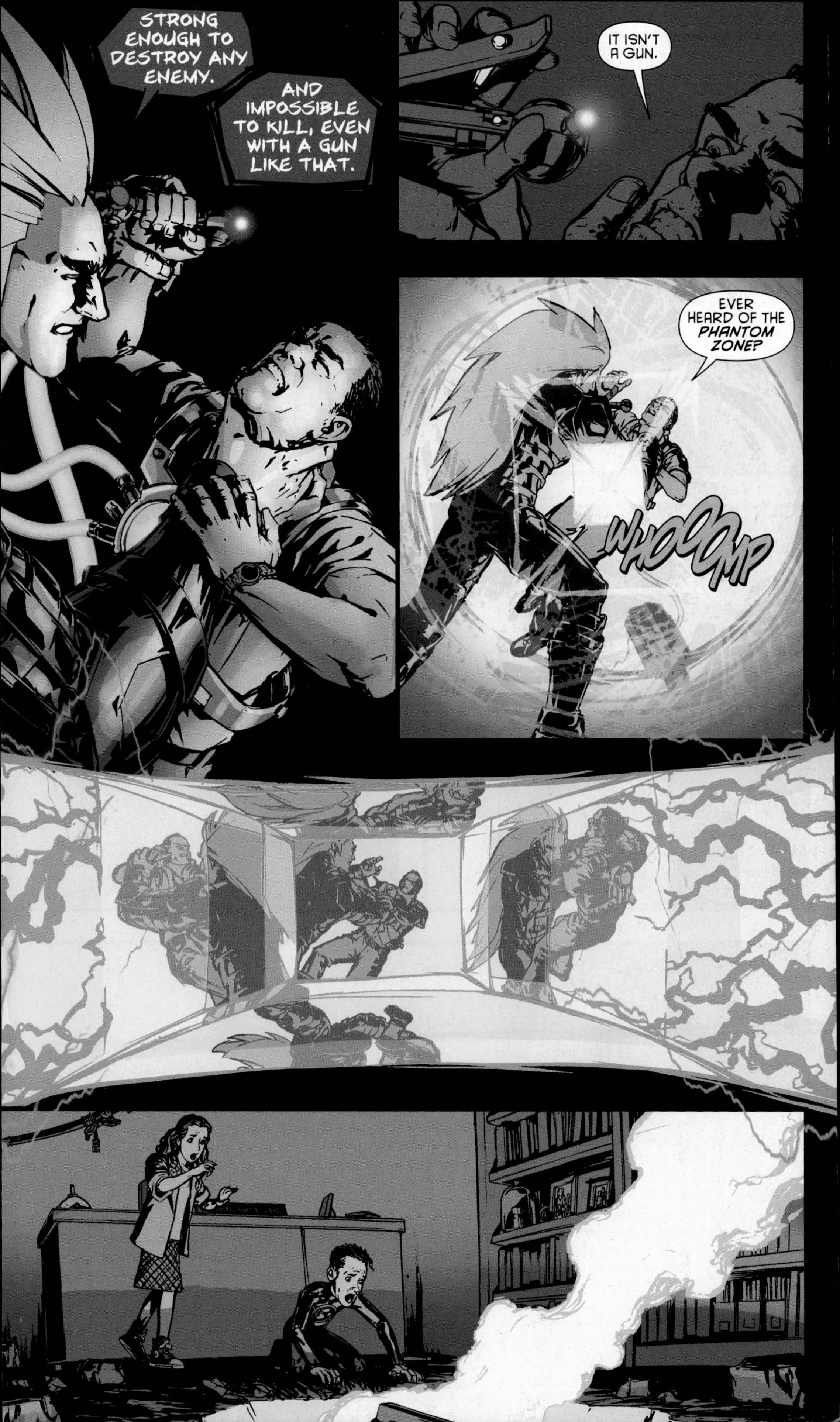
STRONG ENOUGH TO DESTROY ANY ENEMY.
AND IMPOSSIBLE TO KILL, EVEN WITH A GUN LIKE THAT.
IT ISN'T A GUN.
EVER HEARD OF THE PHANTOM ZONE?
WHOOOOMP

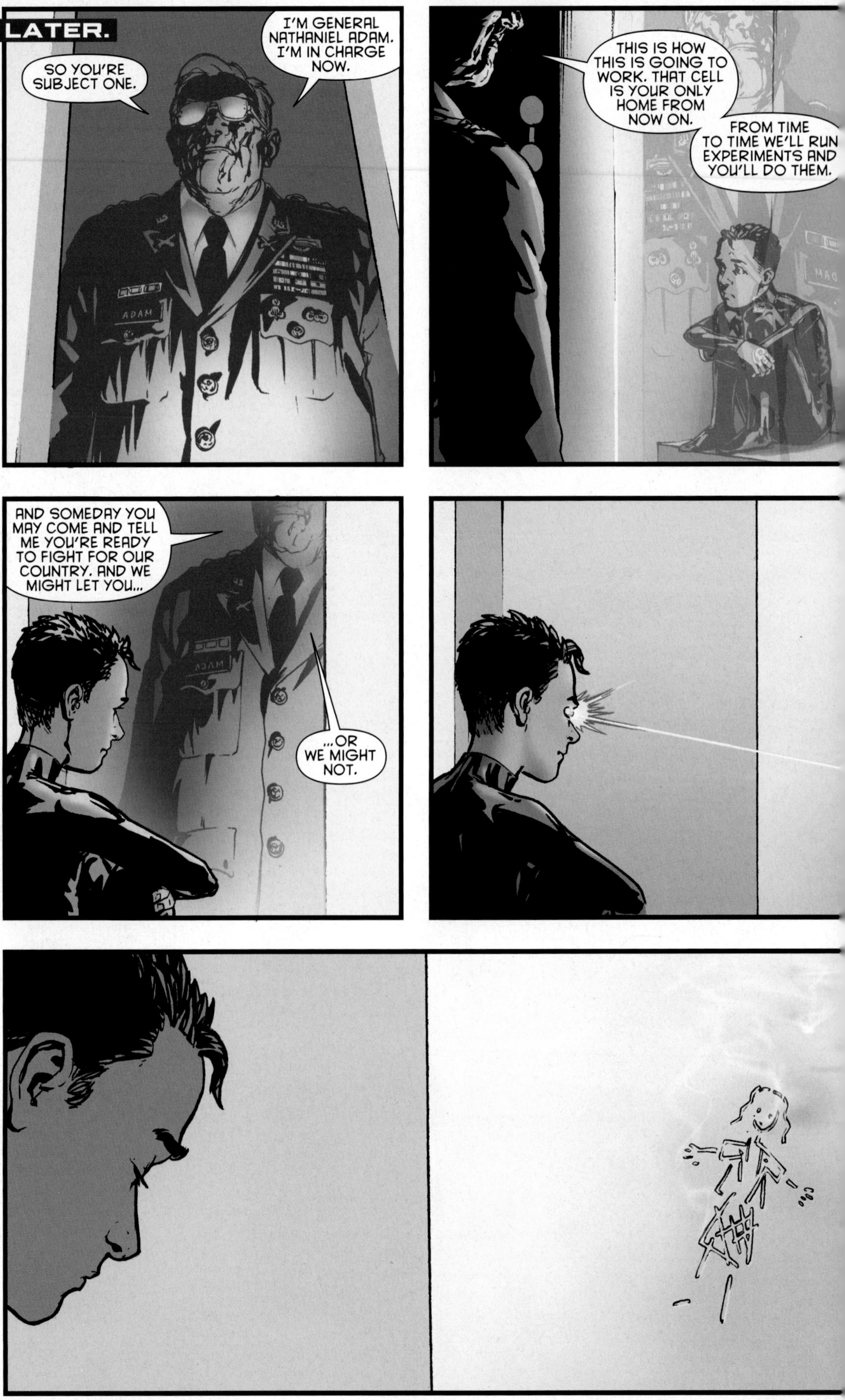
LATER.
SO YOU'RE SUBJECT ONE.
I'M GENERAL NATHANIEL ADAM. I'M IN CHARGE NOW.
ADAM
THIS IS HOW THIS IS GOING TO WORK. THAT CELL IS YOUR ONLY HOME FROM NOW ON.
FROM TIME TO TIME WE'LL RUN EXPERIMENTS AND YOU'LL DO THEM.
AND SOMEDAY YOU MAY COME AND TELL ME YOU'RE READY TO FIGHT FOR OUR COUNTRY. AND WE MIGHT LET YOU...
...OR WE MIGHT NOT.

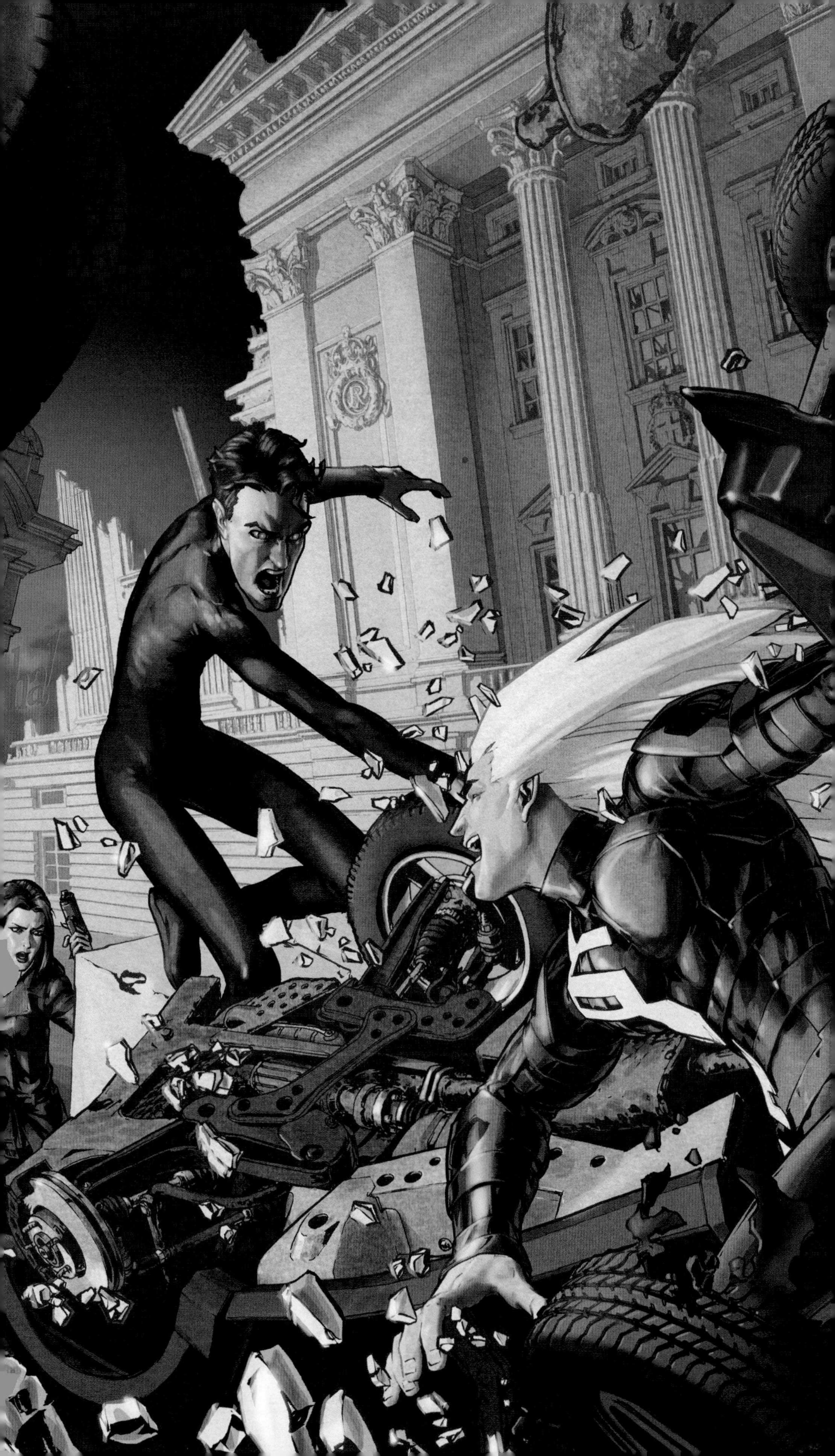

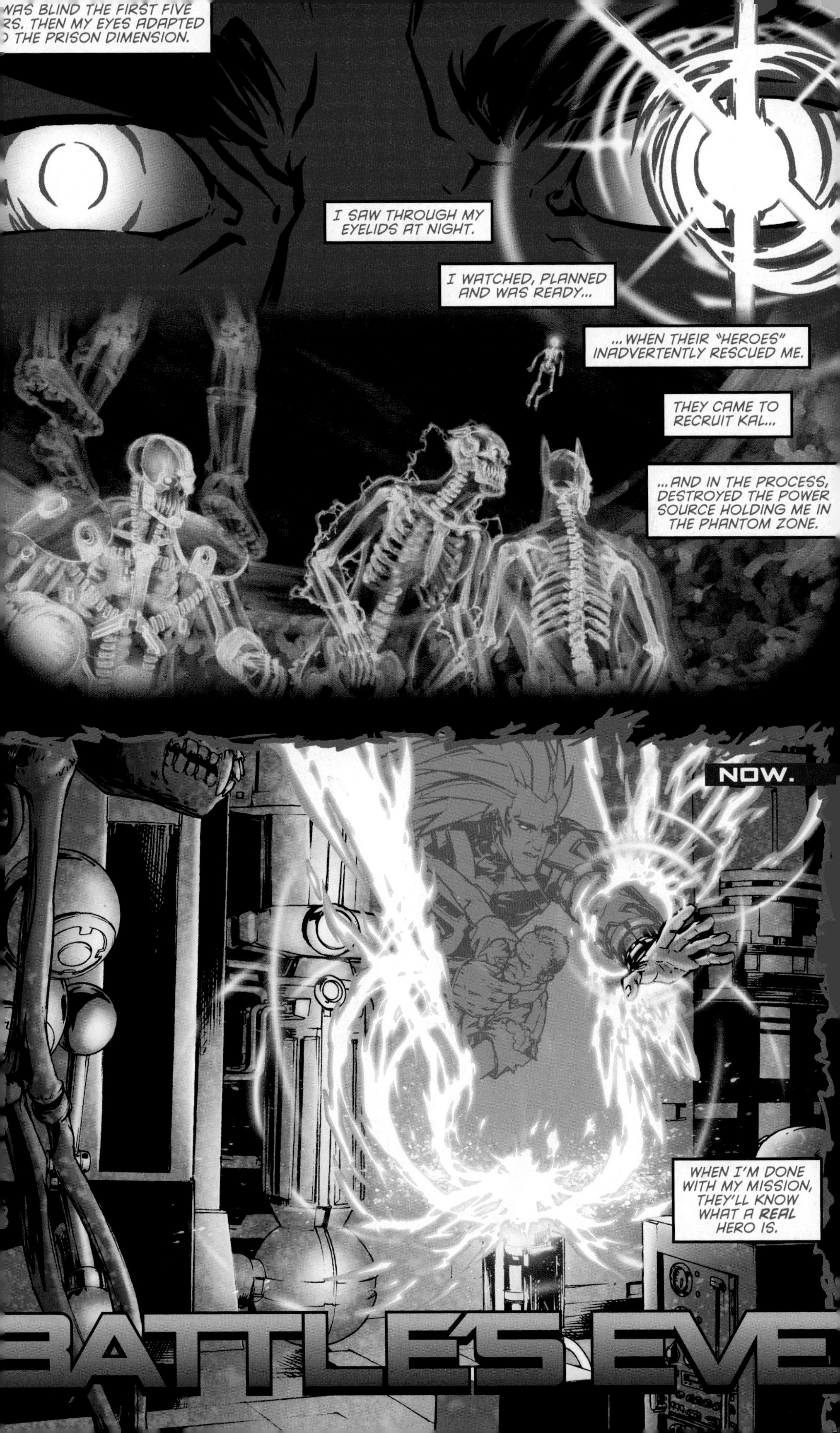
WAS BLIND THE FIRST FIVE
RS. THEN MY EYES ADAPTED
THE PRISON DIMENSION.
I SAW THROUGH MY EYELIDS AT NIGHT.
I WATCHED, PLANNED AND WAS READY...
...WHEN THEIR "HEROES" INADVERTENTLY RESCUED ME.
THEY CAME TO RECRUIT KAL...
...AND IN THE PROCESS, DESTROYED THE POWER SOURCE HOLDING ME IN THE PHANTOM ZONE.
NOW.
WHEN I'M DONE WITH MY MISSION, THEY'LL KNOW WHAT A REAL HERO IS.
BATTLE'S EVE

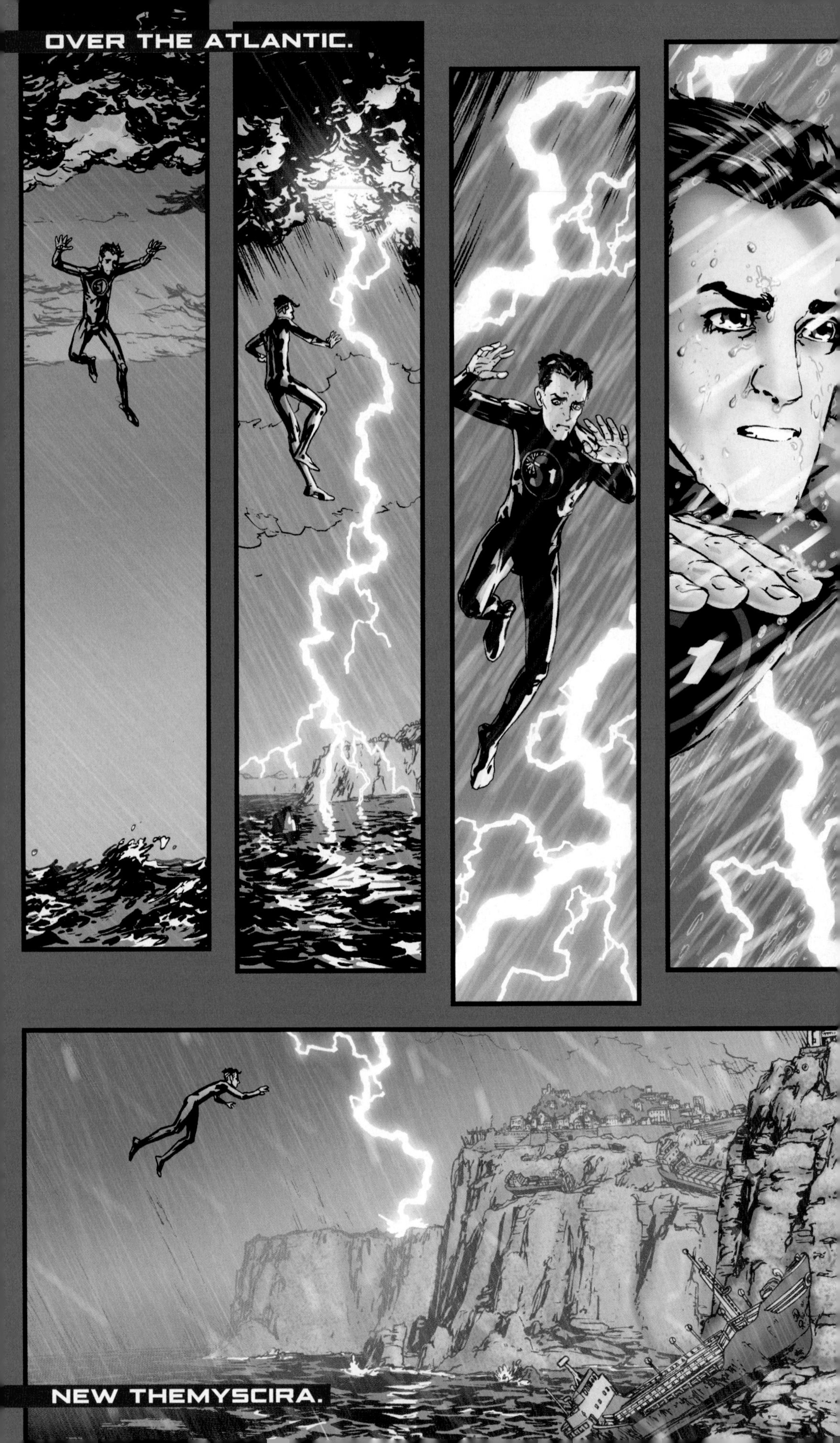
OVER THE ATLANTIC.
NEW THEMYSCIRA.

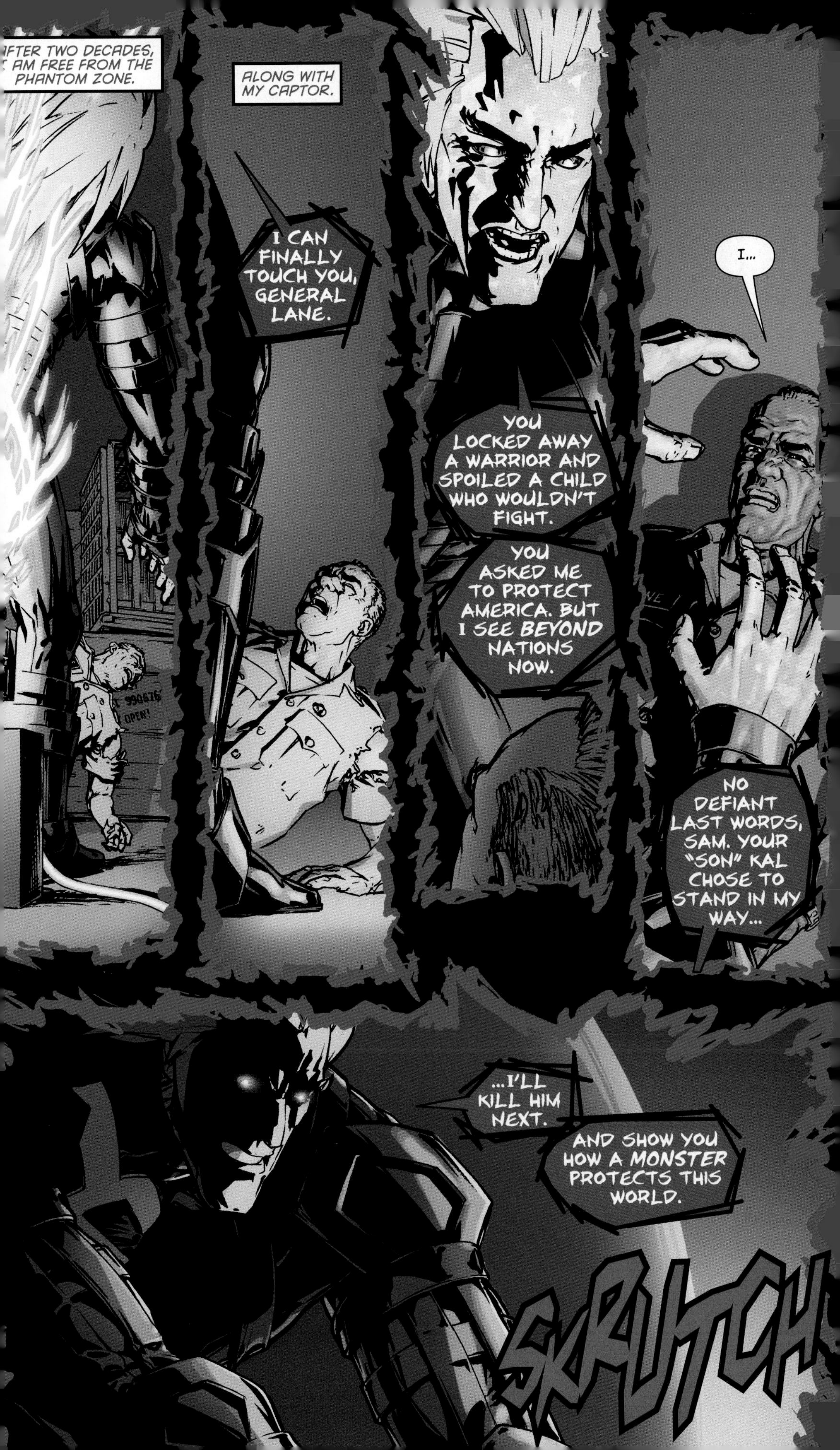

AFTER TWO DECADES, I AM FREE FROM THE PHANTOM ZONE.
ALONG WITH MY CAPTOR.
I CAN FINALLY TOUCH YOU, GENERAL LANE.
YOU LOCKED AWAY A WARRIOR AND SPOILED A CHILD WHO WOULDN'T FIGHT.
YOU ASKED ME TO PROTECT AMERICA. BUT I SEE BEYOND NATIONS NOW.
I...
NO DEFIANT LAST WORDS, SAM. YOUR "SON" KAL CHOSE TO STAND IN MY WAY...
...I'LL KILL HIM NEXT.
AND SHOW YOU HOW A MONSTER PROTECTS THIS WORLD.
SKRUTCH

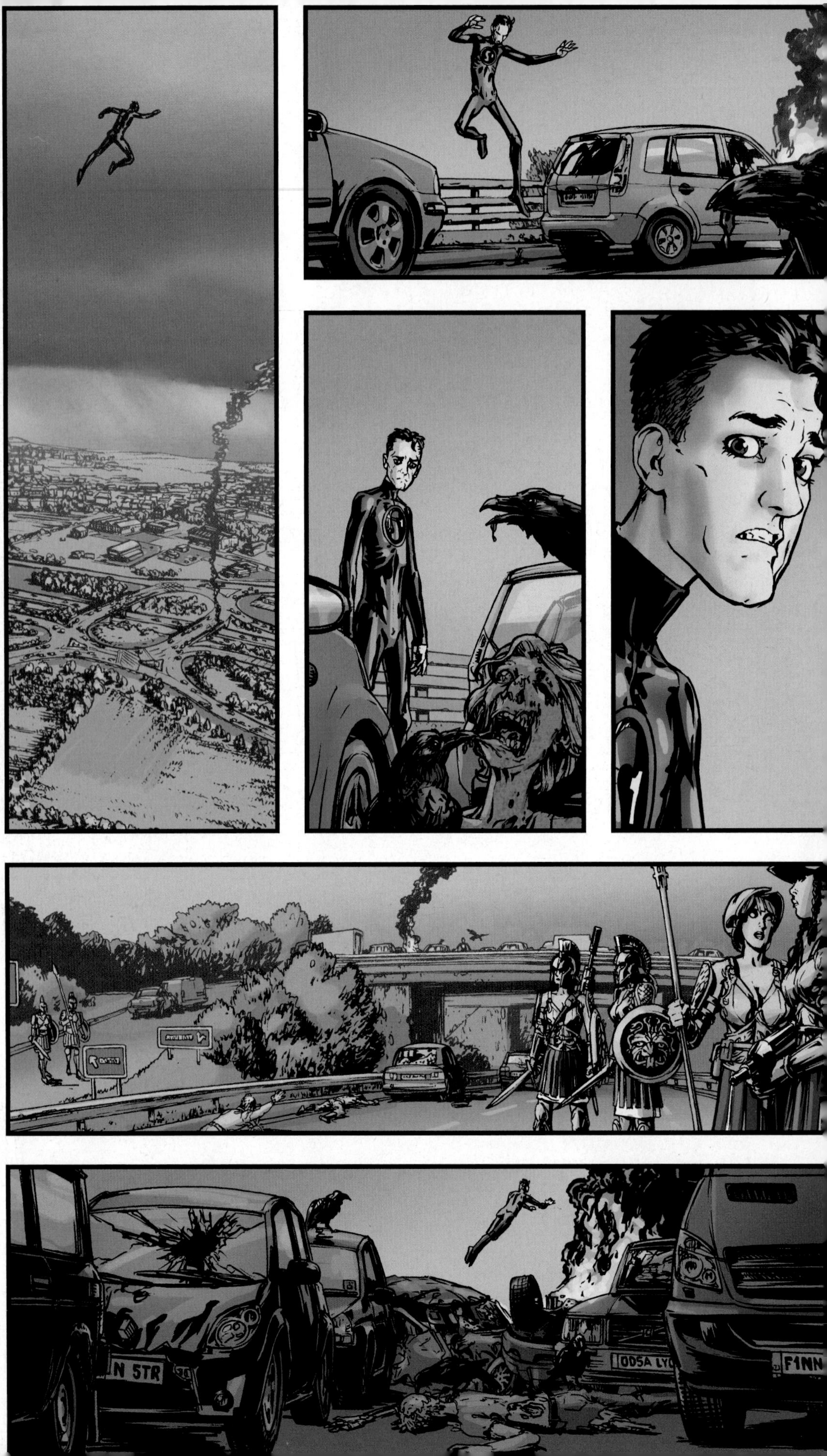
N 5TR
OD5A LY
F1NN

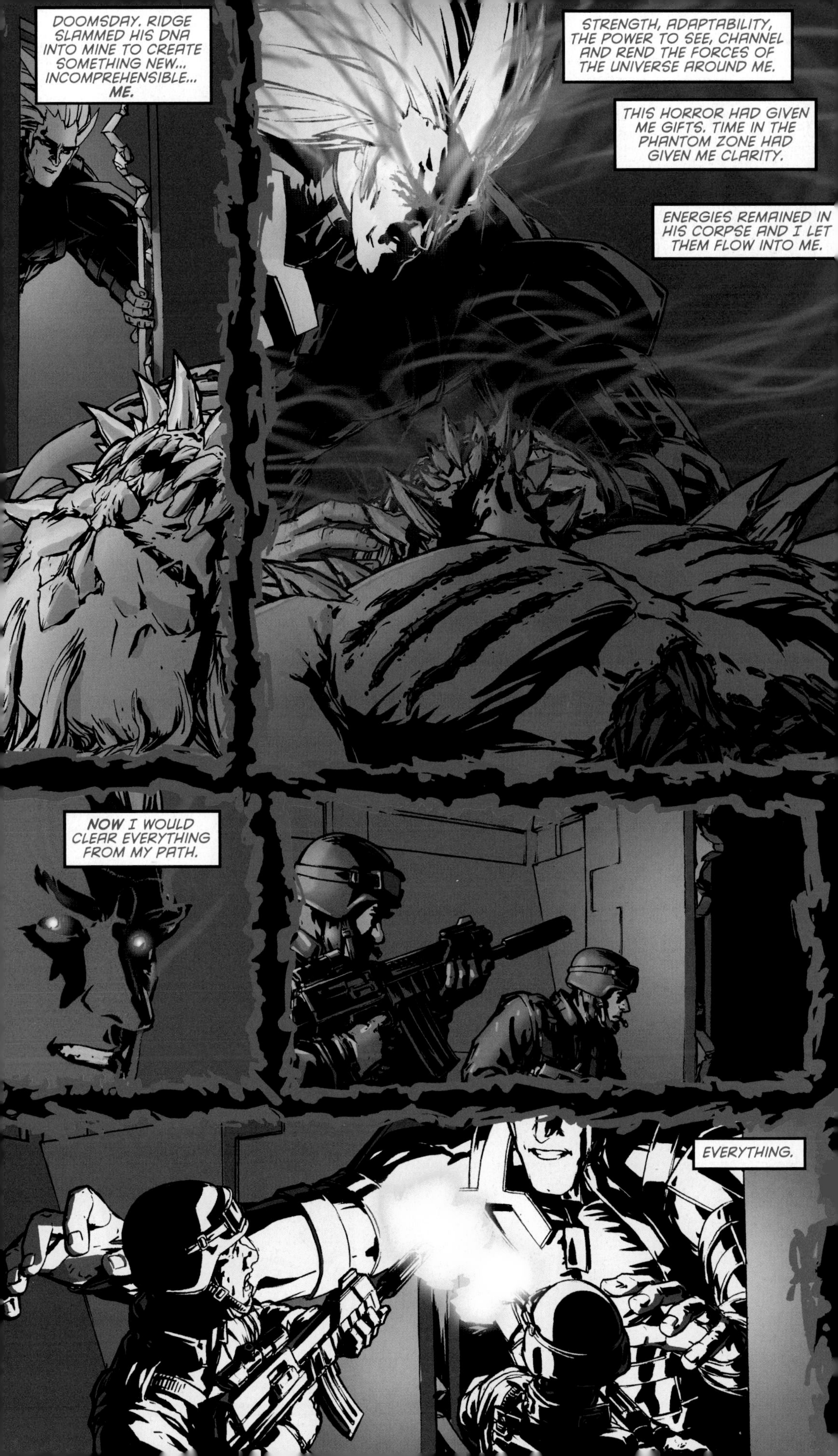
DOOMSDAY. RIDGE SLAMMED HIS DNA INTO MINE TO CREATE SOMETHING NEW... INCOMPREHENSIBLE... ME.
STRENGTH, ADAPTABILITY, THE POWER TO SEE, CHANNEL AND REND THE FORCES OF THE UNIVERSE AROUND ME.
THIS HORROR HAD GIVEN ME GIFTS. TIME IN THE PHANTOM ZONE HAD GIVEN ME CLARITY.
ENERGIES REMAINED IN HIS CORPSE AND I LET THEM FLOW INTO ME.
NOW I WOULD CLEAR EVERYTHING FROM MY PATH.
EVERYTHING.

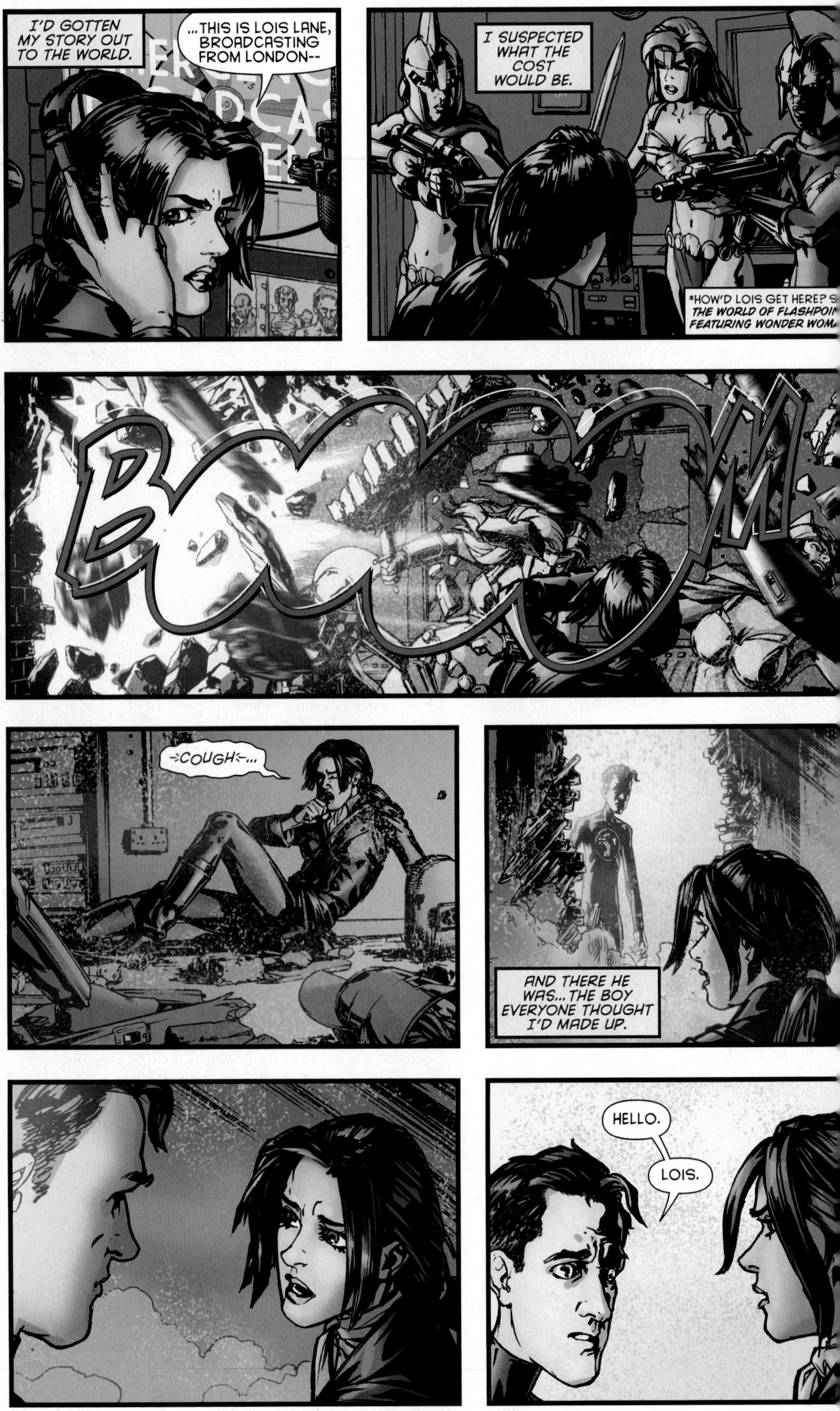
I'D GOTTEN MY STORY OUT TO THE WORLD.
...THIS IS LOIS LANE, BROADCASTING FROM LONDON--
I SUSPECTED WHAT THE COST WOULD BE.
*HOW'D LOIS GET HERE? S
THE WORLD OF FLASHPOI
FEATURING WONDER WOM
BOOM
>COUGH<...
AND THERE HE WAS...THE BOY EVERYONE THOUGHT I'D MADE UP.
HELLO.
LOIS.

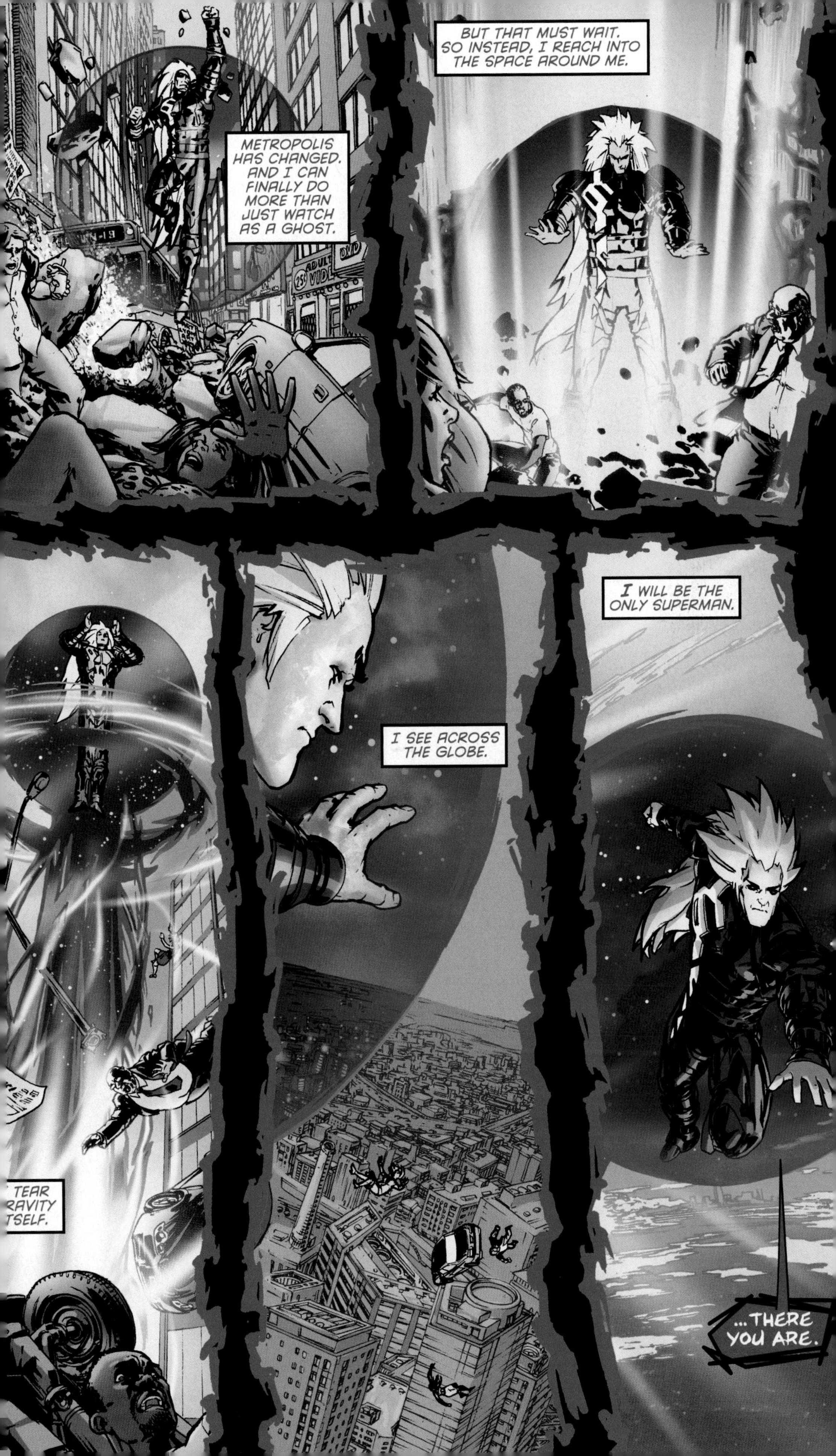
METROPOLIS HAS CHANGED. AND I CAN FINALLY DO MORE THAN JUST WATCH AS A GHOST.
BUT THAT MUST WAIT. SO INSTEAD, I REACH INTO THE SPACE AROUND ME.
TEAR
RAVITY
TSELF.
I SEE ACROSS THE GLOBE.
I WILL BE THE ONLY SUPERMAN.
...THERE YOU ARE.

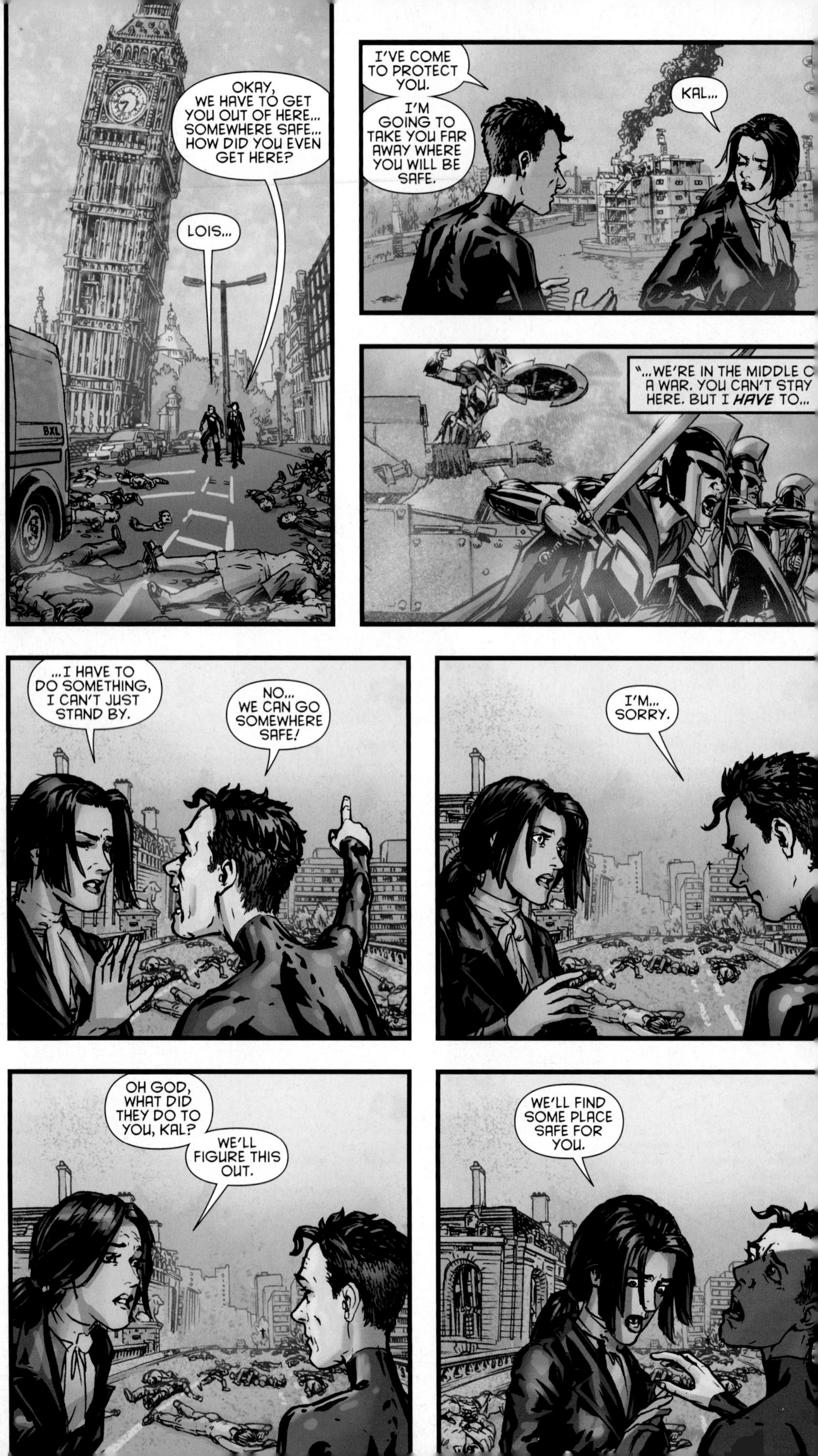
OKAY, WE HAVE TO GET YOU OUT OF HERE... SOMEWHERE SAFE... HOW DID YOU EVEN GET HERE?
LOIS...
BXL
I'VE COME TO PROTECT YOU.
I'M GOING TO TAKE YOU FAR AWAY WHERE YOU WILL BE SAFE.
KAL...
"...WE'RE IN THE MIDDLE O A WAR. YOU CAN'T STAY HERE. BUT I *HAVE* TO...
...I HAVE TO DO SOMETHING, I CAN'T JUST STAND BY.
NO... WE CAN GO SOMEWHERE SAFE!
I'M... SORRY.
OH GOD, WHAT DID THEY DO TO YOU, KAL?
WE'LL FIGURE THIS OUT.
WE'LL FIND SOME PLACE SAFE FOR YOU.

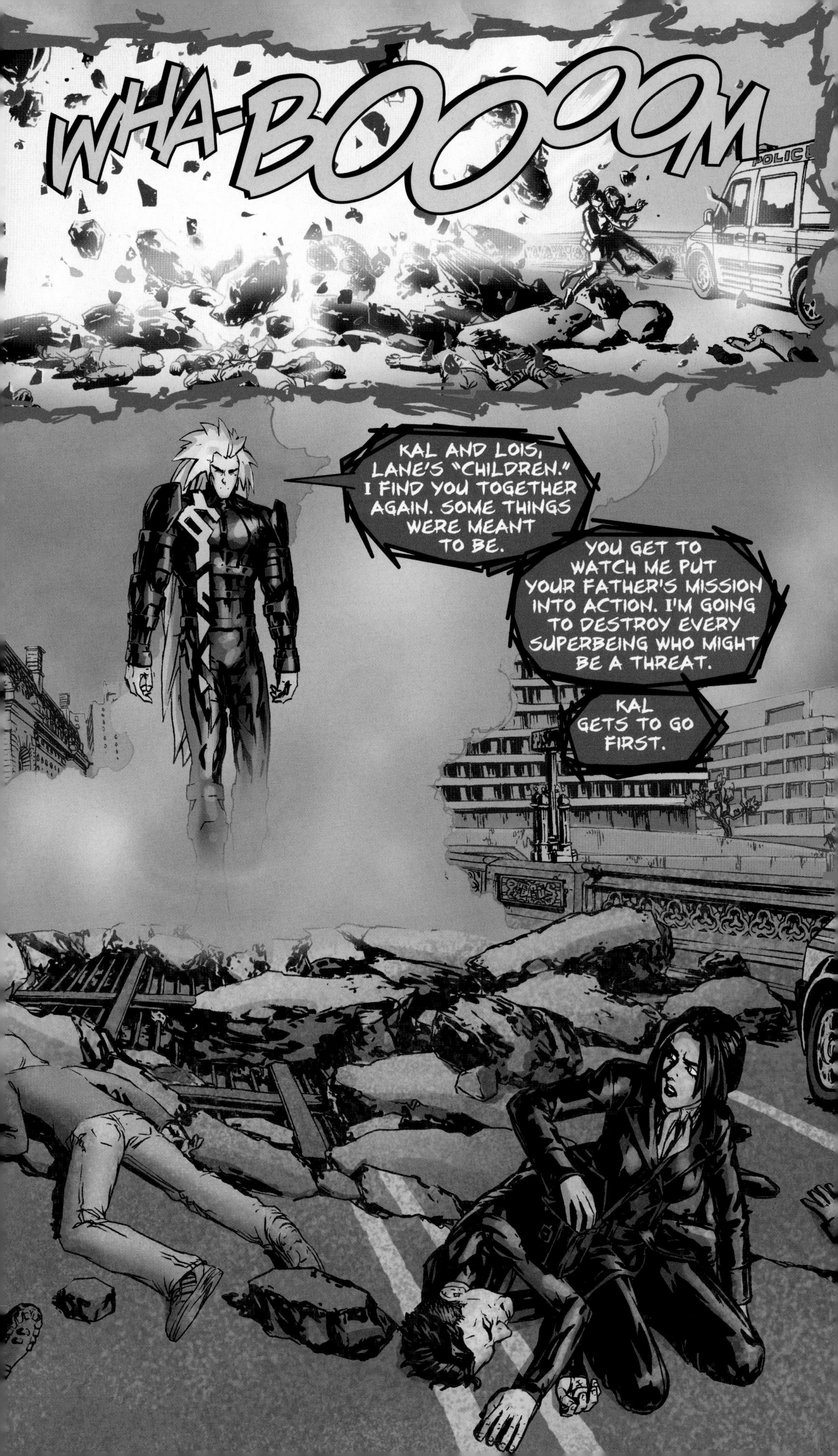
WHA-BOOOOM
POLICE
KAL AND LOIS, LANE'S "CHILDREN." I FIND YOU TOGETHER AGAIN. SOME THINGS WERE MEANT TO BE.
YOU GET TO WATCH ME PUT YOUR FATHER'S MISSION INTO ACTION. I'M GOING TO DESTROY EVERY SUPERBEING WHO MIGHT BE A THREAT.
KAL GETS TO GO FIRST.

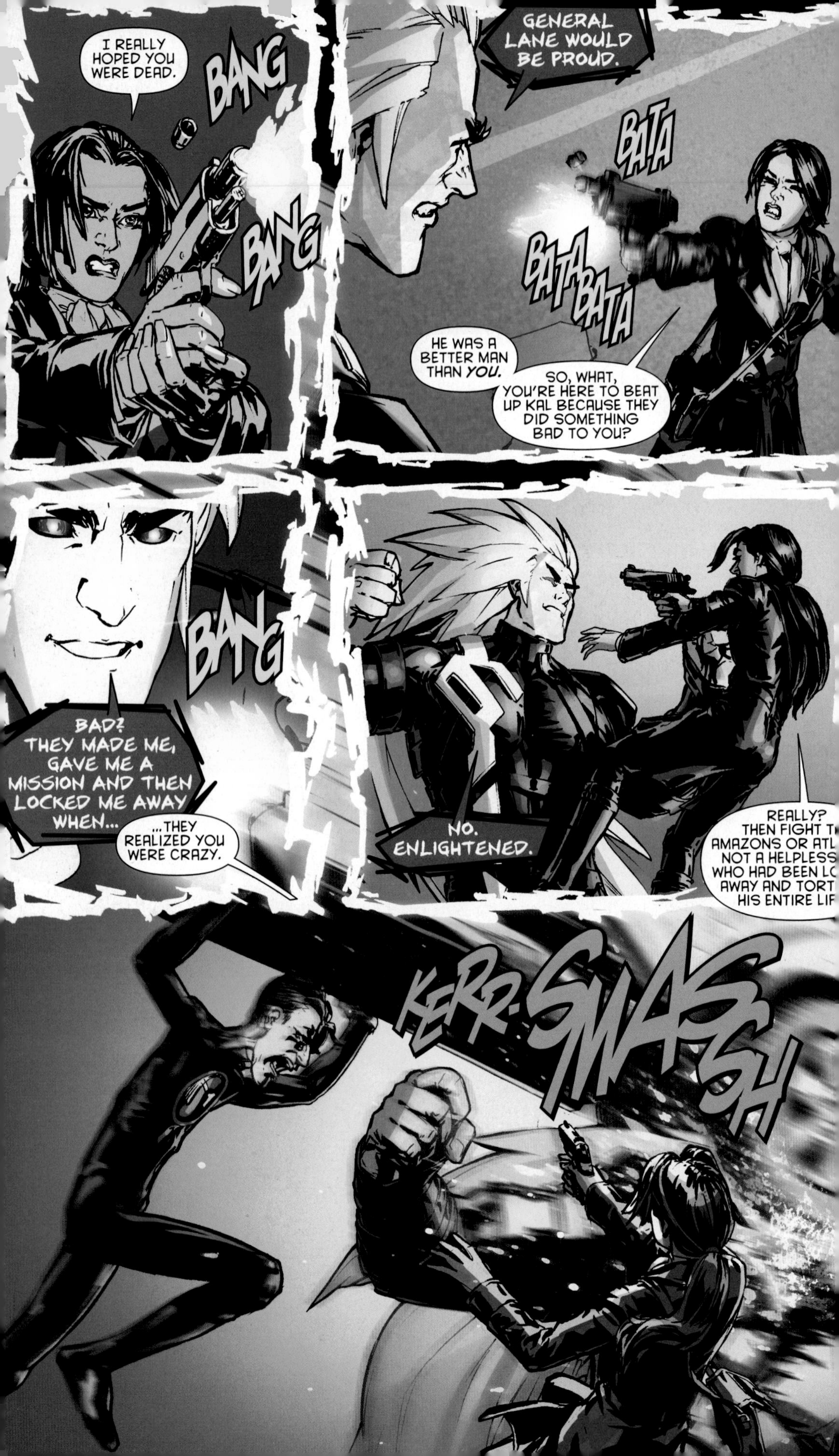

I REALLY HOPED YOU WERE DEAD.
BANG
BANG
GENERAL LANE WOULD BE PROUD.
BATA
BATA BATA
HE WAS A BETTER MAN THAN YOU.
SO, WHAT, YOU'RE HERE TO BEAT UP KAL BECAUSE THEY DID SOMETHING BAD TO YOU?
BANG
BAD? THEY MADE ME, GAVE ME A MISSION AND THEN LOCKED ME AWAY WHEN...
...THEY REALIZED YOU WERE CRAZY.
NO. ENLIGHTENED.
REALLY?
KERR-SMASH

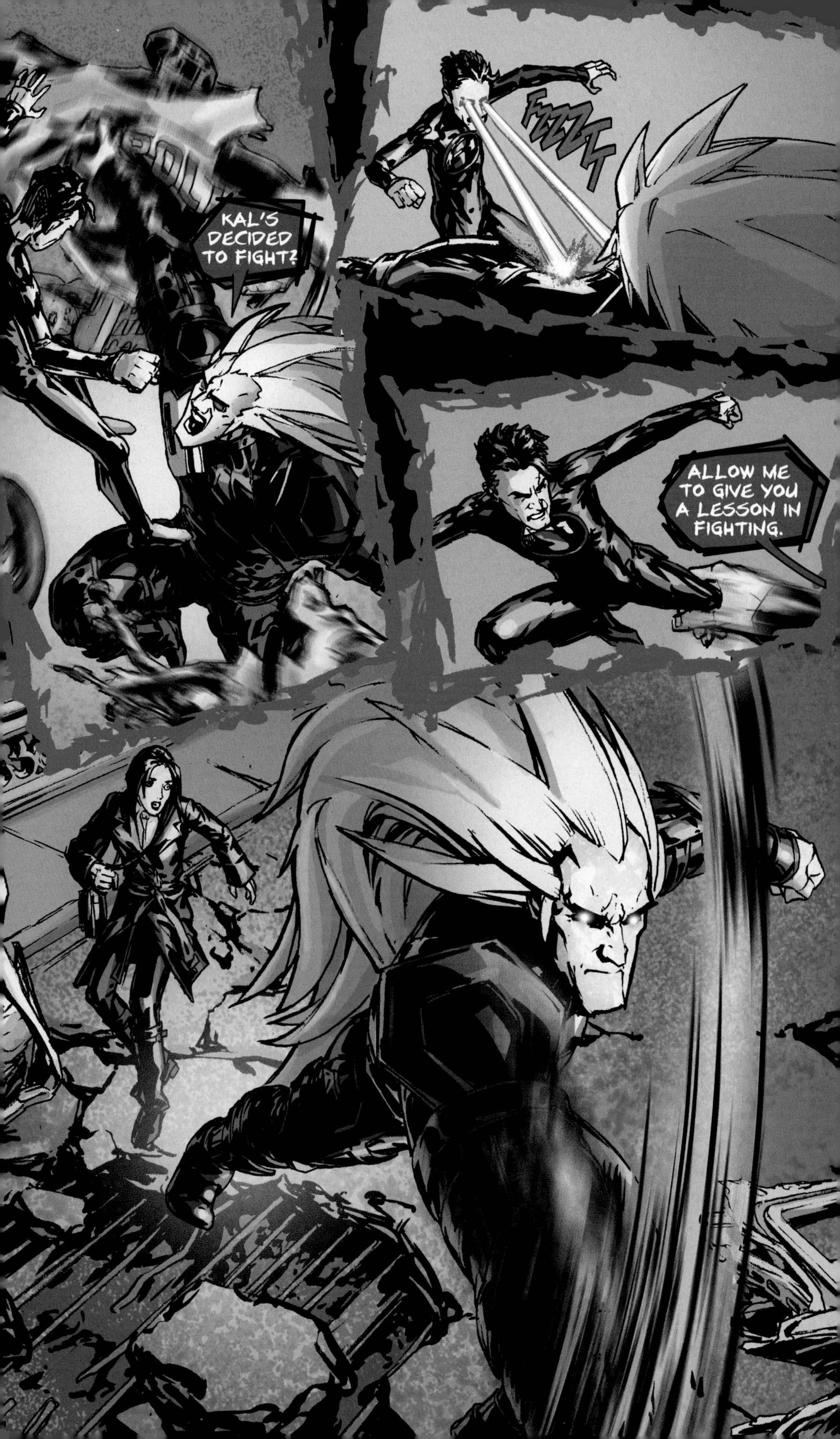
KAL'S DECIDED TO FIGHT?
FZZZZT
ALLOW ME TO GIVE YOU A LESSON IN FIGHTING.

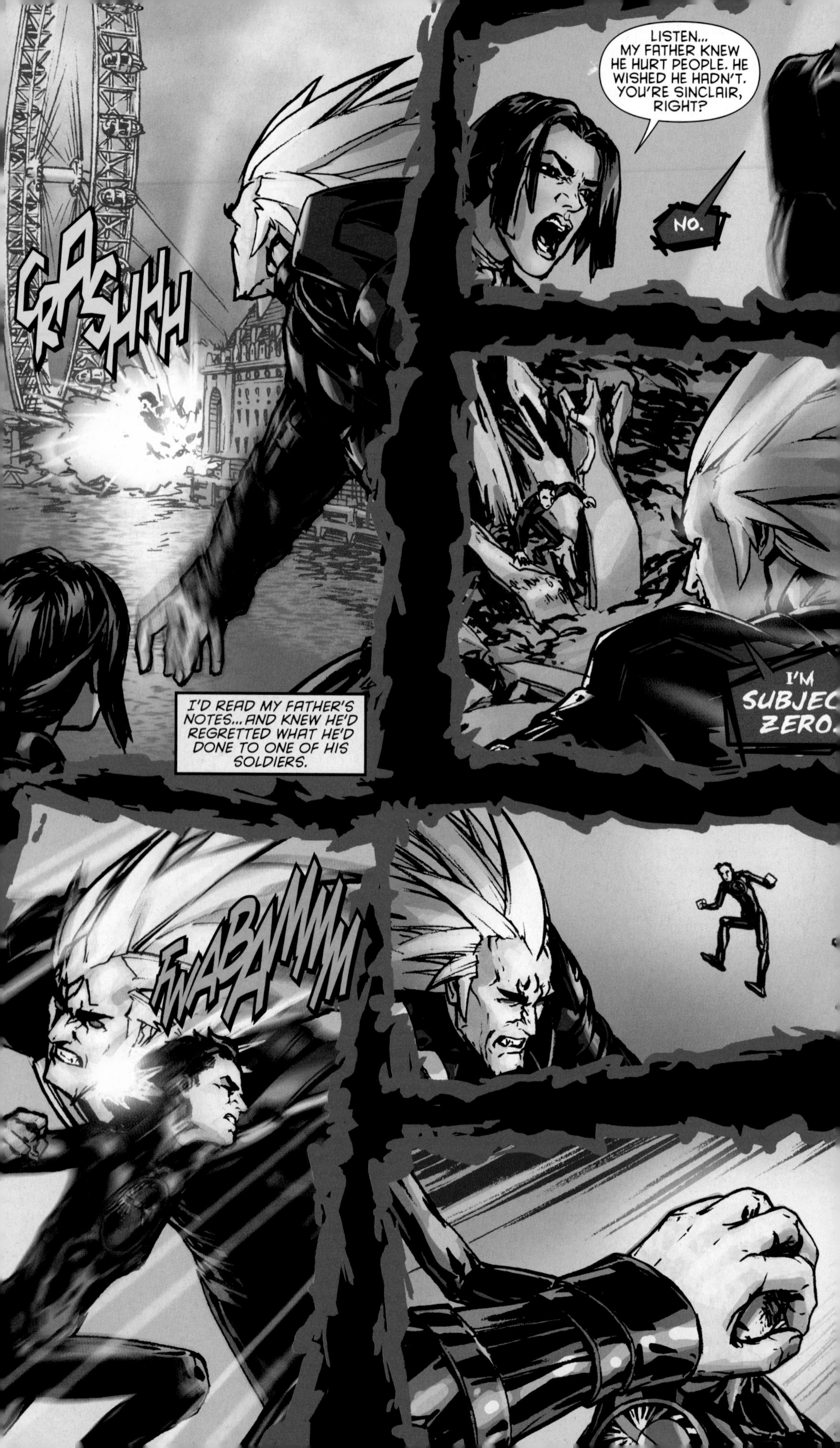
CRASHHH
LISTEN... MY FATHER KNEW HE HURT PEOPLE. HE WISHED HE HADN'T. YOU'RE SINCLAIR, RIGHT?
NO.
I'D READ MY FATHER'S NOTES...AND KNEW HE'D REGRETTED WHAT HE'D DONE TO ONE OF HIS SOLDIERS.
I'M SUBJEC ZERO.
FWABAMMM

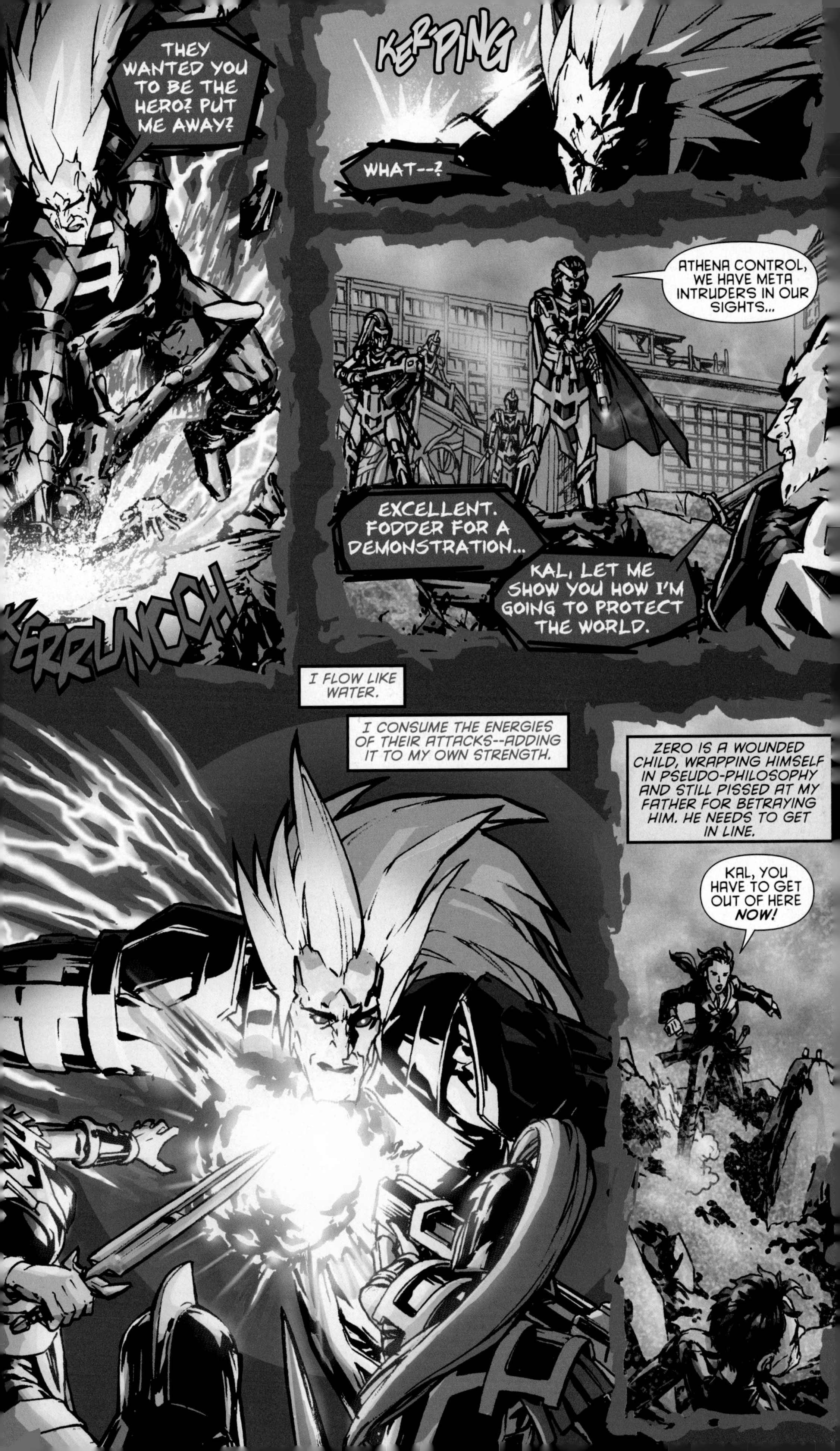
THEY WANTED YOU TO BE THE HERO? PUT ME AWAY?
KERRUNCCH
KERPING
WHAT--?
ATHENA CONTROL, WE HAVE META INTRUDERS IN OUR SIGHTS...
EXCELLENT. FODDER FOR A DEMONSTRATION...
KAL, LET ME SHOW YOU HOW I'M GOING TO PROTECT THE WORLD.
I FLOW LIKE WATER.
I CONSUME THE ENERGIES OF THEIR ATTACKS--ADDING IT TO MY OWN STRENGTH.
ZERO IS A WOUNDED CHILD, WRAPPING HIMSELF IN PSEUDO-PHILOSOPHY AND STILL PISSED AT MY FATHER FOR BETRAYING HIM. HE NEEDS TO GET IN LINE.
KAL, YOU HAVE TO GET OUT OF HERE NOW!

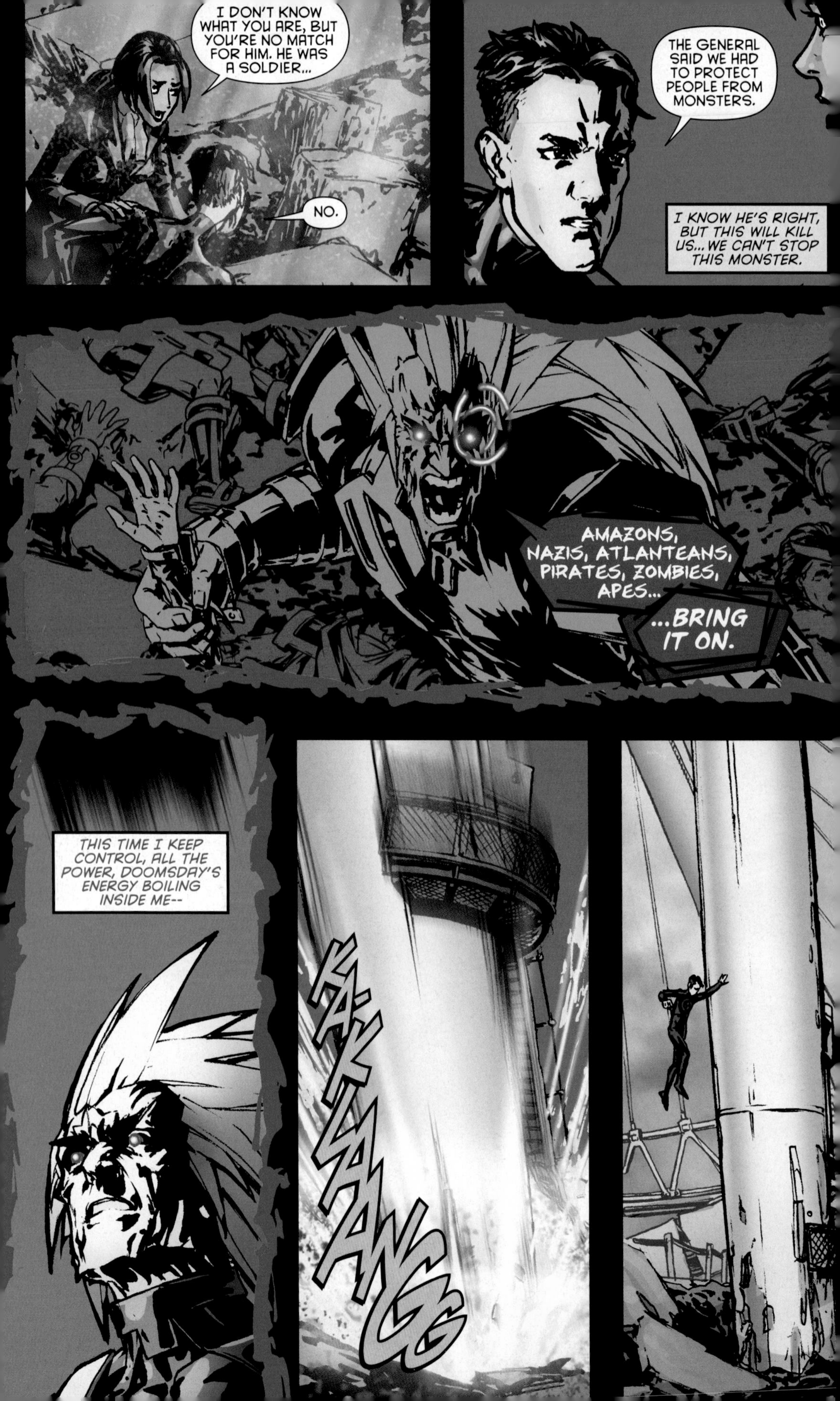
I DON'T KNOW WHAT YOU ARE, BUT YOU'RE NO MATCH FOR HIM. HE WAS A SOLDIER...
NO.
THE GENERAL SAID WE HAD TO PROTECT PEOPLE FROM MONSTERS.
I KNOW HE'S RIGHT, BUT THIS WILL KILL US...WE CAN'T STOP THIS MONSTER.
AMAZONS, NAZIS, ATLANTEANS, PIRATES, ZOMBIES, APES...
...BRING IT ON.
THIS TIME I KEEP CONTROL, ALL THE POWER, DOOMSDAY'S ENERGY BOILING INSIDE ME--
KA-KLANNGG

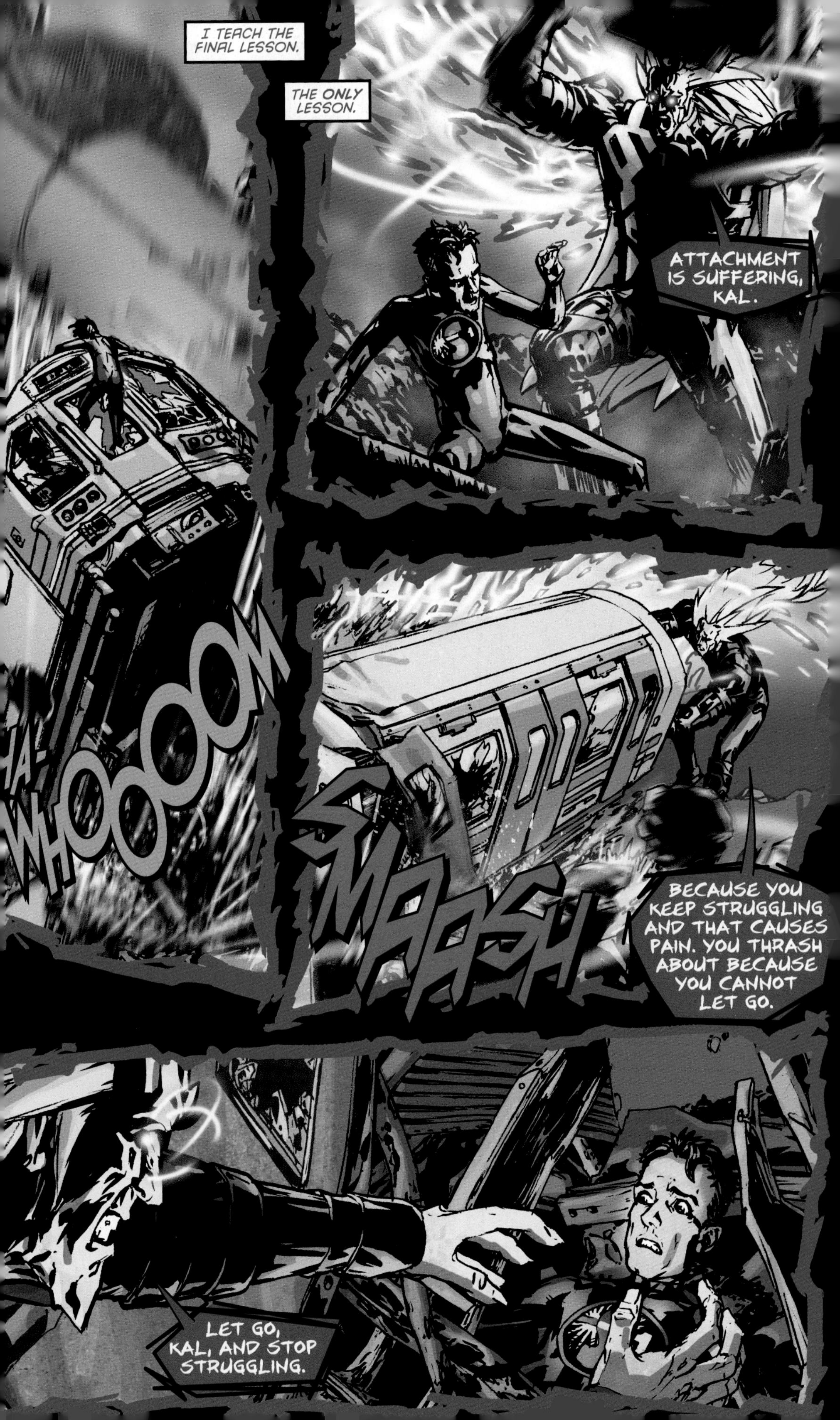
I TEACH THE FINAL LESSON.
THE ONLY LESSON.
ATTACHMENT IS SUFFERING, KAL.
KA-WHOOOOOM
SMASH
BECAUSE YOU KEEP STRUGGLING AND THAT CAUSES PAIN. YOU THRASH ABOUT BECAUSE YOU CANNOT LET GO.
LET GO, KAL, AND STOP STRUGGLING.

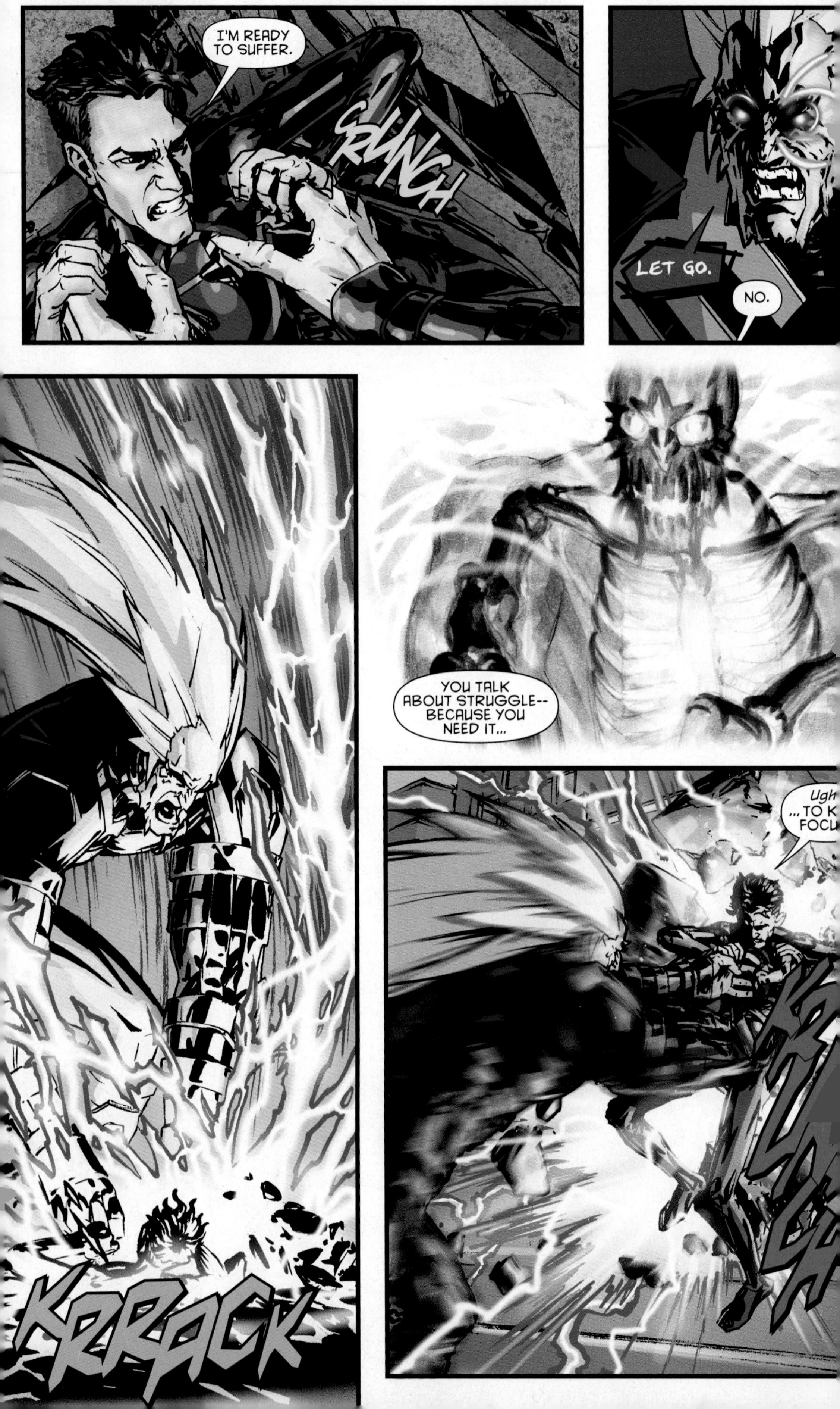
I'M READY TO SUFFER.
CRUNCH
LET GO.
NO.
YOU TALK ABOUT STRUGGLE-- BECAUSE YOU NEED IT...
KRRACK
Ugh
...TO

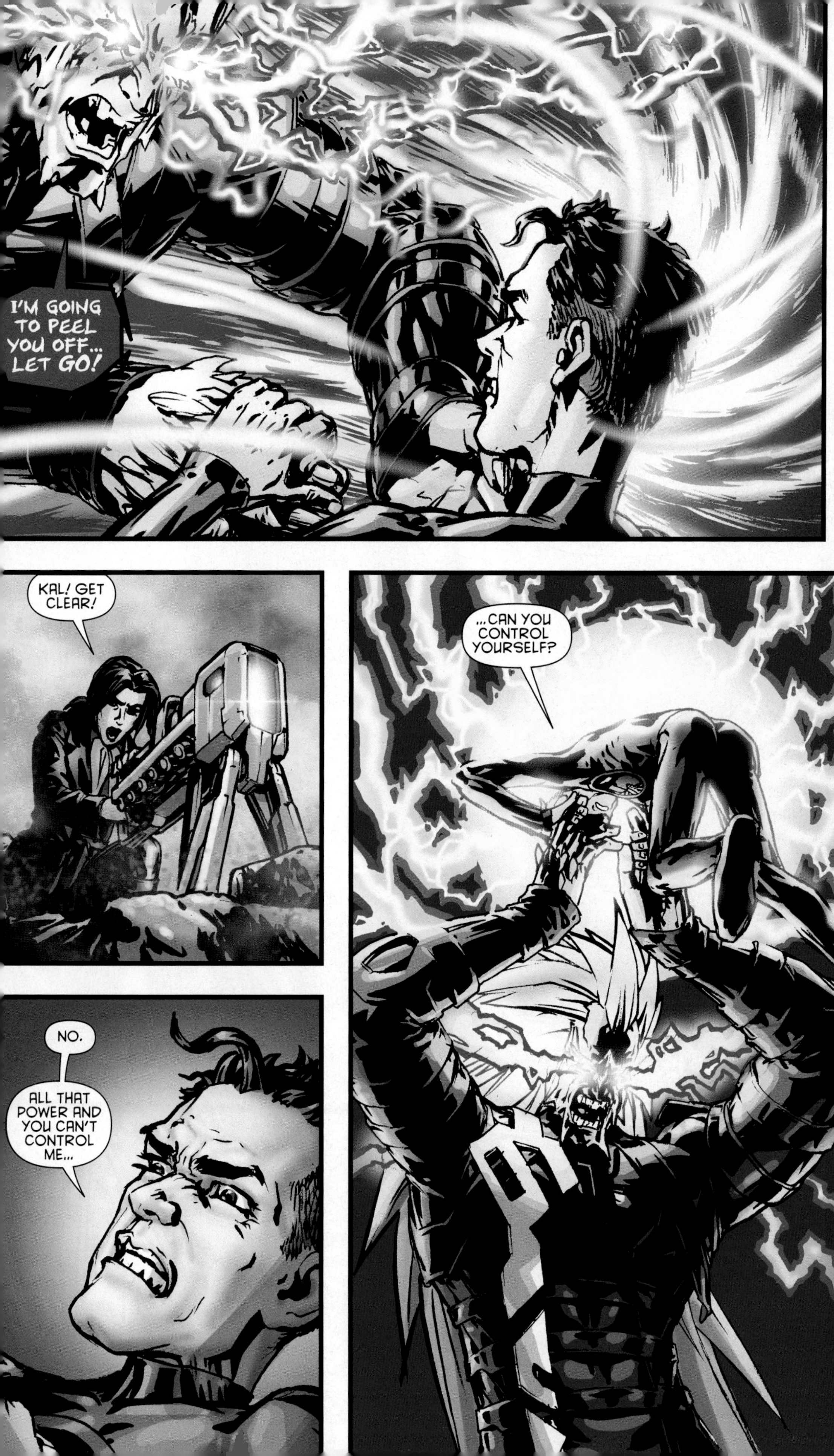
I'M GOING TO PEEL YOU OFF... LET GO!
KAL! GET CLEAR!
...CAN YOU CONTROL YOURSELF?
NO.
ALL THAT POWER AND YOU CAN'T CONTROL ME...

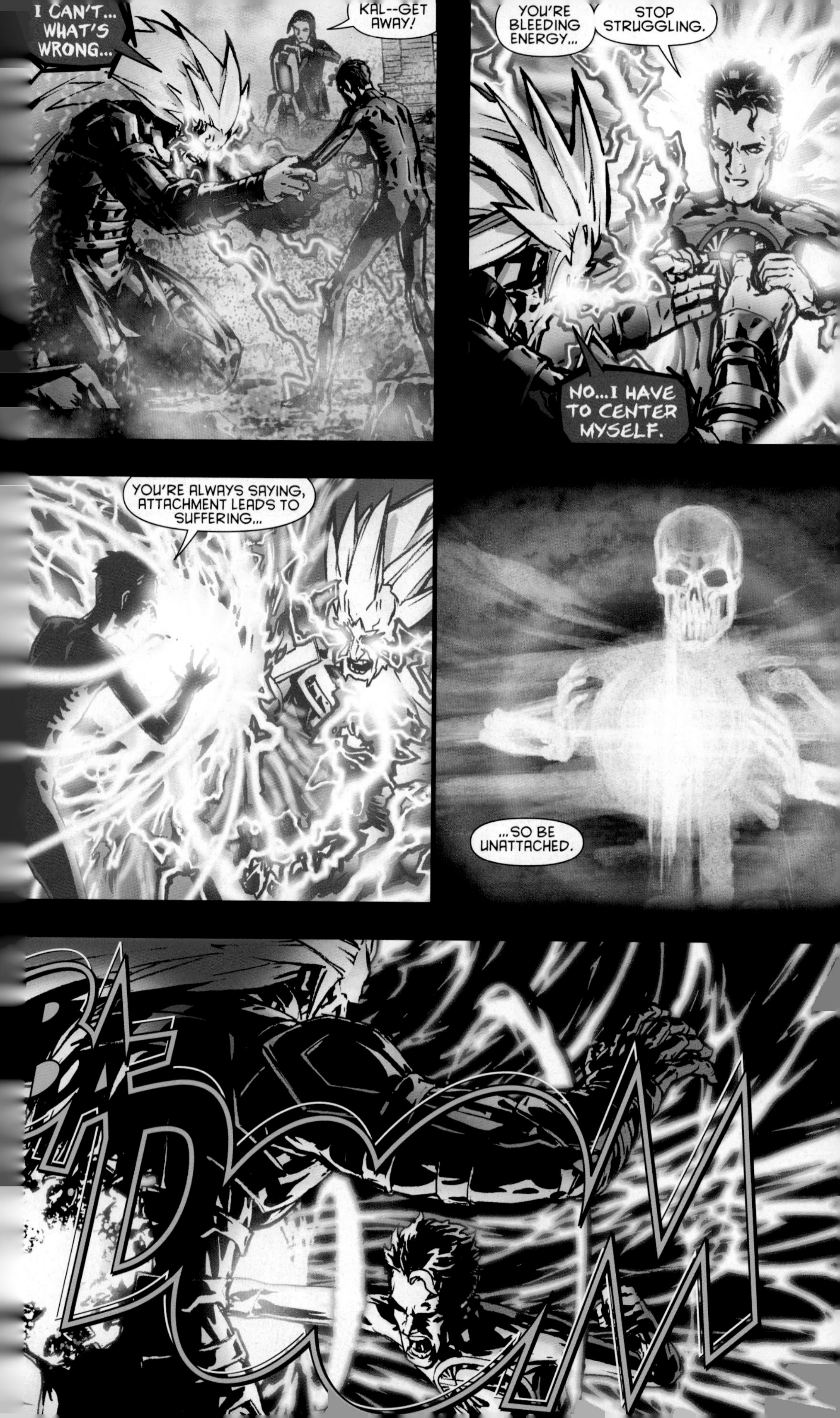
I CAN'T... WHAT'S WRONG...
KAL--GET AWAY!
YOU'RE BLEEDING ENERGY...
STOP STRUGGLING.
NO...I HAVE TO CENTER MYSELF.
YOU'RE ALWAYS SAYING, ATTACHMENT LEADS TO SUFFERING...
...SO BE UNATTACHED.

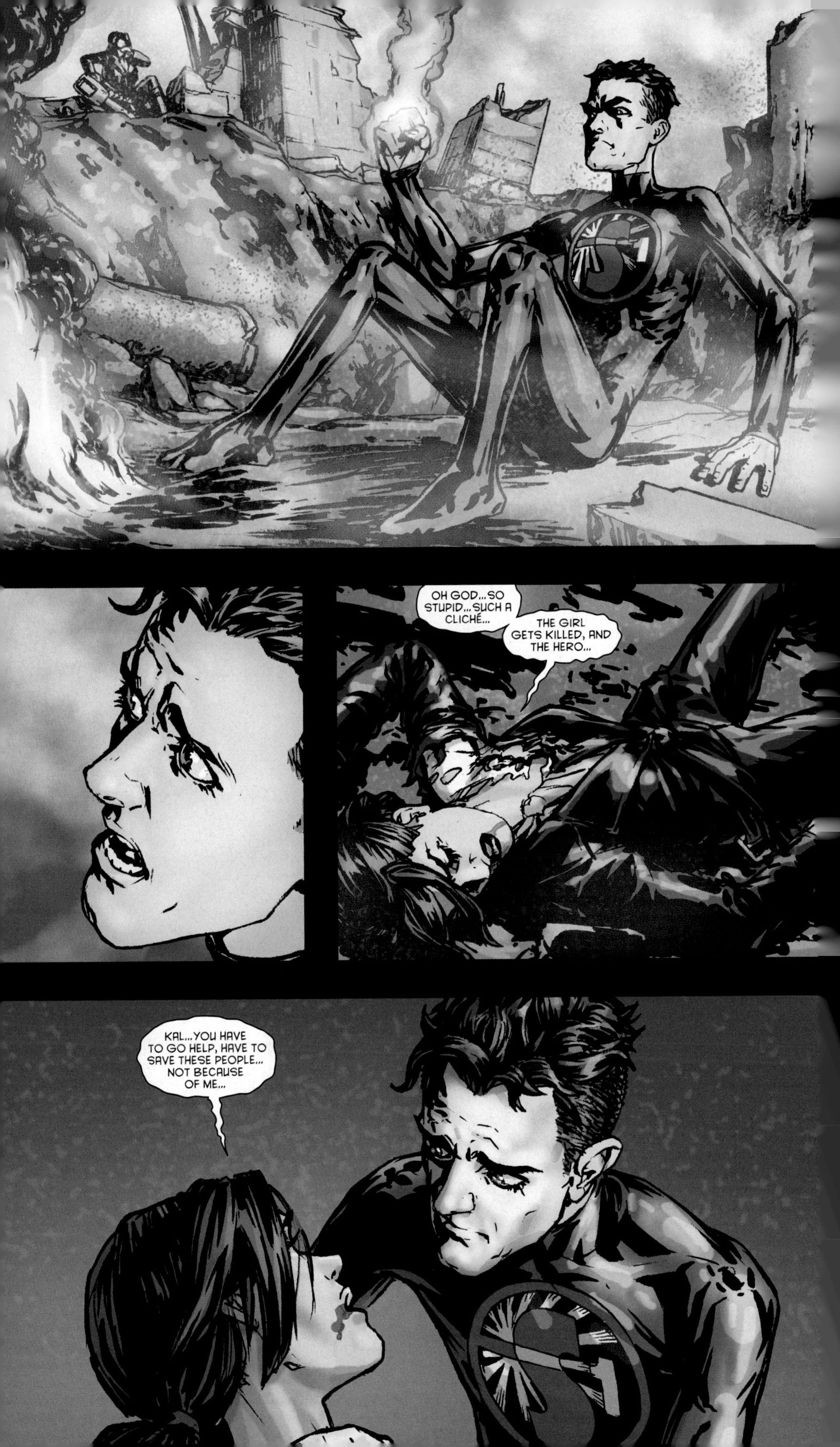
OH GOD... SO STUPID... SUCH A CLICHÉ...
THE GIRL GETS KILLED, AND THE HERO...
KAL... YOU HAVE TO GO HELP, HAVE TO SAVE THESE PEOPLE... NOT BECAUSE OF ME...

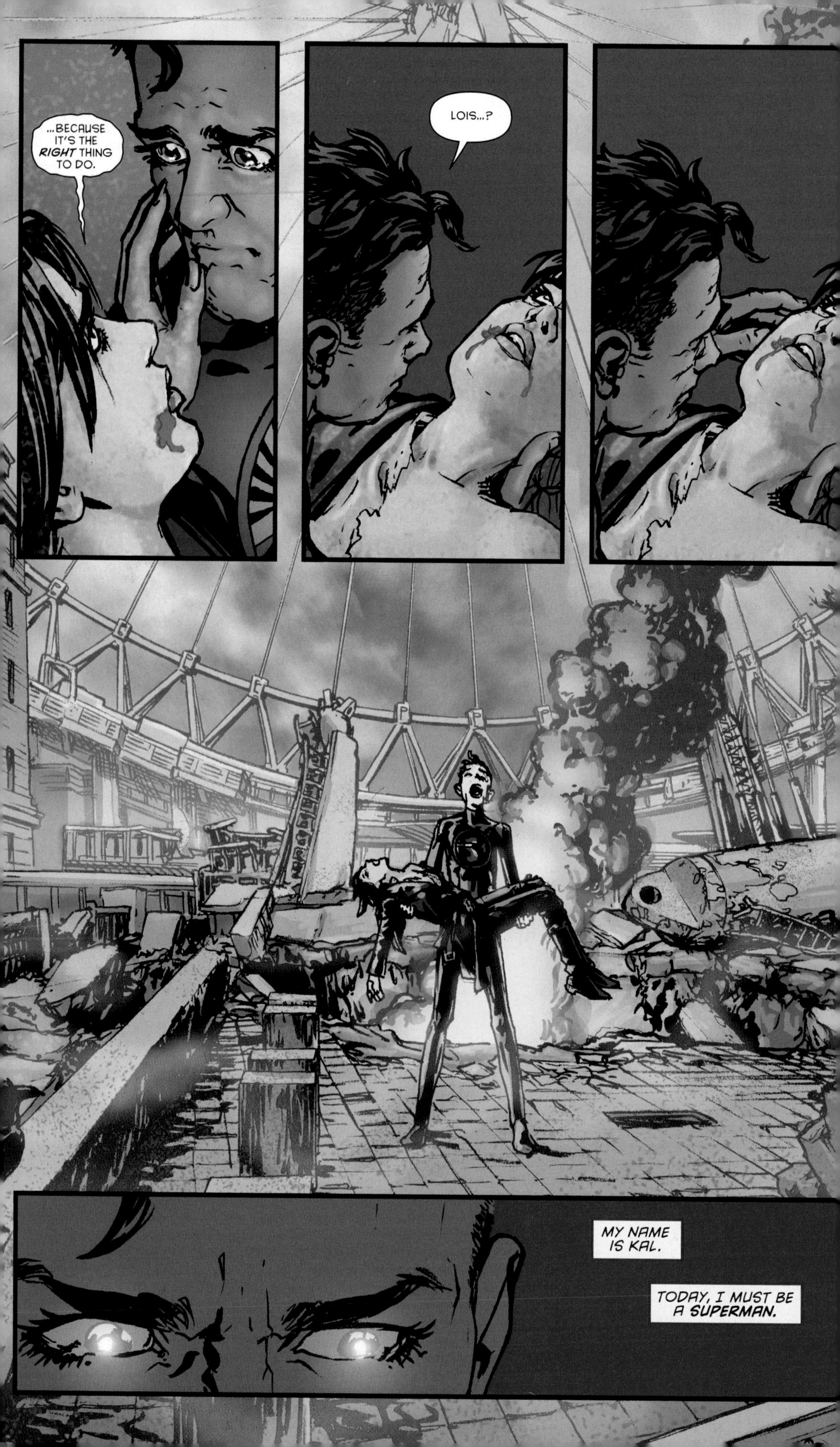

...BECAUSE IT'S THE RIGHT THING TO DO.
LOIS...?
MY NAME IS KAL.
TODAY, I MUST BE A SUPERMAN.

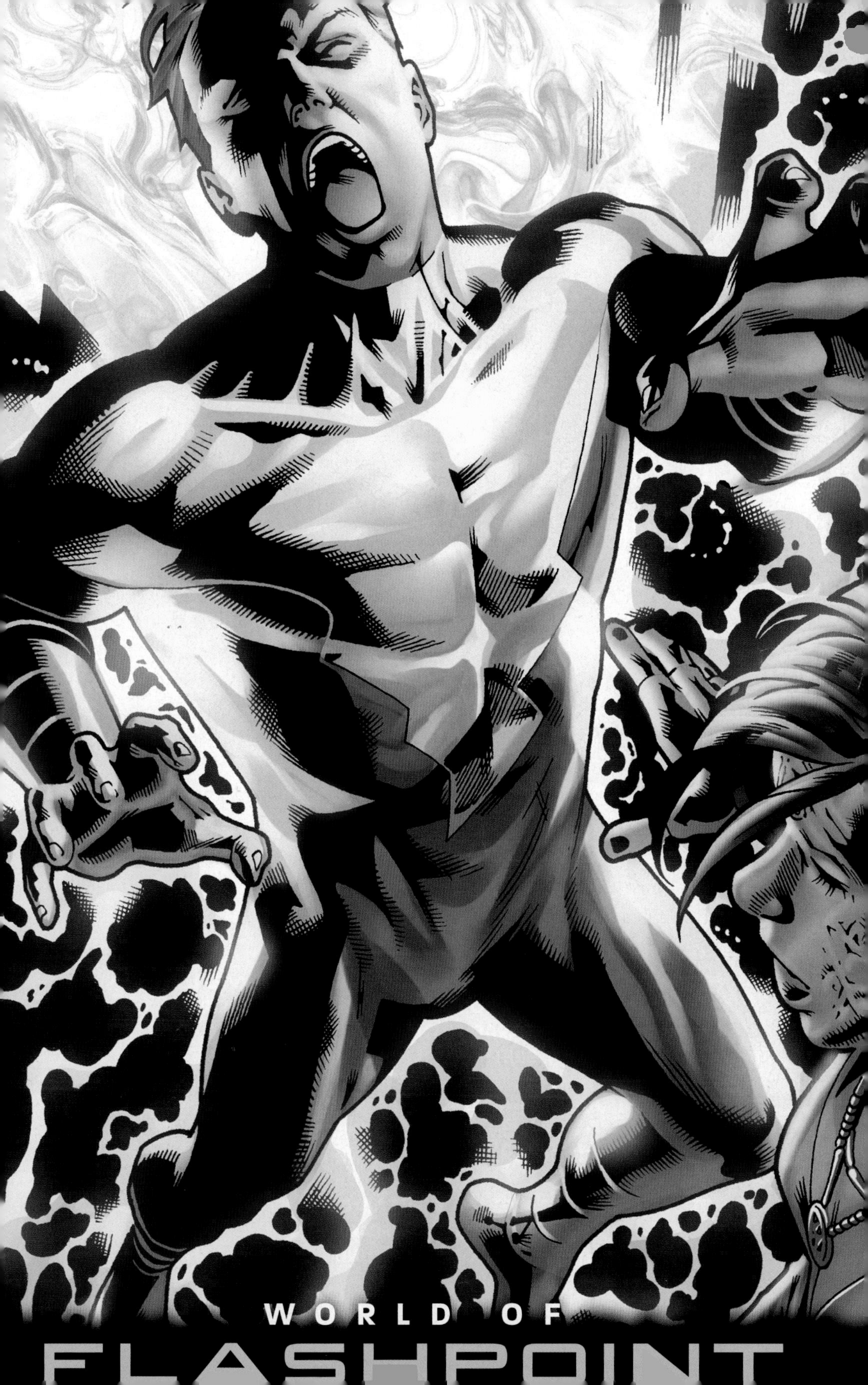
WORLD OF
FLASHPOINT

REX OGLE
Writer

PART ONE: THIS IS THE WORLD WE LIVE IN
Pencils by **EDUARDO FRANCISCO & PAULO SIQUEIRA**
Inks by **EDUARDO FRANCISCO & ROLAND PARIS**
Cover by **BRETT BOOTH & ANDREW DALHOUSE**

PART TWO: THIS IS THE WORLD WE MADE
Art by **EDUARDO FRANCISCO**
Cover by **BRETT BOOTH, NORM RAPMUND & ANDREW DALHOUSE**

PART THREE: THIS IS THE WORLD WE HOPE FOR
Art by **EDUARDO FRANCISCO**
Cover by **BRETT BOOTH, NORM RAPMUND & ANDREW DALHOUSE**

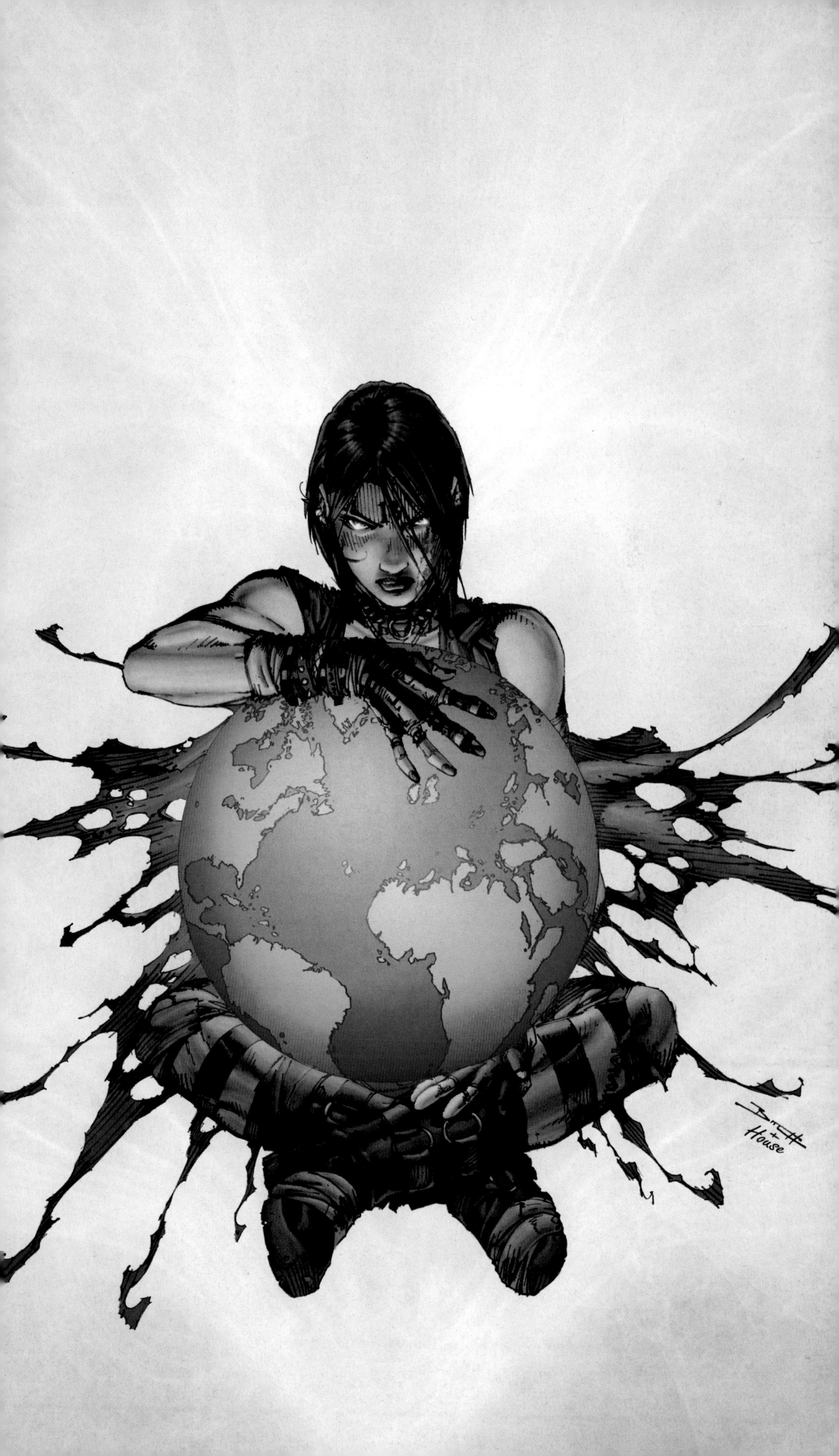
House

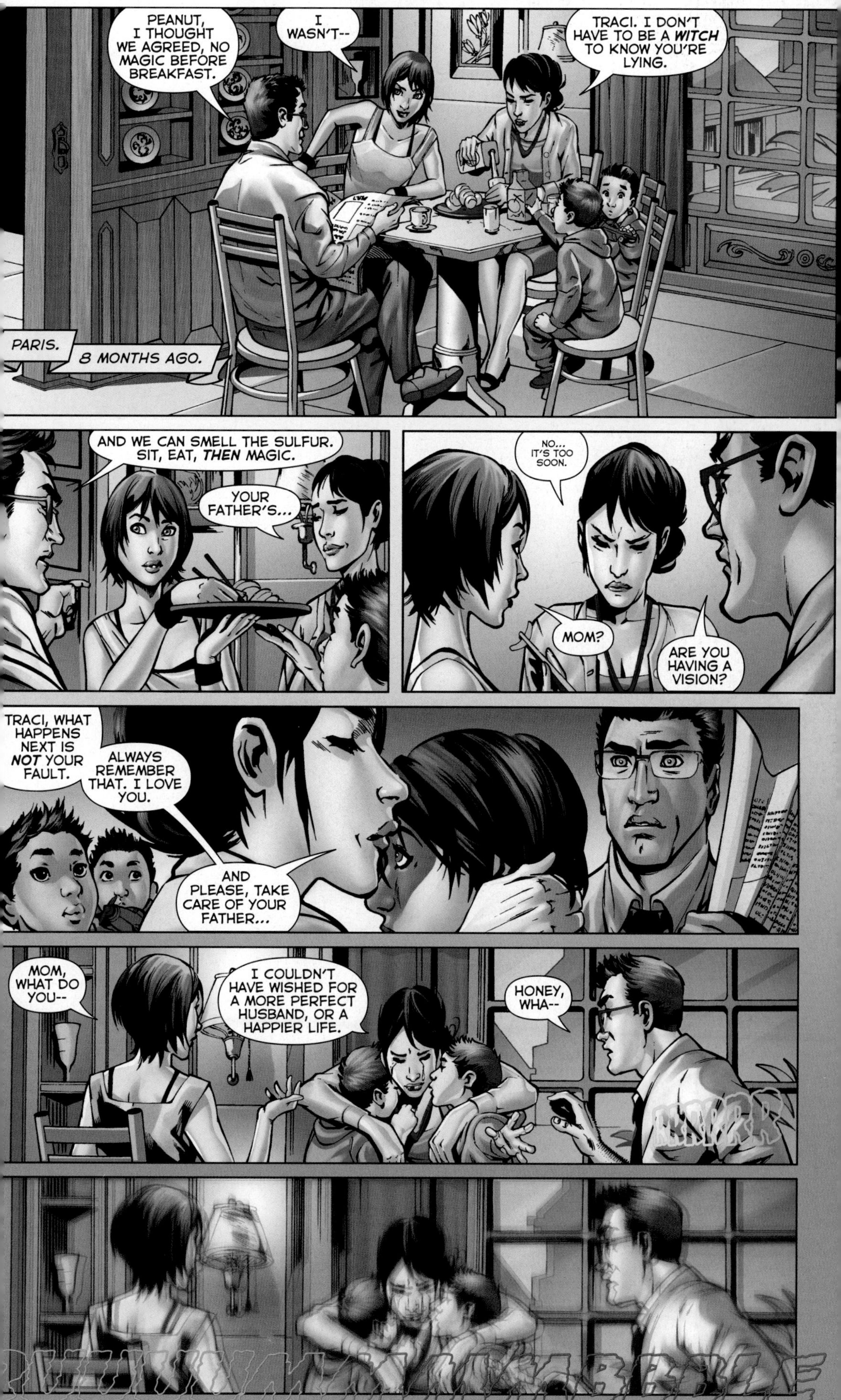
PEANUT, I THOUGHT WE AGREED, NO MAGIC BEFORE BREAKFAST.
I WASN'T--
TRACI. I DON'T HAVE TO BE A *WITCH* TO KNOW YOU'RE LYING.
PARIS.
8 MONTHS AGO.
AND WE CAN SMELL THE SULFUR. SIT, EAT, *THEN* MAGIC.
YOUR FATHER'S...
NO... IT'S TOO SOON.
MOM?
ARE YOU HAVING A VISION?
TRACI, WHAT HAPPENS NEXT IS *NOT* YOUR FAULT.
ALWAYS REMEMBER THAT. I LOVE YOU.
AND PLEASE, TAKE CARE OF YOUR FATHER...
MOM, WHAT DO YOU--
I COULDN'T HAVE WISHED FOR A MORE PERFECT HUSBAND, OR A HAPPIER LIFE.
HONEY, WHA--

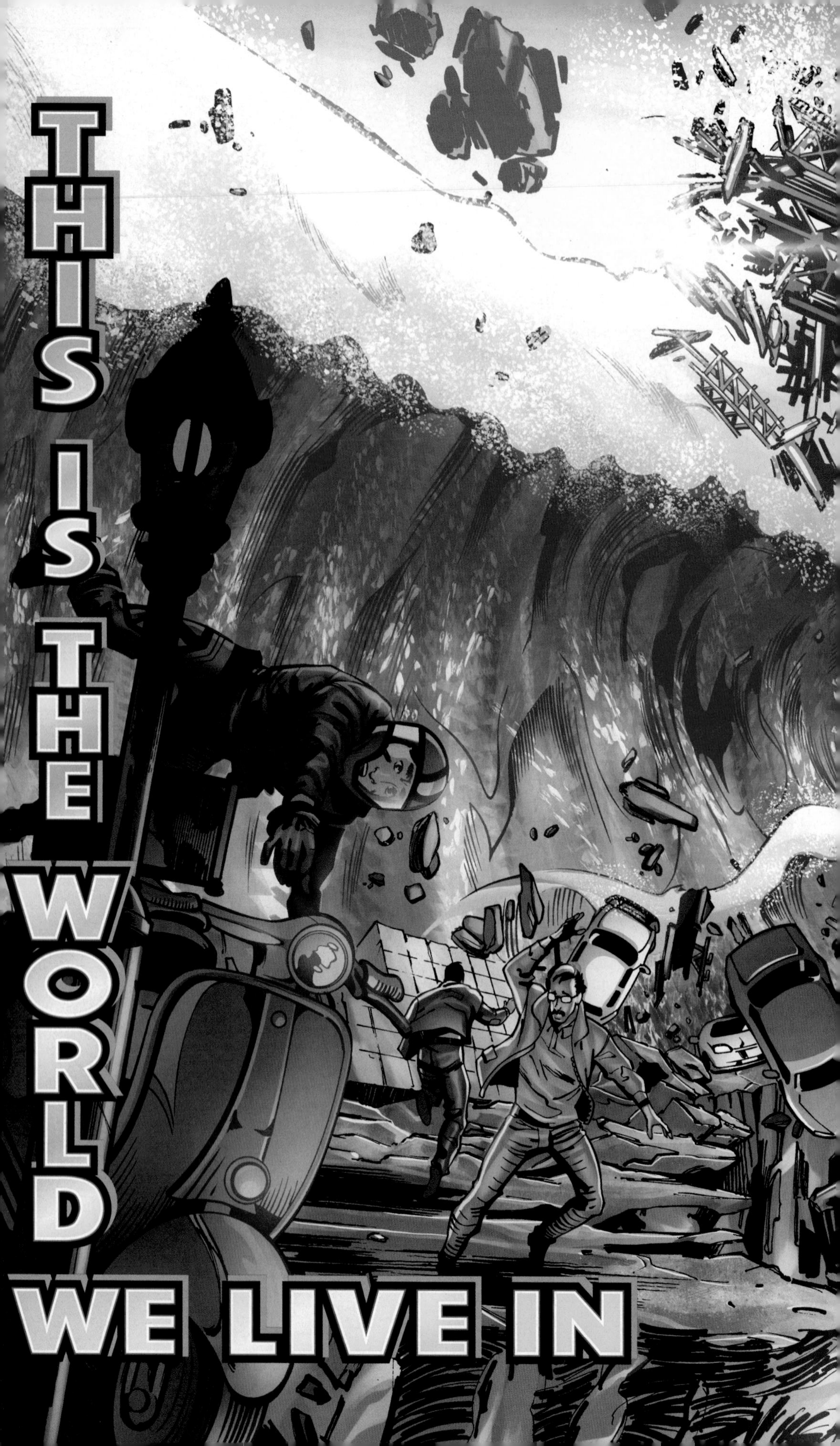
THIS IS THE WORLD
WE LIVE IN

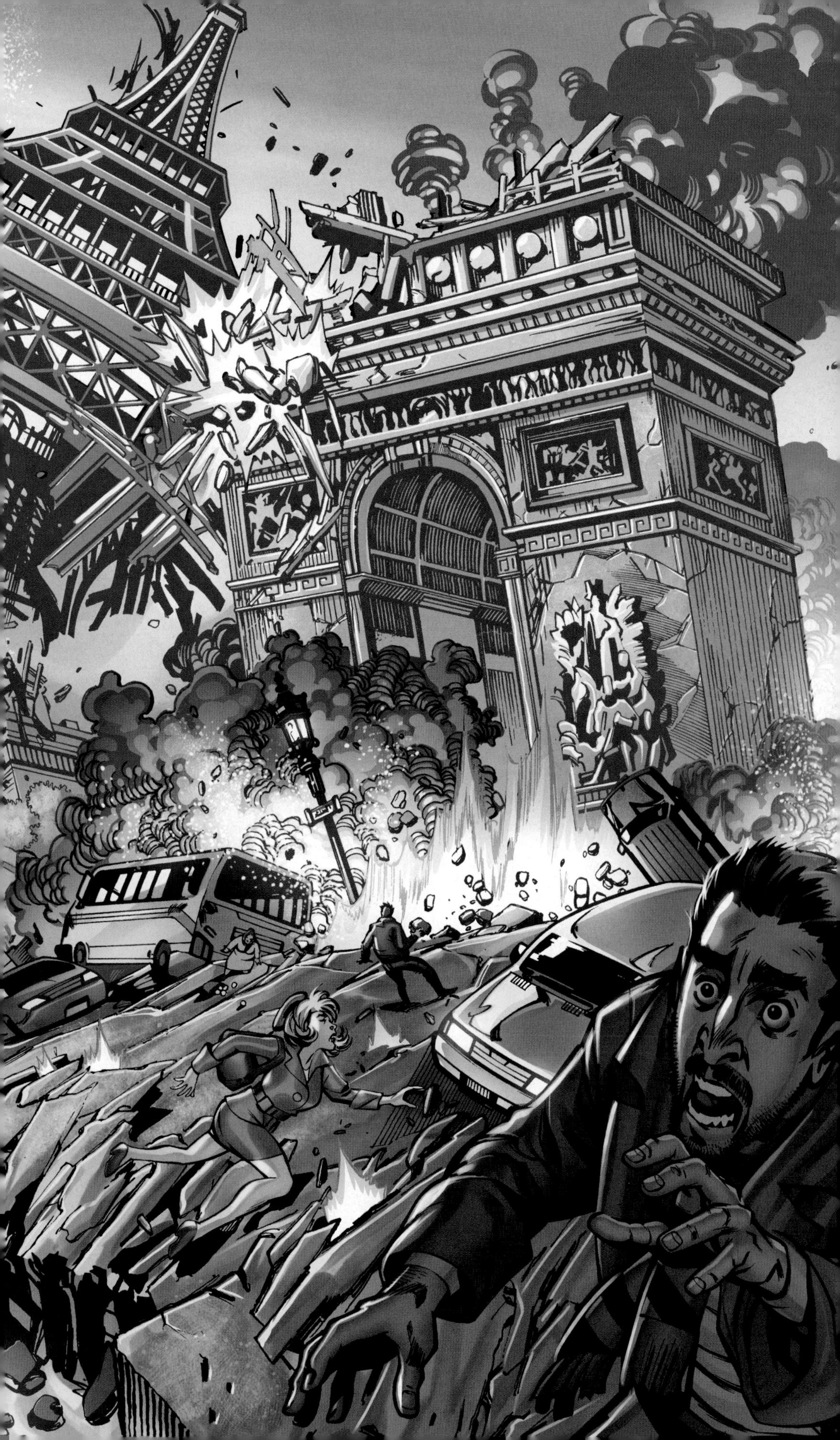

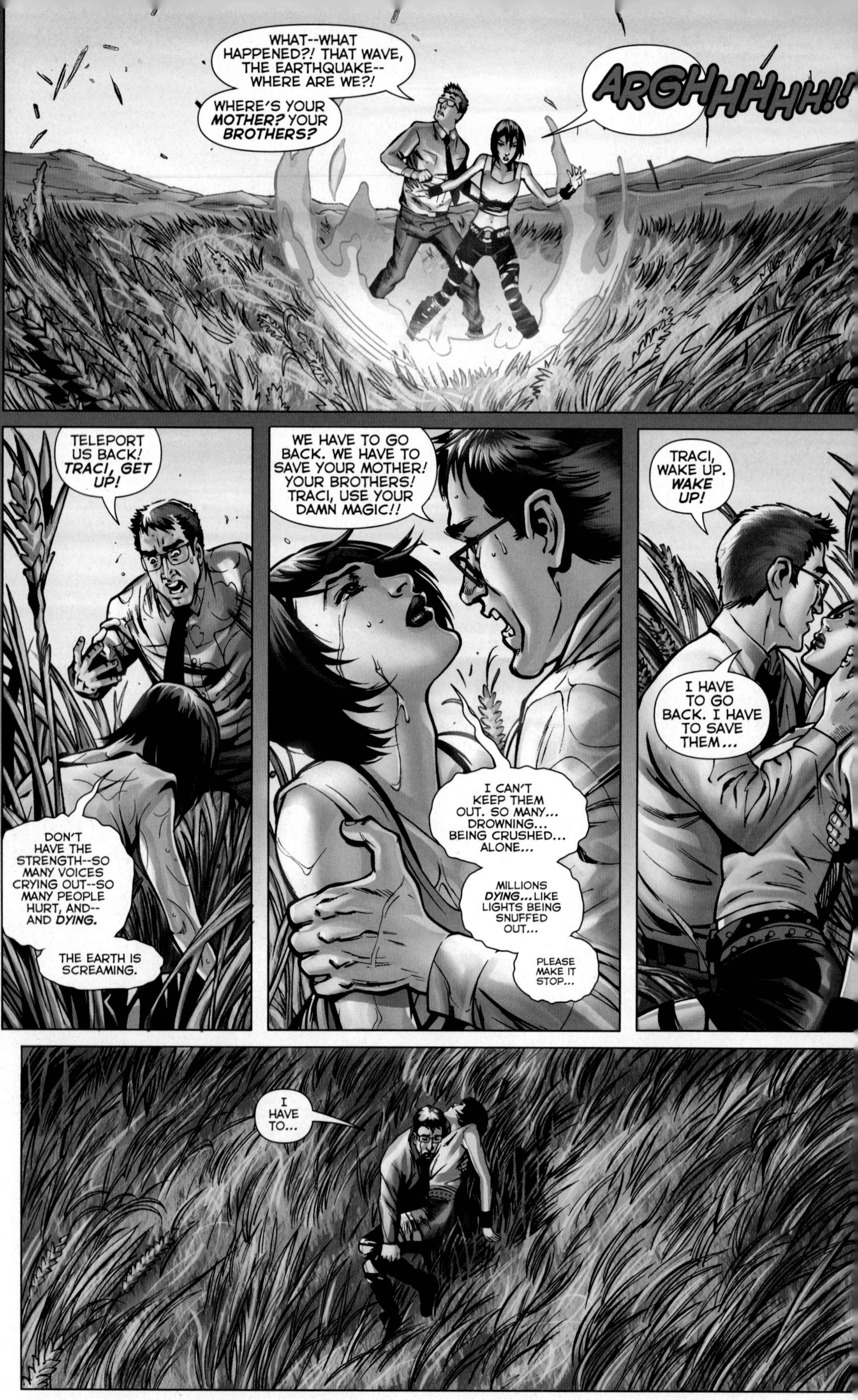
WHAT--WHAT HAPPENED?! THAT WAVE, THE EARTHQUAKE-- WHERE ARE WE?!
WHERE'S YOUR MOTHER? YOUR BROTHERS?
ARGHHHHH!!
TELEPORT US BACK! TRACI, GET UP!
DON'T HAVE THE STRENGTH--SO MANY VOICES CRYING OUT--SO MANY PEOPLE HURT, AND-- AND DYING.
THE EARTH IS SCREAMING.
WE HAVE TO GO BACK. WE HAVE TO SAVE YOUR MOTHER! YOUR BROTHERS! TRACI, USE YOUR DAMN MAGIC!!
I CAN'T KEEP THEM OUT. SO MANY... DROWNING... BEING CRUSHED... ALONE...
MILLIONS DYING... LIKE LIGHTS BEING SNUFFED OUT...
PLEASE MAKE IT STOP...
TRACI, WAKE UP. WAKE UP!
I HAVE TO GO BACK. I HAVE TO SAVE THEM...
I HAVE TO...

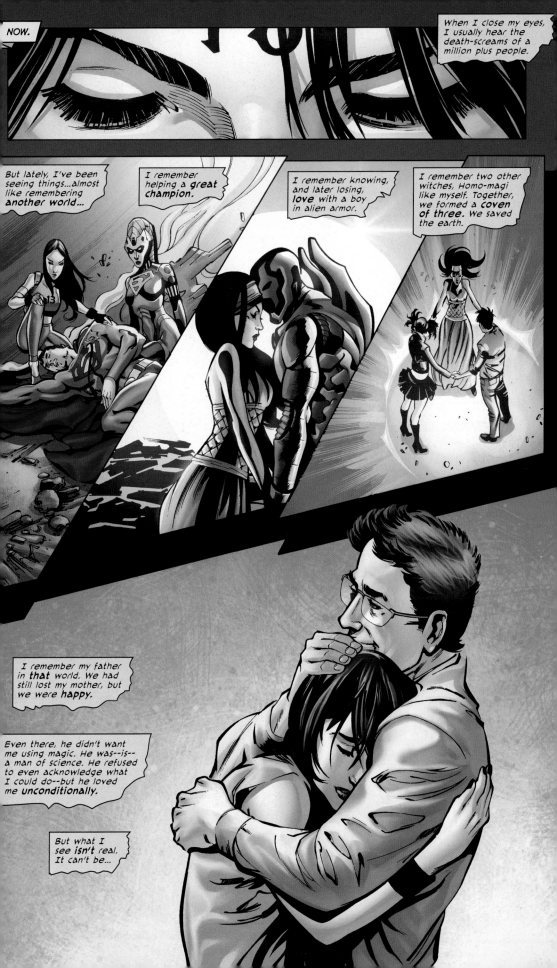

NOW.

When I close my eyes, I usually hear the death-screams of a million plus people.

But lately, I've been seeing things...almost like remembering another world...

I remember helping a great champion.

I remember knowing, and later losing, love with a boy in alien armor.

I remember two other witches, Homo-magi like myself. Together, we formed a coven of three. We saved the earth.

I remember my father in that world. We had still lost my mother, but we were happy.

Even there, he didn't want me using magic. He was--is-- a man of science. He refused to even acknowledge what I could do--but he loved me unconditionally.

But what I see isn't real. It can't be...

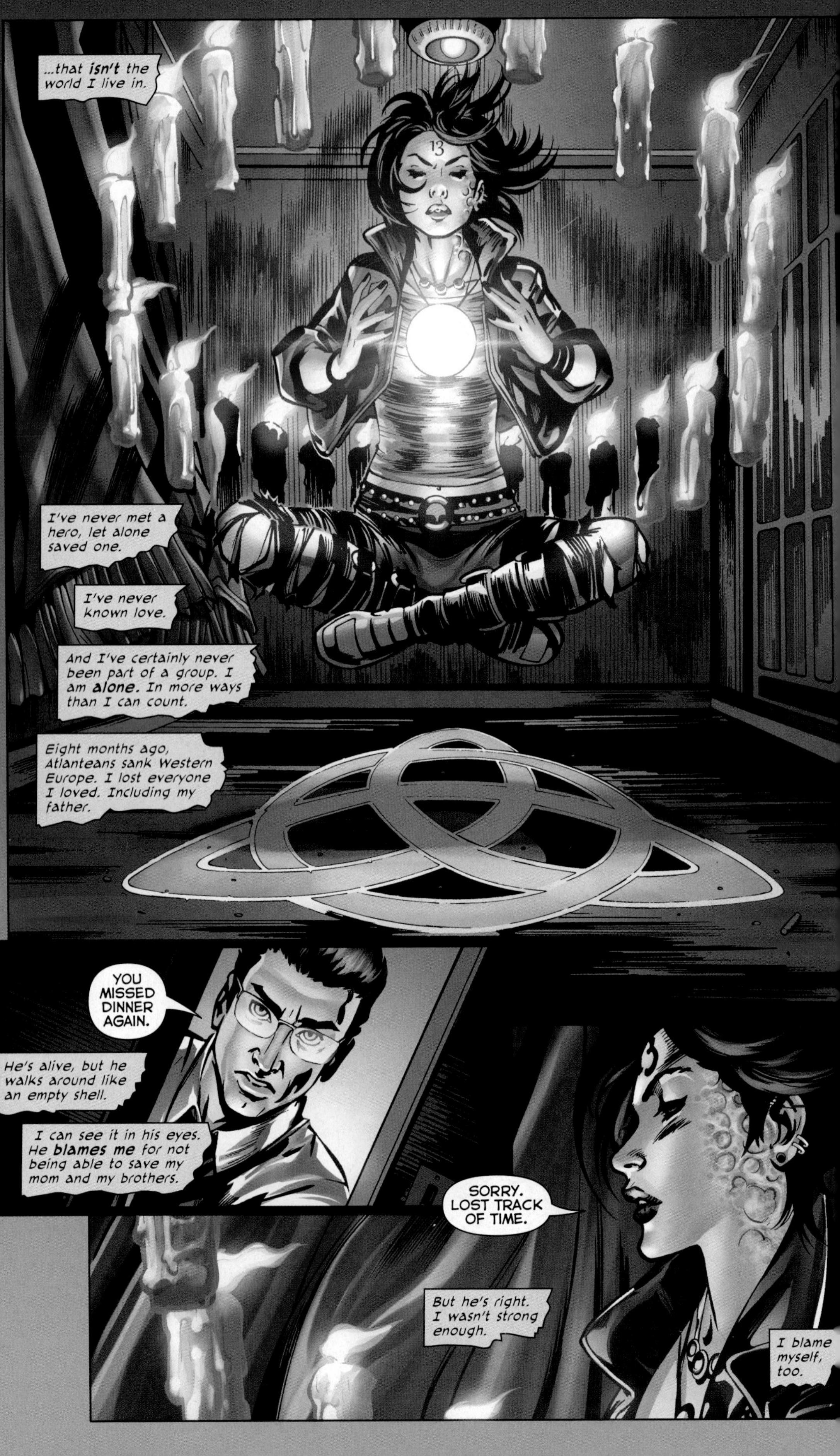
...that isn't the world I live in.
I've never met a hero, let alone saved one.
I've never known love.
And I've certainly never been part of a group. I am alone. In more ways than I can count.
Eight months ago, Atlanteans sank Western Europe. I lost everyone I loved. Including my father.
YOU MISSED DINNER AGAIN.
He's alive, but he walks around like an empty shell.
I can see it in his eyes. He blames me for not being able to save my mom and my brothers.
SORRY. LOST TRACK OF TIME.
But he's right. I wasn't strong enough.
I blame myself, too.

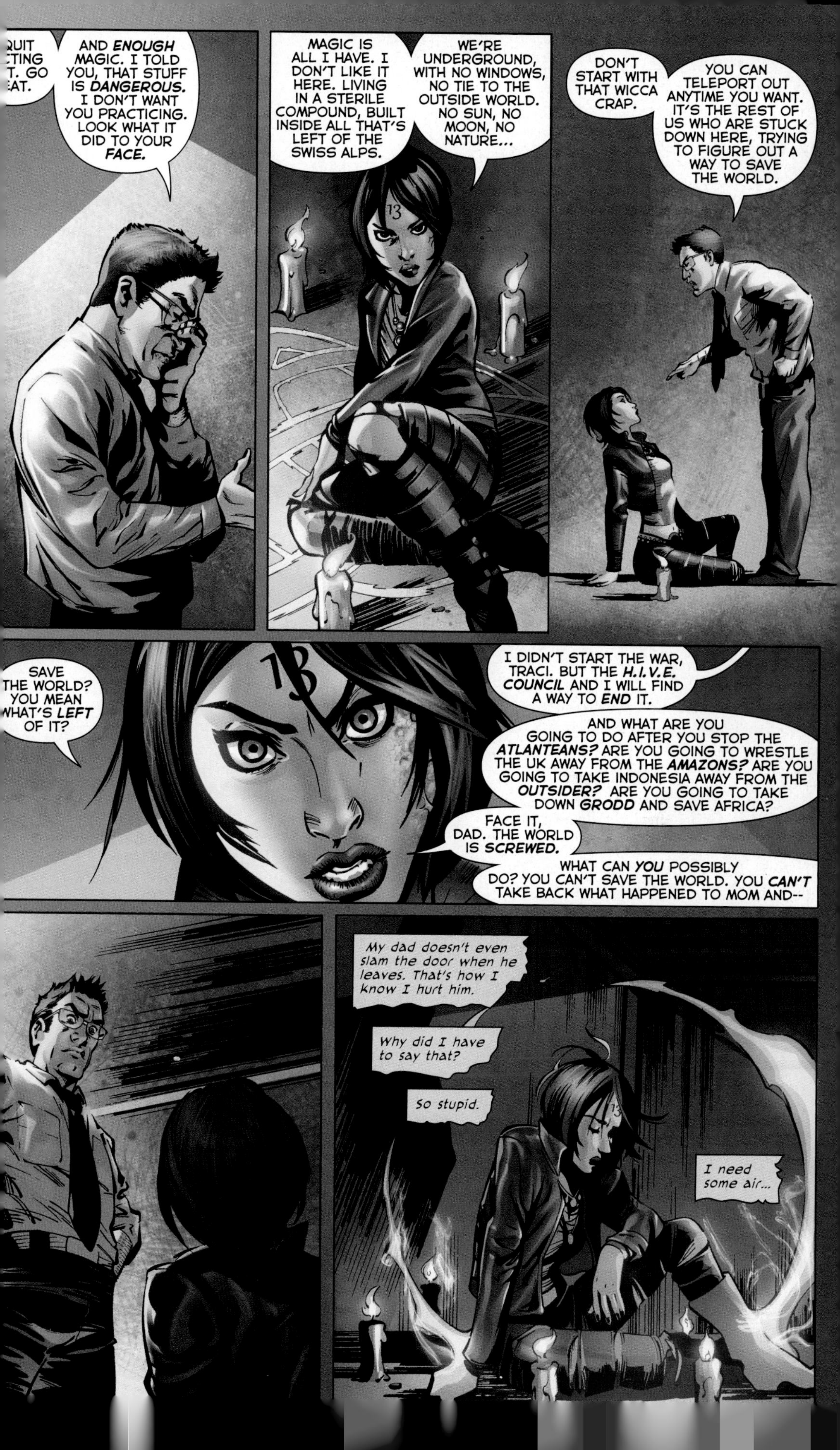

QUIT
CTING
T. GO
EAT.
AND ENOUGH MAGIC. I TOLD YOU, THAT STUFF IS DANGEROUS. I DON'T WANT YOU PRACTICING. LOOK WHAT IT DID TO YOUR FACE.
MAGIC IS ALL I HAVE. I DON'T LIKE IT HERE. LIVING IN A STERILE COMPOUND, BUILT INSIDE ALL THAT'S LEFT OF THE SWISS ALPS.
WE'RE UNDERGROUND, WITH NO WINDOWS, NO TIE TO THE OUTSIDE WORLD. NO SUN, NO MOON, NO NATURE...
DON'T START WITH THAT WICCA CRAP.
YOU CAN TELEPORT OUT ANYTIME YOU WANT. IT'S THE REST OF US WHO ARE STUCK DOWN HERE, TRYING TO FIGURE OUT A WAY TO SAVE THE WORLD.
SAVE THE WORLD? YOU MEAN WHAT'S LEFT OF IT?
I DIDN'T START THE WAR, TRACI. BUT THE H.I.V.E. COUNCIL AND I WILL FIND A WAY TO END IT.
AND WHAT ARE YOU GOING TO DO AFTER YOU STOP THE ATLANTEANS? ARE YOU GOING TO WRESTLE THE UK AWAY FROM THE AMAZONS? ARE YOU GOING TO TAKE INDONESIA AWAY FROM THE OUTSIDER? ARE YOU GOING TO TAKE DOWN GRODD AND SAVE AFRICA?
FACE IT, DAD. THE WORLD IS SCREWED.
WHAT CAN YOU POSSIBLY DO? YOU CAN'T SAVE THE WORLD. YOU CAN'T TAKE BACK WHAT HAPPENED TO MOM AND--
My dad doesn't even slam the door when he leaves. That's how I know I hurt him.
Why did I have to say that?
So stupid.
I need some air...

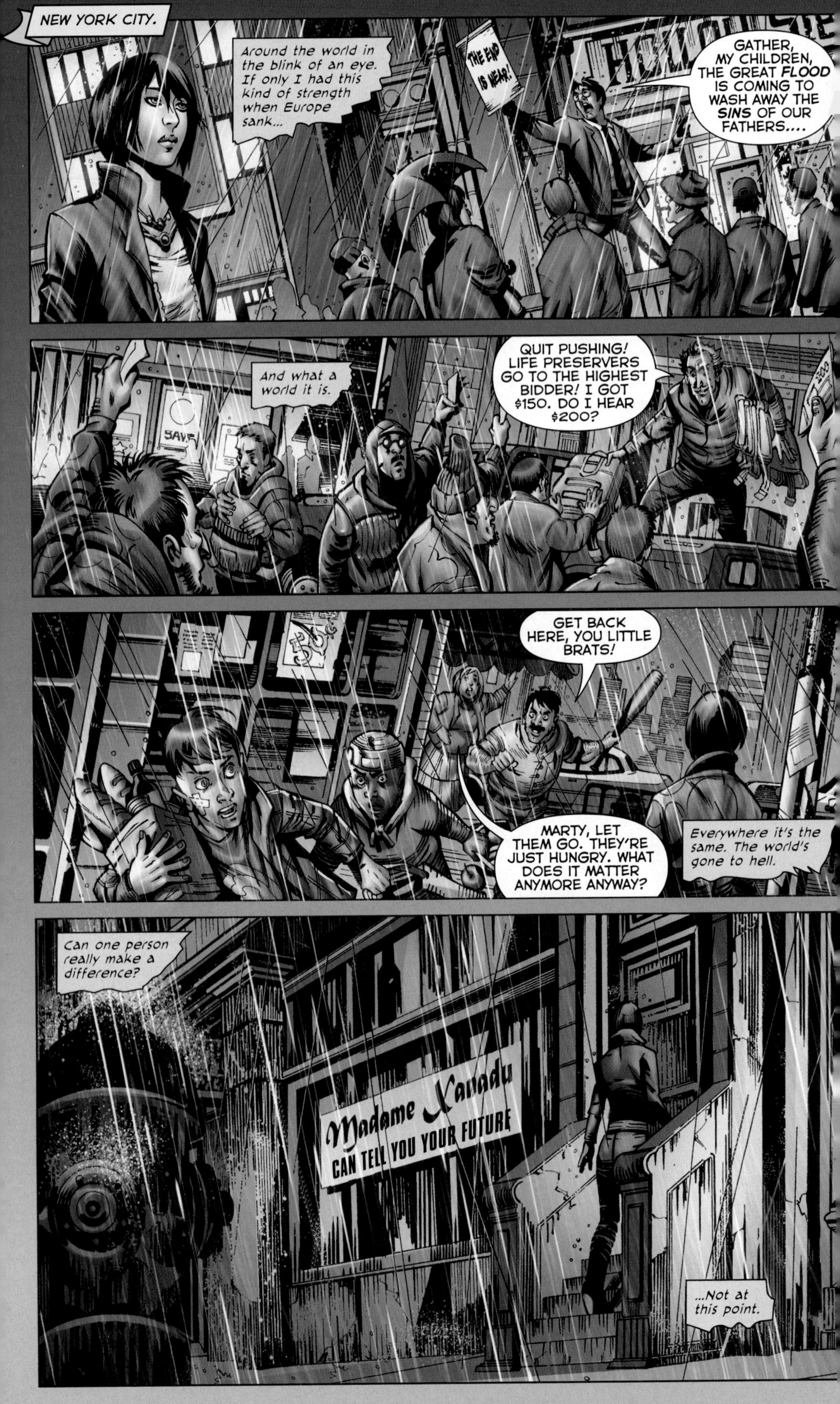
NEW YORK CITY.
Around the world in the blink of an eye. If only I had this kind of strength when Europe sank...
THE END IS NEAR!
GATHER, MY CHILDREN, THE GREAT FLOOD IS COMING TO WASH AWAY THE SINS OF OUR FATHERS....
And what a world it is.
QUIT PUSHING! LIFE PRESERVERS GO TO THE HIGHEST BIDDER! I GOT $150. DO I HEAR $200?
SAVE
GET BACK HERE, YOU LITTLE BRATS!
MARTY, LET THEM GO. THEY'RE JUST HUNGRY. WHAT DOES IT MATTER ANYMORE ANYWAY?
Everywhere it's the same. The world's gone to hell.
Can one person really make a difference?
Madame Xanadu
CAN TELL YOU YOUR FUTURE
...Not at this point.

ANOTHER FIGHT WITH YOUR DAD?

HOW DID--UGH. NIMUE, I HATE WHEN YOU DO THAT.

IT DOESN'T TAKE A *PRECOG* TO KNOW THAT YOU ONLY VISIT THIS OLD CRONE WHEN YOU FIGHT WITH YOUR FATHER.

YOU'RE NOT OLD.

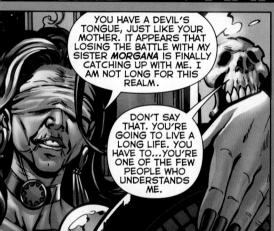

YOU HAVE A DEVIL'S TONGUE, JUST LIKE YOUR MOTHER. IT APPEARS THAT LOSING THE BATTLE WITH MY SISTER *MORGANA* IS FINALLY CATCHING UP WITH ME. I AM NOT LONG FOR THIS REALM.

DON'T SAY THAT. YOU'RE GOING TO LIVE A LONG LIFE. YOU HAVE TO...YOU'RE ONE OF THE FEW PEOPLE WHO UNDERSTANDS ME.

TRUTH IS TRUTH. ALL THINGS HAVE THEIR ENDING.

NOW, TELL ME WHAT'S ON YOUR MIND.

EVERYTHING JUST FEELS SO...SO BIG, SO HEAVY. LIKE THE WORLD IS ON THE VERGE OF COLLAPSING IN ON ITSELF. LIKE WE COULD ALL DIE AT ANY MOMENT.

HOW DID THE WORLD GET THIS BAD?

THIS IS THE WORLD FATE BUILT FOR US.

BUT WHERE IS OPTIMISM? WHERE IS HOPE? WHERE ARE THE HEROES?

THERE ARE HEROES IN THIS WORLD...THEY ARE JUST *HARDER* TO FIND.

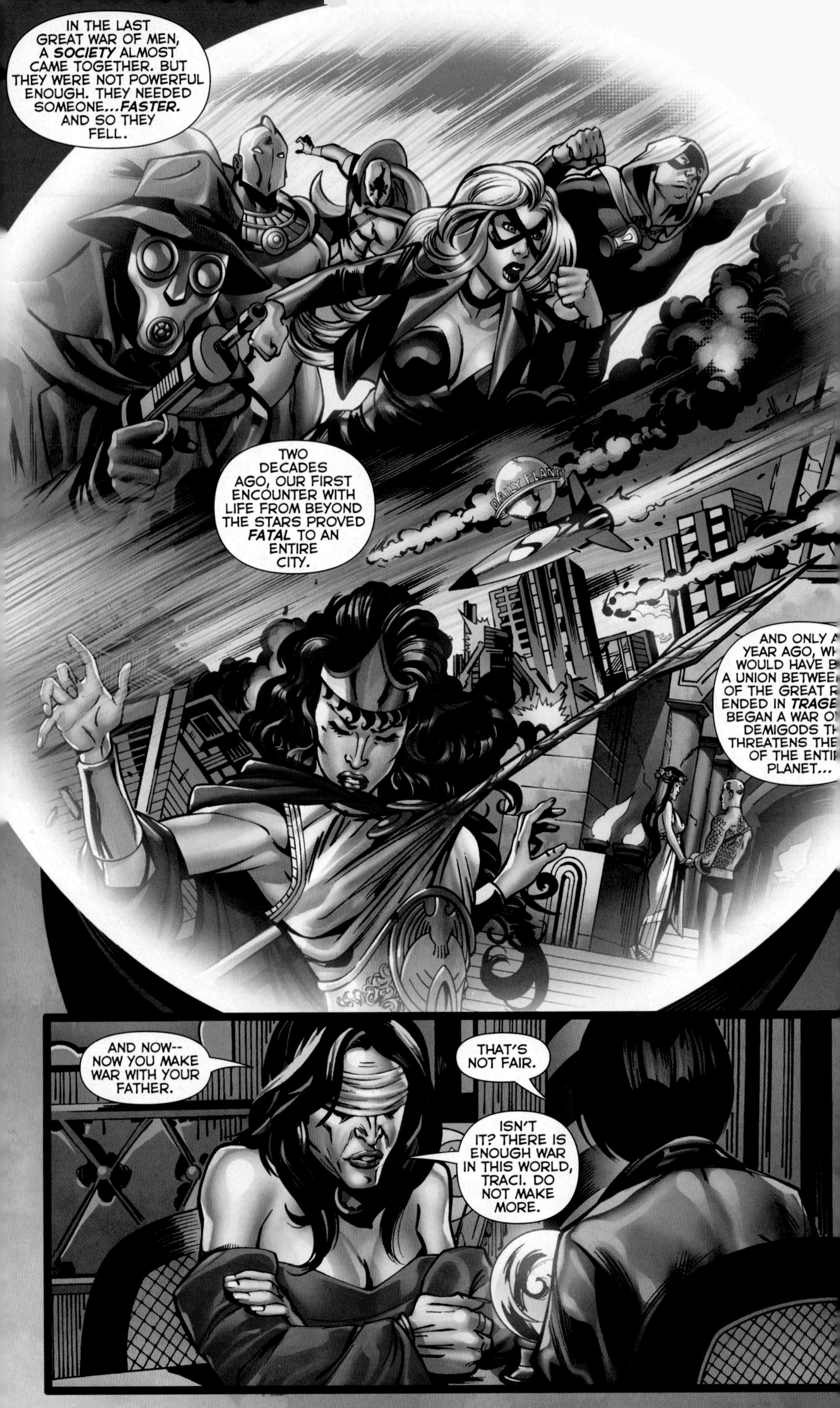
IN THE LAST GREAT WAR OF MEN, A SOCIETY ALMOST CAME TOGETHER. BUT THEY WERE NOT POWERFUL ENOUGH. THEY NEEDED SOMEONE...FASTER. AND SO THEY FELL.
TWO DECADES AGO, OUR FIRST ENCOUNTER WITH LIFE FROM BEYOND THE STARS PROVED FATAL TO AN ENTIRE CITY.
DAILY PLANET
AND ONLY A YEAR AGO, WH WOULD HAVE B A UNION BETWEE OF THE GREAT R ENDED IN TRAGE BEGAN A WAR O DEMIGODS TH THREATENS THE OF THE ENTI PLANET...
AND NOW-- NOW YOU MAKE WAR WITH YOUR FATHER.
THAT'S NOT FAIR.
ISN'T IT? THERE IS ENOUGH WAR IN THIS WORLD, TRACI. DO NOT MAKE MORE.

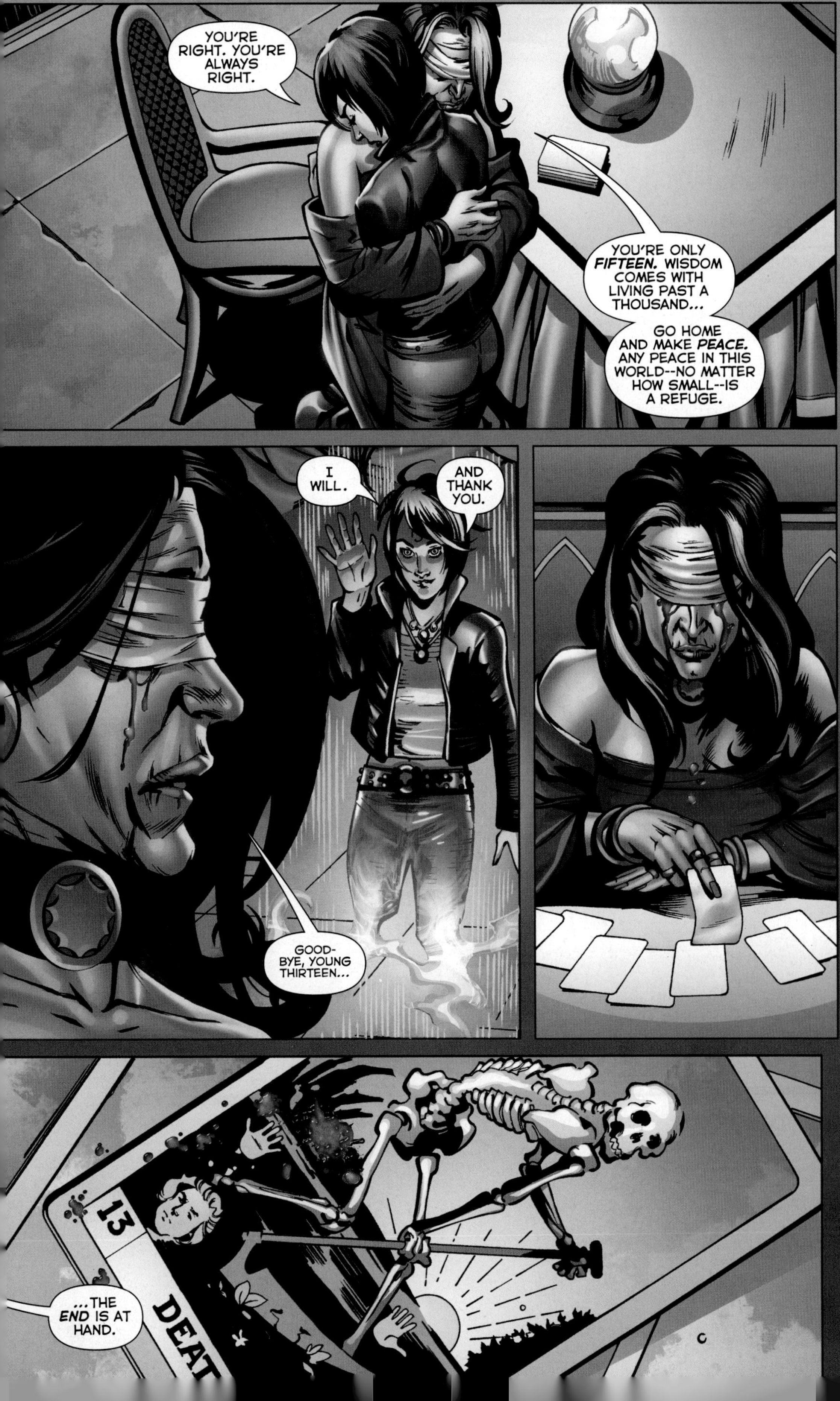
YOU'RE RIGHT. YOU'RE ALWAYS RIGHT.
YOU'RE ONLY FIFTEEN. WISDOM COMES WITH LIVING PAST A THOUSAND...
GO HOME AND MAKE PEACE. ANY PEACE IN THIS WORLD--NO MATTER HOW SMALL--IS A REFUGE.
I WILL.
AND THANK YOU.
GOOD-BYE, YOUNG THIRTEEN...
13
...THE END IS AT HAND.

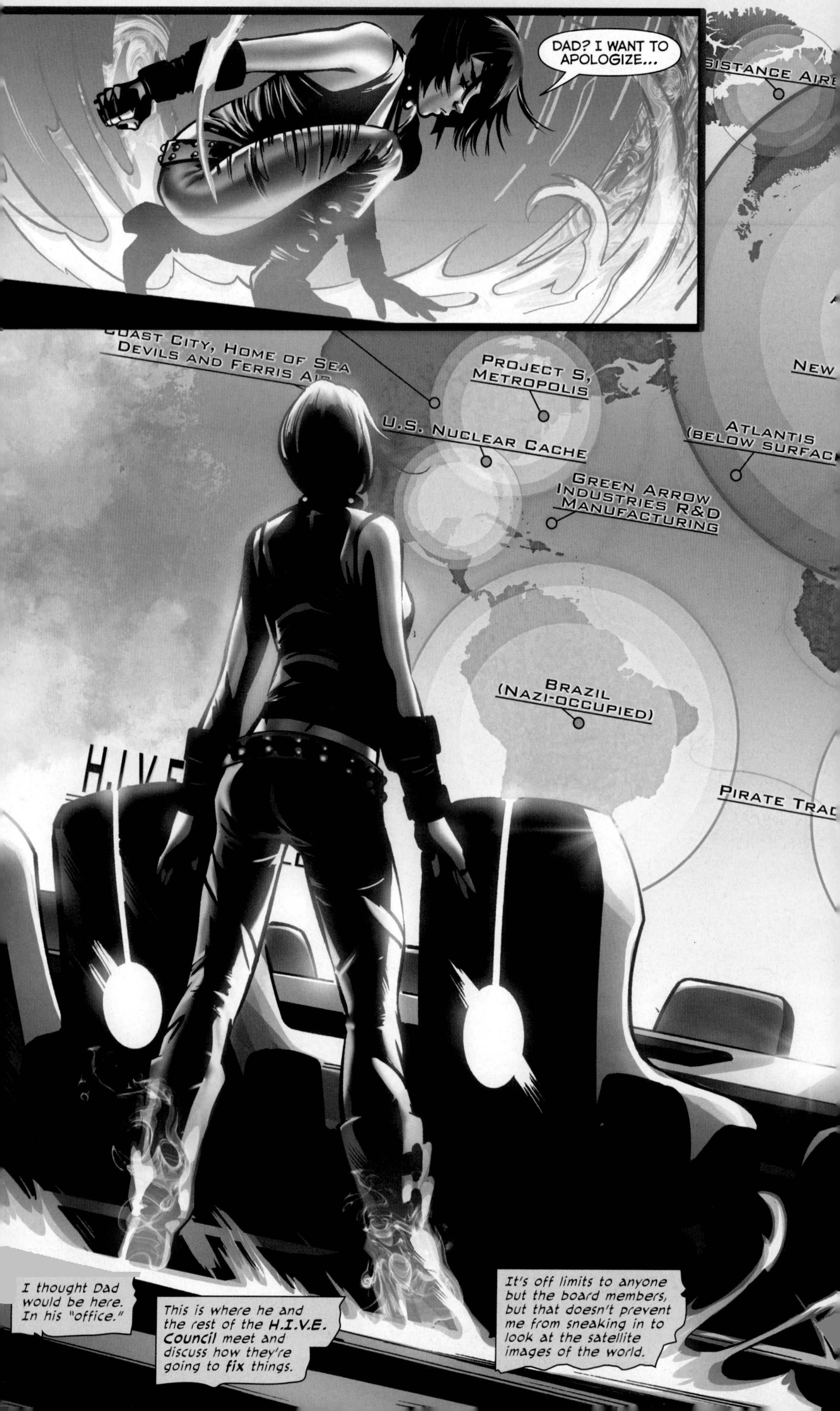
DAD? I WANT TO APOLOGIZE...
SISTANCE AIRE
OAST CITY, HOME OF SEA DEVILS AND FERRIS AI
PROJECT S, METROPOLIS
NEW
U.S. NUCLEAR CACHE
ATLANTIS (BELOW SURFAC
GREEN ARROW INDUSTRIES R&D MANUFACTURING
BRAZIL (NAZI-OCCUPIED)
H.I.V.E
PIRATE TRAD
I thought Dad would be here. In his "office."
This is where he and the rest of the **H.I.V.E. Council** meet and discuss how they're going to **fix** things.
It's off limits to anyone but the board members, but that doesn't prevent me from sneaking in to look at the satellite images of the world.

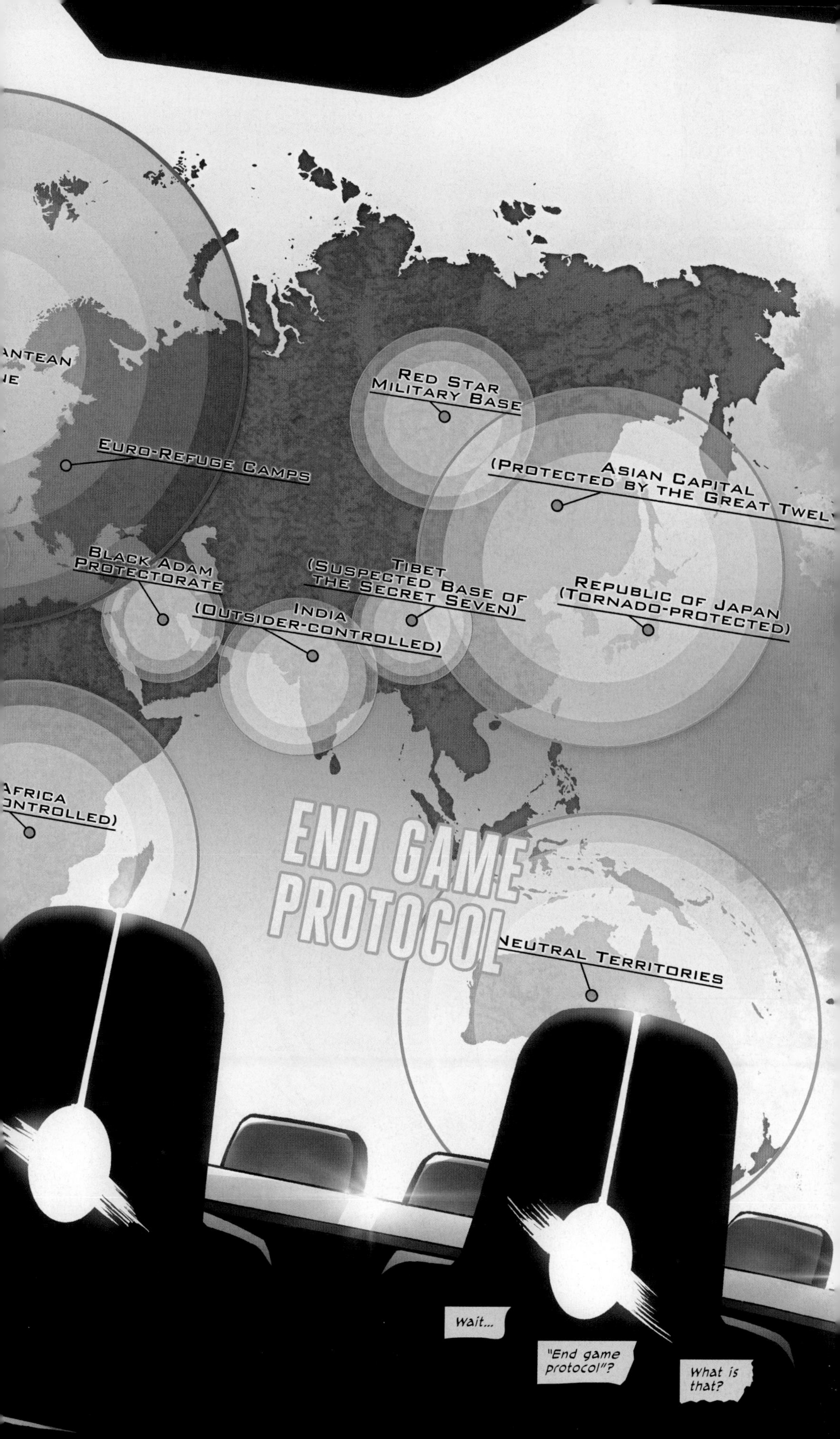

ANTEAN
NE
Red Star
Military Base
Euro-Refuge Camps
Asian Capital
(Protected by the Great Twel
Black Adam
Protectorate
Tibet
(Suspected Base of
the Secret Seven)
India
(Outsider-controlled)
Republic of Japan
(Tornado-protected)
Africa
ONTROLLED)
END GAME
PROTOCOL
Neutral Territories
Wait...
"End game
protocol"?
What is
that?

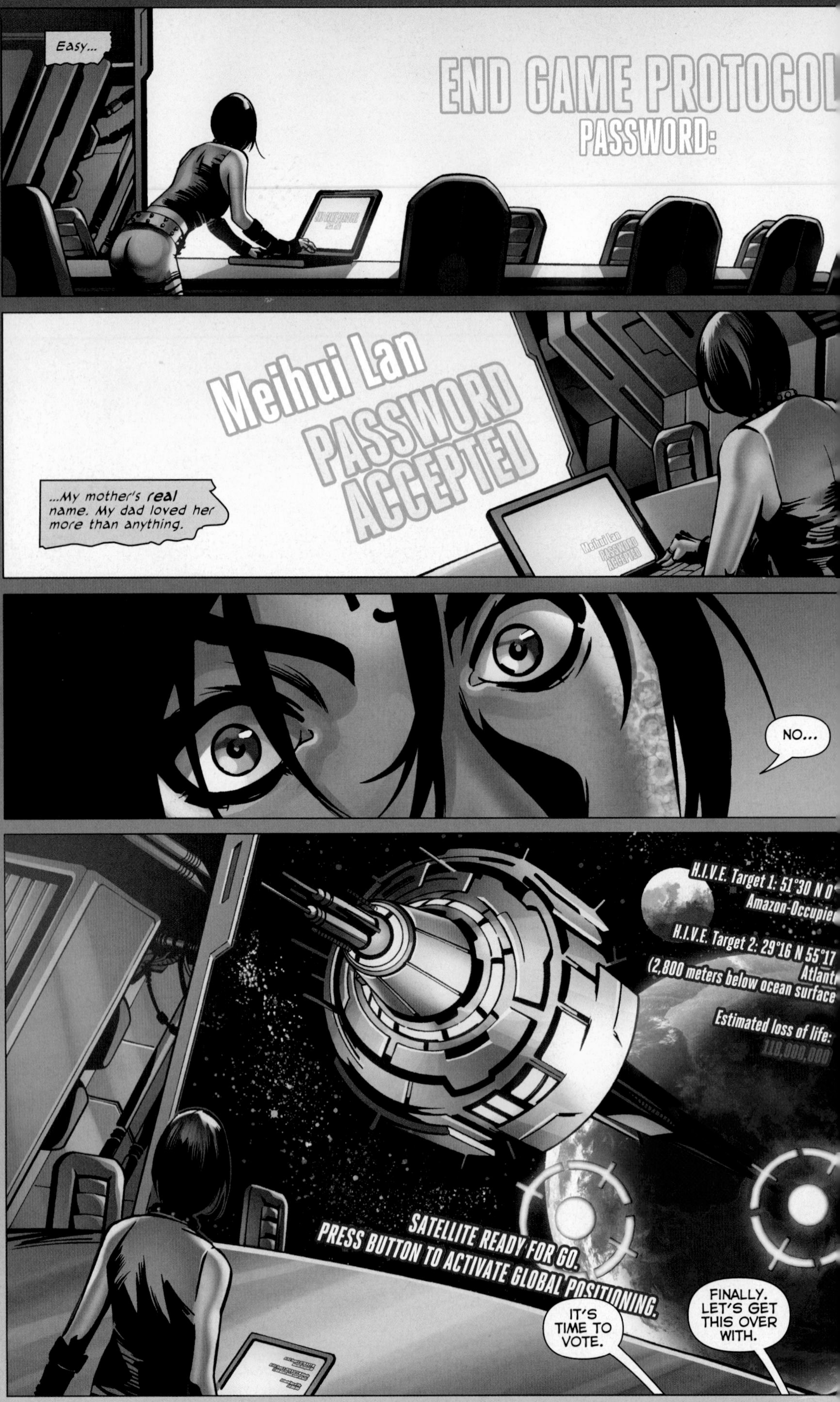

Easy...
END GAME PROTOCOL
PASSWORD:
Meihui Lan
PASSWORD ACCEPTED
...My mother's real name. My dad loved her more than anything.
NO...
H.I.V.E. Target 1: 51°30 N 0
Amazon-Occupie
H.I.V.E. Target 2: 29°16 N 55°17
Atlant
(2,800 meters below ocean surface
Estimated loss of life:
118,000,000
SATELLITE READY FOR GO.
PRESS BUTTON TO ACTIVATE GLOBAL POSITIONING.
IT'S TIME TO VOTE.
FINALLY. LET'S GET THIS OVER WITH.

EVERYONE TAKE THEIR [SEA]TS SO WE CAN [G]ET DOWN TO BUSINESS.

IS ALL THIS PAGEANTRY AND RITUAL REALLY NECESSARY? WE ALL KNOW WHAT WE MUST DO.

WE'RE TRYING TO SAVE THE WORLD, BUT WE'RE STILL SIGNING A DEATH SENTENCE FOR MILLIONS OF PEOPLE. I THINK TAKING AN OFFICIAL VOTE IS THE VERY LEAST WE CAN DO.

I'LL CALL OUT YOUR NAME AND COUNTRY, AND YOU GIVE YOUR VOTE.

VOS [...]AN NON [...]ADVERTO MIHI.

AUGUST GENERAL IN IRON OF CHINA?

THERE IS NOTHING HONORABLE ABOUT DEATH FROM THE SKY. NO.

RED STAR OF RUSSIA?

NO. THERE HAS TO BE ANOTHER WAY.

RA'S AL GHUL OF EGYPT?

MY VOTE IS IN THE AFFIRMATIVE. LET US RESTORE THE BALANCE OF THE EARTH BEFORE THESE INFIDELS WRECK ANY MORE ECO-SYSTEMS.

DR. KIMIYO HOSHI OF JAPAN?

YES.

NAIF AL-SHEIKH OF SAUDI ARABIA?

I SEE NO OTHER WAY, BUT MY ANSWER REMAINS NO.

ADELINE KANE OF THE UNITED STATES?

THE WORLD WILL REMEMBER US AS MONSTERS...

...YES.

CAPTAIN NAZI OF GERMANY?

JA. DO IT.

IMPALA OF SOUTH AFRICA?

THOUGH REASON DICTATES YES, I MUST FOLLOW MY HEART. NO.

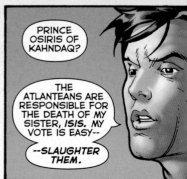

PRINCE OSIRIS OF KAHNDAQ?

THE ATLANTEANS ARE RESPONSIBLE FOR THE DEATH OF MY SISTER, ISIS. MY VOTE IS EASY--

--SLAUGHTER THEM.

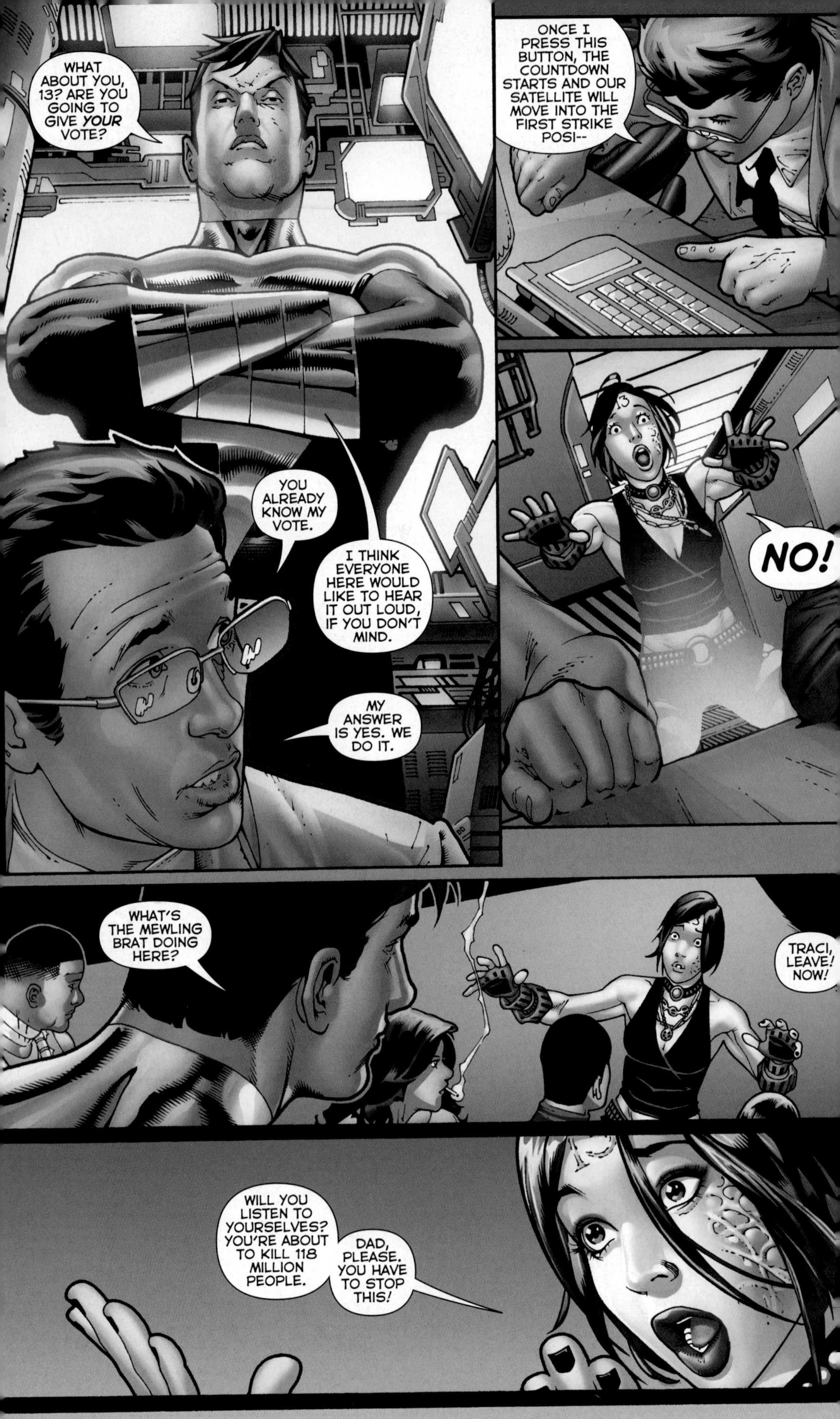
WHAT ABOUT YOU, 13? ARE YOU GOING TO GIVE *YOUR* VOTE?
ONCE I PRESS THIS BUTTON, THE COUNTDOWN STARTS AND OUR SATELLITE WILL MOVE INTO THE FIRST STRIKE POSI--
YOU ALREADY KNOW MY VOTE.
I THINK EVERYONE HERE WOULD LIKE TO HEAR IT OUT LOUD, IF YOU DON'T MIND.
MY ANSWER IS YES. WE DO IT.
NO!
WHAT'S THE MEWLING BRAT DOING HERE?
TRACI, LEAVE! NOW!
WILL YOU LISTEN TO YOURSELVES? YOU'RE ABOUT TO KILL 118 MILLION PEOPLE.
DAD, PLEASE. YOU HAVE TO STOP THIS!

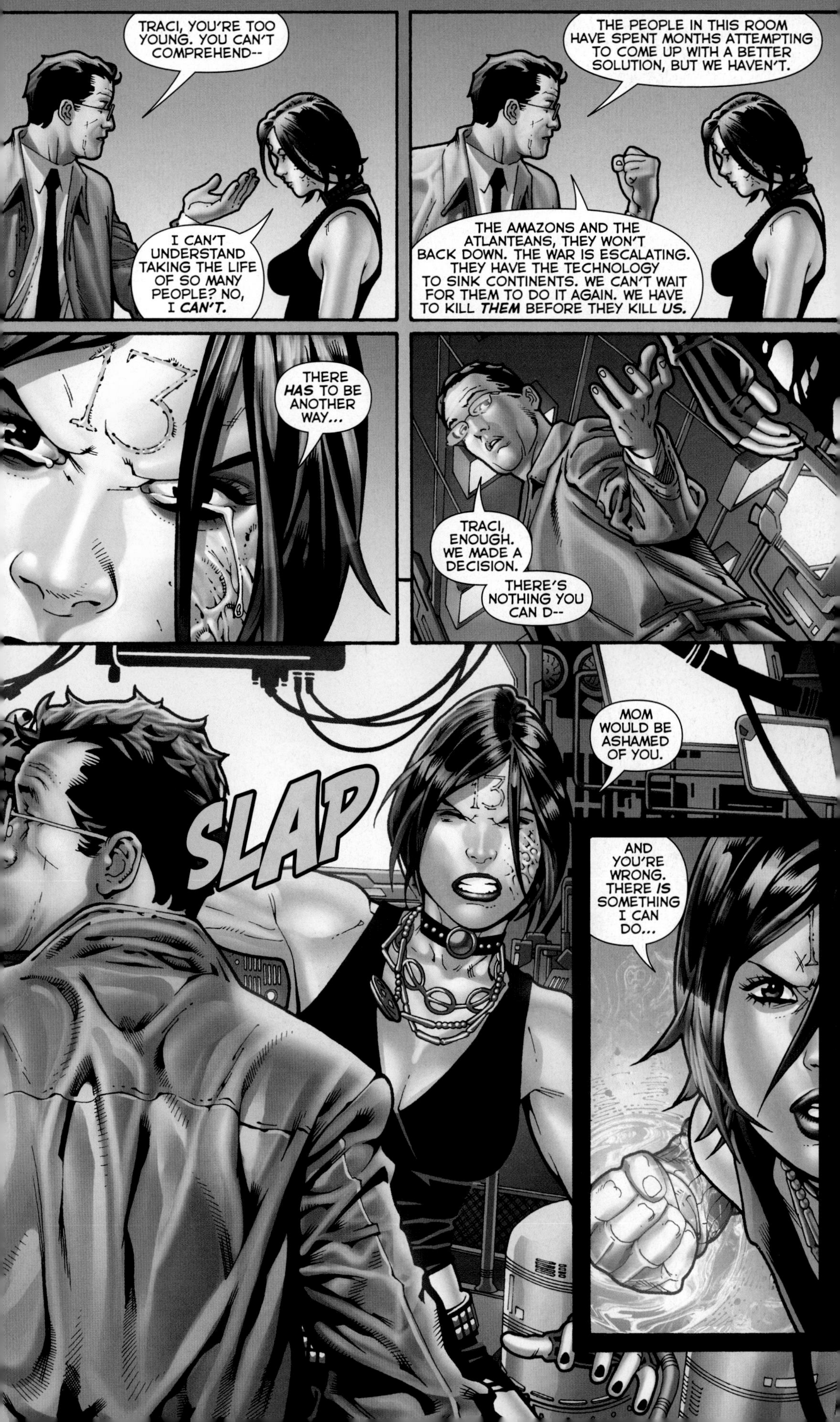
TRACI, YOU'RE TOO YOUNG. YOU CAN'T COMPREHEND--
I CAN'T UNDERSTAND TAKING THE LIFE OF SO MANY PEOPLE? NO, I *CAN'T.*
THE PEOPLE IN THIS ROOM HAVE SPENT MONTHS ATTEMPTING TO COME UP WITH A BETTER SOLUTION, BUT WE HAVEN'T.
THE AMAZONS AND THE ATLANTEANS, THEY WON'T BACK DOWN. THE WAR IS ESCALATING. THEY HAVE THE TECHNOLOGY TO SINK CONTINENTS. WE CAN'T WAIT FOR THEM TO DO IT AGAIN. WE HAVE TO KILL *THEM* BEFORE THEY KILL *US.*
THERE *HAS* TO BE ANOTHER WAY...
TRACI, ENOUGH. WE MADE A DECISION.
THERE'S NOTHING YOU CAN D--
SLAP
MOM WOULD BE ASHAMED OF YOU.
AND YOU'RE WRONG. THERE *IS* SOMETHING I CAN DO...

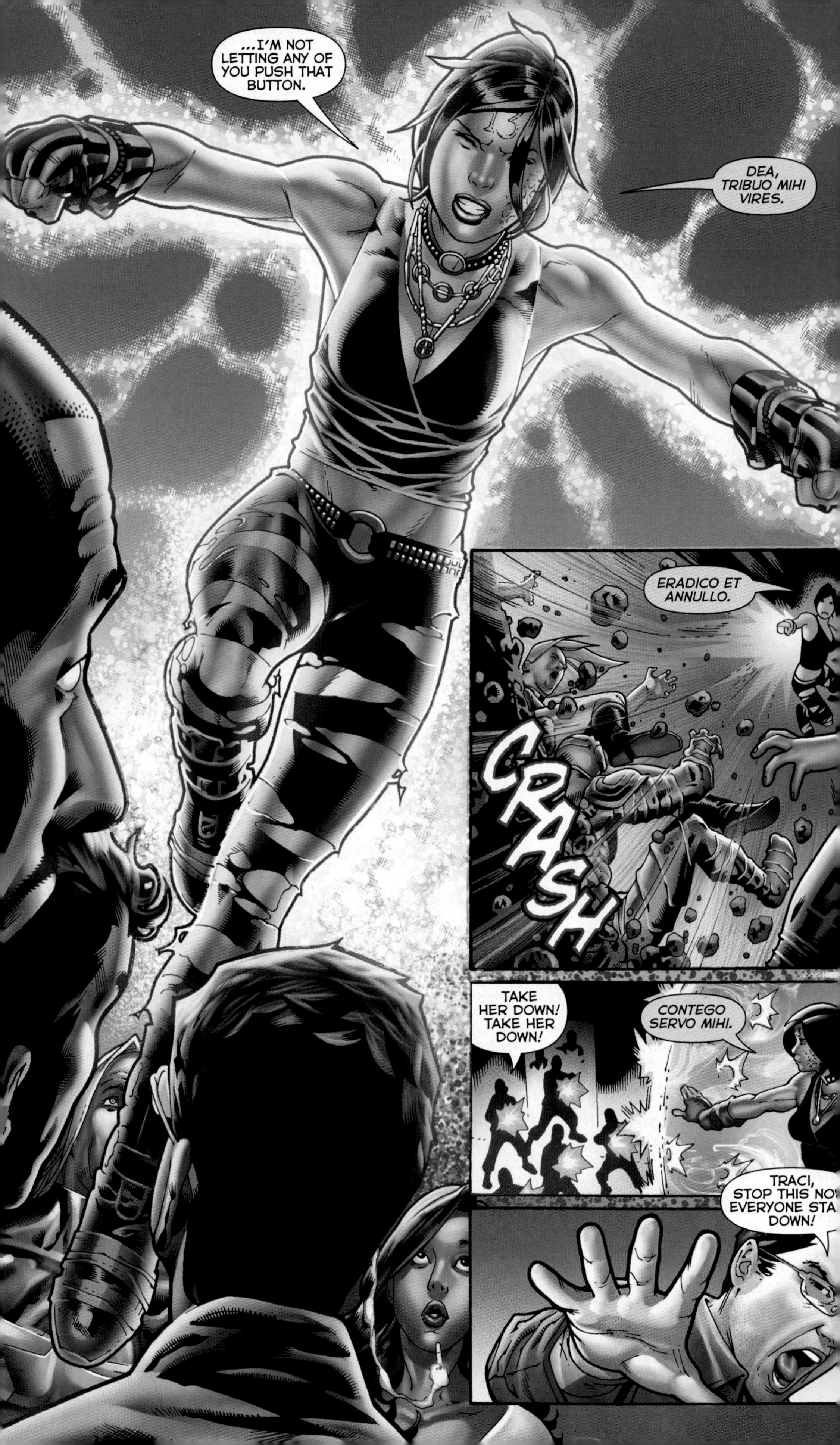
...I'M NOT LETTING ANY OF YOU PUSH THAT BUTTON.
DEA, TRIBUO MIHI VIRES.
ERADICO ET ANNULLO.
CRASH
TAKE HER DOWN! TAKE HER DOWN!
CONTEGO SERVO MIHI.
TRACI, STOP THIS NO
EVERYONE STA
DOWN!

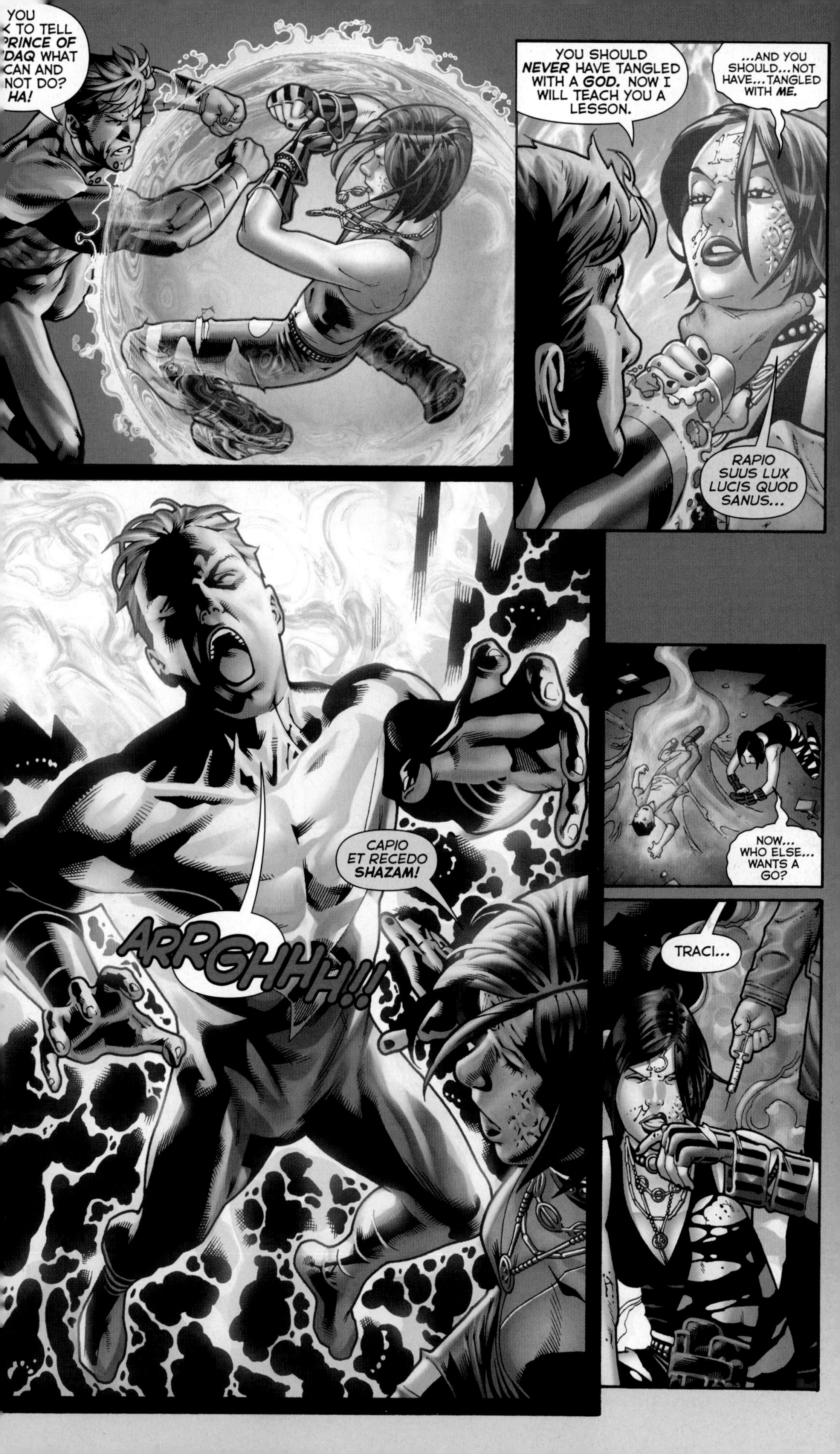
YOU ...K TO TELL PRINCE OF ...DAQ WHAT ...CAN AND NOT DO? HA!
YOU SHOULD NEVER HAVE TANGLED WITH A GOD. NOW I WILL TEACH YOU A LESSON.
...AND YOU SHOULD...NOT HAVE...TANGLED WITH ME.
RAPIO SUUS LUX LUCIS QUOD SANUS...
CAPIO ET RECEDO SHAZAM!
ARRGHHHH!!
NOW... WHO ELSE... WANTS A GO?
TRACI...

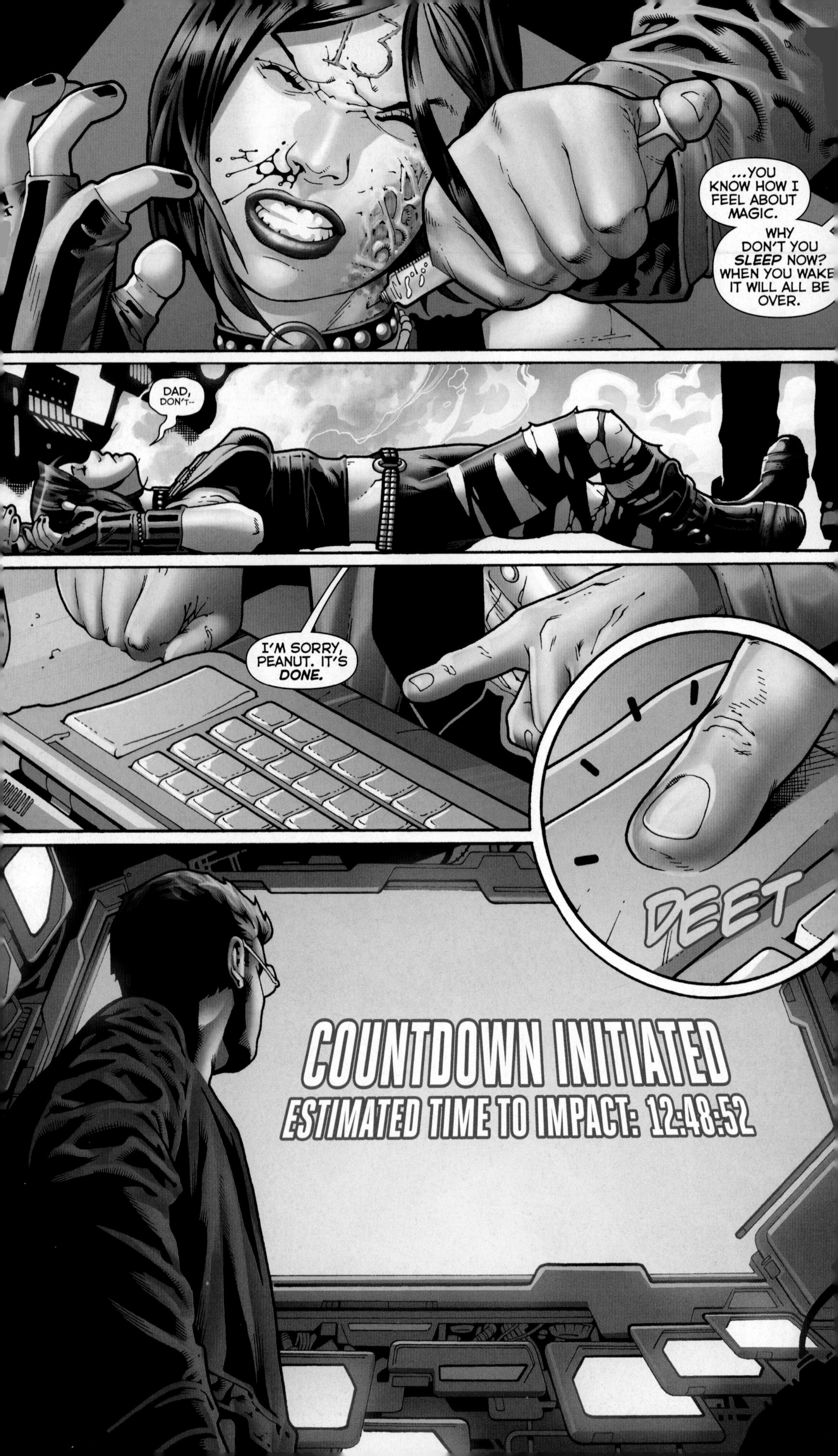
...YOU KNOW HOW I FEEL ABOUT MAGIC.
WHY DON'T YOU SLEEP NOW? WHEN YOU WAKE IT WILL ALL BE OVER.
DAD, DON'T--
I'M SORRY, PEANUT. IT'S DONE.
DEET
COUNTDOWN INITIATED
ESTIMATED TIME TO IMPACT: 12:48:52

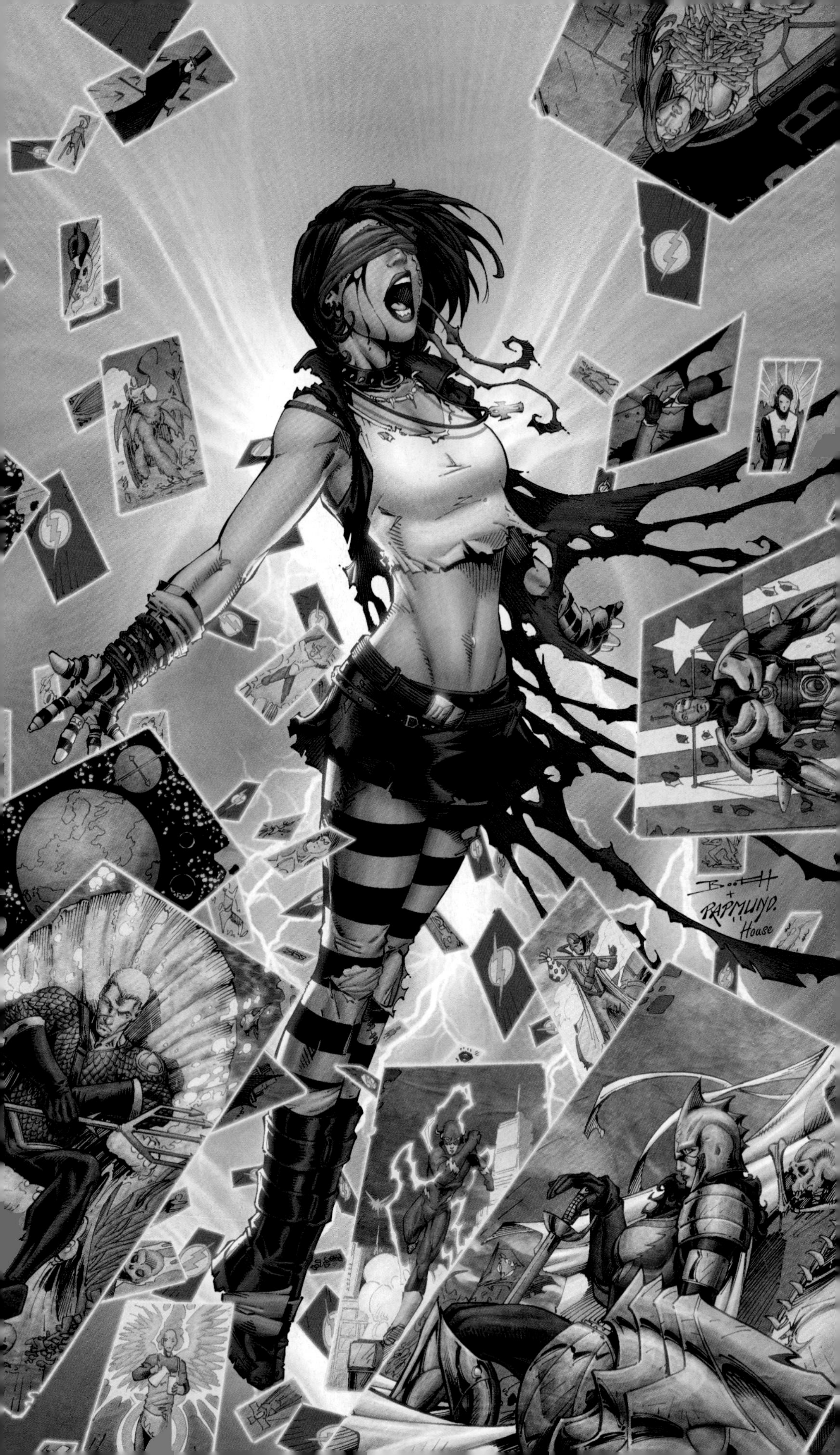
Booth
+
Rapmund.
House

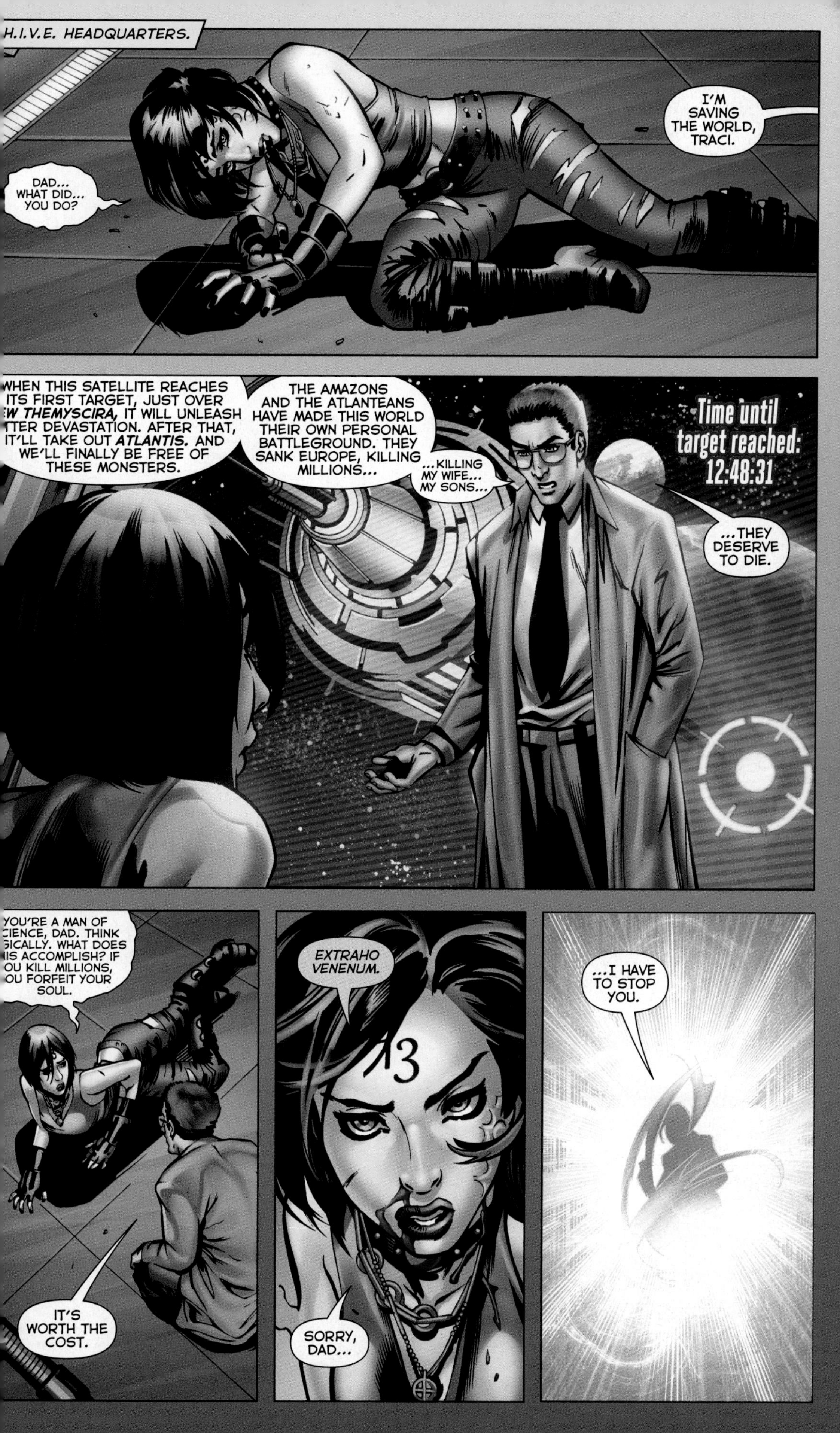
H.I.V.E. HEADQUARTERS.
DAD... WHAT DID... YOU DO?
I'M SAVING THE WORLD, TRACI.
WHEN THIS SATELLITE REACHES ITS FIRST TARGET, JUST OVER EW THEMYSCIRA, IT WILL UNLEASH TTER DEVASTATION. AFTER THAT, IT'LL TAKE OUT ATLANTIS. AND WE'LL FINALLY BE FREE OF THESE MONSTERS.
THE AMAZONS AND THE ATLANTEANS HAVE MADE THIS WORLD THEIR OWN PERSONAL BATTLEGROUND. THEY SANK EUROPE, KILLING MILLIONS...
...KILLING MY WIFE... MY SONS...
Time until target reached: 12:48:31
...THEY DESERVE TO DIE.
YOU'RE A MAN OF CIENCE, DAD. THINK GICALLY. WHAT DOES IS ACCOMPLISH? IF OU KILL MILLIONS, OU FORFEIT YOUR SOUL.
IT'S WORTH THE COST.
EXTRAHO VENENUM.
SORRY, DAD...
...I HAVE TO STOP YOU.

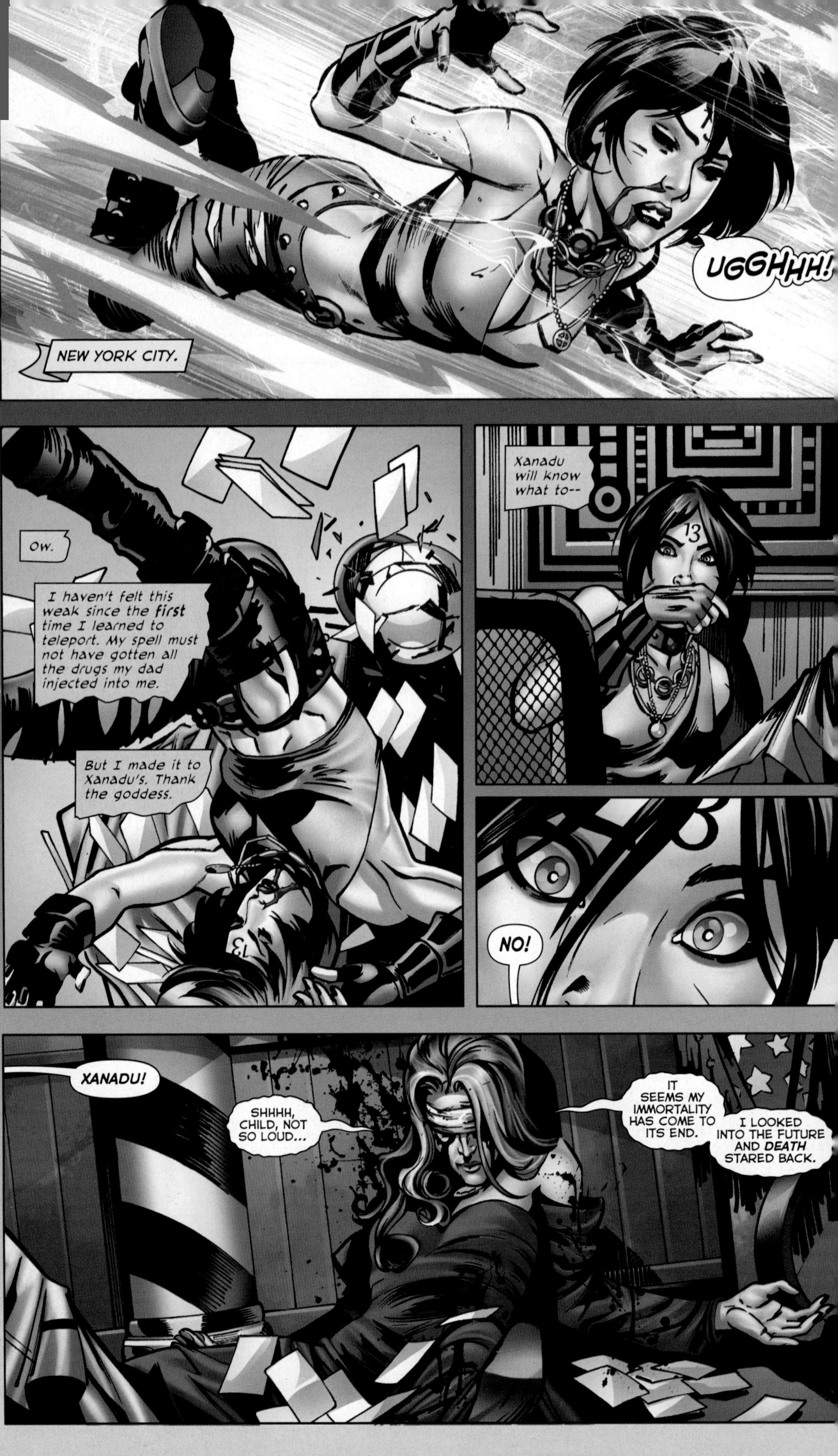
UGGHHH!
NEW YORK CITY.
Ow.
I haven't felt this weak since the first time I learned to teleport. My spell must not have gotten all the drugs my dad injected into me.
But I made it to Xanadu's. Thank the goddess.
Xanadu will know what to--
NO!
XANADU!
SHHHH, CHILD, NOT SO LOUD...
IT SEEMS MY IMMORTALITY HAS COME TO ITS END.
I LOOKED INTO THE FUTURE AND DEATH STARED BACK.

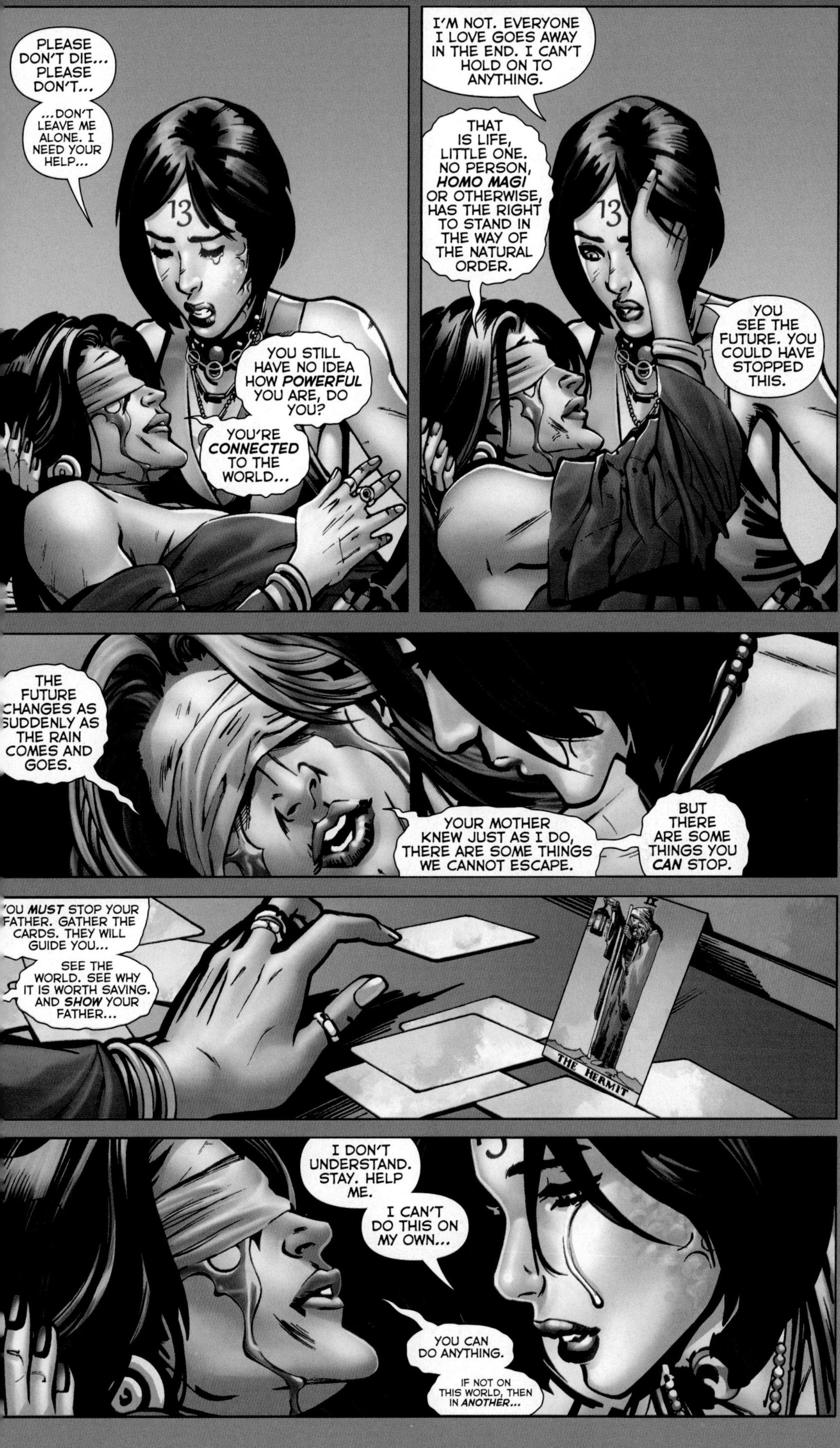
PLEASE DON'T DIE... PLEASE DON'T...
...DON'T LEAVE ME ALONE. I NEED YOUR HELP...
YOU STILL HAVE NO IDEA HOW POWERFUL YOU ARE, DO YOU?
YOU'RE CONNECTED TO THE WORLD...
I'M NOT. EVERYONE I LOVE GOES AWAY IN THE END. I CAN'T HOLD ON TO ANYTHING.
THAT IS LIFE, LITTLE ONE. NO PERSON, HOMO MAGI OR OTHERWISE, HAS THE RIGHT TO STAND IN THE WAY OF THE NATURAL ORDER.
YOU SEE THE FUTURE. YOU COULD HAVE STOPPED THIS.
THE FUTURE CHANGES AS SUDDENLY AS THE RAIN COMES AND GOES.
YOUR MOTHER KNEW JUST AS I DO, THERE ARE SOME THINGS WE CANNOT ESCAPE.
BUT THERE ARE SOME THINGS YOU CAN STOP.
YOU MUST STOP YOUR FATHER. GATHER THE CARDS. THEY WILL GUIDE YOU...
SEE THE WORLD. SEE WHY IT IS WORTH SAVING. AND SHOW YOUR FATHER...
THE HERMIT
I DON'T UNDERSTAND. STAY. HELP ME.
I CAN'T DO THIS ON MY OWN...
YOU CAN DO ANYTHING.
IF NOT ON THIS WORLD, THEN IN ANOTHER...

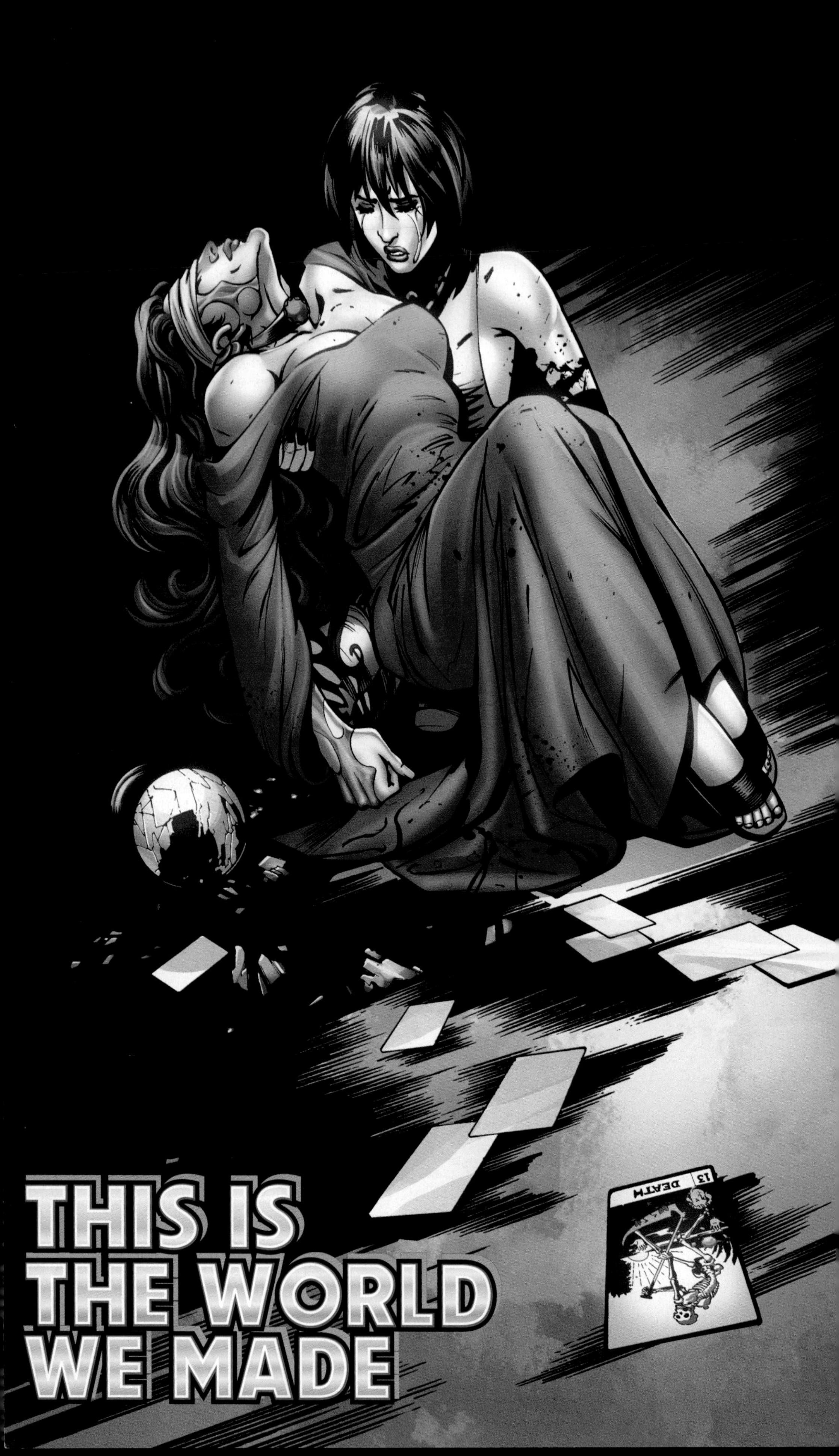
THIS IS
THE WORLD
WE MADE
13 DEATH

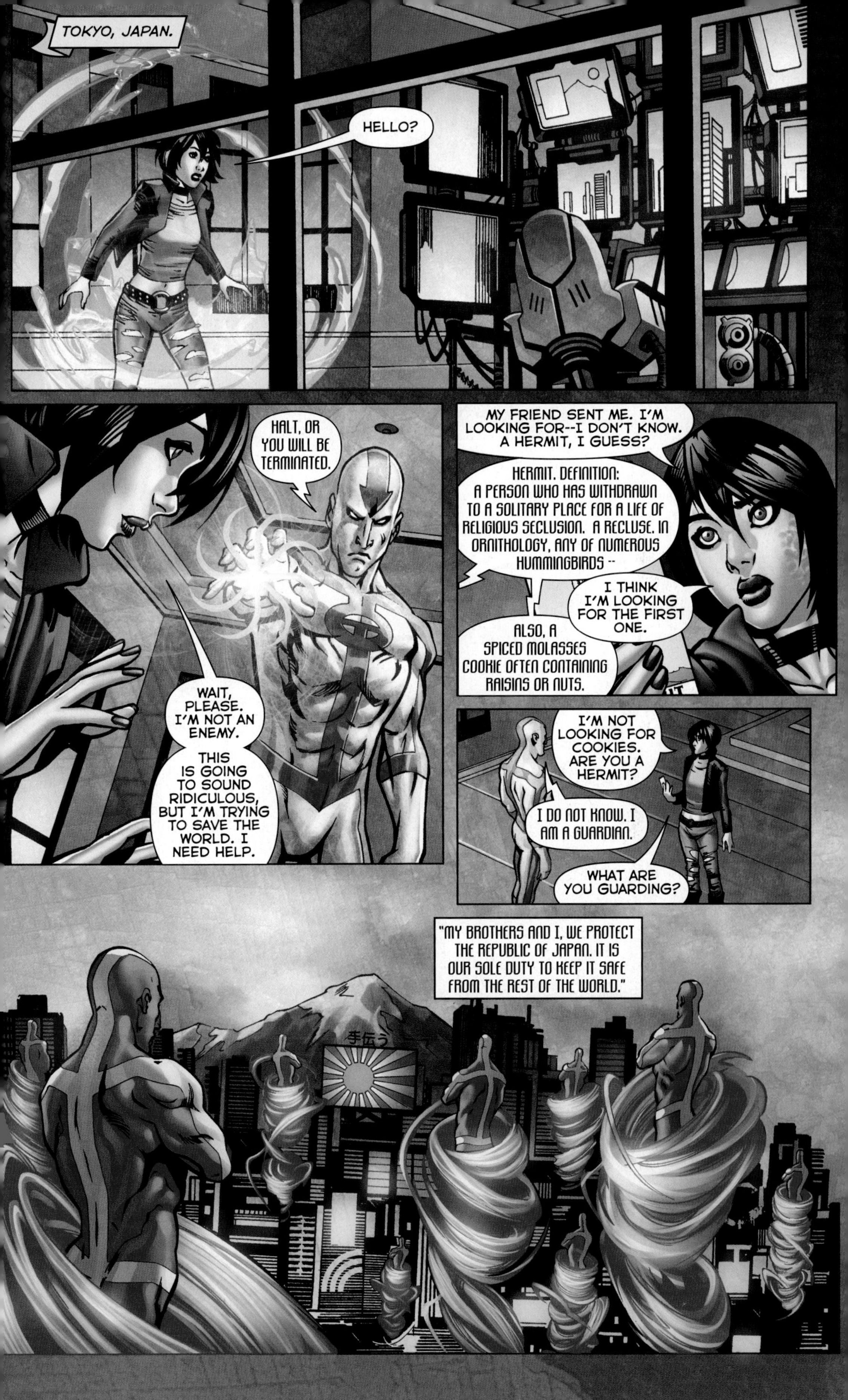
TOKYO, JAPAN.
HELLO?
HALT, OR YOU WILL BE TERMINATED.
WAIT, PLEASE. I'M NOT AN ENEMY.
THIS IS GOING TO SOUND RIDICULOUS, BUT I'M TRYING TO SAVE THE WORLD. I NEED HELP.
MY FRIEND SENT ME. I'M LOOKING FOR--I DON'T KNOW. A HERMIT, I GUESS?
HERMIT. DEFINITION: A PERSON WHO HAS WITHDRAWN TO A SOLITARY PLACE FOR A LIFE OF RELIGIOUS SECLUSION. A RECLUSE. IN ORNITHOLOGY, ANY OF NUMEROUS HUMMINGBIRDS --
I THINK I'M LOOKING FOR THE FIRST ONE.
ALSO, A SPICED MOLASSES COOKIE OFTEN CONTAINING RAISINS OR NUTS.
I'M NOT LOOKING FOR COOKIES. ARE YOU A HERMIT?
I DO NOT KNOW. I AM A GUARDIAN.
WHAT ARE YOU GUARDING?
"MY BROTHERS AND I, WE PROTECT THE REPUBLIC OF JAPAN. IT IS OUR SOLE DUTY TO KEEP IT SAFE FROM THE REST OF THE WORLD."
手伝う

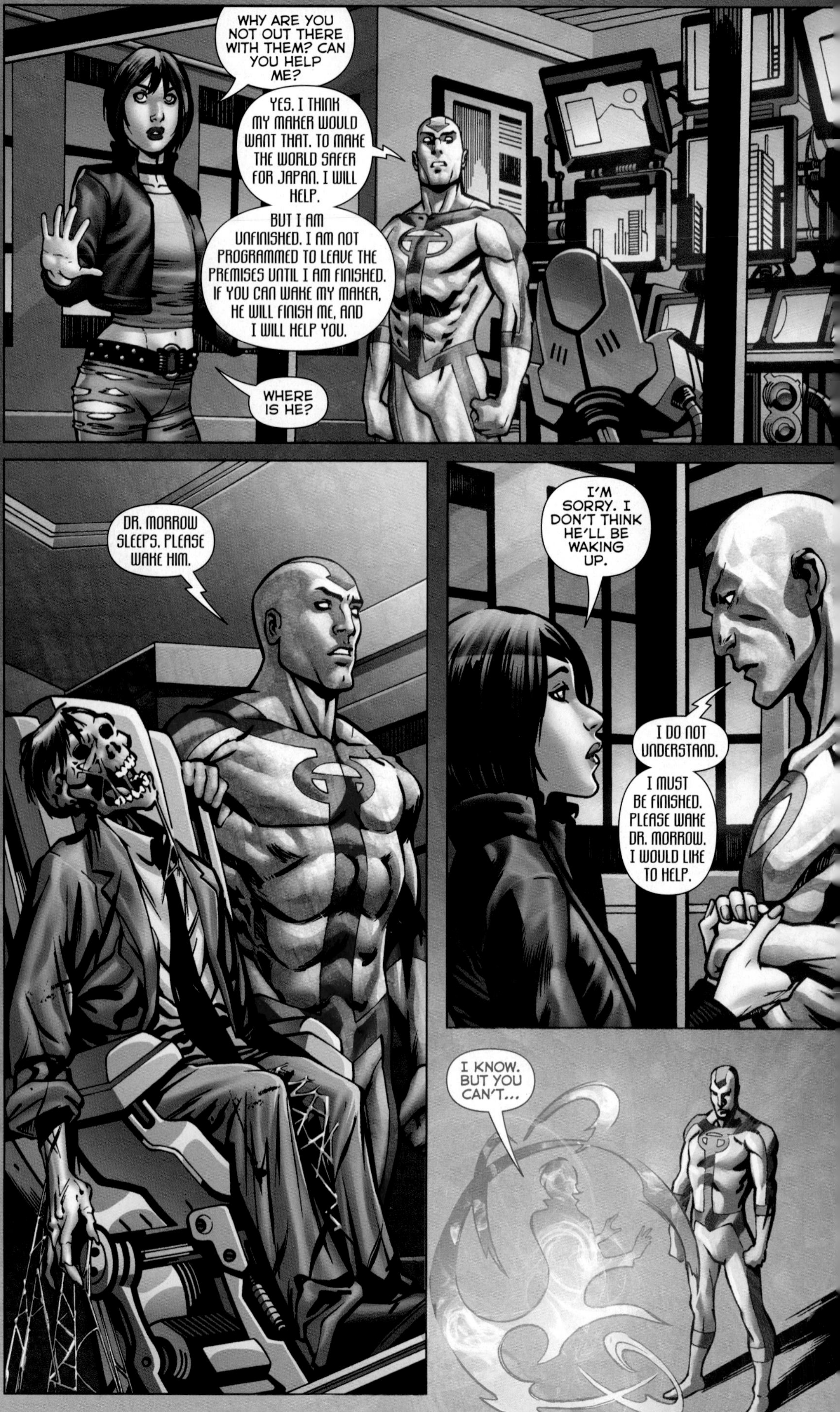
WHY ARE YOU NOT OUT THERE WITH THEM? CAN YOU HELP ME?
YES. I THINK MY MAKER WOULD WANT THAT. TO MAKE THE WORLD SAFER FOR JAPAN. I WILL HELP.
BUT I AM UNFINISHED. I AM NOT PROGRAMMED TO LEAVE THE PREMISES UNTIL I AM FINISHED. IF YOU CAN WAKE MY MAKER, HE WILL FINISH ME, AND I WILL HELP YOU.
WHERE IS HE?
DR. MORROW SLEEPS. PLEASE WAKE HIM.
I'M SORRY. I DON'T THINK HE'LL BE WAKING UP.
I DO NOT UNDERSTAND.
I MUST BE FINISHED. PLEASE WAKE DR. MORROW. I WOULD LIKE TO HELP.
I KNOW. BUT YOU CAN'T...

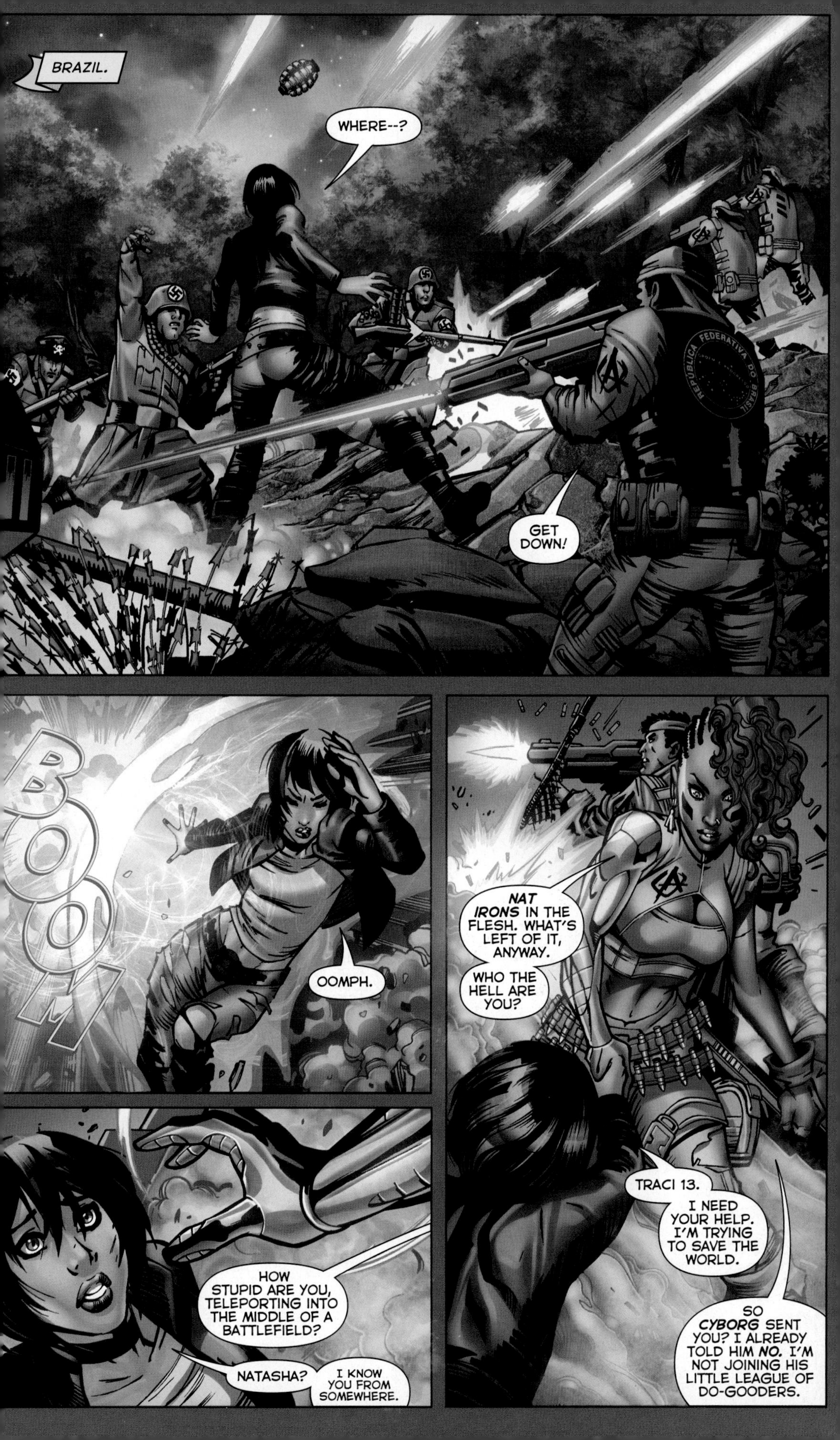

BRAZIL.
WHERE--?
GET DOWN!
BOOOM
OOMPH.
HOW STUPID ARE YOU, TELEPORTING INTO THE MIDDLE OF A BATTLEFIELD?
NATASHA?
I KNOW YOU FROM SOMEWHERE.
NAT IRONS IN THE FLESH. WHAT'S LEFT OF IT, ANYWAY.
WHO THE HELL ARE YOU?
TRACI 13.
I NEED YOUR HELP. I'M TRYING TO SAVE THE WORLD.
SO CYBORG SENT YOU? I ALREADY TOLD HIM NO. I'M NOT JOINING HIS LITTLE LEAGUE OF DO-GOODERS.

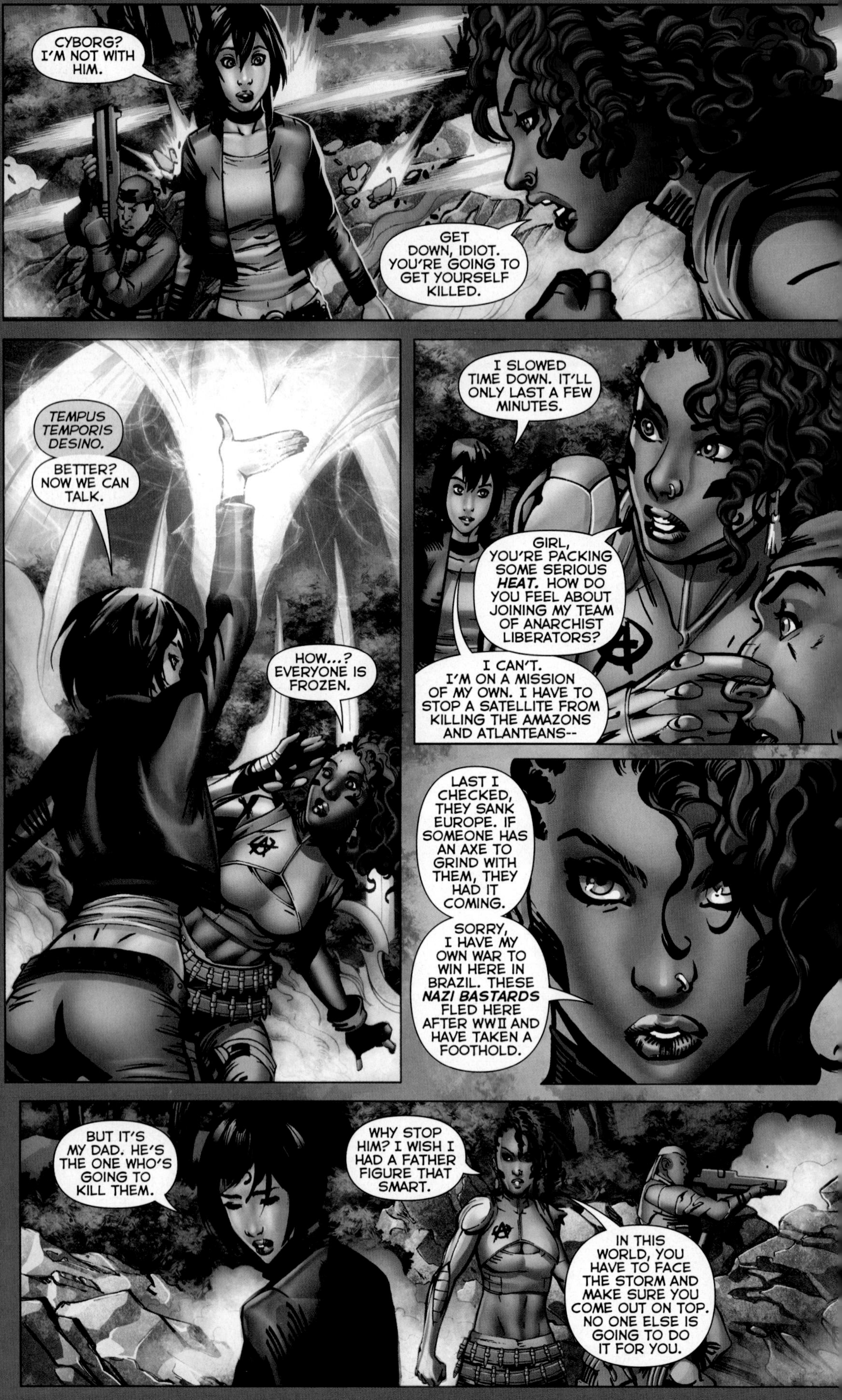
CYBORG? I'M NOT WITH HIM.
GET DOWN, IDIOT. YOU'RE GOING TO GET YOURSELF KILLED.
TEMPUS TEMPORIS DESINO.
BETTER? NOW WE CAN TALK.
HOW...? EVERYONE IS FROZEN.
I SLOWED TIME DOWN. IT'LL ONLY LAST A FEW MINUTES.
GIRL, YOU'RE PACKING SOME SERIOUS ***HEAT.*** HOW DO YOU FEEL ABOUT JOINING MY TEAM OF ANARCHIST LIBERATORS?
I CAN'T. I'M ON A MISSION OF MY OWN. I HAVE TO STOP A SATELLITE FROM KILLING THE AMAZONS AND ATLANTEANS--
LAST I CHECKED, THEY SANK EUROPE. IF SOMEONE HAS AN AXE TO GRIND WITH THEM, THEY HAD IT COMING.
SORRY, I HAVE MY OWN WAR TO WIN HERE IN BRAZIL. THESE ***NAZI BASTARDS*** FLED HERE AFTER WWII AND HAVE TAKEN A FOOTHOLD.
BUT IT'S MY DAD. HE'S THE ONE WHO'S GOING TO KILL THEM.
WHY STOP HIM? I WISH I HAD A FATHER FIGURE THAT SMART.
IN THIS WORLD, YOU HAVE TO FACE THE STORM AND MAKE SURE YOU COME OUT ON TOP. NO ONE ELSE IS GOING TO DO IT FOR YOU.

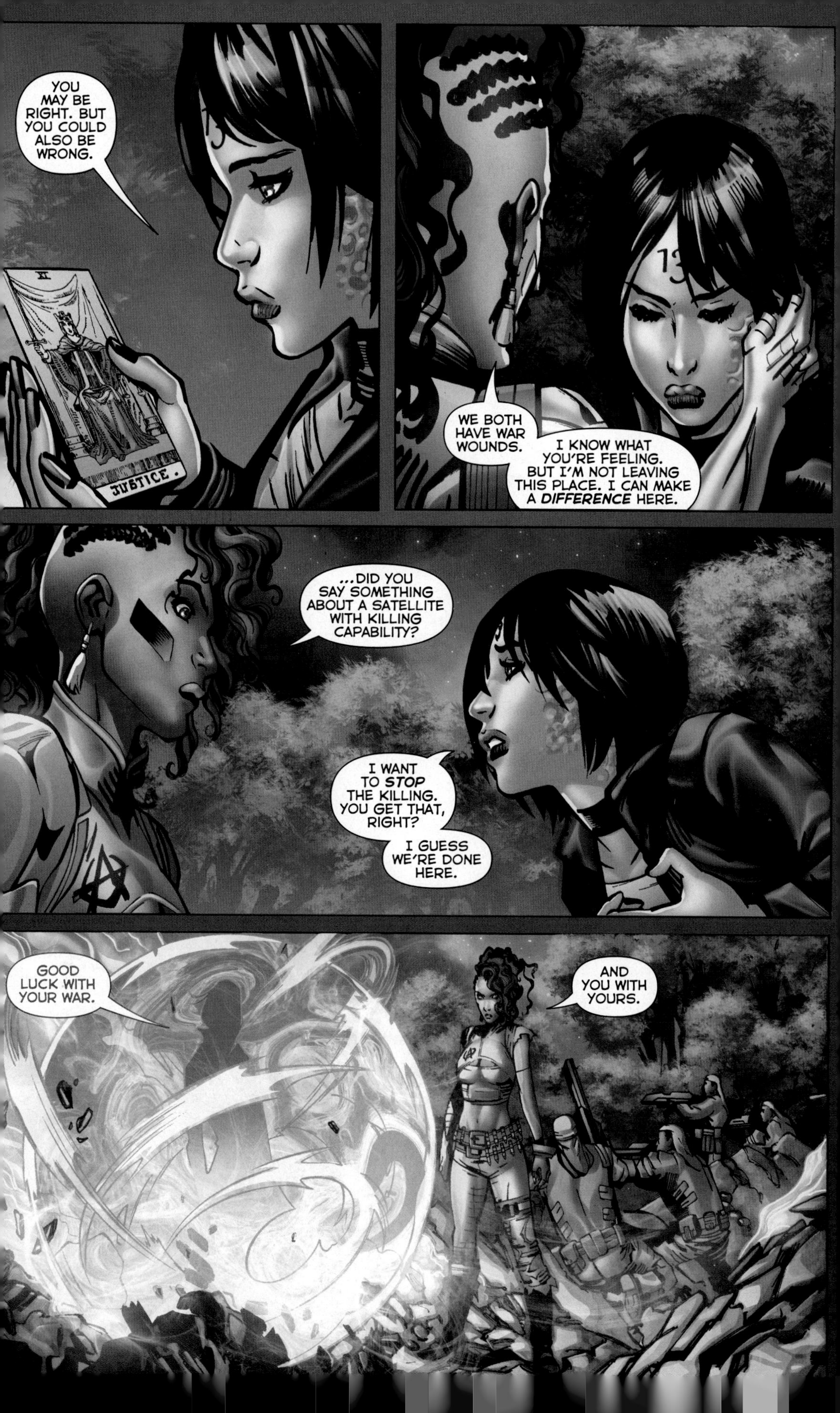
YOU MAY BE RIGHT. BUT YOU COULD ALSO BE WRONG.
JUSTICE.
WE BOTH HAVE WAR WOUNDS.
I KNOW WHAT YOU'RE FEELING. BUT I'M NOT LEAVING THIS PLACE. I CAN MAKE A *DIFFERENCE* HERE.
...DID YOU SAY SOMETHING ABOUT A SATELLITE WITH KILLING CAPABILITY?
I WANT TO ***STOP*** THE KILLING. YOU GET THAT, RIGHT?
I GUESS WE'RE DONE HERE.
GOOD LUCK WITH YOUR WAR.
AND YOU WITH YOURS.

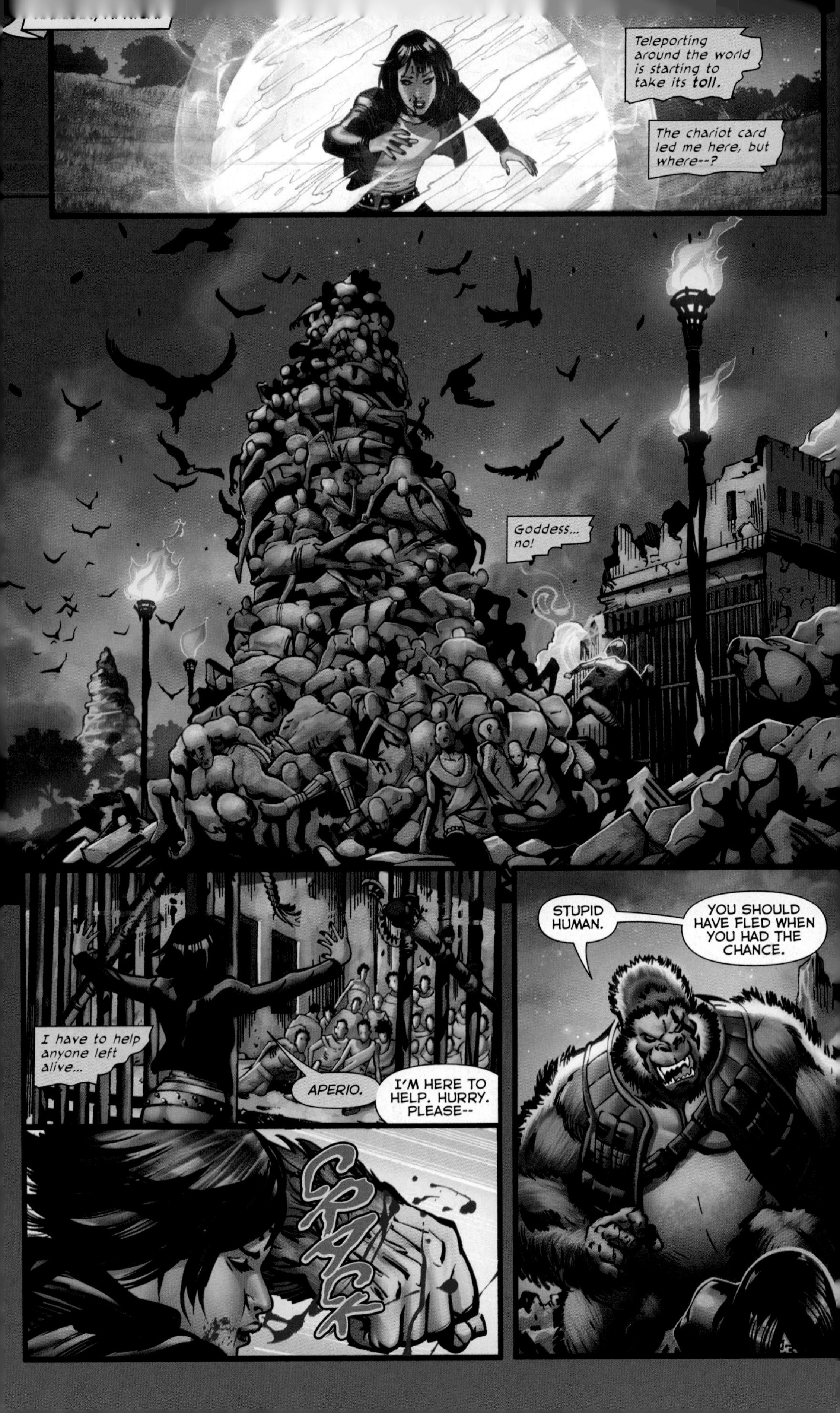

Teleporting around the world is starting to take its toll.
The chariot card led me here, but where--?
Goddess... no!
I have to help anyone left alive...
APERIO.
I'M HERE TO HELP. HURRY. PLEASE--
CRACK
STUPID HUMAN.
YOU SHOULD HAVE FLED WHEN YOU HAD THE CHANCE.

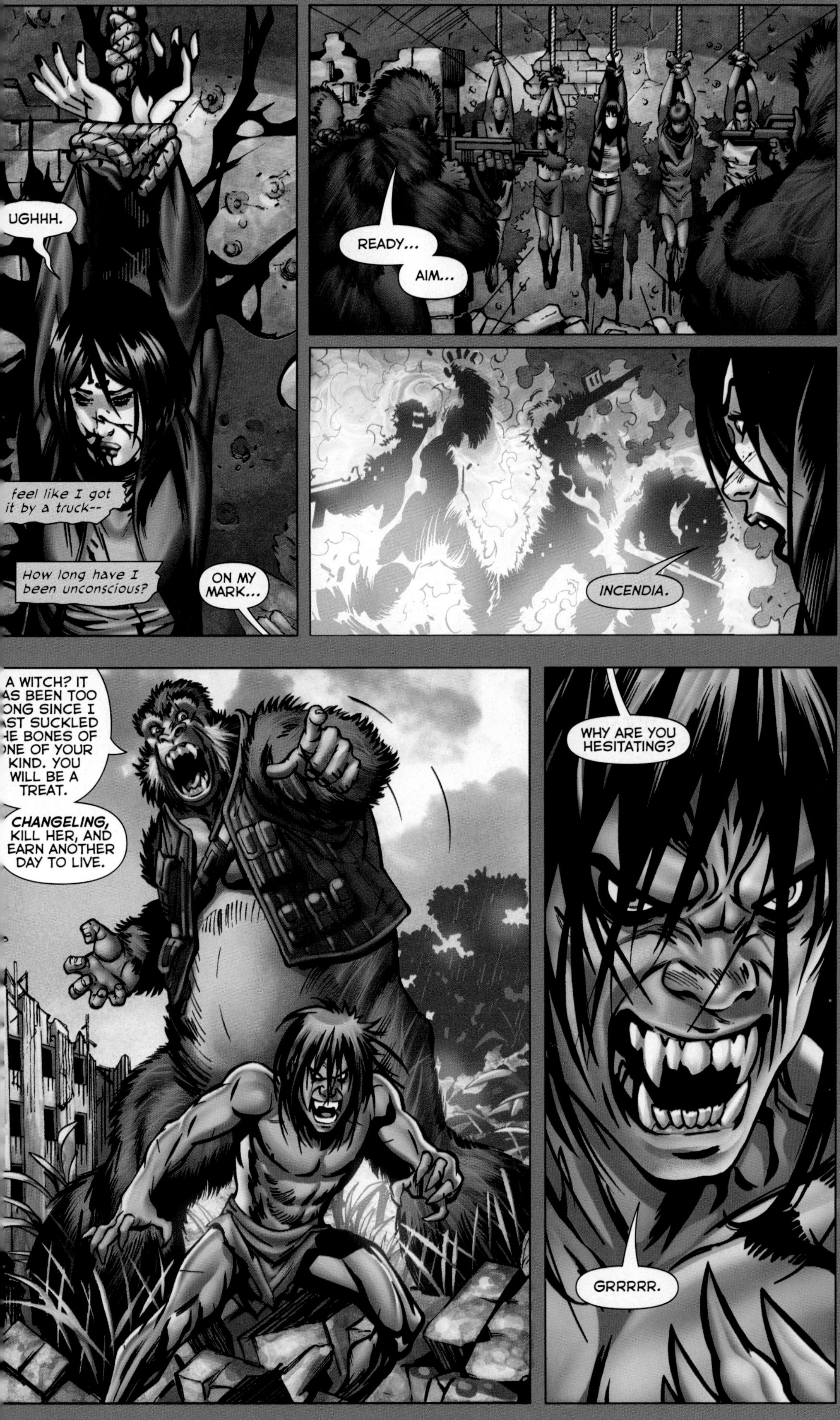
UGHHH.
feel like I got it by a truck--
How long have I been unconscious?
ON MY MARK...
READY...
AIM...
INCENDIA.
A WITCH? IT AS BEEN TOO ONG SINCE I AST SUCKLED HE BONES OF ONE OF YOUR KIND. YOU WILL BE A TREAT.
CHANGELING, KILL HER, AND EARN ANOTHER DAY TO LIVE.
WHY ARE YOU HESITATING?
GRRRRR.

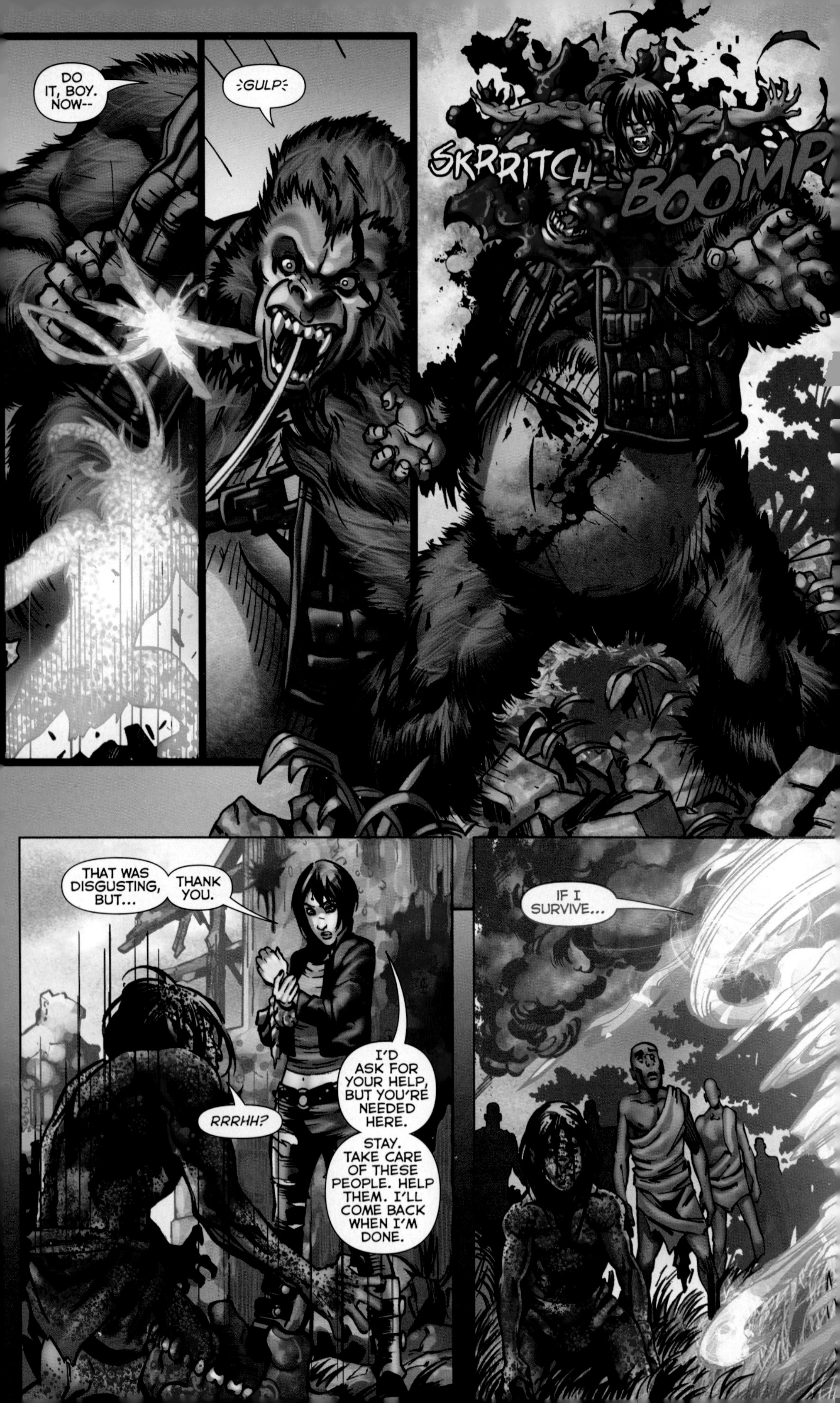
DO IT, BOY. NOW--
GULP
SKRRITCH--
BOOMP!
THAT WAS DISGUSTING, BUT...
THANK YOU.
RRRHH?
I'D ASK FOR YOUR HELP, BUT YOU'RE NEEDED HERE.
STAY. TAKE CARE OF THESE PEOPLE. HELP THEM. I'LL COME BACK WHEN I'M DONE.
IF I SURVIVE...

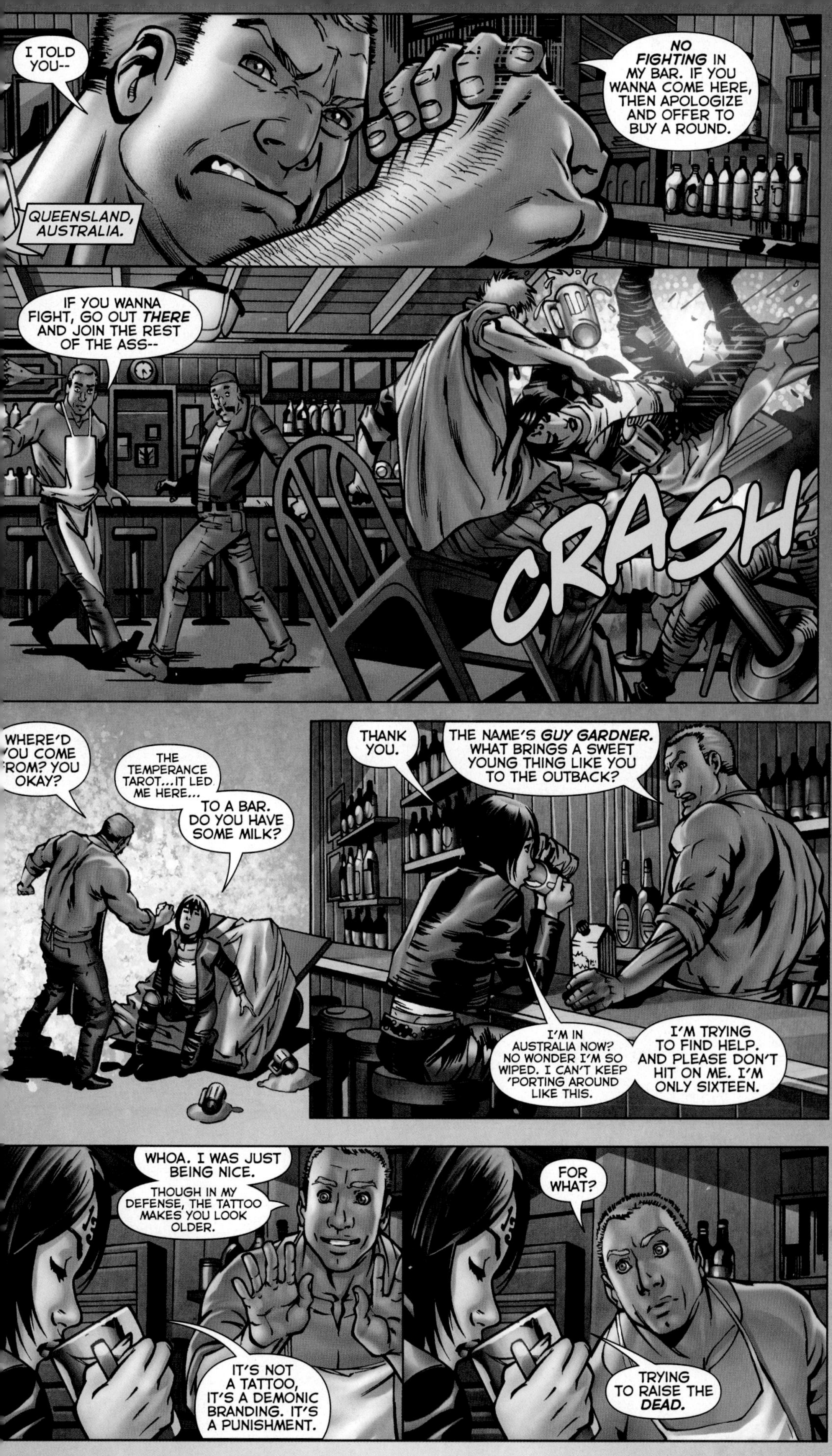
I TOLD YOU--
NO FIGHTING IN MY BAR. IF YOU WANNA COME HERE, THEN APOLOGIZE AND OFFER TO BUY A ROUND.
QUEENSLAND, AUSTRALIA.
IF YOU WANNA FIGHT, GO OUT THERE AND JOIN THE REST OF THE ASS--
CRASH
WHERE'D YOU COME FROM? YOU OKAY?
THE TEMPERANCE TAROT...IT LED ME HERE...
TO A BAR. DO YOU HAVE SOME MILK?
THANK YOU.
THE NAME'S GUY GARDNER. WHAT BRINGS A SWEET YOUNG THING LIKE YOU TO THE OUTBACK?
I'M IN AUSTRALIA NOW? NO WONDER I'M SO WIPED. I CAN'T KEEP 'PORTING AROUND LIKE THIS.
I'M TRYING TO FIND HELP. AND PLEASE DON'T HIT ON ME. I'M ONLY SIXTEEN.
WHOA. I WAS JUST BEING NICE.
THOUGH IN MY DEFENSE, THE TATTOO MAKES YOU LOOK OLDER.
IT'S NOT A TATTOO, IT'S A DEMONIC BRANDING. IT'S A PUNISHMENT.
FOR WHAT?
TRYING TO RAISE THE DEAD.

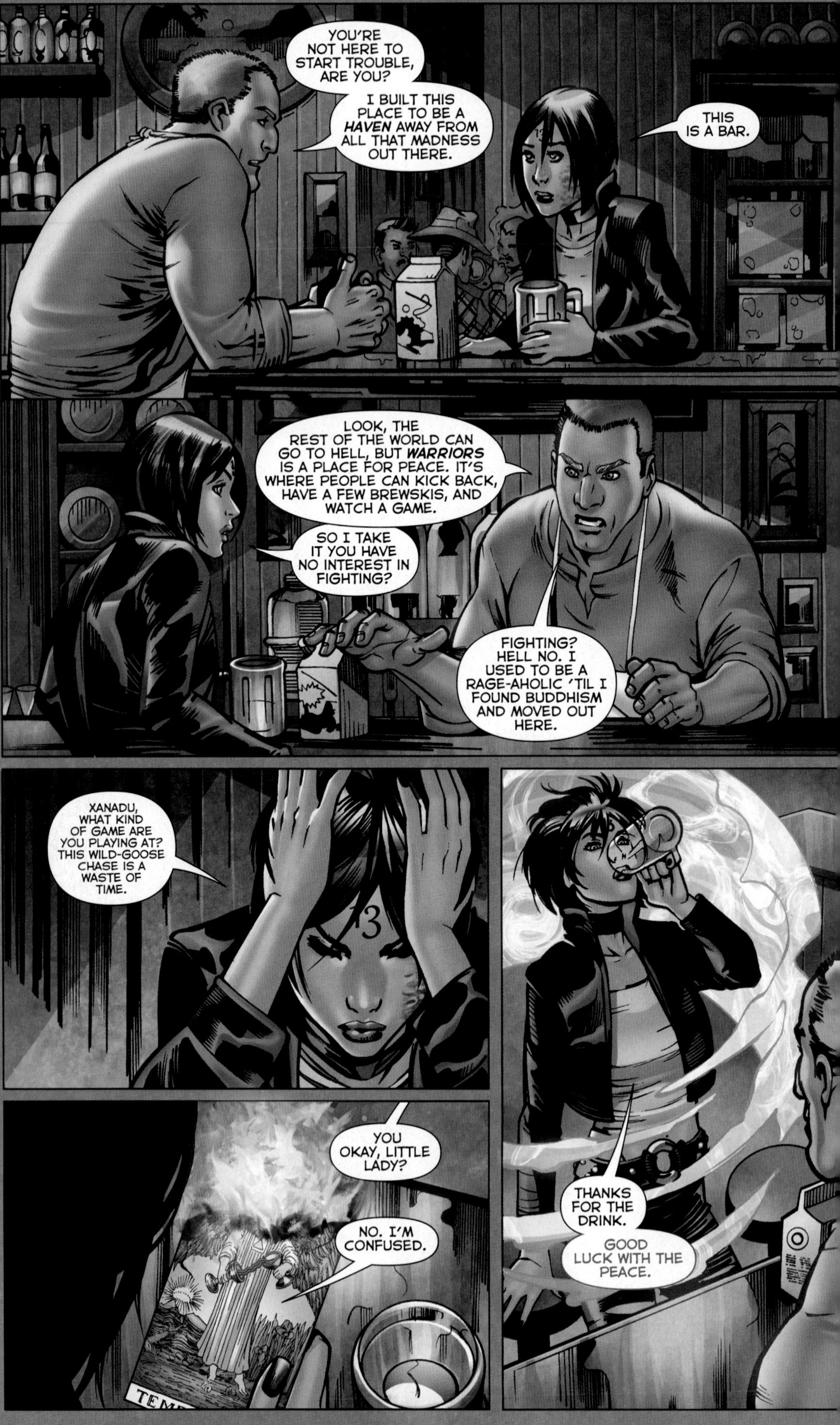
YOU'RE NOT HERE TO START TROUBLE, ARE YOU?
I BUILT THIS PLACE TO BE A *HAVEN* AWAY FROM ALL THAT MADNESS OUT THERE.
THIS IS A BAR.
LOOK, THE REST OF THE WORLD CAN GO TO HELL, BUT *WARRIORS* IS A PLACE FOR PEACE. IT'S WHERE PEOPLE CAN KICK BACK, HAVE A FEW BREWSKIS, AND WATCH A GAME.
SO I TAKE IT YOU HAVE NO INTEREST IN FIGHTING?
FIGHTING? HELL NO. I USED TO BE A RAGE-AHOLIC 'TIL I FOUND BUDDHISM AND MOVED OUT HERE.
XANADU, WHAT KIND OF GAME ARE YOU PLAYING AT? THIS WILD-GOOSE CHASE IS A WASTE OF TIME.
YOU OKAY, LITTLE LADY?
NO. I'M CONFUSED.
THANKS FOR THE DRINK.
GOOD LUCK WITH THE PEACE.

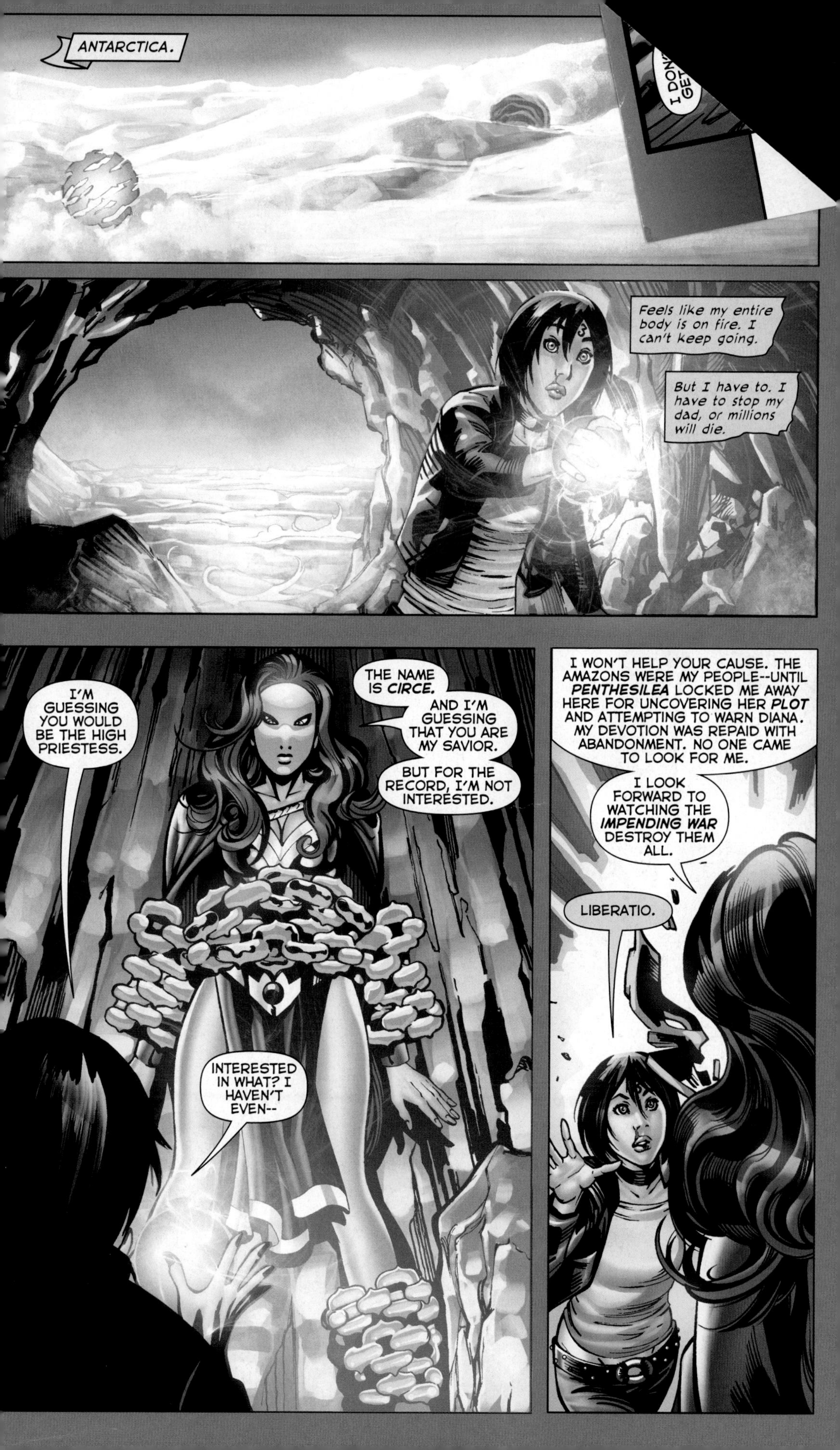
ANTARCTICA.
Feels like my entire body is on fire. I can't keep going.
But I have to. I have to stop my dad, or millions will die.
I'M GUESSING YOU WOULD BE THE HIGH PRIESTESS.
THE NAME IS *CIRCE.*
AND I'M GUESSING THAT YOU ARE MY SAVIOR.
BUT FOR THE RECORD, I'M NOT INTERESTED.
INTERESTED IN WHAT? I HAVEN'T EVEN--
I WON'T HELP YOUR CAUSE. THE AMAZONS WERE MY PEOPLE--UNTIL ***PENTHESILEA*** LOCKED ME AWAY HERE FOR UNCOVERING HER ***PLOT*** AND ATTEMPTING TO WARN DIANA. MY DEVOTION WAS REPAID WITH ABANDONMENT. NO ONE CAME TO LOOK FOR ME.
I LOOK FORWARD TO WATCHING THE ***IMPENDING WAR*** DESTROY THEM ALL.
LIBERATIO.

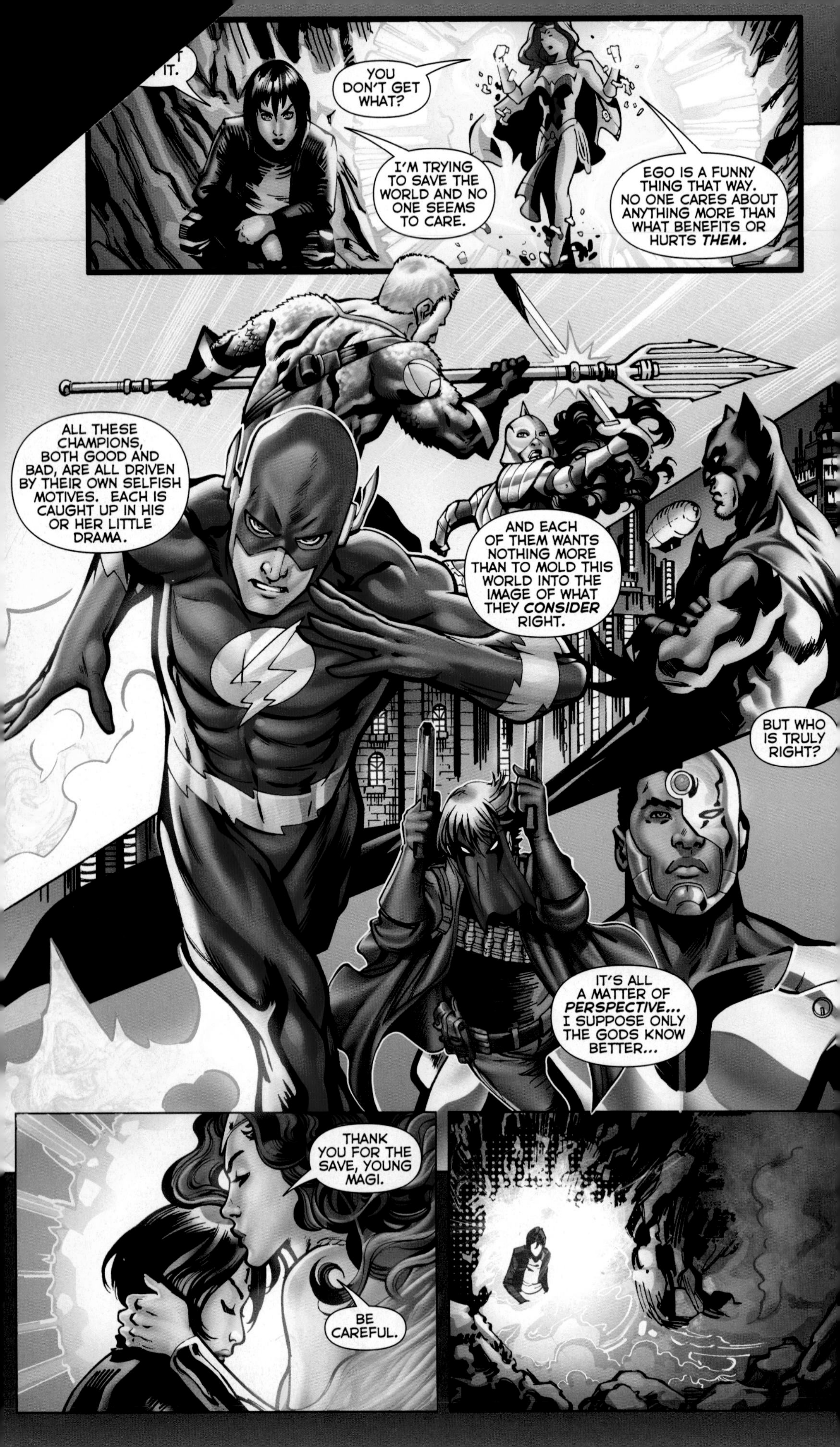
YOU DON'T GET WHAT?
I'M TRYING TO SAVE THE WORLD AND NO ONE SEEMS TO CARE.
EGO IS A FUNNY THING THAT WAY. NO ONE CARES ABOUT ANYTHING MORE THAN WHAT BENEFITS OR HURTS *THEM.*
ALL THESE CHAMPIONS, BOTH GOOD AND BAD, ARE ALL DRIVEN BY THEIR OWN SELFISH MOTIVES. EACH IS CAUGHT UP IN HIS OR HER LITTLE DRAMA.
AND EACH OF THEM WANTS NOTHING MORE THAN TO MOLD THIS WORLD INTO THE IMAGE OF WHAT THEY *CONSIDER* RIGHT.
BUT WHO IS TRULY RIGHT?
IT'S ALL A MATTER OF *PERSPECTIVE...* I SUPPOSE ONLY THE GODS KNOW BETTER...
THANK YOU FOR THE SAVE, YOUNG MAGI.
BE CAREFUL.

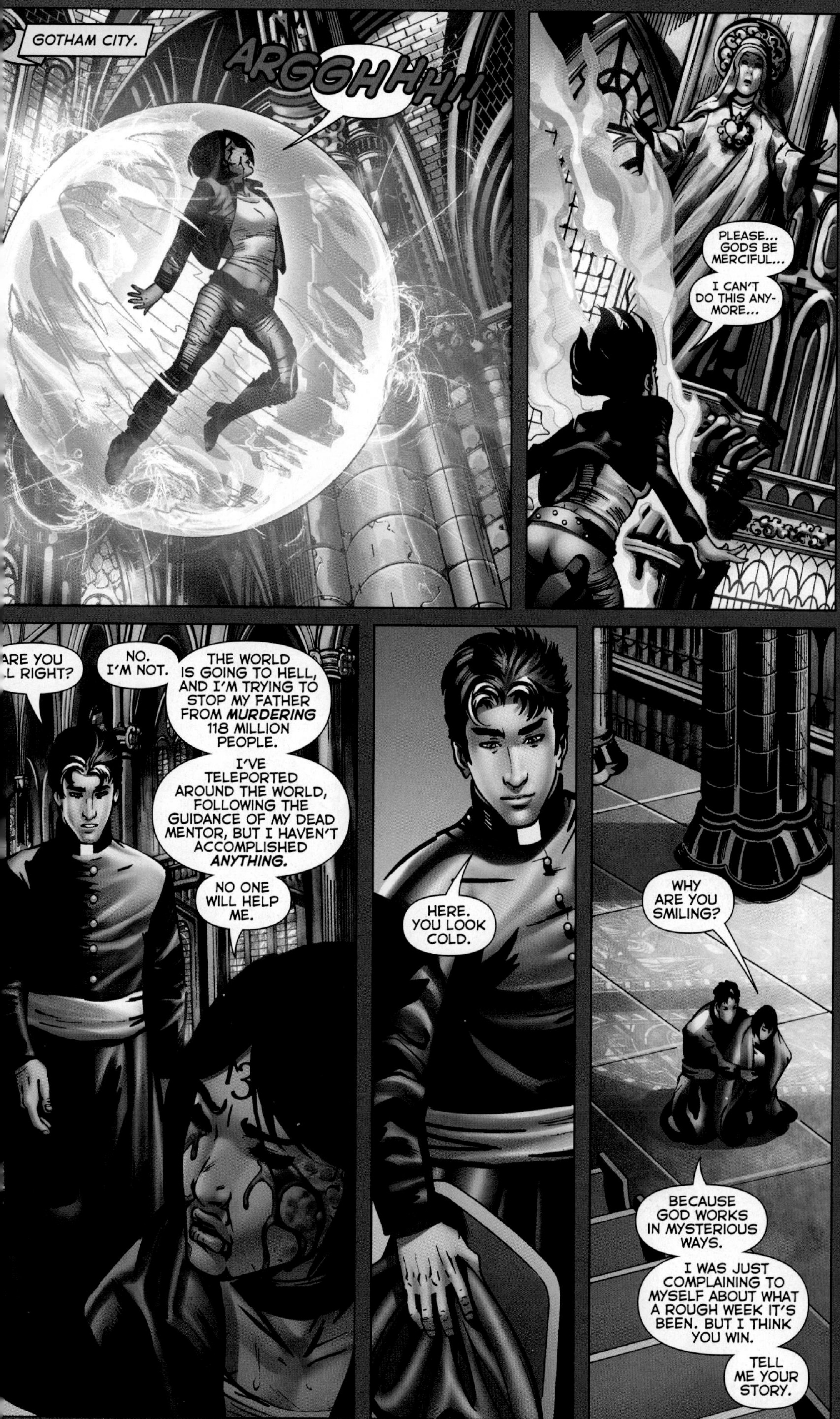
GOTHAM CITY.
ARGGHHH!!
PLEASE... GODS BE MERCIFUL...
I CAN'T DO THIS ANY-MORE...
ARE YOU L RIGHT?
NO. I'M NOT.
THE WORLD IS GOING TO HELL, AND I'M TRYING TO STOP MY FATHER FROM *MURDERING* 118 MILLION PEOPLE.
I'VE TELEPORTED AROUND THE WORLD, FOLLOWING THE GUIDANCE OF MY DEAD MENTOR, BUT I HAVEN'T ACCOMPLISHED *ANYTHING.*
NO ONE WILL HELP ME.
HERE. YOU LOOK COLD.
WHY ARE YOU SMILING?
BECAUSE GOD WORKS IN MYSTERIOUS WAYS.
I WAS JUST COMPLAINING TO MYSELF ABOUT WHAT A ROUGH WEEK IT'S BEEN. BUT I THINK YOU WIN.
TELL ME YOUR STORY.

...AND THEN I LANDED HERE. WITH NOTHING TO SHOW.

YOU KNOW, I USED TO BE A BAD KID, RAN WITH THE WRONG CROWD, STOLE THINGS TO PAY FOR MY DRUG HABIT. EVEN GOT MIXED UP IN AN APOCALYPSE CULT LED BY A NUTJOB NAMED *BROTHER BLOOD*.

DURING THAT TIME, I CAME TO SEE THE WORLD AS A TERRIBLE PLACE. I SAW THINGS...AWFUL THINGS. AND THEN I *DIED*.

BUT I GOT A SECOND CHANCE. AND I DISCOVERED, THE WORLD CAN ALSO BE BEAUTIFUL AND GOOD.

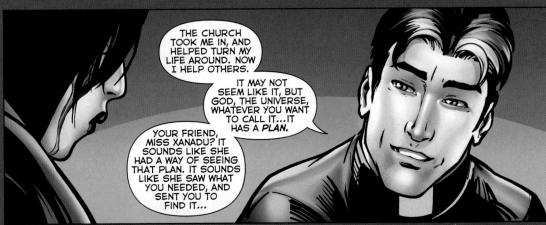

THE CHURCH TOOK ME IN, AND HELPED TURN MY LIFE AROUND. NOW I HELP OTHERS.

IT MAY NOT SEEM LIKE IT, BUT GOD, THE UNIVERSE, WHATEVER YOU WANT TO CALL IT...IT HAS A *PLAN*.

YOUR FRIEND, MISS XANADU? IT SOUNDS LIKE SHE HAD A WAY OF SEEING THAT PLAN. IT SOUNDS LIKE SHE SAW WHAT YOU NEEDED, AND SENT YOU TO FIND IT...

WEREN'T YOU LISTENING? NO ONE HAS HELPED ME. NO ONE...

MAYBE THEY WEREN'T SUPPOSED TO JOIN YOU. MAYBE YOU WERE JUST SUPPOSED TO *LEARN* SOMETHING FROM THEM.

BUT I DON'T HAVE TIME TO FIGURE IT OUT--

WHEN THE TIME IS RIGHT, YOU WILL.

YOU DON'T SEEM VERY WEIRDED OUT TO BE SITTING HERE TALKING WITH A WITCH.

I'M A *GOTHAM CITY* PRIEST. BELIEVE ME, I'VE SEEN WEIRDER.

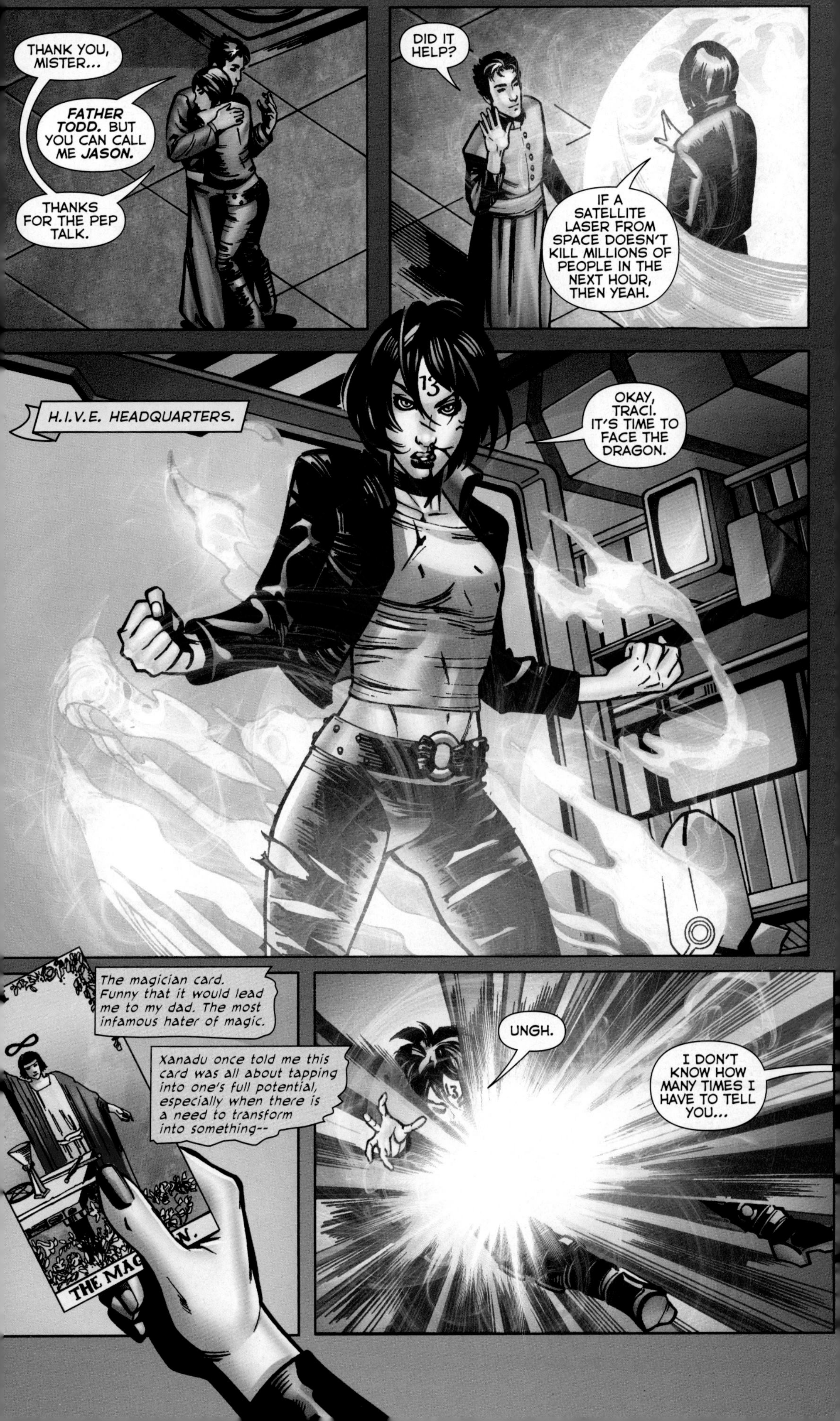
THANK YOU, MISTER...
FATHER TODD. BUT YOU CAN CALL ME JASON.
THANKS FOR THE PEP TALK.
DID IT HELP?
IF A SATELLITE LASER FROM SPACE DOESN'T KILL MILLIONS OF PEOPLE IN THE NEXT HOUR, THEN YEAH.
H.I.V.E. HEADQUARTERS.
OKAY, TRACI. IT'S TIME TO FACE THE DRAGON.
The magician card. Funny that it would lead me to my dad. The most infamous hater of magic.
Xanadu once told me this card was all about tapping into one's full potential, especially when there is a need to transform into something--
UNGH.
I DON'T KNOW HOW MANY TIMES I HAVE TO TELL YOU...

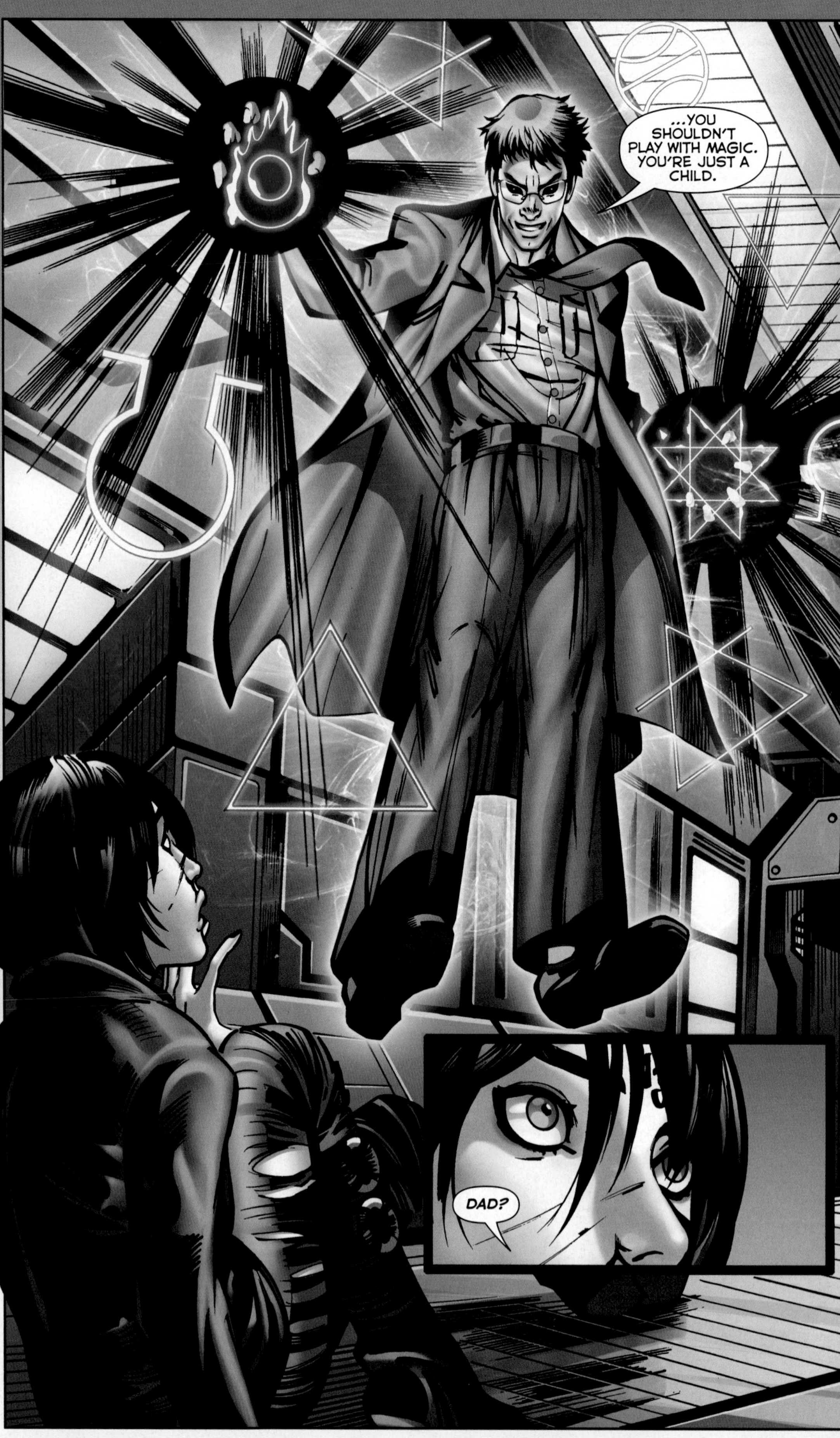
...YOU SHOULDN'T PLAY WITH MAGIC. YOU'RE JUST A CHILD.
DAD?

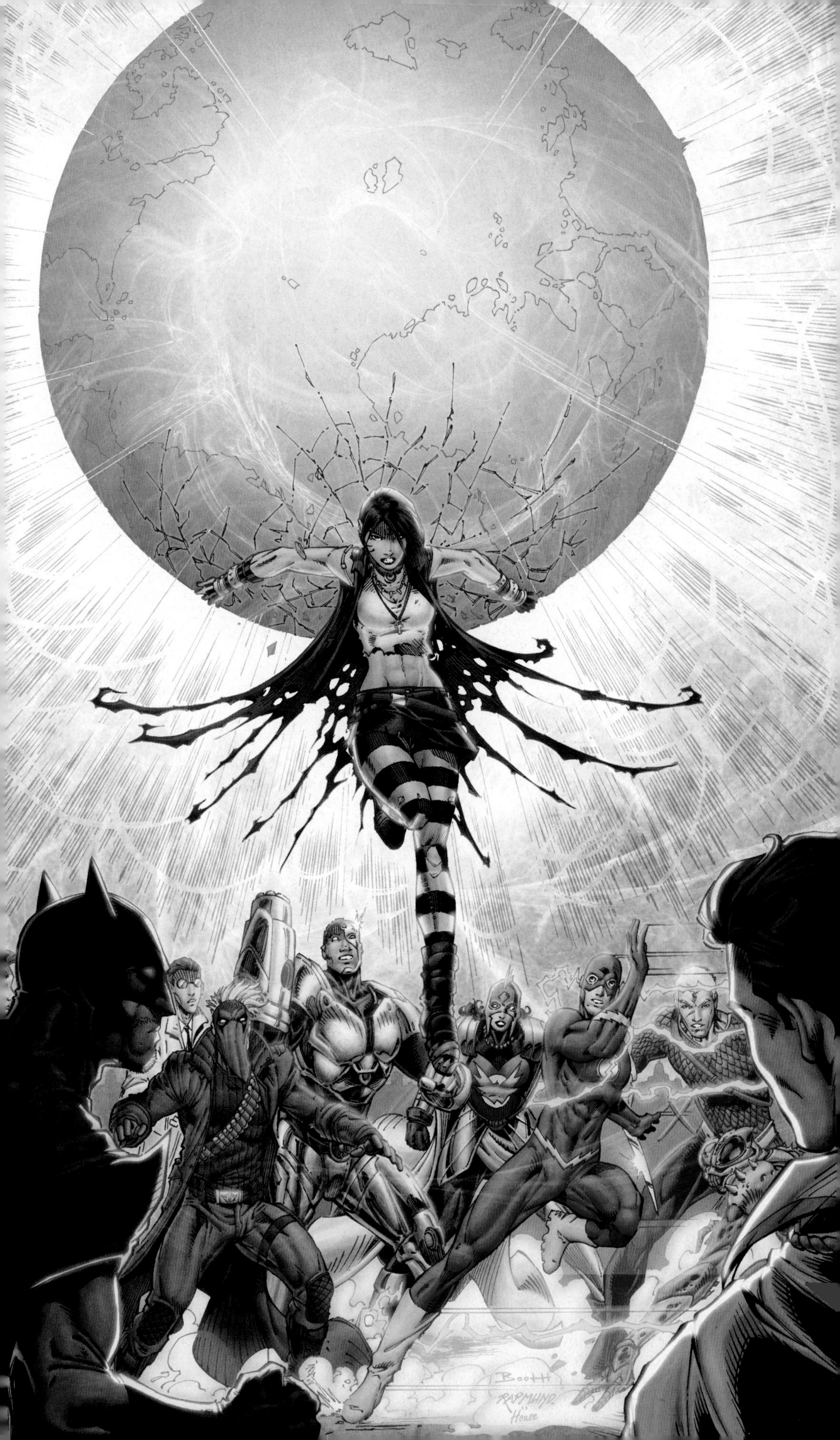
Booth
RAPMUND
House

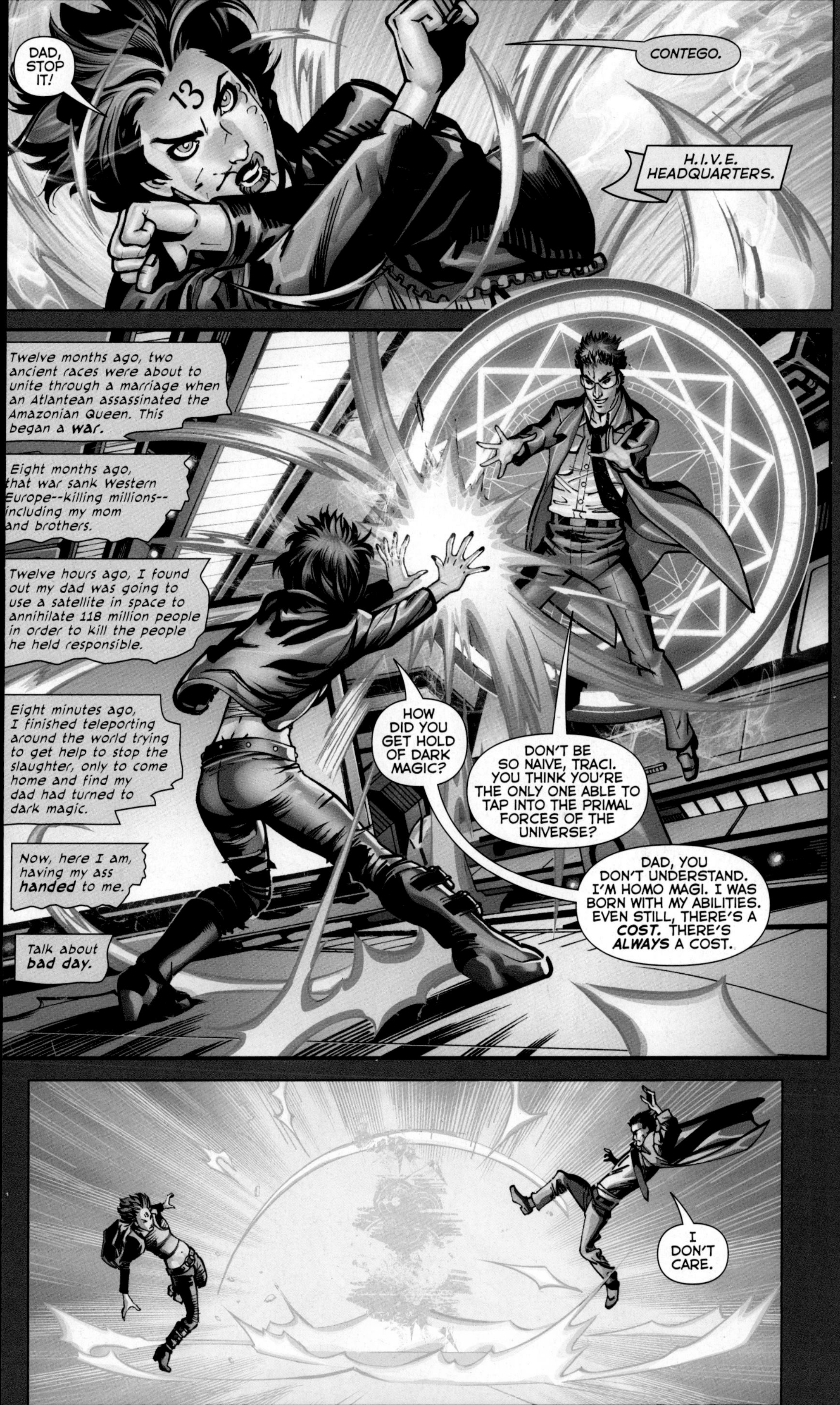
DAD, STOP IT!
CONTEGO.
H.I.V.E. HEADQUARTERS.
Twelve months ago, two ancient races were about to unite through a marriage when an Atlantean assassinated the Amazonian Queen. This began a war.
Eight months ago, that war sank Western Europe--killing millions--including my mom and brothers.
Twelve hours ago, I found out my dad was going to use a satellite in space to annihilate 118 million people in order to kill the people he held responsible.
Eight minutes ago, I finished teleporting around the world trying to get help to stop the slaughter, only to come home and find my dad had turned to dark magic.
Now, here I am, having my ass handed to me.
Talk about bad day.
HOW DID YOU GET HOLD OF DARK MAGIC?
DON'T BE SO NAIVE, TRACI. YOU THINK YOU'RE THE ONLY ONE ABLE TO TAP INTO THE PRIMAL FORCES OF THE UNIVERSE?
DAD, YOU DON'T UNDERSTAND. I'M HOMO MAGI. I WAS BORN WITH MY ABILITIES. EVEN STILL, THERE'S A COST. THERE'S ALWAYS A COST.
I DON'T CARE.

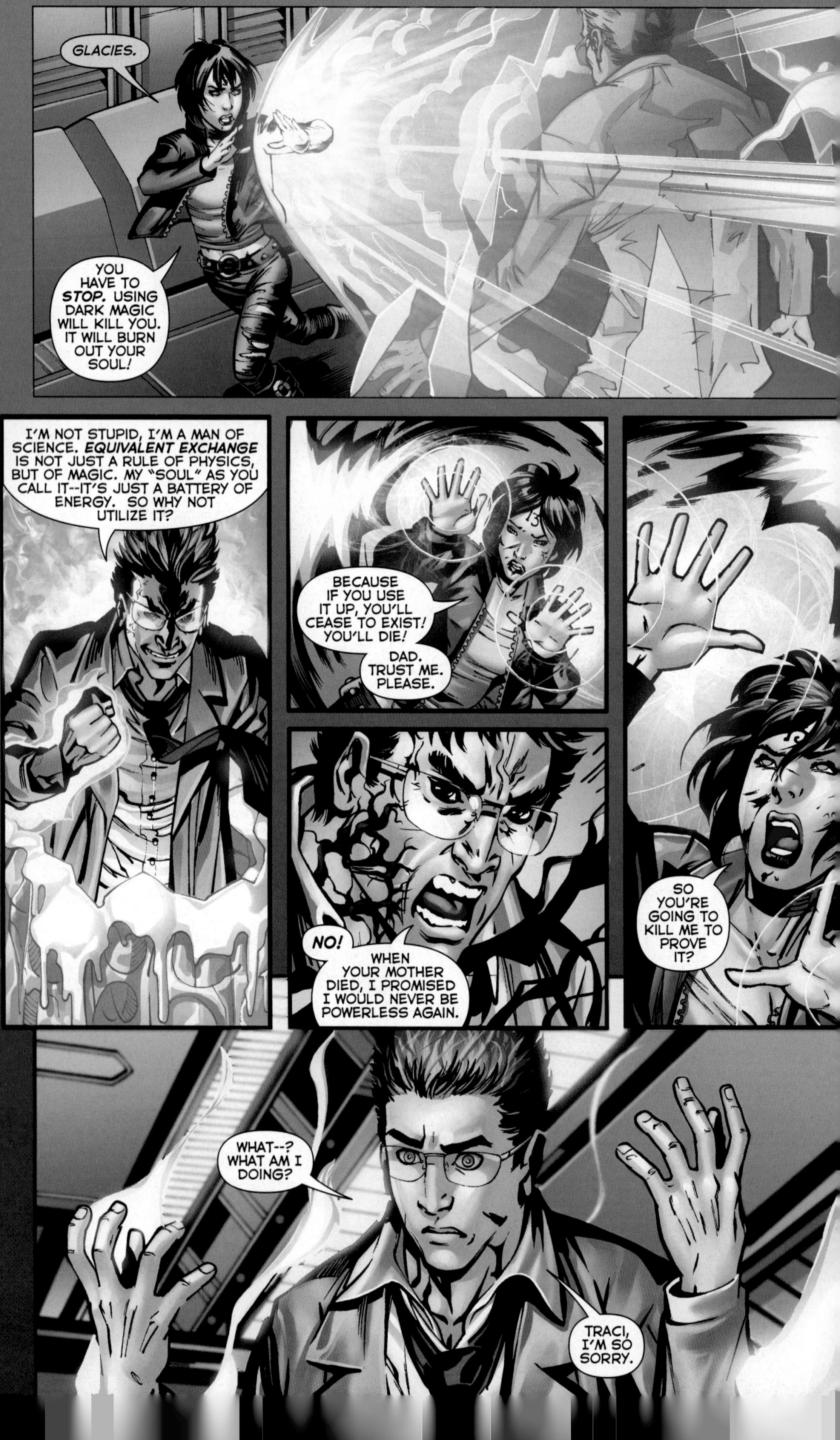

GLACIES.
YOU HAVE TO STOP. USING DARK MAGIC WILL KILL YOU. IT WILL BURN OUT YOUR SOUL!
I'M NOT STUPID, I'M A MAN OF SCIENCE. EQUIVALENT EXCHANGE IS NOT JUST A RULE OF PHYSICS, BUT OF MAGIC. MY "SOUL" AS YOU CALL IT--IT'S JUST A BATTERY OF ENERGY. SO WHY NOT UTILIZE IT?
BECAUSE IF YOU USE IT UP, YOU'LL CEASE TO EXIST! YOU'LL DIE!
DAD. TRUST ME. PLEASE.
NO!
WHEN YOUR MOTHER DIED, I PROMISED I WOULD NEVER BE POWERLESS AGAIN.
SO YOU'RE GOING TO KILL ME TO PROVE IT?
WHAT--? WHAT AM I DOING?
TRACI, I'M SO SORRY.

...DAD?

OH, PEANUT...

...YOU HAVE A LOT TO LEARN.

ARGHHH!!

I DON'T KNOW WHY YOU'RE FIGHTING ME ON THIS. I JUST WANT THE WORLD AT PEACE AGAIN. AND IF IT KILLS YOUR MOTHER'S MURDERERS? EVEN BETTER.

New Themyscira. Targeting... Estimated time until annihilation: 00:12:17

DAD... DON'T...

LOOK AT ALL THOSE PEOPLE FIGHTING. AS IF WAR EVER ACHIEVED ANYTHING BUT MORE WAR.

IN MINUTES, THEY'LL ALL BE DEAD.

New Themyscira. Targeting... Estimated time until annihilation: 00:12:09

YOU WANT TO KILL 118 MILLION PEOPLE?

FINE...

New Themyscira. Targeting... Estimated time until annihil... 11:58

TRACI! NO!

...COUNT ME AS ONE OF THEM.

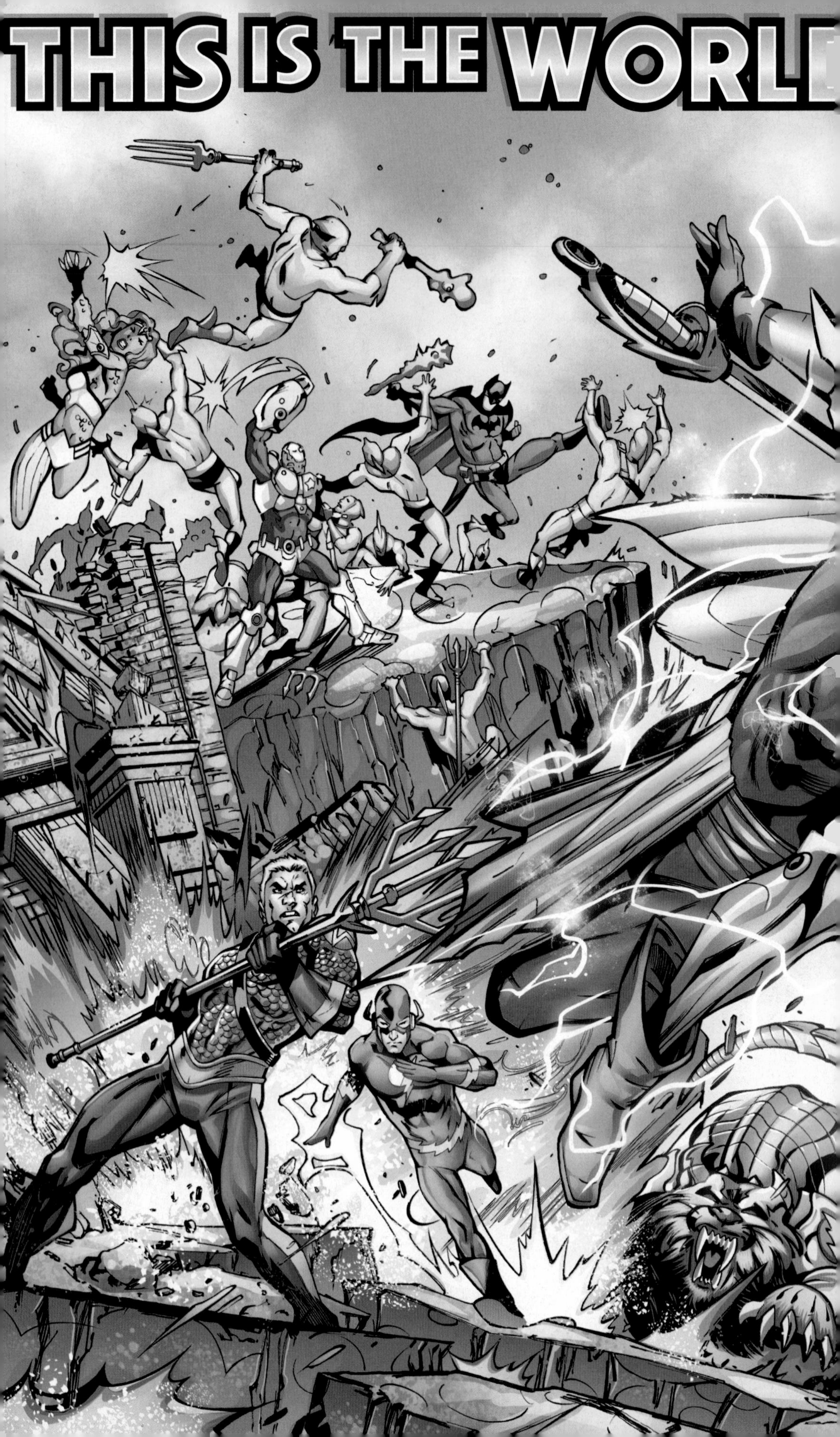
THIS IS THE WORLD

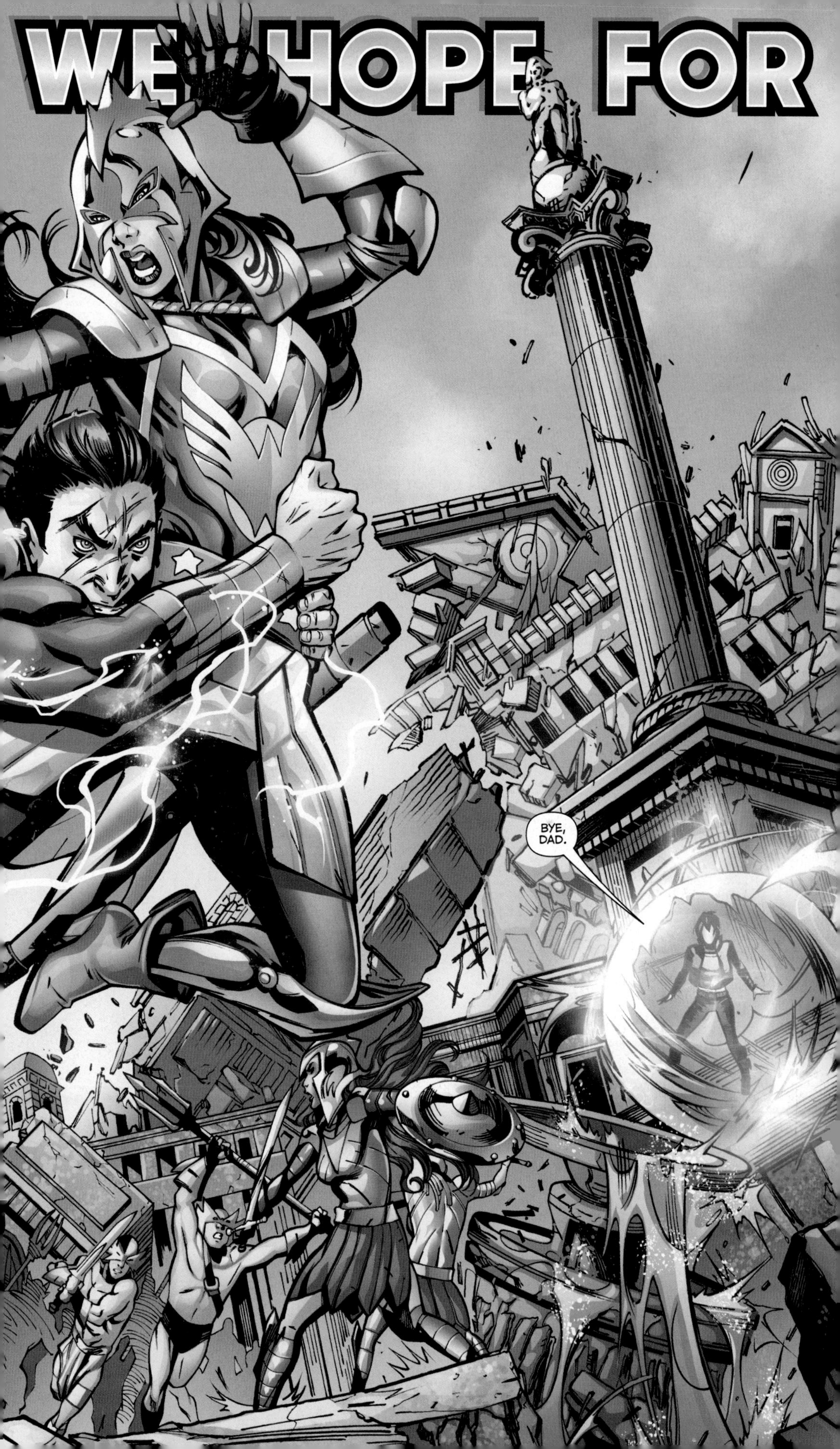
WE HOPE FOR
BYE, DAD.

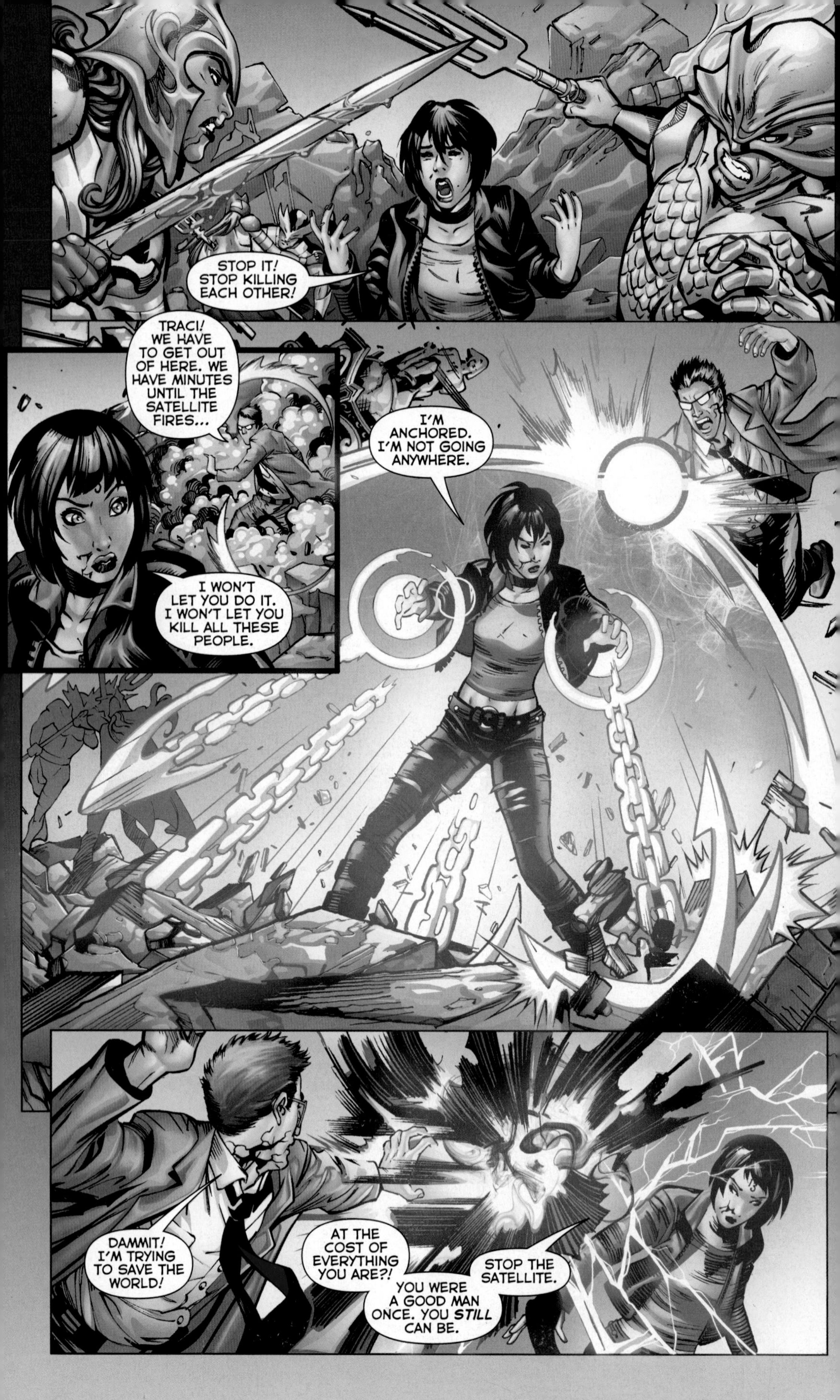
STOP IT! STOP KILLING EACH OTHER!
TRACI! WE HAVE TO GET OUT OF HERE. WE HAVE MINUTES UNTIL THE SATELLITE FIRES...
I WON'T LET YOU DO IT. I WON'T LET YOU KILL ALL THESE PEOPLE.
I'M ANCHORED. I'M NOT GOING ANYWHERE.
DAMMIT! I'M TRYING TO SAVE THE WORLD!
AT THE COST OF EVERYTHING YOU ARE?!
YOU WERE A GOOD MAN ONCE. YOU STILL CAN BE.
STOP THE SATELLITE.

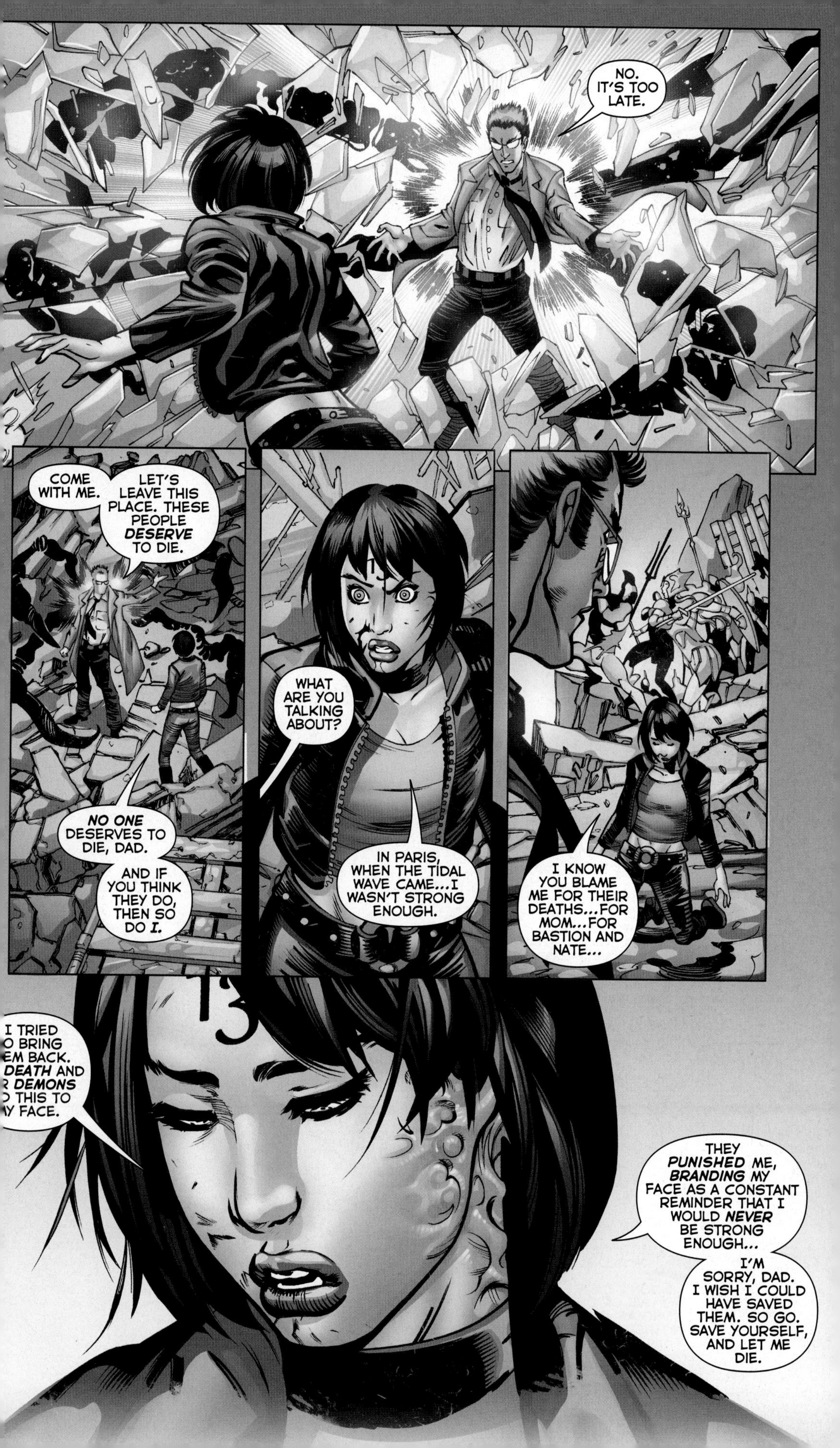
NO. IT'S TOO LATE.
COME WITH ME.
LET'S LEAVE THIS PLACE. THESE PEOPLE *DESERVE* TO DIE.
NO ONE DESERVES TO DIE, DAD.
AND IF YOU THINK THEY DO, THEN SO DO *I*.
WHAT ARE YOU TALKING ABOUT?
IN PARIS, WHEN THE TIDAL WAVE CAME...I WASN'T STRONG ENOUGH.
I KNOW YOU BLAME ME FOR THEIR DEATHS...FOR MOM...FOR BASTION AND NATE...
I TRIED O BRING EM BACK. *DEATH* AND R *DEMONS* D THIS TO Y FACE.
THEY *PUNISHED* ME, *BRANDING* MY FACE AS A CONSTANT REMINDER THAT I WOULD *NEVER* BE STRONG ENOUGH...
I'M SORRY, DAD. I WISH I COULD HAVE SAVED THEM. SO GO. SAVE YOURSELF, AND LET ME DIE.

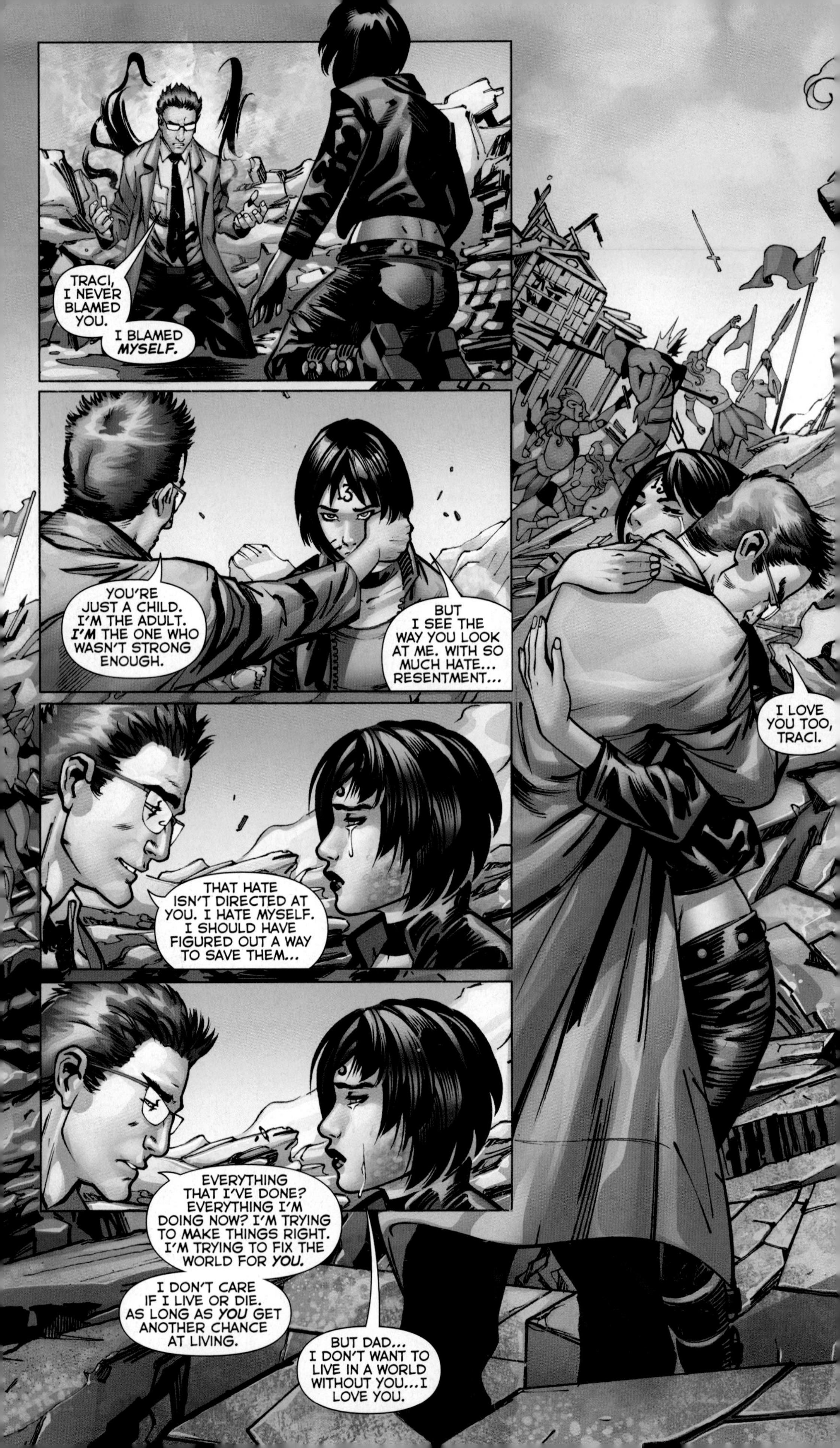
TRACI, I NEVER BLAMED YOU.
I BLAMED *MYSELF.*
YOU'RE JUST A CHILD. I'M THE ADULT. ***I'M*** THE ONE WHO WASN'T STRONG ENOUGH.
BUT I SEE THE WAY YOU LOOK AT ME. WITH SO MUCH HATE... RESENTMENT...
THAT HATE ISN'T DIRECTED AT YOU. I HATE MYSELF. I SHOULD HAVE FIGURED OUT A WAY TO SAVE THEM...
EVERYTHING THAT I'VE DONE? EVERYTHING I'M DOING NOW? I'M TRYING TO MAKE THINGS RIGHT. I'M TRYING TO FIX THE WORLD FOR *YOU.*
I DON'T CARE IF I LIVE OR DIE. AS LONG AS *YOU* GET ANOTHER CHANCE AT LIVING.
BUT DAD... I DON'T WANT TO LIVE IN A WORLD WITHOUT YOU...I LOVE YOU.
I LOVE YOU TOO, TRACI.

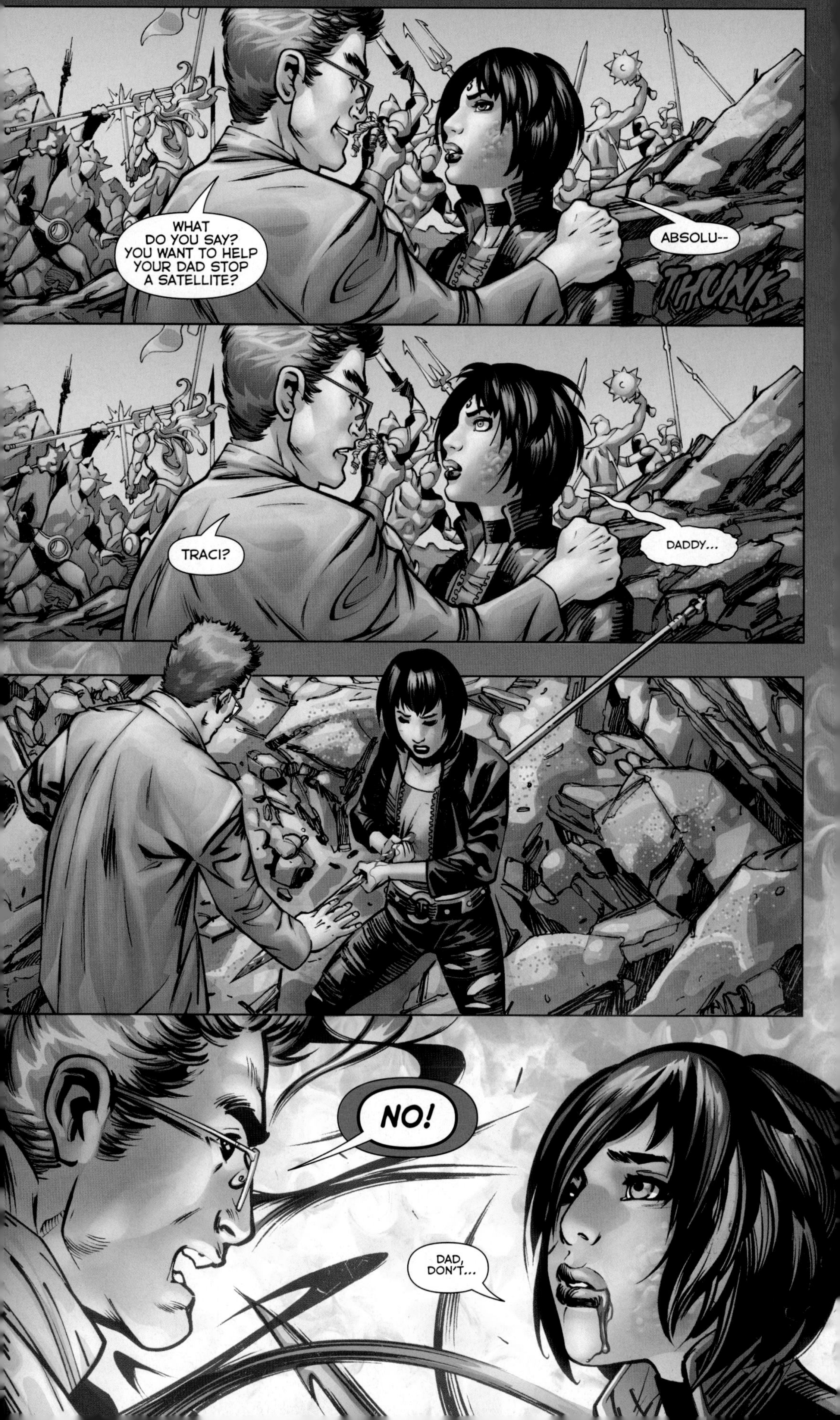
WHAT DO YOU SAY? YOU WANT TO HELP YOUR DAD STOP A SATELLITE?
ABSOLU--
THUNK
TRACI?
DADDY...
NO!
DAD, DON'T...

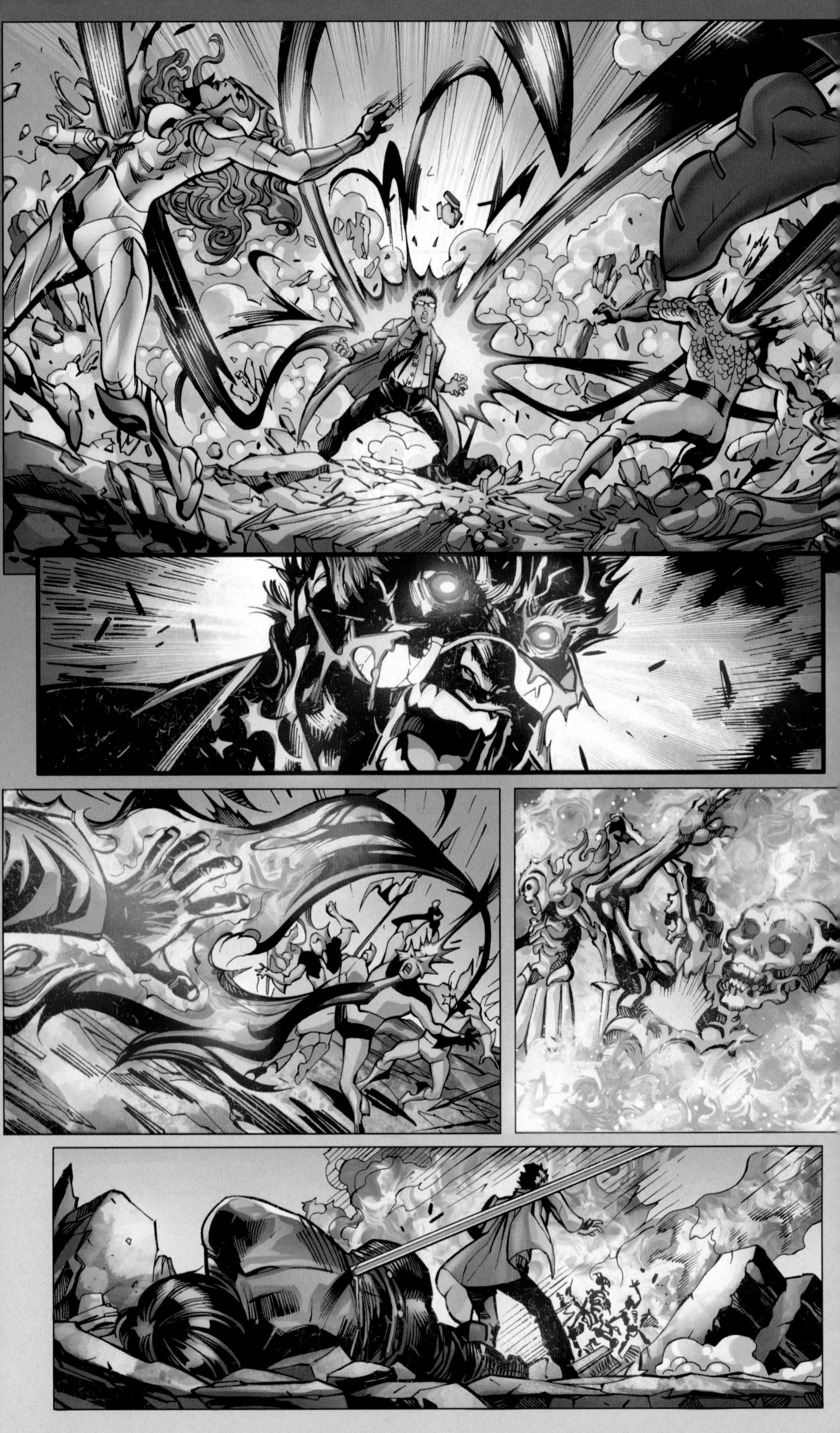

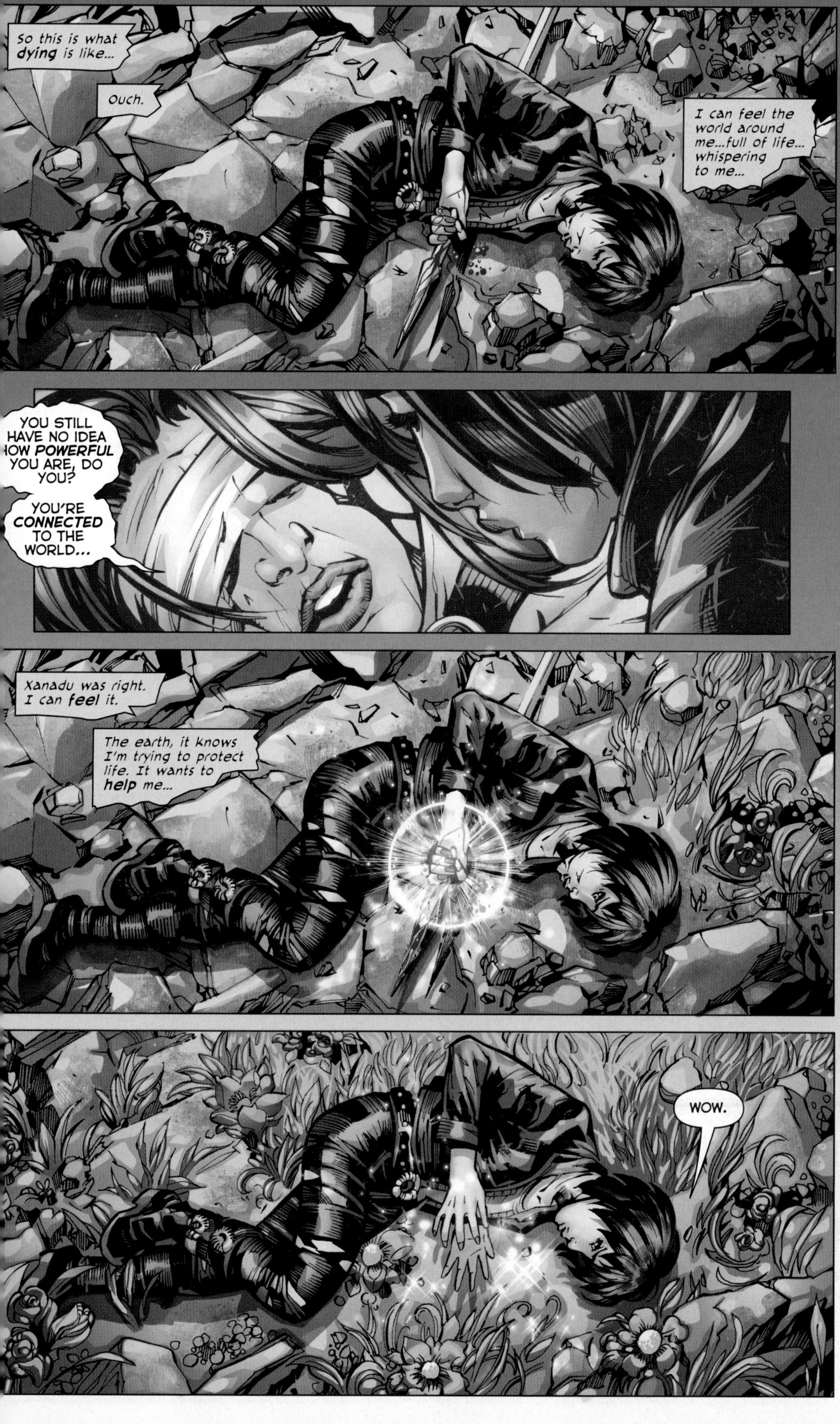

So this is what dying is like...
Ouch.
I can feel the world around me...full of life... whispering to me...
YOU STILL HAVE NO IDEA HOW POWERFUL YOU ARE, DO YOU?
YOU'RE CONNECTED TO THE WORLD...
Xanadu was right. I can feel it.
The earth, it knows I'm trying to protect life. It wants to help me...
WOW.

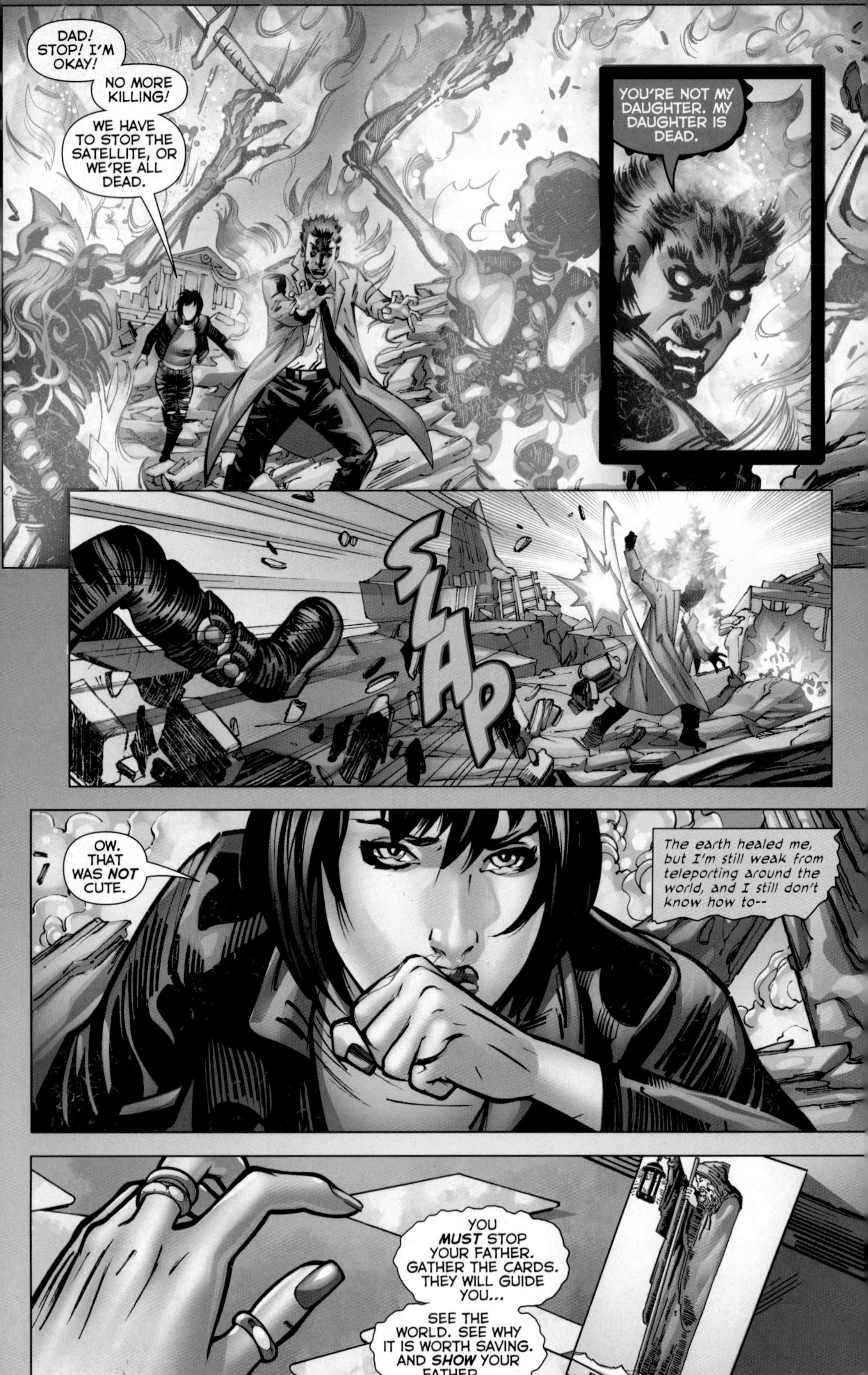
DAD! STOP! I'M OKAY!
NO MORE KILLING!
WE HAVE TO STOP THE SATELLITE, OR WE'RE ALL DEAD.
YOU'RE NOT MY DAUGHTER. MY DAUGHTER IS DEAD.
SLAP
OW. THAT WAS NOT CUTE.
The earth healed me, but I'm still weak from teleporting around the world, and I still don't know how to--
YOU MUST STOP YOUR FATHER. GATHER THE CARDS. THEY WILL GUIDE YOU...
SEE THE WORLD. SEE WHY IT IS WORTH SAVING. AND SHOW YOUR FATHER...

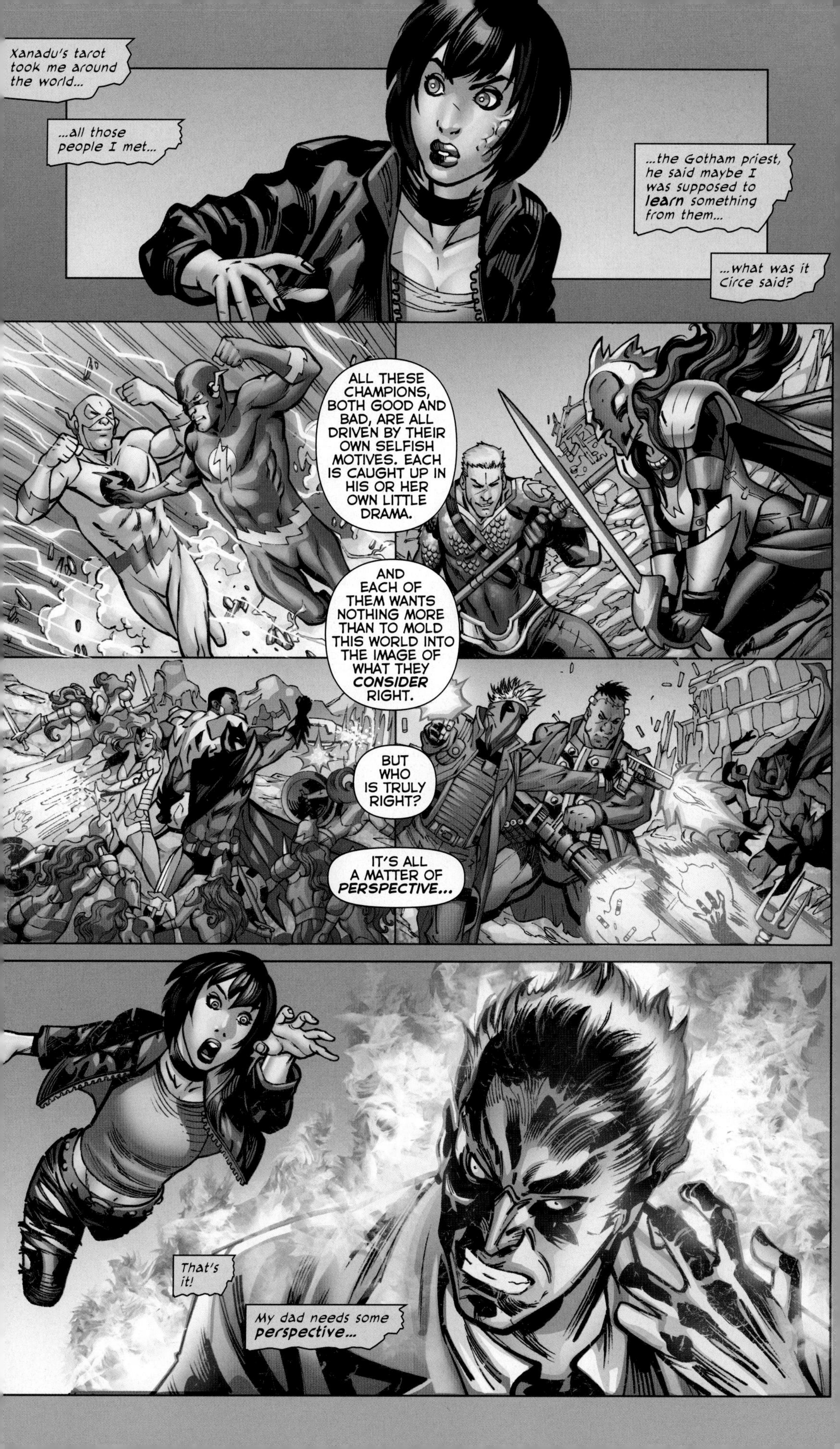
Xanadu's tarot took me around the world...
...all those people I met...
...the Gotham priest, he said maybe I was supposed to learn something from them...
...what was it Circe said?
ALL THESE CHAMPIONS, BOTH GOOD AND BAD, ARE ALL DRIVEN BY THEIR OWN SELFISH MOTIVES. EACH IS CAUGHT UP IN HIS OR HER OWN LITTLE DRAMA.
AND EACH OF THEM WANTS NOTHING MORE THAN TO MOLD THIS WORLD INTO THE IMAGE OF WHAT THEY CONSIDER RIGHT.
BUT WHO IS TRULY RIGHT?
IT'S ALL A MATTER OF PERSPECTIVE...
That's it!
My dad needs some perspective...

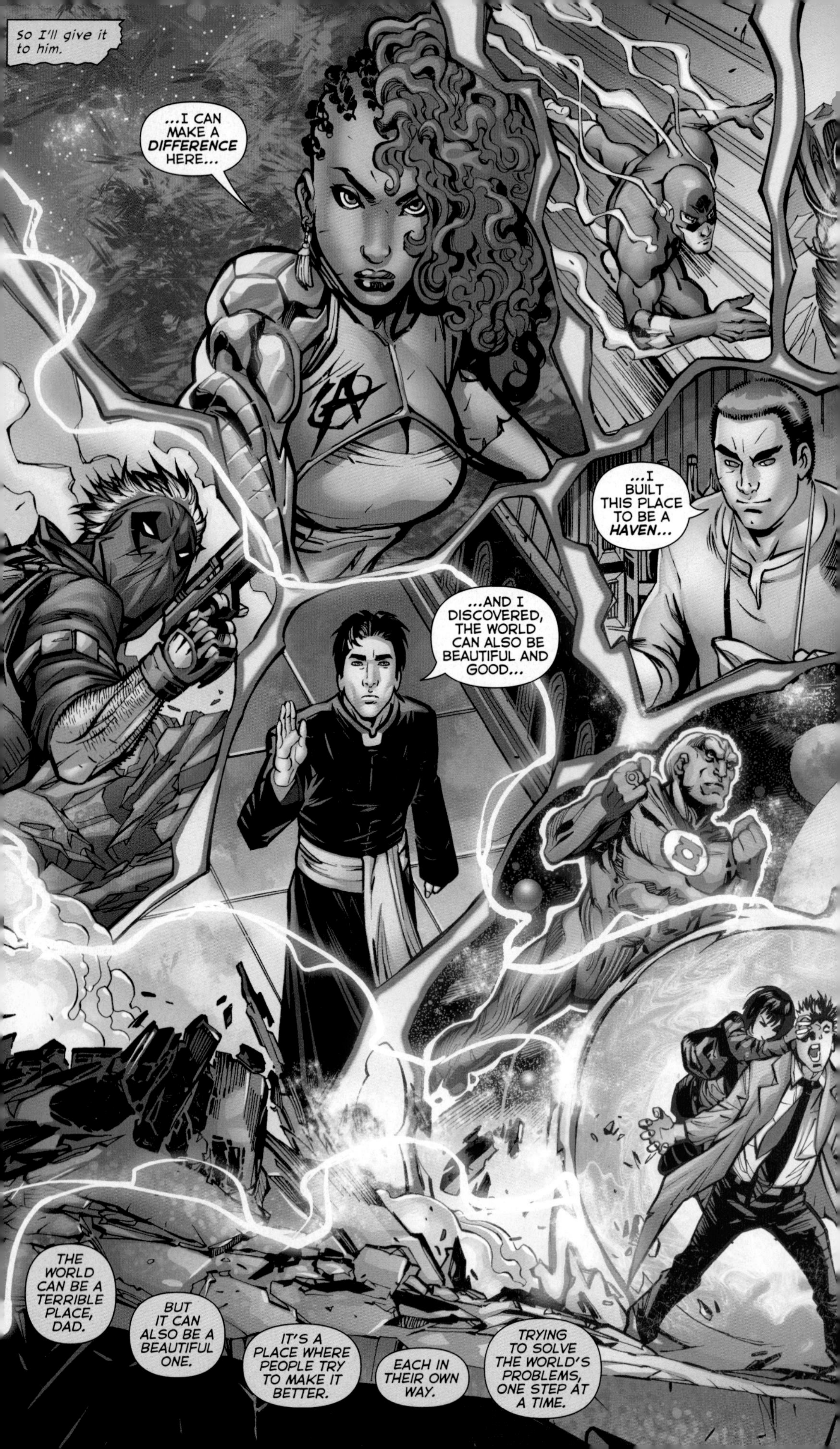
So I'll give it to him.
...I CAN MAKE A *DIFFERENCE* HERE...
...I BUILT THIS PLACE TO BE A *HAVEN*...
...AND I DISCOVERED, THE WORLD CAN ALSO BE BEAUTIFUL AND GOOD...
THE WORLD CAN BE A TERRIBLE PLACE, DAD.
BUT IT CAN ALSO BE A BEAUTIFUL ONE.
IT'S A PLACE WHERE PEOPLE TRY TO MAKE IT BETTER.
EACH IN THEIR OWN WAY.
TRYING TO SOLVE THE WORLD'S PROBLEMS, ONE STEP AT A TIME.

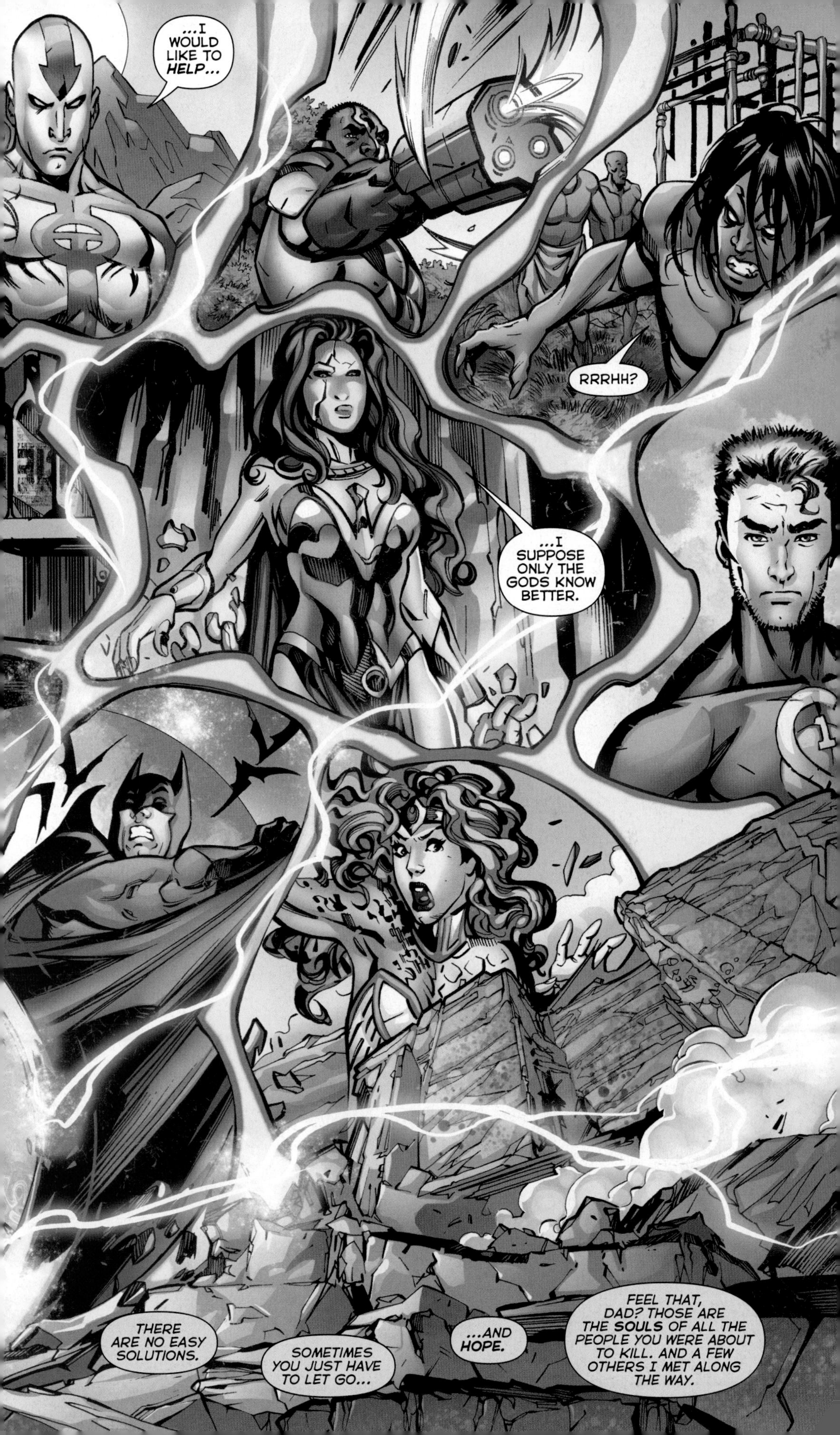
...I WOULD LIKE TO HELP...
RRRHH?
...I SUPPOSE ONLY THE GODS KNOW BETTER.
THERE ARE NO EASY SOLUTIONS.
SOMETIMES YOU JUST HAVE TO LET GO...
...AND HOPE.
FEEL THAT, DAD? THOSE ARE THE SOULS OF ALL THE PEOPLE YOU WERE ABOUT TO KILL. AND A FEW OTHERS I MET ALONG THE WAY.

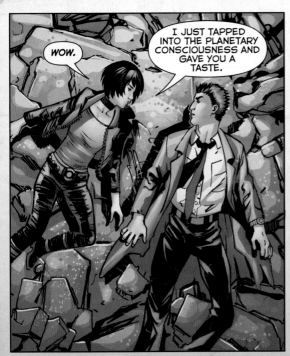

WOW.

I JUST TAPPED INTO THE PLANETARY CONSCIOUSNESS AND GAVE YOU A TASTE.

I HAD NO IDEA YOU WERE THAT POWERFUL.

NEITHER DID I.

THE SATELLITE!

WE HAVE TWO MINUTES.

WHAT? MY MAGIC--

I DON'T THINK I CAN--

YOU DON'T HAVE TO...

"...IT'S MY TURN TO TRY TO DO SOMETHING GOOD WITH ALL THIS DARKNESS IN ME..."

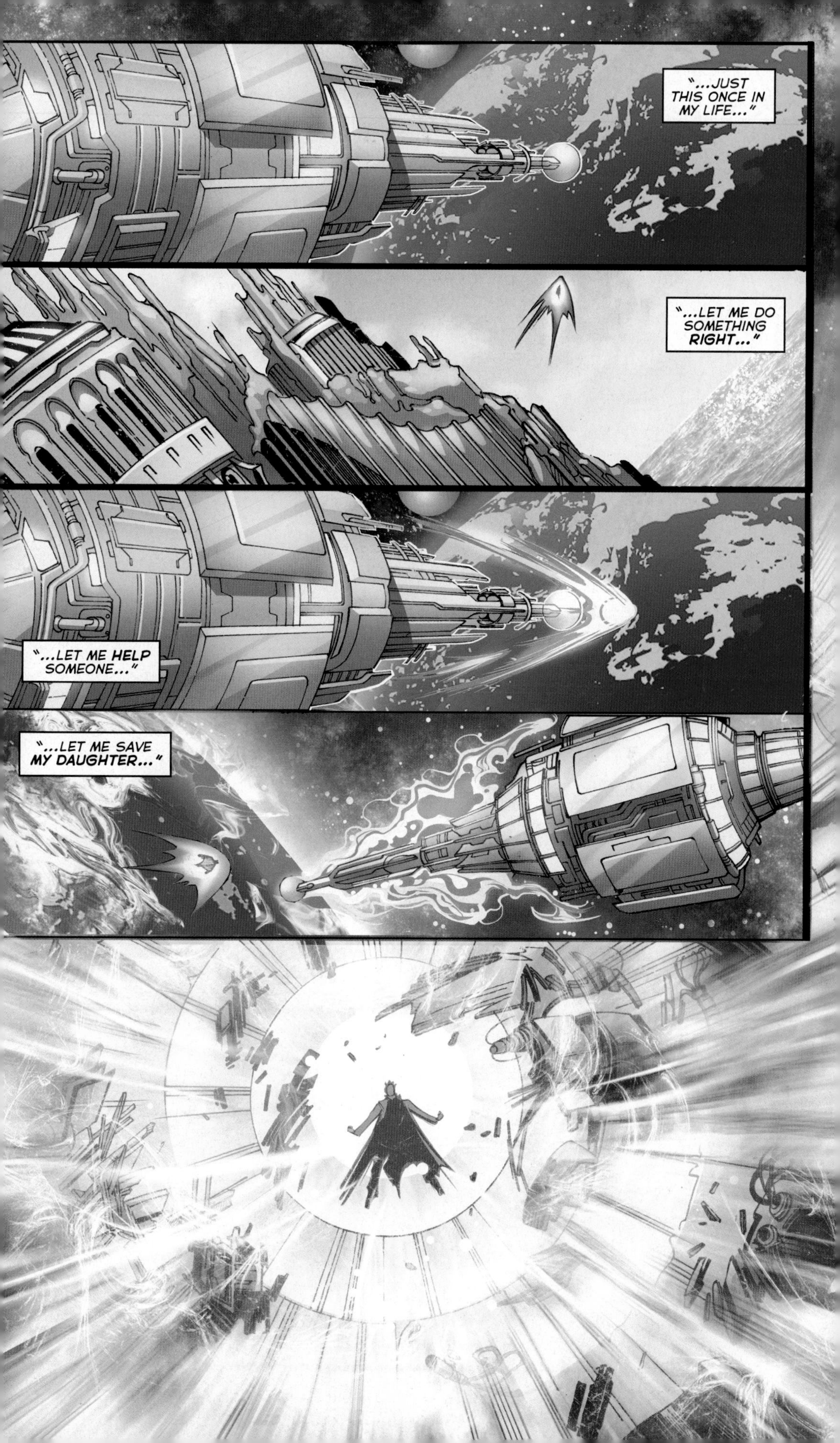
"...JUST THIS ONCE IN MY LIFE..."
"...LET ME DO SOMETHING RIGHT..."
"...LET ME HELP SOMEONE..."
"...LET ME SAVE MY DAUGHTER..."

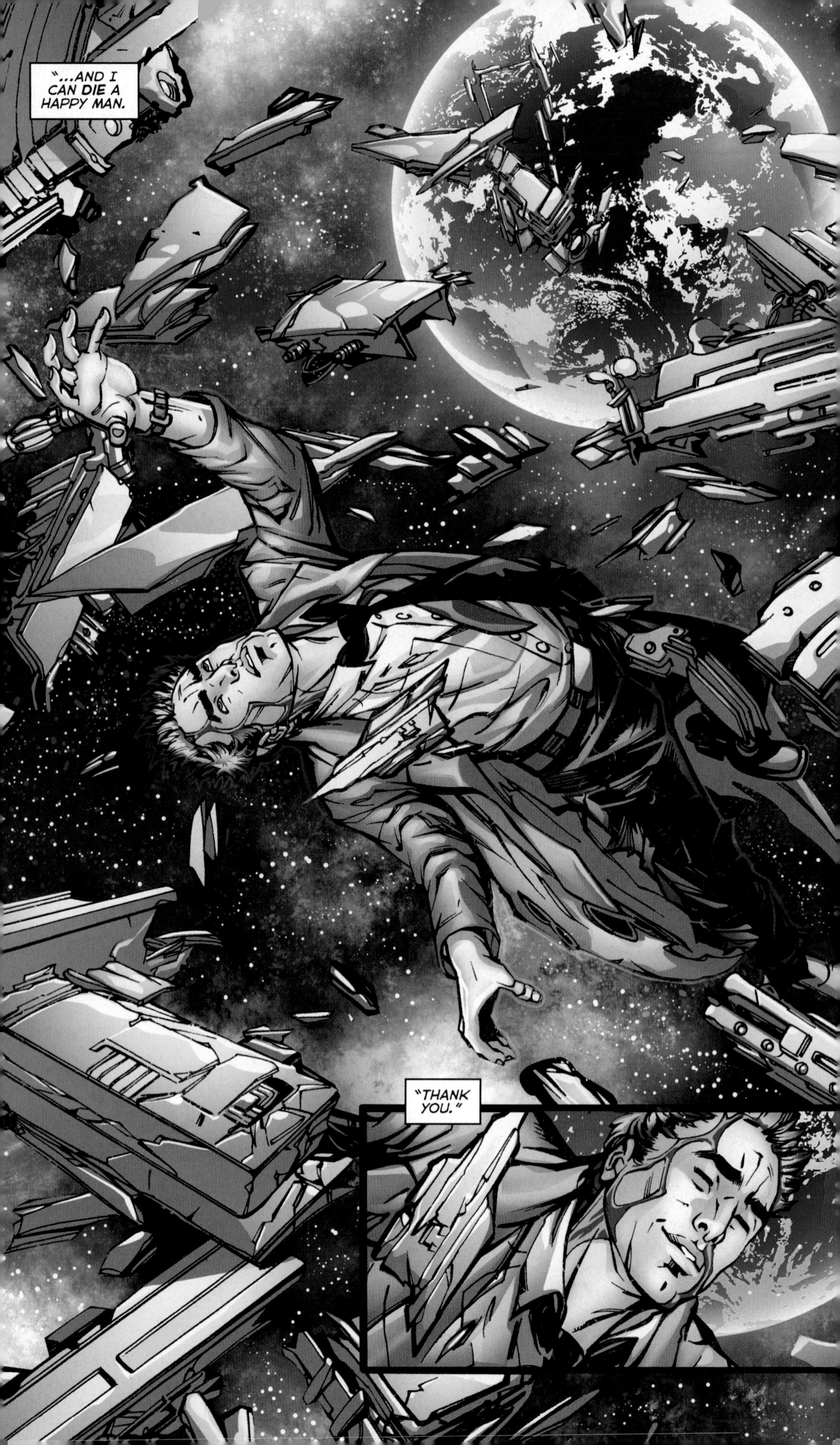
"...AND I CAN DIE A HAPPY MAN.
"THANK YOU."

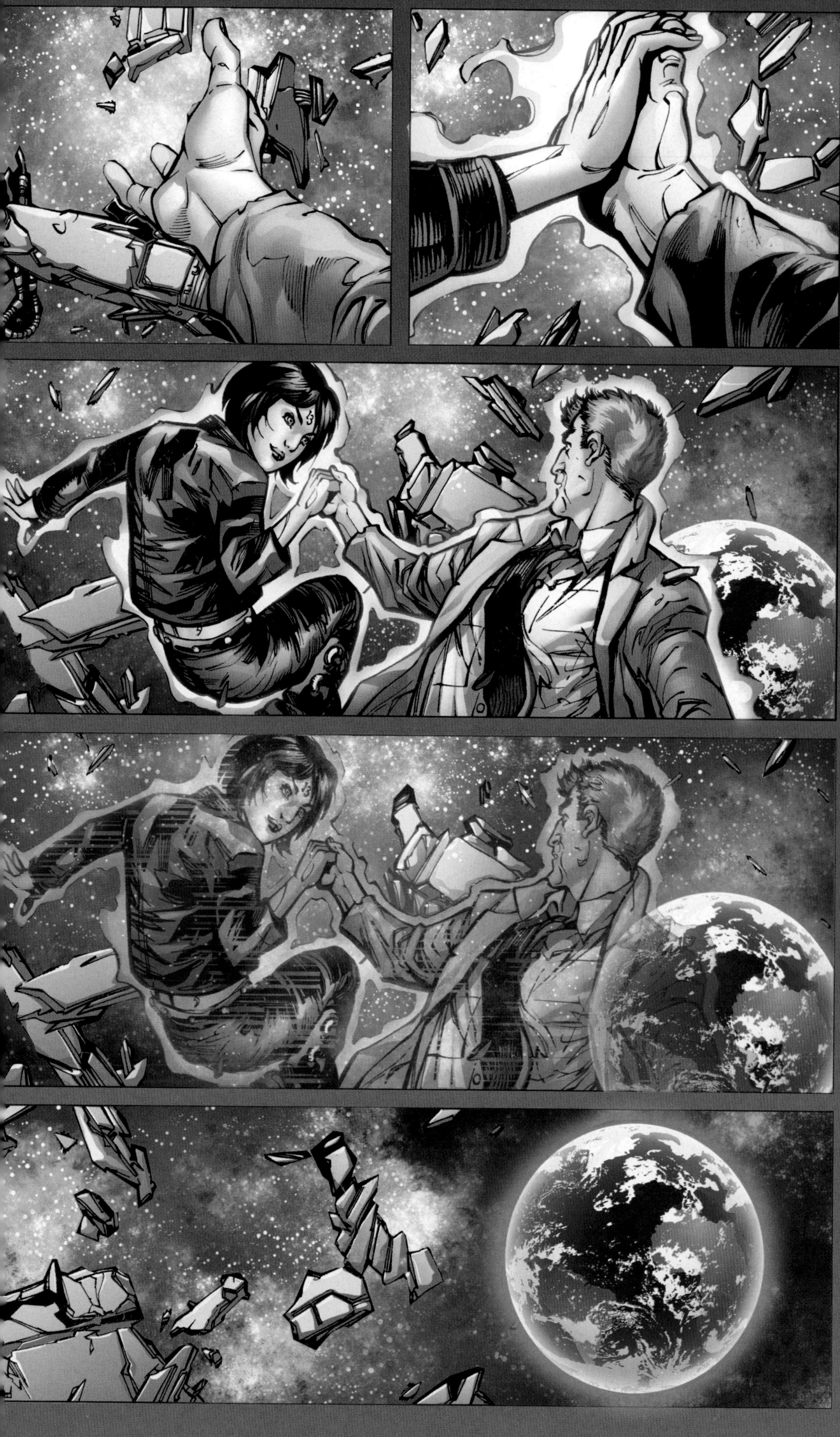

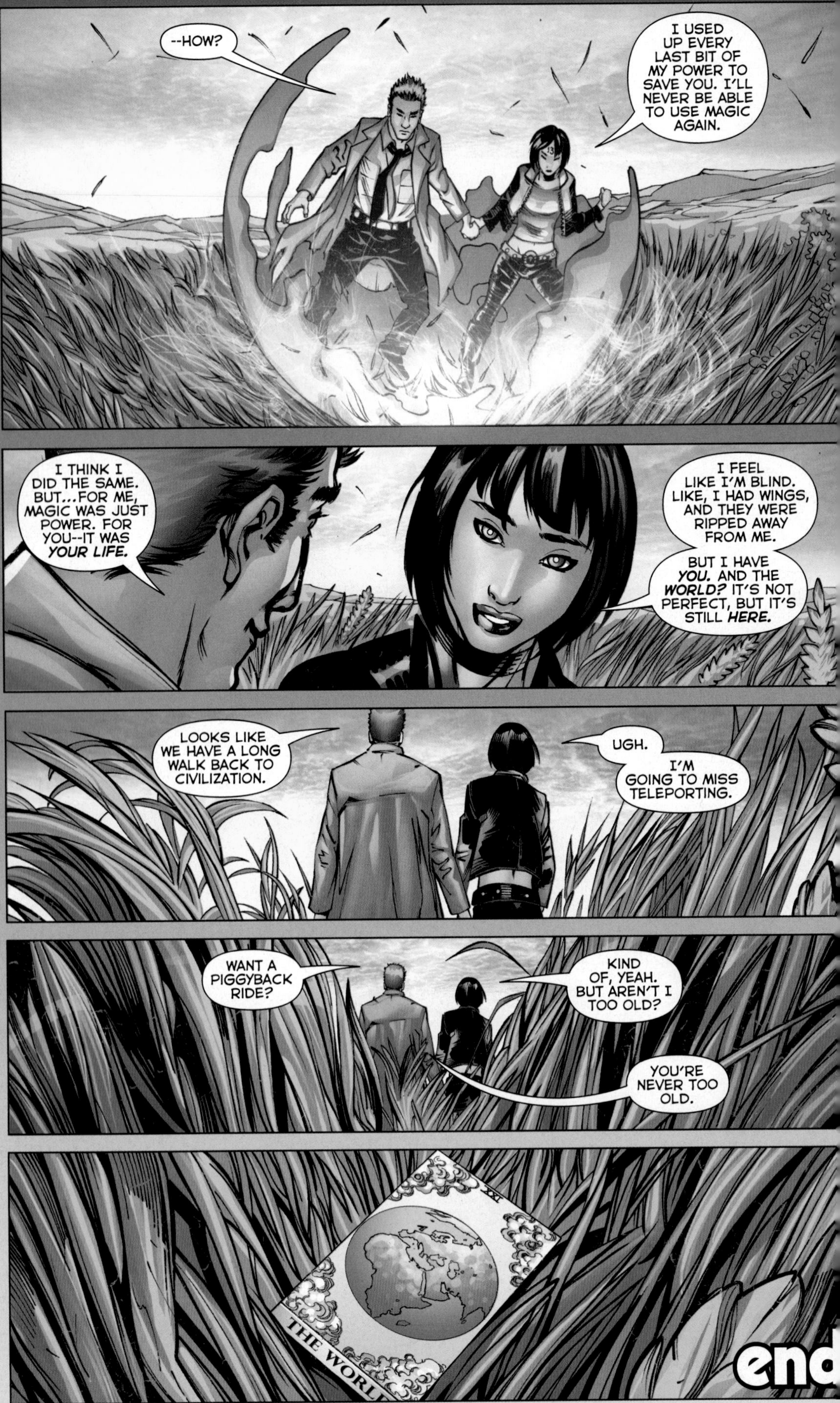
--HOW?
I USED UP EVERY LAST BIT OF MY POWER TO SAVE YOU. I'LL NEVER BE ABLE TO USE MAGIC AGAIN.
I THINK I DID THE SAME. BUT...FOR ME, MAGIC WAS JUST POWER. FOR YOU--IT WAS YOUR LIFE.
I FEEL LIKE I'M BLIND. LIKE, I HAD WINGS, AND THEY WERE RIPPED AWAY FROM ME.
BUT I HAVE YOU. AND THE WORLD? IT'S NOT PERFECT, BUT IT'S STILL HERE.
LOOKS LIKE WE HAVE A LONG WALK BACK TO CIVILIZATION.
UGH.
I'M GOING TO MISS TELEPORTING.
WANT A PIGGYBACK RIDE?
KIND OF, YEAH. BUT AREN'T I TOO OLD?
YOU'RE NEVER TOO OLD.
XXI
THE WORLD
end

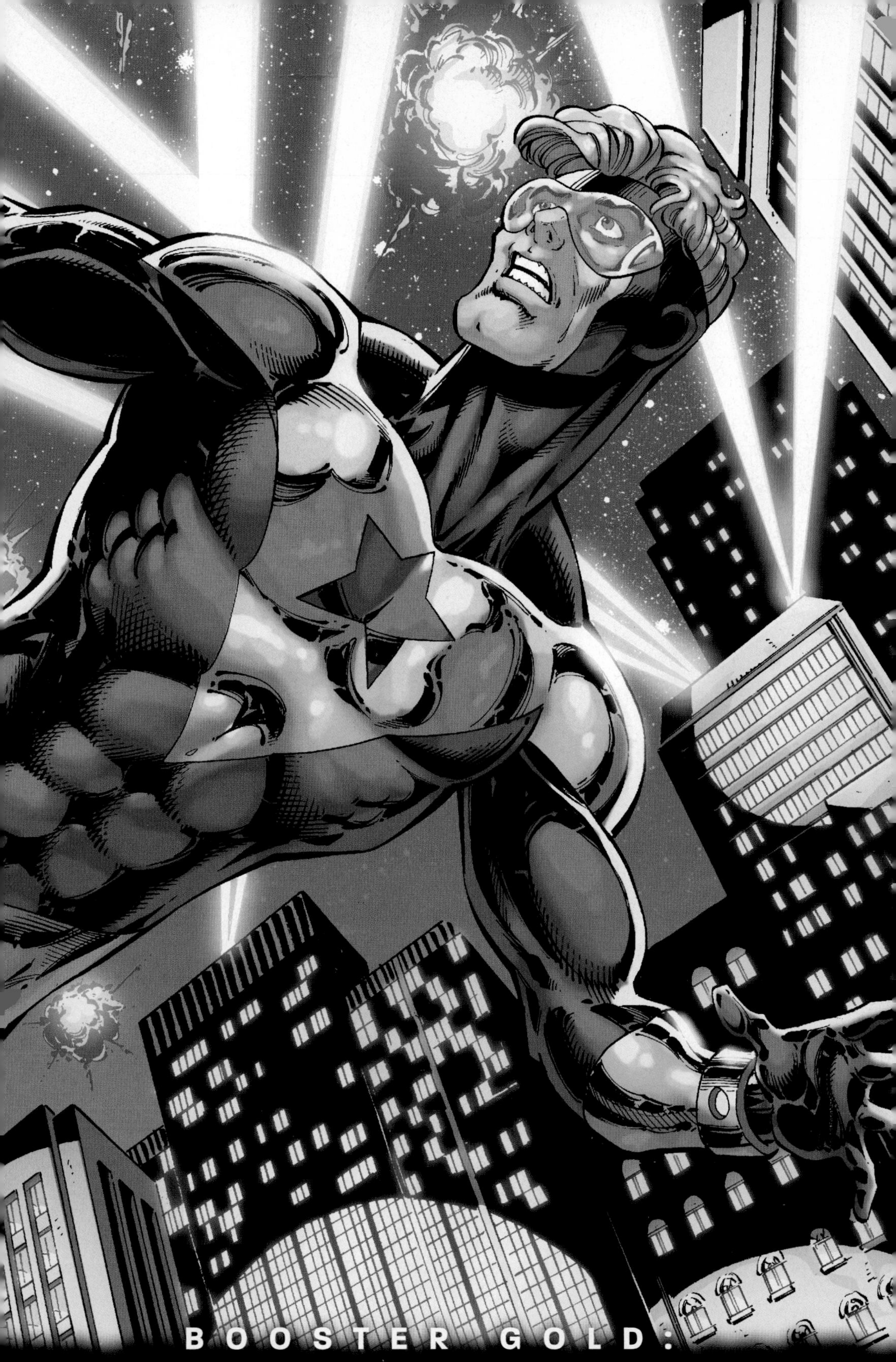

BOOSTER GOLD: TURBULENCE

DAN JURGENS
Writer

PART ONE
Art by **DAN JURGENS** Finishes by **NORM RAPMUND**

PART TWO
Art by **DAN JURGENS** Finishes by **NORM RAPMUND**

PART THREE
Pencils by **DAN JURGENS** and **IG GUARA** Inks by **NORM RAPMUND** and **RUY JOSÉ**

PART FOUR
Pencils by **RICK LEONARDI** and **DAN JURGENS** Inks by **DON HO** and **NORM RAPMUND**

Covers by **DAN JURGENS** and **NORM RAPMUND**

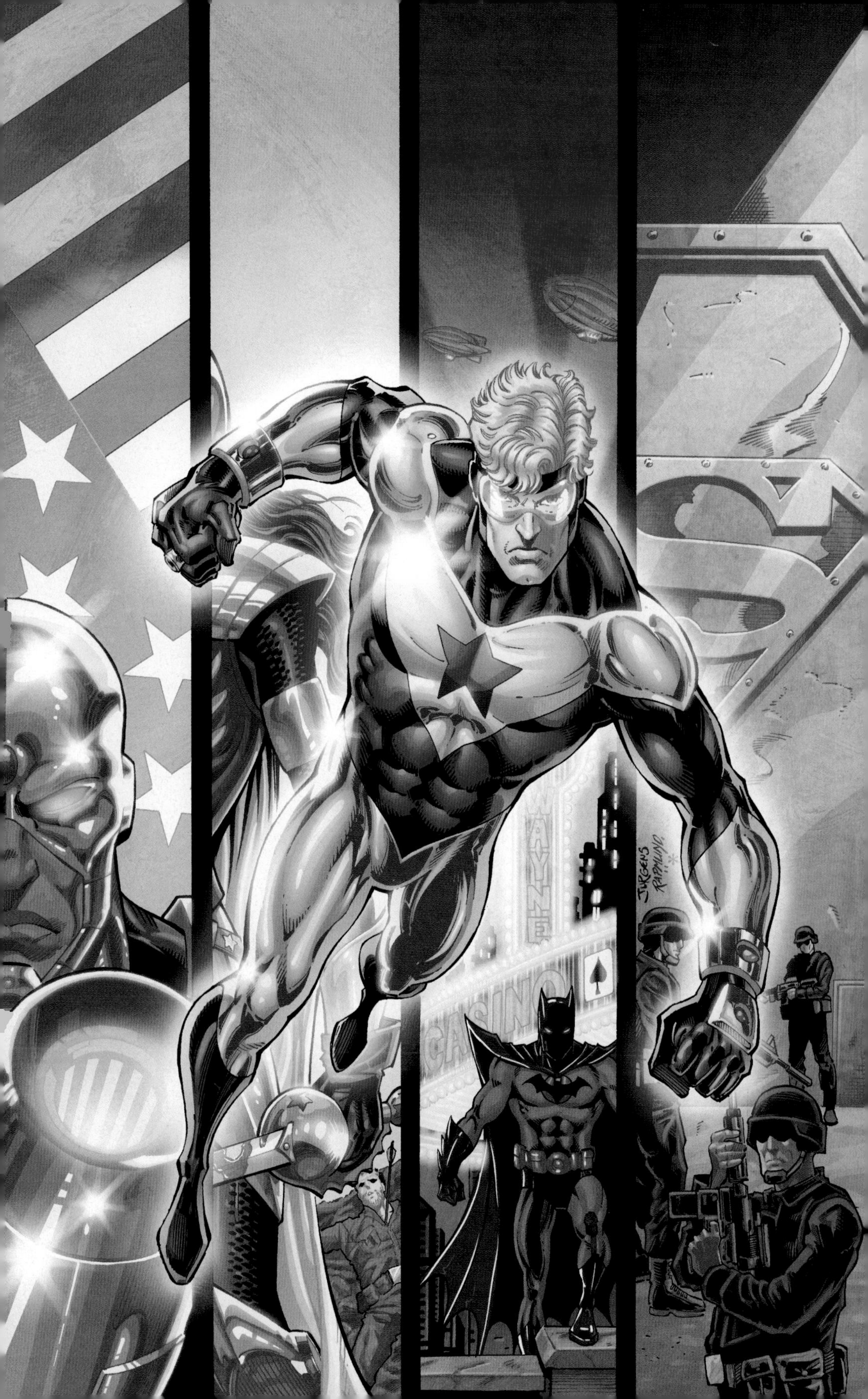
WAYNE
CASINO
JURGENS
RAPMUND

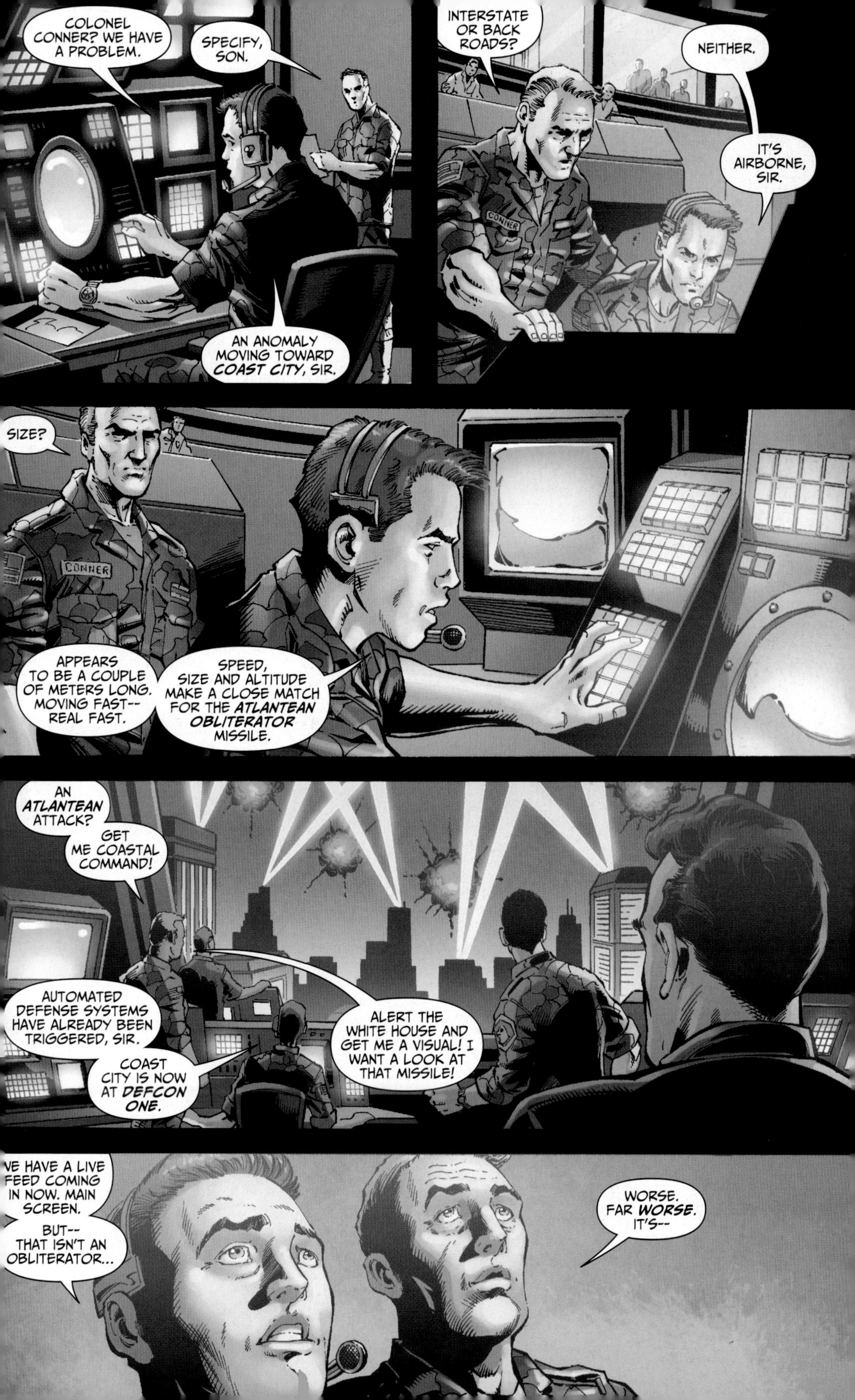
COLONEL CONNER? WE HAVE A PROBLEM.
SPECIFY, SON.
AN ANOMALY MOVING TOWARD COAST CITY, SIR.
INTERSTATE OR BACK ROADS?
NEITHER.
IT'S AIRBORNE, SIR.
SIZE?
APPEARS TO BE A COUPLE OF METERS LONG. MOVING FAST-- REAL FAST.
SPEED, SIZE AND ALTITUDE MAKE A CLOSE MATCH FOR THE ATLANTEAN OBLITERATOR MISSILE.
AN ATLANTEAN ATTACK? GET ME COASTAL COMMAND!
AUTOMATED DEFENSE SYSTEMS HAVE ALREADY BEEN TRIGGERED, SIR.
COAST CITY IS NOW AT DEFCON ONE.
ALERT THE WHITE HOUSE AND GET ME A VISUAL! I WANT A LOOK AT THAT MISSILE!
VE HAVE A LIVE FEED COMING IN NOW. MAIN SCREEN.
BUT-- THAT ISN'T AN OBLITERATOR...
WORSE. FAR WORSE. IT'S--

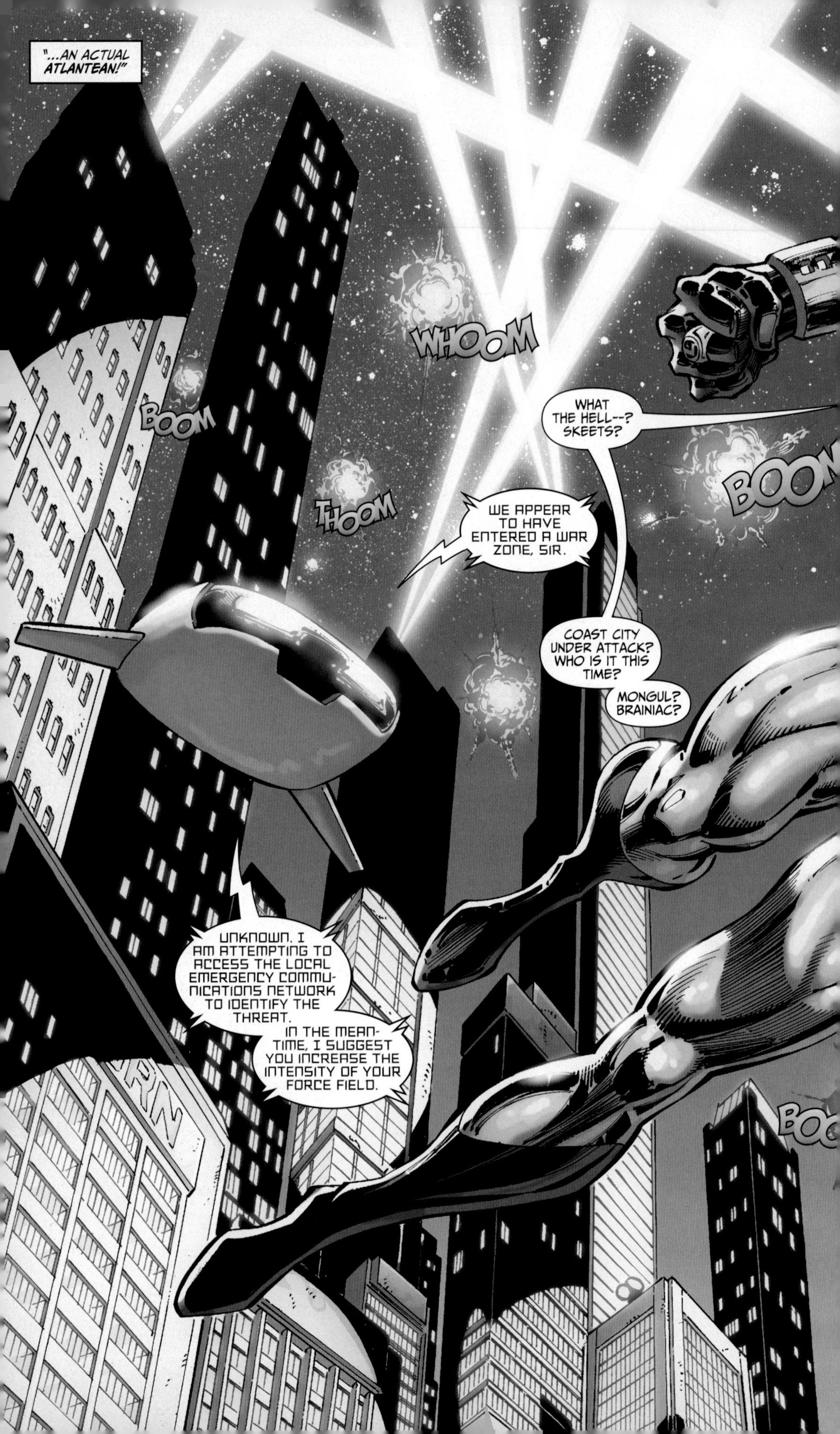

"...AN ACTUAL ATLANTEAN!"
WHOOM
BOOM
WHAT THE HELL--? SKEETS?
BOOM
THOOM
WE APPEAR TO HAVE ENTERED A WAR ZONE, SIR.
COAST CITY UNDER ATTACK? WHO IS IT THIS TIME?
MONGUL? BRAINIAC?
UNKNOWN. I AM ATTEMPTING TO ACCESS THE LOCAL EMERGENCY COMMUNICATIONS NETWORK TO IDENTIFY THE THREAT.
IN THE MEANTIME, I SUGGEST YOU INCREASE THE INTENSITY OF YOUR FORCE FIELD.

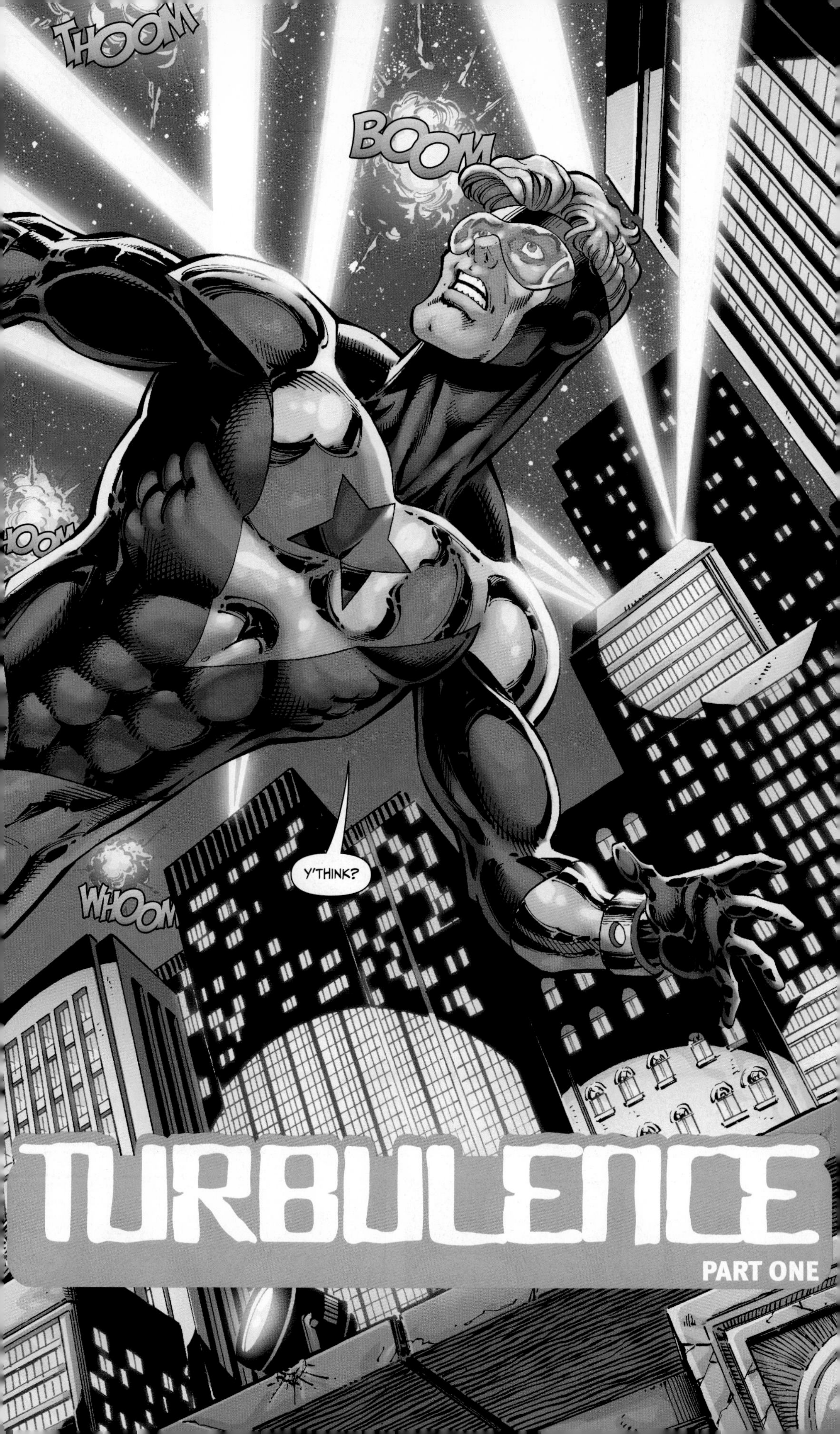
THOOM
BOOM
WHOOM
Y'THINK?
WHOOM
TURBULENCE
PART ONE

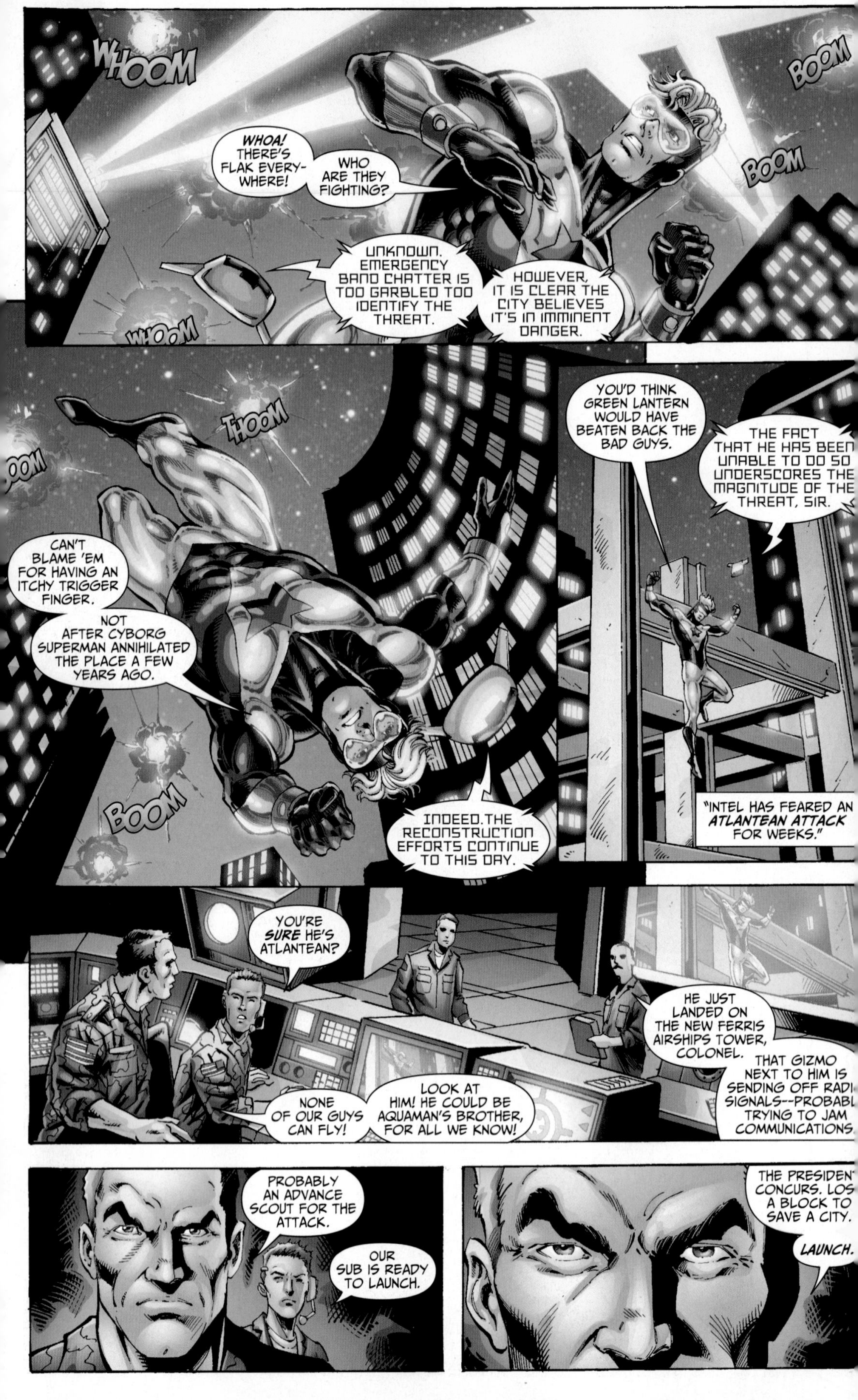

WHOOM
BOOM
WHOA! THERE'S FLAK EVERY-WHERE!
WHO ARE THEY FIGHTING?
BOOM
UNKNOWN. EMERGENCY BAND CHATTER IS TOO GARBLED TOO IDENTIFY THE THREAT.
HOWEVER, IT IS CLEAR THE CITY BELIEVES IT'S IN IMMINENT DANGER.
WHOOM
THOOM
CAN'T BLAME 'EM FOR HAVING AN ITCHY TRIGGER FINGER.
NOT AFTER CYBORG SUPERMAN ANNIHILATED THE PLACE A FEW YEARS AGO.
BOOM
INDEED. THE RECONSTRUCTION EFFORTS CONTINUE TO THIS DAY.
YOU'D THINK GREEN LANTERN WOULD HAVE BEATEN BACK THE BAD GUYS.
THE FACT THAT HE HAS BEEN UNABLE TO DO SO UNDERSCORES THE MAGNITUDE OF THE THREAT, SIR.
"INTEL HAS FEARED AN ATLANTEAN ATTACK FOR WEEKS."
YOU'RE SURE HE'S ATLANTEAN?
HE JUST LANDED ON THE NEW FERRIS AIRSHIPS TOWER, COLONEL.
THAT GIZMO NEXT TO HIM IS SENDING OFF RADI SIGNALS--PROBABL TRYING TO JAM COMMUNICATIONS.
NONE OF OUR GUYS CAN FLY!
LOOK AT HIM! HE COULD BE AQUAMAN'S BROTHER, FOR ALL WE KNOW!
PROBABLY AN ADVANCE SCOUT FOR THE ATTACK.
OUR SUB IS READY TO LAUNCH.
THE PRESIDEN CONCURS. LOS A BLOCK TO SAVE A CITY.
LAUNCH.

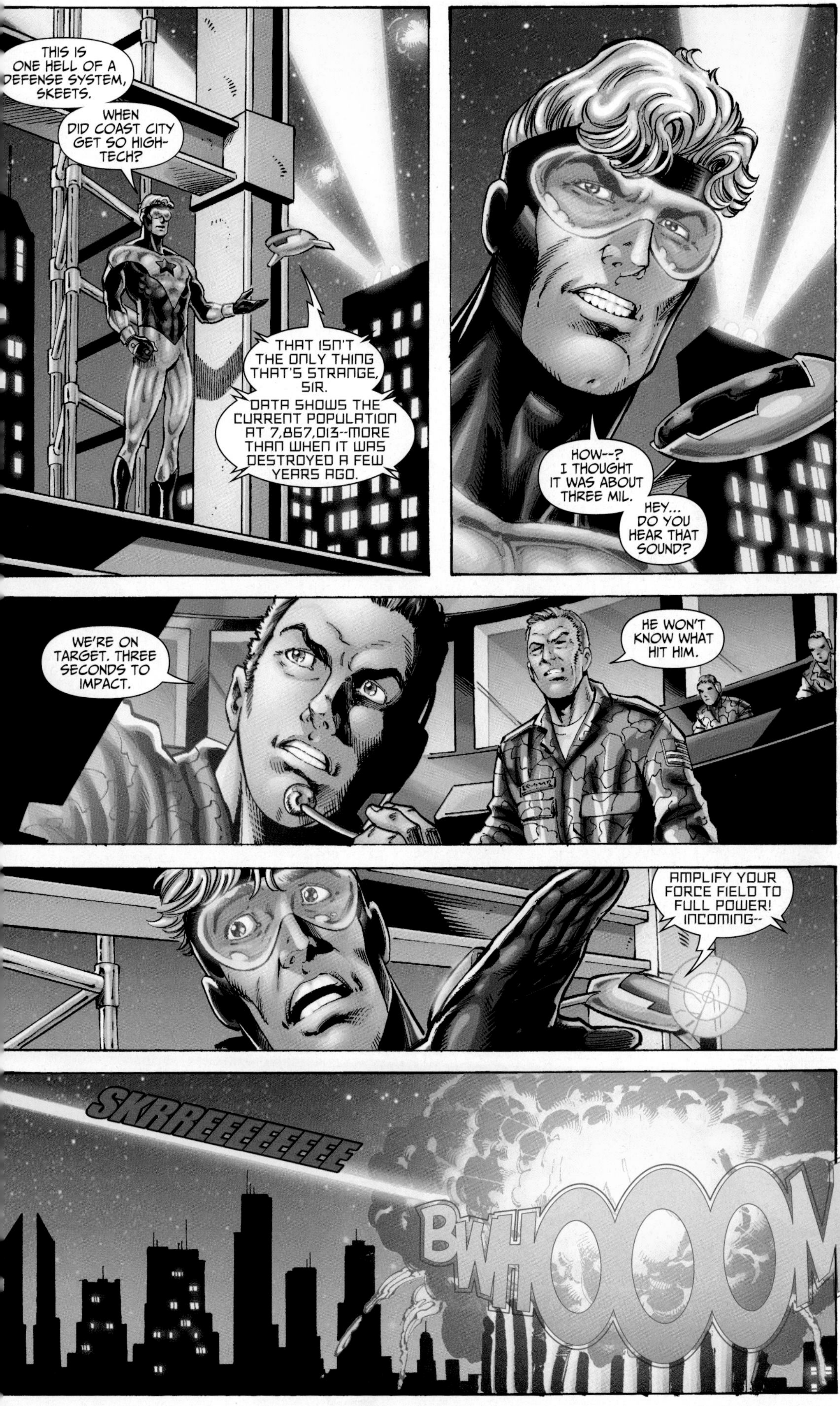
THIS IS ONE HELL OF A DEFENSE SYSTEM, SKEETS.
WHEN DID COAST CITY GET SO HIGH-TECH?
THAT ISN'T THE ONLY THING THAT'S STRANGE, SIR.
DATA SHOWS THE CURRENT POPULATION AT 7,867,013--MORE THAN WHEN IT WAS DESTROYED A FEW YEARS AGO.
HOW--? I THOUGHT IT WAS ABOUT THREE MIL.
HEY... DO YOU HEAR THAT SOUND?
WE'RE ON TARGET. THREE SECONDS TO IMPACT.
HE WON'T KNOW WHAT HIT HIM.
AMPLIFY YOUR FORCE FIELD TO FULL POWER! INCOMING--
SKRREEEEEEEEE
BWHOOOM

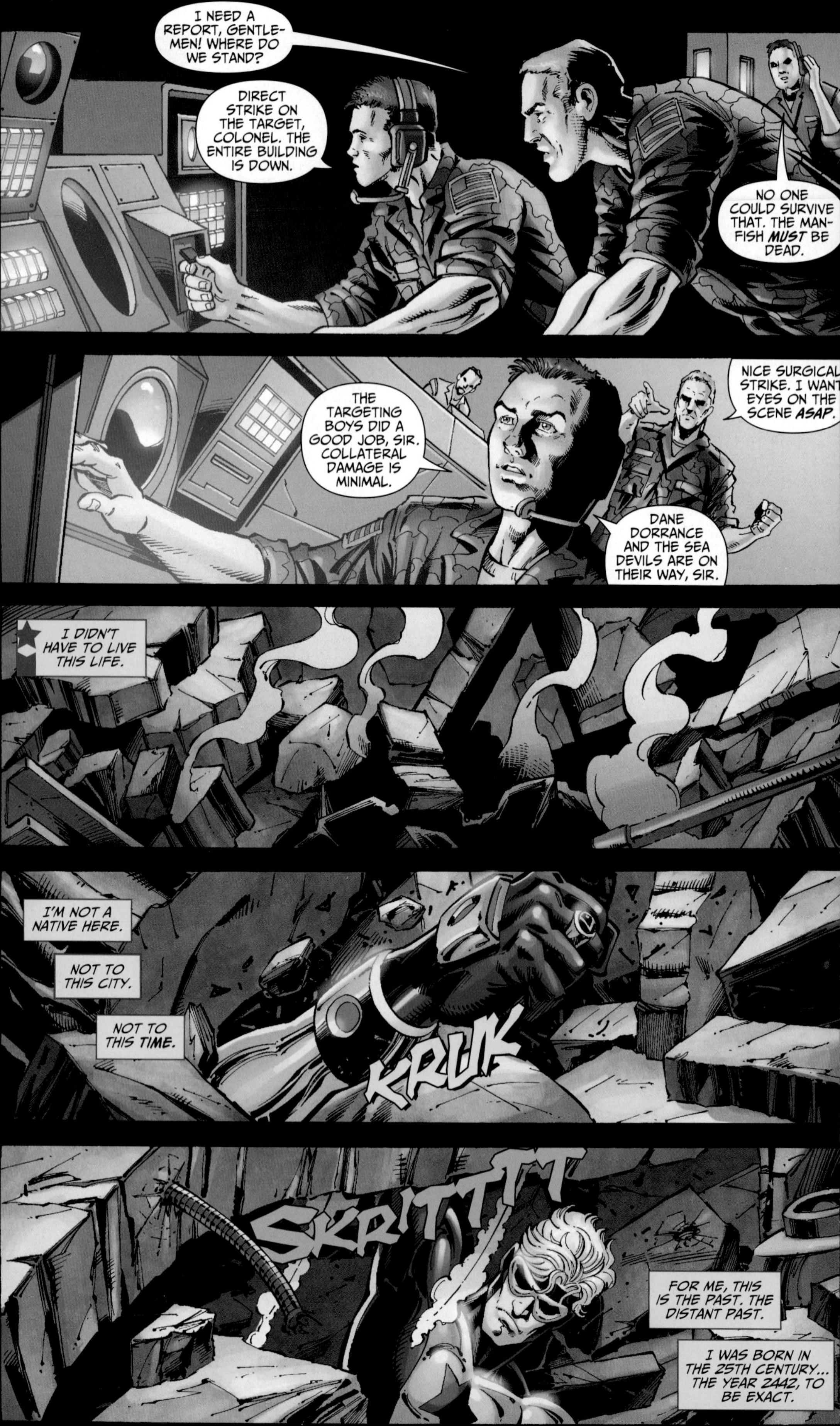

I NEED A REPORT, GENTLE-MEN! WHERE DO WE STAND?
DIRECT STRIKE ON THE TARGET, COLONEL. THE ENTIRE BUILDING IS DOWN.
NO ONE COULD SURVIVE THAT. THE MAN-FISH *MUST* BE DEAD.
THE TARGETING BOYS DID A GOOD JOB, SIR. COLLATERAL DAMAGE IS MINIMAL.
NICE SURGICAL STRIKE. I WANT EYES ON THE SCENE *ASAP*.
DANE DORRANCE AND THE SEA DEVILS ARE ON THEIR WAY, SIR.
I DIDN'T HAVE TO LIVE THIS LIFE.
I'M NOT A NATIVE HERE.
NOT TO THIS CITY.
NOT TO THIS TIME.
KRUK
SKRITTTTT
FOR ME, THIS IS THE PAST. THE DISTANT PAST.
I WAS BORN IN THE 25TH CENTURY... THE YEAR 2442, TO BE EXACT.

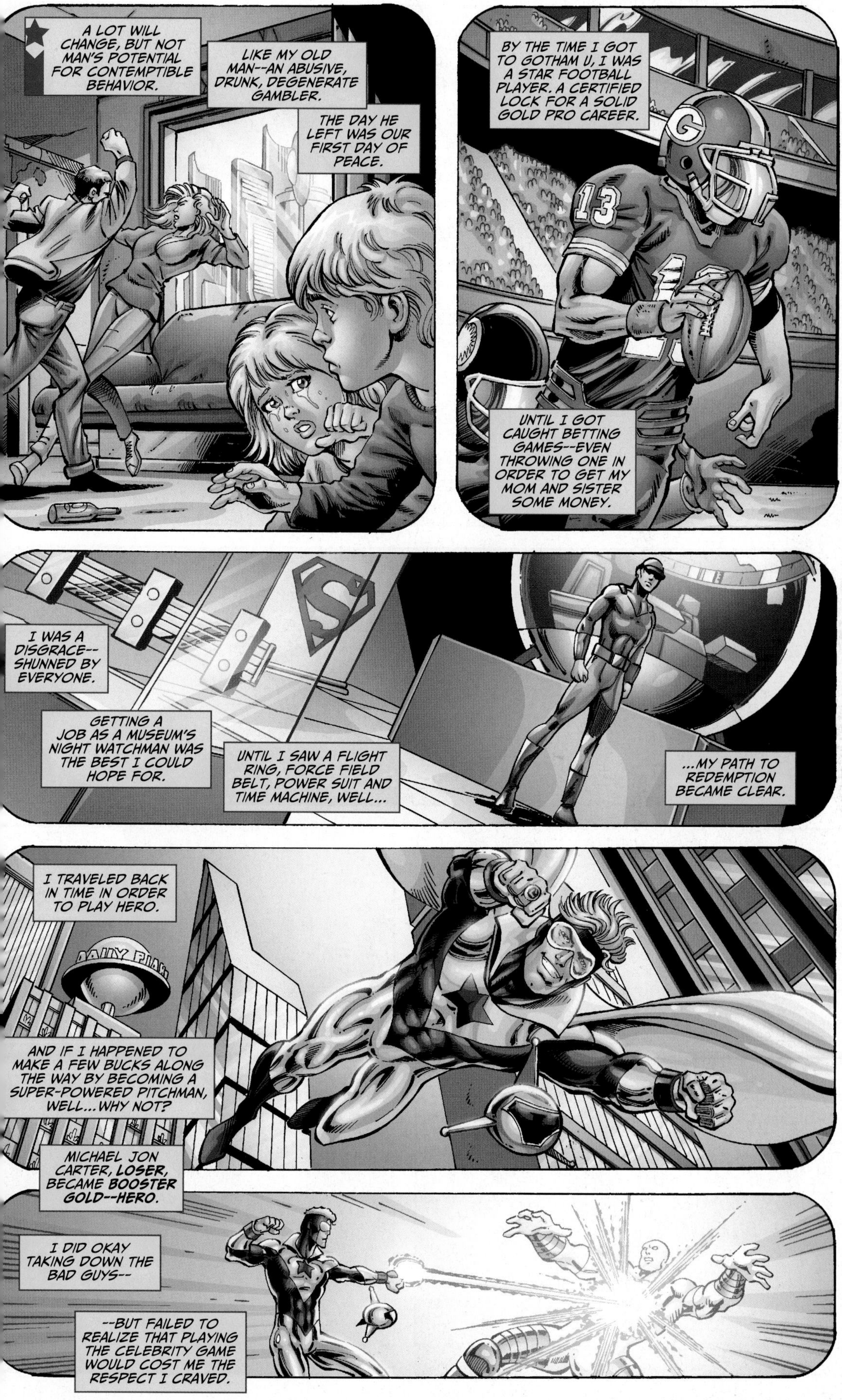
A LOT WILL CHANGE, BUT NOT MAN'S POTENTIAL FOR CONTEMPTIBLE BEHAVIOR.
LIKE MY OLD MAN--AN ABUSIVE, DRUNK, DEGENERATE GAMBLER.
THE DAY HE LEFT WAS OUR FIRST DAY OF PEACE.
BY THE TIME I GOT TO GOTHAM U, I WAS A STAR FOOTBALL PLAYER. A CERTIFIED LOCK FOR A SOLID GOLD PRO CAREER.
UNTIL I GOT CAUGHT BETTING GAMES--EVEN THROWING ONE IN ORDER TO GET MY MOM AND SISTER SOME MONEY.
I WAS A DISGRACE-- SHUNNED BY EVERYONE.
GETTING A JOB AS A MUSEUM'S NIGHT WATCHMAN WAS THE BEST I COULD HOPE FOR.
UNTIL I SAW A FLIGHT RING, FORCE FIELD BELT, POWER SUIT AND TIME MACHINE, WELL...
...MY PATH TO REDEMPTION BECAME CLEAR.
I TRAVELED BACK IN TIME IN ORDER TO PLAY HERO.
AND IF I HAPPENED TO MAKE A FEW BUCKS ALONG THE WAY BY BECOMING A SUPER-POWERED PITCHMAN, WELL...WHY NOT?
MICHAEL JON CARTER, **LOSER**, BECAME **BOOSTER GOLD--HERO**.
I DID OKAY TAKING DOWN THE BAD GUYS--
--BUT FAILED TO REALIZE THAT PLAYING THE CELEBRITY GAME WOULD COST ME THE RESPECT I CRAVED.

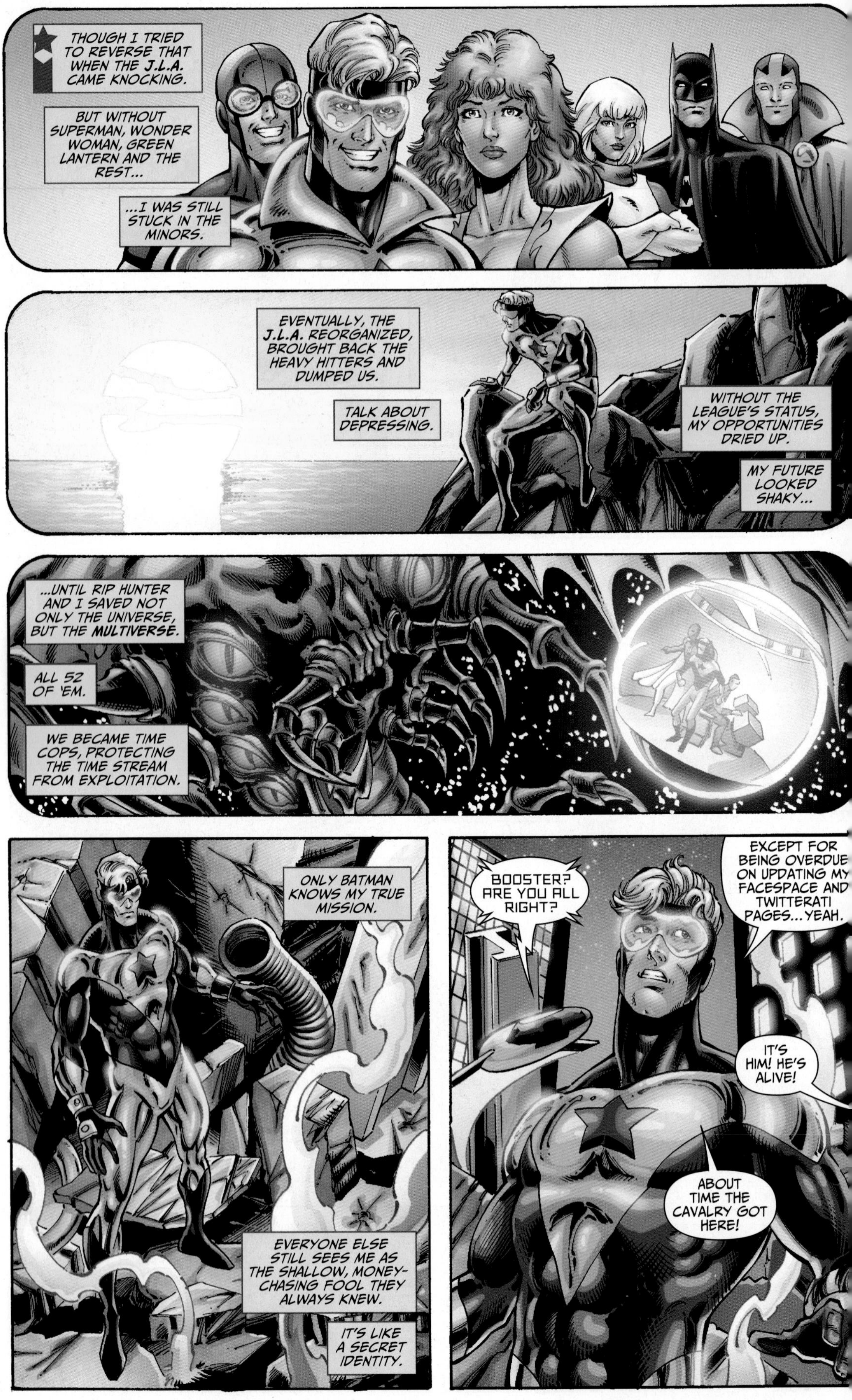
THOUGH I TRIED TO REVERSE THAT WHEN THE J.L.A. CAME KNOCKING.
BUT WITHOUT SUPERMAN, WONDER WOMAN, GREEN LANTERN AND THE REST...
...I WAS STILL STUCK IN THE MINORS.
EVENTUALLY, THE J.L.A. REORGANIZED, BROUGHT BACK THE HEAVY HITTERS AND DUMPED US.
TALK ABOUT DEPRESSING.
WITHOUT THE LEAGUE'S STATUS, MY OPPORTUNITIES DRIED UP.
MY FUTURE LOOKED SHAKY...
...UNTIL RIP HUNTER AND I SAVED NOT ONLY THE UNIVERSE, BUT THE MULTIVERSE.
ALL 52 OF 'EM.
WE BECAME TIME COPS, PROTECTING THE TIME STREAM FROM EXPLOITATION.
ONLY BATMAN KNOWS MY TRUE MISSION.
EVERYONE ELSE STILL SEES ME AS THE SHALLOW, MONEY-CHASING FOOL THEY ALWAYS KNEW.
IT'S LIKE A SECRET IDENTITY.
BOOSTER? ARE YOU ALL RIGHT?
EXCEPT FOR BEING OVERDUE ON UPDATING MY FACESPACE AND TWITTERATI PAGES...YEAH.
IT'S HIM! HE'S ALIVE!
ABOUT TIME THE CAVALRY GOT HERE!

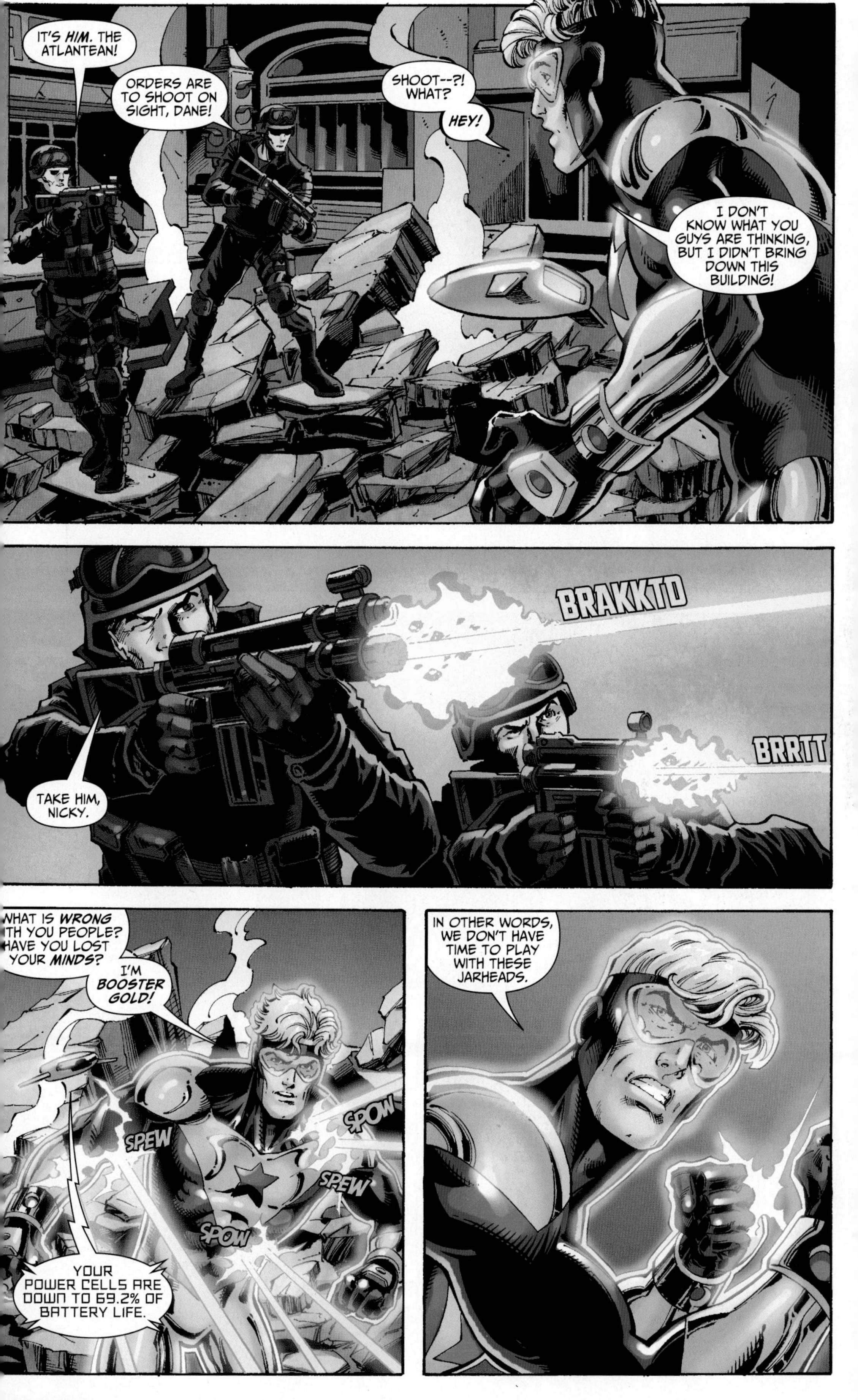
IT'S HIM. THE ATLANTEAN!
ORDERS ARE TO SHOOT ON SIGHT, DANE!
SHOOT--?! WHAT?
HEY!
I DON'T KNOW WHAT YOU GUYS ARE THINKING, BUT I DIDN'T BRING DOWN THIS BUILDING!
BRAKKTD
BRRTT
TAKE HIM, NICKY.
WHAT IS WRONG ITH YOU PEOPLE? HAVE YOU LOST YOUR MINDS?
I'M BOOSTER GOLD!
SPOW
SPEW
SPEW
SPOW
YOUR POWER CELLS ARE DOWN TO 69.2% OF BATTERY LIFE.
IN OTHER WORDS, WE DON'T HAVE TIME TO PLAY WITH THESE JARHEADS.

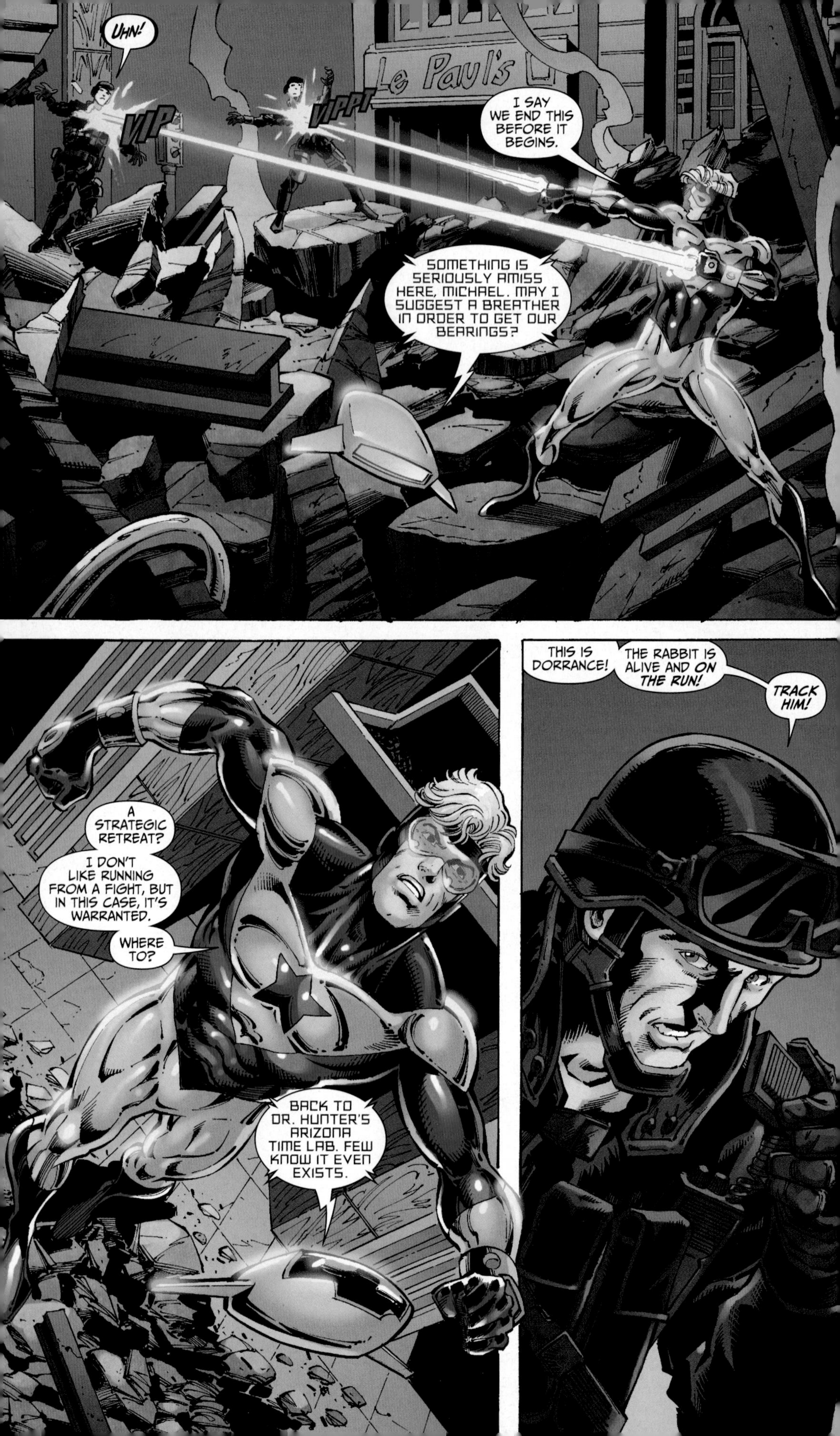
UHN!
VIP
VIPPT
Le Paul's
I SAY WE END THIS BEFORE IT BEGINS.
SOMETHING IS SERIOUSLY AMISS HERE, MICHAEL. MAY I SUGGEST A BREATHER IN ORDER TO GET OUR BEARINGS?
A STRATEGIC RETREAT?
I DON'T LIKE RUNNING FROM A FIGHT, BUT IN THIS CASE, IT'S WARRANTED.
WHERE TO?
BACK TO DR. HUNTER'S ARIZONA TIME LAB. FEW KNOW IT EVEN EXISTS.
THIS IS DORRANCE!
THE RABBIT IS ALIVE AND *ON THE RUN!*
TRACK HIM!

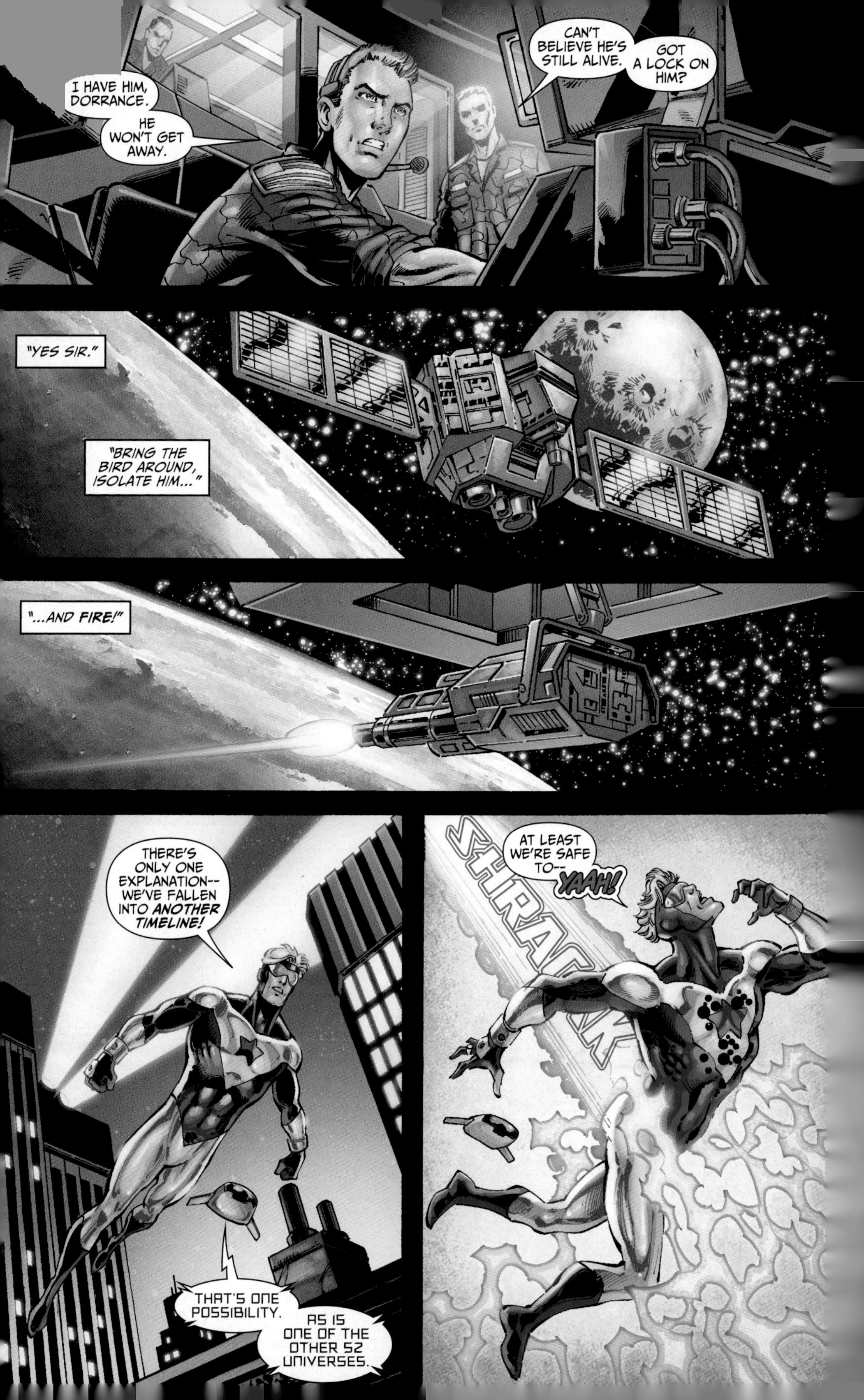
I HAVE HIM, DORRANCE.
HE WON'T GET AWAY.
CAN'T BELIEVE HE'S STILL ALIVE.
GOT A LOCK ON HIM?
"YES SIR."
"BRING THE BIRD AROUND, ISOLATE HIM..."
"...AND FIRE!"
THERE'S ONLY ONE EXPLANATION-- WE'VE FALLEN INTO ANOTHER TIMELINE!
THAT'S ONE POSSIBILITY.
AS IS ONE OF THE OTHER 52 UNIVERSES.
AT LEAST WE'RE SAFE TO--
YAAH!

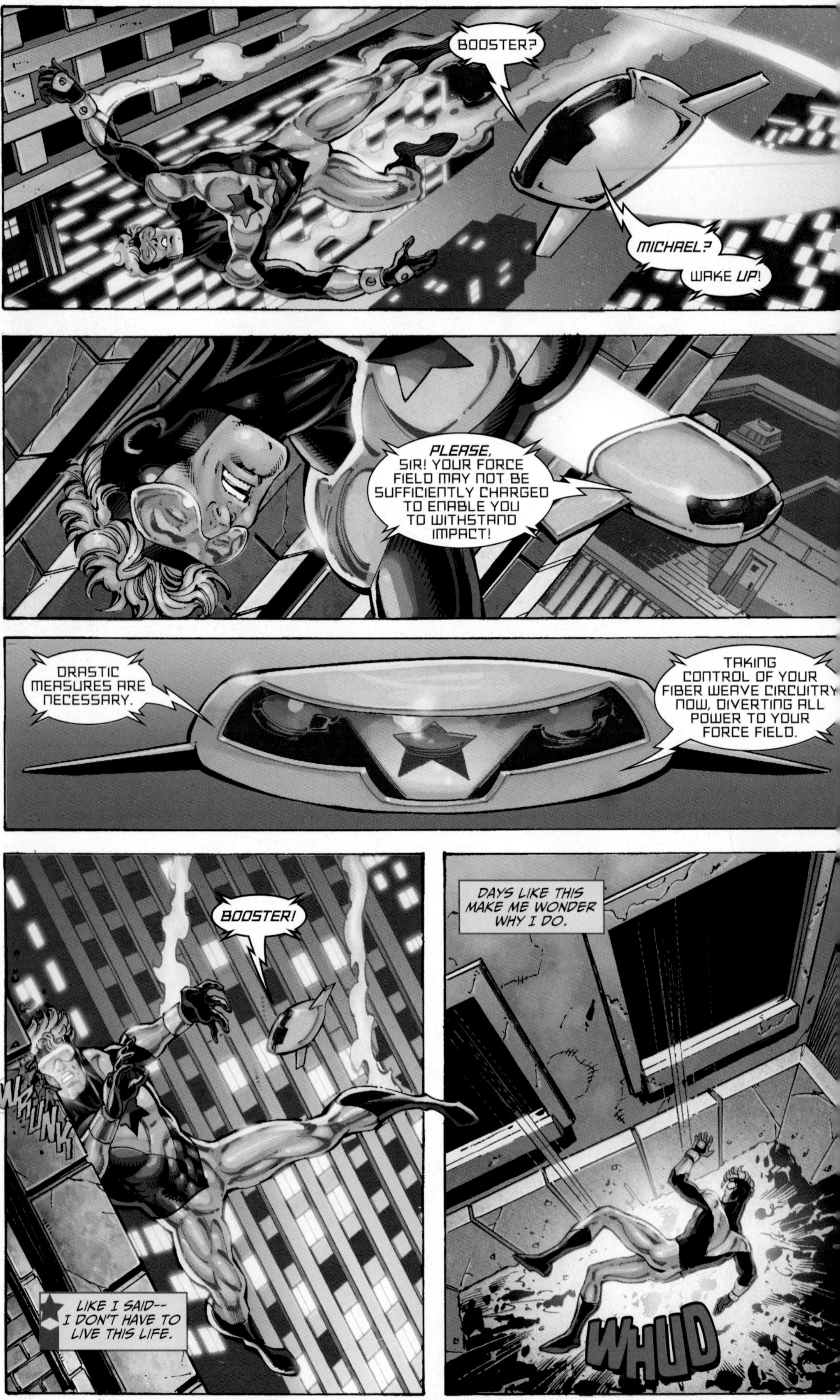
BOOSTER?
MICHAEL?
WAKE UP!
PLEASE, SIR! YOUR FORCE FIELD MAY NOT BE SUFFICIENTLY CHARGED TO ENABLE YOU TO WITHSTAND IMPACT!
DRASTIC MEASURES ARE NECESSARY.
TAKING CONTROL OF YOUR FIBER WEAVE CIRCUITRY NOW, DIVERTING ALL POWER TO YOUR FORCE FIELD.
BOOSTER!
WHUNK
LIKE I SAID-- I DON'T HAVE TO LIVE THIS LIFE.
DAYS LIKE THIS MAKE ME WONDER WHY I DO.
WHUD

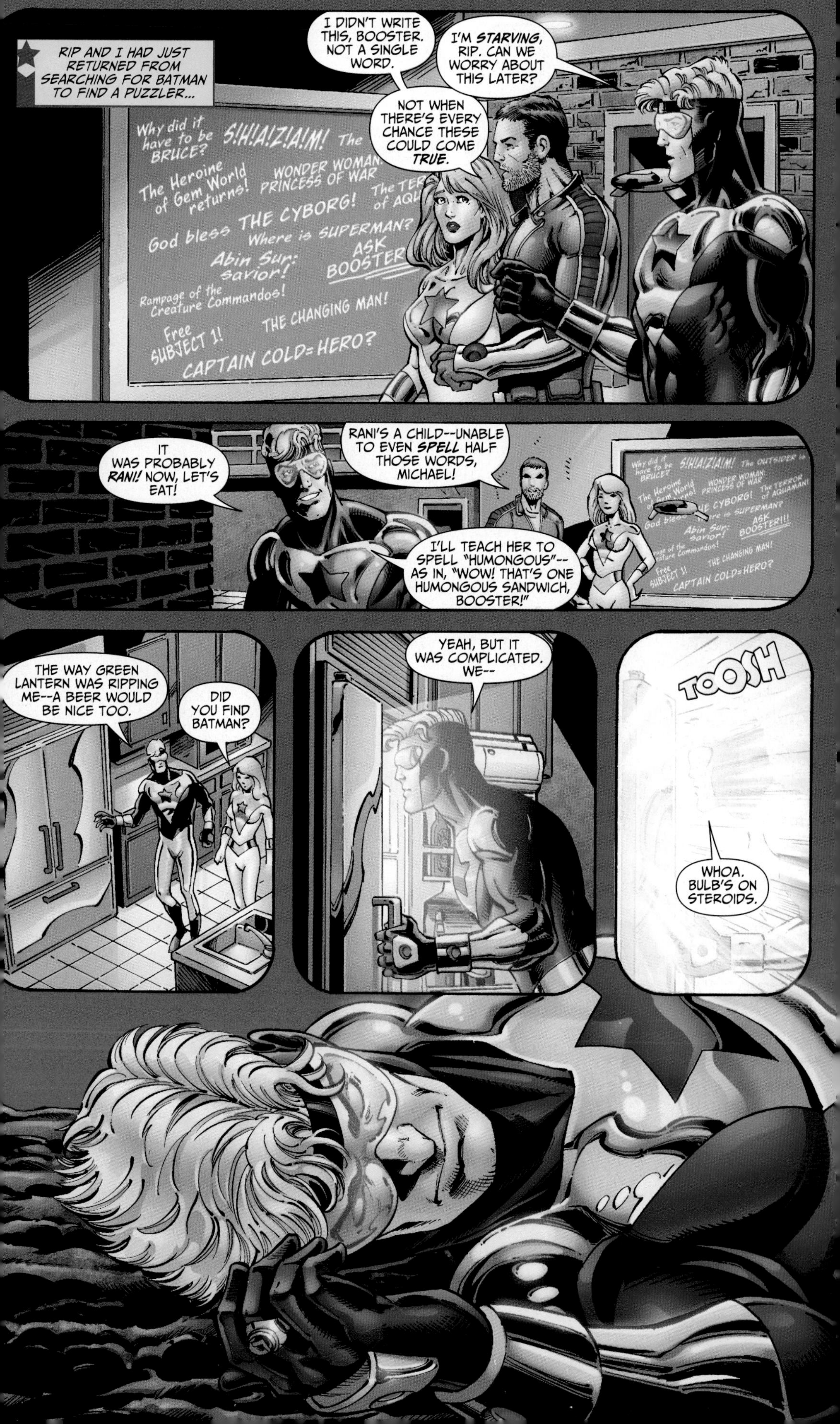

RIP AND I HAD JUST RETURNED FROM SEARCHING FOR BATMAN TO FIND A PUZZLER...
Why did it have to be BRUCE?
S!H!A!Z!A!M!
The Heroine of Gem World returns!
WONDER WOMAN: PRINCESS OF WAR
God bless THE CYBORG!
Where is SUPERMAN?
Abin Sur: savior!
ASK BOOSTER
Rampage of the Creature Commandos!
Free SUBJECT 1!
THE CHANGING MAN!
CAPTAIN COLD=HERO?
I DIDN'T WRITE THIS, BOOSTER. NOT A SINGLE WORD.
I'M STARVING, RIP. CAN WE WORRY ABOUT THIS LATER?
NOT WHEN THERE'S EVERY CHANCE THESE COULD COME TRUE.
IT WAS PROBABLY RANI! NOW, LET'S EAT!
RANI'S A CHILD--UNABLE TO EVEN SPELL HALF THOSE WORDS, MICHAEL!
I'LL TEACH HER TO SPELL "HUMONGOUS"--AS IN, "WOW! THAT'S ONE HUMONGOUS SANDWICH, BOOSTER!"
THE WAY GREEN LANTERN WAS RIPPING ME--A BEER WOULD BE NICE TOO.
DID YOU FIND BATMAN?
YEAH, BUT IT WAS COMPLICATED. WE--
TOOSH
WHOA. BULB'S ON STEROIDS.

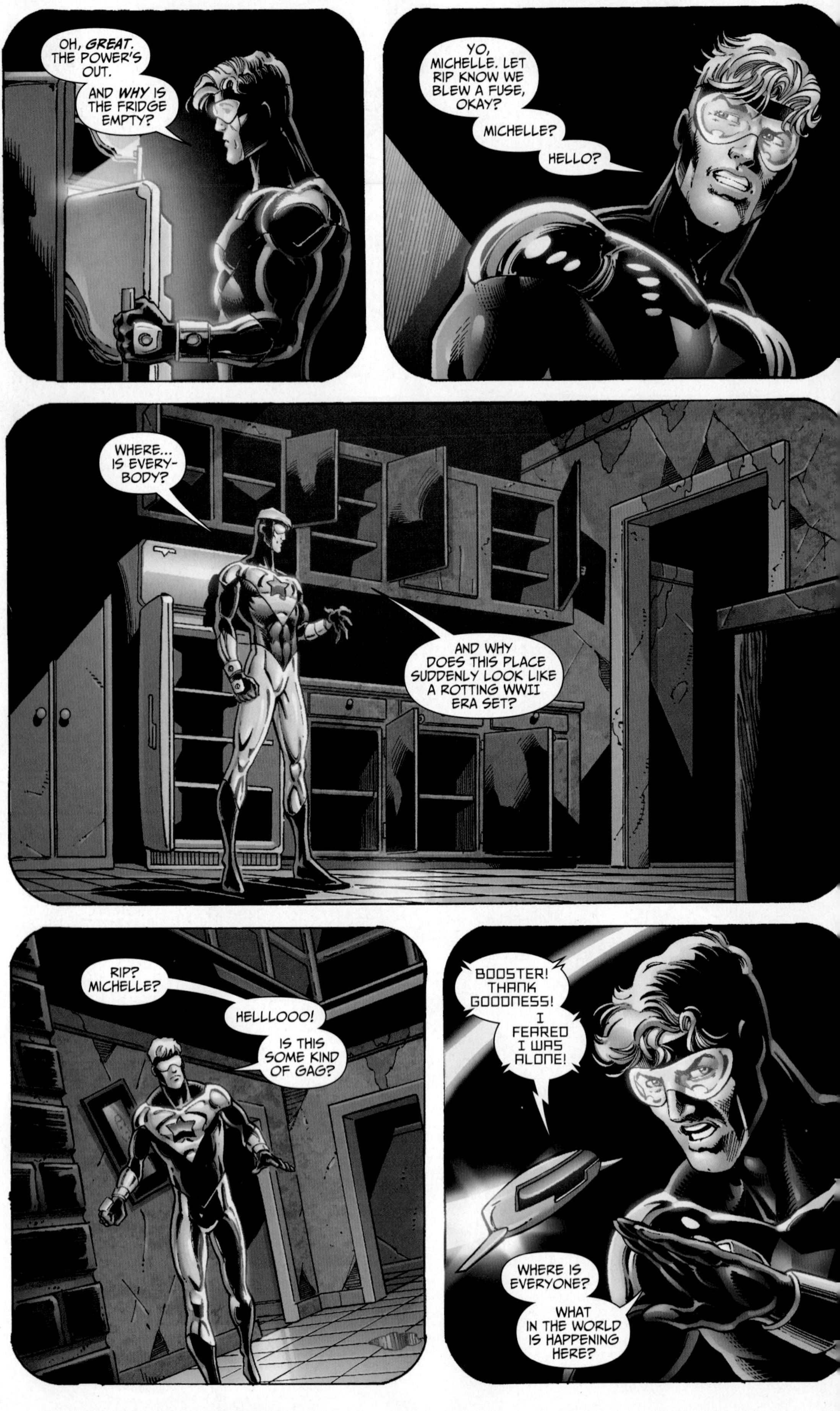
OH, GREAT. THE POWER'S OUT.
AND WHY IS THE FRIDGE EMPTY?
YO, MICHELLE. LET RIP KNOW WE BLEW A FUSE, OKAY?
MICHELLE?
HELLO?
WHERE... IS EVERY-BODY?
AND WHY DOES THIS PLACE SUDDENLY LOOK LIKE A ROTTING WWII ERA SET?
RIP? MICHELLE?
HELLLOOO!
IS THIS SOME KIND OF GAG?
BOOSTER! THANK GOODNESS!
I FEARED I WAS ALONE!
WHERE IS EVERYONE?
WHAT IN THE WORLD IS HAPPENING HERE?

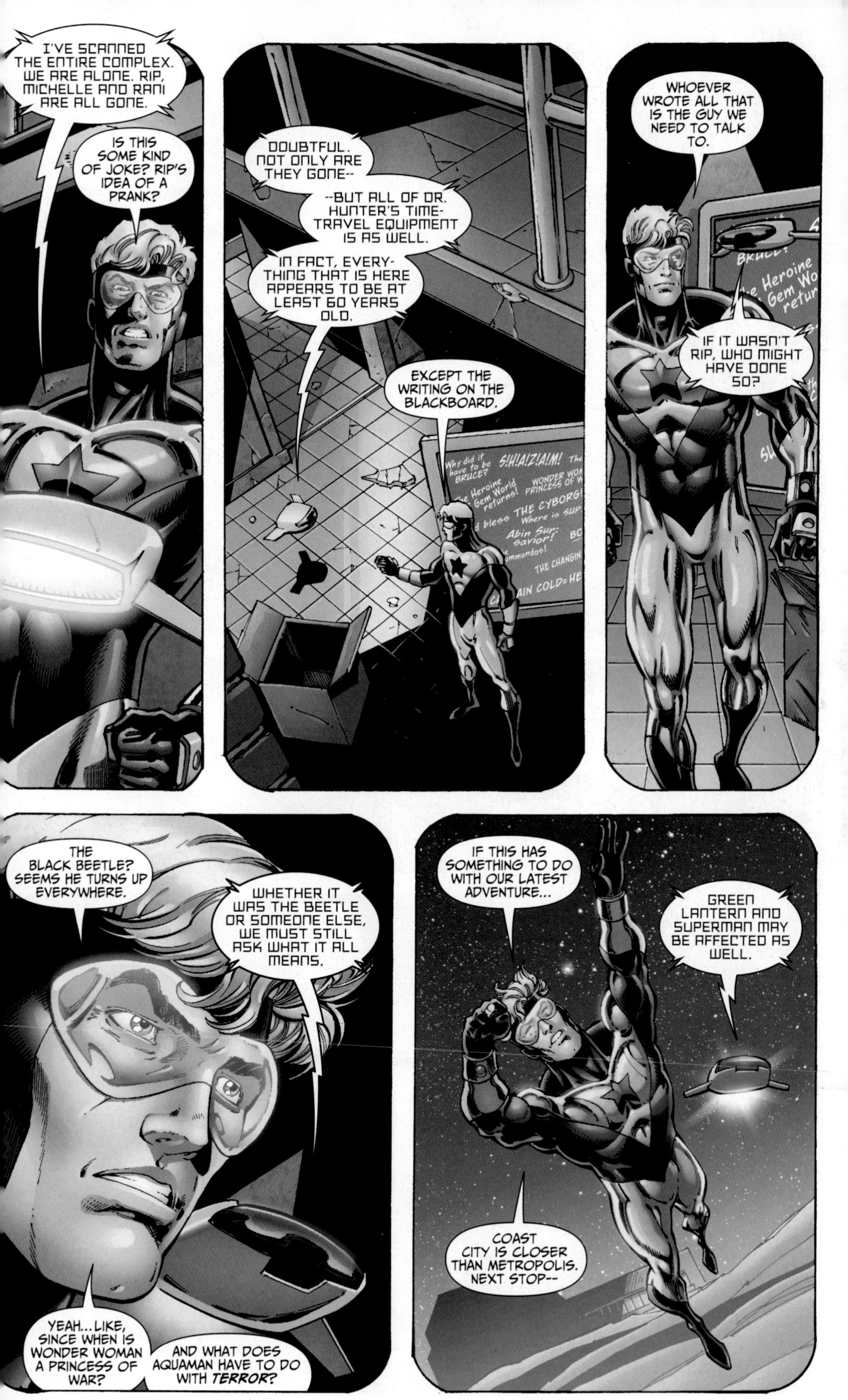
I'VE SCANNED THE ENTIRE COMPLEX. WE ARE ALONE. RIP, MICHELLE AND RANI ARE ALL GONE.
IS THIS SOME KIND OF JOKE? RIP'S IDEA OF A PRANK?
DOUBTFUL. NOT ONLY ARE THEY GONE--
--BUT ALL OF DR. HUNTER'S TIME-TRAVEL EQUIPMENT IS AS WELL.
IN FACT, EVERY-THING THAT IS HERE APPEARS TO BE AT LEAST 60 YEARS OLD.
EXCEPT THE WRITING ON THE BLACKBOARD.
Why did it have to be BRUCE?
S!H!A!Z!A!M!
THE CYBORG!
Abin Sur: Savior!
WHOEVER WROTE ALL THAT IS THE GUY WE NEED TO TALK TO.
IF IT WASN'T RIP, WHO MIGHT HAVE DONE SO?
THE BLACK BEETLE? SEEMS HE TURNS UP EVERYWHERE.
WHETHER IT WAS THE BEETLE OR SOMEONE ELSE, WE MUST STILL ASK WHAT IT ALL MEANS.
YEAH... LIKE, SINCE WHEN IS WONDER WOMAN A PRINCESS OF WAR?
AND WHAT DOES AQUAMAN HAVE TO DO WITH *TERROR*?
IF THIS HAS SOMETHING TO DO WITH OUR LATEST ADVENTURE...
GREEN LANTERN AND SUPERMAN MAY BE AFFECTED AS WELL.
COAST CITY IS CLOSER THAN METROPOLIS. NEXT STOP--

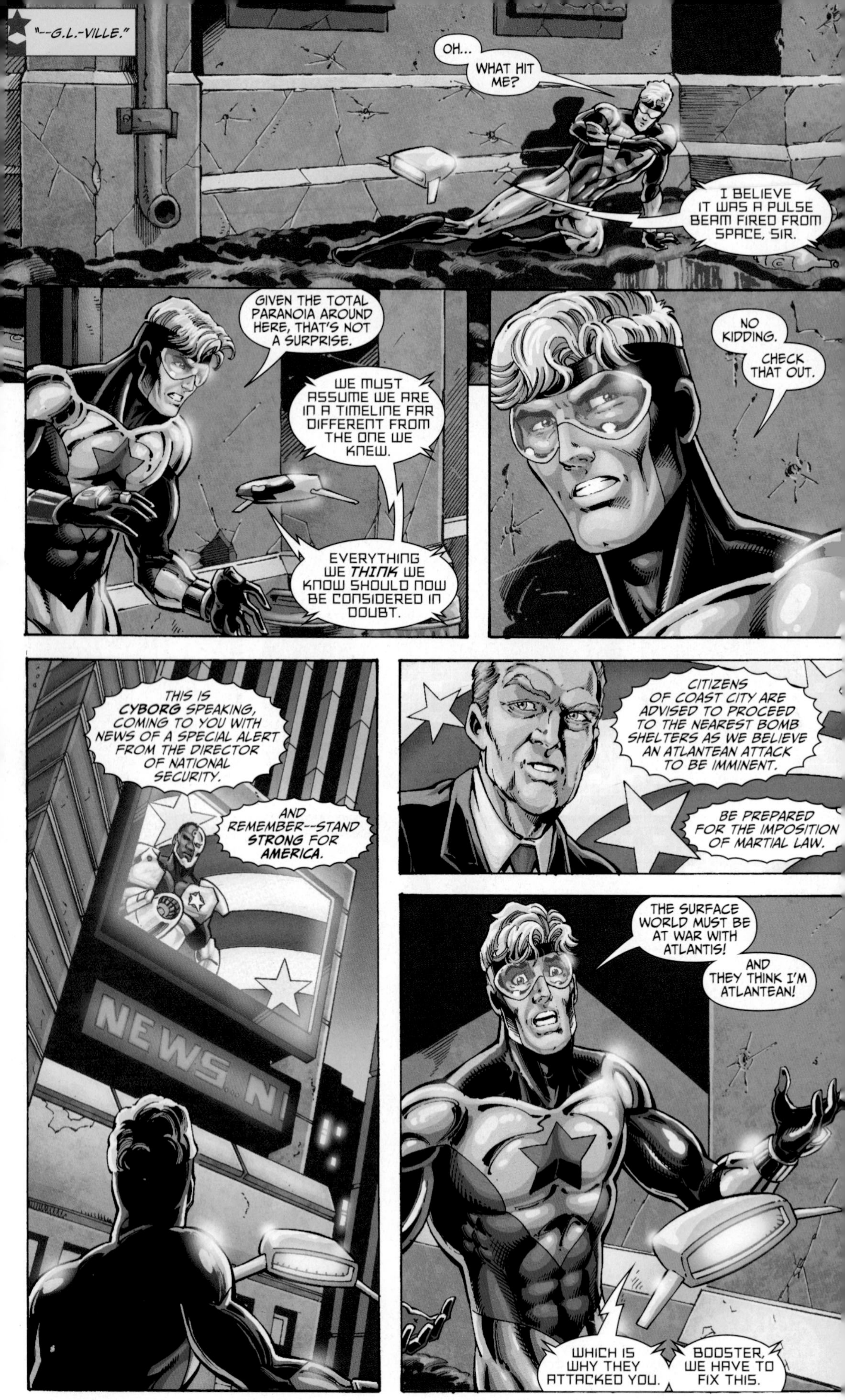
"--G.L.-VILLE."
OH...
WHAT HIT ME?
I BELIEVE IT WAS A PULSE BEAM FIRED FROM SPACE, SIR.
GIVEN THE TOTAL PARANOIA AROUND HERE, THAT'S NOT A SURPRISE.
WE MUST ASSUME WE ARE IN A TIMELINE FAR DIFFERENT FROM THE ONE WE KNEW.
EVERYTHING WE *THINK* WE KNOW SHOULD NOW BE CONSIDERED IN DOUBT.
NO KIDDING.
CHECK THAT OUT, SIR.
THIS IS **CYBORG** SPEAKING, COMING TO YOU WITH NEWS OF A SPECIAL ALERT FROM THE DIRECTOR OF NATIONAL SECURITY.
AND REMEMBER--STAND **STRONG** FOR **AMERICA.**
NEWS N
CITIZENS OF COAST CITY ARE ADVISED TO PROCEED TO THE NEAREST BOMB SHELTERS AS WE BELIEVE AN ATLANTEAN ATTACK TO BE IMMINENT.
BE PREPARED FOR THE IMPOSITION OF MARTIAL LAW.
THE SURFACE WORLD MUST BE AT WAR WITH ATLANTIS!
AND THEY THINK I'M ATLANTEAN!
WHICH IS WHY THEY ATTACKED YOU.
BOOSTER, WE HAVE TO FIX THIS.

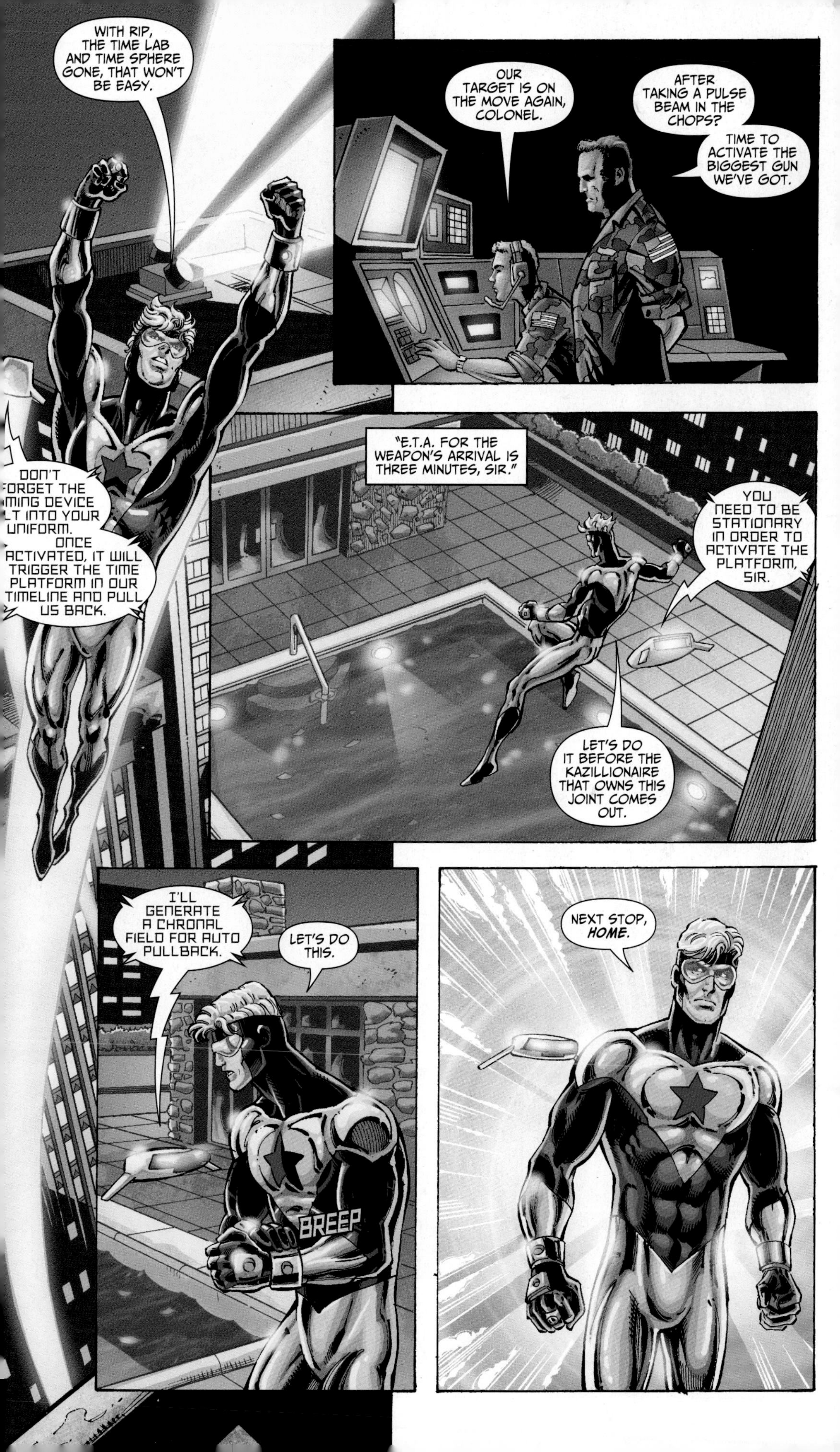
WITH RIP, THE TIME LAB AND TIME SPHERE GONE, THAT WON'T BE EASY.
OUR TARGET IS ON THE MOVE AGAIN, COLONEL.
AFTER TAKING A PULSE BEAM IN THE CHOPS?
TIME TO ACTIVATE THE BIGGEST GUN WE'VE GOT.
DON'T FORGET THE MING DEVICE LT INTO YOUR UNIFORM. ONCE ACTIVATED, IT WILL TRIGGER THE TIME PLATFORM IN OUR TIMELINE AND PULL US BACK.
"E.T.A. FOR THE WEAPON'S ARRIVAL IS THREE MINUTES, SIR."
YOU NEED TO BE STATIONARY IN ORDER TO ACTIVATE THE PLATFORM, SIR.
LET'S DO IT BEFORE THE KAZILLIONAIRE THAT OWNS THIS JOINT COMES OUT.
I'LL GENERATE A CHRONAL FIELD FOR AUTO PULLBACK.
LET'S DO THIS.
BREEP
NEXT STOP, *HOME*.

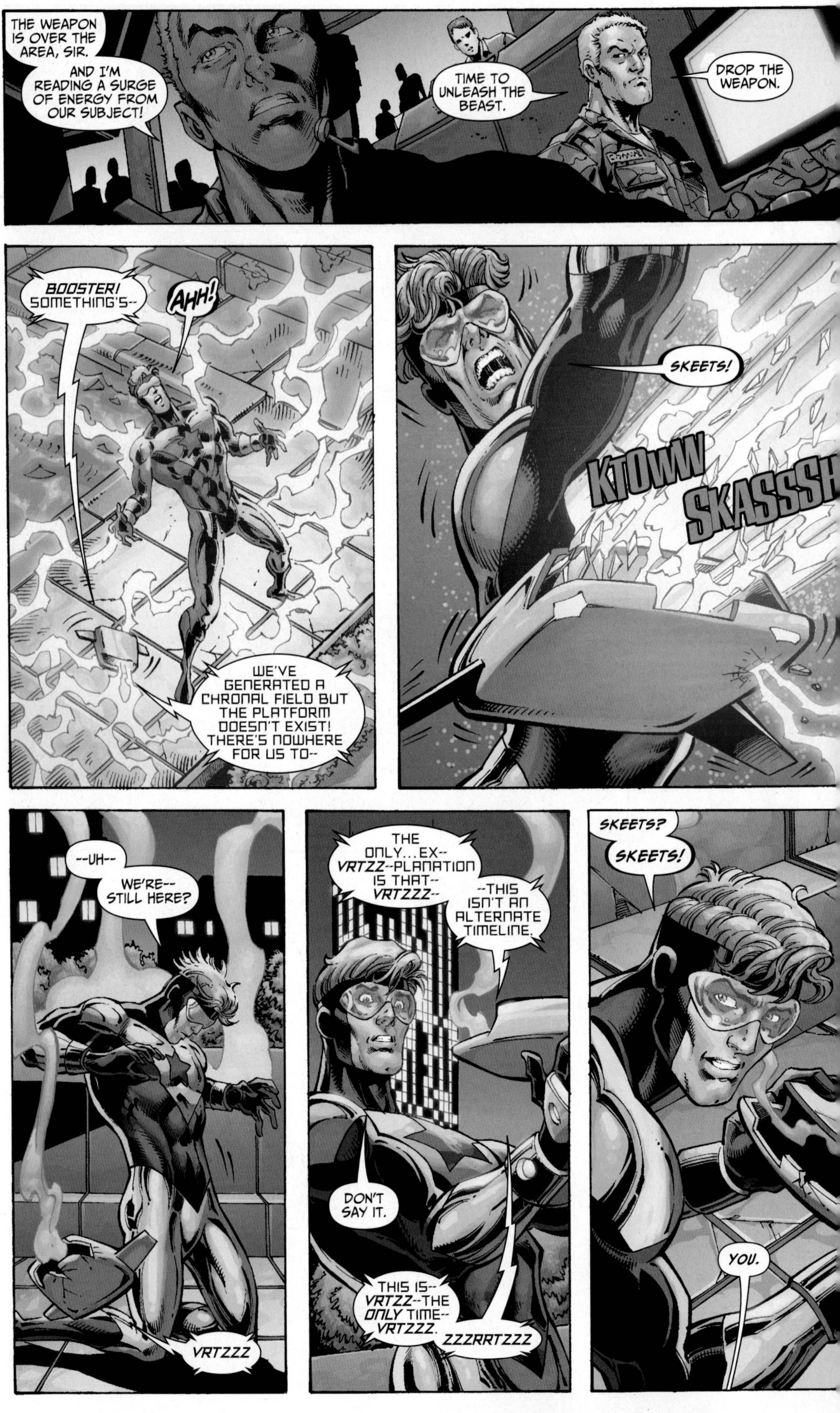
THE WEAPON IS OVER THE AREA, SIR.
AND I'M READING A SURGE OF ENERGY FROM OUR SUBJECT!
TIME TO UNLEASH THE BEAST.
DROP THE WEAPON.
BOOSTER! SOMETHING'S--
AHH!
WE'VE GENERATED A CHRONAL FIELD BUT THE PLATFORM DOESN'T EXIST! THERE'S NOWHERE FOR US TO--
SKEETS!
KTOWW
SKASSSH
--UH--
WE'RE-- STILL HERE?
VRTZZZ
THE ONLY... EX-- VRTZZ--PLANATION IS THAT-- VRTZZZ--
--THIS ISN'T AN ALTERNATE TIMELINE.
DON'T SAY IT.
THIS IS-- VRTZZ--THE ONLY TIME-- VRTZZZ.
ZZZRRTZZZ
SKEETS?
SKEETS!
YOU.

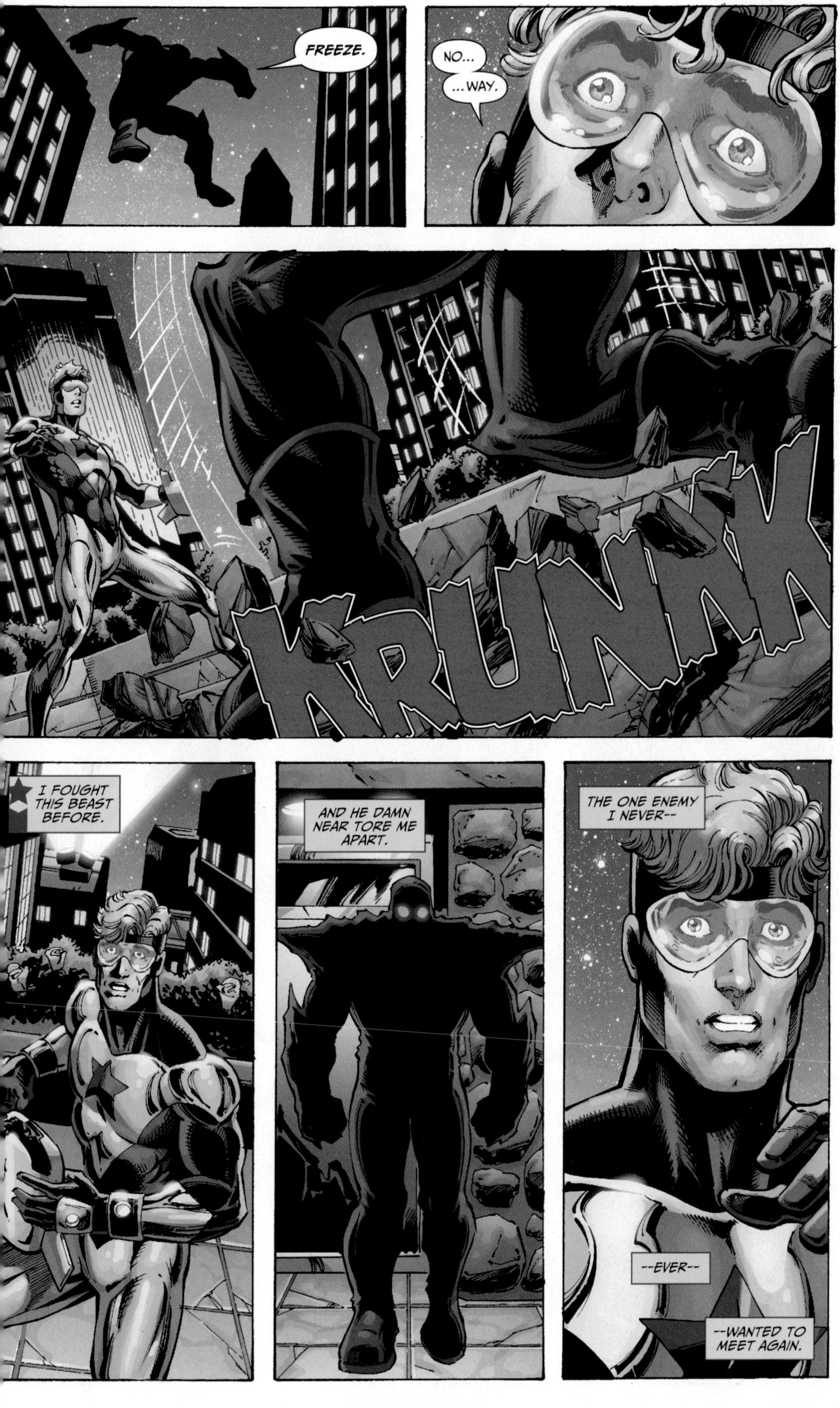
FREEZE.
NO...
...WAY.
KRUNKK
I FOUGHT THIS BEAST BEFORE.
AND HE DAMN NEAR TORE ME APART.
THE ONE ENEMY I NEVER--
--EVER--
--WANTED TO MEET AGAIN.

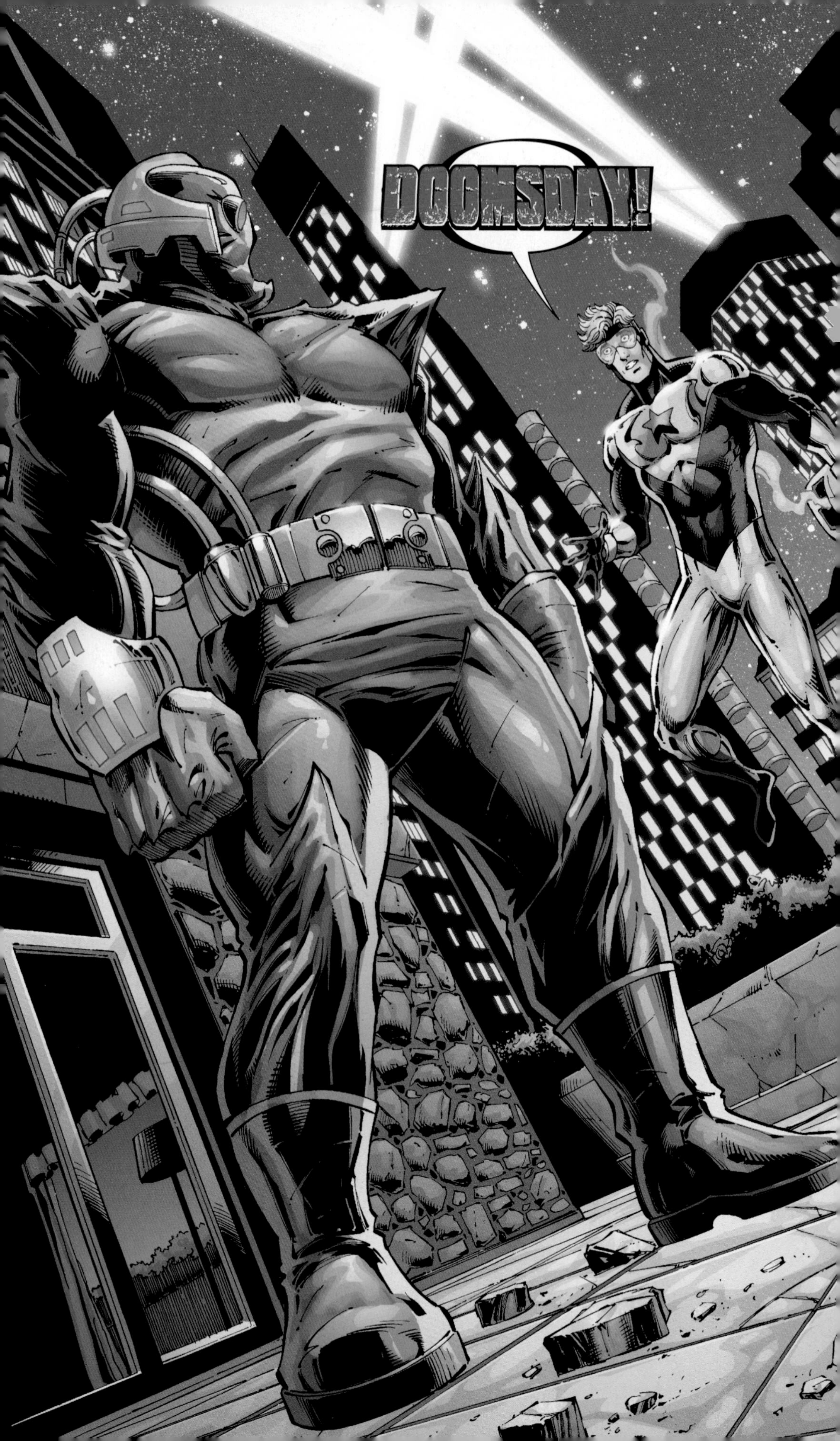
DOOMSDAY!

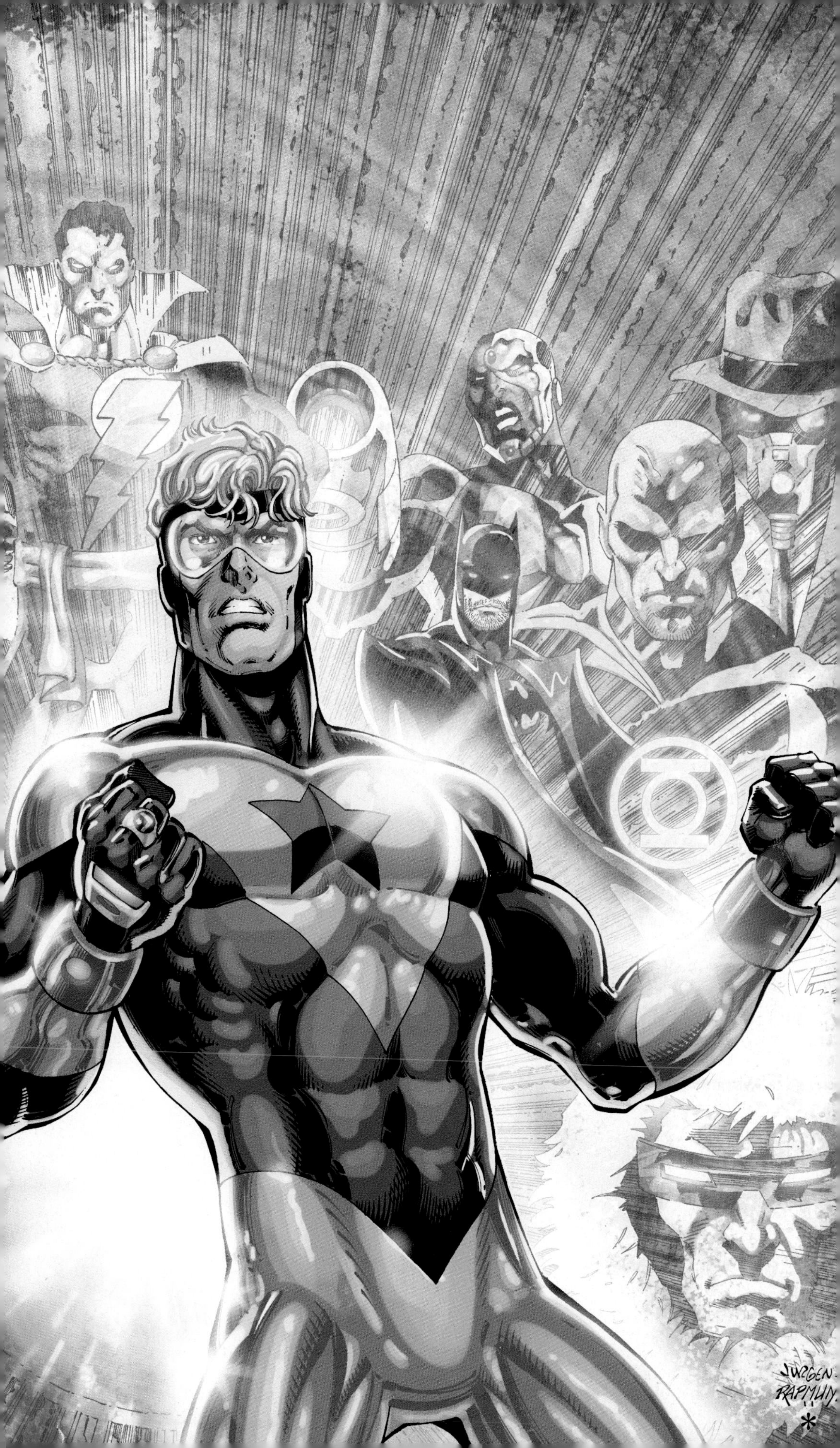

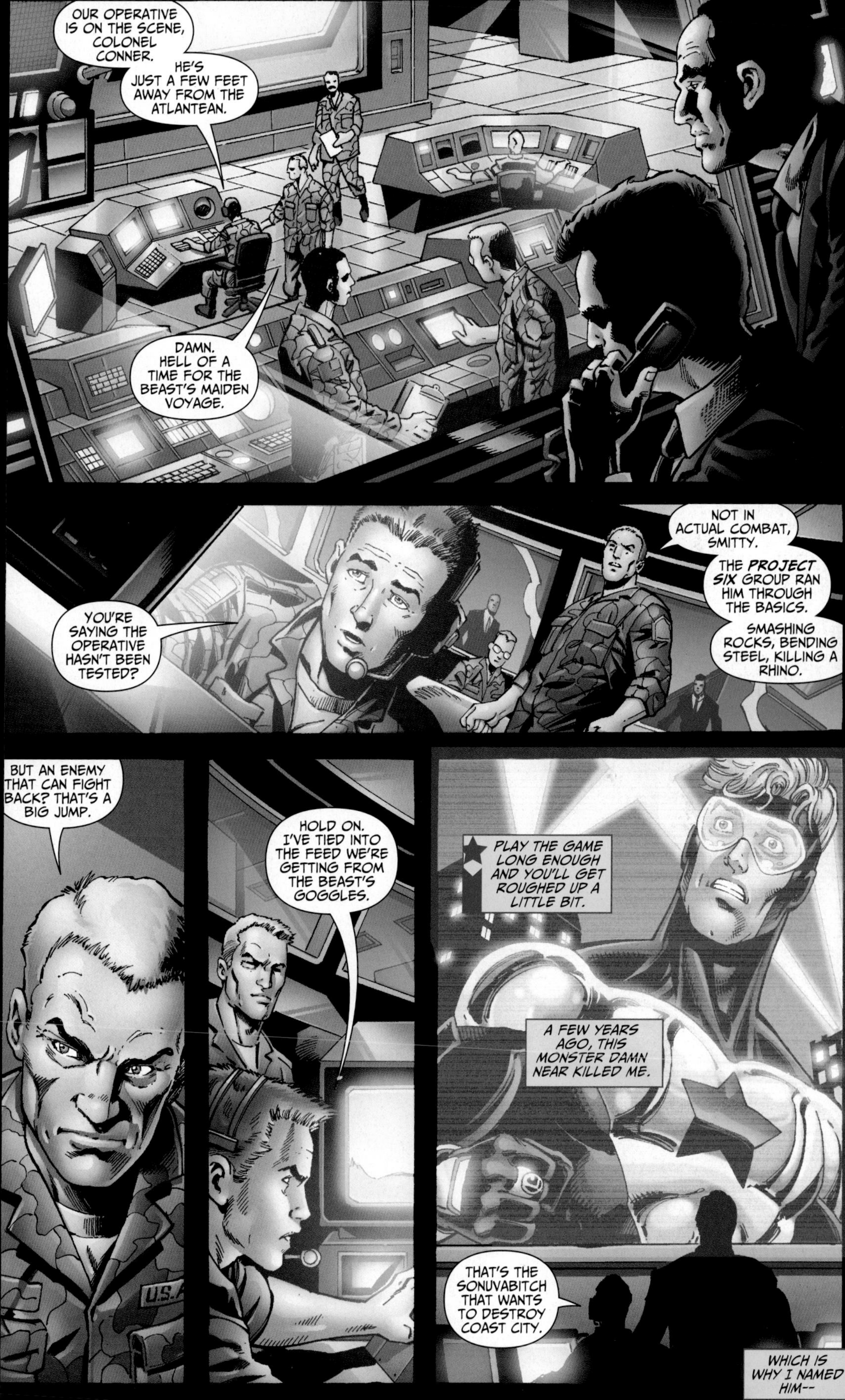

OUR OPERATIVE IS ON THE SCENE, COLONEL CONNER.
HE'S JUST A FEW FEET AWAY FROM THE ATLANTEAN.
DAMN. HELL OF A TIME FOR THE BEAST'S MAIDEN VOYAGE.
YOU'RE SAYING THE OPERATIVE HASN'T BEEN TESTED?
NOT IN ACTUAL COMBAT, SMITTY.
THE PROJECT SIX GROUP RAN HIM THROUGH THE BASICS.
SMASHING ROCKS, BENDING STEEL, KILLING A RHINO.
BUT AN ENEMY THAT CAN FIGHT BACK? THAT'S A BIG JUMP.
HOLD ON. I'VE TIED INTO THE FEED WE'RE GETTING FROM THE BEAST'S GOGGLES.
PLAY THE GAME LONG ENOUGH AND YOU'LL GET ROUGHED UP A LITTLE BIT.
A FEW YEARS AGO, THIS MONSTER DAMN NEAR KILLED ME.
THAT'S THE SONUVABITCH THAT WANTS TO DESTROY COAST CITY.
WHICH IS WHY I NAMED HIM--
U.S.A

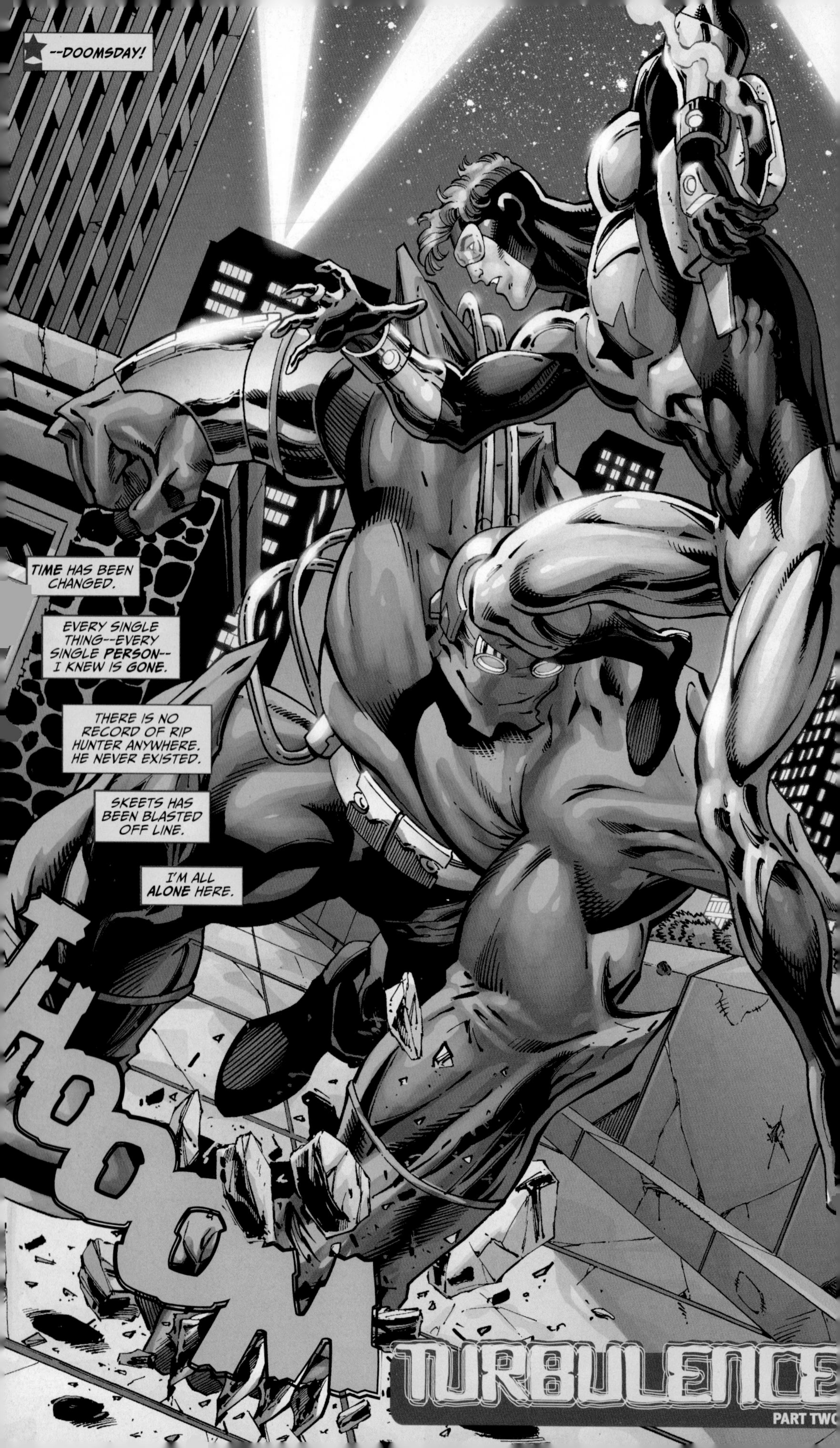
--DOOMSDAY!
TIME HAS BEEN CHANGED.
EVERY SINGLE THING--EVERY SINGLE PERSON--I KNEW IS GONE.
THERE IS NO RECORD OF RIP HUNTER ANYWHERE. HE NEVER EXISTED.
SKEETS HAS BEEN BLASTED OFF LINE.
I'M ALL ALONE HERE.
TURBULENCE
PART TWO

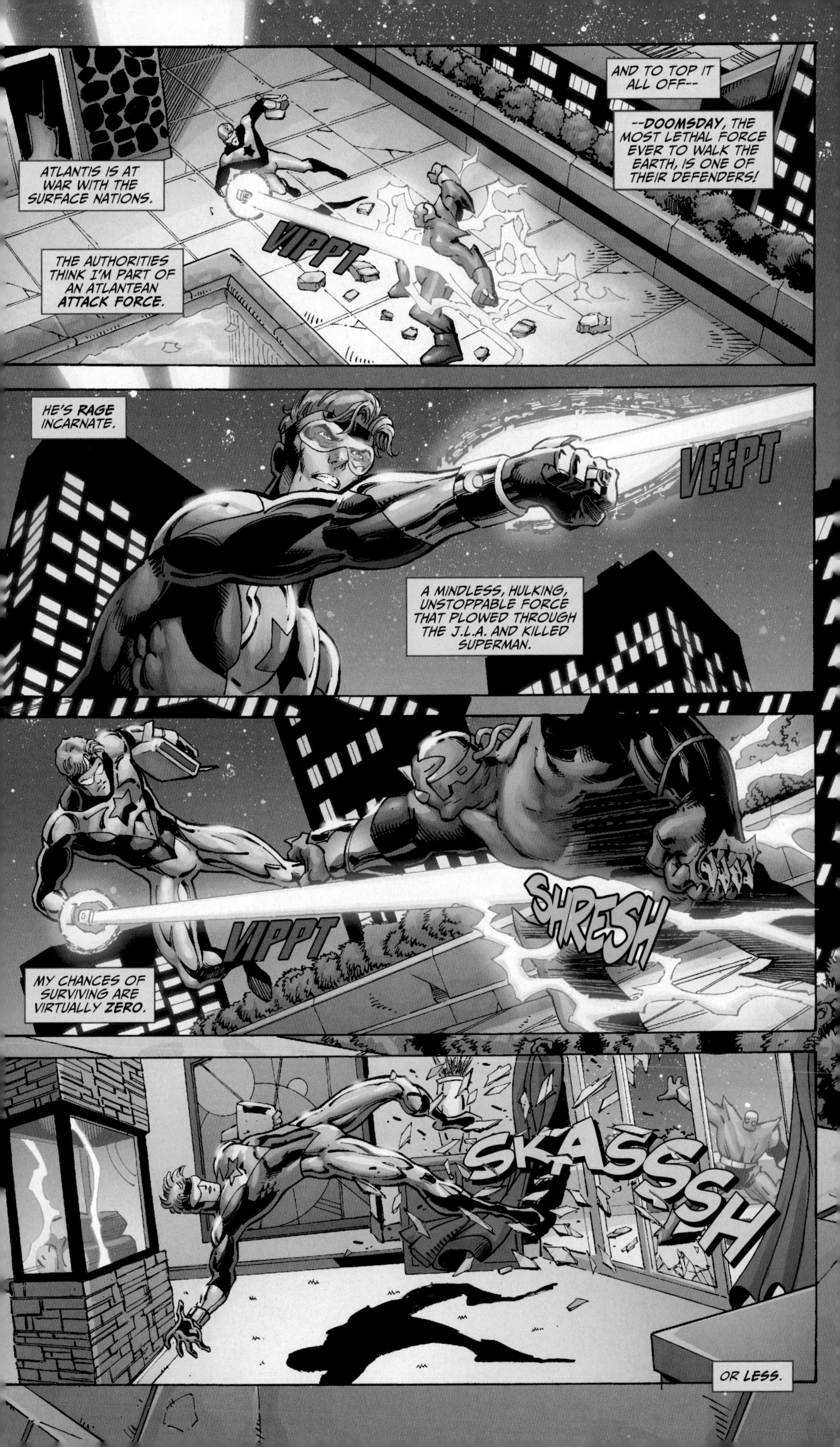
ATLANTIS IS AT WAR WITH THE SURFACE NATIONS.
THE AUTHORITIES THINK I'M PART OF AN ATLANTEAN ATTACK FORCE.
VIPPT
AND TO TOP IT ALL OFF--
--DOOMSDAY, THE MOST LETHAL FORCE EVER TO WALK THE EARTH, IS ONE OF THEIR DEFENDERS!
HE'S RAGE INCARNATE.
VEEPT
A MINDLESS, HULKING, UNSTOPPABLE FORCE THAT PLOWED THROUGH THE J.L.A. AND KILLED SUPERMAN.
VIPPT
SHRESH
MY CHANCES OF SURVIVING ARE VIRTUALLY ZERO.
SKASSSH
OR LESS.

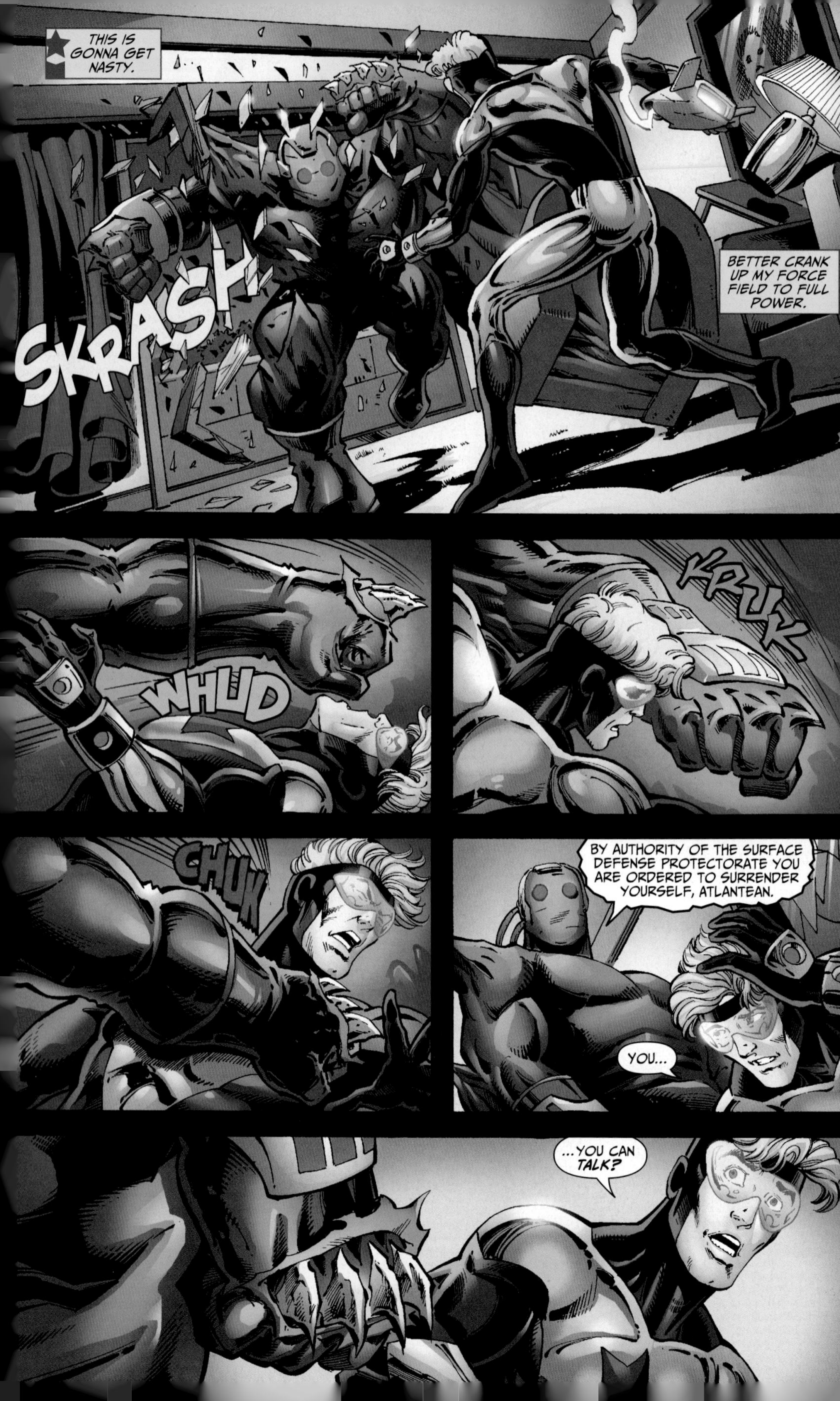
THIS IS GONNA GET NASTY.
SKRASH
BETTER CRANK UP MY FORCE FIELD TO FULL POWER.
WHUD
KRUK
CHUK
BY AUTHORITY OF THE SURFACE DEFENSE PROTECTORATE YOU ARE ORDERED TO SURRENDER YOURSELF, ATLANTEAN.
YOU...
...YOU CAN TALK?

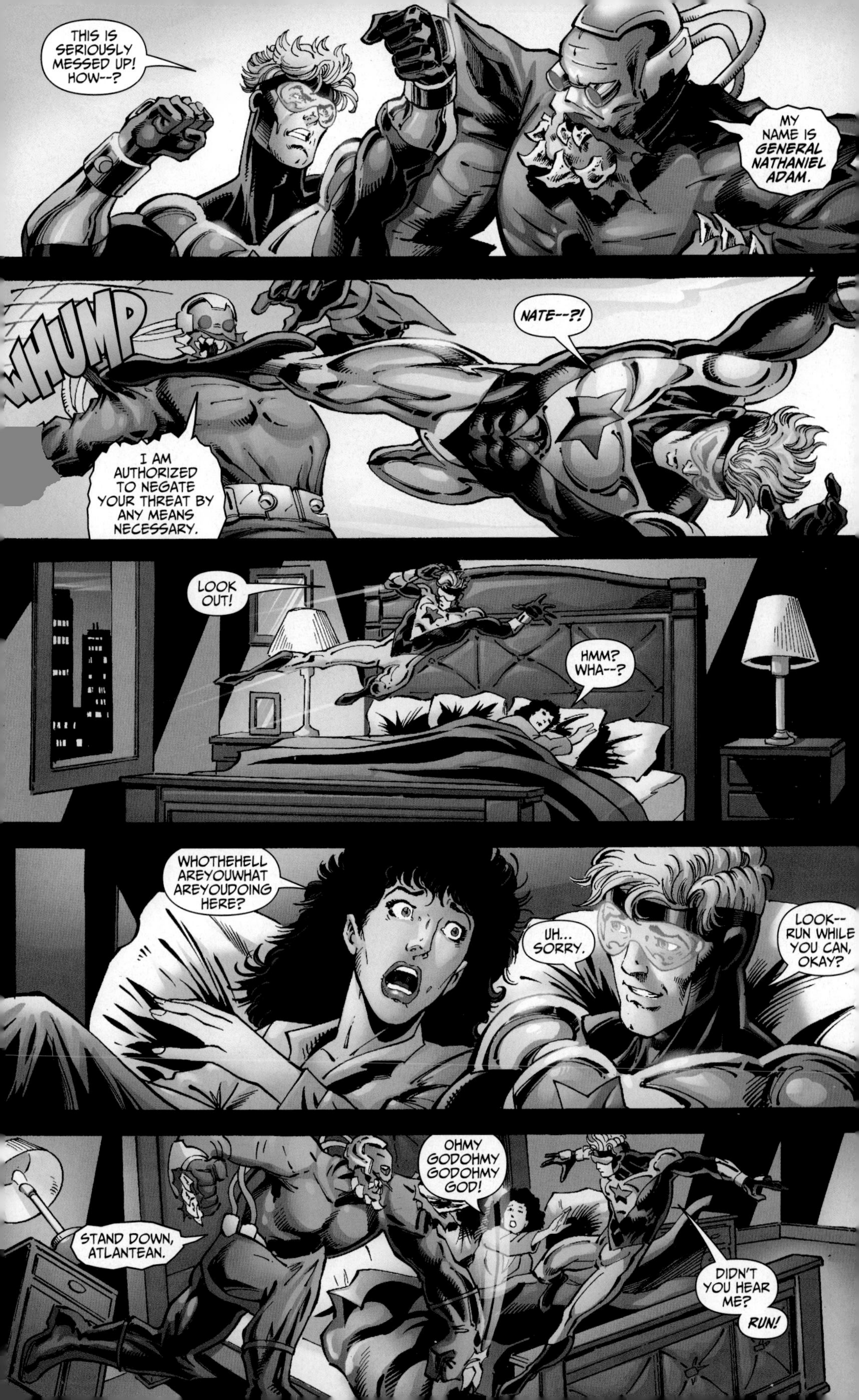

THIS IS SERIOUSLY MESSED UP! HOW--?
MY NAME IS GENERAL NATHANIEL ADAM.
WHUMP
NATE--?!
I AM AUTHORIZED TO NEGATE YOUR THREAT BY ANY MEANS NECESSARY.
LOOK OUT!
HMM? WHA--?
WHOTHEHELL AREYOUWHAT AREYOUDOING HERE?
UH... SORRY.
LOOK-- RUN WHILE YOU CAN, OKAY?
STAND DOWN, ATLANTEAN.
OHMY GODOHMY GODOHMY GOD!
DIDN'T YOU HEAR ME? RUN!

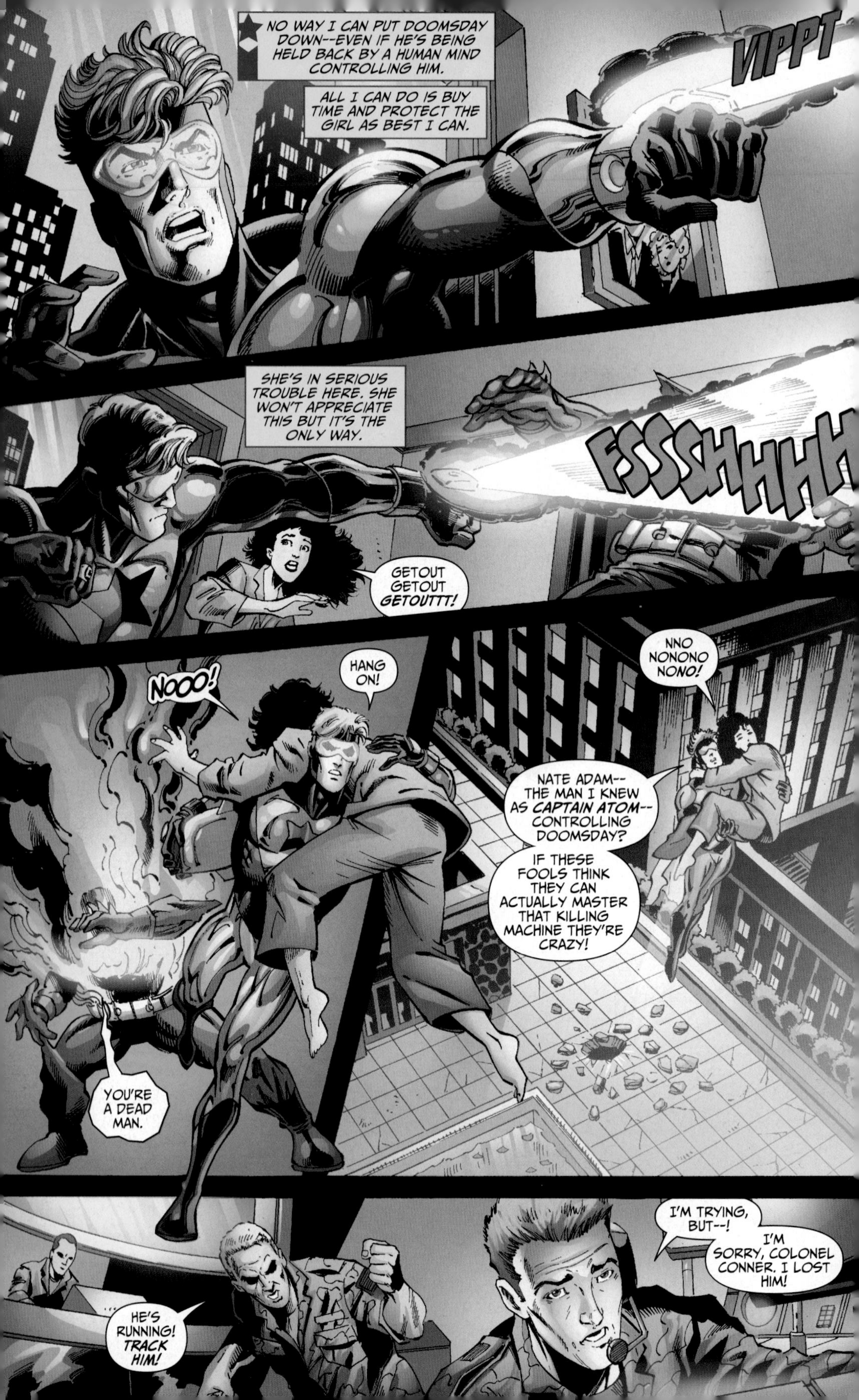
NO WAY I CAN PUT DOOMSDAY DOWN--EVEN IF HE'S BEING HELD BACK BY A HUMAN MIND CONTROLLING HIM.
ALL I CAN DO IS BUY TIME AND PROTECT THE GIRL AS BEST I CAN.
VIPPT
SHE'S IN SERIOUS TROUBLE HERE. SHE WON'T APPRECIATE THIS BUT IT'S THE ONLY WAY.
FSSSHHHH
GETOUT GETOUT GETOUTTT!
NOOO!
HANG ON!
NNO NONONO NONO!
NATE ADAM-- THE MAN I KNEW AS CAPTAIN ATOM-- CONTROLLING DOOMSDAY?
IF THESE FOOLS THINK THEY CAN ACTUALLY MASTER THAT KILLING MACHINE THEY'RE CRAZY!
YOU'RE A DEAD MAN.
HE'S RUNNING! TRACK HIM!
I'M TRYING, BUT--!
I'M SORRY, COLONEL CONNER. I LOST HIM!

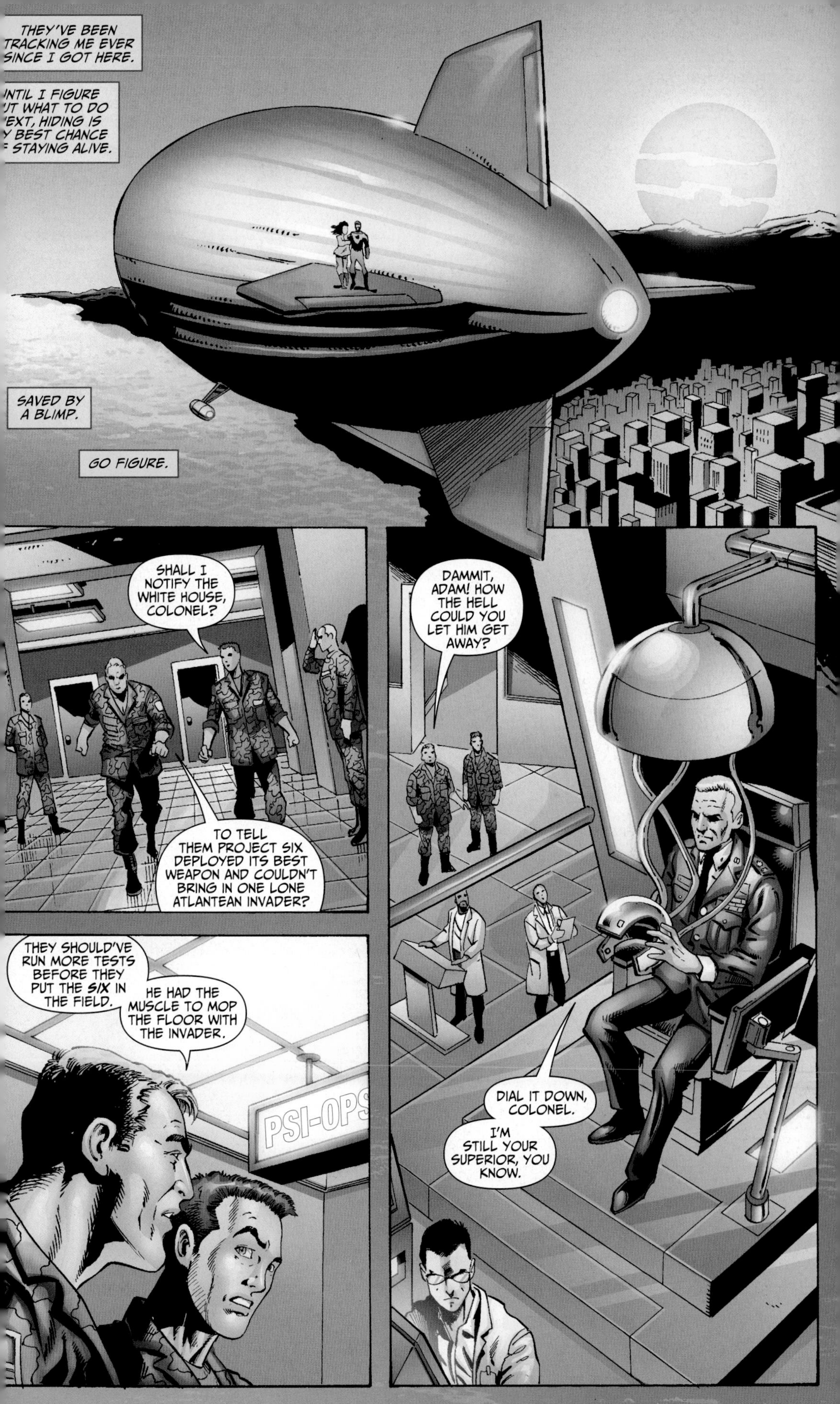

THEY'VE BEEN TRACKING ME EVER SINCE I GOT HERE.
UNTIL I FIGURE OUT WHAT TO DO NEXT, HIDING IS MY BEST CHANCE OF STAYING ALIVE.
SAVED BY A BLIMP.
GO FIGURE.
SHALL I NOTIFY THE WHITE HOUSE, COLONEL?
TO TELL THEM PROJECT SIX DEPLOYED ITS BEST WEAPON AND COULDN'T BRING IN ONE LONE ATLANTEAN INVADER?
DAMMIT, ADAM! HOW THE HELL COULD YOU LET HIM GET AWAY?
DIAL IT DOWN, COLONEL.
I'M STILL YOUR SUPERIOR, YOU KNOW.
THEY SHOULD'VE RUN MORE TESTS BEFORE THEY PUT THE SIX IN THE FIELD.
HE HAD THE MUSCLE TO MOP THE FLOOR WITH THE INVADER.
PSI-OPS

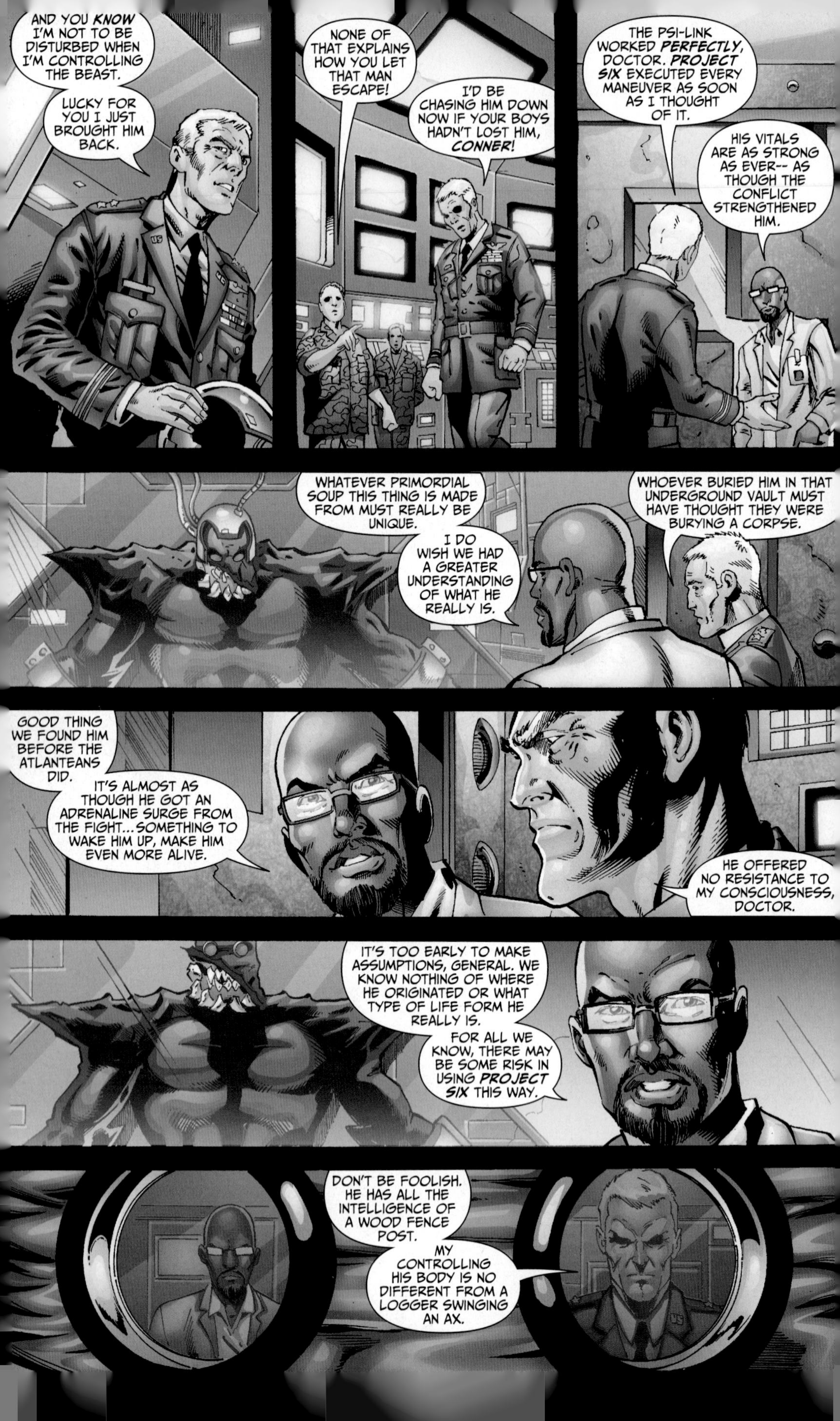
AND YOU *KNOW* I'M NOT TO BE DISTURBED WHEN I'M CONTROLLING THE BEAST.
LUCKY FOR YOU I JUST BROUGHT HIM BACK.
NONE OF THAT EXPLAINS HOW YOU LET THAT MAN ESCAPE!
I'D BE CHASING HIM DOWN NOW IF YOUR BOYS HADN'T LOST HIM, *CONNER!*
THE PSI-LINK WORKED *PERFECTLY*, DOCTOR. *PROJECT SIX* EXECUTED EVERY MANEUVER AS SOON AS I THOUGHT OF IT.
HIS VITALS ARE AS STRONG AS EVER-- AS THOUGH THE CONFLICT STRENGTHENED HIM.
WHATEVER PRIMORDIAL SOUP THIS THING IS MADE FROM MUST REALLY BE UNIQUE.
I DO WISH WE HAD A GREATER UNDERSTANDING OF WHAT HE REALLY IS.
WHOEVER BURIED HIM IN THAT UNDERGROUND VAULT MUST HAVE THOUGHT THEY WERE BURYING A CORPSE.
GOOD THING WE FOUND HIM BEFORE THE ATLANTEANS DID.
IT'S ALMOST AS THOUGH HE GOT AN ADRENALINE SURGE FROM THE FIGHT...SOMETHING TO WAKE HIM UP, MAKE HIM EVEN MORE ALIVE.
HE OFFERED NO RESISTANCE TO MY CONSCIOUSNESS, DOCTOR.
IT'S TOO EARLY TO MAKE ASSUMPTIONS, GENERAL. WE KNOW NOTHING OF WHERE HE ORIGINATED OR WHAT TYPE OF LIFE FORM HE REALLY IS.
FOR ALL WE KNOW, THERE MAY BE SOME RISK IN USING *PROJECT SIX* THIS WAY.
DON'T BE FOOLISH. HE HAS ALL THE INTELLIGENCE OF A WOOD FENCE POST.
MY CONTROLLING HIS BODY IS NO DIFFERENT FROM A LOGGER SWINGING AN AX.

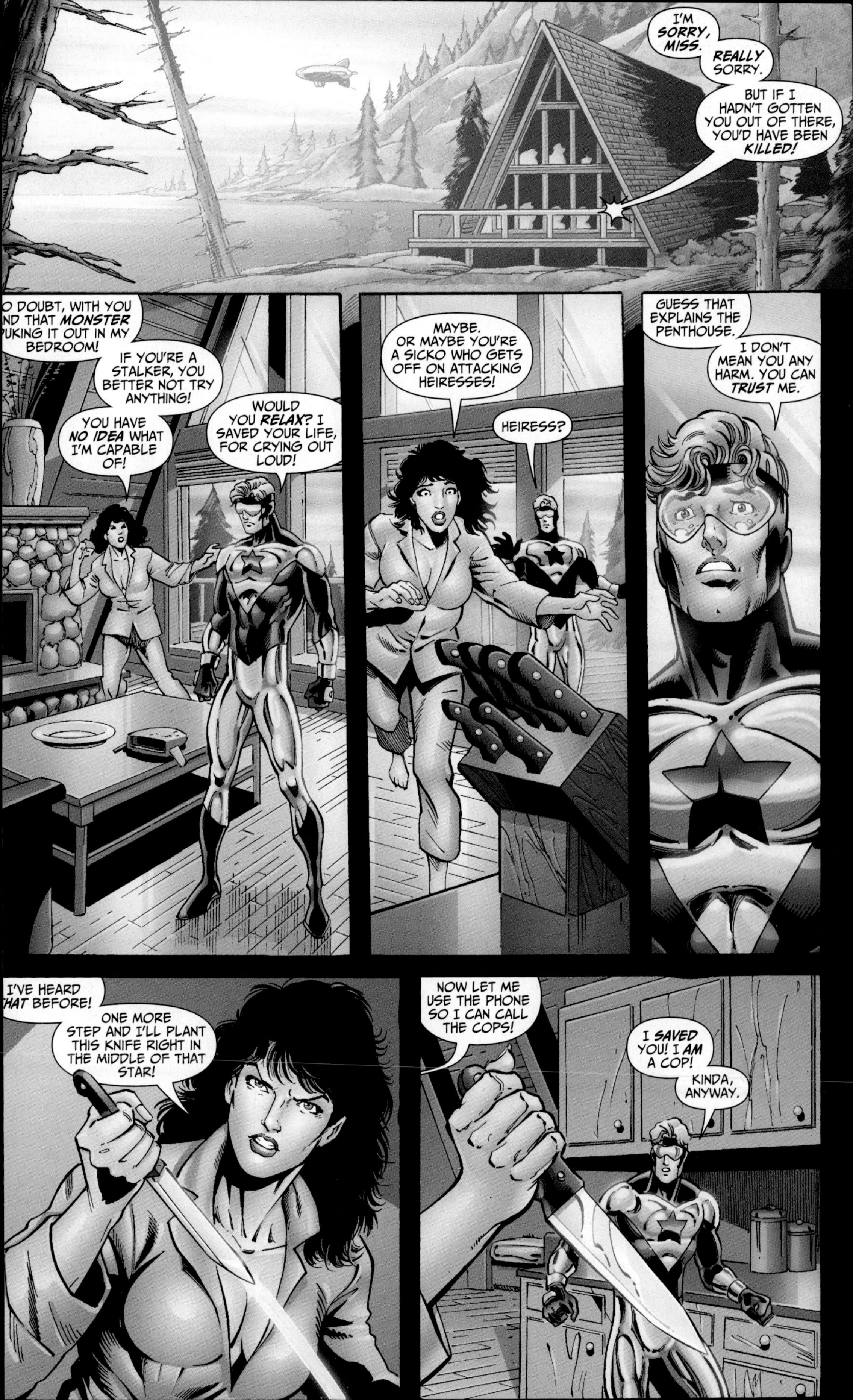
I'M SORRY, MISS. REALLY SORRY.
BUT IF I HADN'T GOTTEN YOU OUT OF THERE, YOU'D HAVE BEEN KILLED!
O DOUBT, WITH YOU ND THAT MONSTER PUKING IT OUT IN MY BEDROOM!
IF YOU'RE A STALKER, YOU BETTER NOT TRY ANYTHING!
YOU HAVE NO IDEA WHAT I'M CAPABLE OF!
WOULD YOU RELAX? I SAVED YOUR LIFE, FOR CRYING OUT LOUD!
MAYBE. OR MAYBE YOU'RE A SICKO WHO GETS OFF ON ATTACKING HEIRESSES!
HEIRESS?
GUESS THAT EXPLAINS THE PENTHOUSE.
I DON'T MEAN YOU ANY HARM. YOU CAN TRUST ME.
I'VE HEARD THAT BEFORE!
ONE MORE STEP AND I'LL PLANT THIS KNIFE RIGHT IN THE MIDDLE OF THAT STAR!
NOW LET ME USE THE PHONE SO I CAN CALL THE COPS!
I SAVED YOU! I AM A COP!
KINDA, ANYWAY.

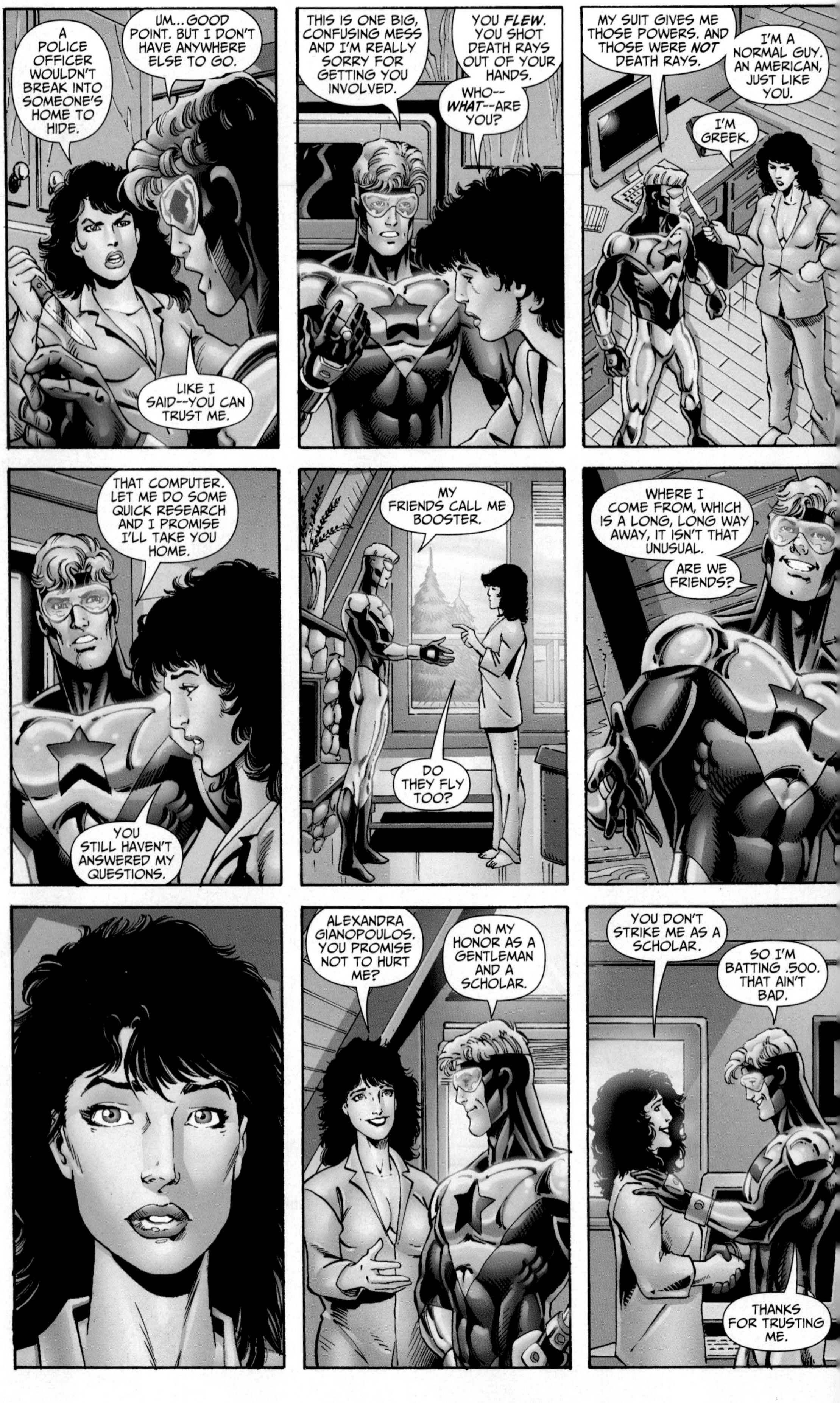

A POLICE OFFICER WOULDN'T BREAK INTO SOMEONE'S HOME TO HIDE.
UM...GOOD POINT. BUT I DON'T HAVE ANYWHERE ELSE TO GO.
LIKE I SAID--YOU CAN TRUST ME.
THIS IS ONE BIG, CONFUSING MESS AND I'M REALLY SORRY FOR GETTING YOU INVOLVED.
YOU *FLEW*. YOU SHOT DEATH RAYS OUT OF YOUR HANDS.
WHO--*WHAT*--ARE YOU?
MY SUIT GIVES ME THOSE POWERS. AND THOSE WERE *NOT* DEATH RAYS.
I'M A NORMAL GUY. AN AMERICAN, JUST LIKE YOU.
I'M GREEK.
THAT COMPUTER. LET ME DO SOME QUICK RESEARCH AND I PROMISE I'LL TAKE YOU HOME.
YOU STILL HAVEN'T ANSWERED MY QUESTIONS.
MY FRIENDS CALL ME BOOSTER.
DO THEY FLY TOO?
WHERE I COME FROM, WHICH IS A LONG, LONG WAY AWAY, IT ISN'T THAT UNUSUAL.
ARE WE FRIENDS?
ALEXANDRA GIANOPOULOS. YOU PROMISE NOT TO HURT ME?
ON MY HONOR AS A GENTLEMAN AND A SCHOLAR.
YOU DON'T STRIKE ME AS A SCHOLAR.
SO I'M BATTING .500. THAT AIN'T BAD.
THANKS FOR TRUSTING ME.

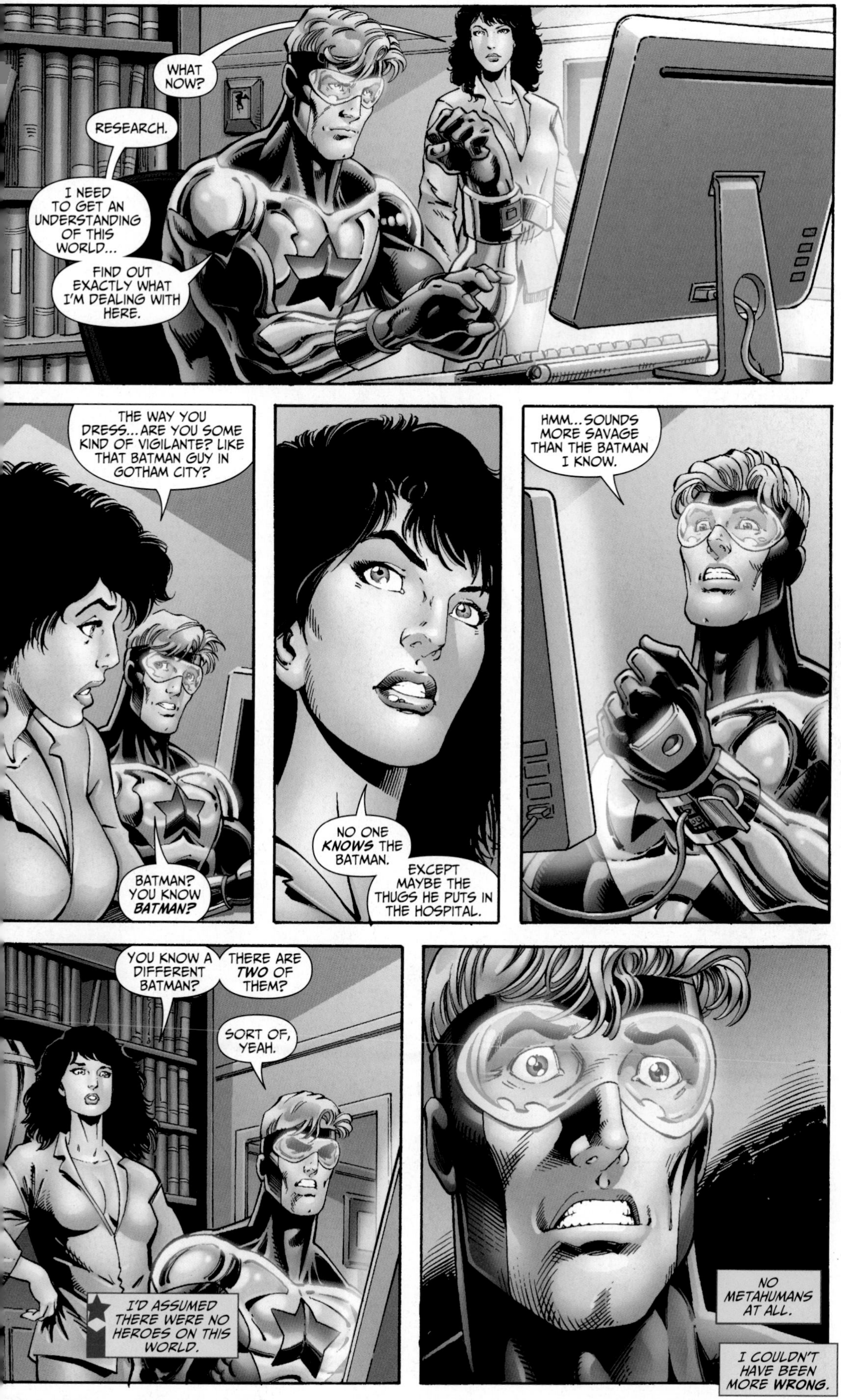
WHAT NOW?
RESEARCH.
I NEED TO GET AN UNDERSTANDING OF THIS WORLD...
FIND OUT EXACTLY WHAT I'M DEALING WITH HERE.
THE WAY YOU DRESS...ARE YOU SOME KIND OF VIGILANTE? LIKE THAT BATMAN GUY IN GOTHAM CITY?
BATMAN? YOU KNOW BATMAN?
NO ONE KNOWS THE BATMAN.
EXCEPT MAYBE THE THUGS HE PUTS IN THE HOSPITAL.
HMM...SOUNDS MORE SAVAGE THAN THE BATMAN I KNOW.
YOU KNOW A DIFFERENT BATMAN?
THERE ARE TWO OF THEM?
SORT OF, YEAH.
I'D ASSUMED THERE WERE NO HEROES ON THIS WORLD.
NO METAHUMANS AT ALL.
I COULDN'T HAVE BEEN MORE WRONG.

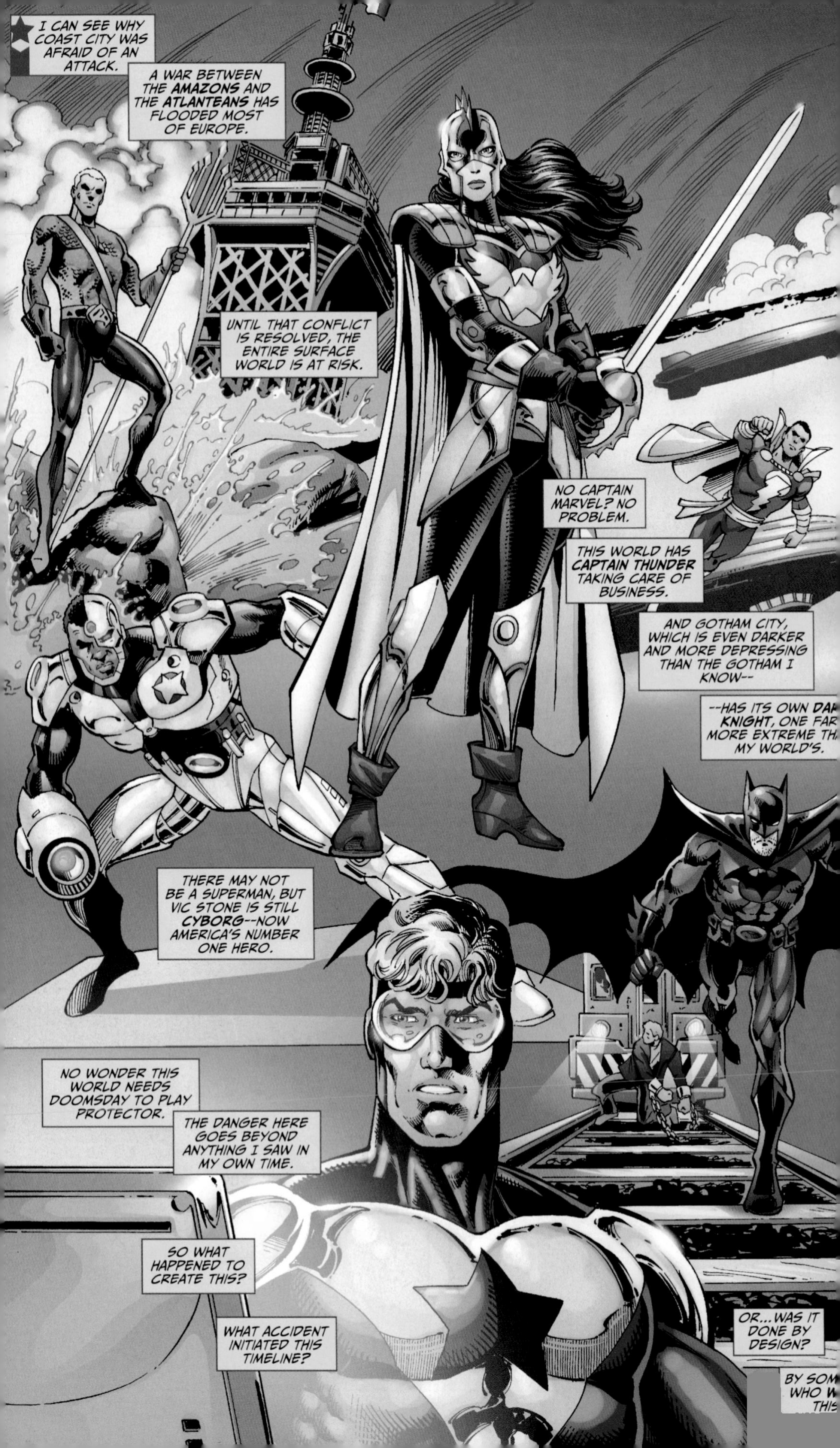
I CAN SEE WHY COAST CITY WAS AFRAID OF AN ATTACK.
A WAR BETWEEN THE **AMAZONS** AND THE **ATLANTEANS** HAS FLOODED MOST OF EUROPE.
UNTIL THAT CONFLICT IS RESOLVED, THE ENTIRE SURFACE WORLD IS AT RISK.
NO CAPTAIN MARVEL? NO PROBLEM.
THIS WORLD HAS **CAPTAIN THUNDER** TAKING CARE OF BUSINESS.
AND GOTHAM CITY, WHICH IS EVEN DARKER AND MORE DEPRESSING THAN THE GOTHAM I KNOW--
--HAS ITS OWN **DA** **KNIGHT**, ONE FAR MORE EXTREME TH MY WORLD'S.
THERE MAY NOT BE A SUPERMAN, BUT VIC STONE IS STILL **CYBORG**--NOW AMERICA'S NUMBER ONE HERO.
NO WONDER THIS WORLD NEEDS DOOMSDAY TO PLAY PROTECTOR.
THE DANGER HERE GOES BEYOND ANYTHING I SAW IN MY OWN TIME.
SO WHAT HAPPENED TO CREATE THIS?
WHAT ACCIDENT INITIATED THIS TIMELINE?
OR...WAS IT DONE BY DESIGN?
BY SOM WHO W THIS

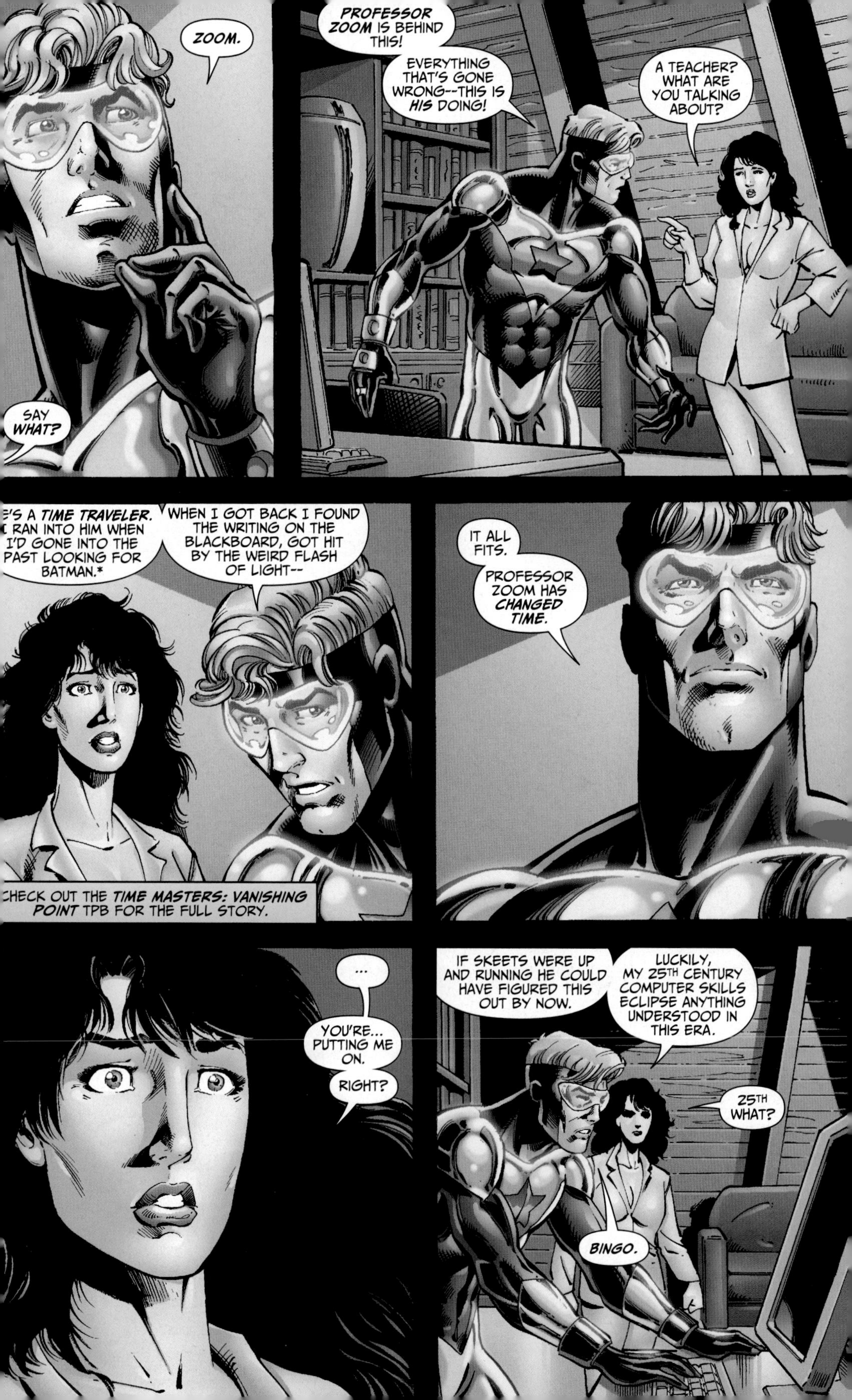

ZOOM.
SAY *WHAT?*
PROFESSOR ZOOM IS BEHIND THIS!
EVERYTHING THAT'S GONE WRONG--THIS IS *HIS* DOING!
A TEACHER? WHAT ARE YOU TALKING ABOUT?
'S A *TIME TRAVELER.* RAN INTO HIM WHEN I'D GONE INTO THE PAST LOOKING FOR BATMAN.*
WHEN I GOT BACK I FOUND THE WRITING ON THE BLACKBOARD, GOT HIT BY THE WEIRD FLASH OF LIGHT--
CHECK OUT THE *TIME MASTERS: VANISHING POINT* TPB FOR THE FULL STORY.
IT ALL FITS.
PROFESSOR ZOOM HAS *CHANGED TIME.*
...
YOU'RE... PUTTING ME ON.
RIGHT?
IF SKEETS WERE UP AND RUNNING HE COULD HAVE FIGURED THIS OUT BY NOW.
LUCKILY, MY 25TH CENTURY COMPUTER SKILLS ECLIPSE ANYTHING UNDERSTOOD IN THIS ERA.
25TH WHAT?
BINGO.

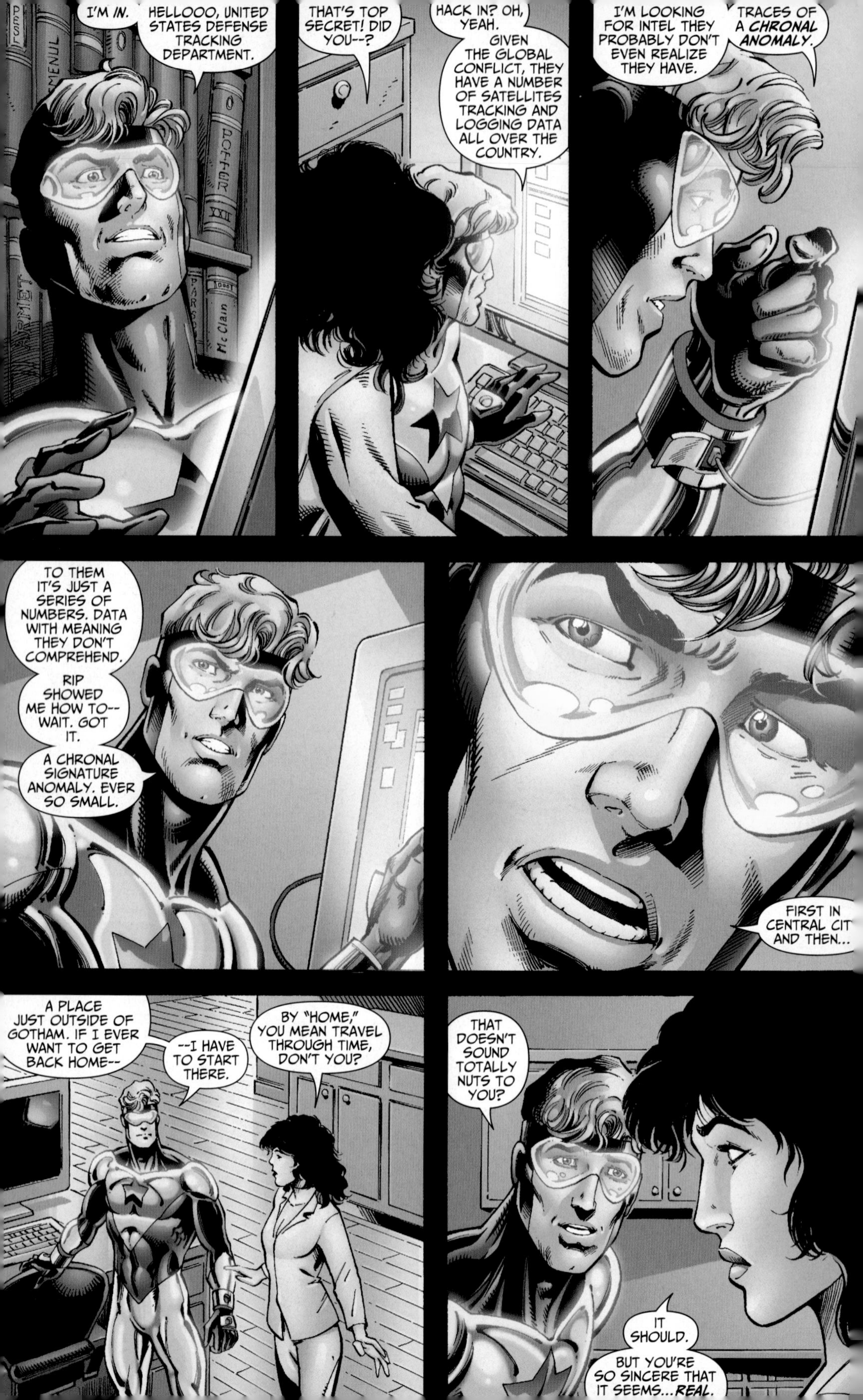
I'M *IN.*
HELLOOO, UNITED STATES DEFENSE TRACKING DEPARTMENT.
THAT'S TOP SECRET! DID YOU--?
HACK IN? OH, YEAH.
GIVEN THE GLOBAL CONFLICT, THEY HAVE A NUMBER OF SATELLITES TRACKING AND LOGGING DATA ALL OVER THE COUNTRY.
I'M LOOKING FOR INTEL THEY PROBABLY DON'T EVEN REALIZE THEY HAVE.
TRACES OF A ***CHRONAL ANOMALY.***
TO THEM IT'S JUST A SERIES OF NUMBERS. DATA WITH MEANING THEY DON'T COMPREHEND.
RIP SHOWED ME HOW TO-- WAIT. GOT IT.
A CHRONAL SIGNATURE ANOMALY. EVER SO SMALL.
FIRST IN CENTRAL CIT AND THEN...
A PLACE JUST OUTSIDE OF GOTHAM. IF I EVER WANT TO GET BACK HOME--
--I HAVE TO START THERE.
BY "HOME," YOU MEAN TRAVEL THROUGH TIME, DON'T YOU?
THAT DOESN'T SOUND TOTALLY NUTS TO YOU?
IT SHOULD.
BUT YOU'RE SO SINCERE THAT IT SEEMS... ***REAL.***

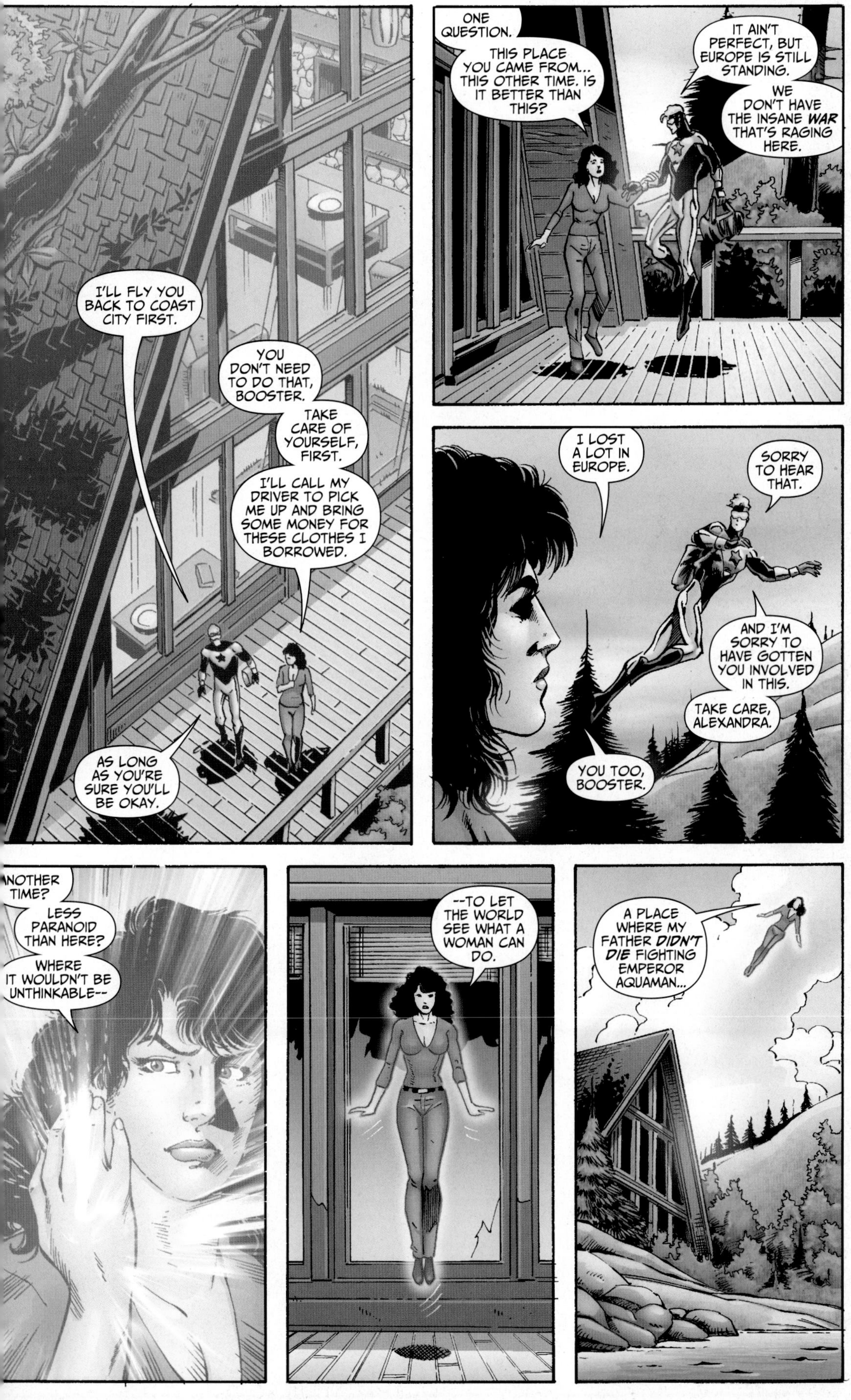
I'LL FLY YOU BACK TO COAST CITY FIRST.
YOU DON'T NEED TO DO THAT, BOOSTER.
TAKE CARE OF YOURSELF, FIRST.
I'LL CALL MY DRIVER TO PICK ME UP AND BRING SOME MONEY FOR THESE CLOTHES I BORROWED.
AS LONG AS YOU'RE SURE YOU'LL BE OKAY.
ONE QUESTION.
THIS PLACE YOU CAME FROM... THIS OTHER TIME. IS IT BETTER THAN THIS?
IT AIN'T PERFECT, BUT EUROPE IS STILL STANDING.
WE DON'T HAVE THE INSANE WAR THAT'S RAGING HERE.
I LOST A LOT IN EUROPE.
SORRY TO HEAR THAT.
AND I'M SORRY TO HAVE GOTTEN YOU INVOLVED IN THIS.
TAKE CARE, ALEXANDRA.
YOU TOO, BOOSTER.
NOTHER TIME?
LESS PARANOID THAN HERE?
WHERE IT WOULDN'T BE UNTHINKABLE--
--TO LET THE WORLD SEE WHAT A WOMAN CAN DO.
A PLACE WHERE MY FATHER DIDN'T DIE FIGHTING EMPEROR AQUAMAN...

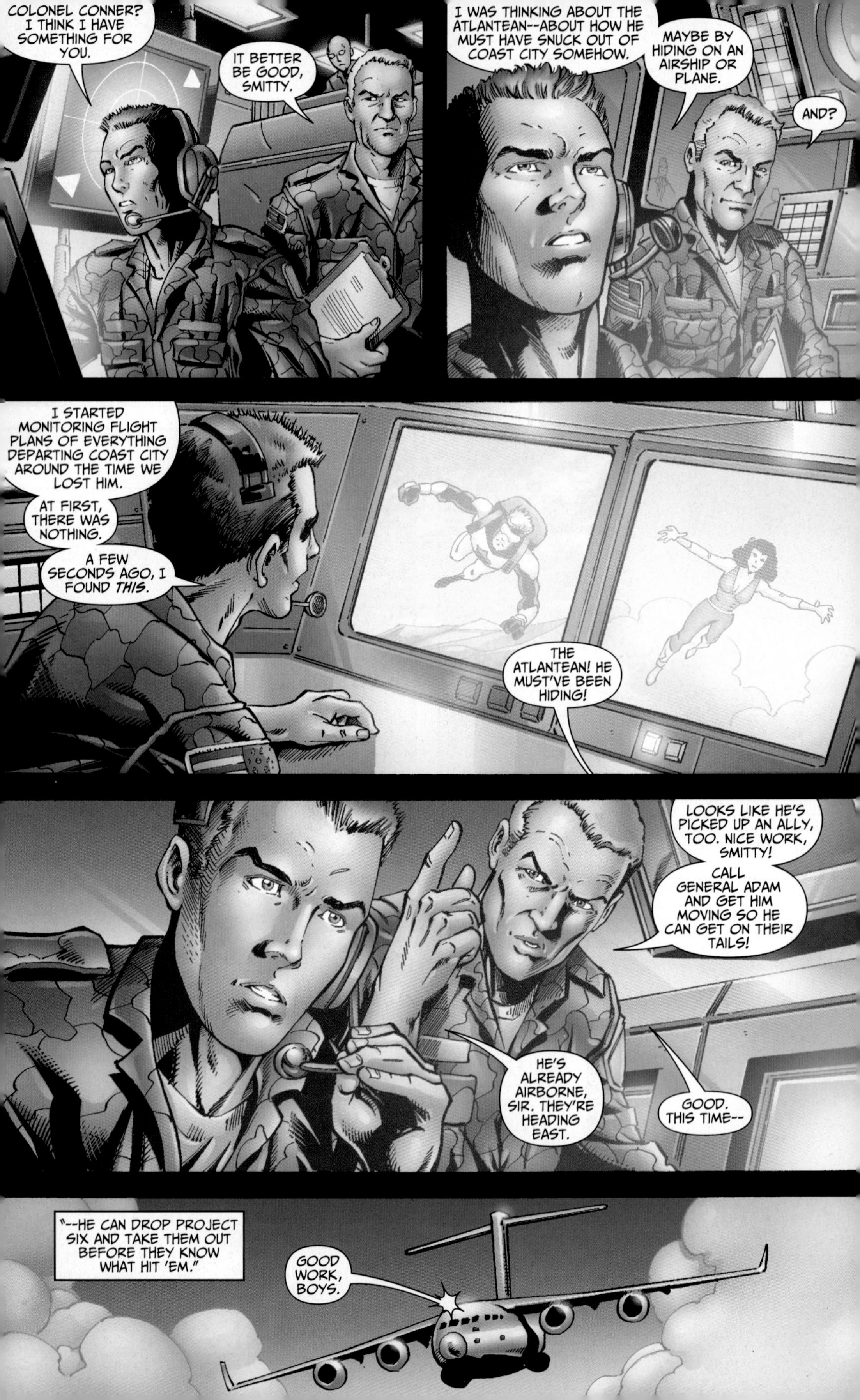
COLONEL CONNER? I THINK I HAVE SOMETHING FOR YOU.
IT BETTER BE GOOD, SMITTY.
I WAS THINKING ABOUT THE ATLANTEAN--ABOUT HOW HE MUST HAVE SNUCK OUT OF COAST CITY SOMEHOW.
MAYBE BY HIDING ON AN AIRSHIP OR PLANE.
AND?
I STARTED MONITORING FLIGHT PLANS OF EVERYTHING DEPARTING COAST CITY AROUND THE TIME WE LOST HIM.
AT FIRST, THERE WAS NOTHING.
A FEW SECONDS AGO, I FOUND *THIS*.
THE ATLANTEAN! HE MUST'VE BEEN HIDING!
LOOKS LIKE HE'S PICKED UP AN ALLY, TOO. NICE WORK, SMITTY!
CALL GENERAL ADAM AND GET HIM MOVING SO HE CAN GET ON THEIR TAILS!
HE'S ALREADY AIRBORNE, SIR. THEY'RE HEADING EAST.
GOOD. THIS TIME--
"--HE CAN DROP PROJECT SIX AND TAKE THEM OUT BEFORE THEY KNOW WHAT HIT 'EM."
GOOD WORK, BOYS.

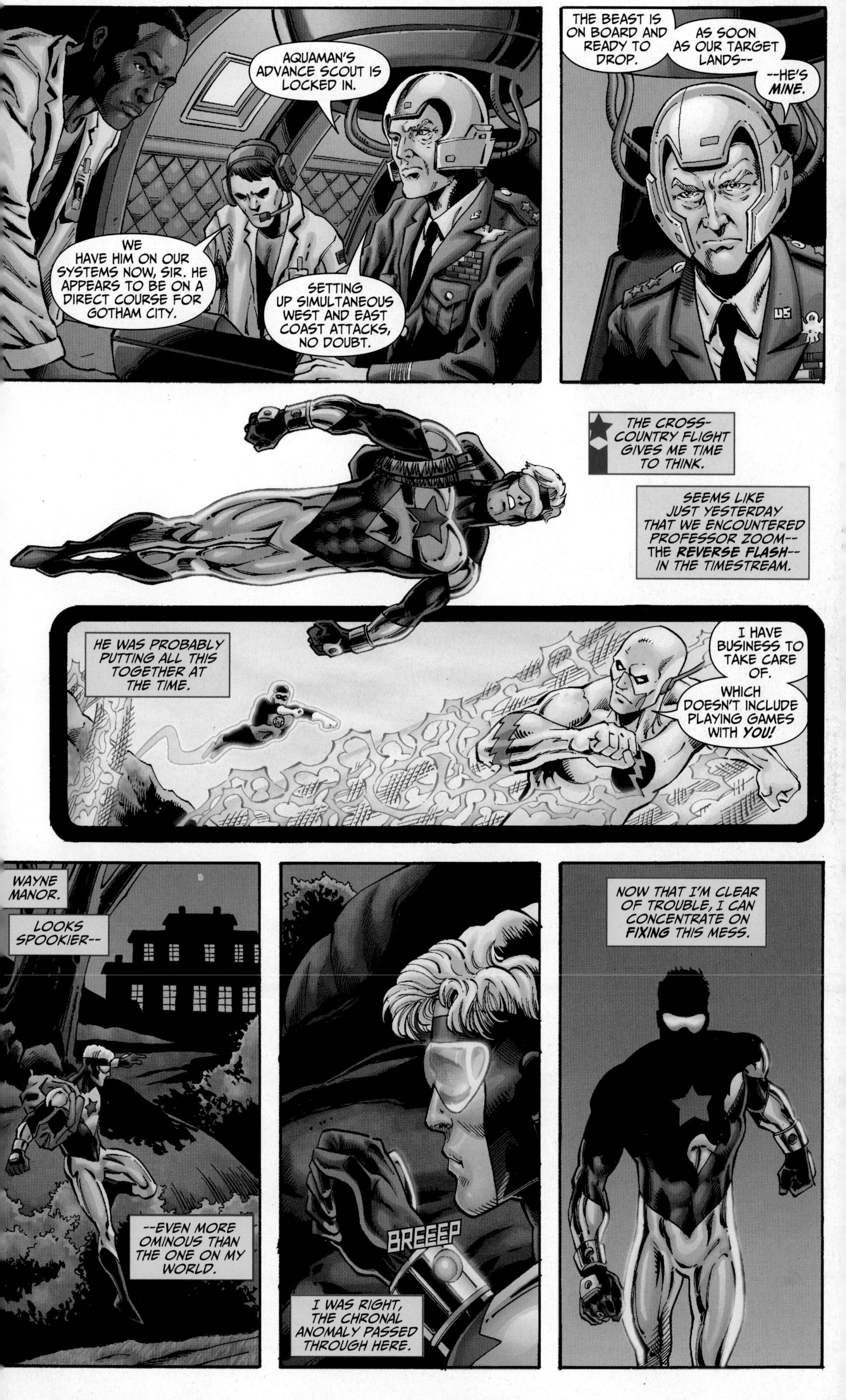
AQUAMAN'S ADVANCE SCOUT IS LOCKED IN.
WE HAVE HIM ON OUR SYSTEMS NOW, SIR. HE APPEARS TO BE ON A DIRECT COURSE FOR GOTHAM CITY.
SETTING UP SIMULTANEOUS WEST AND EAST COAST ATTACKS, NO DOUBT.
THE BEAST IS ON BOARD AND READY TO DROP.
AS SOON AS OUR TARGET LANDS--
--HE'S MINE.
THE CROSS-COUNTRY FLIGHT GIVES ME TIME TO THINK.
SEEMS LIKE JUST YESTERDAY THAT WE ENCOUNTERED PROFESSOR ZOOM-- THE REVERSE FLASH-- IN THE TIMESTREAM.
HE WAS PROBABLY PUTTING ALL THIS TOGETHER AT THE TIME.
I HAVE BUSINESS TO TAKE CARE OF.
WHICH DOESN'T INCLUDE PLAYING GAMES WITH YOU!
WAYNE MANOR.
LOOKS SPOOKIER--
--EVEN MORE OMINOUS THAN THE ONE ON MY WORLD.
BREEEP
I WAS RIGHT, THE CHRONAL ANOMALY PASSED THROUGH HERE.
NOW THAT I'M CLEAR OF TROUBLE, I CAN CONCENTRATE ON FIXING THIS MESS.

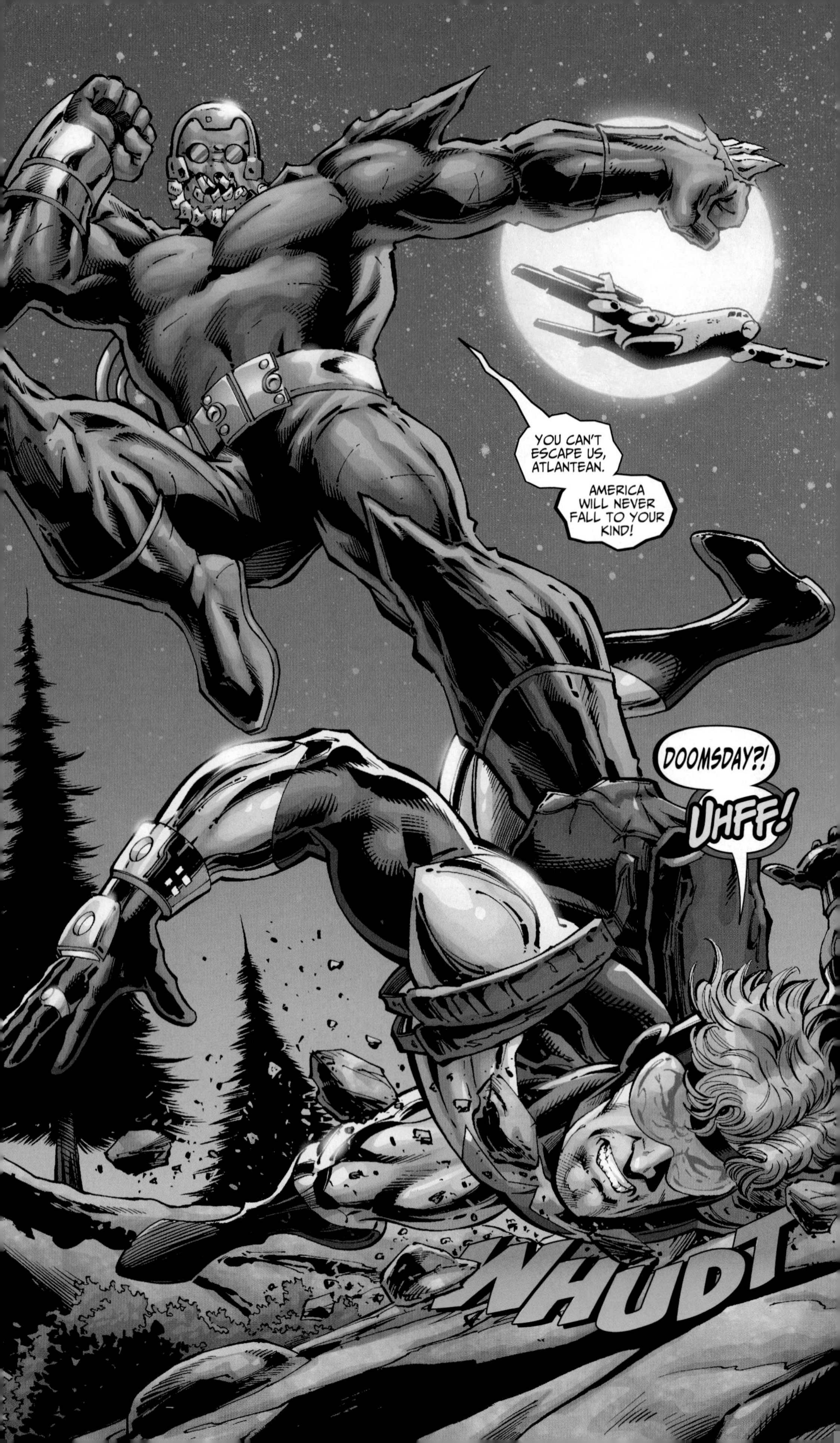

YOU CAN'T ESCAPE US, ATLANTEAN.
AMERICA WILL NEVER FALL TO YOUR KIND!
DOOMSDAY?!
UHFF!
WHUDT

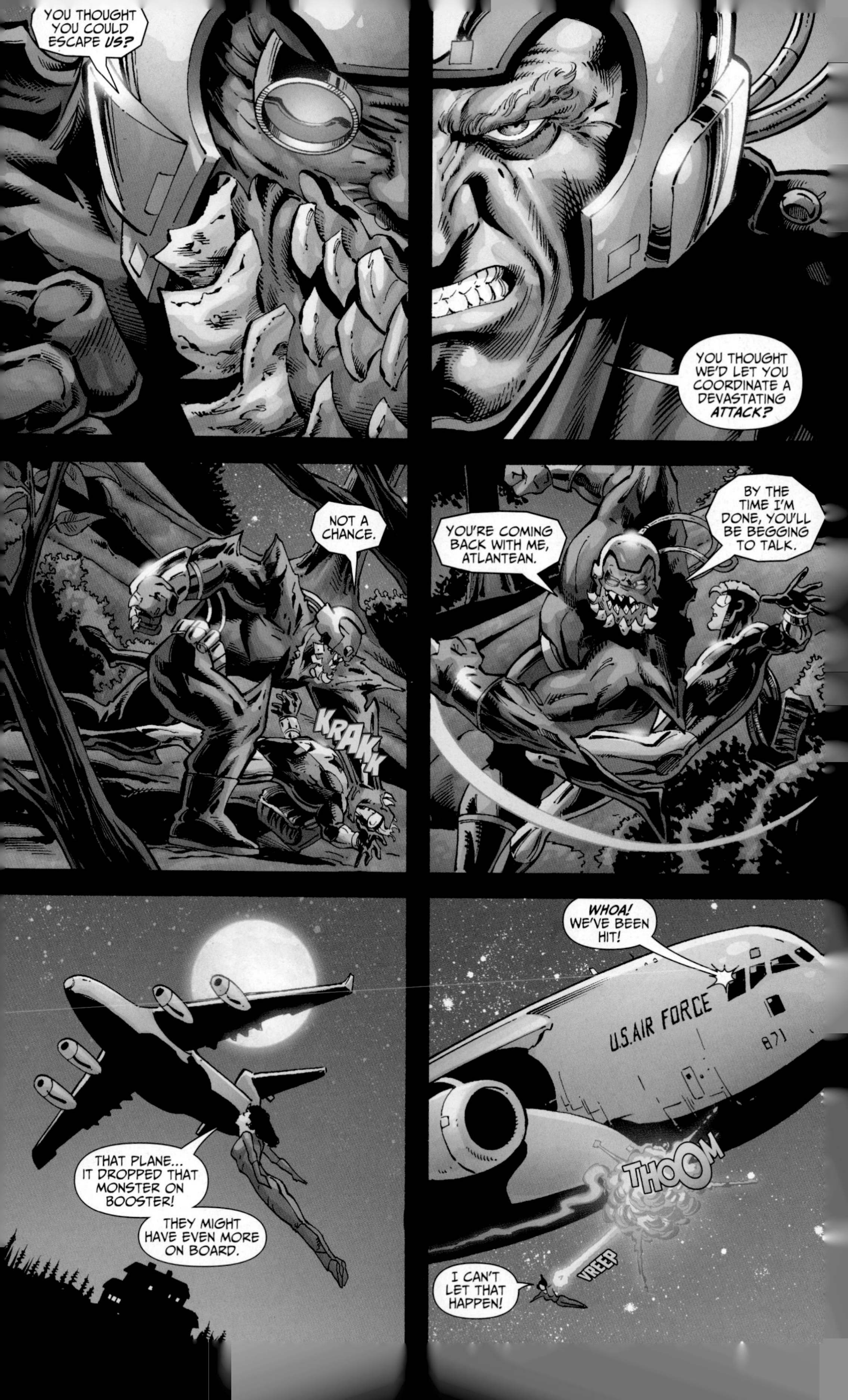
YOU THOUGHT YOU COULD ESCAPE *US?*
YOU THOUGHT WE'D LET YOU COORDINATE A DEVASTATING *ATTACK?*
NOT A CHANCE.
KRAKK
YOU'RE COMING BACK WITH ME, ATLANTEAN.
BY THE TIME I'M DONE, YOU'LL BE BEGGING TO TALK.
THAT PLANE... IT DROPPED THAT MONSTER ON BOOSTER!
THEY MIGHT HAVE EVEN MORE ON BOARD.
WHOA! WE'VE BEEN HIT!
U.S. AIR FORCE
871
THOOM
VREEP
I CAN'T LET THAT HAPPEN!

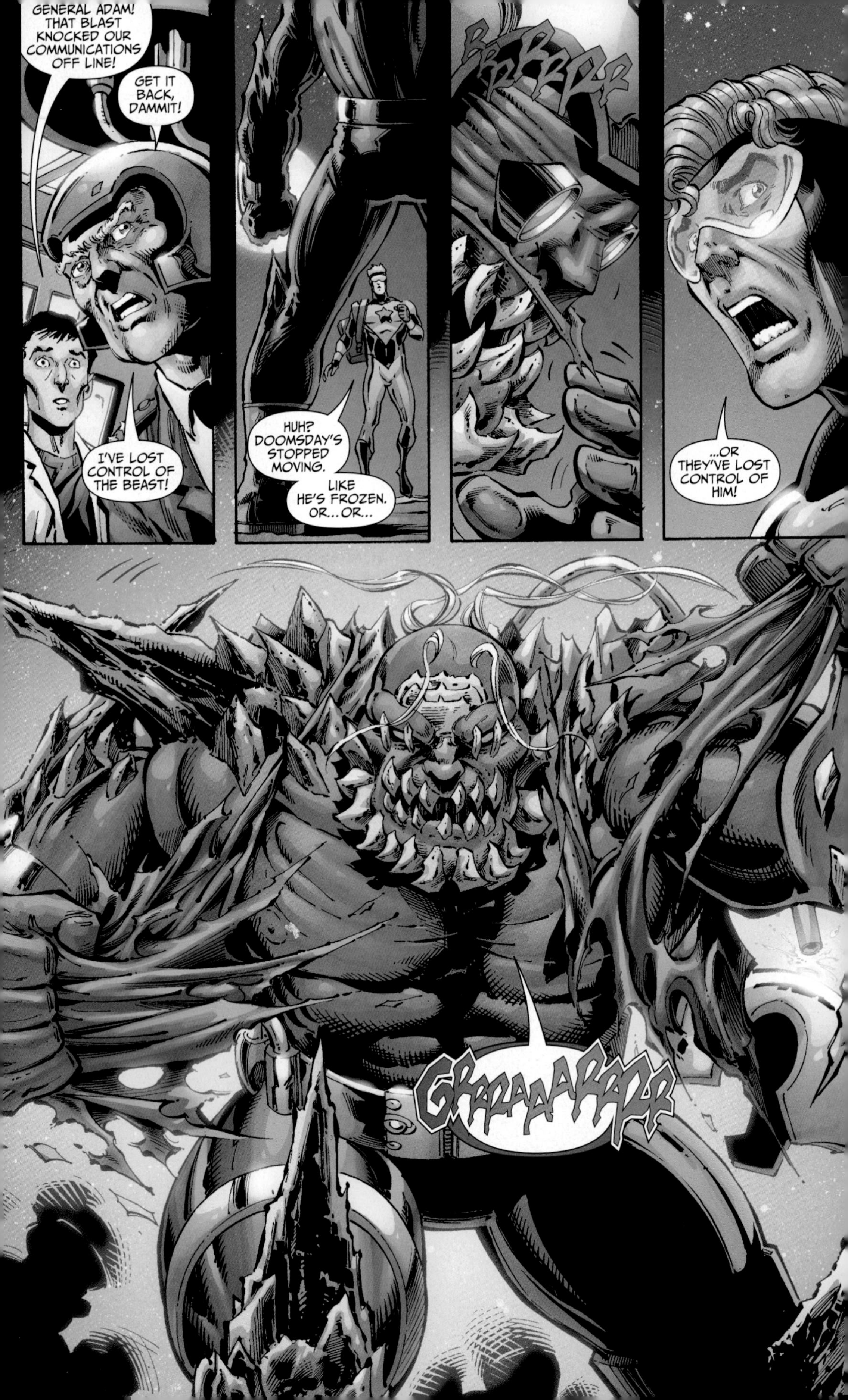
GENERAL ADAM! THAT BLAST KNOCKED OUR COMMUNICATIONS OFF LINE!
GET IT BACK, DAMMIT!
I'VE LOST CONTROL OF THE BEAST!
HUH? DOOMSDAY'S STOPPED MOVING.
LIKE HE'S FROZEN. OR...OR...
BRZRRRZRR
...OR THEY'VE LOST CONTROL OF HIM!
GRAAARRRR

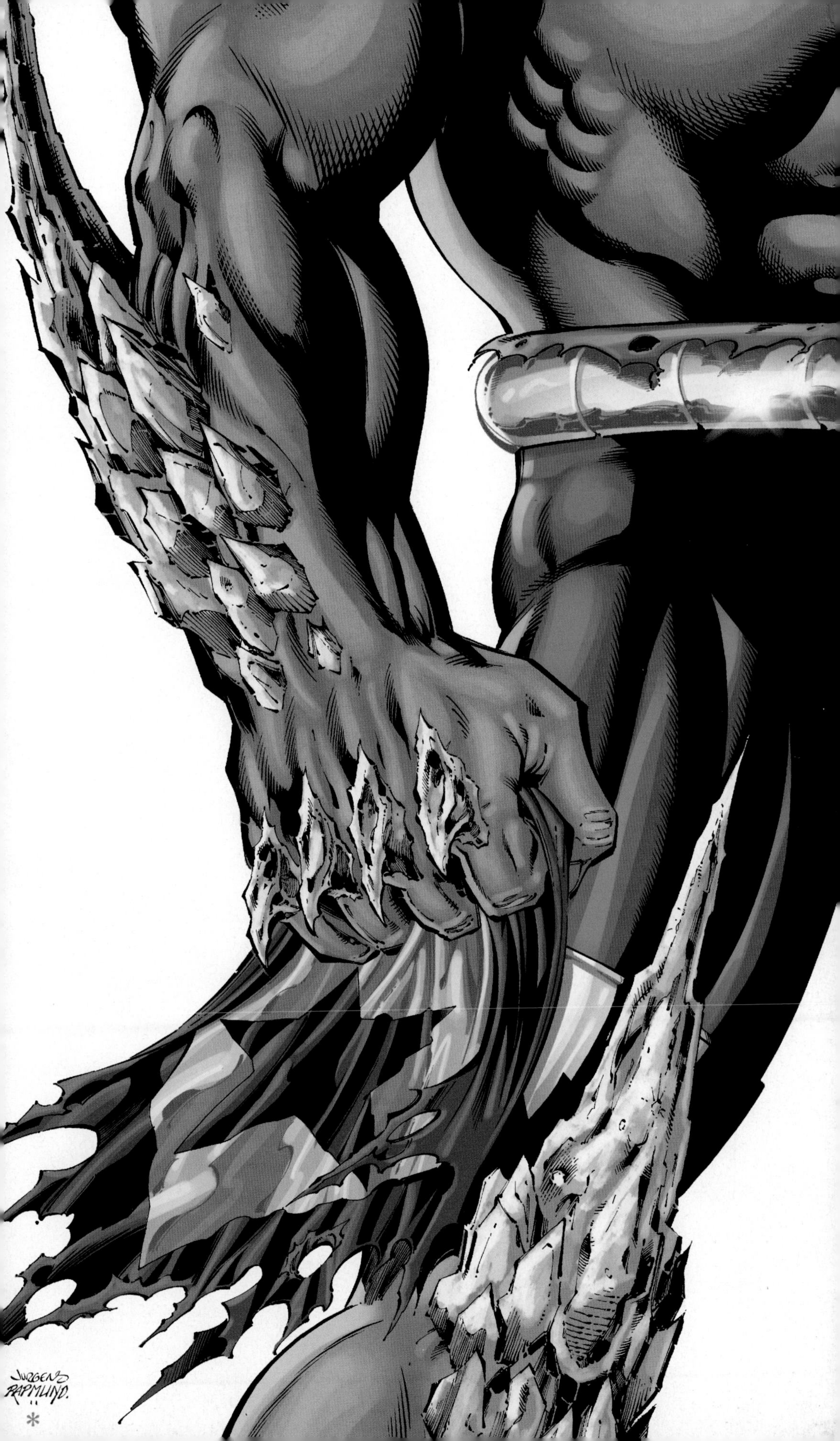
JURGENS
RAPMUND.

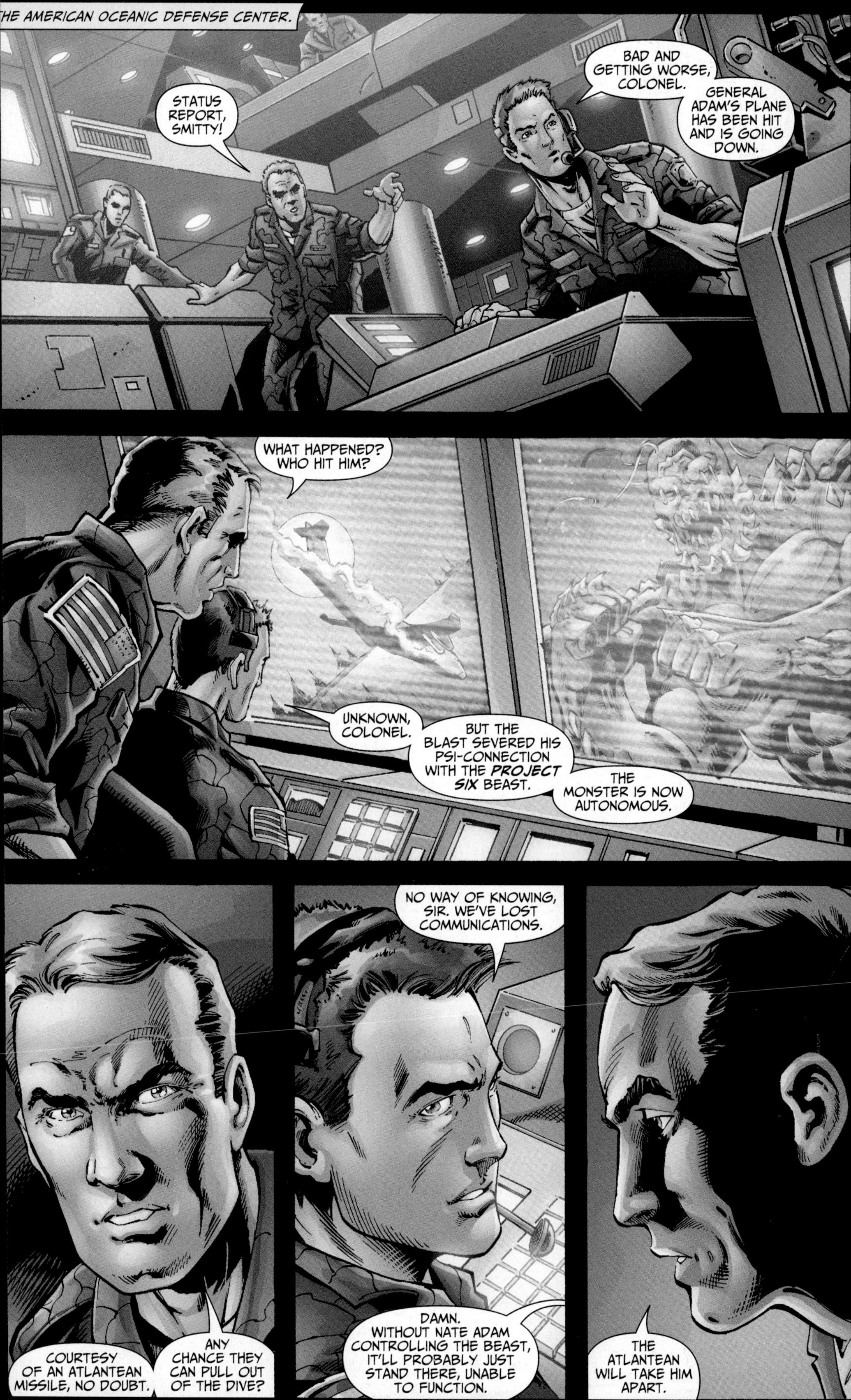
THE AMERICAN OCEANIC DEFENSE CENTER.
STATUS REPORT, SMITTY!
BAD AND GETTING WORSE, COLONEL.
GENERAL ADAM'S PLANE HAS BEEN HIT AND IS GOING DOWN.
WHAT HAPPENED? WHO HIT HIM?
UNKNOWN, COLONEL.
BUT THE BLAST SEVERED HIS PSI-CONNECTION WITH THE PROJECT SIX BEAST.
THE MONSTER IS NOW AUTONOMOUS.
COURTESY OF AN ATLANTEAN MISSILE, NO DOUBT.
ANY CHANCE THEY CAN PULL OUT OF THE DIVE?
NO WAY OF KNOWING, SIR. WE'VE LOST COMMUNICATIONS.
DAMN. WITHOUT NATE ADAM CONTROLLING THE BEAST, IT'LL PROBABLY JUST STAND THERE, UNABLE TO FUNCTION.
THE ATLANTEAN WILL TAKE HIM APART.

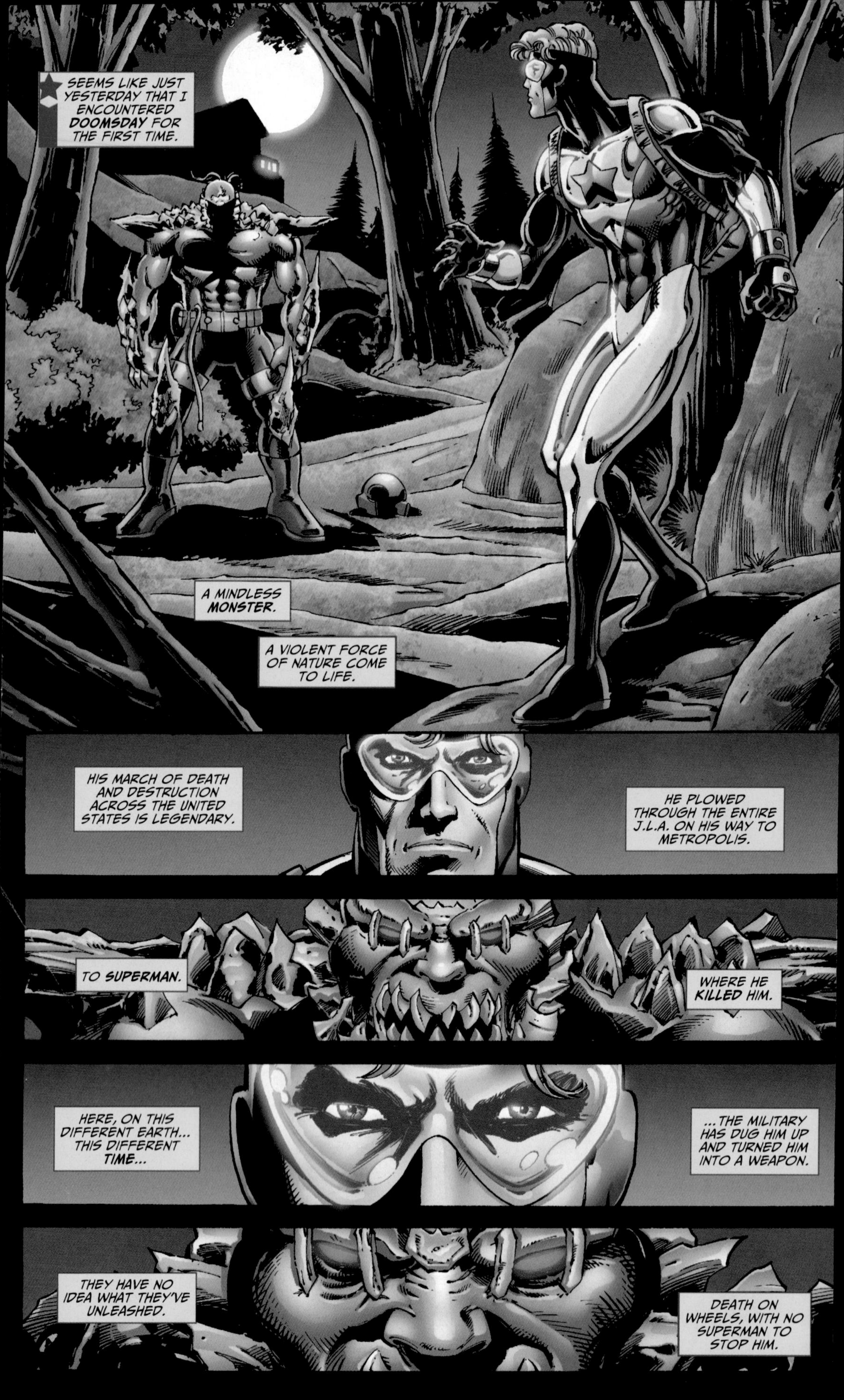
SEEMS LIKE JUST YESTERDAY THAT I ENCOUNTERED DOOMSDAY FOR THE FIRST TIME.
A MINDLESS MONSTER.
A VIOLENT FORCE OF NATURE COME TO LIFE.
HIS MARCH OF DEATH AND DESTRUCTION ACROSS THE UNITED STATES IS LEGENDARY.
HE PLOWED THROUGH THE ENTIRE J.L.A. ON HIS WAY TO METROPOLIS.
TO SUPERMAN.
WHERE HE KILLED HIM.
HERE, ON THIS DIFFERENT EARTH... THIS DIFFERENT TIME...
...THE MILITARY HAS DUG HIM UP AND TURNED HIM INTO A WEAPON.
THEY HAVE NO IDEA WHAT THEY'VE UNLEASHED.
DEATH ON WHEELS, WITH NO SUPERMAN TO STOP HIM.

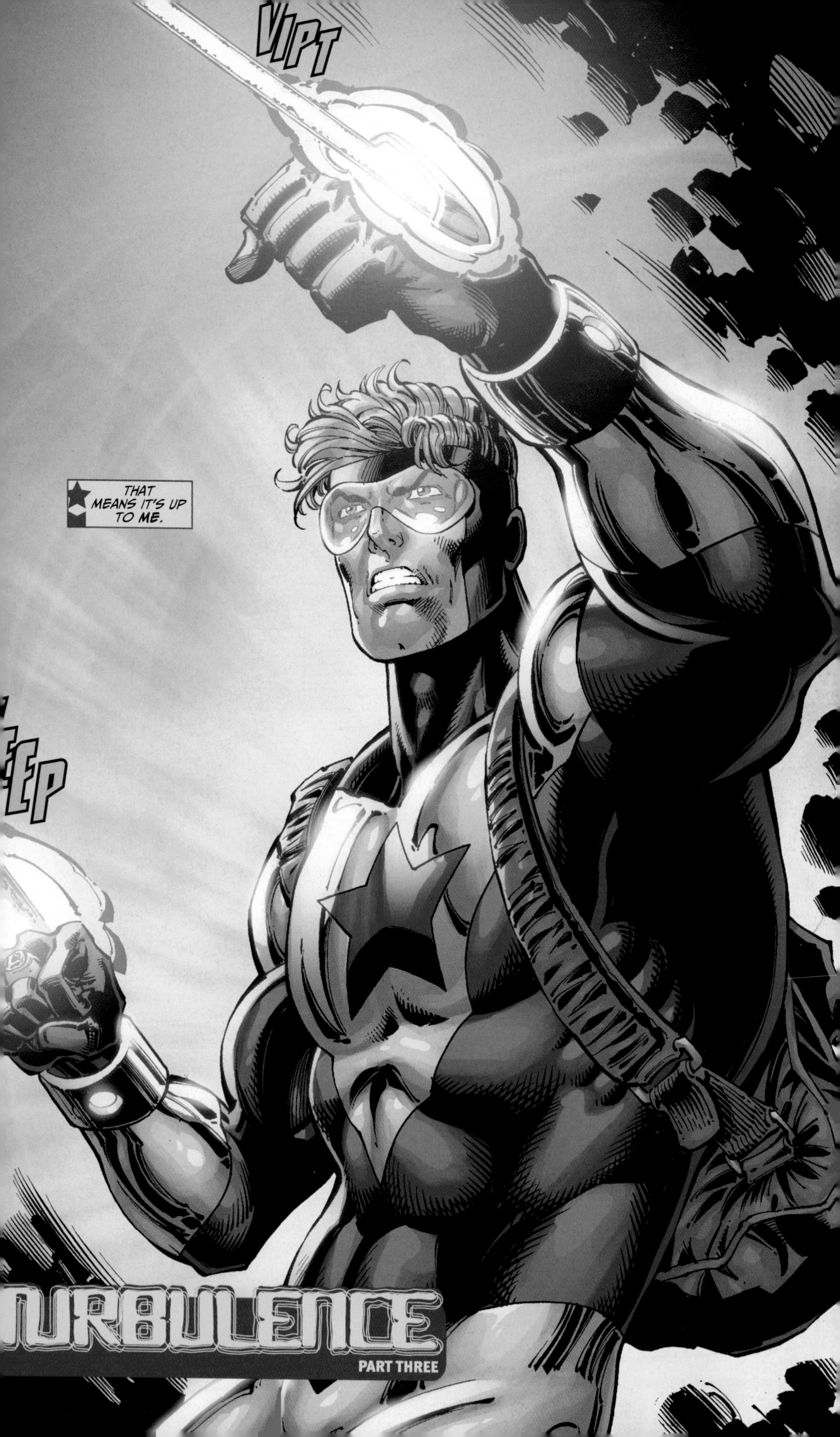
VIPT
THAT MEANS IT'S UP TO ME.
EEP
URBULENCE
PART THREE

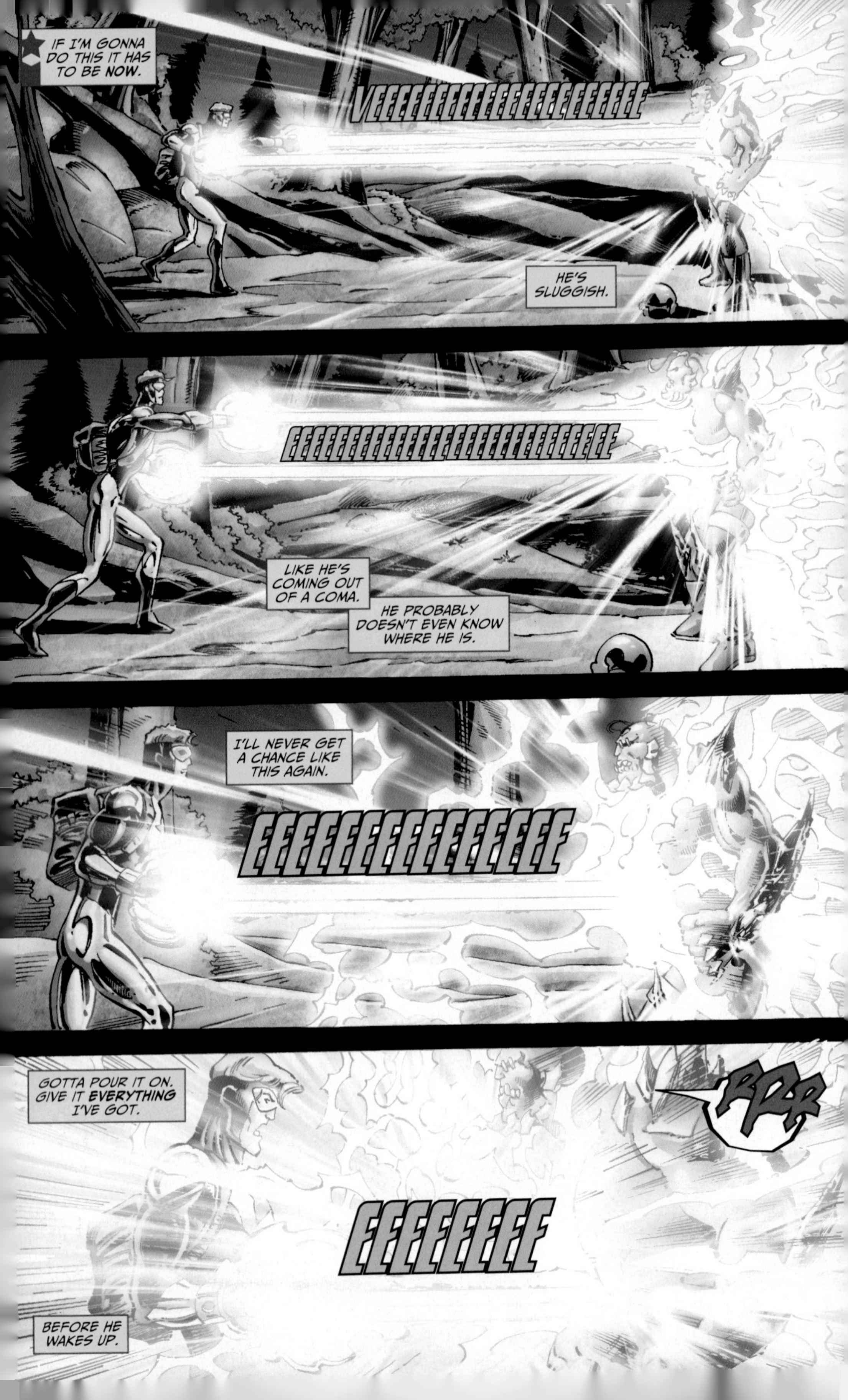
IF I'M GONNA DO THIS IT HAS TO BE NOW.
VEEEEEEEEEEEEEEEEEEEEE
HE'S SLUGGISH.
EEEEEEEEEEEEEEEEEEEEEEEEEEEEE
LIKE HE'S COMING OUT OF A COMA.
HE PROBABLY DOESN'T EVEN KNOW WHERE HE IS.
I'LL NEVER GET A CHANCE LIKE THIS AGAIN.
EEEEEEEEEEEEEEEE
GOTTA POUR IT ON. GIVE IT EVERYTHING I'VE GOT.
RRR
EEEEEEEE
BEFORE HE WAKES UP.

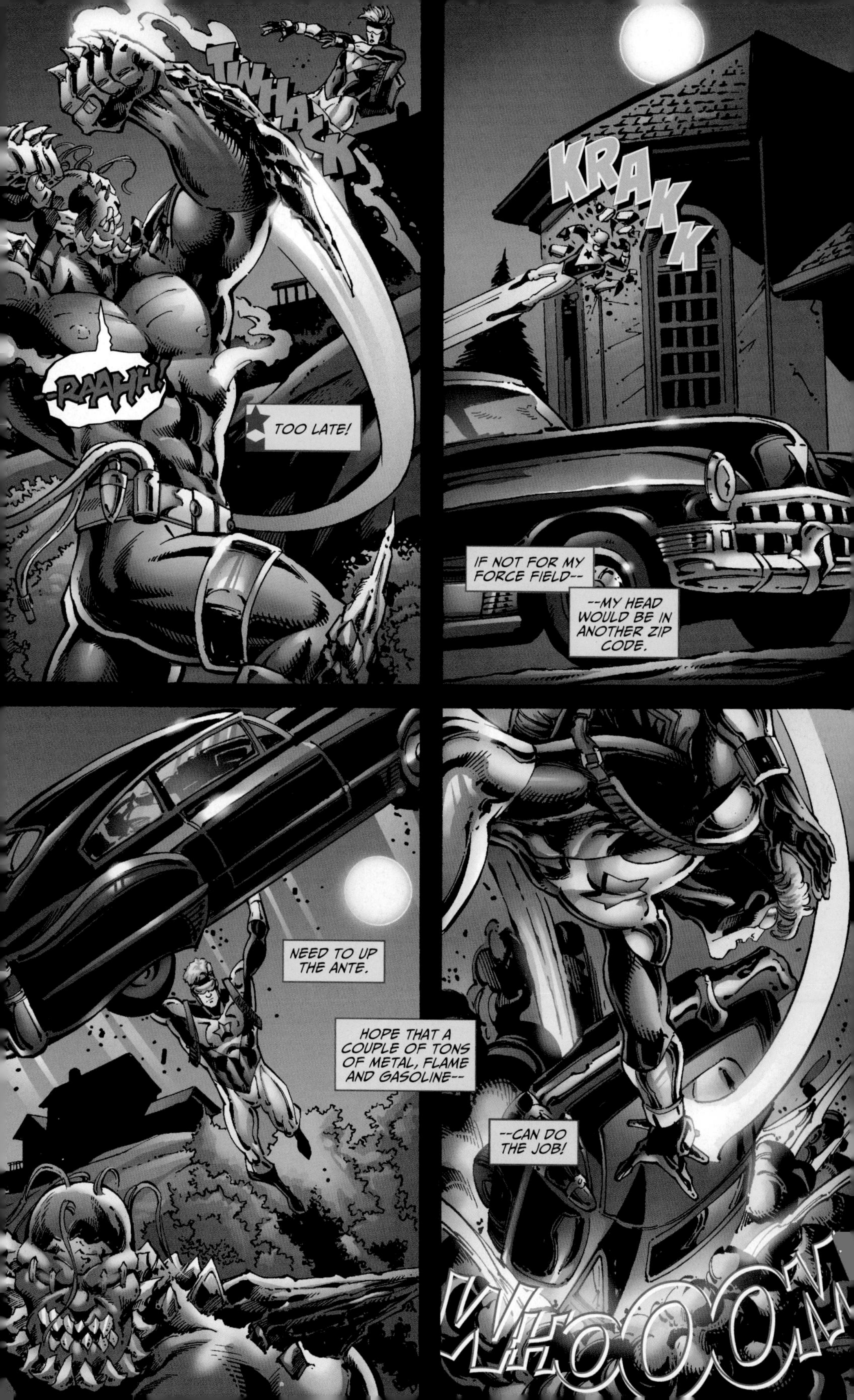

TWHACK
RAAHH!
TOO LATE!
KRAKK
IF NOT FOR MY FORCE FIELD--
--MY HEAD WOULD BE IN ANOTHER ZIP CODE.
NEED TO UP THE ANTE.
HOPE THAT A COUPLE OF TONS OF METAL, FLAME AND GASOLINE--
--CAN DO THE JOB!
WHOOOOM

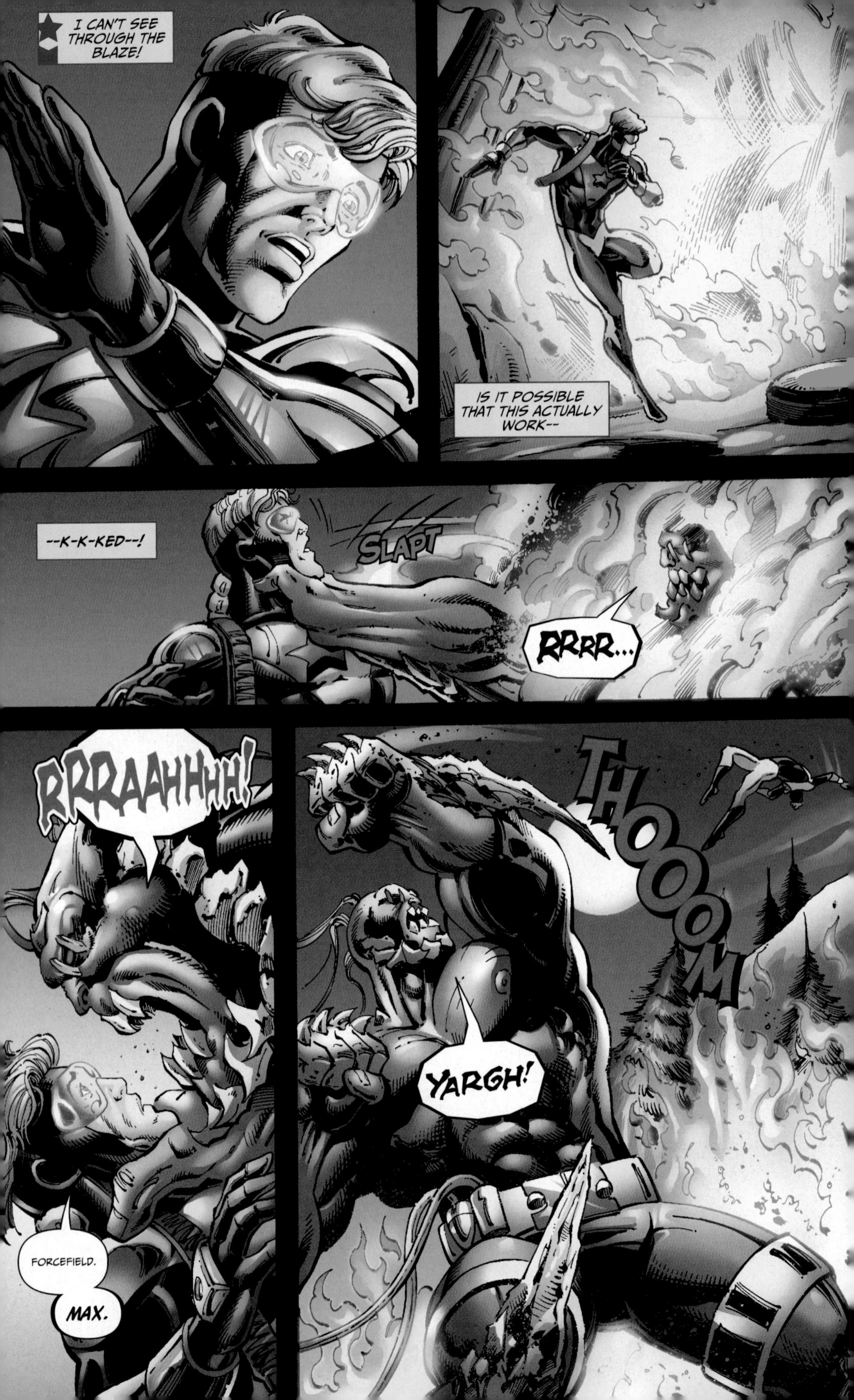
I CAN'T SEE THROUGH THE BLAZE!
IS IT POSSIBLE THAT THIS ACTUALLY WORK--
--K-K-KED--!
SLAPT
RRRR...
RRRAAHHHH!
FORCEFIELD.
MAX.
THOOOOM
YARGH!

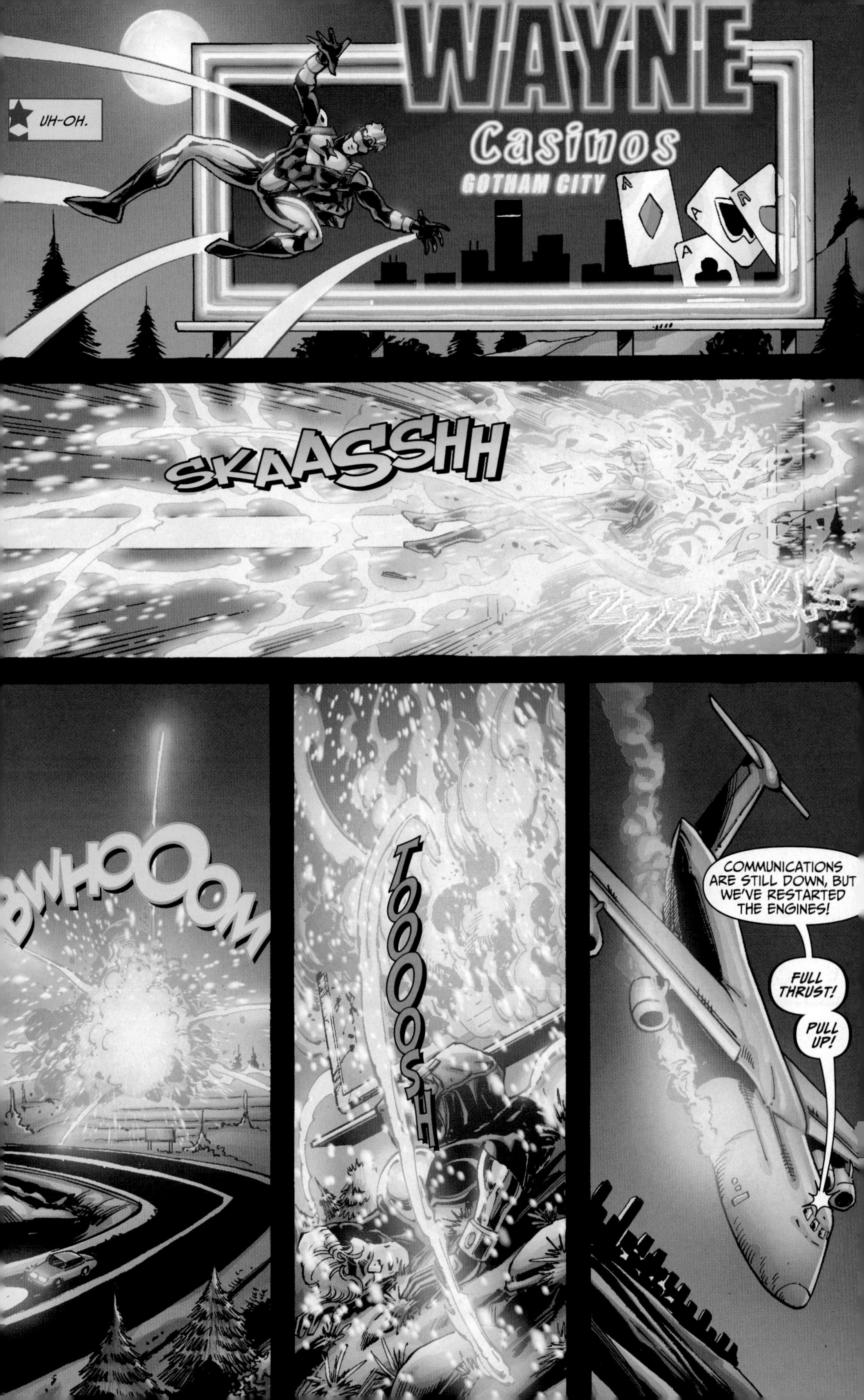
WAYNE
Casinos
GOTHAM CITY
UH-OH.
SKAASSHH
ZZZAKK
BWHOOOOM
TOOOOOSH
COMMUNICATIONS ARE STILL DOWN, BUT WE'VE RESTARTED THE ENGINES!
FULL THRUST!
PULL UP!

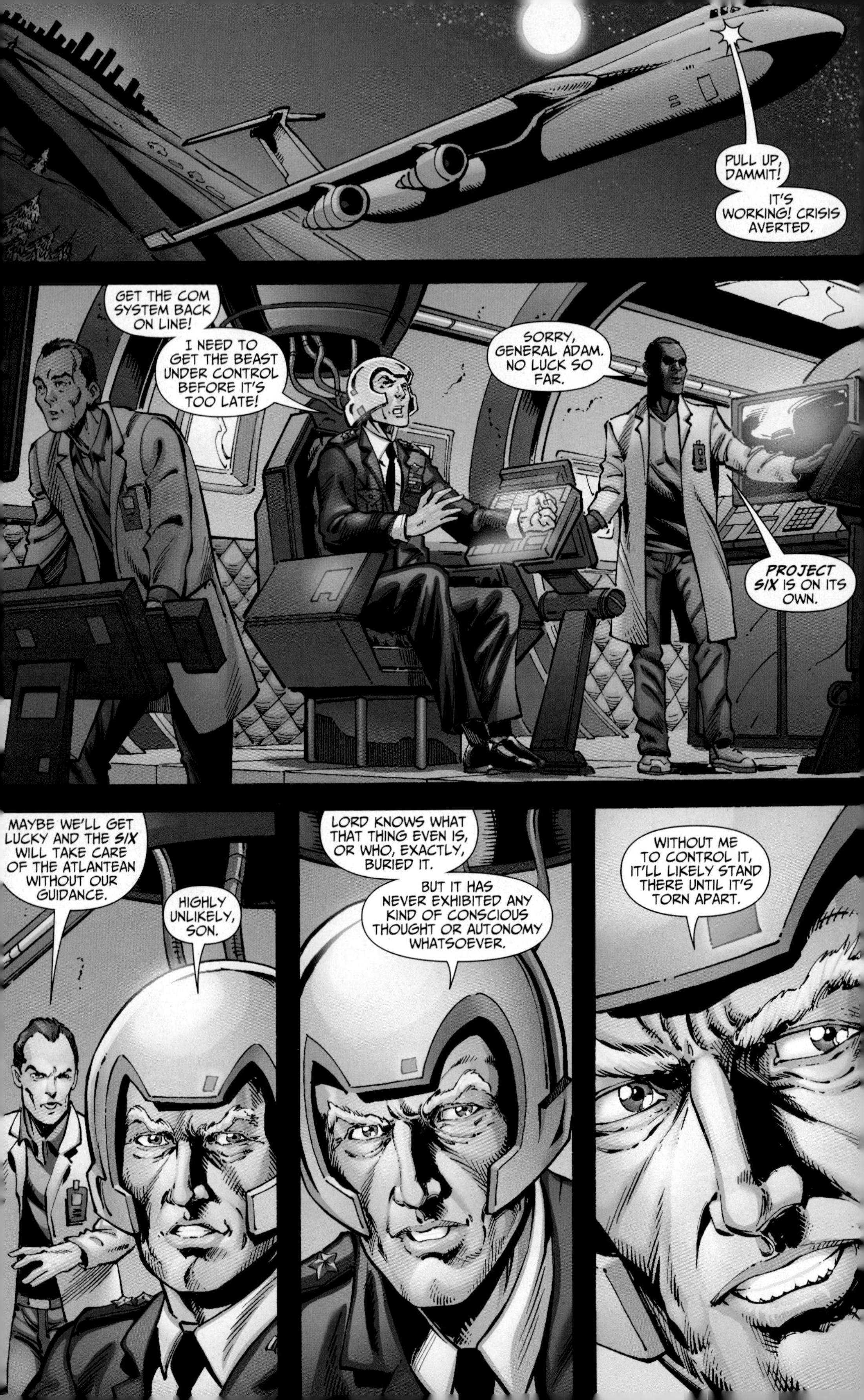
PULL UP, DAMMIT!
IT'S WORKING! CRISIS AVERTED.
GET THE COM SYSTEM BACK ON LINE!
I NEED TO GET THE BEAST UNDER CONTROL BEFORE IT'S TOO LATE!
SORRY, GENERAL ADAM. NO LUCK SO FAR.
PROJECT SIX IS ON ITS OWN.
MAYBE WE'LL GET LUCKY AND THE SIX WILL TAKE CARE OF THE ATLANTEAN WITHOUT OUR GUIDANCE.
HIGHLY UNLIKELY, SON.
LORD KNOWS WHAT THAT THING EVEN IS, OR WHO, EXACTLY, BURIED IT.
BUT IT HAS NEVER EXHIBITED ANY KIND OF CONSCIOUS THOUGHT OR AUTONOMY WHATSOEVER.
WITHOUT ME TO CONTROL IT, IT'LL LIKELY STAND THERE UNTIL IT'S TORN APART.

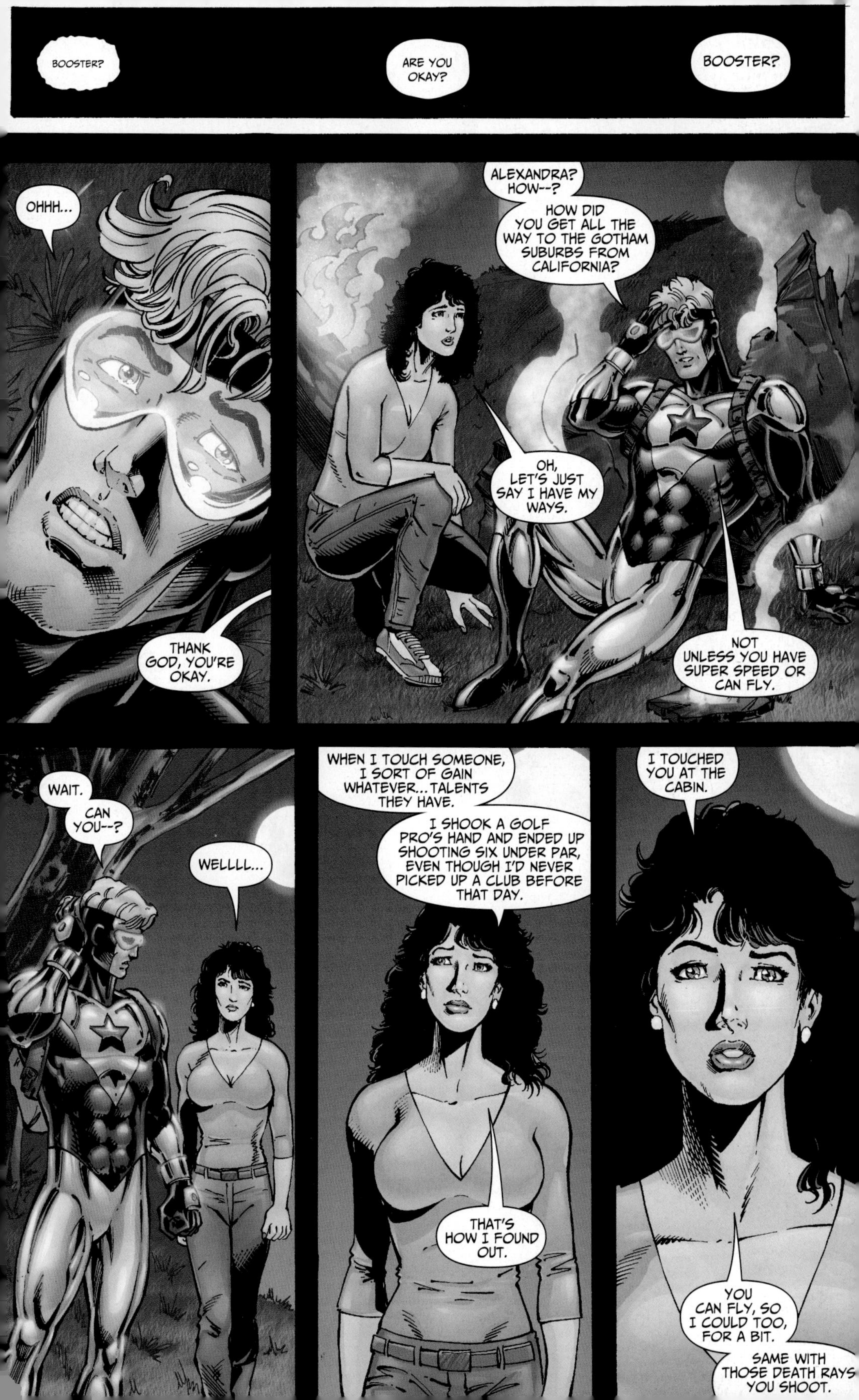
BOOSTER?
ARE YOU OKAY?
BOOSTER?
OHHH...
THANK GOD, YOU'RE OKAY.
ALEXANDRA? HOW--?
HOW DID YOU GET ALL THE WAY TO THE GOTHAM SUBURBS FROM CALIFORNIA?
OH, LET'S JUST SAY I HAVE MY WAYS.
NOT UNLESS YOU HAVE SUPER SPEED OR CAN FLY.
WAIT.
CAN YOU--?
WELLLL...
WHEN I TOUCH SOMEONE, I SORT OF GAIN WHATEVER...TALENTS THEY HAVE.
I SHOOK A GOLF PRO'S HAND AND ENDED UP SHOOTING SIX UNDER PAR, EVEN THOUGH I'D NEVER PICKED UP A CLUB BEFORE THAT DAY.
THAT'S HOW I FOUND OUT.
I TOUCHED YOU AT THE CABIN.
YOU CAN FLY, SO I COULD TOO, FOR A BIT.
SAME WITH THOSE DEATH RAYS YOU SHOOT.

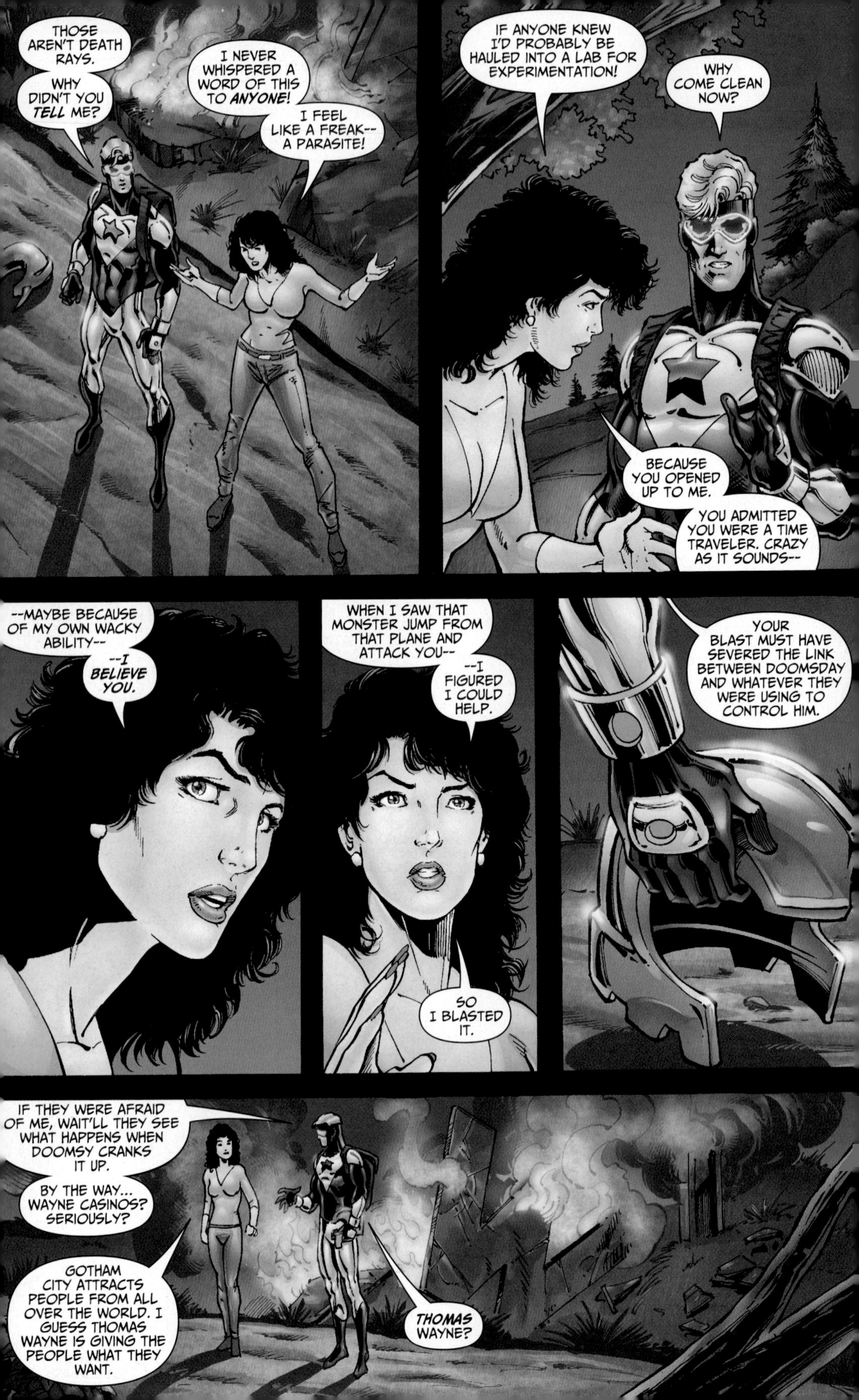
THOSE AREN'T DEATH RAYS.
WHY DIDN'T YOU *TELL* ME?
I NEVER WHISPERED A WORD OF THIS TO *ANYONE*!
I FEEL LIKE A FREAK-- A PARASITE!
IF ANYONE KNEW I'D PROBABLY BE HAULED INTO A LAB FOR EXPERIMENTATION!
WHY COME CLEAN NOW?
BECAUSE YOU OPENED UP TO ME.
YOU ADMITTED YOU WERE A TIME TRAVELER. CRAZY AS IT SOUNDS--
--MAYBE BECAUSE OF MY OWN WACKY ABILITY--
--I *BELIEVE YOU.*
WHEN I SAW THAT MONSTER JUMP FROM THAT PLANE AND ATTACK YOU--
--I FIGURED I COULD HELP.
SO I BLASTED IT.
YOUR BLAST MUST HAVE SEVERED THE LINK BETWEEN DOOMSDAY AND WHATEVER THEY WERE USING TO CONTROL HIM.
IF THEY WERE AFRAID OF ME, WAIT'LL THEY SEE WHAT HAPPENS WHEN DOOMSY CRANKS IT UP.
BY THE WAY... WAYNE CASINOS? SERIOUSLY?
GOTHAM CITY ATTRACTS PEOPLE FROM ALL OVER THE WORLD. I GUESS THOMAS WAYNE IS GIVING THE PEOPLE WHAT THEY WANT.
THOMAS WAYNE?

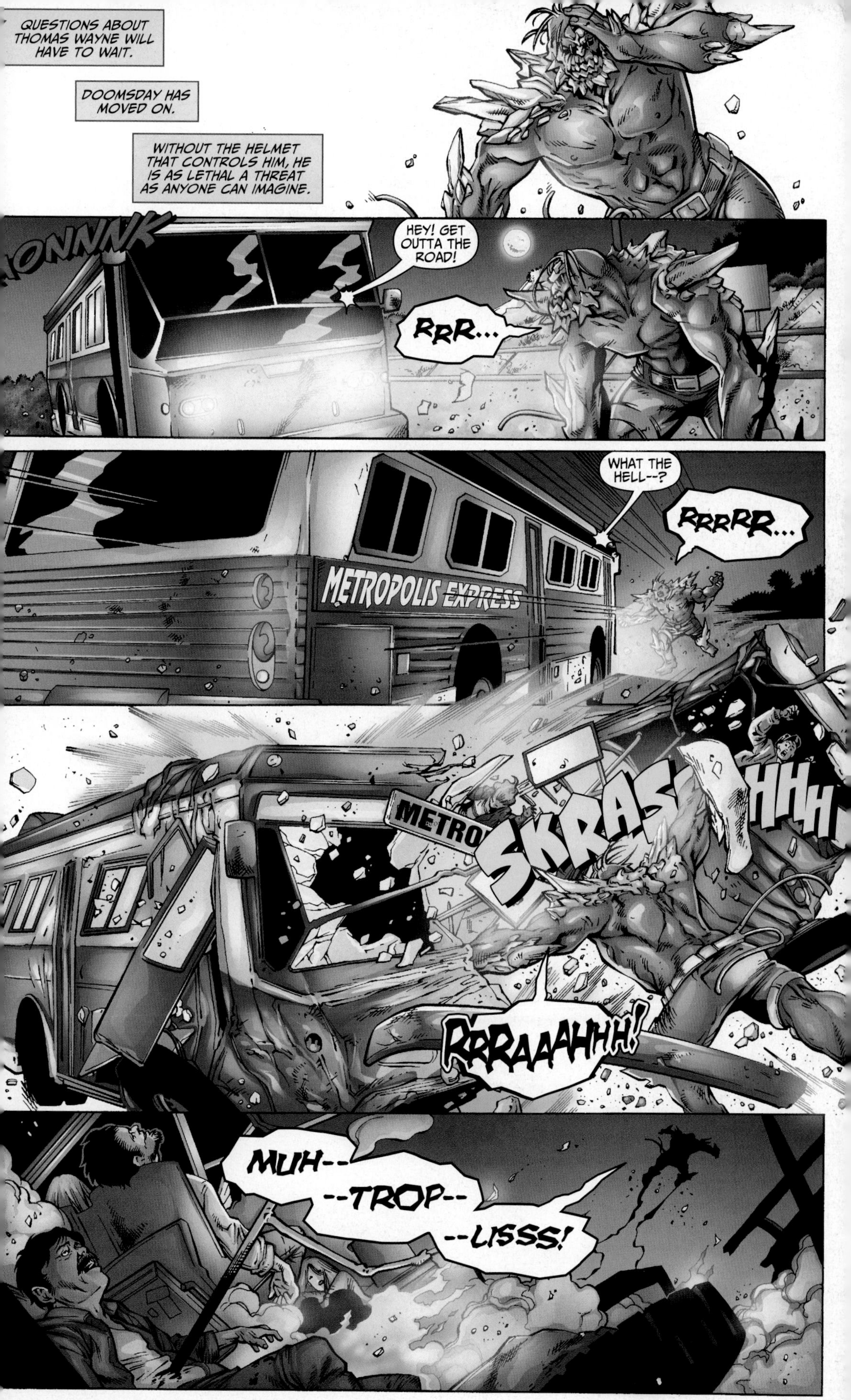
QUESTIONS ABOUT THOMAS WAYNE WILL HAVE TO WAIT.
DOOMSDAY HAS MOVED ON.
WITHOUT THE HELMET THAT CONTROLS HIM, HE IS AS LETHAL A THREAT AS ANYONE CAN IMAGINE.
HONNNK
HEY! GET OUTTA THE ROAD!
RRR...
WHAT THE HELL--?
RRRRR...
METROPOLIS EXPRESS
METRO
SKRASHHHH
RRRAAAHHH!
MUH--
--TROP--
--LISSS!

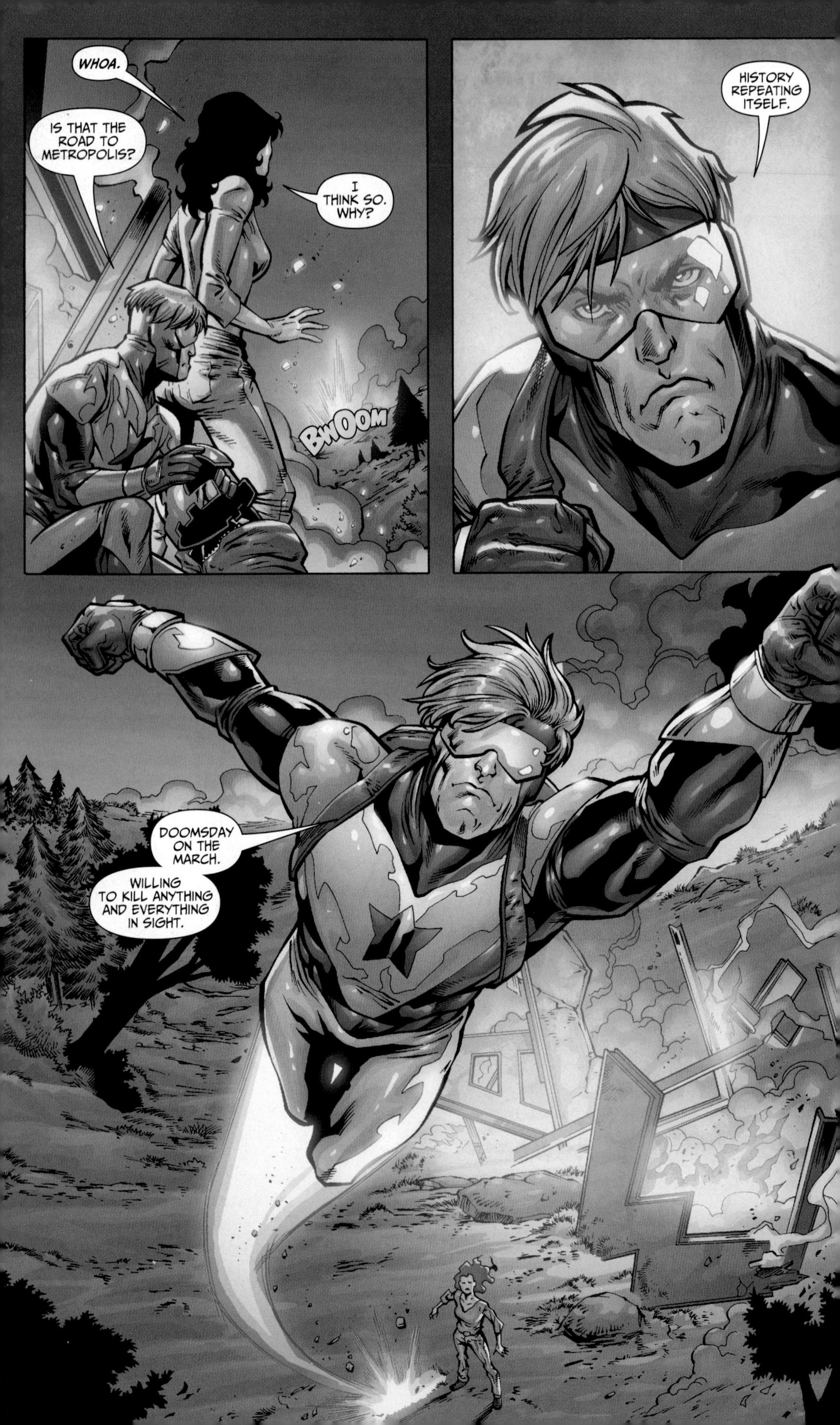
WHOA.
IS THAT THE ROAD TO METROPOLIS?
I THINK SO. WHY?
BWOOM
HISTORY REPEATING ITSELF.
DOOMSDAY ON THE MARCH.
WILLING TO KILL ANYTHING AND EVERYTHING IN SIGHT.

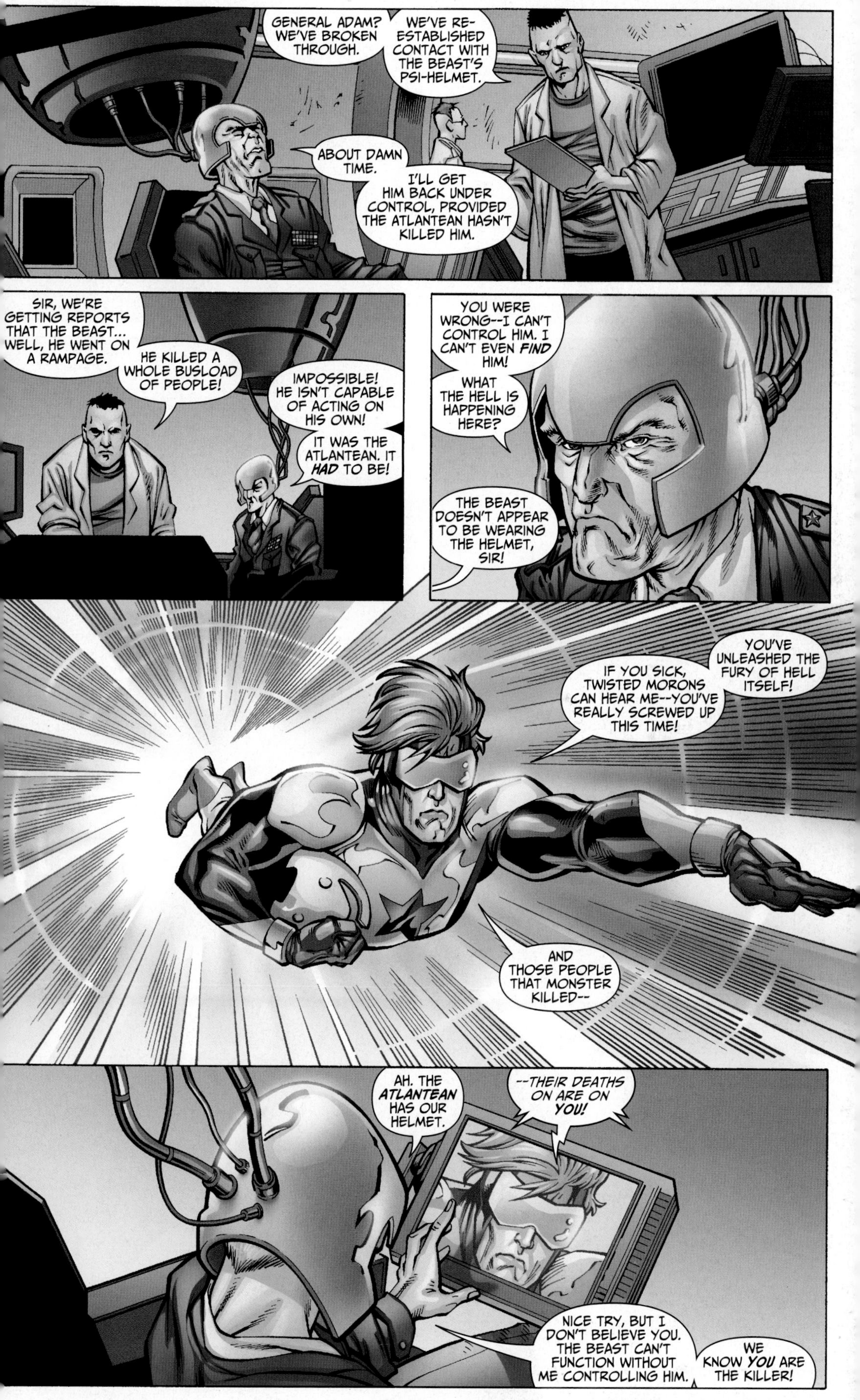
GENERAL ADAM? WE'VE BROKEN THROUGH.
WE'VE RE-ESTABLISHED CONTACT WITH THE BEAST'S PSI-HELMET.
ABOUT DAMN TIME.
I'LL GET HIM BACK UNDER CONTROL, PROVIDED THE ATLANTEAN HASN'T KILLED HIM.
SIR, WE'RE GETTING REPORTS THAT THE BEAST... WELL, HE WENT ON A RAMPAGE.
HE KILLED A WHOLE BUSLOAD OF PEOPLE!
IMPOSSIBLE! HE ISN'T CAPABLE OF ACTING ON HIS OWN!
IT WAS THE ATLANTEAN. IT *HAD* TO BE!
YOU WERE WRONG--I CAN'T CONTROL HIM. I CAN'T EVEN *FIND* HIM!
WHAT THE HELL IS HAPPENING HERE?
THE BEAST DOESN'T APPEAR TO BE WEARING THE HELMET, SIR!
IF YOU SICK, TWISTED MORONS CAN HEAR ME--YOU'VE REALLY SCREWED UP THIS TIME!
YOU'VE UNLEASHED THE FURY OF HELL ITSELF!
AND THOSE PEOPLE THAT MONSTER KILLED--
AH. THE *ATLANTEAN* HAS OUR HELMET.
--THEIR DEATHS ON ARE ON *YOU!*
NICE TRY, BUT I DON'T BELIEVE YOU. THE BEAST CAN'T FUNCTION WITHOUT ME CONTROLLING HIM.
WE KNOW *YOU* ARE THE KILLER!

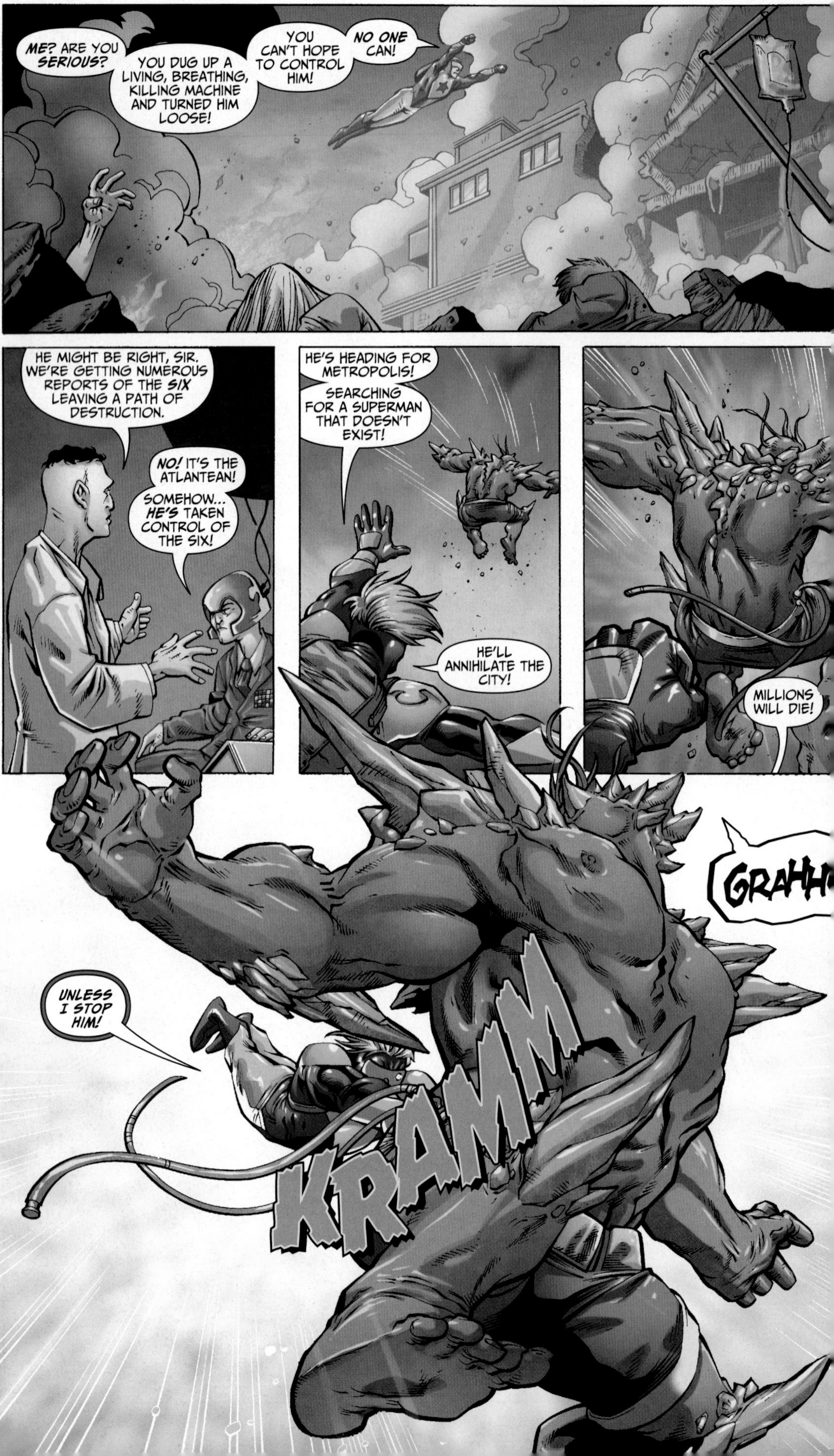

ME? ARE YOU SERIOUS?
YOU DUG UP A LIVING, BREATHING, KILLING MACHINE AND TURNED HIM LOOSE!
YOU CAN'T HOPE TO CONTROL HIM!
NO ONE CAN!
HE MIGHT BE RIGHT, SIR. WE'RE GETTING NUMEROUS REPORTS OF THE SIX LEAVING A PATH OF DESTRUCTION.
NO! IT'S THE ATLANTEAN!
SOMEHOW... HE'S TAKEN CONTROL OF THE SIX!
HE'S HEADING FOR METROPOLIS!
SEARCHING FOR A SUPERMAN THAT DOESN'T EXIST!
HE'LL ANNIHILATE THE CITY!
MILLIONS WILL DIE!
UNLESS I STOP HIM!
KRAMM

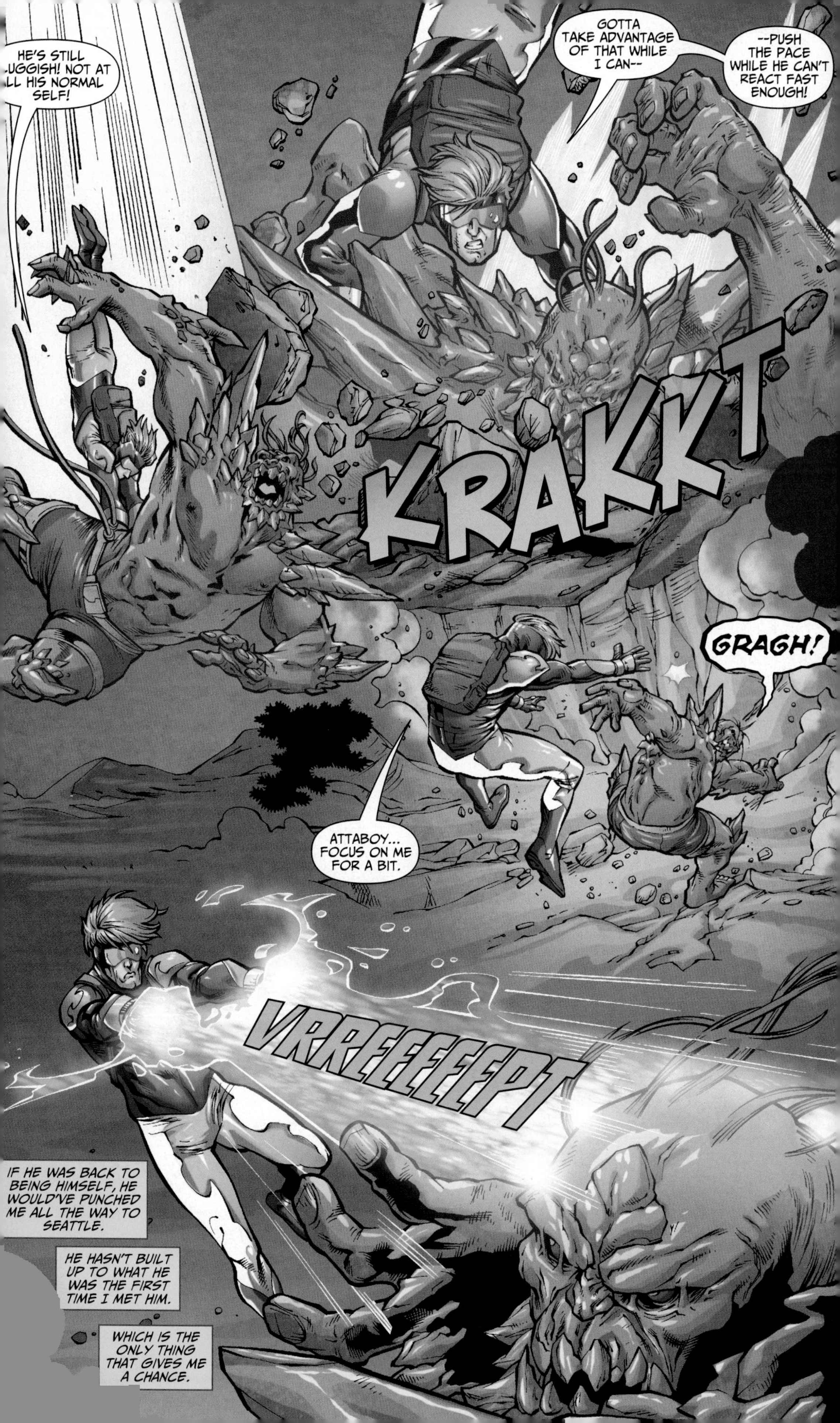
HE'S STILL LUGGISH! NOT AT LL HIS NORMAL SELF!
GOTTA TAKE ADVANTAGE OF THAT WHILE I CAN--
--PUSH THE PACE WHILE HE CAN'T REACT FAST ENOUGH!
KRAKKT
GRAGH!
ATTABOY... FOCUS ON ME FOR A BIT.
VRREEEEEPT
IF HE WAS BACK TO BEING HIMSELF, HE WOULD'VE PUNCHED ME ALL THE WAY TO SEATTLE.
HE HASN'T BUILT UP TO WHAT HE WAS THE FIRST TIME I MET HIM.
WHICH IS THE ONLY THING THAT GIVES ME A CHANCE.

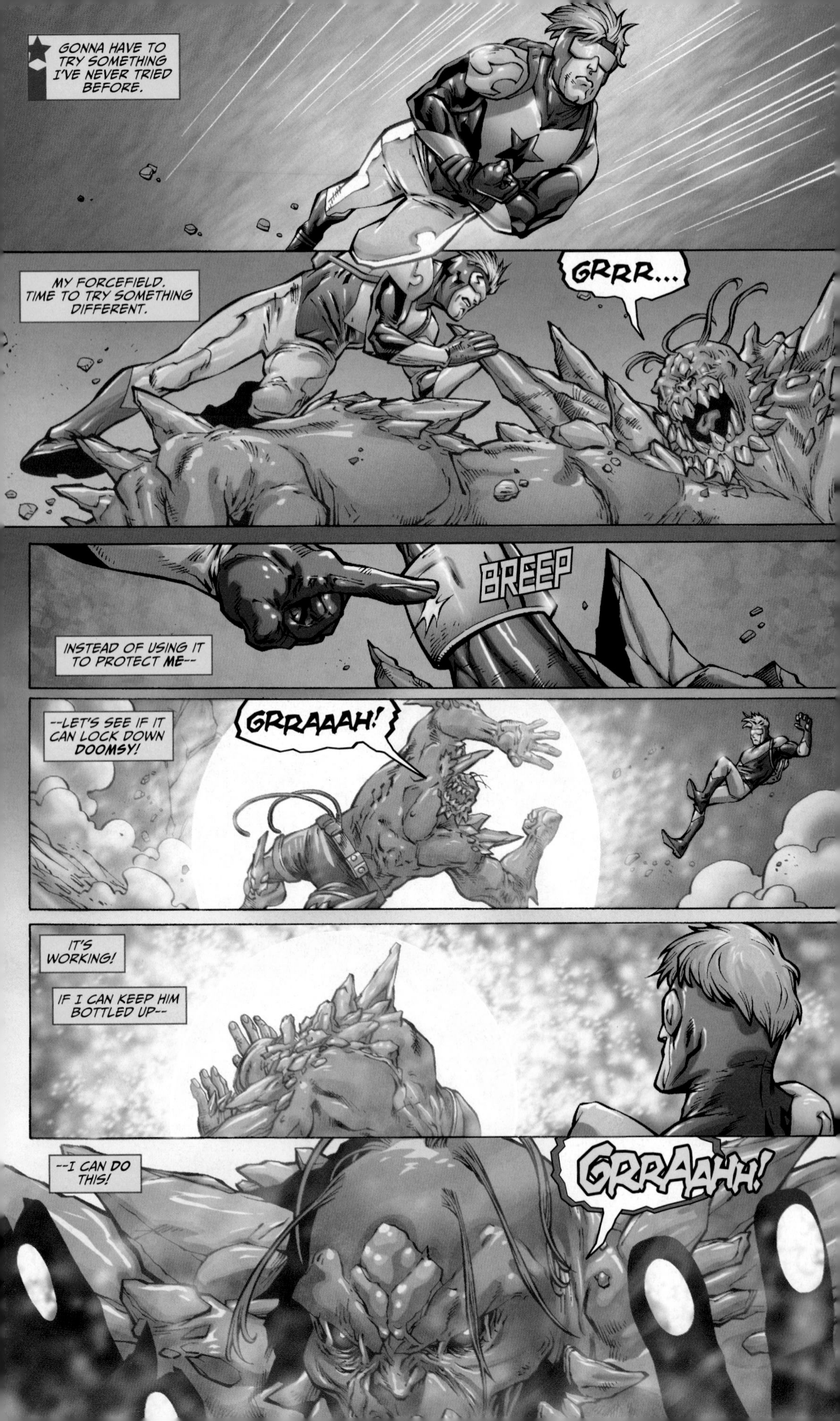
GONNA HAVE TO TRY SOMETHING I'VE NEVER TRIED BEFORE.
MY FORCEFIELD. TIME TO TRY SOMETHING DIFFERENT.
GRRR...
BREEP
INSTEAD OF USING IT TO PROTECT ME--
--LET'S SEE IF IT CAN LOCK DOWN DOOMSY!
GRRAAAH!
IT'S WORKING!
IF I CAN KEEP HIM BOTTLED UP--
--I CAN DO THIS!
GRRAAHH!

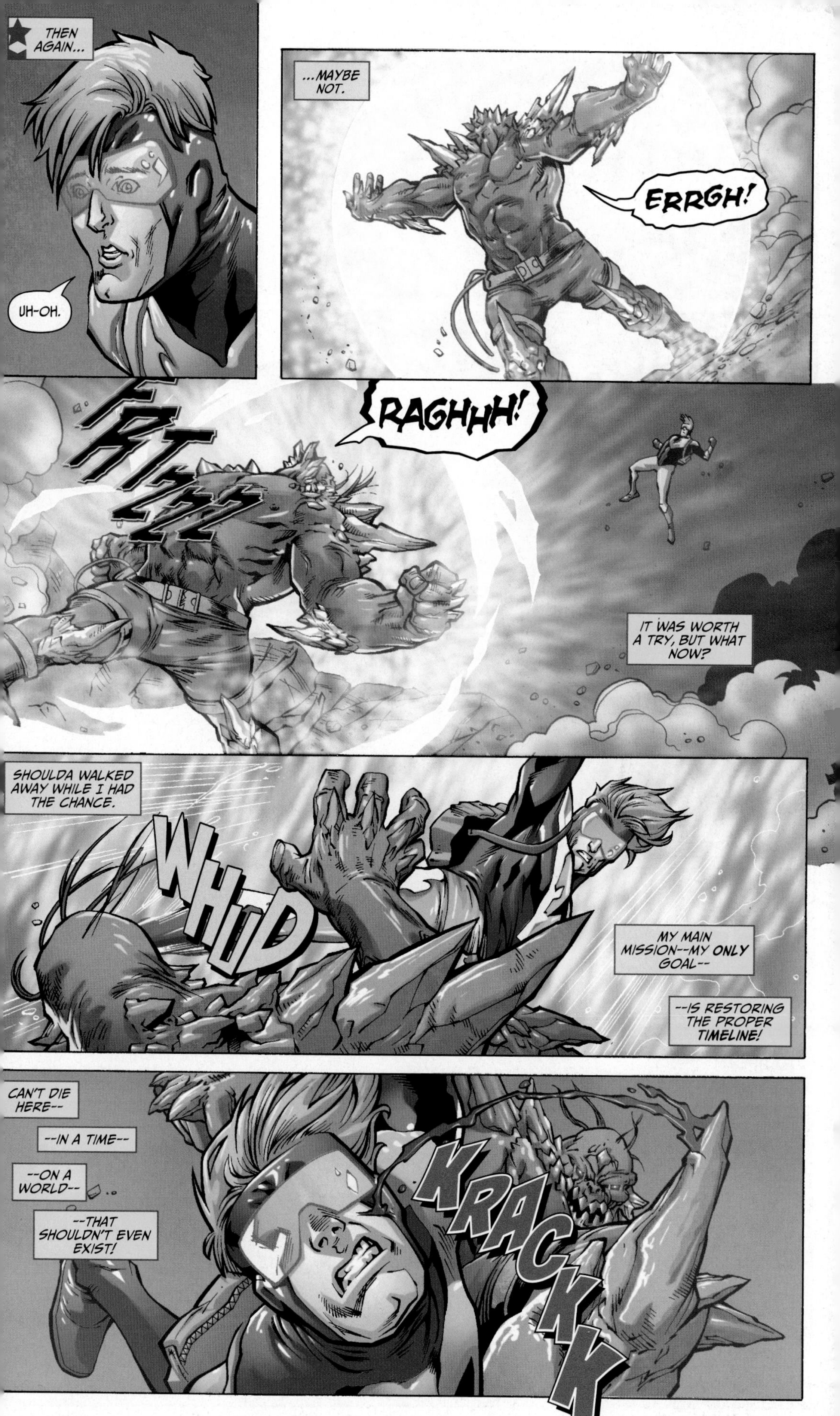
THEN AGAIN...
UH-OH.
...MAYBE NOT.
ERRGH!
FRTZZZ
RAGHHH!
IT WAS WORTH A TRY, BUT WHAT NOW?
SHOULDA WALKED AWAY WHILE I HAD THE CHANCE.
WHUD
MY MAIN MISSION--MY ONLY GOAL--
--IS RESTORING THE PROPER TIMELINE!
CAN'T DIE HERE--
--IN A TIME--
--ON A WORLD--
--THAT SHOULDN'T EVEN EXIST!
KRACKK

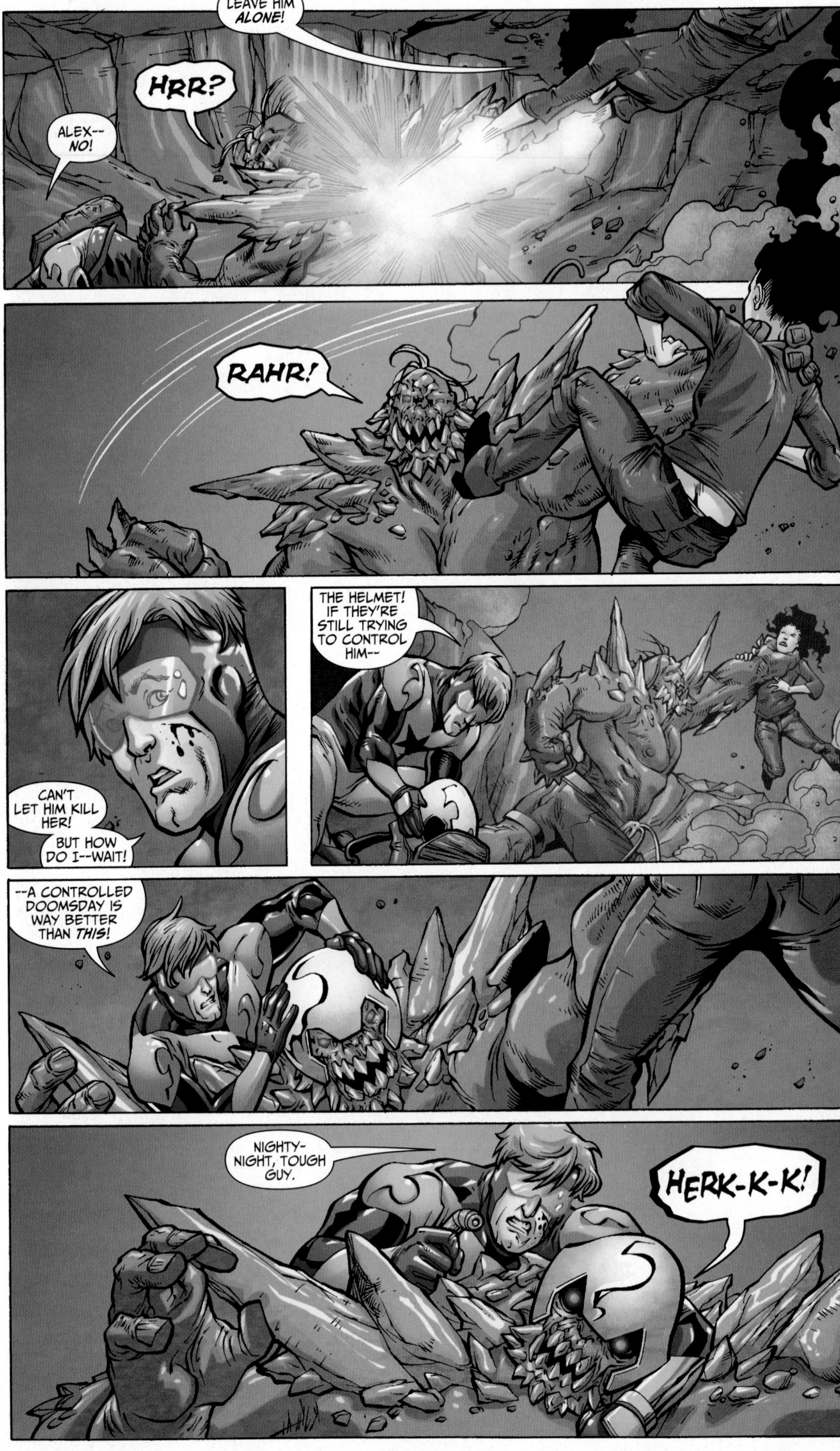
LEAVE HIM ALONE!
HRR?
ALEX-- NO!
RAHR!
THE HELMET! IF THEY'RE STILL TRYING TO CONTROL HIM--
CAN'T LET HIM KILL HER!
BUT HOW DO I--WAIT!
--A CONTROLLED DOOMSDAY IS WAY BETTER THAN THIS!
NIGHTY-NIGHT, TOUGH GUY.
HERK-K-K!

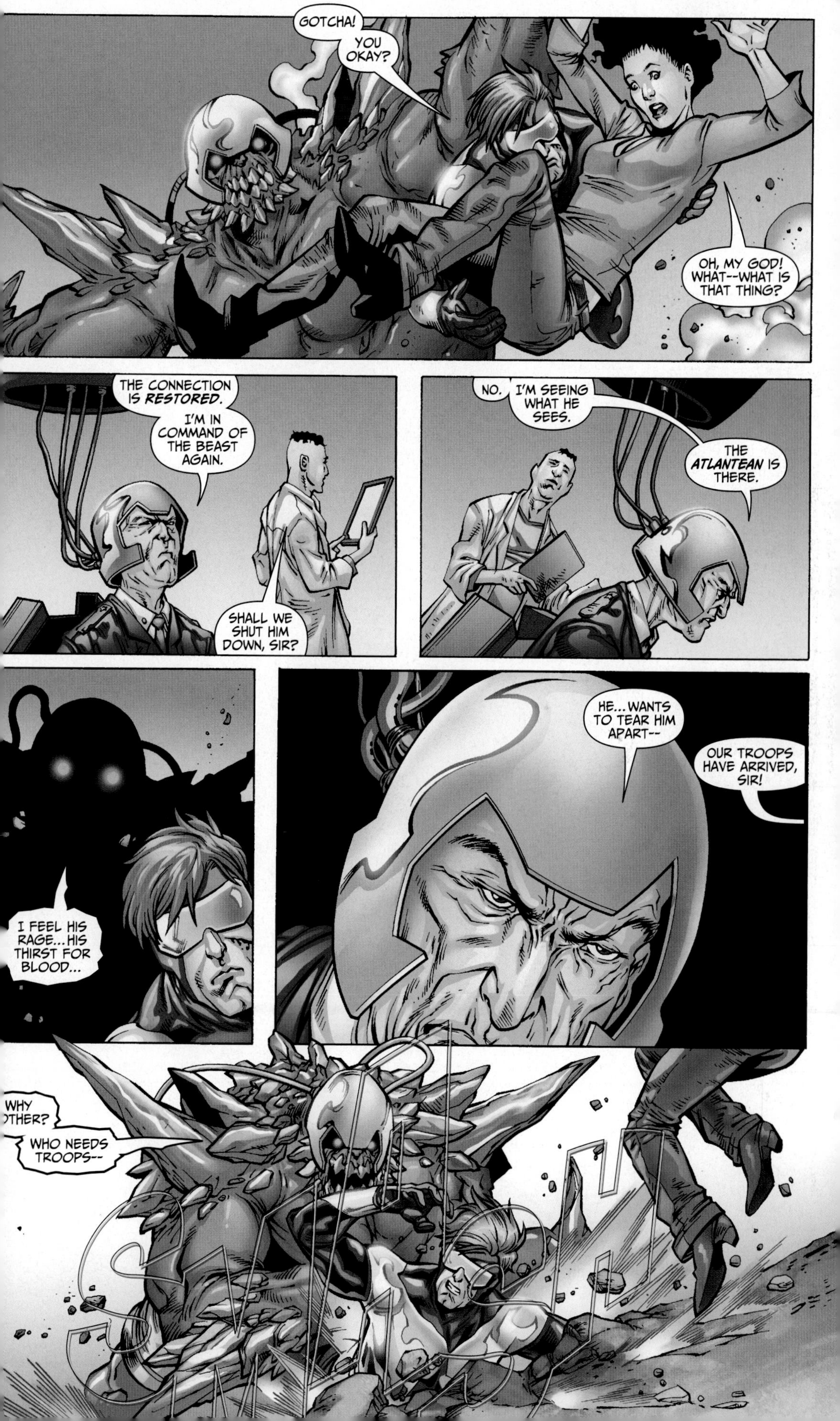
GOTCHA!
YOU OKAY?
OH, MY GOD! WHAT--WHAT IS THAT THING?
THE CONNECTION IS RESTORED.
I'M IN COMMAND OF THE BEAST AGAIN.
SHALL WE SHUT HIM DOWN, SIR?
NO.
I'M SEEING WHAT HE SEES.
THE ATLANTEAN IS THERE.
I FEEL HIS RAGE...HIS THIRST FOR BLOOD...
HE...WANTS TO TEAR HIM APART--
OUR TROOPS HAVE ARRIVED, SIR!
WHY BOTHER?
WHO NEEDS TROOPS--

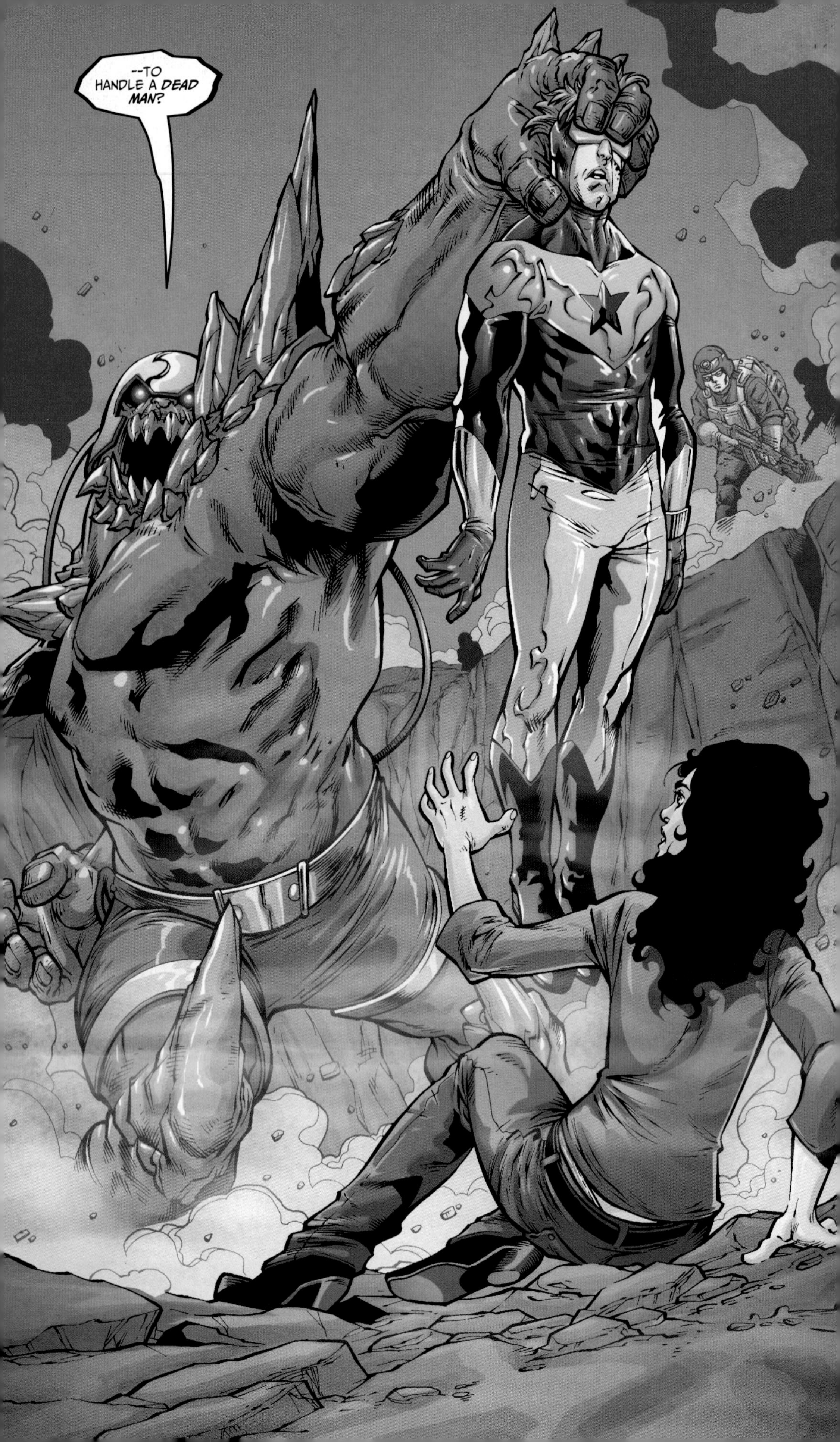
--TO HANDLE A *DEAD MAN?*

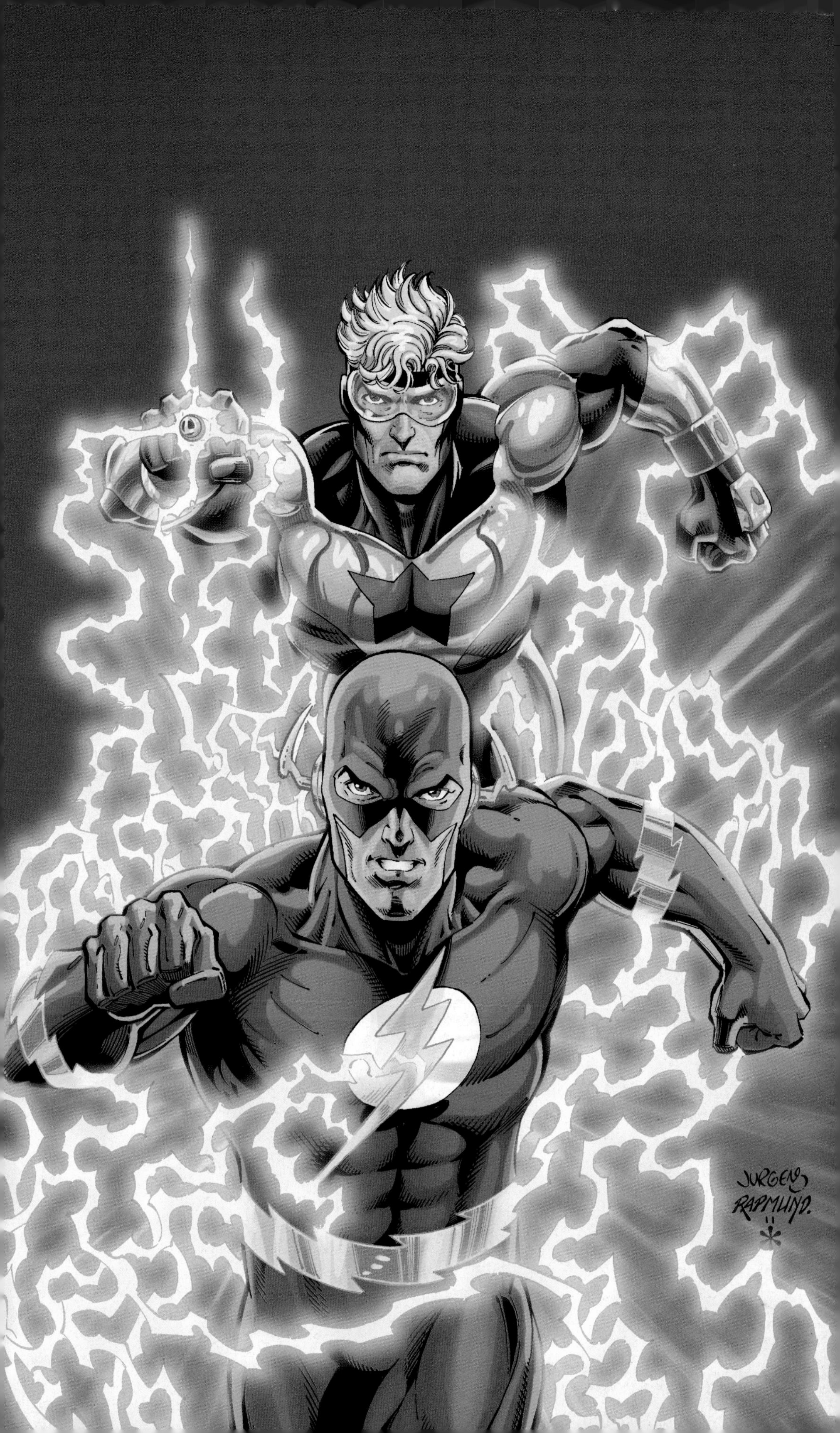

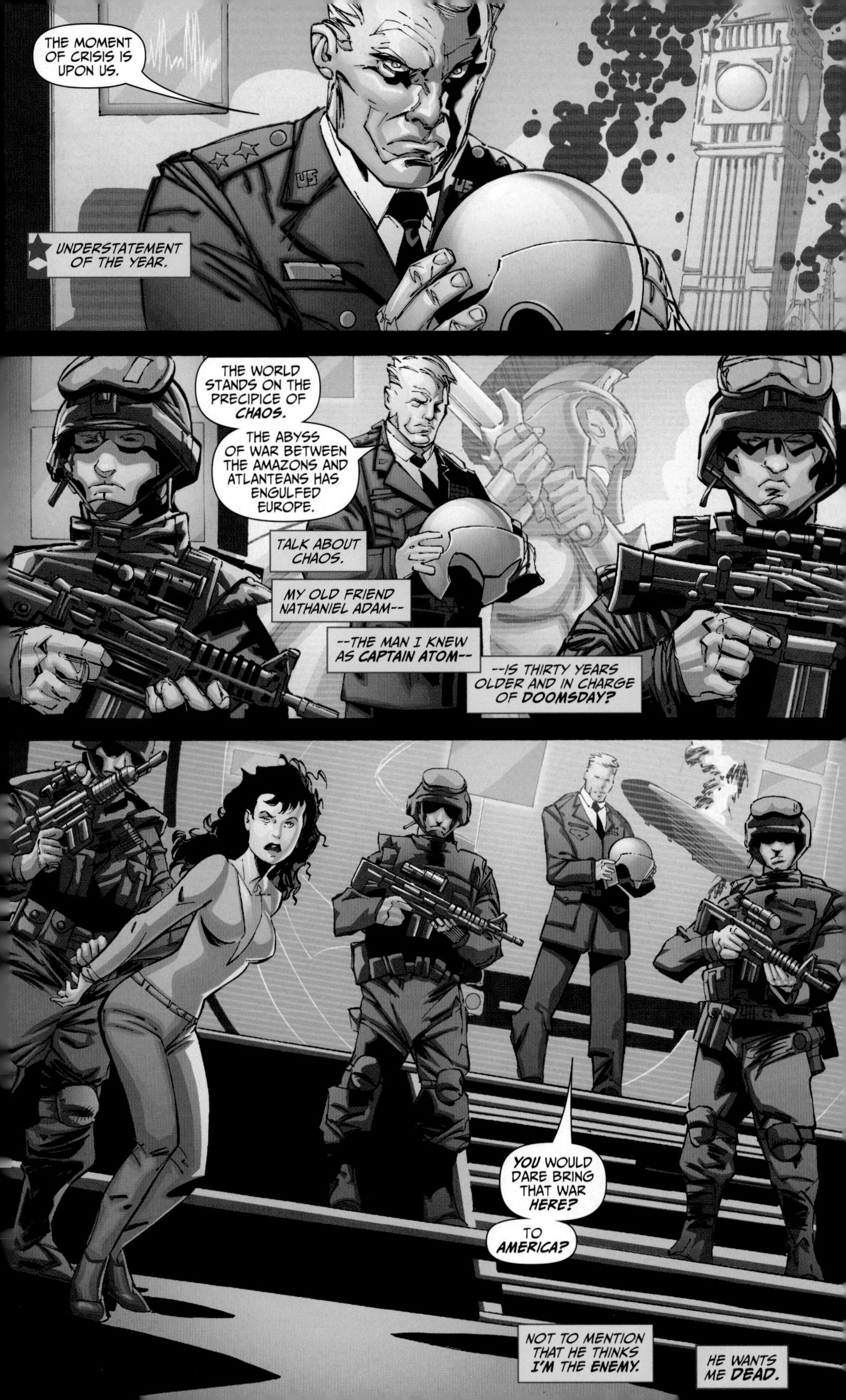
THE MOMENT OF CRISIS IS UPON US.
UNDERSTATEMENT OF THE YEAR.
THE WORLD STANDS ON THE PRECIPICE OF CHAOS.
THE ABYSS OF WAR BETWEEN THE AMAZONS AND ATLANTEANS HAS ENGULFED EUROPE.
TALK ABOUT CHAOS.
MY OLD FRIEND NATHANIEL ADAM--
--THE MAN I KNEW AS CAPTAIN ATOM--
--IS THIRTY YEARS OLDER AND IN CHARGE OF DOOMSDAY?
YOU WOULD DARE BRING THAT WAR HERE?
TO AMERICA?
NOT TO MENTION THAT HE THINKS I'M THE ENEMY.
HE WANTS ME DEAD.

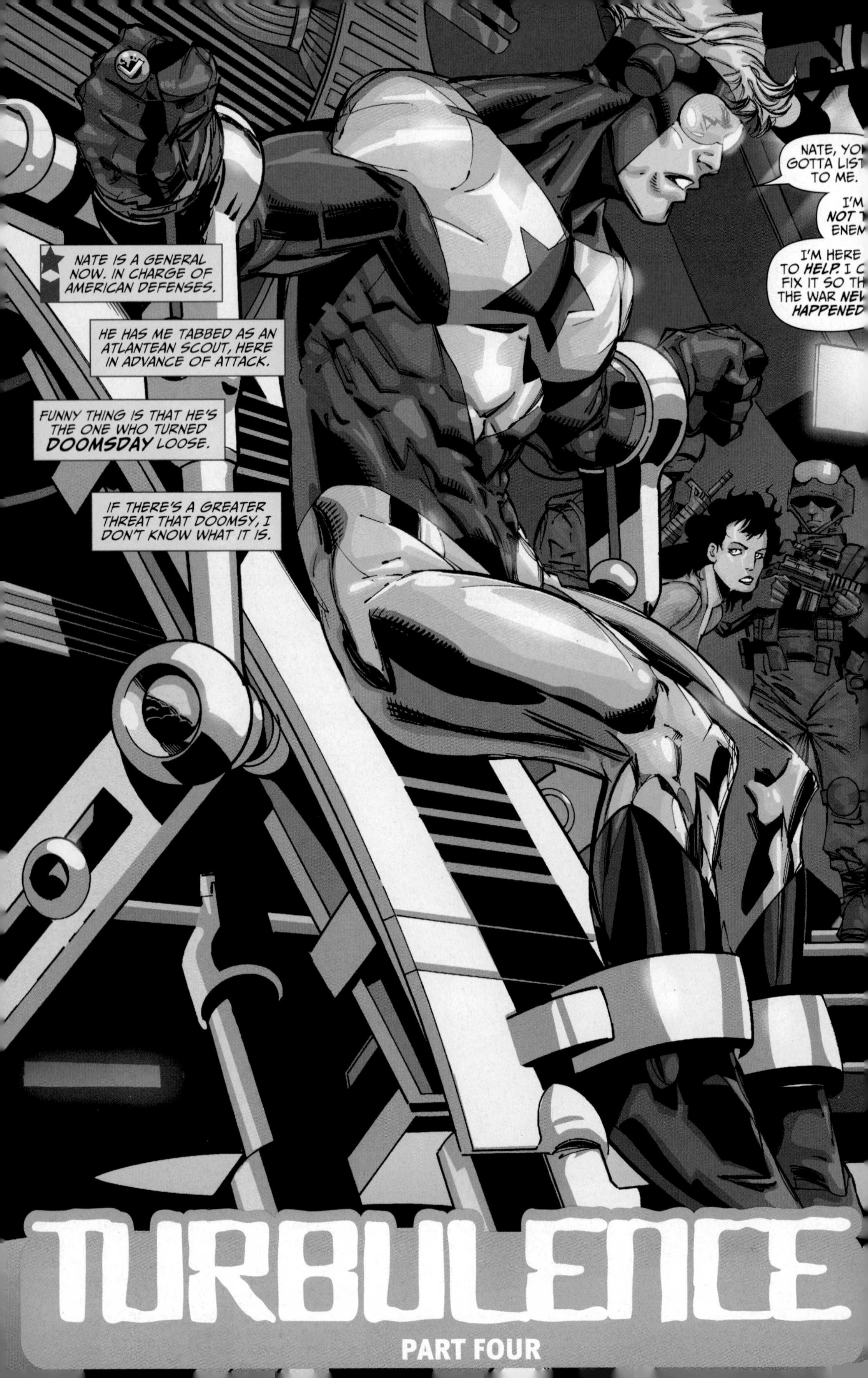
NATE IS A GENERAL NOW. IN CHARGE OF AMERICAN DEFENSES.
HE HAS ME TABBED AS AN ATLANTEAN SCOUT, HERE IN ADVANCE OF ATTACK.
FUNNY THING IS THAT HE'S THE ONE WHO TURNED DOOMSDAY LOOSE.
IF THERE'S A GREATER THREAT THAT DOOMSY, I DON'T KNOW WHAT IT IS.
NATE, YO GOTTA LIST TO ME.
I'M NOT T ENEM
I'M HERE TO HELP. I C FIX IT SO TH THE WAR NEV HAPPENED
TURBULENCE
PART FOUR

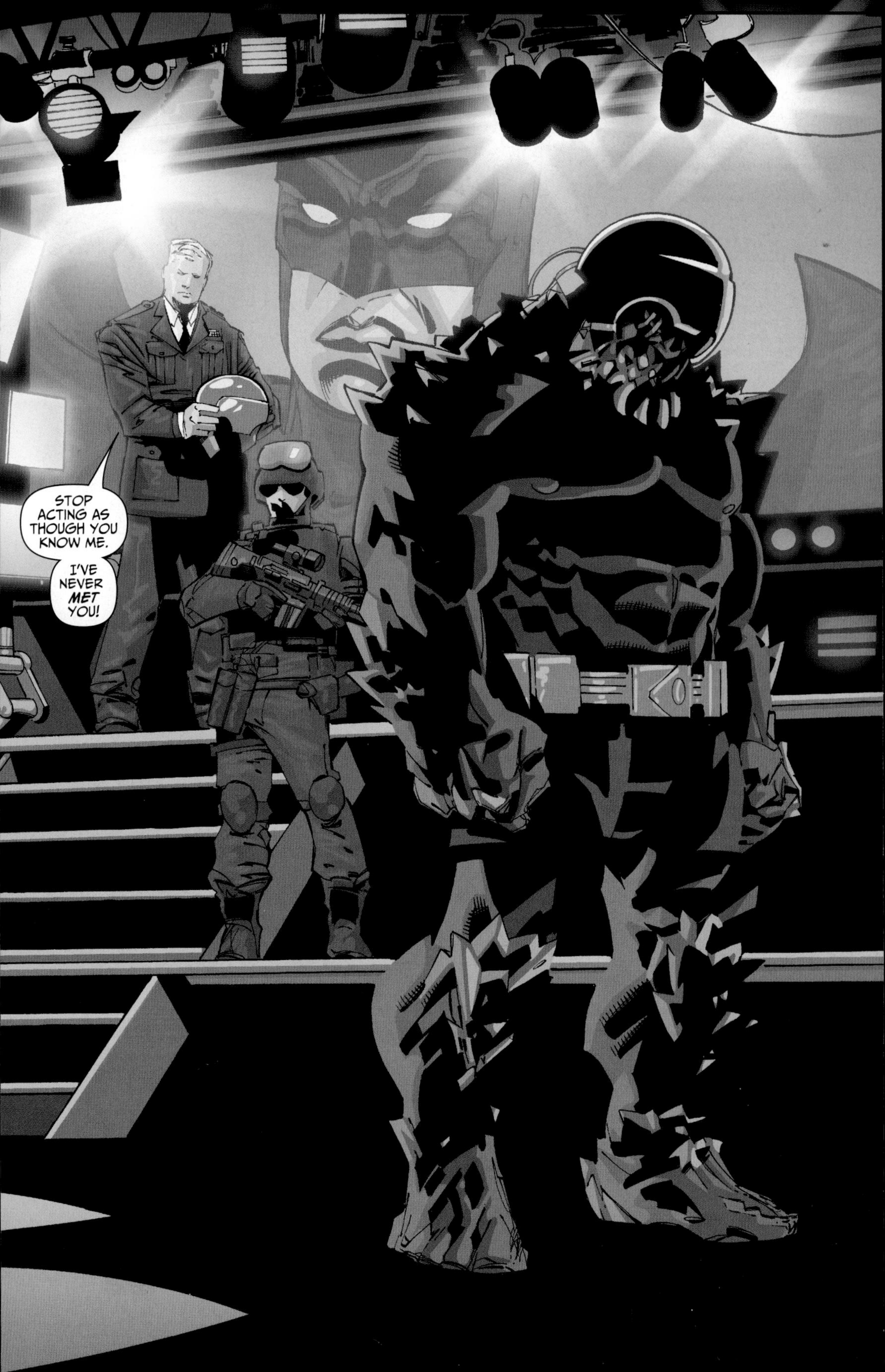
STOP ACTING AS THOUGH YOU KNOW ME.
I'VE NEVER ***MET*** YOU!

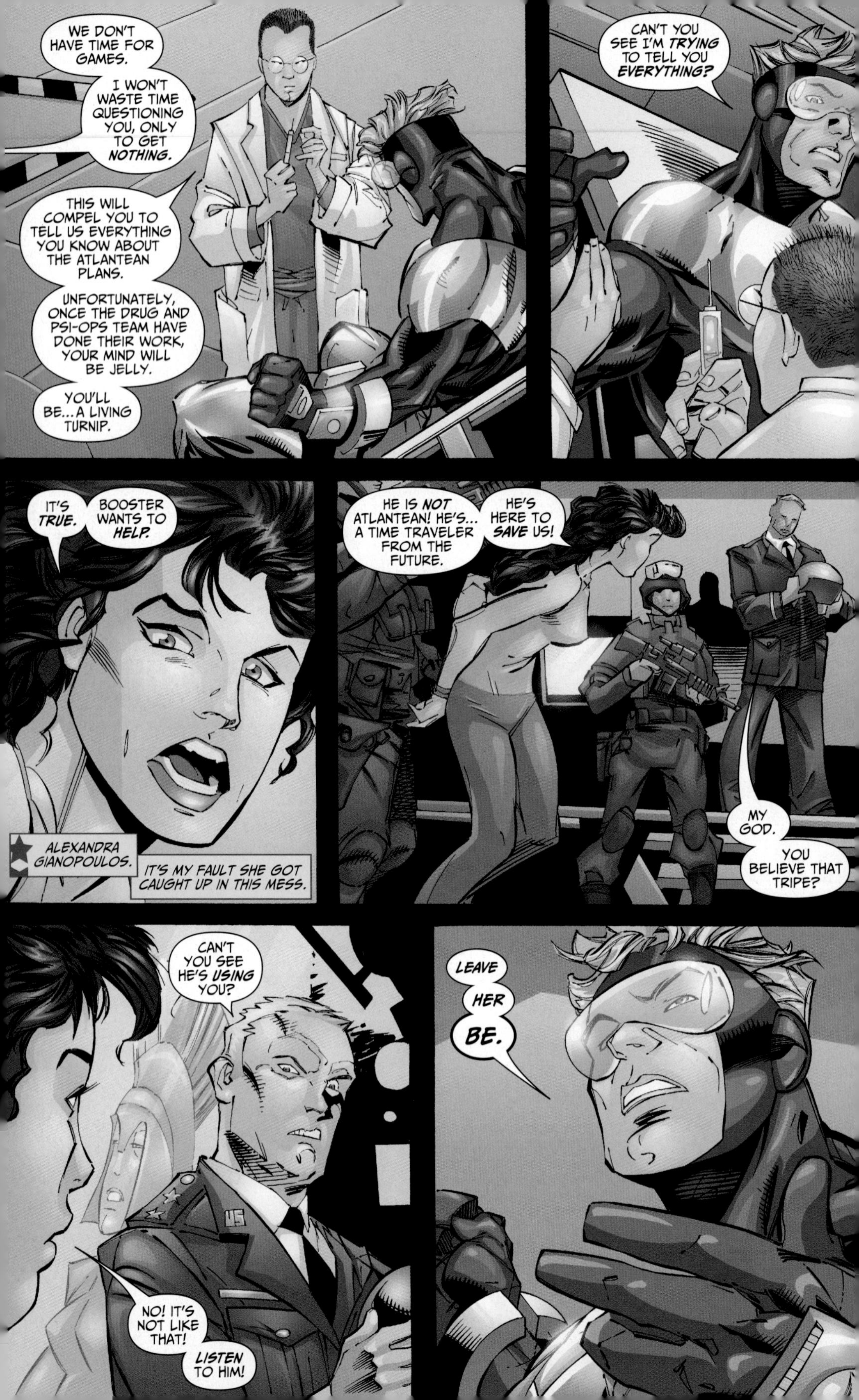

WE DON'T HAVE TIME FOR GAMES.
I WON'T WASTE TIME QUESTIONING YOU, ONLY TO GET NOTHING.
THIS WILL COMPEL YOU TO TELL US EVERYTHING YOU KNOW ABOUT THE ATLANTEAN PLANS.
UNFORTUNATELY, ONCE THE DRUG AND PSI-OPS TEAM HAVE DONE THEIR WORK, YOUR MIND WILL BE JELLY.
YOU'LL BE...A LIVING TURNIP.
CAN'T YOU SEE I'M TRYING TO TELL YOU EVERYTHING?
IT'S TRUE.
BOOSTER WANTS TO HELP.
ALEXANDRA GIANOPOULOS.
IT'S MY FAULT SHE GOT CAUGHT UP IN THIS MESS.
HE IS NOT ATLANTEAN! HE'S... A TIME TRAVELER FROM THE FUTURE.
HE'S HERE TO SAVE US!
MY GOD.
YOU BELIEVE THAT TRIPE?
CAN'T YOU SEE HE'S USING YOU?
NO! IT'S NOT LIKE THAT!
LISTEN TO HIM!
LEAVE HER BE.

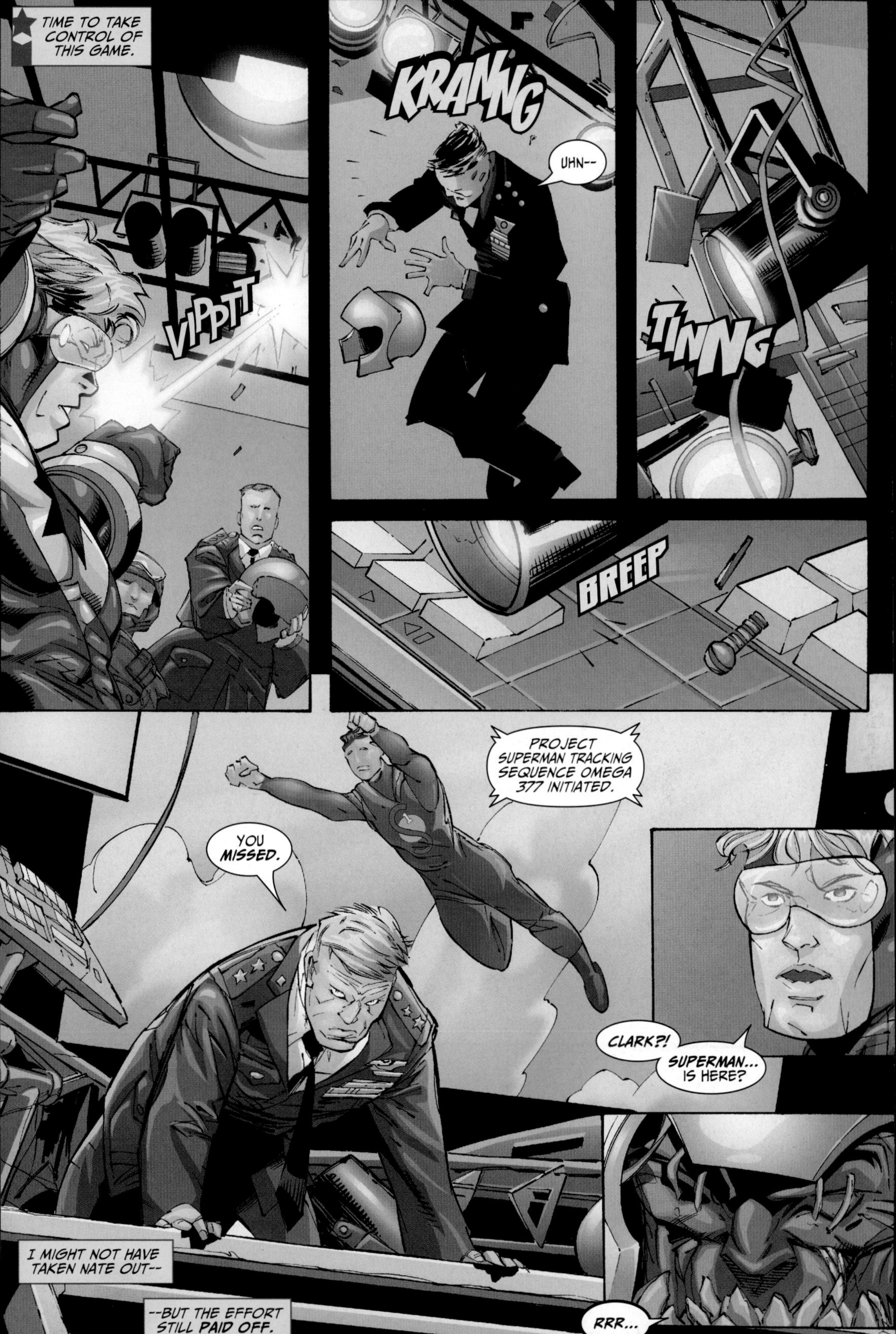
TIME TO TAKE CONTROL OF THIS GAME.
VIPPTT
KRANNG
UHN--
TINNG
BREEP
PROJECT SUPERMAN TRACKING SEQUENCE OMEGA 377 INITIATED.
YOU MISSED.
CLARK?!
SUPERMAN... IS HERE?
I MIGHT NOT HAVE TAKEN NATE OUT--
--BUT THE EFFORT STILL PAID OFF.
RRR...

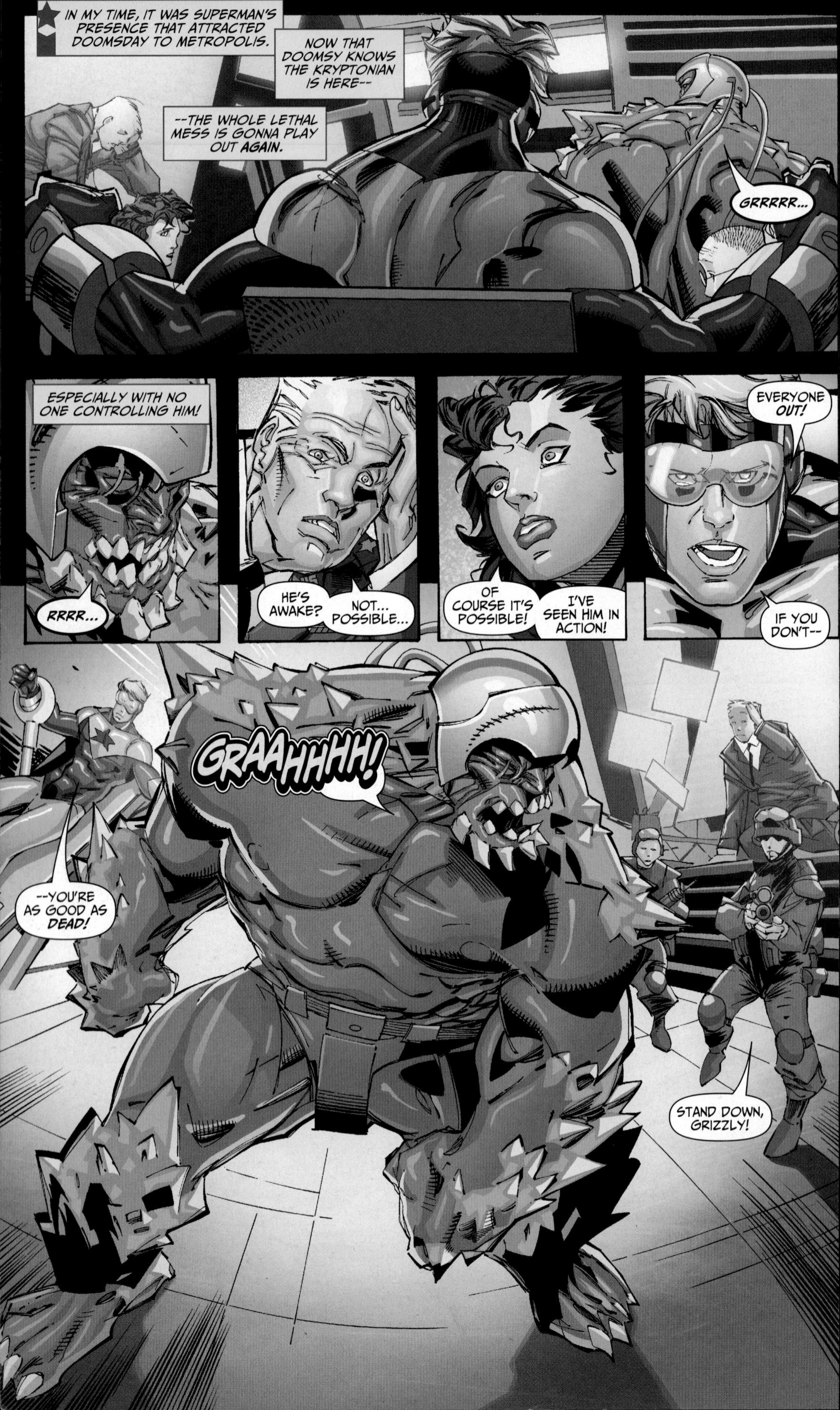

IN MY TIME, IT WAS SUPERMAN'S PRESENCE THAT ATTRACTED DOOMSDAY TO METROPOLIS.
NOW THAT DOOMSY KNOWS THE KRYPTONIAN IS HERE--
--THE WHOLE LETHAL MESS IS GONNA PLAY OUT AGAIN.
GRRRRR...
ESPECIALLY WITH NO ONE CONTROLLING HIM!
RRRR...
HE'S AWAKE?
NOT... POSSIBLE...
OF COURSE IT'S POSSIBLE!
I'VE SEEN HIM IN ACTION!
EVERYONE OUT!
IF YOU DON'T--
GRAAHHHH!
--YOU'RE AS GOOD AS DEAD!
STAND DOWN, GRIZZLY!

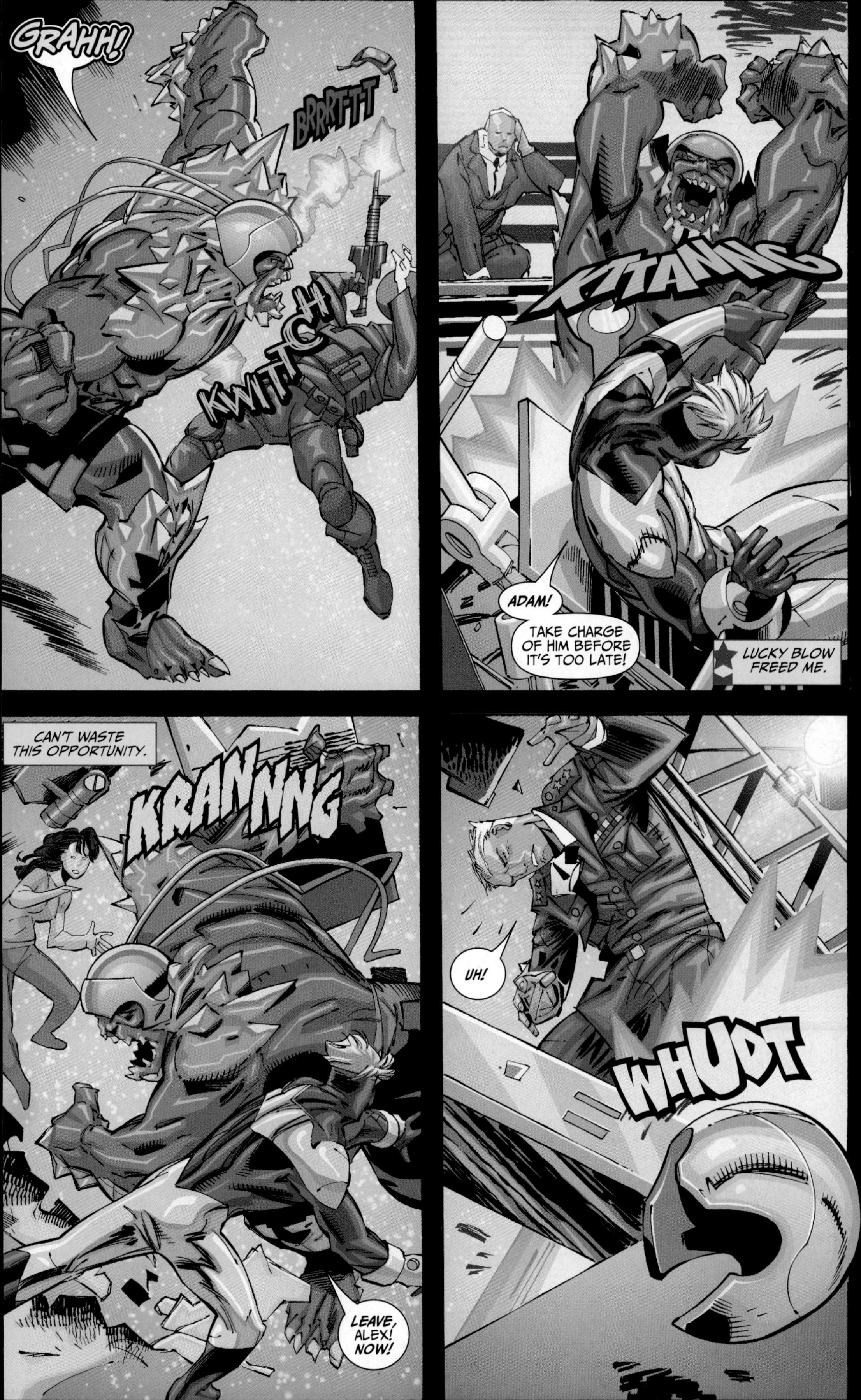
GRAHH!
BRRRT-T-T
KWITTCH
KTTANNG
ADAM!
TAKE CHARGE OF HIM BEFORE IT'S TOO LATE!
LUCKY BLOW FREED ME.
CAN'T WASTE THIS OPPORTUNITY.
KRANNNG
LEAVE, ALEX! NOW!
UH!
WHUDT

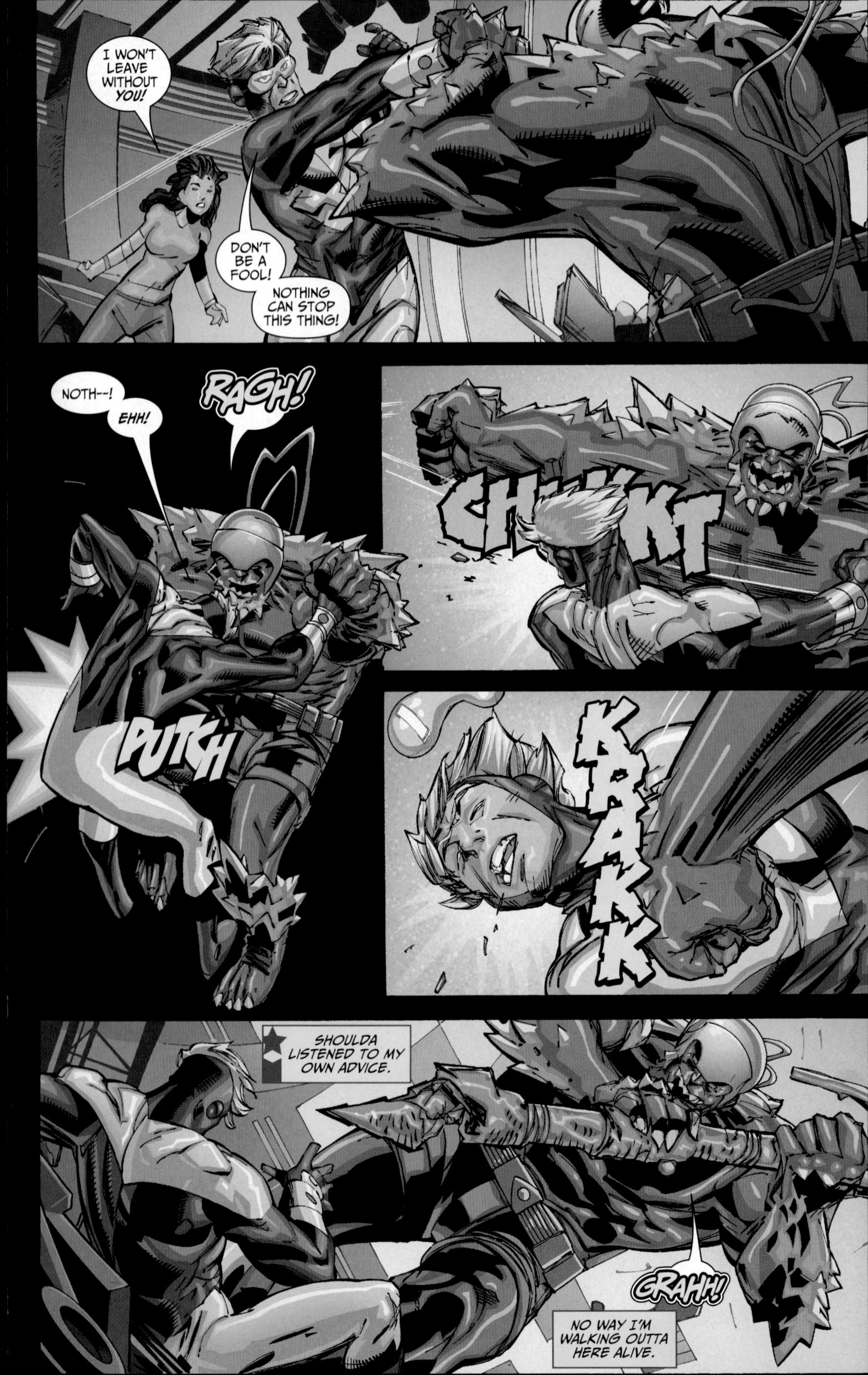

I WON'T LEAVE WITHOUT YOU!
DON'T BE A FOOL!
NOTHING CAN STOP THIS THING!
NOTH--!
EHH!
RAGH!
PUTCH
KRAKK
SHOULDA LISTENED TO MY OWN ADVICE.
GRAHH!
NO WAY I'M WALKING OUTTA HERE ALIVE.

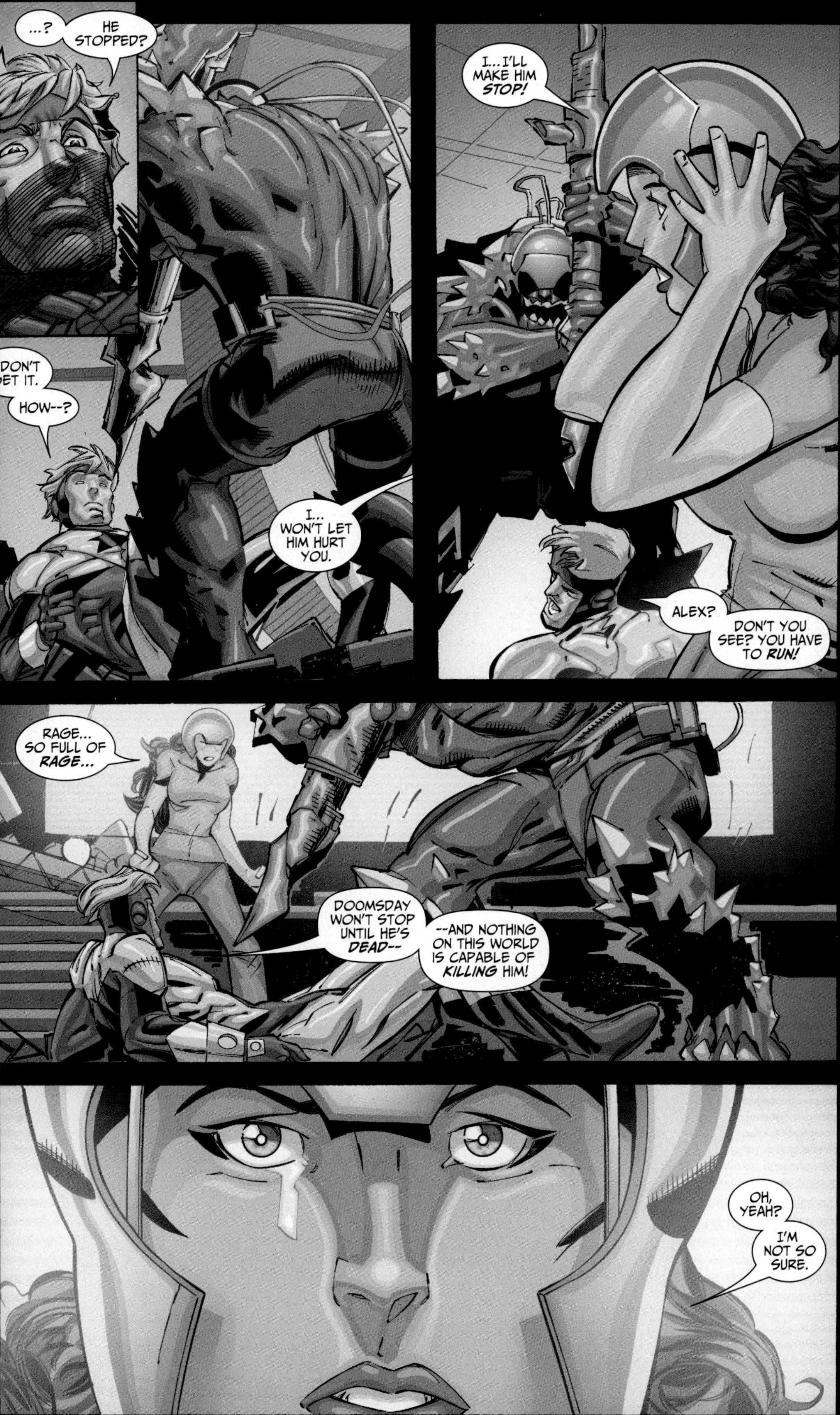
...?
HE STOPPED?
I...I'LL MAKE HIM STOP!
DON'T GET IT.
HOW--?
I... WON'T LET HIM HURT YOU.
ALEX?
DON'T YOU SEE? YOU HAVE TO RUN!
RAGE... SO FULL OF RAGE...
DOOMSDAY WON'T STOP UNTIL HE'S DEAD--
--AND NOTHING ON THIS WORLD IS CAPABLE OF KILLING HIM!
OH, YEAH?
I'M NOT SO SURE.

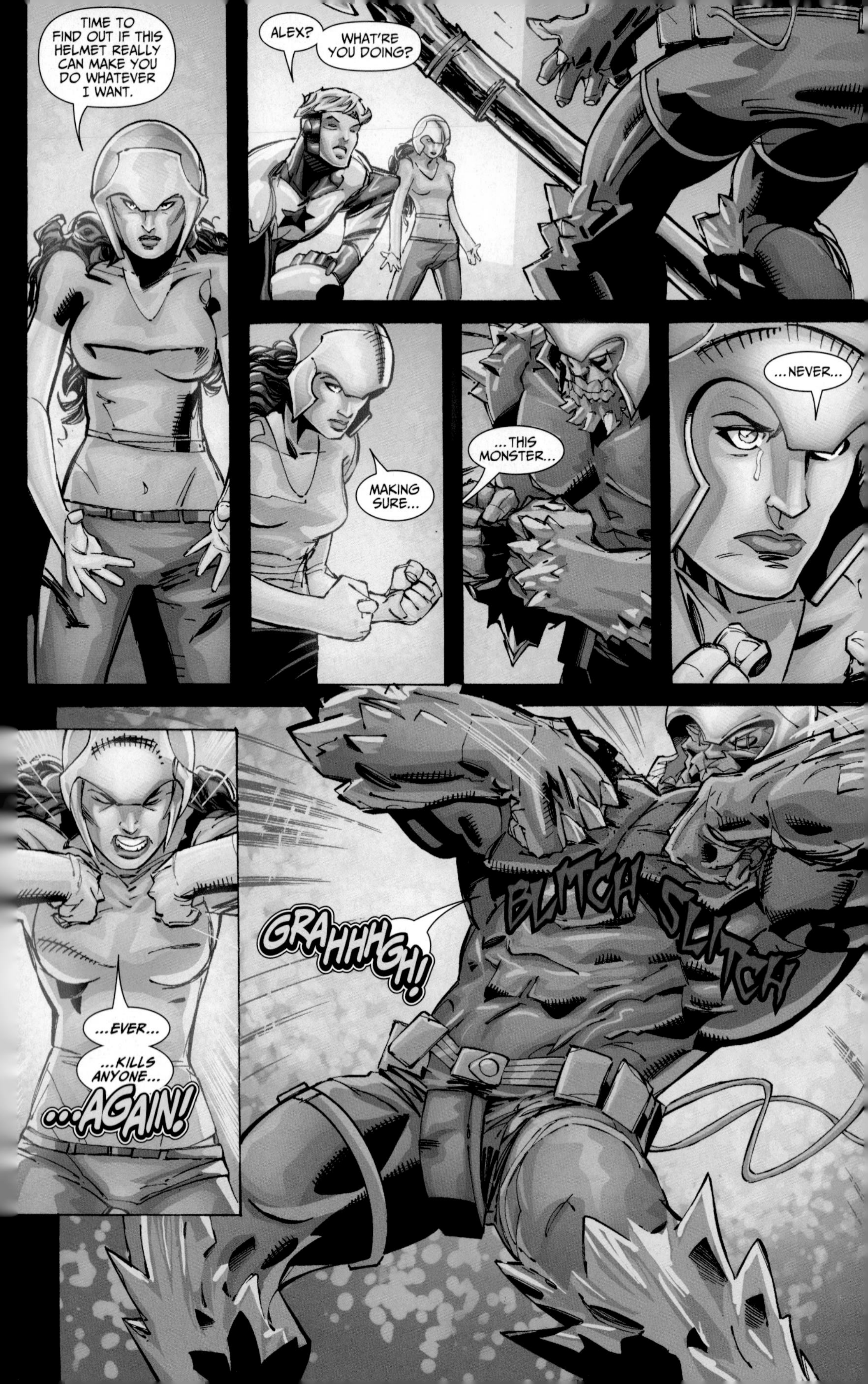
TIME TO FIND OUT IF THIS HELMET REALLY CAN MAKE YOU DO WHATEVER I WANT.
ALEX?
WHAT'RE YOU DOING?
MAKING SURE...
...THIS MONSTER...
...NEVER...
...EVER...
...KILLS ANYONE...
...AGAIN!
GRAHHHGH!
BLTCH
SLTCH

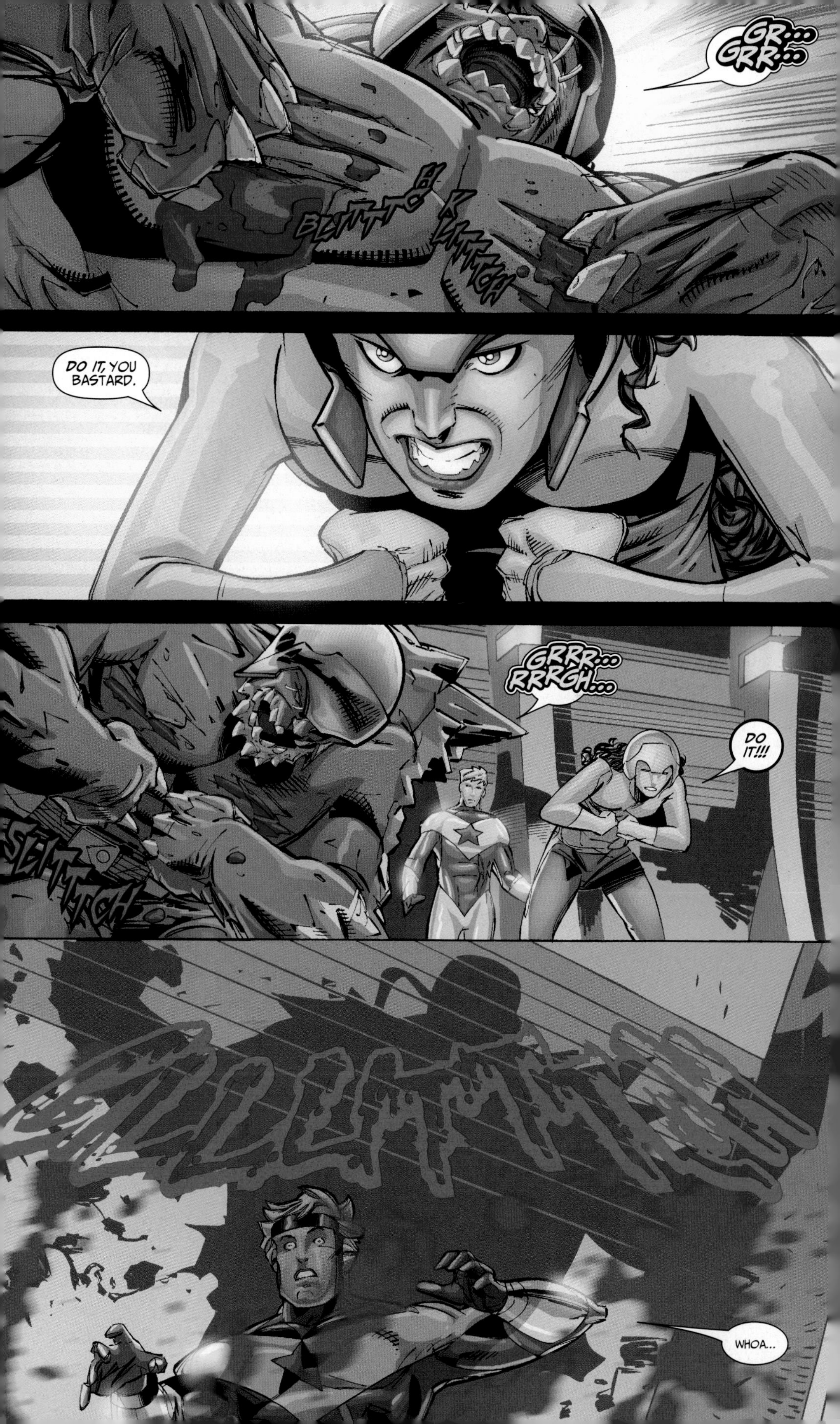
GR...
GRR...
BLITTCH KLITTCH
DO IT, YOU BASTARD.
GRRR...
RRRGH...
DO IT!!!
WHOA...

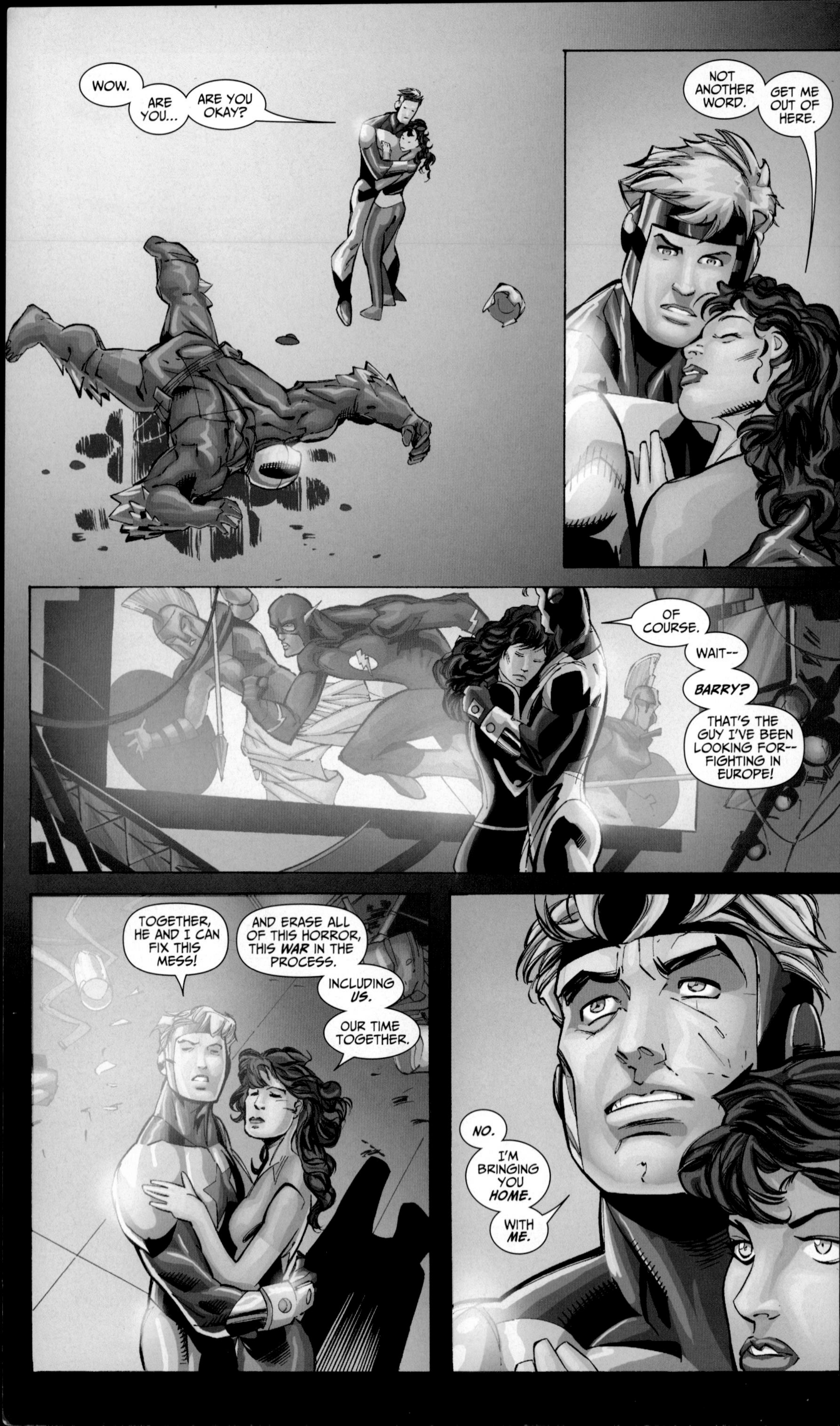
WOW.
ARE YOU...
ARE YOU OKAY?
NOT ANOTHER WORD.
GET ME OUT OF HERE.
OF COURSE.
WAIT--
BARRY?
THAT'S THE GUY I'VE BEEN LOOKING FOR-- FIGHTING IN EUROPE!
TOGETHER, HE AND I CAN FIX THIS MESS!
AND ERASE ALL OF THIS HORROR, THIS WAR IN THE PROCESS.
INCLUDING US.
OUR TIME TOGETHER.
NO.
I'M BRINGING YOU HOME.
WITH ME.

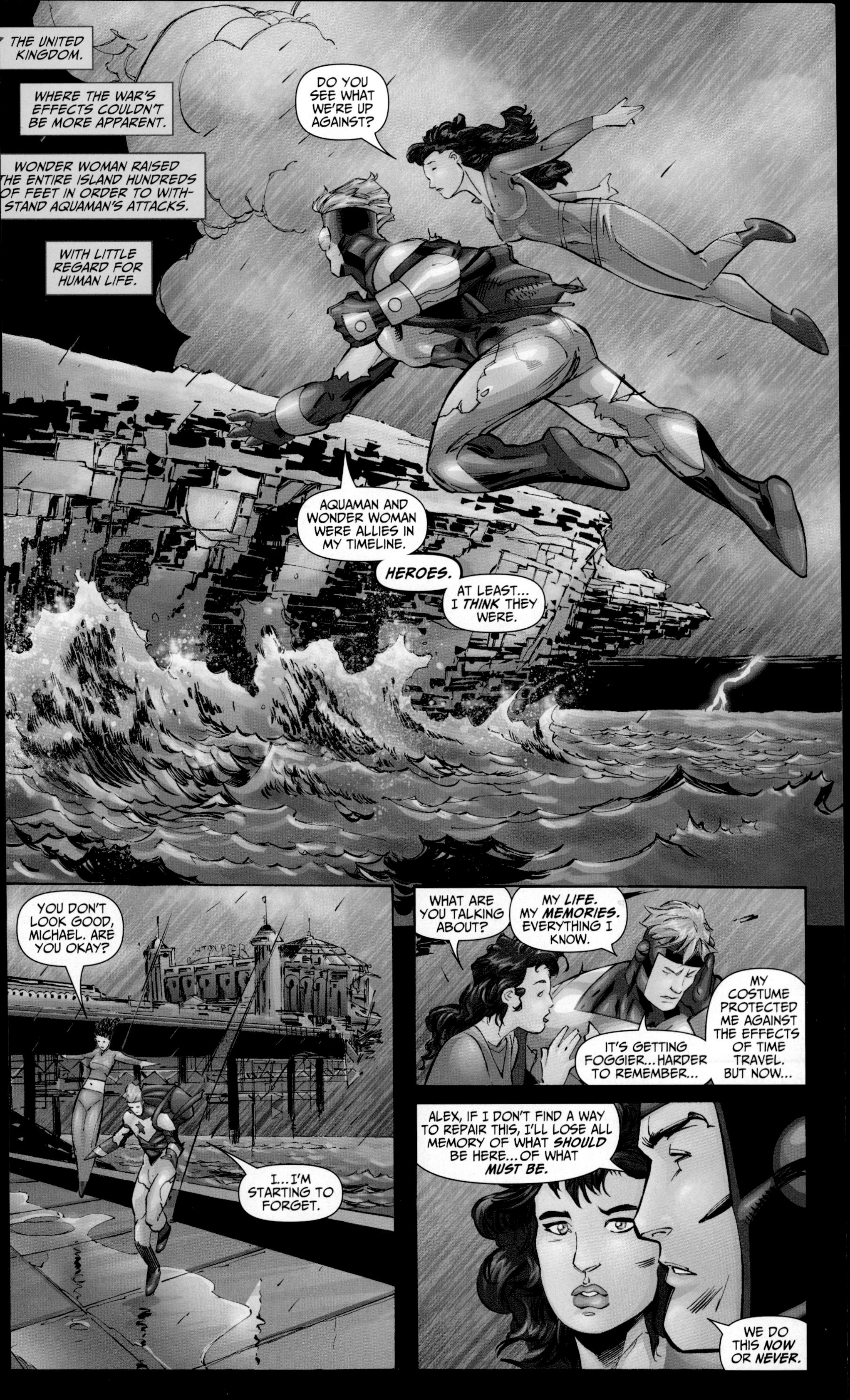
THE UNITED KINGDOM.
WHERE THE WAR'S EFFECTS COULDN'T BE MORE APPARENT.
WONDER WOMAN RAISED THE ENTIRE ISLAND HUNDREDS OF FEET IN ORDER TO WITH-STAND AQUAMAN'S ATTACKS.
WITH LITTLE REGARD FOR HUMAN LIFE.
DO YOU SEE WHAT WE'RE UP AGAINST?
AQUAMAN AND WONDER WOMAN WERE ALLIES IN MY TIMELINE.
HEROES.
AT LEAST... I THINK THEY WERE.
YOU DON'T LOOK GOOD, MICHAEL. ARE YOU OKAY?
I...I'M STARTING TO FORGET.
WHAT ARE YOU TALKING ABOUT?
MY LIFE. MY MEMORIES. EVERYTHING I KNOW.
IT'S GETTING FOGGIER...HARDER TO REMEMBER...
MY COSTUME PROTECTED ME AGAINST THE EFFECTS OF TIME TRAVEL. BUT NOW...
ALEX, IF I DON'T FIND A WAY TO REPAIR THIS, I'LL LOSE ALL MEMORY OF WHAT SHOULD BE HERE...OF WHAT MUST BE.
WE DO THIS NOW OR NEVER.

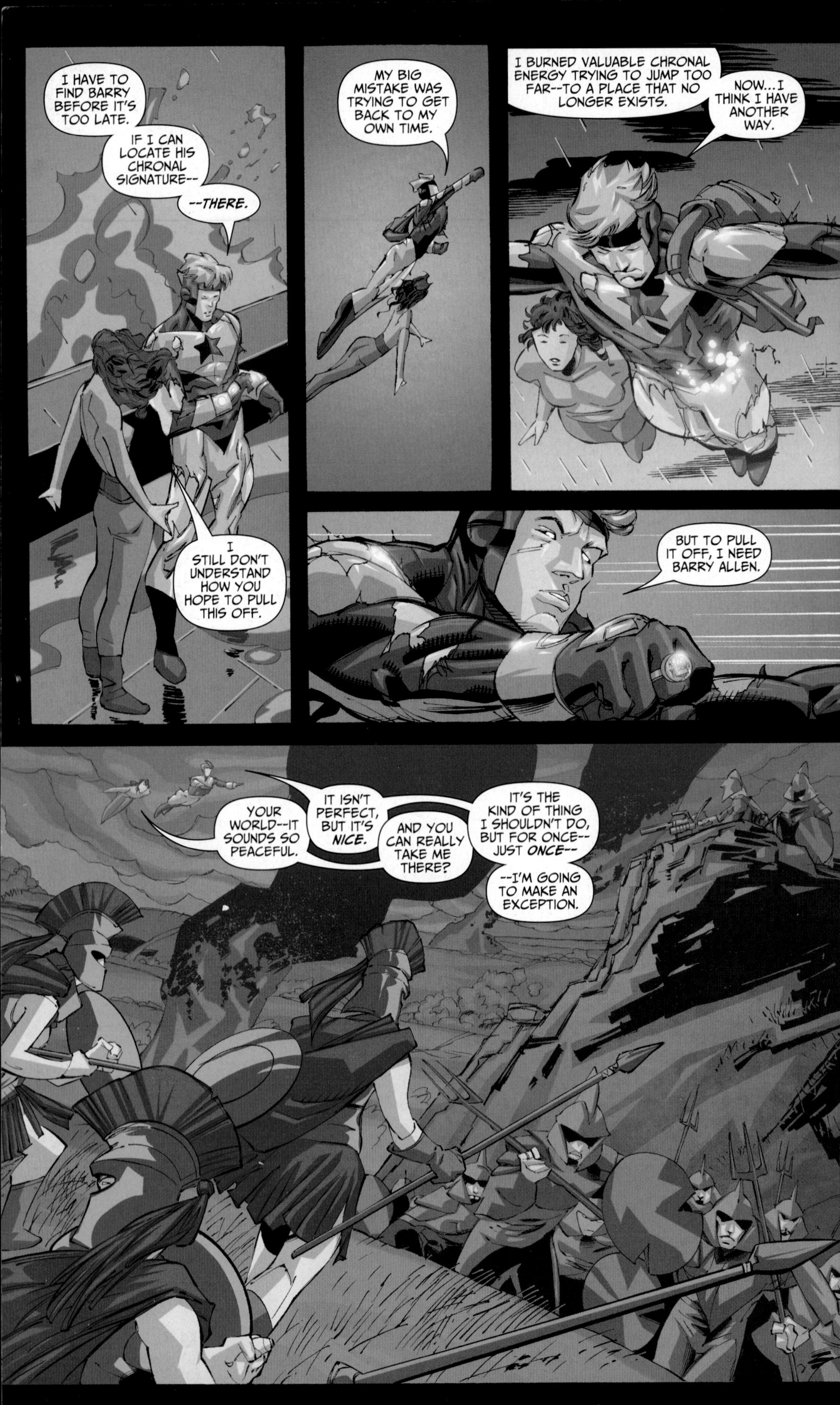

I HAVE TO FIND BARRY BEFORE IT'S TOO LATE.
IF I CAN LOCATE HIS CHRONAL SIGNATURE--
--THERE.
I STILL DON'T UNDERSTAND HOW YOU HOPE TO PULL THIS OFF.
MY BIG MISTAKE WAS TRYING TO GET BACK TO MY OWN TIME.
I BURNED VALUABLE CHRONAL ENERGY TRYING TO JUMP TOO FAR--TO A PLACE THAT NO LONGER EXISTS.
NOW...I THINK I HAVE ANOTHER WAY.
BUT TO PULL IT OFF, I NEED BARRY ALLEN.
YOUR WORLD--IT SOUNDS SO PEACEFUL.
IT ISN'T PERFECT, BUT IT'S NICE.
AND YOU CAN REALLY TAKE ME THERE?
IT'S THE KIND OF THING I SHOULDN'T DO, BUT FOR ONCE--JUST ONCE--
--I'M GOING TO MAKE AN EXCEPTION.

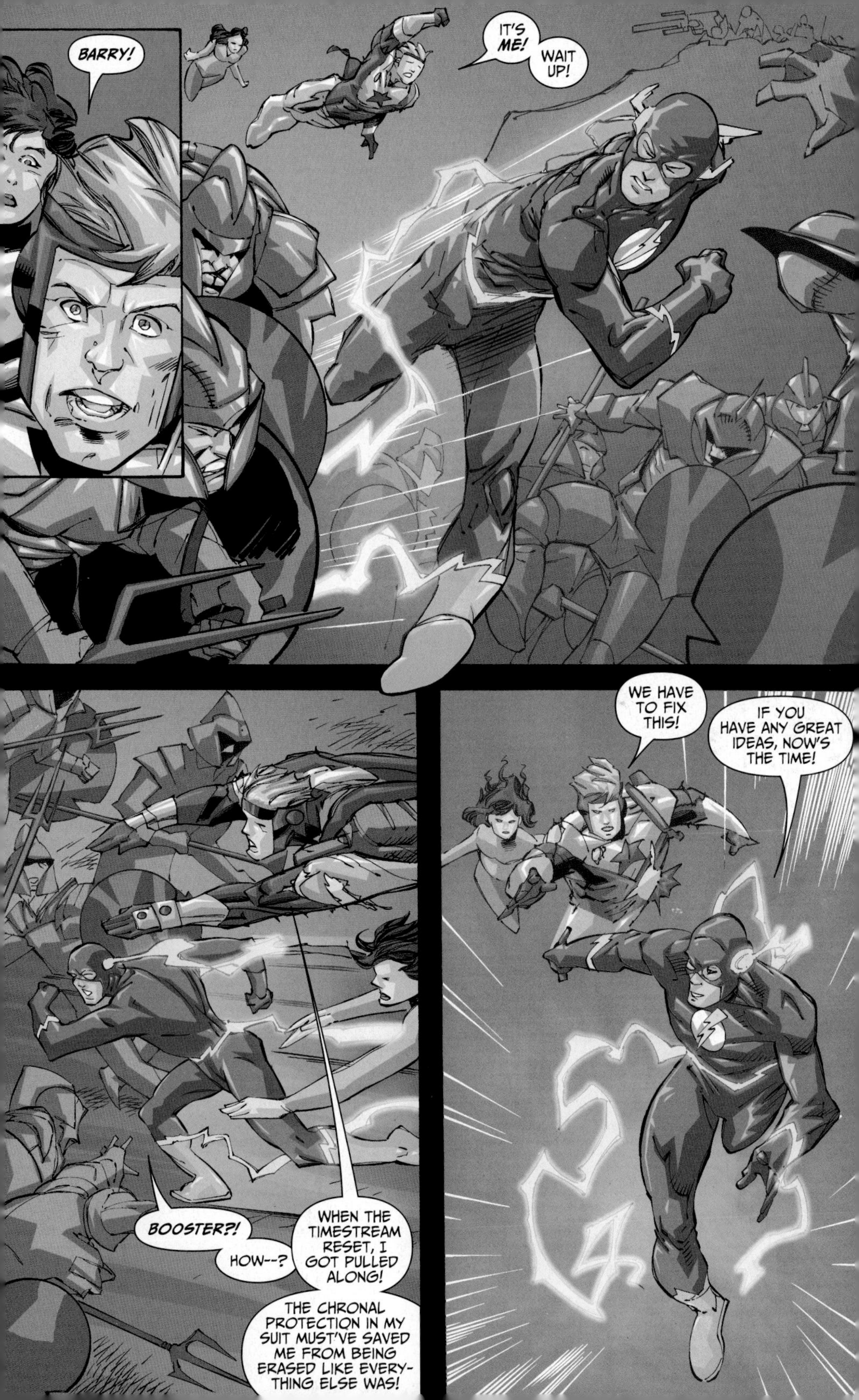
BARRY!
IT'S ME!
WAIT UP!
BOOSTER?!
HOW--?
WHEN THE TIMESTREAM RESET, I GOT PULLED ALONG!
THE CHRONAL PROTECTION IN MY SUIT MUST'VE SAVED ME FROM BEING ERASED LIKE EVERY-THING ELSE WAS!
WE HAVE TO FIX THIS!
IF YOU HAVE ANY GREAT IDEAS, NOW'S THE TIME!

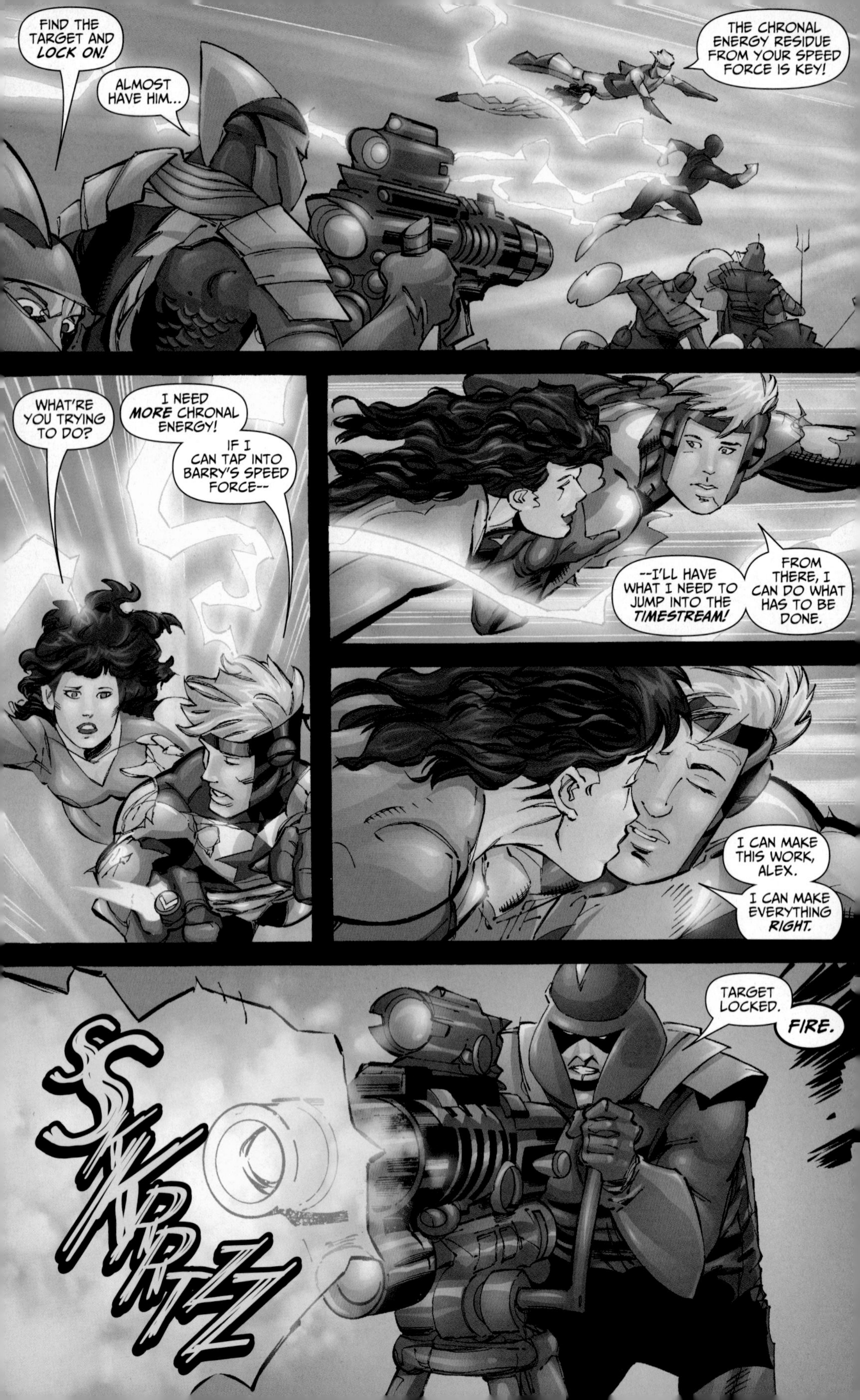
FIND THE TARGET AND LOCK ON!
ALMOST HAVE HIM...
THE CHRONAL ENERGY RESIDUE FROM YOUR SPEED FORCE IS KEY!
WHAT'RE YOU TRYING TO DO?
I NEED MORE CHRONAL ENERGY!
IF I CAN TAP INTO BARRY'S SPEED FORCE--
--I'LL HAVE WHAT I NEED TO JUMP INTO THE TIMESTREAM!
FROM THERE, I CAN DO WHAT HAS TO BE DONE.
I CAN MAKE THIS WORK, ALEX.
I CAN MAKE EVERYTHING RIGHT.
TARGET LOCKED.
FIRE.
SKKRRTZZ

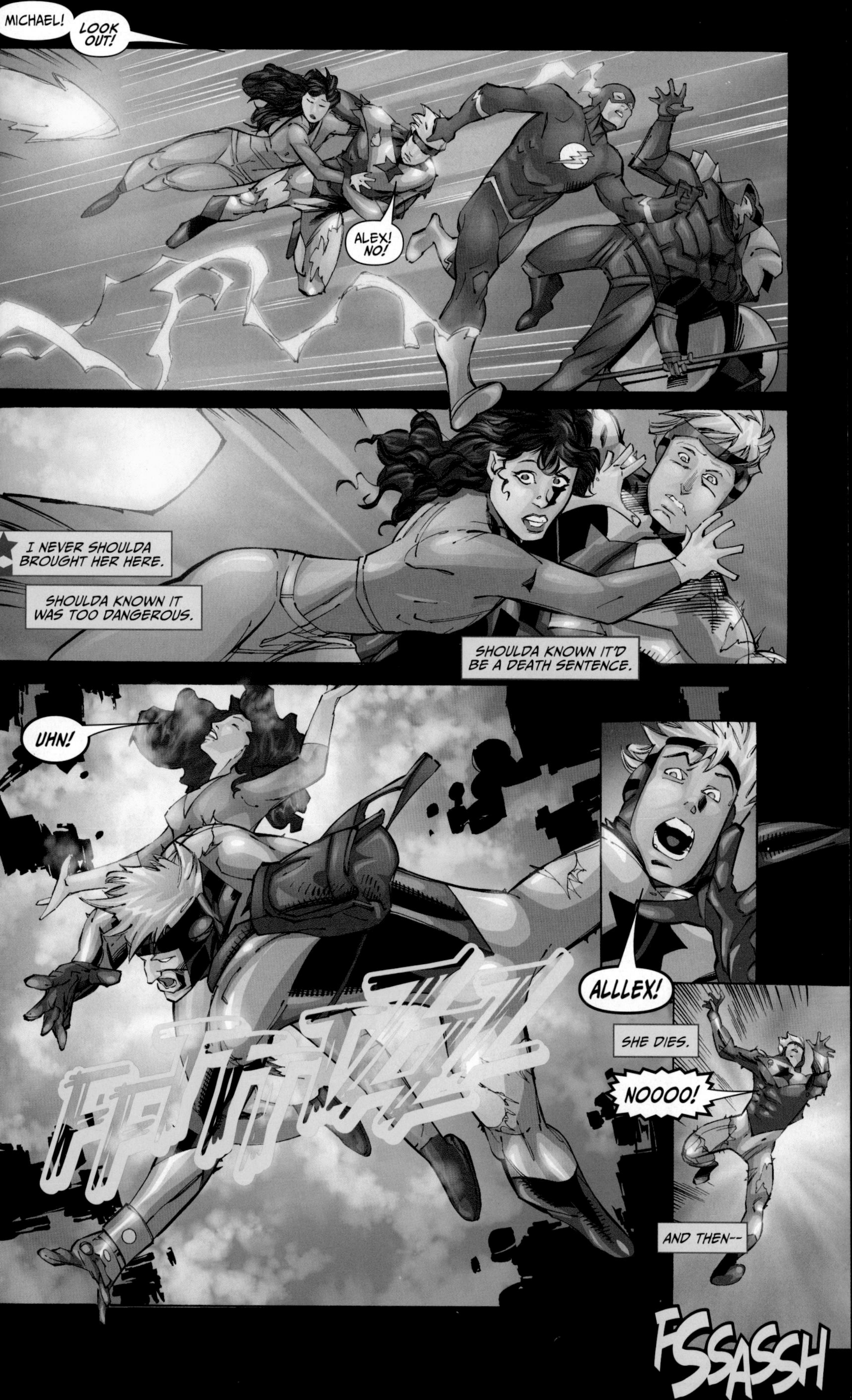
MICHAEL!
LOOK OUT!
ALEX! NO!
I NEVER SHOULDA BROUGHT HER HERE.
SHOULDA KNOWN IT WAS TOO DANGEROUS.
SHOULDA KNOWN IT'D BE A DEATH SENTENCE.
UHN!
ALLLEX!
SHE DIES.
NOOOO!
AND THEN--
FSSASSH

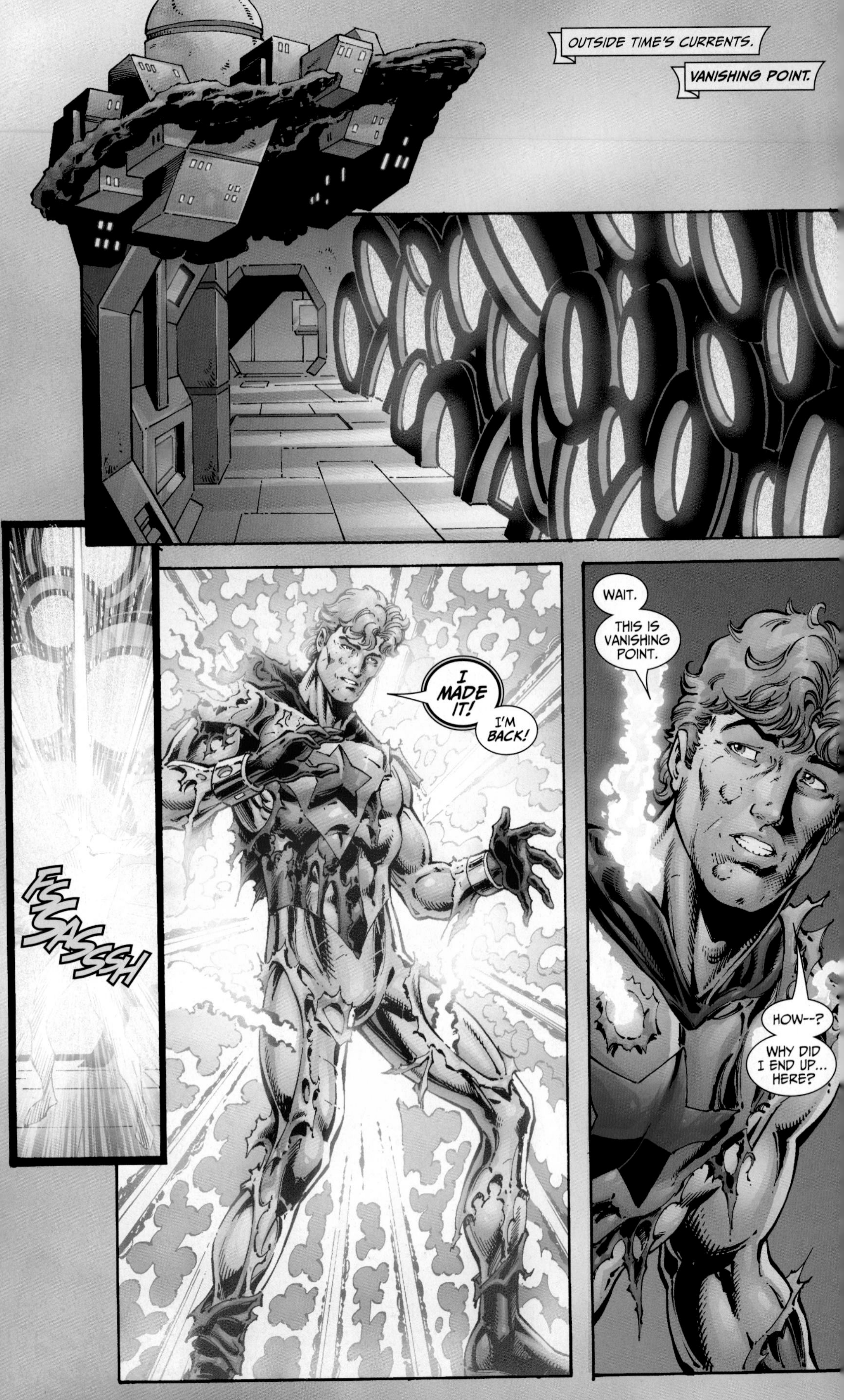
OUTSIDE TIME'S CURRENTS.
VANISHING POINT.
FSSASSSH
I MADE IT!
I'M BACK!
WAIT.
THIS IS VANISHING POINT.
HOW--?
WHY DID I END UP... HERE?

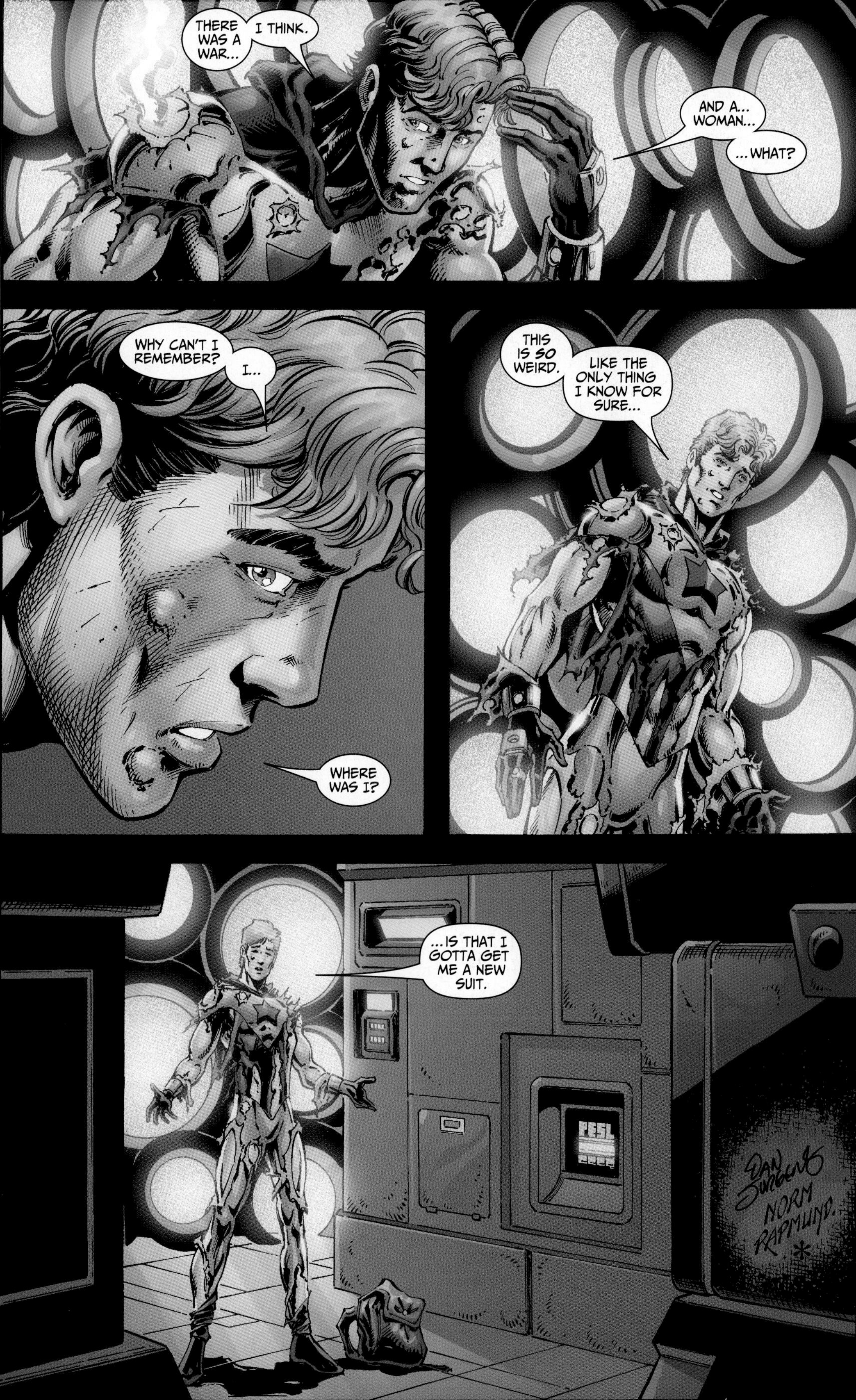

THERE WAS A WAR...
I THINK.
AND A... WOMAN...
...WHAT?
WHY CAN'T I REMEMBER?
I...
WHERE WAS I?
THIS IS SO WEIRD.
LIKE THE ONLY THING I KNOW FOR SURE...
...IS THAT I GOTTA GET ME A NEW SUIT.
PESL
DAN JURGENS
NORM RAPMUND.

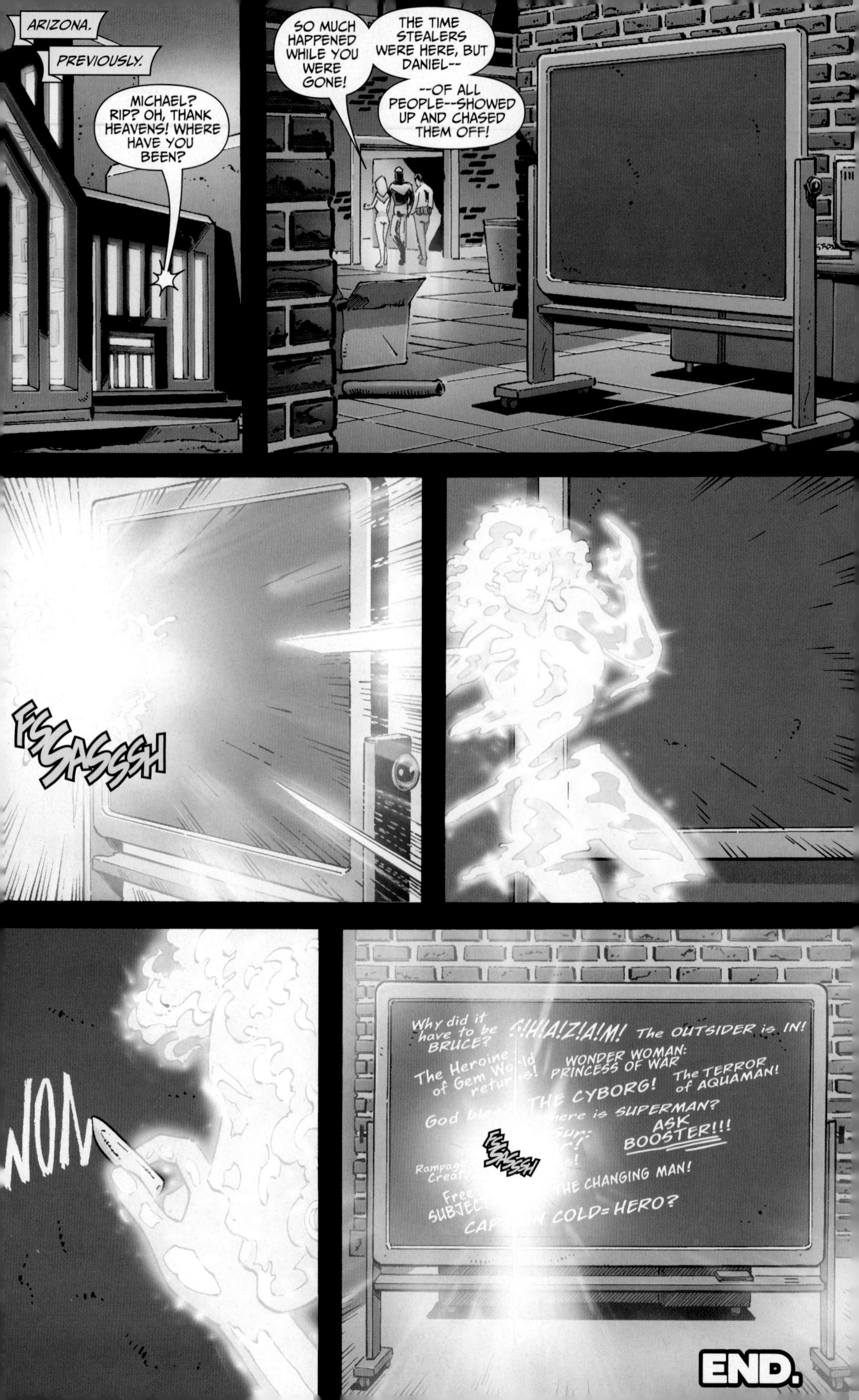
ARIZONA.
PREVIOUSLY.
MICHAEL? RIP? OH, THANK HEAVENS! WHERE HAVE YOU BEEN?
SO MUCH HAPPENED WHILE YOU WERE GONE!
THE TIME STEALERS WERE HERE, BUT DANIEL--
--OF ALL PEOPLE--SHOWED UP AND CHASED THEM OFF!
FSSASSSH
WOM
Why did it have to be BRUCE?
S!H!A!Z!A!M!
The OUTSIDER is IN!
WONDER WOMAN: PRINCESS OF WAR
The TERROR of AQUAMAN!
THE CYBORG!
SUPERMAN?
ASK BOOSTER!!!
FSSASSSH
THE CHANGING MAN!
COLD=HERO?
END.

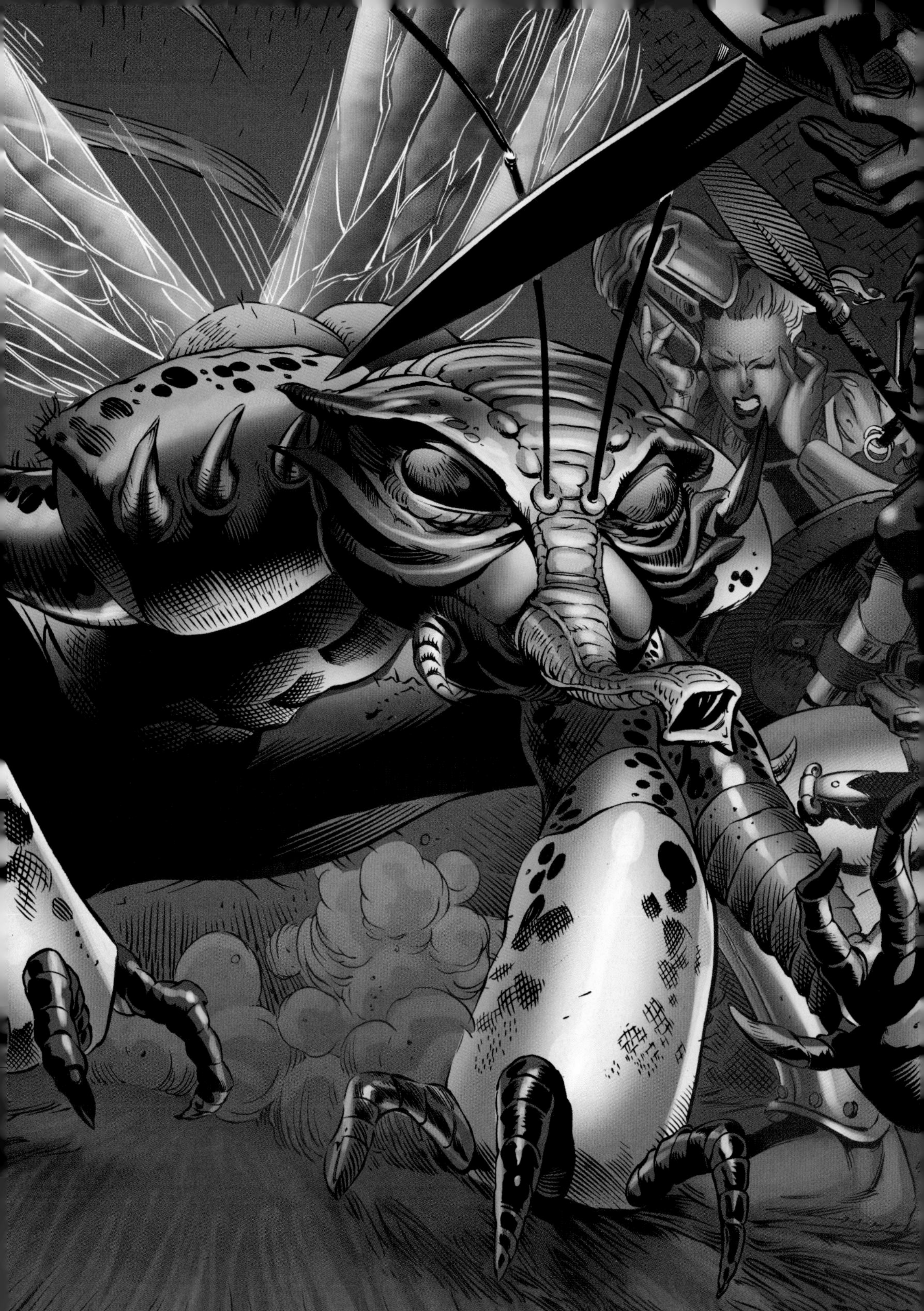

THE CANTERBURY

CRICKET

MIKE CARLIN
Writer

RAGS MORALES
Artist

RICK BRYANT
Inker

Cover by
RAGS MORALES AND **NEI RUFFINO**

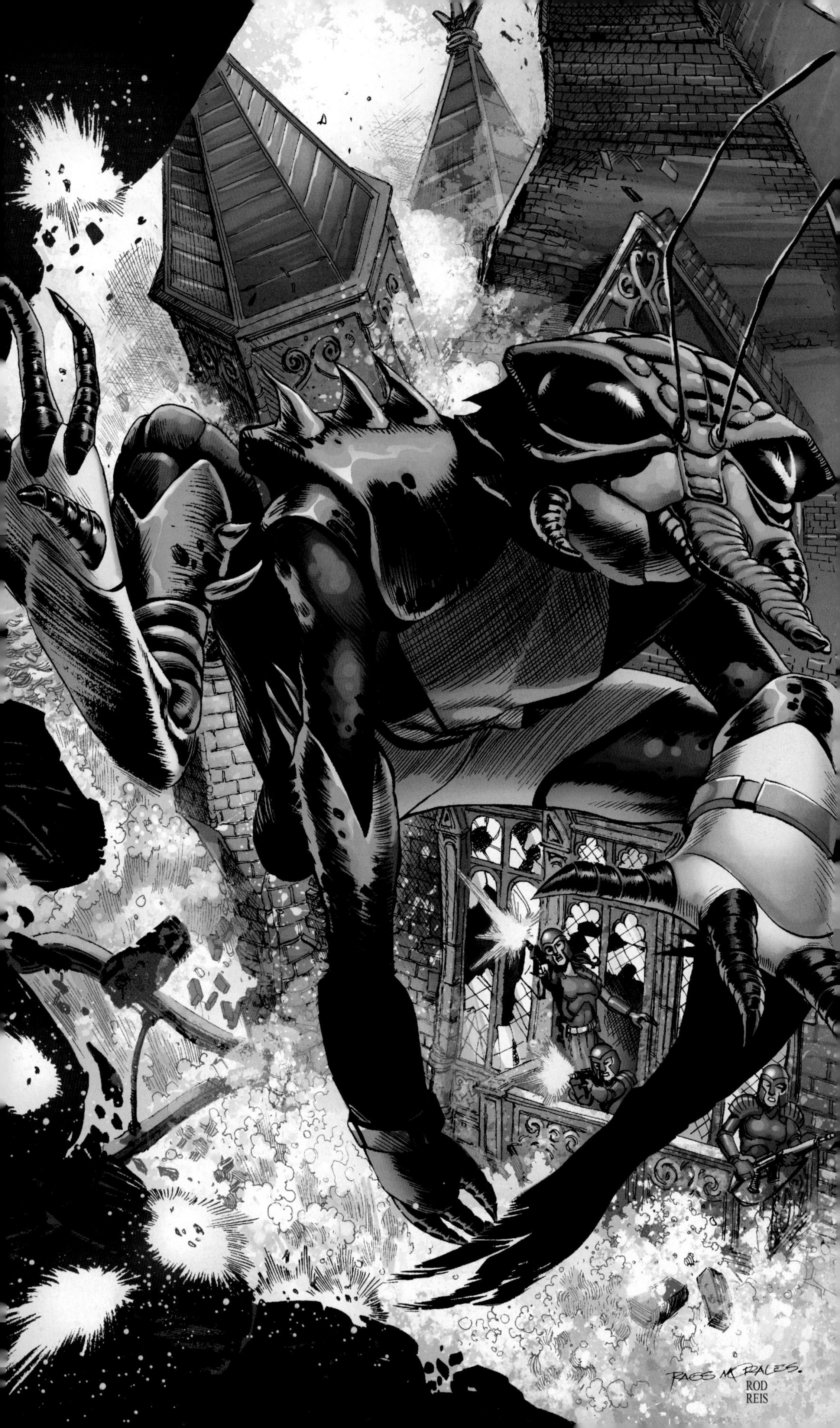
RAGS MORALES.
ROD
REIS

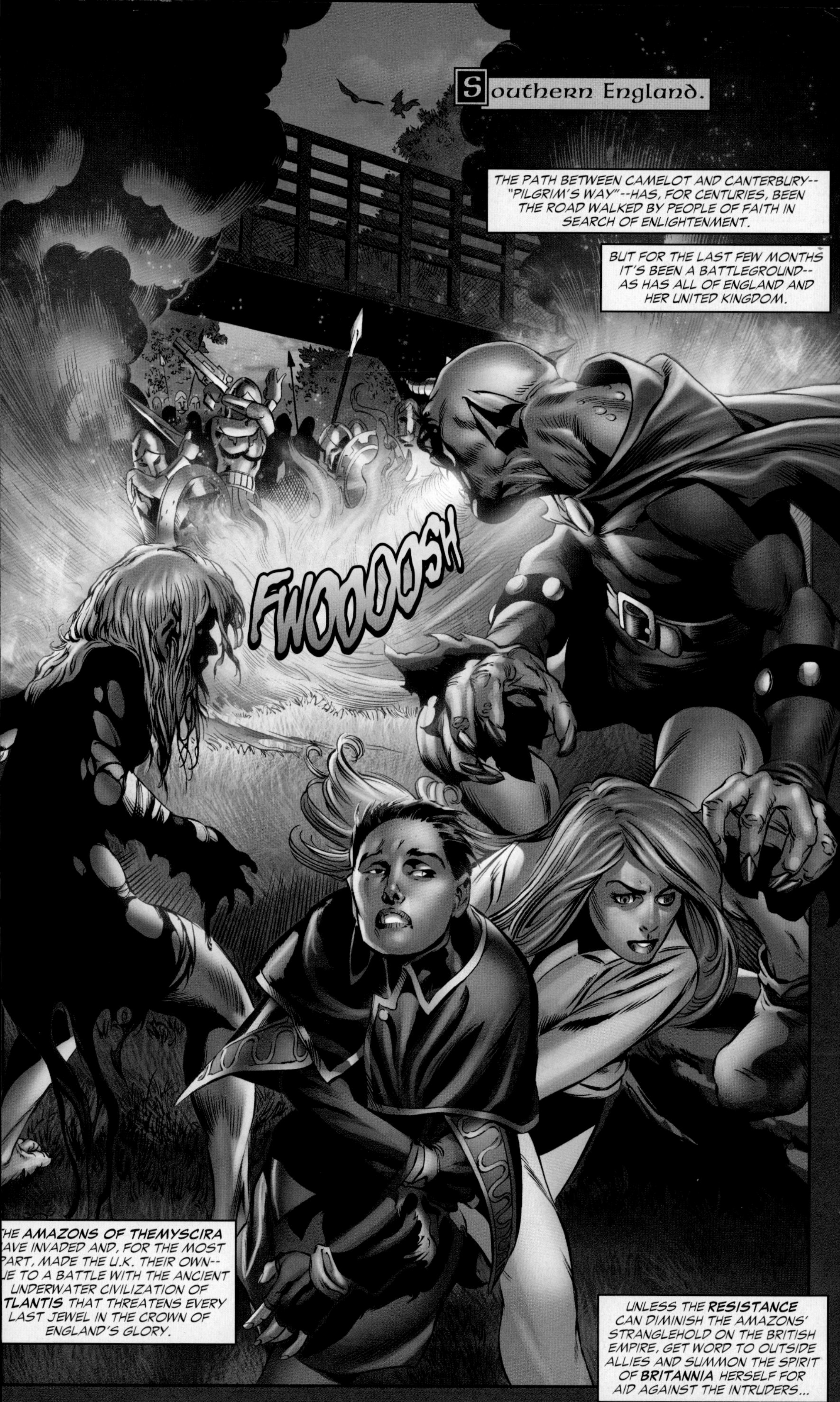
Southern England.
THE PATH BETWEEN CAMELOT AND CANTERBURY-- "PILGRIM'S WAY"--HAS, FOR CENTURIES, BEEN THE ROAD WALKED BY PEOPLE OF FAITH IN SEARCH OF ENLIGHTENMENT.
BUT FOR THE LAST FEW MONTHS IT'S BEEN A BATTLEGROUND-- AS HAS ALL OF ENGLAND AND HER UNITED KINGDOM.
FWOOOOSH
THE AMAZONS OF THEMYSCIRA AVE INVADED AND, FOR THE MOST PART, MADE THE U.K. THEIR OWN-- UE TO A BATTLE WITH THE ANCIENT UNDERWATER CIVILIZATION OF TLANTIS THAT THREATENS EVERY LAST JEWEL IN THE CROWN OF ENGLAND'S GLORY.
UNLESS THE RESISTANCE CAN DIMINISH THE AMAZONS' STRANGLEHOLD ON THE BRITISH EMPIRE, GET WORD TO OUTSIDE ALLIES AND SUMMON THE SPIRIT OF BRITANNIA HERSELF FOR AID AGAINST THE INTRUDERS...

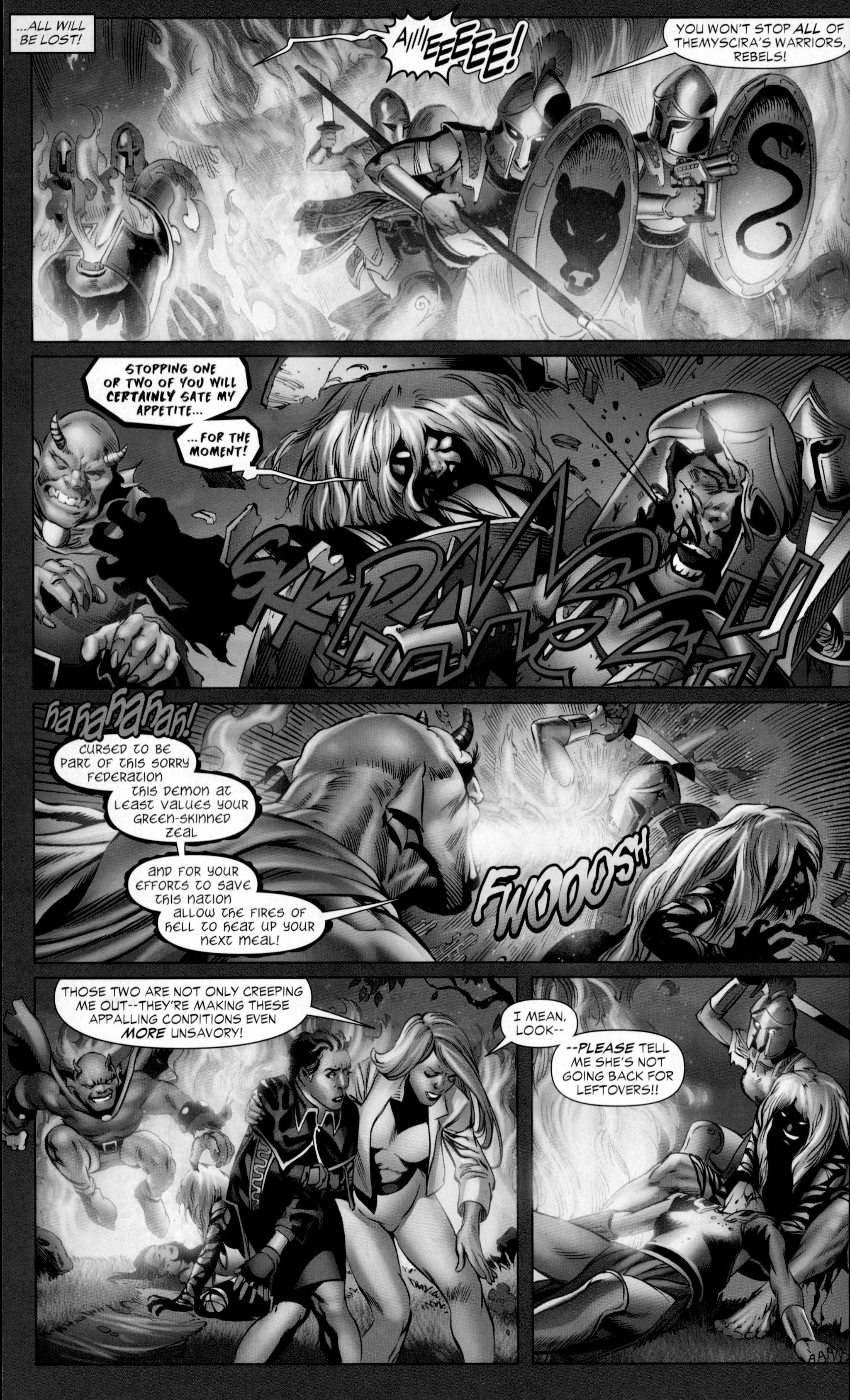

...ALL WILL BE LOST!
AIIIEEEEEE!
YOU WON'T STOP ALL OF THEMYSCIRA'S WARRIORS, REBELS!
STOPPING ONE OR TWO OF YOU WILL CERTAINLY SATE MY APPETITE...
...FOR THE MOMENT!
HAHAHAHAH!
CURSED TO BE PART OF THIS SORRY FEDERATION
THIS DEMON AT LEAST VALUES YOUR GREEN-SKINNED ZEAL
AND FOR YOUR EFFORTS TO SAVE THIS NATION
ALLOW THE FIRES OF HELL TO HEAT UP YOUR NEXT MEAL!
FWOOOSH
THOSE TWO ARE NOT ONLY CREEPING ME OUT--THEY'RE MAKING THESE APPALLING CONDITIONS EVEN MORE UNSAVORY!
I MEAN, LOOK--
--PLEASE TELL ME SHE'S NOT GOING BACK FOR LEFTOVERS!!

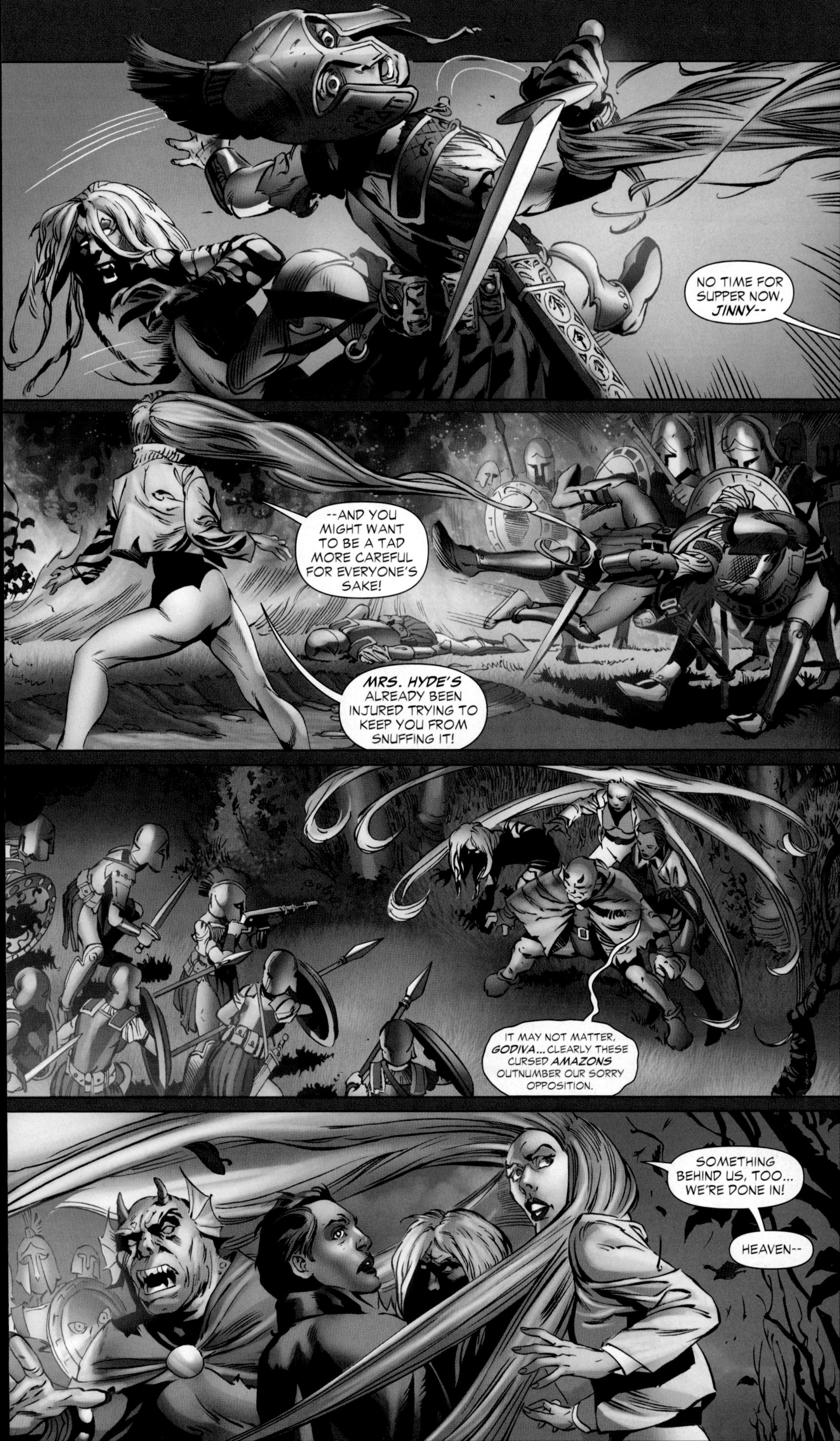
NO TIME FOR SUPPER NOW, *JINNY*--
--AND YOU MIGHT WANT TO BE A TAD MORE CAREFUL FOR EVERYONE'S SAKE!
MRS. HYDE'S ALREADY BEEN INJURED TRYING TO KEEP YOU FROM SNUFFING IT!
IT MAY NOT MATTER, *GODIVA*... CLEARLY THESE CURSED *AMAZONS* OUTNUMBER OUR SORRY OPPOSITION.
SOMETHING BEHIND US, TOO... WE'RE DONE IN!
HEAVEN--

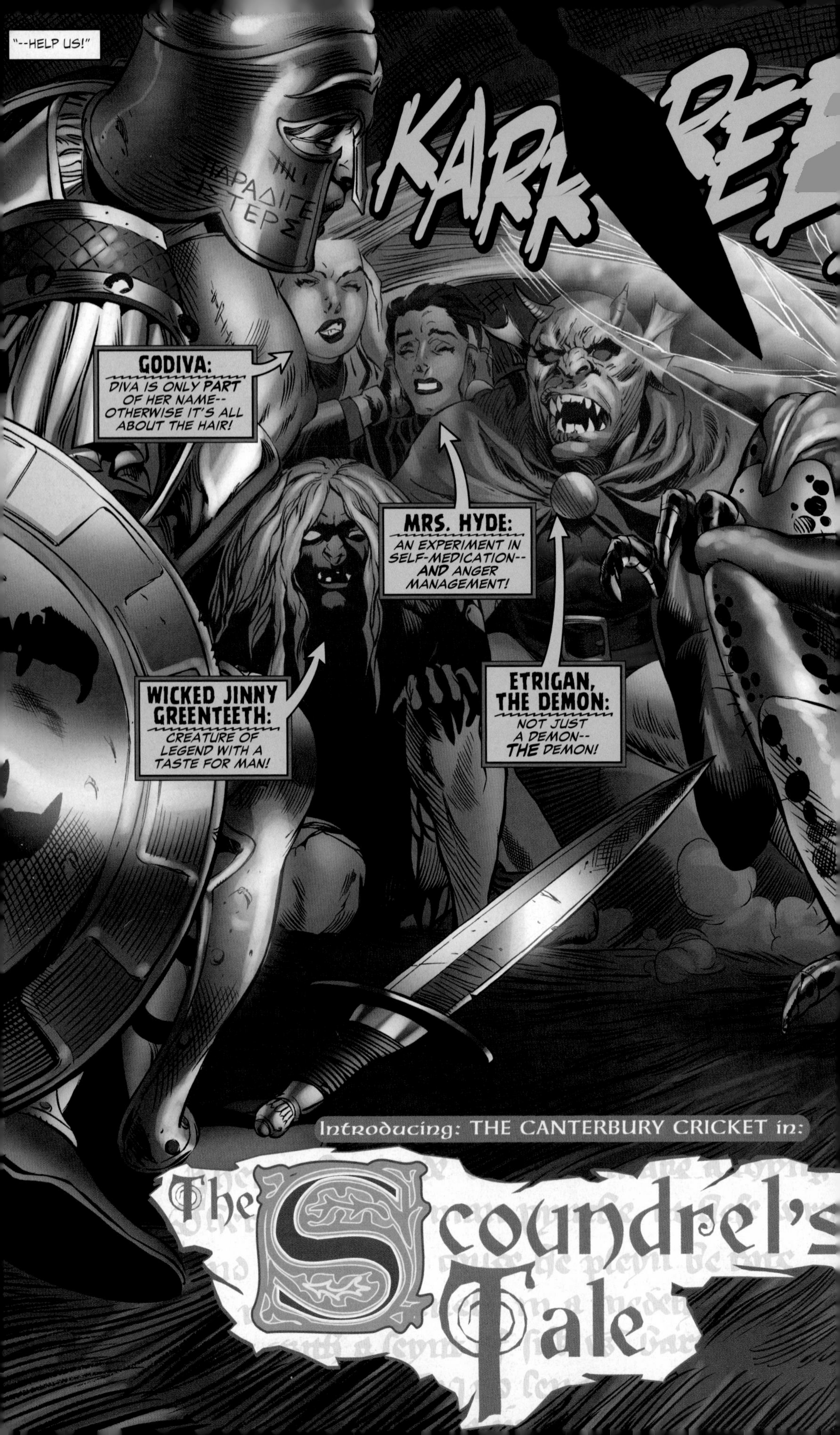
"--HELP US!"
KARR
GODIVA: DIVA IS ONLY PART OF HER NAME-- OTHERWISE IT'S ALL ABOUT THE HAIR!
MRS. HYDE: AN EXPERIMENT IN SELF-MEDICATION-- AND ANGER MANAGEMENT!
WICKED JINNY GREENTEETH: CREATURE OF LEGEND WITH A TASTE FOR MAN!
ETRIGAN, THE DEMON: NOT JUST A DEMON-- THE DEMON!
Introducing: THE CANTERBURY CRICKET in:
The Scoundrel's Tale

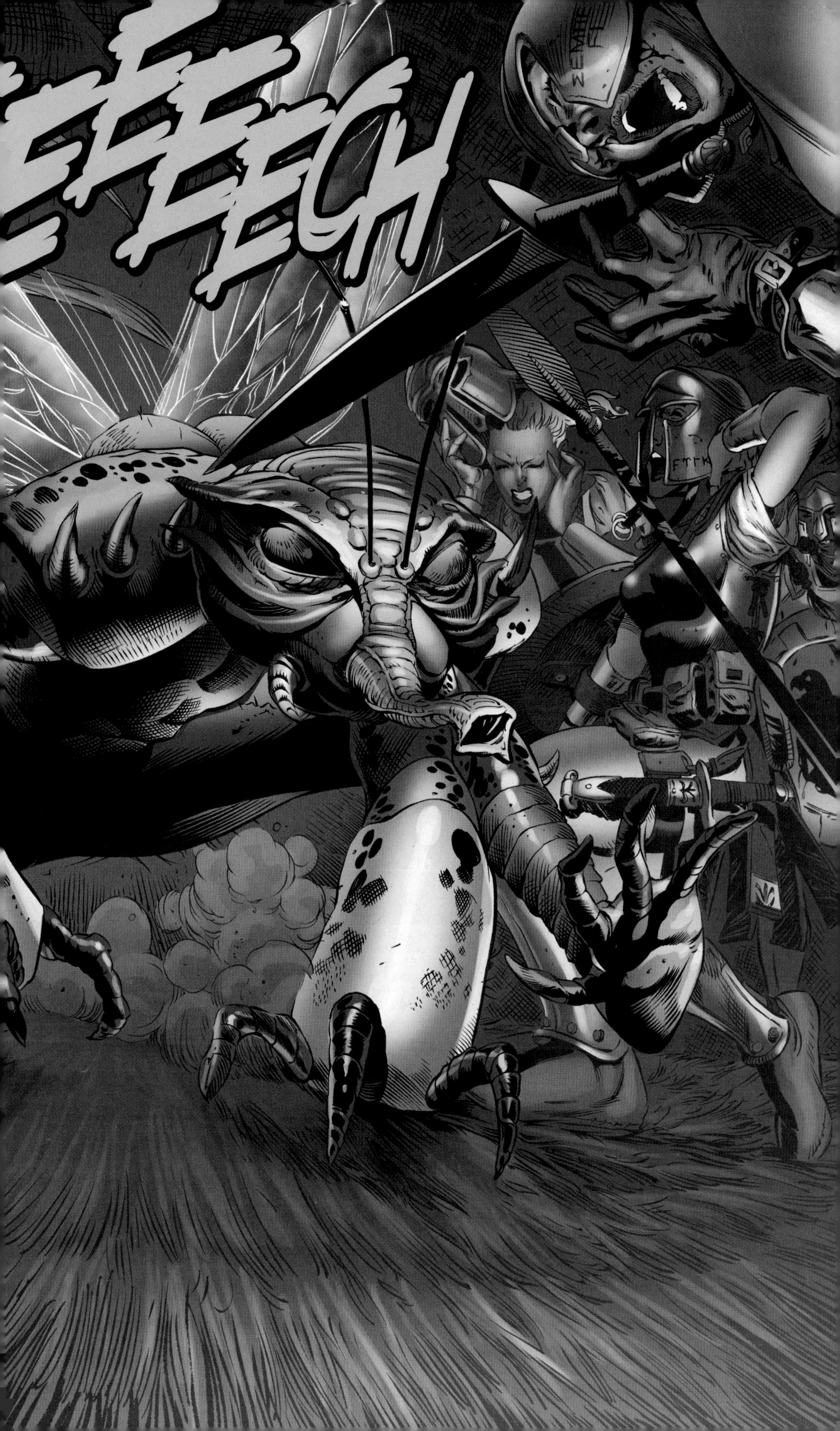
EEEECH

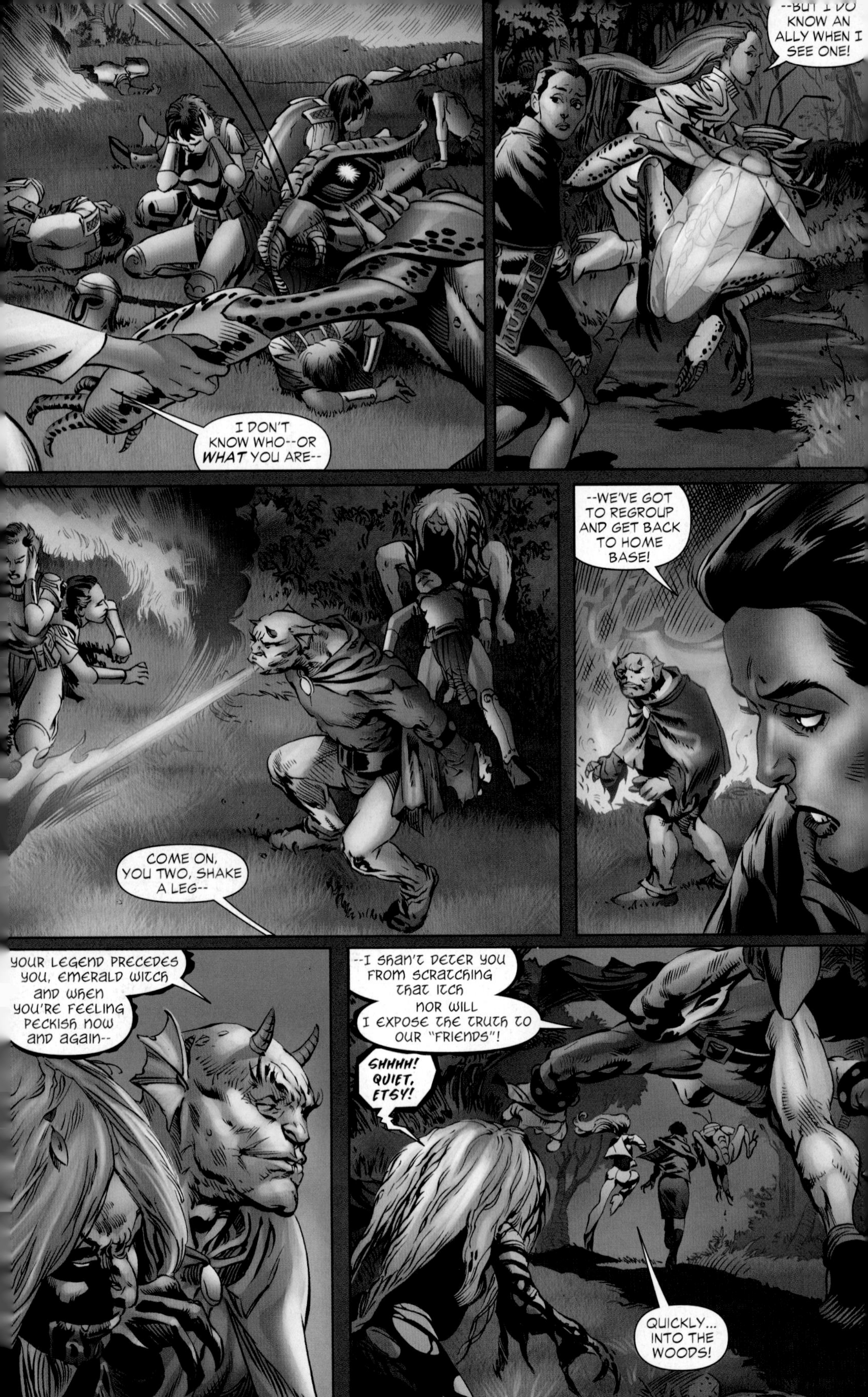

I DON'T KNOW WHO--OR *WHAT* YOU ARE--
--BUT I DO KNOW AN ALLY WHEN I SEE ONE!
COME ON, YOU TWO, SHAKE A LEG--
--WE'VE GOT TO REGROUP AND GET BACK TO HOME BASE!
YOUR LEGEND PRECEDES YOU, EMERALD WITCH AND WHEN YOU'RE FEELING PECKISH NOW AND AGAIN--
--I SHAN'T DETER YOU FROM SCRATCHING THAT ITCH NOR WILL I EXPOSE THE TRUTH TO OUR "FRIENDS"!
SHHHH! QUIET, ETSY!
QUICKLY... INTO THE WOODS!

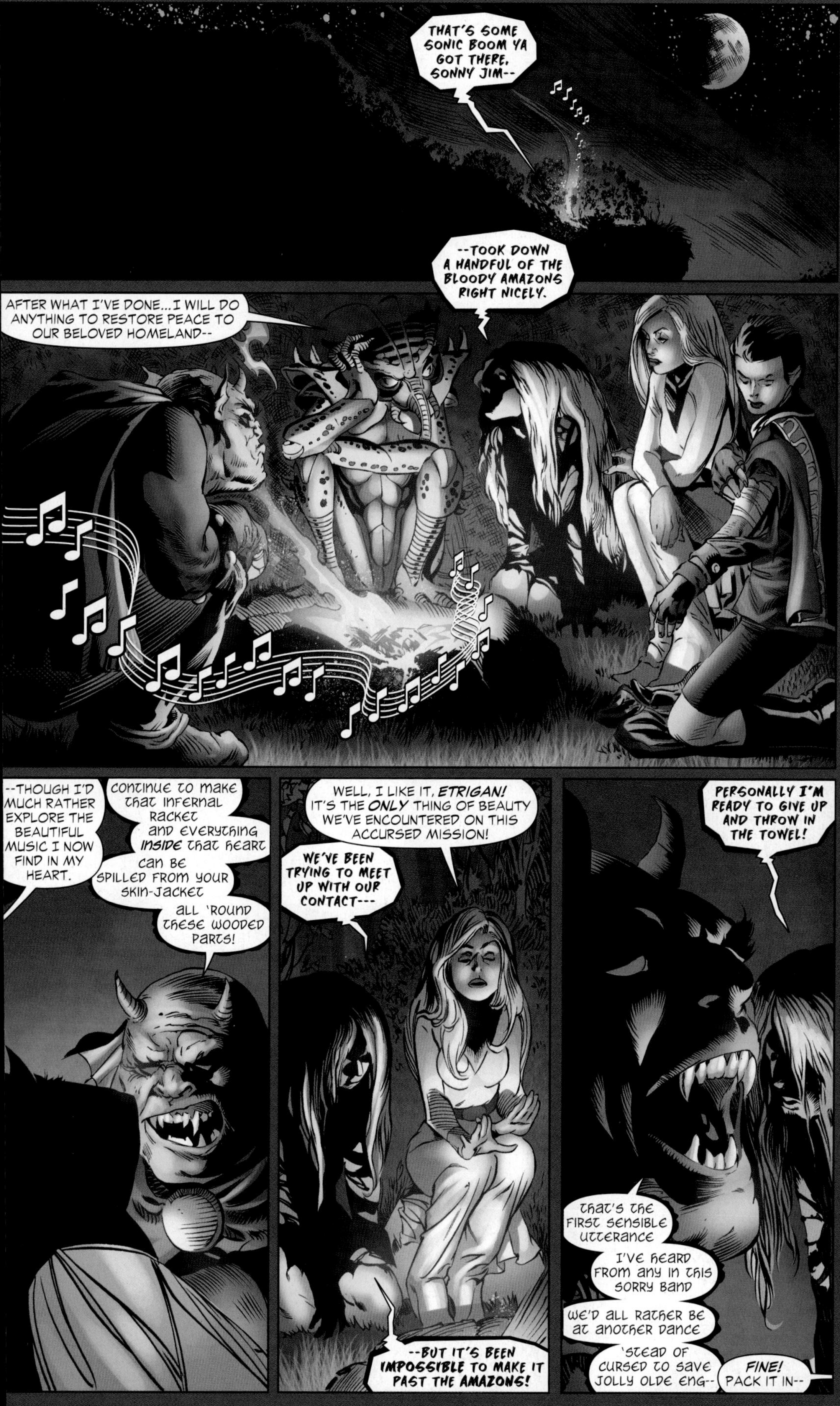

THAT'S SOME SONIC BOOM YA GOT THERE, SONNY JIM--
--TOOK DOWN A HANDFUL OF THE BLOODY AMAZONS RIGHT NICELY.
AFTER WHAT I'VE DONE... I WILL DO ANYTHING TO RESTORE PEACE TO OUR BELOVED HOMELAND--
--THOUGH I'D MUCH RATHER EXPLORE THE BEAUTIFUL MUSIC I NOW FIND IN MY HEART.
CONTINUE TO MAKE THAT INFERNAL RACKET
AND EVERYTHING INSIDE THAT HEART
CAN BE SPILLED FROM YOUR SKIN-JACKET
ALL 'ROUND THESE WOODED PARTS!
WELL, I LIKE IT, ETRIGAN! IT'S THE ONLY THING OF BEAUTY WE'VE ENCOUNTERED ON THIS ACCURSED MISSION!
WE'VE BEEN TRYING TO MEET UP WITH OUR CONTACT---
--BUT IT'S BEEN IMPOSSIBLE TO MAKE IT PAST THE AMAZONS!
PERSONALLY I'M READY TO GIVE UP AND THROW IN THE TOWEL!
THAT'S THE FIRST SENSIBLE UTTERANCE
I'VE HEARD FROM ANY IN THIS SORRY BAND
WE'D ALL RATHER BE AT ANOTHER DANCE
'STEAD OF CURSED TO SAVE JOLLY OLDE ENG--
FINE! PACK IT IN--

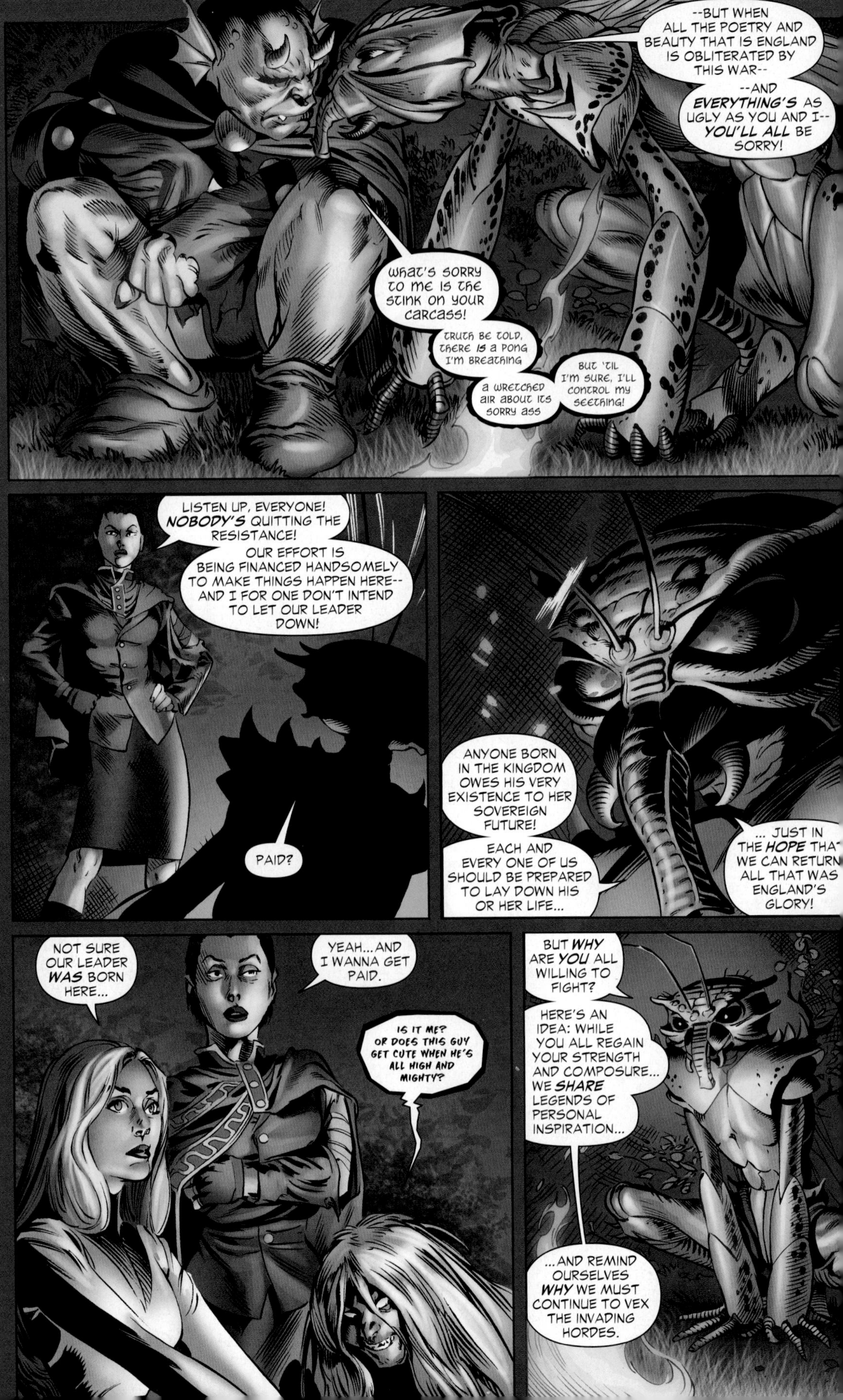
--BUT WHEN ALL THE POETRY AND BEAUTY THAT IS ENGLAND IS OBLITERATED BY THIS WAR--
--AND EVERYTHING'S AS UGLY AS YOU AND I-- YOU'LL ALL BE SORRY!
WHAT'S SORRY TO ME IS THE STINK ON YOUR CARCASS!
TRUTH BE TOLD, THERE IS A PONG I'M BREATHING
A WRETCHED AIR ABOUT ITS SORRY ASS
BUT 'TIL I'M SURE, I'LL CONTROL MY SEETHING!
LISTEN UP, EVERYONE! NOBODY'S QUITTING THE RESISTANCE!
OUR EFFORT IS BEING FINANCED HANDSOMELY TO MAKE THINGS HAPPEN HERE-- AND I FOR ONE DON'T INTEND TO LET OUR LEADER DOWN!
PAID?
ANYONE BORN IN THE KINGDOM OWES HIS VERY EXISTENCE TO HER SOVEREIGN FUTURE!
EACH AND EVERY ONE OF US SHOULD BE PREPARED TO LAY DOWN HIS OR HER LIFE...
... JUST IN THE HOPE THAT WE CAN RETURN ALL THAT WAS ENGLAND'S GLORY!
NOT SURE OUR LEADER WAS BORN HERE...
YEAH... AND I WANNA GET PAID.
IS IT ME? OR DOES THIS GUY GET CUTE WHEN HE'S ALL HIGH AND MIGHTY?
BUT WHY ARE YOU ALL WILLING TO FIGHT?
HERE'S AN IDEA: WHILE YOU ALL REGAIN YOUR STRENGTH AND COMPOSURE... WE SHARE LEGENDS OF PERSONAL INSPIRATION...
...AND REMIND OURSELVES WHY WE MUST CONTINUE TO VEX THE INVADING HORDES.

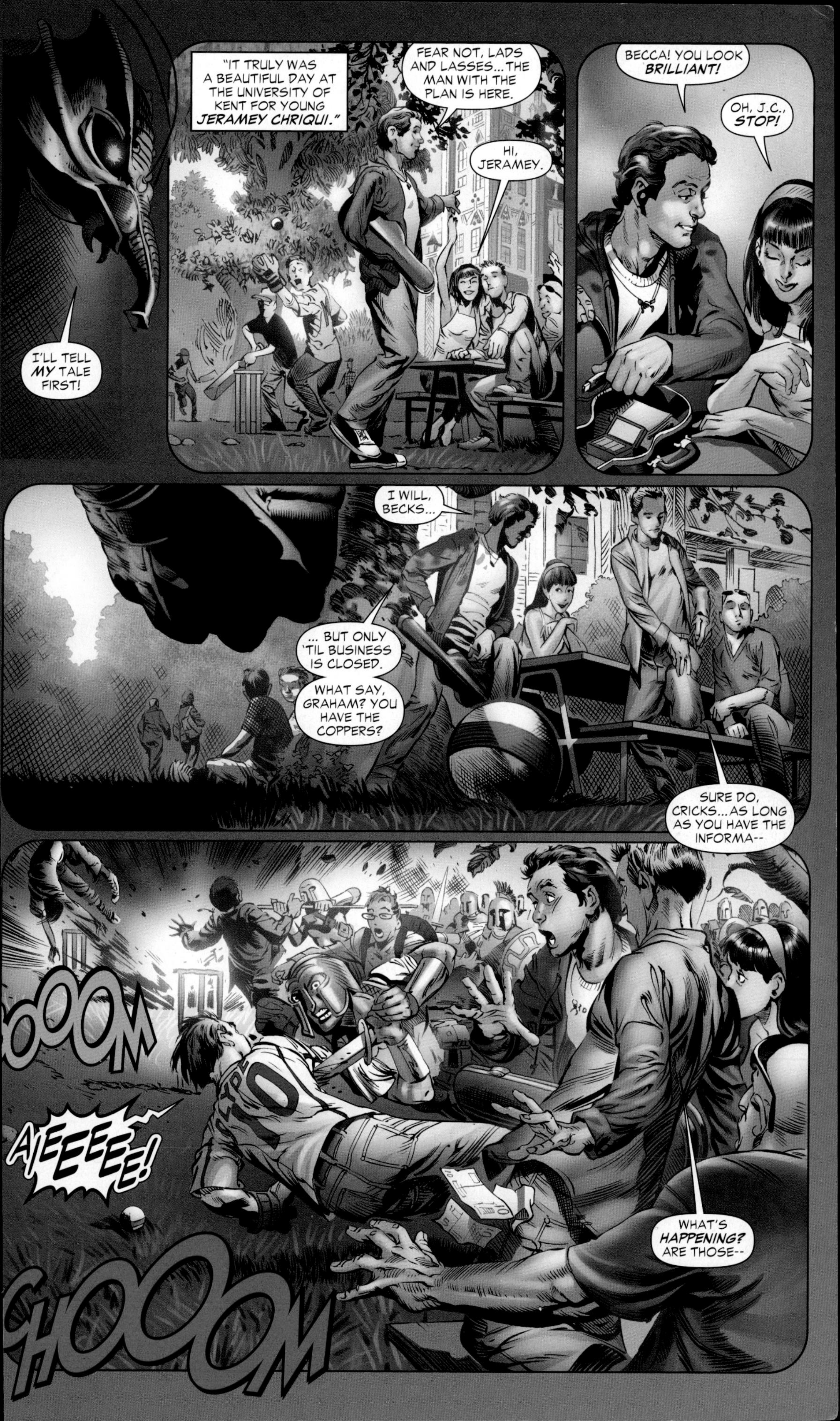
I'LL TELL MY TALE FIRST!
"IT TRULY WAS A BEAUTIFUL DAY AT THE UNIVERSITY OF KENT FOR YOUNG JERAMEY CHRIQUI."
FEAR NOT, LADS AND LASSES... THE MAN WITH THE PLAN IS HERE.
HI, JERAMEY.
BECCA! YOU LOOK BRILLIANT!
OH, J.C., STOP!
I WILL, BECKS...
... BUT ONLY 'TIL BUSINESS IS CLOSED.
WHAT SAY, GRAHAM? YOU HAVE THE COPPERS?
SURE DO, CRICKS... AS LONG AS YOU HAVE THE INFORMA--
BOOOM
AIEEEEEE!
WHAT'S HAPPENING? ARE THOSE--
CHOOOM

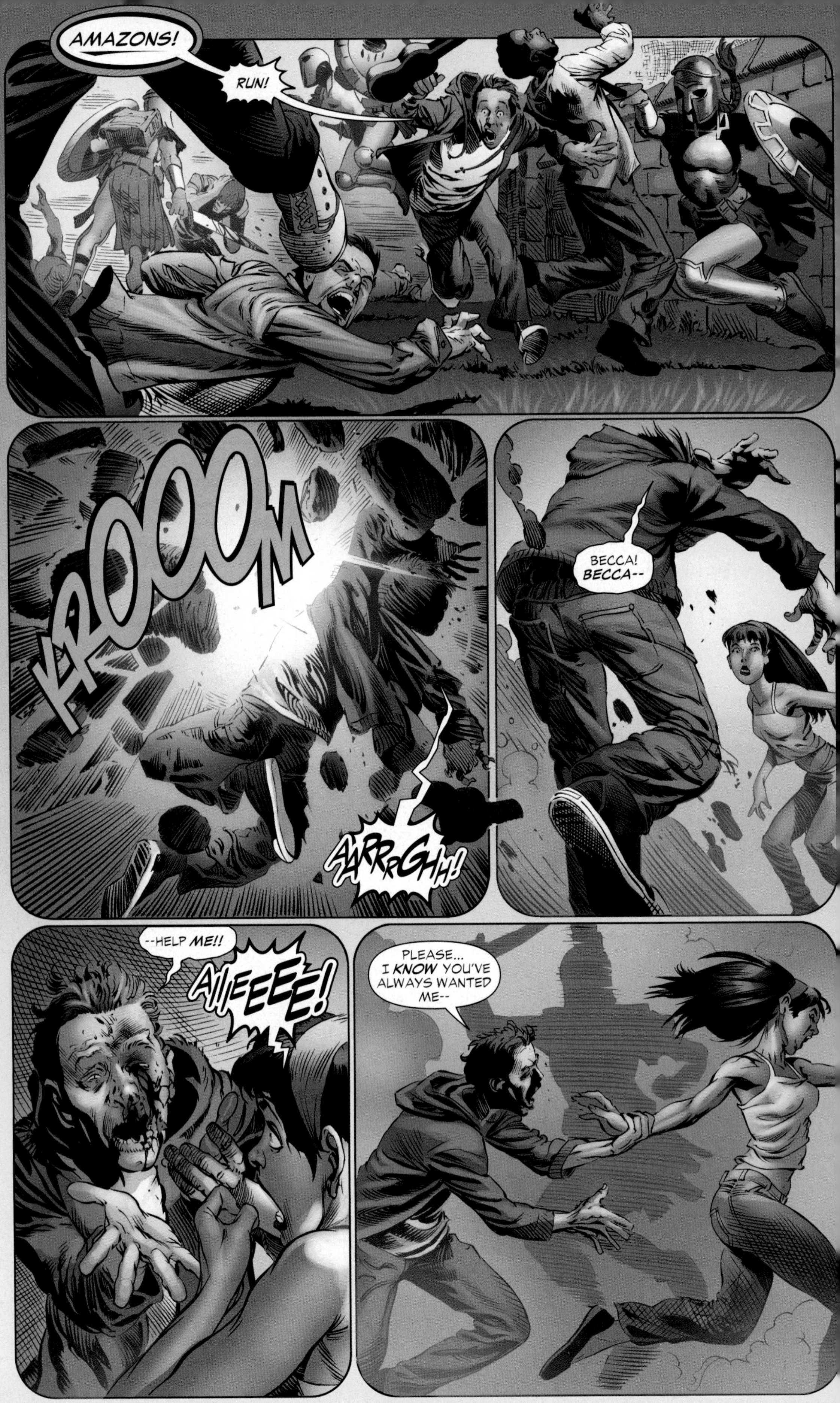
AMAZONS!
RUN!
KROOOM
AARRRGHH!
BECCA! BECCA--
--HELP ME!!
AIIEEEE!
PLEASE... I KNOW YOU'VE ALWAYS WANTED ME--

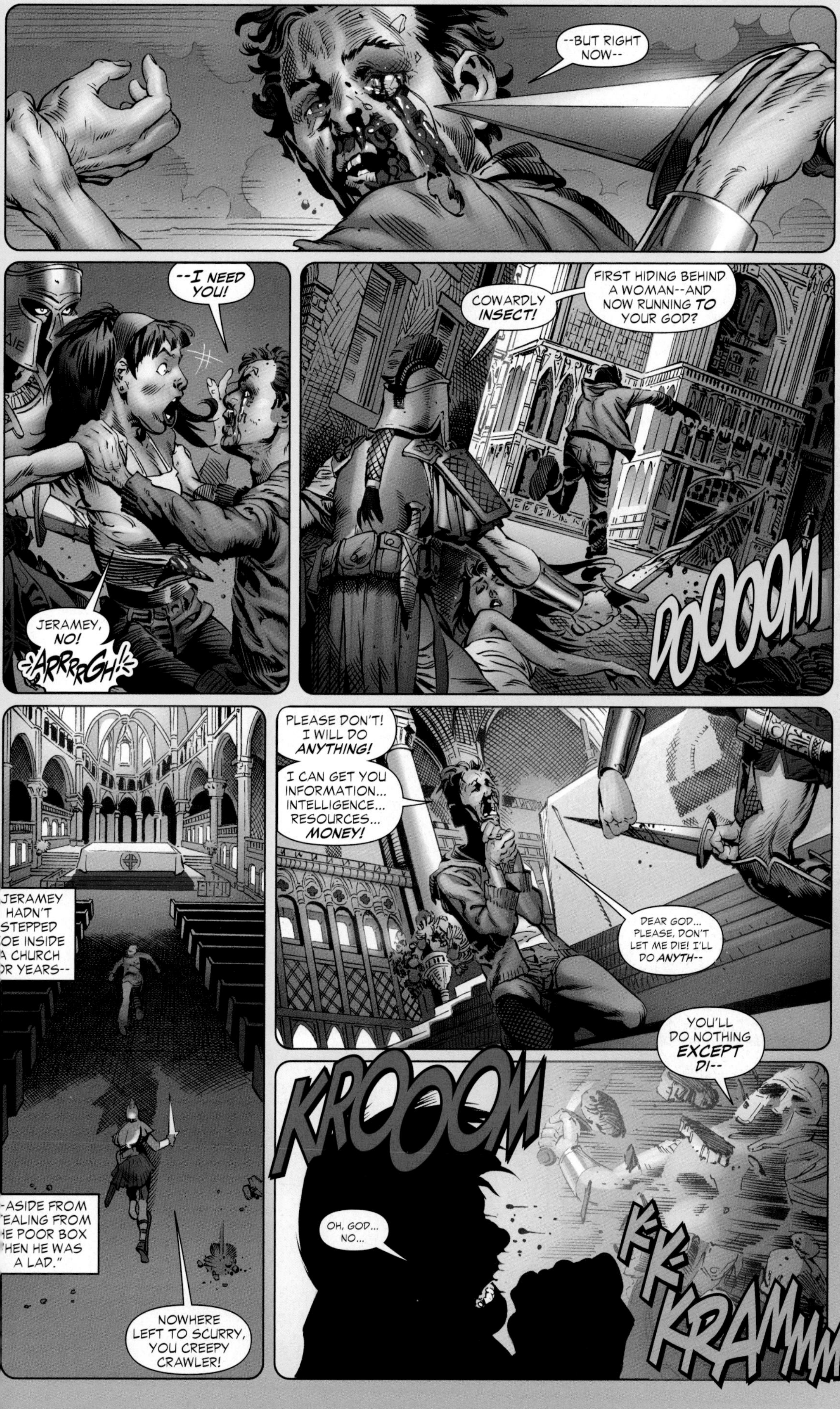
--BUT RIGHT NOW--
--I NEED YOU!
JERAMEY, NO!
ARRRRGH!
COWARDLY INSECT!
FIRST HIDING BEHIND A WOMAN--AND NOW RUNNING TO YOUR GOD?
DOOOOM
JERAMEY HADN'T STEPPED OOE INSIDE A CHURCH OR YEARS--
-ASIDE FROM TEALING FROM HE POOR BOX HEN HE WAS A LAD."
NOWHERE LEFT TO SCURRY, YOU CREEPY CRAWLER!
PLEASE DON'T! I WILL DO ANYTHING!
I CAN GET YOU INFORMATION... INTELLIGENCE... RESOURCES... MONEY!
DEAR GOD... PLEASE, DON'T LET ME DIE! I'LL DO ANYTH--
YOU'LL DO NOTHING EXCEPT DI--
KROOOM
OH, GOD... NO...
K-K-KRAMMMM

"JERAMEY STOOD... SPARED...

"AND...IN STARK CONTRAST TO THE SOUNDS OF WAR AROUND HIM...HE HEARD SOMETHING.

"SOMETHING... SMALL.

KRRKT KRRKT KRRK

BARROOOM

"SOMETHING... UNNERVING.

KRRRKT

"FACE TO FACE WITH THE PAST...

KRRKT

KRRKT

KRRKT

"...AND SUDDENLY FACING THE FUTURE...

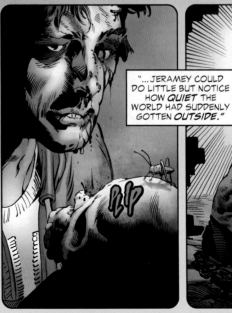

RIP

"...JERAMEY COULD DO LITTLE BUT NOTICE HOW QUIET THE WORLD HAD SUDDENLY GOTTEN OUTSIDE."

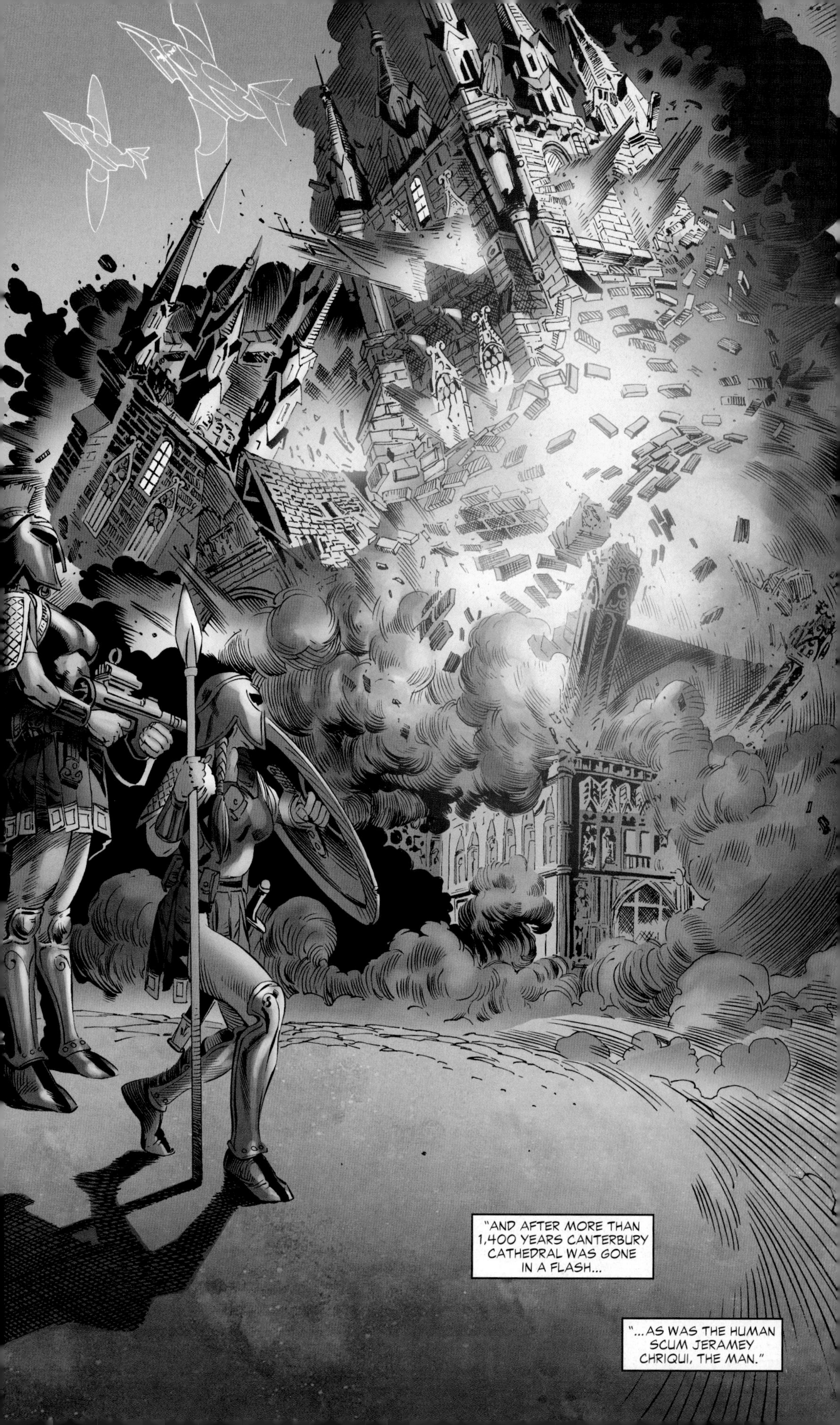
"AND AFTER MORE THAN 1,400 YEARS CANTERBURY CATHEDRAL WAS GONE IN A FLASH...
"...AS WAS THE HUMAN SCUM JERAMEY CHRIQUI, THE MAN."

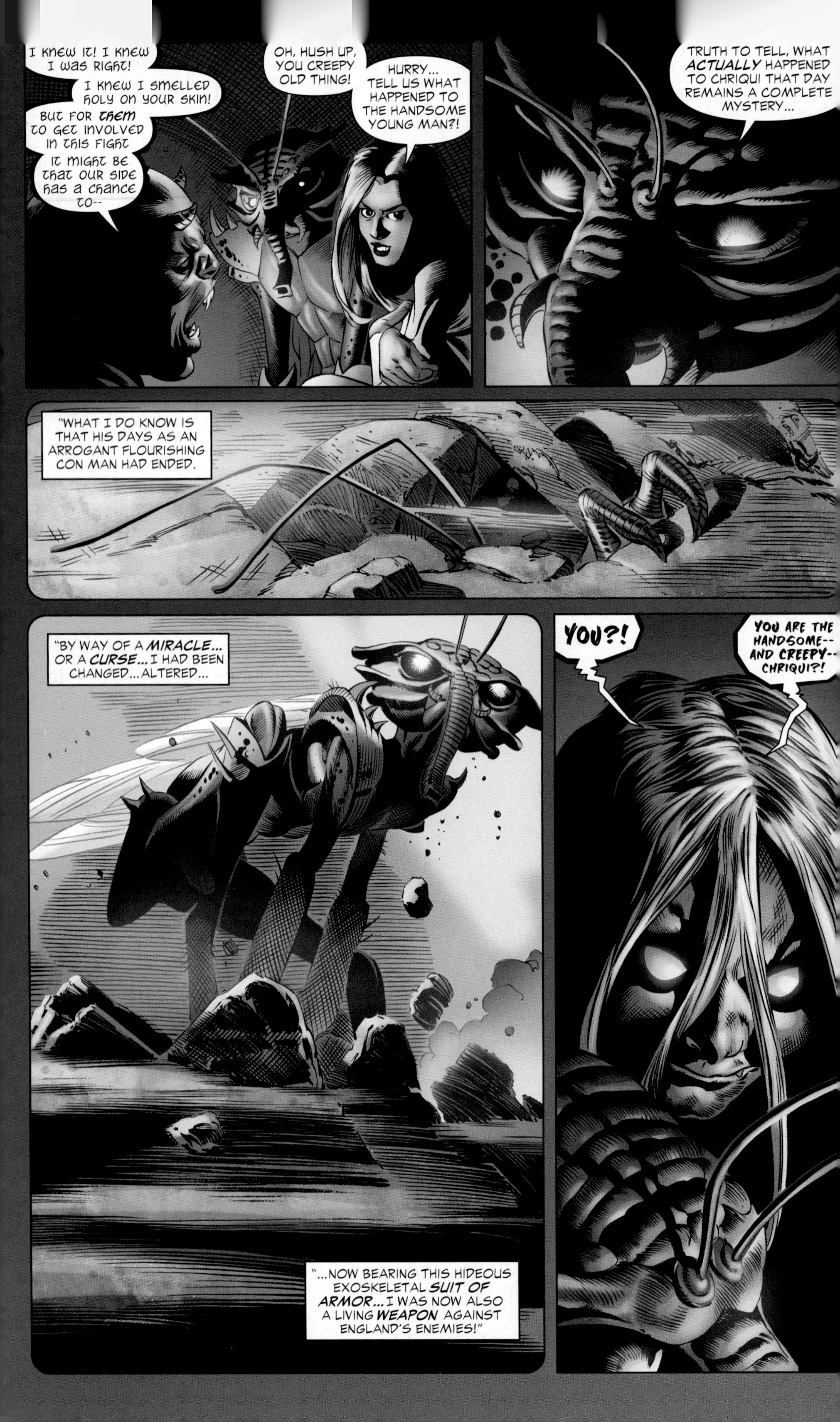
I KNEW IT! I KNEW I WAS RIGHT!
I KNEW I SMELLED HOLY ON YOUR SKIN!
BUT FOR THEM TO GET INVOLVED IN THIS FIGHT
IT MIGHT BE THAT OUR SIDE HAS A CHANCE TO--
OH, HUSH UP, YOU CREEPY OLD THING!
HURRY... TELL US WHAT HAPPENED TO THE HANDSOME YOUNG MAN?!
TRUTH TO TELL, WHAT ACTUALLY HAPPENED TO CHRIQUI THAT DAY REMAINS A COMPLETE MYSTERY...
"WHAT I DO KNOW IS THAT HIS DAYS AS AN ARROGANT FLOURISHING CON MAN HAD ENDED.
"BY WAY OF A MIRACLE... OR A CURSE... I HAD BEEN CHANGED... ALTERED...
"...NOW BEARING THIS HIDEOUS EXOSKELETAL SUIT OF ARMOR... I WAS NOW ALSO A LIVING WEAPON AGAINST ENGLAND'S ENEMIES!"
YOU?!
YOU ARE THE HANDSOME-- AND CREEPY-- CHRIQUI?!

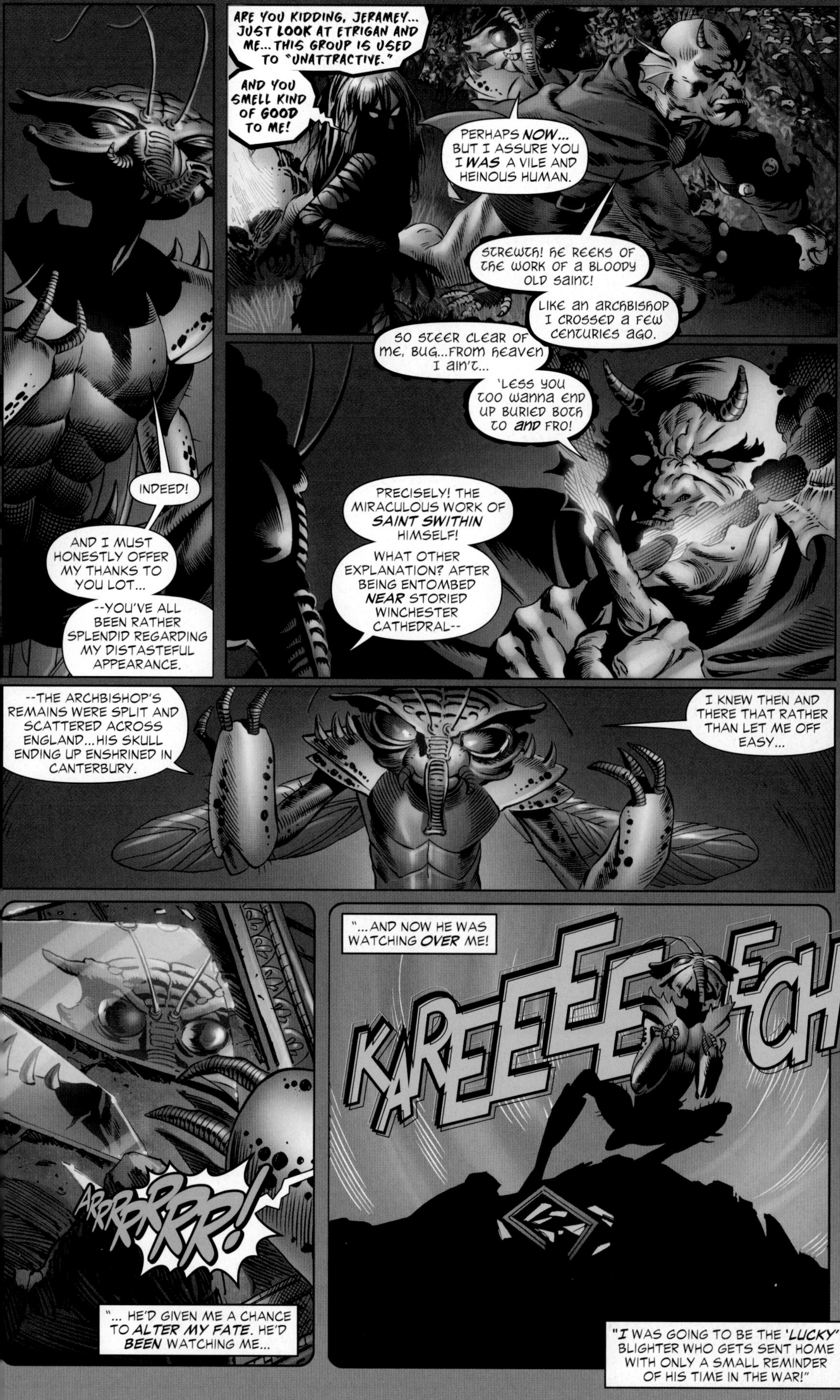
ARE YOU KIDDING, JERAMEY... JUST LOOK AT ETRIGAN AND ME... THIS GROUP IS USED TO "UNATTRACTIVE."
AND YOU SMELL KIND OF GOOD TO ME!
PERHAPS NOW... BUT I ASSURE YOU I WAS A VILE AND HEINOUS HUMAN.
STREWTH! HE REEKS OF THE WORK OF A BLOODY OLD SAINT!
LIKE AN ARCHBISHOP I CROSSED A FEW CENTURIES AGO.
SO STEER CLEAR OF ME, BUG...FROM HEAVEN I AIN'T...
'LESS YOU TOO WANNA END UP BURIED BOTH TO AND FRO!
INDEED!
AND I MUST HONESTLY OFFER MY THANKS TO YOU LOT...
--YOU'VE ALL BEEN RATHER SPLENDID REGARDING MY DISTASTEFUL APPEARANCE.
PRECISELY! THE MIRACULOUS WORK OF SAINT SWITHIN HIMSELF!
WHAT OTHER EXPLANATION? AFTER BEING ENTOMBED NEAR STORIED WINCHESTER CATHEDRAL--
--THE ARCHBISHOP'S REMAINS WERE SPLIT AND SCATTERED ACROSS ENGLAND...HIS SKULL ENDING UP ENSHRINED IN CANTERBURY.
I KNEW THEN AND THERE THAT RATHER THAN LET ME OFF EASY...
ARRRRRRRR!
"... HE'D GIVEN ME A CHANCE TO ALTER MY FATE. HE'D BEEN WATCHING ME...
"...AND NOW HE WAS WATCHING OVER ME!
KAREEEEECH
"I WAS GOING TO BE THE 'LUCKY' BLIGHTER WHO GETS SENT HOME WITH ONLY A SMALL REMINDER OF HIS TIME IN THE WAR!"

I DIDN'T KNOW IT THEN...BUT I'D BEEN GIVEN A CHANCE TO MAKE MY INSIDES BETTER WHILE MY OUTSIDES...WELL... YOU CAN SEE...
"SO I SEIZED THIS OPPORTUNITY TO REDEEM MYSELF...
"...BY ALLYING WITH THE FINEST BATTALION OF AMBUSH BUGS ON GOD'S EARTH.
"ALL WITH THE SAME SACRED MISSION: TAKE DOWN THE ENEMY!
"QUEEN BEE! THE COCKROACH! FIREFLY! AND BLUE BEETLE!
"AN INTERNATIONAL GATHERING OF CONDEMNED SOULS WITH LITERALLY NOTHING TO LOSE--
"--SAVE OUR HIDEOUS LIVES!

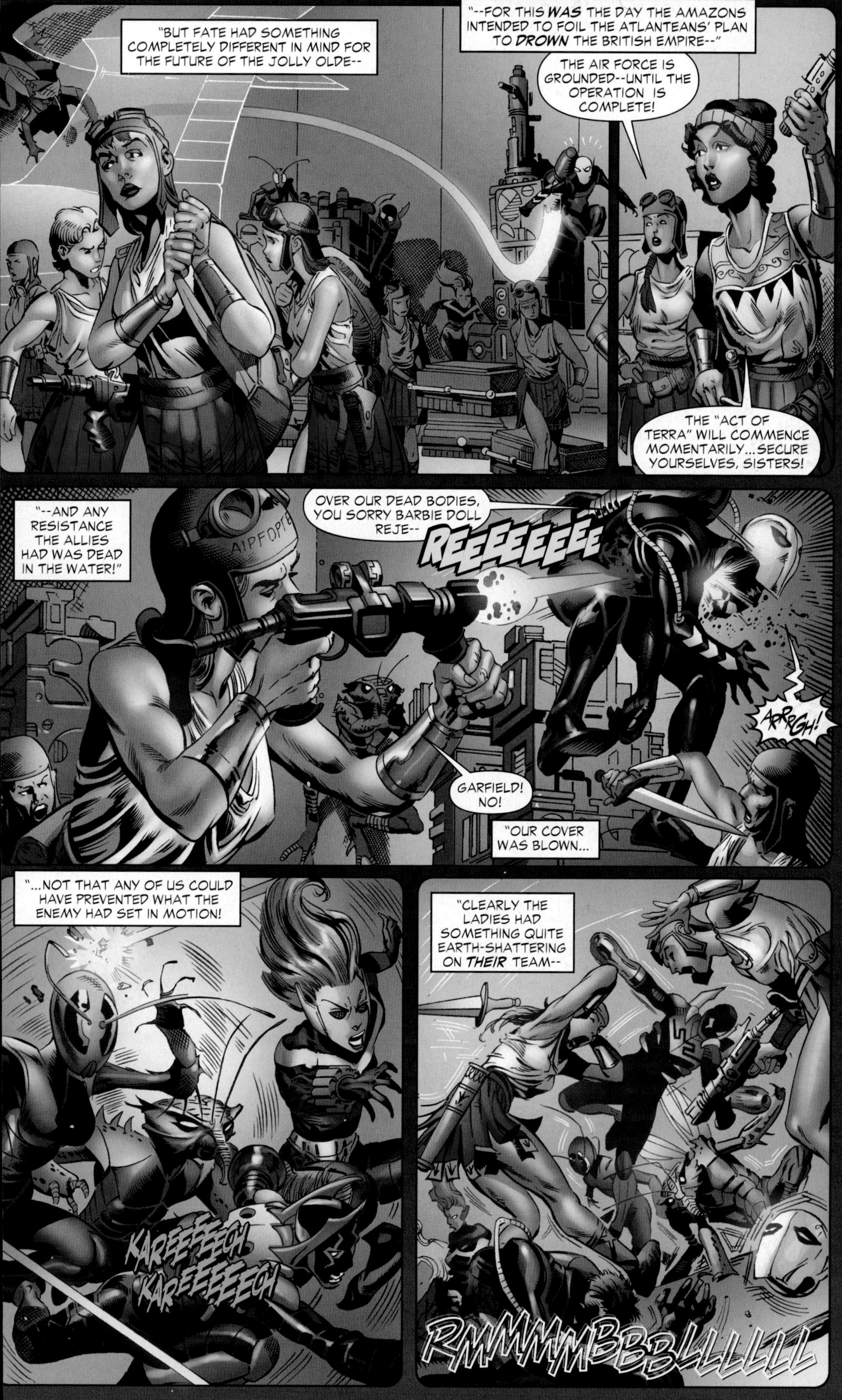
"BUT FATE HAD SOMETHING COMPLETELY DIFFERENT IN MIND FOR THE FUTURE OF THE JOLLY OLDE--
"--FOR THIS WAS THE DAY THE AMAZONS INTENDED TO FOIL THE ATLANTEANS' PLAN TO DROWN THE BRITISH EMPIRE--"
THE AIR FORCE IS GROUNDED--UNTIL THE OPERATION IS COMPLETE!
THE "ACT OF TERRA" WILL COMMENCE MOMENTARILY...SECURE YOURSELVES, SISTERS!
"--AND ANY RESISTANCE THE ALLIES HAD WAS DEAD IN THE WATER!"
OVER OUR DEAD BODIES, YOU SORRY BARBIE DOLL REJE--
REEEEEEEE
ARRRGH!
GARFIELD! NO!
"OUR COVER WAS BLOWN...
"...NOT THAT ANY OF US COULD HAVE PREVENTED WHAT THE ENEMY HAD SET IN MOTION!
KAREEEEECH
KAREEEEEECH
"CLEARLY THE LADIES HAD SOMETHING QUITE EARTH-SHATTERING ON THEIR TEAM--
RMMMMBBBLLLLLL

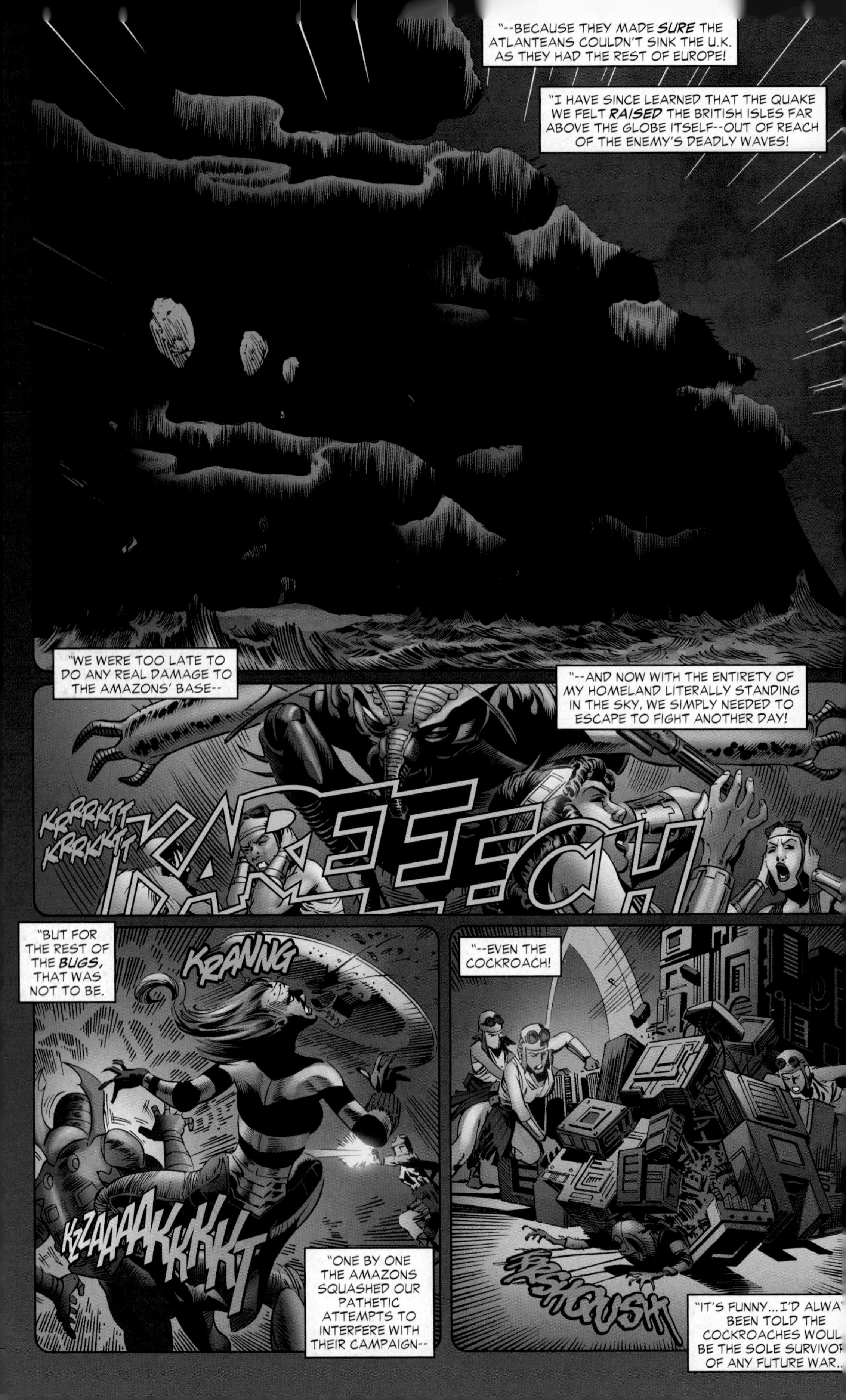
"--BECAUSE THEY MADE *SURE* THE ATLANTEANS COULDN'T SINK THE U.K. AS THEY HAD THE REST OF EUROPE!
"I HAVE SINCE LEARNED THAT THE QUAKE WE FELT *RAISED* THE BRITISH ISLES FAR ABOVE THE GLOBE ITSELF--OUT OF REACH OF THE ENEMY'S DEADLY WAVES!
"WE WERE TOO LATE TO DO ANY REAL DAMAGE TO THE AMAZONS' BASE--
"--AND NOW WITH THE ENTIRETY OF MY HOMELAND LITERALLY STANDING IN THE SKY, WE SIMPLY NEEDED TO ESCAPE TO FIGHT ANOTHER DAY!
KRRRKTT
KRRKKTT
"BUT FOR THE REST OF THE *BUGS,* THAT WAS NOT TO BE.
KRANNG
KZZAAAAKKKKT
"ONE BY ONE THE AMAZONS SQUASHED OUR PATHETIC ATTEMPTS TO INTERFERE WITH THEIR CAMPAIGN--
"--EVEN THE COCKROACH!
"IT'S FUNNY...I'D ALWA BEEN TOLD THE COCKROACHES WOUL BE THE SOLE SURVIVOR OF ANY FUTURE WAR...

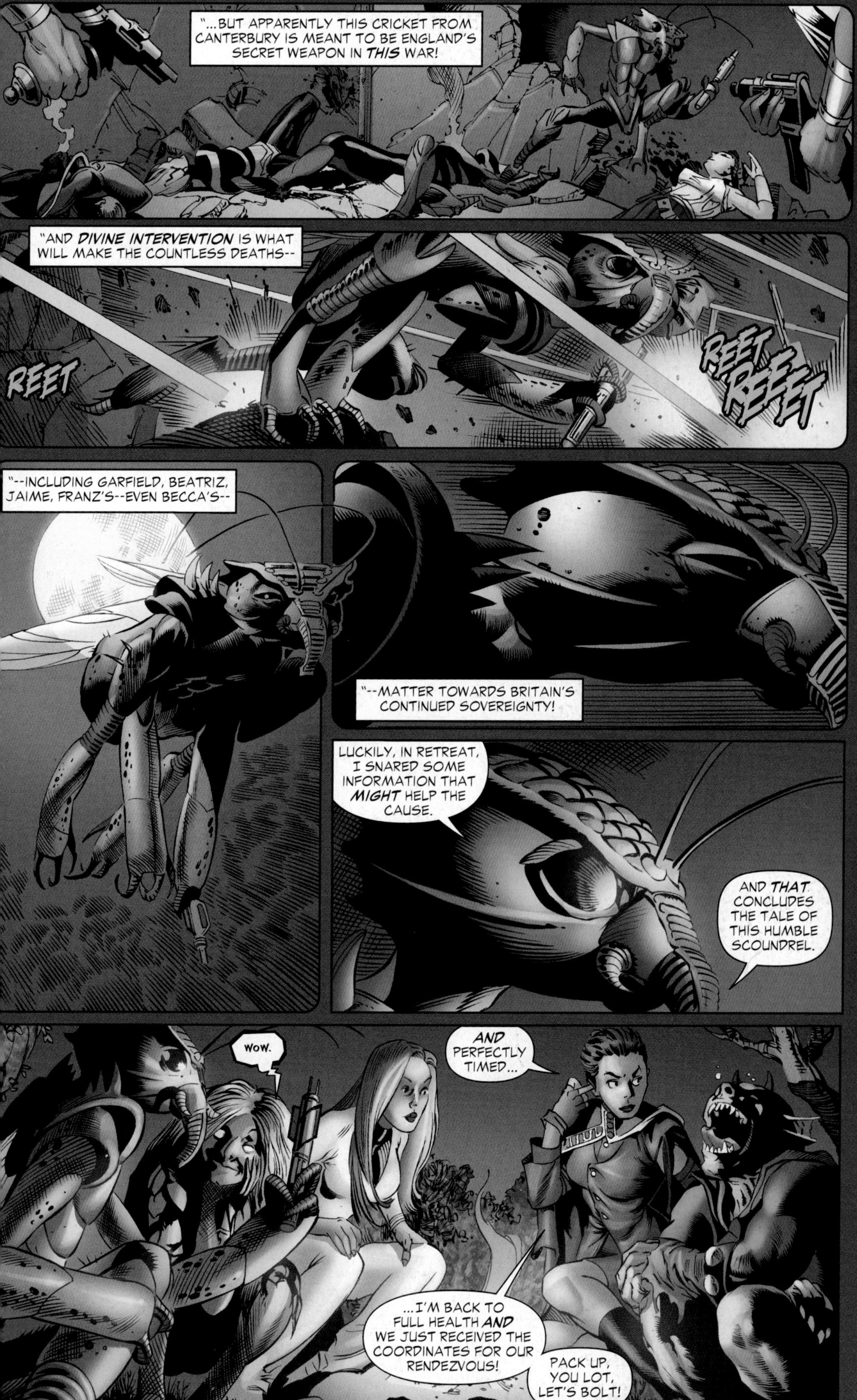
"...BUT APPARENTLY THIS CRICKET FROM CANTERBURY IS MEANT TO BE ENGLAND'S SECRET WEAPON IN *THIS* WAR!
"AND *DIVINE INTERVENTION* IS WHAT WILL MAKE THE COUNTLESS DEATHS--
REET
REET REEET
"--INCLUDING GARFIELD, BEATRIZ, JAIME, FRANZ'S--EVEN BECCA'S--
"--MATTER TOWARDS BRITAIN'S CONTINUED SOVEREIGNTY!
LUCKILY, IN RETREAT, I SNARED SOME INFORMATION THAT *MIGHT* HELP THE CAUSE.
AND *THAT* CONCLUDES THE TALE OF THIS HUMBLE SCOUNDREL.
WOW.
AND PERFECTLY TIMED...
...I'M BACK TO FULL HEALTH *AND* WE JUST RECEIVED THE COORDINATES FOR OUR RENDEZVOUS!
PACK UP, YOU LOT, LET'S BOLT!

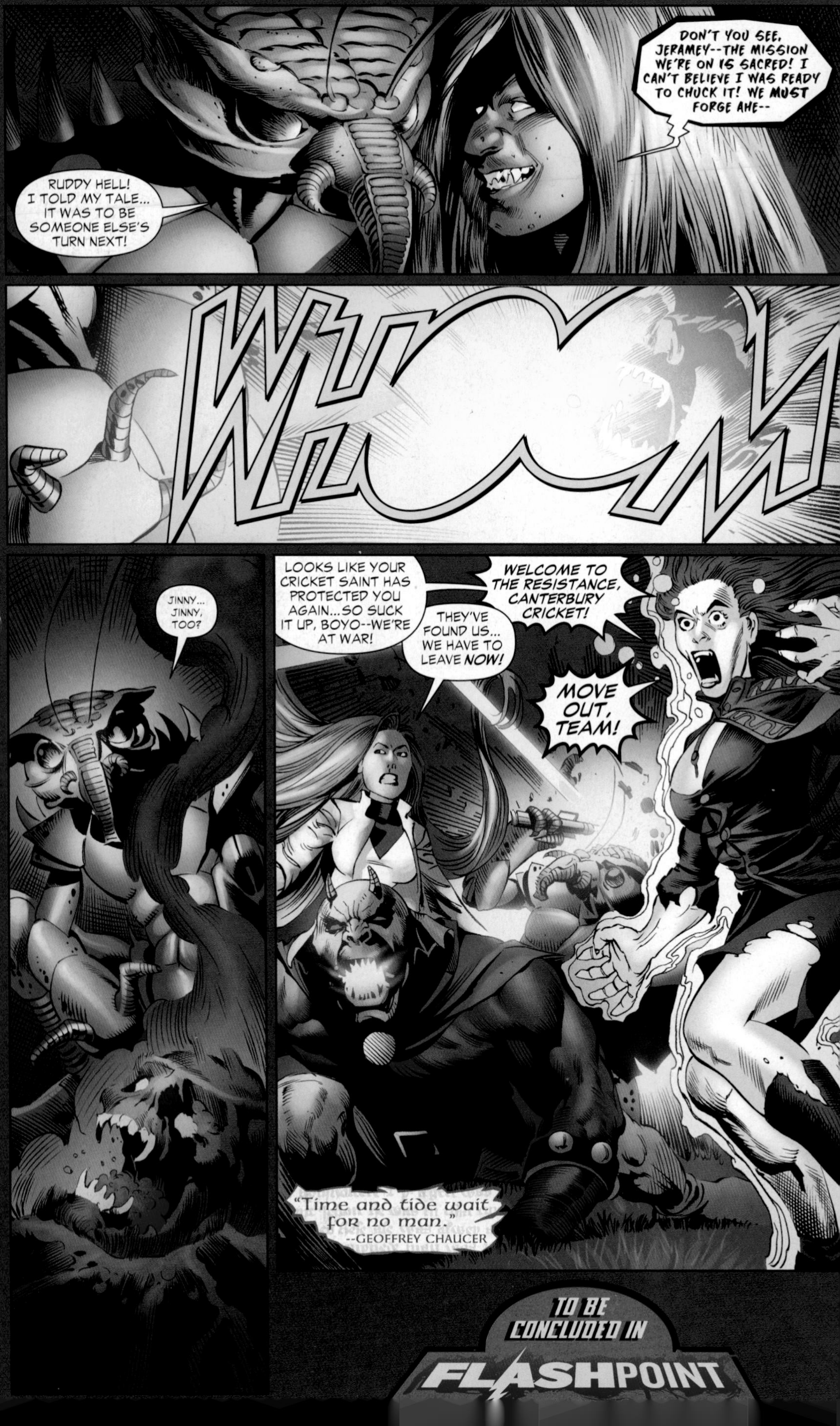
DON'T YOU SEE, JERAMEY--THE MISSION WE'RE ON IS SACRED! I CAN'T BELIEVE I WAS READY TO CHUCK IT! WE MUST FORGE AHE--
RUDDY HELL! I TOLD MY TALE... IT WAS TO BE SOMEONE ELSE'S TURN NEXT!
WHOOM
JINNY... JINNY, TOO?
LOOKS LIKE YOUR CRICKET SAINT HAS PROTECTED YOU AGAIN...SO SUCK IT UP, BOYO--WE'RE AT WAR!
WELCOME TO THE RESISTANCE, CANTERBURY CRICKET!
THEY'VE FOUND US... WE HAVE TO LEAVE NOW!
MOVE OUT, TEAM!
"Time and tide wait for no man."
--GEOFFREY CHAUCER
TO BE CONCLUDED IN
FLASHPOINT